W9-CNA-652

Hitchcock's Motifs

Hitchcock's Motifs

Michael Walker

AMSTERDAM UNIVERSITY PRESS

Cover illustration: (front) To Catch a Thief: Food motif. The picnic: Francie (Grace Kelly) and Robie (Cary Grant share a chicken. (back) poster for To Catch a Thief

Cover design: Kok Korpershoek, Amsterdam
Layout: JAPES, Amsterdam

ISBN 90 5356 772 0 (paperback)
ISBN 90 5356 773 9 (hardcover)
NUR 674

For Robin Wood, not only a seminal Hitchcock critic, but also a friend

Contents

Acknowledgements

Hitchcock's Motifs has been researched and written over many years, expanding in the process from an essay to a book. I would like to thank first those who read drafts and sections during the early stages, and who provided helpful and encouraging feedback: the late Bob Baker, Charles Barr, Peter Evans, Ed Gallafent, Derek Owen, Neil Sinyard, Keith Withall and Robin Wood. As the project developed, Sheldon Hall, Ken Mogg, John Oliver and Victor Perkins all helped track down copies of the rarer films/TV episodes; Richard Lippe supplied some vital stills. Ken Mogg was also invaluable in answering factual questions. I am especially indebted to Richard Chatten, who checked the filmography with great care, and Tony Brereton, who was an assiduous arbiter of my prose style. Thomas Elsaesser then provided encouragement and very useful feedback as the book neared completion.

For more specific help, I would like to thank Stella Bruzzi, who tutored me on the nuances of hair colour and styling for 'Blondes and brunettes', Susan Smith, who sent me the chapter on 'Hitchcock and Food' from her PhD, Sarah Street, who supplied me with a copy of her article on 'Hitchcockian Haberdashery', and two of my sisters: Jenny Winter, who translated Hartmut Redottée's article on Hitchcock's motifs from the German, and Susie Wardell, who produced the book's diagrams in a professional manner. Bob Quaif advised me on the subtleties of the soundtrack of REAR WINDOW; my nephew Keith Winter provided unfailing technical support for any computer problems.

I watched and discussed many of the films over the years with Stephen Blumenthal and Natasha Broad, and I am sure that some of their insights will have found their way into the text. Likewise, generations of students on the FEDAS Course at Hounslow Borough College (latterly West Thames College) and on the Media Arts Course at Royal Holloway, University of London, have contributed to my understanding of film in general and Hitchcock in particular.

Finally, I am grateful above all to Leighton Grist. Not only have his ideas on Hitchcock helped shape my own, but he has read (almost) every word of the text, and been exacting in his criticism of anything that he felt was not as clear as it should be.

Introduction

> A *leitmotif* can be understood not as literary technique, but as the expression
> of an obsession.
>
> (Klaus Theweleit: *Male Fantasies Volume 2* 1989: 383)

This book examines Alfred Hitchcock's work through his recurring motifs. Motifs in general are a neglected area of Film Studies. Although the decade by decade multi-volume *American Film Institute Catalog of Motion Pictures Produced in the United States* (see Munden 1997; Krafsur 1997; Hanson 1988, 1993 & 1999) includes a 'Subject Index' for each decade, and several film guides have either a 'Category Index' or a 'General Subject Index' – all of which include motifs – these are no more than listings of the films in which a specific feature occurs. Actual discussions of motifs in the cinema are rare, and there is only one publication in this area which I have found useful to this project and would like to acknowledge at the outset: Michel Cieutat's two-volume *Les grands thèmes du cinéma américain* (1988 & 1991). Despite the title, Cieutat includes motifs as well as themes, and he looks at the ways in which recurring elements in Hollywood films reveal (sometimes hidden) aspects of the culture which produced them. Nevertheless – to anticipate one of my arguments – whenever Cieutat's categories overlap with those in Hitchcock's films, there is a clash: Hitchcock's motifs do not fit the general pattern: see, for example, *Milk* in Part I and STAIR-CASES in Part II.

I have had a substantive interest in motifs in the cinema for many years. This book arose out of my research. Although it is confined to Hitchcock's films, it is also informed by an awareness of the functioning of motifs in films generally. In cases where one of the Hitchcock motifs has resonances with examples elsewhere, I discuss the similarities and differences. My response to the not unreasonable question: 'why another book on Hitchcock?' would be that (a) this aspect of his films has been surprisingly ignored and (b) approaching Hitchcock's films from the point of view of his recurring motifs offers a different slant on his work, one which I hope will reveal new insights.

My project here is not without precedent: there was an article on Hitchcock's motifs published in *Cahiers du Cinéma* as long ago as 1956. Written by Philippe Demonsablon and entitled *Lexique mythologique pour l'oeuvre de Hitchcock* (Demonsablon 1956: 18-29 & 54-55), this considered twenty recurring motifs in Hitchcock's films up to THE MAN WHO KNEW TOO MUCH (1955): for details, see

Appendix II. But this was in the days when *Sight and Sound* – as the key representative of British film criticism of the period – considered the ideas of these
French critics to be slightly batty, as is shown by Richard Roud's survey of their
criticism in 'The French Line' (Roud 1960: 166-171). After quoting an admittedly
rather mystical passage from Eric Rohmer and Claude Chabrol's *Hitchcock*
(1957), Roud adds, 'If this were not enough, *Cahiers* once devoted fourteen
pages to a thematic index of objects in Hitchcock's films: glasses, throats, clocks,
cats, eyes, knives, keys...' (Roud 1960: 169). Although he has invented the
throats, clocks and eyes, he has grasped the principle: they would not have
been out of place.

Roud was fighting a rearguard action; it was *Cahiers du Cinéma's* enthusiasm
for Hitchcock as auteur which prevailed, and which spread rapidly throughout
the cinéphile world. No other film director has prompted so many books and
articles on his work: the annotated bibliography in Jane Sloan's *Alfred Hitchcock:
a Filmography and Bibliography* (1995) has some 1100 separate entries – up to
1994, and excluding contemporary reviews – and runs to almost two hundred
pages. With such a wealth of material, one would have anticipated some reference to further articles on Hitchcock's motifs. Indeed, this seemed such an obvious area for scholarship that, in a short piece on Hitchcock for *Film Dope* in
1982, I was moved to speculate:

> even now, one has visions of a student somewhere painstakingly working on Hitch's
> 'master-code', under such headings as false arrest, voyeurism, mother figures,
> blondes versus brunettes, the law, guilt and confession, pursuit, public disturbances,
> murder weapons, staircases, falls, birds, keys etc., each with its sub-divisions and
> variations.
>
> (Walker, M. 1982a: 39)

But, although there have been articles on Hitchcock's themes, and a few on individual motifs, to my knowledge not until 2000 was one published (in German) on Hitchcock's motifs in general: Hartmut W. Redottée: *Leid-Motive: Das
Universum des Alfred Hitchcock* (Redottée 2000: 19-50). This book takes up the
project I outlined in 1982 and looks in detail at the director's motifs.

In *Hitchcock's Films Revisited*, Robin Wood looks at one area of the 'master-
code': Hitchcock's 'plot formations' (Wood 1989: 239-248). He discusses five recurring stories in the films: those of the falsely accused man; the guilty woman;
the psychopath; the spy intrigue; the marriage. In part, I conceived *Hitchcock's
Motifs* as an albeit somewhat expanded complement to this chapter. Robin
Wood looks at Hitchcock's most significant plots; this book returns to the spirit
of the original *Cahiers* lexicon and focuses on those recurring elements in
Hitchcock which, for the most part, one would call motifs. Here I am following
Northrop Frye in *Anatomy of Criticism* (Frye 1957: 73-74) and taking the term

motif from the more familiar musical term *leitmotif*, or 'leading motif'. But, as well as amending and extending the original *Cahiers du Cinéma* categories, I have also incorporated a few examples which should more properly be termed themes, e.g. EXHIBITIONISM / VOYEURISM / THE LOOK, GUILT AND CONFESSION and HOMOSEXUALITY, which I included because I was dissatisfied with the discussions of them elsewhere. In context, I have referred to these as themes, but in the book generally, reversing the usual practice, these few themes are subsumed under the general rubric of motifs, and 'motifs' should be read as short for 'themes and motifs'.

In *Hitchcock – The Murderous Gaze*, William Rothman refers en passant to several Hitchcock motifs (Rothman 1982). But his examples are for the most part recurring *visual* motifs, e.g. the parallel vertical lines '////' which he traces throughout Hitchcock's work: he introduces this motif on page 33. In a more recent article, Rothman has helpfully summarised the Hitchcock motifs which he cites throughout his 1982 book:

> 'curtain raisings'; 'eclipses'; 'tunnel shots'; white flashes; frames-within-frames; profile shots; symbolically charged objects (e.g., lamps, staircases, birds); symbolically charged colours (red, white, blue-green, brown)
>
> (Rothman 1999: 32)

Only the symbolically charged objects overlap with my project. This is not to say that visual motifs are not equally important to Hitchcock's work, and one could cite others: e.g. circles and spirals, the colour yellow. But, for reasons of space, I have excluded visual motifs: they could indeed form the subject of another book. And so, for example, LIGHT(S) in this book refers to a diegetic light or lights, i.e. light sources within the film's narrative world, such as light bulbs, candles and the sun, rather than to a film's lighting scheme (➤ APPENDIX III for a fuller definition of diegetic).

Since I am also making a distinction between themes and motifs, I should clarify what I mean. Motifs are recurring elements of a certain kind in a narrative or a series of narratives: in Hitchcock's case they include objects (e.g. keys), types of character (e.g. mothers), settings (e.g. trains), actions (e.g. entrances through a window) and events (e.g. public disturbances). They are usually denoted by concrete nouns, but occasionally by a gerund, e.g. falling.

A theme is more abstract: it incorporates a point of view and implies that the film is saying something about this matter. Themes are denoted by abstract nouns. However, because of the complexity and density of Hitchcock's work, I would argue that there is in practice little or no functional difference between themes and motifs in his films. A theme in any work is necessarily articulated, inflected in a certain way. Or, from the point of view of the critic: 'We apprehend the theme by inference – it is the rationale of the images and sym-

bols (i.e. motifs)' (Sage 1987: 248). But I would say the same of Hitchcock's motifs: they are not simply recurring elements, but elements which are articulated
and recur in patterns of meaning. The significance of these patterns may then be
critically inferred: it is my purpose here to investigate and explicate them.

As will be apparent, and as is the common practice in auteur studies, I am
attributing the ways in which the individual motifs are inflected in the films to
Hitchcock himself. Of course, some of the specific examples will have originated
elsewhere, and of course there may be other directors – or, indeed, literary
authors – whose work shows similar inflections of a given motif. Collectively,
however, they are Hitchcock's motifs: they provide another facet to his more
familiar themes and preoccupations; one whose significance only fully emerges
when the examples are considered in toto. In approaching his work from this
point of view, my underlying premise is that little (nothing?) in his films is accidental, and so if he chooses, for example, to include a scene in or on a bed in
most of his films, there will, consciously or unconsciously, be a purpose and
pattern to this. Occasionally, a particular manifestation of a motif might seem to
be merely incidental, but I would argue that this is rare. I hope that the examples themselves will provide the evidence to support this argument.

The interaction of an artist with his or her culture can be a complex and difficult one; this is perhaps especially so with an artist as sophisticated as Hitchcock. Investigating Hitchcock's films through their motifs – particularly in the
cases where the motifs are widespread in other works – thus becomes in part an
exploration of Hitchcock's relationship to his culture. As with motifs in films
generally, some of the examples discussed here function in a way which seems
quite unconscious. An exploration of their meanings should thus also reveal
something of the 'Hitchcockian unconscious', the hidden/unconscious patterns
underlying his works. I should stress that the concept of the Hitchcockian unconscious is not meant to refer to the psychology of Hitchcock himself, but to a
feature of his films: it arises, again, from the complex interaction of Hitchcock
the artist with his culture. In many respects, Hitchcock is an elusive figure:
critics have noted how guarded he usually sounds in interviews. But the films
are a different matter: they offer themselves as subjects for analysis.

A few words about the structure of the book. Part I constitutes a general discussion of the significance and meaning of motifs, with selected examples. The
theoretical material here is designed to underpin and contextualise the discussions of the individual motifs. The examples in Part I have been selected to illustrate aspects of the theoretical arguments, but also to probe more deeply into
the whole issue of Hitchcock's motifs by looking at a small number of instances
of a given motif in detail. The examples have also been chosen to illustrate two
basic points I wish to make about Hitchcock's use of motifs. First, that his articulation of a given motif tends to be more sophisticated (and/or distinctive)

than the norm. Second, that there are Hitchcock films in which a motif is woven into the narrative to such an extent that one can use the motif itself as a starting point to investigate the film's concerns. All this material is in turn designed to explore the issue of why an investigation of the motifs in Hitchcock's work in particular is so rewarding.

Part II constitutes an alphabetical listing of what I have termed the Key Motifs. These are all elements which occur in a substantial number of films, rather than just a few. Some of the categories will be familiar from the Hitchcock literature; others less so. I have necessarily been selective, but I hope that no significant motifs have been overlooked. Where I have excluded motifs cited by Demonsablon – and indeed a couple on my own 1982 list – this is because I decided that they were ultimately less important to Hitchcock's work overall than those that I have included. One example, the Police, is covered in a different manner from the rest. There are two motifs – ENDINGS AND THE POLICE and HANDCUFFS AND BONDAGE – in which the police feature throughout the discussions. Otherwise, their special place in Hitchcock's cinema is recorded in a note at the end of each motif which cites their specific contributions to that particular motif.

I have also sought to be comprehensive with regard to the films. Although, inevitably, some titles crop up frequently, some rarely, and the majority in between, each of Hitchcock's fifty-two extant feature films as director has a number of entries. In two motifs, PAINTERS and STAIRCASES, I also refer to a film Hitchcock scripted and designed, THE BLACKGUARD (Graham Cutts, 1925). In addition, Appendix I looks at nine TV episodes Hitchcock directed which include a significant example of one of the key motifs. The spread of the motifs across Hitchcock's whole oeuvre is in fact a strong measure of his consistency as auteur. Whilst there may be a shift in the prominence or inflection of a motif between his British and Hollywood films, none of those discussed in Part II is confined to only one of the periods.

For reference purposes, Appendix II lists the motifs covered in the original article by Philippe Demonsablon and the recent one by Hartmut W. Redottée, together with brief comments. It also lists the themes and motifs included in Thomas Leitch's *The Encyclopedia of Alfred Hitchcock* (2002). For published articles on individual motifs, the reader is referred to Jane Sloan's excellent bibliography index: Sloan 1995: 599-614. Finally, in Appendix III I define two technical terms used throughout the book which could perhaps prove troublesome: diegesis and point-of-view editing.

I should like to acknowledge a general indebtedness to the writings of Robin Wood. One manifestation of this is my adoption of his notion of the 'chaos world' to specify the world of threat and disorder into which Hitchcock's characters are almost invariably plunged. Underlying the mundane, everyday world inhabited by most of the characters at the beginnings of the films, the chaos world emphasises how precarious the surface veneer of 'civilisation' can be. Extending from the experience of injustice of the falsely accused figures (both men and women), through the world of espionage in the spy movies, to specific locations such as the Bates Motel (PSYCHO), or Bodega Bay (THE BIRDS), the chaos world is, perhaps, the master metaphor for Hitchcock's films. Robin Wood's own comments on the concept recur throughout the original 1965 edition of *Hitchcock's Films*: see, for example, Wood, 1989: 84, 94, 107, 117, 134, 145.

Overall, I have sought, as far as possible, to avoid repetition; instead, I have used cross-referencing. The essay under each motif is intended to be self-contained, but where there is further relevant material elsewhere, this is indicated. Obviously, some scenes or elements in a Hitchcock film could be included under more than one motif. For example, what happens in the bell tower in VERTIGO has material relevant to no less than six motifs. I have discussed the events from the different points of view quite fully in four of these (THE CORPSE, GUILT AND CONFESSION, HEIGHTS AND FALLING and STAIRCASES) and in the others (CONFINED SPACES and DOUBLES) included briefer comments. But under each of these six discussions, cross-references to one or more of the other five motifs indicates that there is material there which provides further details. Such cross-referencing serves two additional functions. It highlights the inter-connectedness of the motifs and, by extension, the density of Hitchcock's work – in Freudian terms, the 'overdetermination' of the elements in his films. And it serves to guide the reader from motif to motif for further comments about a given scene.

Identification of the characters. The filmography includes a full listing of the actors who play the various characters, but during the discussions I refer to the characters purely by their names. In most cases, what to call someone is self-evident, but there are exceptions. Joan Fontaine in REBECCA plays a woman who is nameless; in Robert E. Sherwood and Joan Harrison's screenplay (1940/ 1959), she is designated as 'I'. I usually refer to her simply as 'the heroine of REBECCA', but occasionally as 'Maxim's young wife' or 'Maxim's bride'. The hero in SPELLBOUND is amnesiac, and he does not learn his name, John Ballyntine, until close to the end. Ben Hecht's screenplay (1946) calls him Edwardes, the name of the man he is unconsciously impersonating, in the early scenes, and then – when he realises that he is not Edwardes – J.B., from the initials on his cigarette case. I call him J.B. throughout.

For other impersonations, where there are in effect two characters called by the same name, and confusions can arise, I have adopted a convention: Madeleine (VERTIGO) refers to the real Madeleine Elster, unseen alive, 'Madeleine' to Judy's impersonation of her; Mrs Bates (PSYCHO) to the real Mrs Bates, now a

corpse, 'Mrs Bates' to Norman's psychotic version of her and Van Meer (FOR-
EIGN CORRESPONDENT) to the real diplomat, 'Van Meer' to his impersonator.

The stills. The still at the beginning of each of the key motifs is intended,
where possible, to be 'emblematic': to condense that motif into an image which
dramatises the motif in a particularly vivid or relevant way. Other stills within a
given motif are included to illustrate different sorts of example. But sometimes a
still could have been placed under more than one motif: in such cases, both
relevant motifs are mentioned in the captions.

In general, stills are better than frames from the films to illustrate the motifs.
Taken on set during filming, a still does not show exactly what we see in the
film, but it almost always includes more of a given scene, and thus sets the elements, including any motifs, in context. This is particularly true of Hitchcock,
where in the films themselves the individual elements tend to be broken down
into separate shots. In some stills, the characters are also repositioned from the
way they are in the film, but this may well convey the essence of the scene more
effectively than a single frame. For example, the JEWELLERY still from NOTOR-
IOUS (Fig. 35). In the film, when Prescott fastens the necklace on Alicia, Devlin is
on the right and his back is to the camera: a frame of that moment might not
suggest his feelings. In the still, where he is repositioned behind the other two
characters and we can see his face, his sense of exclusion and jealousy – established throughout the scene as a whole – are readily visible.

Finally, a note on FAMILY PLOT. I was surprised how often Hitchcock's last
film served to round off a particular motif and provide a satisfying sense of
closure to the discussion. FAMILY PLOT is not generally considered to be one of
the major works, but in terms of motifs it is crucial. It also contains a Hitchcock
couple I find particularly endearing: Blanche and George. My inclusion of
Barbara Harris and Bruce Dern in a still (Fig. 5) is a little tribute: it's not a particularly exciting still, but I wanted them to be there.

Part I

Hitchcock, Motifs and Melodrama

Introduction

In an article on LETTER FROM AN UNKNOWN WOMAN (Max Ophuls, 1948), I wrote of objects in melodrama that:

> they become charged with internally generated meaning. Flowers (e.g. Lisa's white roses), jewellery (e.g. Madame de's ear-rings), photographs, music-boxes, handker-chiefs, letters, indeed any objects which evoke romantic/nostalgic/symbolic associa-tions for the protagonists function within the films less to convey generic information than to contribute a wealth of internally accumulated significance.
>
> (Walker M. 1982c: 44)

In other words, as certain sorts of object circulate within a melodrama narrative, they generate associations deriving from the different contexts in which they are found. My project here is an extension of this notion. First, motifs are not con-fined to objects, but include other features in the films as well. Second, I am looking at the circulation and function of these motifs not just in individual films, but across Hitchcock's work overall, i.e. intertextually. Third, this intertex-tual context includes films (and other narratives) in general and, in some cases, I compare Hitchcock's inflections of a given motif with those typically found else-where. Fourth, although I would now extend my observation about circulating objects to include not just melodramas but all types of popular narrative, the-ories of melodrama are particularly useful in the analysis of both Hitchcock's films and the individual motifs. Motifs tend to function like 'melodramatic ele-ments' within the films, and they may be analysed accordingly. A final point is that the density of meanings generated by the use of motifs varies: a given motif may possess quite striking resonances in some narratives, and seem of little in-terest in others. In Hitchcock, I would maintain, the associations generated are almost always remarkably rich. A few examples where he has used a motif which is relatively common in other works will help illustrate these points.

Three motifs

Home movies

Home movies viewed within a film are traditionally used to evoke the past, usually with a sense of loss, as in the home movie Charles (Michel Duchaussoy) watches of his dead wife and son in QUE LA BÊTE MEURE (Claude Chabrol, 1969), or the one the middle-aged Salvatore (Jacques Perrin) watches of his lost love, filmed when both of them were teenagers, in CINEMA PARADISO (Giuseppe Tornatore, 1988). These are strong examples of the motif: we are being told a great deal about the man who obsessively shows himself the films, and both scenes are very poignant.

Neither example, however, approaches the complexity of the scene in REBEC-CA, when Maxim and his young wife watch the home movie of their French honeymoon. Here the sense of loss is present in a more astringent way: the con-trast between the couple's happiness in the movie and the tension and unease between them in the present. The tension arises from a number of factors, but one is the consequence of Maxim's contradictory behaviour towards the her-oine. On the one hand, she is supposed to be sweet and self-effacing (as in the home movie) and not dress in a glamorous evening gown (as in the present) and so remind him of Rebecca, his first wife; on the other, she is supposed to be the mistress of the house, and handle domestic matters with Rebecca's control and savoir faire, which she has just failed, rather embarrassingly, to do. As I will argue in detail later, here a motif which was unfamiliar in 1940, but is common today, is employed with a sophistication which has possibly never been bet-tered.

Cigarette case / lighter

Although there are nuances to the way each of these objects functions in films generally, depending on whether it is a case or a lighter, for the purposes of the discussion here they may be combined. The essential point is that the case or lighter is originally a gift from a woman to a man. In most such cases, the gift signals the woman's – frequently rather possessive – desire. For example, the case given by Norma (Gloria Swanson) to Joe (William Holden) in SUNSET BLVD. (Billy Wilder, 1950), inscribed 'Mad about the boy', or that given by an ex-girlfriend to Nickie Ferrante (Cary Grant) in AN AFFAIR TO REMEMBER (Leo McCarey, 1957); Terry McKay (Deborah Kerr), reading its inscription, says that she understands just enough French to be embarrassed. Both these gifts refer to a rather unfortunate sexual relationship which the hero feels the need to explain to the woman he later comes to love. We could call this the sexual-romantic use of the motif.

In other films, the sexual connotations to the gift are more muted, and the case/lighter serves, rather, to introduce another thread into the film: it becomes evidence in a murder investigation. In BEYOND A REASONABLE DOUBT (Fritz Lang, 1956), the hero plants his lighter (a gift from his fiancée) at a murder scene as part of an anti-capital punishment project: he and his fiancée's father wish to draw attention to the unreliability of circumstantial evidence. In LE BOUCHER (Claude Chabrol, 1969), the heroine discovers the lighter she gave the hero lying next to a murdered woman – and conceals this evidence from the police. This may be called the criminal use of the motif. In both these films, the lighter is then used or referred to in later scenes, so that the associations linked to it become more developed. It serves to raise or focus issues relevant to each of the films: issues such as guilt, responsibility and the deceptiveness of appearances. Appropriating a concept from Basil Bernstein, who has written of restricted and elaborated codes in verbal and written discourse (Bernstein 1973: 144-153), we could say that the use of the motif here is elaborated. This may be contrasted with a restricted use of the motif, where it operates in an essentially conventional way. For example, in A KISS BEFORE DYING (James Dearden, 1991), after a man has killed a woman, he takes her monogrammed lighter. But this serves no other purpose than to reveal, to the woman's sister who later finds the lighter, that her own husband is her sister's murderer.

In STRANGERS ON A TRAIN, however, both the sexual-romantic and the criminal threads to the motif are even more elaborated. Again, the lighter was originally a gift from a woman (Anne Morton) to a man (Guy Haines), and is inscribed 'A to G', with two crossed tennis rackets. The design hints at Guy's virility as a successful sportsman: Anne is signalling what she finds particularly attractive about him. But Bruno Antony, who buttonholes Guy on a train, not only knows the story behind the gift – Anne is Senator Morton's daughter, but Guy is already married – he also signals his own attraction to Guy. And so, as critics have noted, when Guy 'accidentally' leaves the lighter behind in Bruno's compartment, this may be seen as a 'Freudian slip': unconsciously, he wants Bruno to have it, because unconsciously he, too, is attracted – the film's gay subtext (➤ BED SCENE and LIGHTS). Certainly, Bruno himself handles the lighter with a fetishistic pleasure which makes it seem like a lover's gift: he always carries it with him, and repeatedly takes it out. In particular, he uses it to check the identity of Miriam, Guy's present wife, before strangling her on the Magic Isle, and, at the end of the movie, he holds it in his hand as he dies.

However, the lighter does not function simply as a love token, but also connects Guy and Bruno as accomplices in Miriam's murder: Guy wanted it; Bruno enacted it. Robin Wood says of Guy's slip in leaving the lighter behind:

Guy's forgetfulness ... belies his dismissive joking air when Bruno asks if he agrees to the exchange of murders ... He is leaving in Bruno's keeping his link with Anne, his possibility of climbing into the ordered existence to which he aspires.

(Wood 1989: 87)

It's as if Guy is unconsciously giving Bruno a sign to go ahead and carry out the murder. Hitchcock's stress on the lighter during the murder scene emphasises Guy's presence behind the murder: in using the lighter to illuminate Miriam's face, Bruno is stressing, almost consciously, that he is doing this for Guy; in picking it up after the murder, he is – quite consciously this time – protecting Guy.

The two threads to the use of the motif are thus combined from an early stage in the narrative. They are combined in a different way when, in the third act of the film, Bruno decides to plant the lighter back on the island as a way of incriminating Guy. He now seeks to use the 'love token' to revenge himself on the – to his mind – fickle Guy. As if to emphasise the lighter's place here in an implicit sexual triangle, Bruno signals his intent in a scene with Anne, whom he reduces to tears as he savours his power over her and Guy. It is the lighter which gives him this power, as Hitchcock emphasises by once more showing it in Bruno's hands in close-up as he talks to Anne. But Bruno is also seeking to return the lighter to where it originally fell; in other words, he is insisting on Guy's (moral) responsibility for the murder.

The lighter is then crucial to the famous sequence in which Hitchcock cross-cuts between Guy's tennis match and Bruno – en route to the island – reaching down into a drain to recover the accidentally dropped lighter. Robin Wood has discussed the contrasts between the two settings and activities, contrasts which characterise the worlds of the two men (Wood 1989: 97). But, so far as the lighter is concerned, here too, the sexual-romantic and the criminal threads are combined: in Bruno's desperation to retrieve it, the lighter seems, once more, like a prized possession, but his real motivation is to use it to incriminate Guy.

Overall, Hitchcock's use of the motif goes significantly beyond the associations in the other movies cited. Not only does the lighter function in a more extended way than usual as a love token – from Anne to Guy to Bruno – but it also serves to bind the two men together; to stress Bruno as Guy's alter ego (➤ DOUBLES). When Guy and Bruno fight on the merry-go-round at the film's climax, this is an archetypal scene of the hero doing battle with his dark alter ego, and what prompts it is Guy seeking to repossess the lighter. That he in fact fails – the lighter, as evidence, passes into the hands of the police – suggests an unresolved quality to the film's ending: as if Guy's inability to reclaim the love token points to a failure of enthusiasm in his relationship with Anne.

A further point is that the lighter is only one of four objects which pass between the two men. The others are Miriam's spectacles, a Luger automatic and a key, and these, too, are relevant to the dynamics of their relationship. For example, when Bruno gives Guy Miriam's spectacles – to show that he has murdered her – this looks like a gift in exchange for the lighter. I discuss the resonances to this gift under SPECTACLES and LIGHT(S), and the implications of the circulation of the key under KEYS AND HANDBAGS. What happens to the Luger automatic is mentioned more briefly under LIGHT(S). The cigarette lighter is nevertheless the most telling 'symbolically charged object' here. Typically of an elaborated motif, it circulates through the narrative, drawing attention to issues, weaving together different strands, prompting additional lines of critical investigation – in general, enriching the film with the associations it generates.

Milk

Michel Cieutat writes of milk: 'In the cinema, milk is a symbol of faith in the future, and therefore of optimism' (Cieutat 1991: 182). His key example to illustrate this is when Jim (James Dean) in REBEL WITHOUT A CAUSE (Nicholas Ray, 1955) returns home after the 'chicken run' and drinks milk, signifying his wish to make a new start in his troubled life. He cites other films in which drinking milk is therapeutic or optimistic, e.g. THE LAST TIME I SAW PARIS (Richard Brooks, 1954) (as cure for a hangover); THE BEST YEARS OF OUR LIVES (William Wyler, 1946) (as the prelude to a moving reconciliation scene). He notes however that the use of milk is given an apparently sinister twist in SUSPICION, when Lina fears that the milk Johnnie brings to her in bed is poisoned: 'But everyone knows this is only an illusion. [Hitchcock] … could not really betray the mythology of milk, the staple drink of his adopted country' (184).

I beg to differ. We know that Hitchcock fully intended the milk to be poisoned. In the ending he insists that he wanted for the film, Lina would realise that it was poisoned, but nevertheless drink it, having first written a letter incriminating Johnnie to her mother. Johnnie would then post the letter. He claims that he couldn't film this ending because Cary Grant couldn't play a murderer (Truffaut 1968: 11). In an essay on SUSPICION, I discuss the finished film taking account of Hitchcock's difficulties in finding a satisfactory ending ('Can Cary Grant Be a Murderer?' in Unexplored Hitchcock, ed. Ian Cameron, forthcoming). My conclusion is that, although the murder-cum-suicide of Lina was quite properly rejected, Hitchcock has still contrived to smuggle his original wishes into the film as it stands, so that Johnnie really is a murderer and the milk really is poisoned. Crucial to this reading is that Lina does not drink the milk. Nevertheless, Johnnie continues to try and kill her (➤ HEIGHTS AND FALLING), and although in the final scene he seems to persuade her of his innocence, I am convinced that he is lying and that this is, in effect, a 'false happy ending' (➤ GUILT AND CONFESSION). In an interview with Peter Bogdanovich, Hitchcock himself has in fact agreed that the ending of the film leaves the question of Johnnie's real intentions towards Lina open: 'He could have killed her when he got home' (Bogdanovich 1997: 509). For more on the poisoning of the milk, see *Food and marriage* and LIGHT(S).

Nor is this the only example of Hitchcock's desecration of the milk motif. In FOREIGN CORRESPONDENT, the journalist Stebbins, obliged to go on the wagon, enviously watches Johnny drink a Scotch and soda and then grimaces as he sips the milk he has ordered for himself: 'Doesn't taste the way it did when I was a baby – that's got poison in it.' In SPELLBOUND, Dr Brulov courteously invites J.B. to join him in a late night glass of milk, but his motive is to knock J.B. out: he laces the milk with bromides. In each case, Hitchcock has taken what Cieutat calls the 'sacrosanct image of milk' (Cieutat 1991: 184) and quite deliberately violated it. In *Hitchcock and Selznick*, Leonard J. Leff recounts an amusing anecdote in this regard:

> The National Creamery Buttermakers' Association had condemned FOREIGN CORRESPONDENT for showing people drinking milk and suggesting 'that milk drinking is an object of ridicule'. Hitchcock responded by associating milk with Mickey Finns in both SUSPICION and [SPELLBOUND].
>
> (Leff 1988: 157)

A later milk reference seems more innocent, but is in fact deceptive. When Norman in PSYCHO offers Marion sandwiches and milk, he obviously means well, but behind this apparently altruistic gesture lies the psychotic shadow of 'Mrs Bates', who has already declared her hostility to Marion's 'appeasing her ugly appetite with my food' and will shortly murder her. Hitchcock's reinflection of a traditionally positive motif, turning it in a darker or more sinister direction, is a characteristic feature of his motifs.

Melodrama and Hitchcock's motifs

Hitchcock's use of the Milk motif is by no means as sophisticated as his use of the cigarette lighter in STRANGERS ON A TRAIN, but it illustrates the distinctiveness of his point of view. Within the cinema generally, motifs could be said to operate across two broad continua: from conventional to unconventional and from simple to complex. Hitchcock's motifs consistently gravitate towards the unconventional and/or the complex, with milk illustrating the former and the cigarette lighter both features.

In particular, Hitchcock's motifs continue to accumulate significance throughout the individual films, and throughout his films overall. In order to explore this further, I would like to pursue the notion that the resonances of a given motif may be analysed through theories of melodrama. In its direct appeal to the emotions of the audience, and in the way that it charges acts, gestures, statements with a wider symbolic significance, melodrama is particularly relevant to an understanding of Hitchcock's films. Equally, the condensed, emotionally resonant signification typical of melodrama may be seen operating in many motifs. Viewed as melodramatic elements in a narrative, motifs serve to crystallise issues and preoccupations.

The role of melodrama in articulating the motifs invites a psychoanalytical approach. In his seminal article 'Hitchcock's Vision', Peter Wollen runs through a number of Hitchcock's themes and motifs, discussing them from a Freudian point of view. I would like to quote one passage in some detail:

> Childhood memories, according to Freud, are always of a visual character, even for those whose memories are not generally visual. (In fact, 'they resemble plastically depicted scenes, comparable only to stage settings': perhaps this is a justification which could be argued in defence of the notorious backdrops in MARNIE, which depict her childhood home.) Evidently, the sense of sight is essential, not only to the cinema, but also to memory and dream: the images on the screen can trigger repressed memories and through them the unconscious can speak as in a dream. It is clear how often Hitchcock evokes childhood fears: anxieties rooted in early phases of sexual development. Indeed, Hitchcock himself seems to see films as like dreams. In SABOTAGE, which is set in a cinema, we only once see any film on the screen, when, at the climactic moment of the action, the heroine has just learned that her husband was responsible for her son's (sic) death: she goes into the cinema and sees on the screen part of a Walt Disney cartoon of WHO KILLED COCK ROBIN?, a distorted version of her own anxieties. She gets up, returns to her husband and kills him. The fragment of film fulfils the same role as the dream sequences in SPELLBOUND and VERTIGO: all three are animated, that in SPELLBOUND by Salvador Dalí.... In the end we discover that to be a 'master technician' in the cinema is to speak a rhetoric which is none other than the rhetoric of the unconscious, the world which surges up beneath the thin protection offered us by civilization.
>
> (Wollen 1969: 4)

Wollen suggests that a Freudian reading of Hitchcock's films should prove particularly rewarding, and this course has since been followed by numerous critics. So far as his motifs are concerned, a psychoanalytical approach leads one to see something of the unconscious patterns in Hitchcock's work. But I would like to broaden the theoretical base by linking such an approach to melodrama. Melodrama, too, has been investigated from a psychoanalytical point of view, an approach again prompted by a seminal article: Thomas Elsaesser's 'Tales of Sound and Fury'. The Freudian concepts which Elsaesser suggests are particularly relevant here are condensation and displacement. With reference to Hollywood melodramas, he writes:

> I have in mind the kind of 'condensation' of motivation into metaphoric images or sequences of images…, the relation that exists in Freudian dream-work between manifest dream material and latent dream content. Just as in dreams certain gestures and incidents mean something by their structure and sequence, rather than by what they literally represent, the melodrama often works … by a displaced emphasis, by substitute acts, by parallel situations and metaphoric connections.
>
> (Elsaesser 1972: 11)

I would like to refer back to the three motifs so far considered in the context of these ideas. Home movies could serve as a test case for Wollen's theory of the importance of the visual in Hitchcock. The other films cited which use the motif lay the stress on the *emotional* gap between the events in the home movie and the situation now: contrasting the happiness of past family life, or the intensity of first love, against the emptiness of a man's life in the present. The home movie sequence in REBECCA does not exclude this dimension, but also depends upon the way in which the visual elements in the home movie – notably the way the heroine is dressed – serve to exacerbate the strain between husband and wife in the present. Ed Gallafent's description is exemplary:

> the sequence begins by offering two images of Fontaine. A magazine drawing of a gown for the 'gala evening' dissolves to Fontaine entering the room wearing the identical gown, and then her image on the home movie screen, kneeling, facing the camera in dowdy clothes, cowering even as she tries to feed the geese. The relative status of the two images for Maxim is explicit in his manifestly insincere praise for the new dress (which drives Fontaine into a physical agony of embarrassment), and his approval of her home movie image as potential mother: 'Won't our grandchildren be delighted when they see how lovely you were?'
>
> (Gallafent 1988: 95)

In other words, through juxtaposing a loaded comment (it's the dowdy image which Maxim characterises as 'lovely') over a particular shot in the home movie, Hitchcock creates a tension within the scene itself between the two images of the heroine. It is also relevant to Wollen's thesis that the glamorous image was produced out of a drawing in a fashion magazine, i.e. out of a visual reproduction. Moments later in the scene, the home movie shows the heroine sitting at an outdoor café table – an iconic image of France – and in the present she comments: 'I wish our honeymoon could have lasted forever, Maxim.' At this point, the home movie breaks. The timing is precise: it's as if the break registers Maxim's unconscious hostility to the sexual intimations of the heroine's wish.

The scene is then interrupted by an interlude with the servants, in which the heroine's social inadequacy is once more emphasised. She has kept quiet about a china cupid she broke, which has caused the housekeeper, Mrs Danvers, to blame another servant, and Maxim is angry with her both for her failure to mention the original incident and for her awkwardness and embarrassment in front of Mrs Danvers in this scene. When the home movie restarts, the heroine is hurt and resentful at the way she has been treated, and she begins to speculate about why Maxim should have married her: 'You knew I was dull and gauche and inexperienced and there could never be any gossip about me.' Once more, the home movie is interrupted, this time by Maxim standing aggressively in the projector beam and glaring at the heroine: 'Gossip? What do you mean?' The heroine has not only put her finger on the truth, but implicitly referred to Rebecca, who simply cannot be mentioned in his presence. Throughout all this, the fact that the heroine is dressed glamorously, like Rebecca before her, adds to the irony: her failure to face up to Mrs Danvers; her sense of herself as gauche and inexperienced.

Overall, the scene works by incorporating the imagery and associations of the home movie into the dynamics of the scene in the present. Like the examples Peter Wollen cites – the cartoon in SABOTAGE, the dreams in SPELLBOUND and VERTIGO – the home movie serves to trigger a chain of 'forbidden' ideas. Although these are not, strictly speaking, repressed, they are certainly thoughts which the survival of the marriage depends upon not being spoken: Maxim's sexual-romantic failings; the heroine's awkwardness in the role of mistress of Manderley; Rebecca. As in the other films which include a home movie scene, the home movie itself represents a 'lost ideal'. But here it is a very different ideal for the two people who watch it. For Maxim, it depicts his bride, away from Manderley, as a simple, inexperienced girl whom he can indulge for her inno- cence and sweetness. For the heroine, it is her honeymoon, and the togetherness of them as a couple in love – the image with which the home movie and the scene ends – has patently not continued in their life together at Manderley, where all the signs are that Maxim no longer sleeps with her. Even the china cupid has its place in the dynamics of the scene, its earlier consignment, broken, to the back of a drawer a metaphorical comment on the infertility of the mar- riage. In sum, this is a very remarkable sequence indeed, with resonances far beyond any other home movie scene I've seen in the cinema.

The cigarette lighter in STRANGERS ON A TRAIN is a good example of a motif which is the product of condensation: a focusing, in one object, of a number of the film's concerns. First, as discussed, it serves to lay out the implicit sexual triangle. Second, it functions as potential criminal evidence: both in Bruno's plan to use it to incriminate Guy (part of the familiar falsely accused man plot) and in Bruno's possession of the lighter, which bears testament to his friendship with Guy – Guy, in effect, gave him the lighter. Indeed, in the initial transaction, when Guy first produces the lighter for Bruno's cigarette, it *looks* as if he is giving him it. Third, Robin Wood links the lighter to Guy's political ambitions: referring to the two crossed rackets on the lighter, he notes: 'it is through his tennis that Guy's entry into politics has become possible' (Wood 1989: 87). Finally, one needs to take account of the crucial intertextual point about the motif: as a signifier of a woman's desire for a man. It is implied, here, that Anne's passion for Guy considerably exceeds his own for her; Bruno may indeed be right when he comments about Guy being 'smart' in 'marrying the boss's daughter'. Guy's statement to Bruno just before he produces the lighter – 'I don't smoke much' – could serve as a coded reference to his sexual reticence with Anne. As in a dream, all these meanings are condensed on the lighter.

Milk is the most familiar of these three motifs, because it has archetypal as well as maternal associations. Barbara G. Walker mentions the large number of creation myths based on milk (Walker B.G. 1995: 489). Here one does not need a psychoanalytical reading: the traditional nurturing associations of milk are entirely familiar, a feature of every culture. Hitchcock's hostility towards milk would seem to be of a piece with his suspicion of the maternal: he does not believe in the nurturing capacity of either (➤ MOTHERS AND HOUSES). In the four instances cited, the only person who actually drinks the milk is the hero in SPELLBOUND, and he promptly passes out. On the other hand, as Susan Smith points out, the examples of potentially poisoned (SUSPICION) and drugged (SPELLBOUND) milk do not derive from an inherent property of the milk itself, but from a man having tampered with it (Smith 2000: 99).

Nevertheless, my argument about Hitchcock's attitude towards milk stands. There are other references to milk in his films, but I have been unable to find any which are positive. On arrival at the Buntings' boarding house, the Lodger dismisses the garrulous Mrs Bunting with a request for 'some bread and butter and a glass of milk'. Ivor Novello delivers the line in his best camp manner, loftily waving his hand to signify the dismissal, and I conclude that the reason Hitchcock wanted the line was to emphasise the Lodger as an effete gentleman who would find the consumption of anything more robust than bread and butter and milk quite beyond him. In other words, even this reference is essentially parodic. In THE 39 STEPS, Hannay orders milk for Pamela which she does not drink; in REAR WINDOW, Jeff likewise ignores his glass of milk. In TO CATCH A THIEF, a man in Bertani's restaurant offers Robie milk in a saucer. He is insinuating that Robie is 'the Cat', but he is also taunting him: the offer is like an insulting gesture. Finally, after the ghost town episode in SABOTEUR, Pat is given sandwiches and milk by the sheriff she reports to – and she does drink some of the milk. But the sheriff is, in fact, in league with the saboteurs: in other words, his friendliness is not just deceptive, but positively dangerous – precisely the sort of suspect figure who would offer the heroine milk.

An elaborated motif: the Bed Scene in Rebecca and Marnie

I would like to extend the discussion of melodrama in the motifs by looking at the ways in which one motif – the BED SCENE – is elaborated to the point where it opens up an investigative path through two films, Rebecca and Marnie. Here both condensation and displacement are in evidence in the workings of the motif.

In Part II, I discuss the BED SCENE in Hitchcock. Most of his films have at least one such scene, and their associations are nearly always negative, to do with pain and suffering. The bed scenes in Rebecca and Marnie are typical in this respect, but they also function in a more developed way. First, Hitchcock here uses the scenes in a subjective sense, to explore the inner world of each film's heroine. Both Rebecca and Marnie belong to Hitchcock's 'stories about a marriage', one of Robin Wood's five plot formations. By telling this story in a crucial sense through the bed scenes, and from the heroine's point of view, Hitchcock achieves a distinctive insight into the workings of each film's marriage. Second, the bed scenes enable Hitchcock to focus on female sexuality in the complex and suggestive manner of the finest Hollywood melodramas. This has to be done through intimation rather than directly – hence the use, in Rebecca in particular, of displacement – but it is nevertheless implicit, woven into the details of the scenes.

In each film, there is an early bed scene in which the heroine has a disturbing dream, prompted in each case by her mother (figure). Each film then has later bed scenes which elaborate on the fears in the dream. In Rebecca, the dream – which is rendered purely aurally – is about Maxim and Rebecca or, rather, what Mrs Van Hopper, the heroine's employer (and her first mother figure), has said about them: Rebecca's beauty; Maxim being a 'broken man' since her death. In *The Women Who Knew Too Much*, Tania Modleski discusses the Oedipal material of Rebecca (Modleski 1988: 46-52) and elements of it are already implicit in these early scenes: the heroine feels that she can never compete with Rebecca (structurally another mother figure) in terms of beauty and the winning of Maxim's love.

The later bed scenes at Manderley extend the heroine's anxieties about Rebecca's power. First, her tour of Rebecca's bedroom, guided by the housekeeper Mrs Danvers, who used to be Rebecca's maid and who functions as yet another mother figure. As Modleski points out 'Mrs Danvers wants the heroine to feel the full force of her difference from – her inferiority to – Rebecca' (Modleski 1988: 48), and, at one point, even sits the heroine at Rebecca's dressing-table and pretends to brush her hair as she used to brush Rebecca's. This, crucially, introduces the second bed scene. The task Hitchcock faced was to stress the sense – in the heroine's imagination – of Rebecca's sexual power, and he effects this, necessarily, by coded intimations. (Necessarily, because Joseph Breen and the Production Code Administration had to pass the scene.) Danvers has been telling the heroine about the social life the couple used to lead: 'Sometimes she and Mr de Winter didn't come home until dawn.' And now, as her voice (off) says 'Then she would say "Goodnight Danny" and step into her bed', the camera tracks in to emphasise the photograph of a more youthful Maxim on the dressing-table. The juxtaposition of the photograph – what the heroine is looking at – and Danvers's words enables us to infer the heroine's thoughts. The track in suggests, melodramatically, her own yearning for Maxim, but a yearning exacerbated by her fantasies of Rebecca as the woman he really loved and desired. At this point, Hitchcock cuts to show Danvers inviting the heroine to come over to Rebecca's imposing four-poster bed. What she wants to show her is Rebecca's see-through nightgown, which further emphasises Rebecca's sexuality.

The displacements are from the bed itself, as a site of fantasised sexual activity, to other elements in the scene: a photograph accompanied by a spoken line; an item of clothing displayed in a suggestive manner (Mrs Danvers holds it to emphasise its see-through features). But they make the point: they communicate what is going on in the heroine's imagination. Not only does she feel unable to compete with Rebecca as mistress of Manderley – as in the home movie scene – but she is also completely overshadowed by Rebecca's sexual power. The Oedipal overtones are emphasised in the youthfulness of Maxim in the portrait: this was how the father figure looked when he was in his prime, married to the charismatic mother figure. The sense of the mise-en-scène (the décor; the clothes) as contributing to our understanding of the inner world of the heroine is typical of the workings of melodrama.

Another point here is that Danvers is coded as a lesbian: her butch appearance; her obsessive devotion to Rebecca. This helps account for her hostility towards the meek, heterosexual heroine. This hostility finds its most venomous expression in subsequent developments and, again, these are articulated around bed scenes. We never see the heroine in bed in Manderley, but we do see her on her bed, when she is doing sketches for her ball costume. Mrs Danvers enters and, having ascertained her purpose, suggests that she look at the costumes in the family portraits. In retrospect, we realise that Danvers is being duplicitous:

she wants to put the heroine once more in Rebecca's place in order to humiliate her with her failure to carry it off (➢ PORTRAITS and EXHIBITIONISM / VOYEURISM). After her humiliation, the heroine confronts Danvers, but she ends up sobbing on Rebecca's bed. As she lifts her head and sees where she is – her face has been resting on Rebecca's nightgown case – she recoils, and, in the ensuing scene, Danvers almost persuades her to commit suicide by jumping out the window.

The first of these scenes shows Mrs Danvers approach the heroine when she is lying on her bed and arouse her – through her suggestion about the ball dress – in order to humiliate her in the potent female arena of costume and display. The matching bed scene at the end of this section of the film registers Danvers's triumph: on behalf of Rebecca, she has dealt with the usurper. The man's role in all this is merely to throw a fit when he sees his wife dressed as Rebecca. He is excluded from the dynamics of what is really going on, just as he is absent from all the female spaces in Manderley, including his wife's bedroom (an indication of the non-sexual nature of the marriage). There would seem to be a charged sexual scenario being enacted here, and Hitchcock's judicious use of the beds adroitly draws attention to it.

We can now see that the anxieties registered in the film's first bed scene echo through all the subsequent ones. It is in the bed scenes that the inner world of the heroine – which would also include her sketches for her costume: her wish to be glamorous and original – is most comprehensively charted. After the last of these scenes, the heroine learns 'the truth' about Maxim's feelings about Rebecca, which enables her anxieties, finally, to be put to rest. Nevertheless, Manderley is still too strongly associated with Rebecca's power for the heroine to feel comfortable living there. In a late scene, Danvers recasts Rebecca's power as derision, but she still associates it with her bed: 'She used to sit on her bed and rock with laughter at the lot of you.' Accordingly, when Danvers – like the ghost of Rebecca – burns Manderley down, it is significant that the last shot of the film returns us to Rebecca's bed, to show her nightgown case, symbol of her sexuality, being consumed in the flames.

In Marnie, the first bed scene – the heroine's disturbing dream – is signalled by a tapping on the window and Marnie talking in her sleep, saying to her mother that she doesn't want to move: it's cold. Here her mother is actually standing in the doorway, a shadowy, sinister presence, telling Marnie to wake up. When Marnie wakes, she starts to tell her mother about the recurring dream, but Mrs Edgar interrupts her, clearly not wanting to know. But Marnie does say, 'It's always when you come to the door; that's when the cold starts.'

Here, even more directly than in Rebecca, the disturbing dream is activated by the mother (figure). Hitchcock alerts us in the first two scenes between Marnie and her mother – the bed scene is the second – to the likelihood that

Mrs Edgar is the source of her daughter's psychological disturbance: her com-
pulsion to steal; her frigidity. The mother/daughter relationship is one of the
most privileged in melodrama, particularly in the sub-genre of melodrama
called the woman's film. But only occasionally – another famous example is
Now, Voyager (Irving Rapper, 1942) – is the relationship as pathologised as it
is in Marnie. The first bed scene in Marnie ends with a shot through the door
of the sinister figure of Mrs Edgar going downstairs, her slow descent marked
by the tapping of her stick; an image which Hitchcock holds before the fade to
black in order to stress its emblematic quality. This is Marnie's abiding memory
of her mother – almost a witch-like figure.

Marnie has a number of links with Rebecca: the focus on the heroine; early
scenes with her mother (figure); her meeting with the rich, upper-class hero (in
both films a widower), which leads to a highly improbable proposal of marriage; the honeymoon; the return to the hero's family mansion, where a hostile
female figure from the first wife's past is in residence (in Marnie, the figure is
Lil, Mark's sister-in-law, who has her own designs on him). The story told within this structure is however quite different in the two films, and the bed scenes
help chart this. In Rebecca, the scenes suggest that the power of the first wife
casts such a shadow over the hero's second marriage that, the moment the couple return to Manderley, their relationship ceases to be sexual. In Marnie, the
outcome is much the same – Mark and Marnie do not sleep together in
Wykwyn, the Rutland mansion – but the reasons are quite different. Here, guaranteed by the casting of Sean Connery, the husband is a highly sexual figure,
whereas the wife is frigid. Again, however, this is dramatised through the bed
scenes. The next two occur on the honeymoon: the first, when Mark discovers
the extent of Marnie's frigidity (she becomes completely hysterical at the
thought of sex); the second, when he rapes her. As he does this, the camera
moves from Marnie's face to a porthole showing the sea outside; the image conveys something of the desolation Marnie is feeling. We can also connect this
shot with the equivalent traumatic scene in Rebecca, when, after her humiliation by Danvers, the heroine herself moves from the bed to the window – with
the sea in the distance – and is almost persuaded by Danvers to kill herself.
After her violation, Marnie – it would seem – really does attempt suicide,
throwing herself into the ship's swimming pool. In both films, then, Hitchcock
uses the traumatic associations of the bed scenes to push the heroine to the
brink of suicide. In Marnie, this actually occurs on the honeymoon itself, which
ensures that, when the couple return to Wykwyn, their relationship is non-sexual.

In Marnie, the melodramatic material lies not in the heroine's fears of her
social and domestic inadequacies as wife, but in her own disturbed psyche. Accordingly, dreams and free association become the pathways to uncovering the

nature of the disturbance, which stems from a repressed childhood trauma. And, just as the childhood trauma itself occurred in and around a bed scene, so the key dream and free association sequence occurs in an extended bed scene. Immediately preceding this scene, Mark speaks on the telephone to a private detective he has hired to enquire into Marnie's mother: the conversation includes his comment, 'I want to know what happened to the little girl – the daughter.' The ensuing bed scene, at one level, answers that question: it shows us what happened to the little girl. It begins as Marnie again has her recurring dream, but on this occasion Hitchcock partly visualises it: she is asleep in a makeshift bed – that of her childhood – and a man's hand taps at the window. As the camera pans around the room, it changes into her bedroom in Wykwyn with Mark, now, knocking at her door. He enters, and for a moment he, too, is visualised as a shadowy presence in the doorway. He even uses the same words as Mrs Edgar when she stood in the doorway: 'Wake up, Marnie.' However it is Lil, not Mark, who succeeds in getting her to wake up.

The free association session follows this, with Marnie still in her bed and Mark 'playing doctor' by supplying the words to trigger the associations. It's as if Hitchcock has situated the scene with Marnie still in bed as a way of re-emphasising the nature of her 'problem'. Robin Wood has outlined the key developments in the scene (Wood 1989: 195), but I would like to note a feature of its contents: that, as Marnie free associates, she goes back to childhood, but in a way which seeks to deflect any tensions the words might evoke. 'Water' prompts a series of associations to do with cleansing, culminating with a Baptist preacher's rhetoric ('"And his tears shall wash away thy sins and make thee over again" – Mother used to take me to church twice on Sundays'). 'Air' prompts a critique of Mark masked by a childhood rhyme ('Stare: that's what you do. You stare and blare and say you care but you're unfair ...'), a rhyme which surely refers to the childhood resentment of being stared at (see Opie, I. & P. 1959: 184). 'Sex', as Wood notes, begins to break down her resistance: after the defensive responses ('Masculine, feminine. Adam and Eve. Jack and Jill'), Marnie suddenly feels vulnerable and – still in the language of the playground – is much more aggressive: 'I'll slap your filthy face if you come near me again, Jack.' The scene then moves swiftly to the point where Mark's 'Red!' produces a distraught reaction from Marnie, who keeps repeating 'White!' hysterically, whilst climbing up the headboard to bury her face in the fabric behind it. As V.F. Perkins observes:

> the action is a very childish one, closely analogous to hiding one's head in one's mother's skirt, and is related to a childish belief ... that by making oneself blind one becomes invisible, that one cannot be harmed by something one refuses to see.
>
> (Perkins 1972: 77)

In other words, just as Marnie's verbal responses suggest her 'regression' to childhood, so, here, does her physical response. It is this point that Mark rushes over to reassure and comfort her, and the scene ends with Marnie crying out: 'Oh God, somebody help me!' The free association has served its purpose in making her realise that, as Mark has suggested, she is indeed 'sick', and for the first time she genuinely cries out for help.

The childhood trauma is dramatised towards the end of the film through fragmented flashbacks. I would like to look at this final bed scene to propose a reinflection of Robin Wood's argument, in which he suggests that the five-year-old Marnie has already been 'indoctrinated' by her prostitute mother 'with a belief in the filthiness of sex and the evilness of men' (Wood 1989: 177). I would go further. I think the film shows a mother-daughter relationship in which the child has been emotionally abused, and this is symbolised in the ritual of the young Marnie being taken from her mother's bed – hence the cold – each time a client came for sex. Far from trying to protect her young daughter from knowledge of her activities as a prostitute, Bernice Edgar made her suffer because of them. And when one night a storm frightened Marnie, and Bernice's client tried to comfort the upset child, Bernice interpreted the man's concern as sinister, and violently assaulted him.

It is true that this scene is Marnie's memory: it is possible that certain details are still 'censored'. Perhaps the sailor kissing the sobbing Marnie on the neck was intended to hint at a childhood molestation which could not be shown. Nevertheless, what we actually see of the man's behaviour does not seem sinister. Instead, the flashbacks show Mrs Edgar in a state of hysteria, pulling her client away from Marnie and beating him with her fists. In the present, remembering the incident, Marnie says 'He hit my Mama!' But, although the sailor threatened to hit Bernice, what we see are his desperate attempts to control Bernice's own violence, which escalated to belabouring him with a poker. Accordingly, when Marnie, in response to her mother's cries for help, leapt out of bed and herself hit the man with the poker, she was merely continuing what her mother had started.

Estela V. Welldon's *Mother, Madonna, Whore* deals extensively with the ways in which a mother can act in perverse ways towards her child, which can lead in turn to the child growing up to have his or her own 'perverse' symptoms. (Welldon uses 'perversion' in the psychoanalytical sense, where 'it means simply a dysfunction of the sexual component of personality development': Welldon 1988: 6.) One passage in particular has clear resonances for the character of Marnie:

> The main feature of perversion is that, symbolically, the individual through her perverse action tries to conquer a tremendous fear of losing her mother. As a baby she never felt safe with her mother, but instead at her most vulnerable, experiencing her

mother as a very dangerous person. Consequently the underlying motivation in per-version is a hostile, sadistic one. This unconscious mechanism is characteristic of the perverse mind.

(Welldon 1988: 9)

I would argue that Marnie's behaviour as an adult – stealing from a succession of male employers in order to try and 'buy' her mother's love – may be seen as reflecting the 'hostile, sadistic' motivation Welldon mentions. On the one hand, she is re-enacting, in symbolic terms, the hostility towards the father figure her mother drummed into her. On the other, it was her mother's behaviour which made her 'cold'; one senses that Marnie also feels an unconscious hostility – masked by an anxious seeking of love and approval – directed at Bernice. The film complicates matters further by associating Mark with both the sailors who 'want in' (the knocking at the door; the struggle with Bernice which precipitates Marnie's flashback memory) *and* Bernice (the shadowy figure in the doorway). Marnie's unconscious fear of and hostility towards her husband is thus doubly motivated. Hence the importance of the struggle between Mark and Bernice in triggering the flashback: it enables Marnie, psychically, to separate the two fig-ures, helping to release her repressed memory.

Further insight into Bernice's pathology may be seen in the way in which the little girl Jessie has replaced the adult Marnie in her mother's affections (➢ CHILDREN). Indeed, the sequence in which Bernice lovingly brushes Jessie's hair may be paralleled with its equivalent in REBECCA: when Mrs Dan-vers recalls how she used to brush Rebecca's hair. Just as grooming Rebecca enabled Mrs Danvers to express covert erotic feelings towards her mistress, so Bernice seems motivated by a similar impulse towards Jessie. And just as the scene in REBECCA includes a track in to Maxim's photograph from the heroine's point of view to express her yearning, so Hitchcock repeats the effect in MARNIE, tracking in to towards Jessie's hair as Bernice brushes it to express Marnie's yearning. But when she goes to touch her mother's hand, Bernice abruptly recoils. Then, in the film's final scene, even after the revelation of the childhood trauma, and even though Bernice has just said to Marnie: 'You're the only thing in this world I ever did love', she still cannot bring herself to touch Marnie's hair. The strong implication is that Bernice has erotic feelings for a little girl, but is subtly repelled by her adult daughter.

Also implied by these and other details in the film – notably her pathological hatred of men – is Bernice's (repressed?) lesbianism. And this, together with the nature of the childhood trauma, has repercussions for the heroine's own sexual-ity. In killing the sailor, Marnie in effect enacted the Oedipal crime of patricide. (Five is the typical age at which a child undergoes the Oedipal trauma.) But the crime relates to the negative Oedipus complex (to use Freud's loaded term): it was the father figure who was killed by the daughter, not the mother. Moreover, it's as if she killed him so that she would no longer be displaced from her mother's bed. This suggests that the lesbian overtones should also be extended to Marnie herself. Together with the moment when Lil wakes Marnie after her nightmare, the Oedipal material contributes to a compelling lesbian subtext to the film (➤ HOMOSEXUALITY).

My purpose here has been to illustrate the ways in which the bed scenes may be used to trace an interpretative path through the film. The honeymoon rape scene is obviously crucial in this context; it shows the realisation of Marnie's fears about men – as indicated in her childhood response to the sailor – in a direct, physical form. In contrast to REBECCA, where the bed scenes are dominated by the heroine's fantasies about Rebecca, the bed scenes in MARNIE show the heroine being *bodily* affected by experiences she has no control over: recurring bad dreams, sexual violation, a sobbing breakdown. The reason lies in the nature of the repressed childhood trauma at the root of Marnie's disturbed psyche. Just as the moments in the film when she reacts to the colour red are registering the threatened return of the repressed memory of the sailor's blood, so the bed scenes register the threatened return of her childhood sexual fears. The overt Freudian nature of the subject matter means that it is Marnie's body which is the primary conduit for the repressed material.

In both REBECCA and MARNIE, the bed scenes dramatise the sexual problems in the marriage: in the former through the emphasis on Rebecca's power (it's as if she has usurped the sexual role in Manderley); in the latter through tracing the repercussions of the heroine's own disturbed sexual history. Both films climax with a return to the bed which is the (original) site of the disturbance: Rebecca's bed; Marnie's childhood bed. The return also results in a severing of the power of the repressive mother (figure): through Mrs Danvers' death; through Marnie's remembering her childhood trauma, and recognising her mother's role in the damaging consequences of keeping this memory from her. This severing is crucial to the heroine being able to come to terms with her fears in order to look forward – with the usual qualifications one finds in Hitchcock – to a happier marriage. However, perhaps the most remarkable connection between the two films is that both of them concern the heroine negotiating a version of the Oedipus complex (positive in REBECCA; negative in MARNIE) before her 'happy ending' with the hero. Tracing the bed scenes through each of the films thus takes us to the heart of the psychoanalytical material.

A melodramatic motif: hands

With some Hitchcock motifs, melodrama is infused directly into the expression of the motif in the sense that it is presented in a heightened, stylised form. This is perhaps a corollary of Hitchcock's visual style: the assembling of pre-visualised shots according to a precise editing plan. As a result of this style, certain elements are focused upon in a manner which is 'expressive', charged with affect. In an article published in 1937, Hitchcock himself discusses this aspect of his style. I would like to quote two extracts.

> What I like to do always is to photograph just the little bits of a scene that I really need for building up a visual sequence. I want to put my film together on the screen, not simply to photograph something that has been put together already in the form of a long piece of stage acting. This is what gives an effect of life to a picture – the feeling that when you see it on the screen you are watching something that has been conceived and brought to birth directly in visual terms.
>
> (Hitchcock 1937/1995: 255)

The example he then uses to illustrate this method is the meal scene which ends with Mrs Verloc stabbing her husband in Sabotage, which I discuss under *Food and murder*. After describing the sequence, Hitchcock comments:

> So you build up the psychological situation, piece by piece, using the camera to emphasise first one detail, then another. The point is to draw the audience right inside the situation instead of leaving them to watch it from outside, from a distance. And you can do this only by breaking the action up into details and cutting from one to the other, so that each detail is forced in turn on the attention of the audience and reveals its psychological meaning.
>
> (Hitchcock 1937/1995: 256-57)

As well as commenting on his editing style in general, Hitchcock's remarks indicate that it is the way in which he incorporates certain details into a scene which gives them such a charge. For example, the so-called 'British version' of Strangers on a Train (➤ FILMOGRAPHY) betrays its status as an earlier cut of the film in that it lacks some of the fine detail present in the 1951 release version. One example is the absence of the close-up of the lighter in Bruno's hand as he talks to Anne. Evidently this shot was inserted by Hitchcock at a late stage, but – as noted – it adds a great deal to the underlying sense of what is going on in the scene. In a discussion of the 'unscripted close-ups' in Notorious, Bill Krohn comments on how they '[enter] into the evolving visual paradigm of "the close-up of a detail revealing a hidden drama going on within a scene"' (Krohn 2000: 98).

Many of these unscripted close-ups in NOTORIOUS and in Hitchcock's work generally are of hands. I would like to take hands as my main example to examine the ways in which Hitchcock's staging of action and his editing style serve to charge his motifs with affect. Hands are a peculiarly 'eloquent' motif: not only can they be isolated in close-up, they are also open to a range of gestural meanings. They thus serve as an excellent illustration of the ways in which the 'details' Hitchcock mentions contribute to the overall impact of a scene.

Hitchcock's films are full of images of hands, in close-up and otherwise, and repeatedly they are shown in a manner which is 'expressive', going beyond the naturalistic gestures considered appropriate for the cinema into a more theatrical style of gesture. In nineteenth-century theatrical melodrama, hand gestures were coded: in *Stars*, Richard Dyer illustrates 'The Delsarte codification of melodrama's repertoire of gestures' (Dyer 1979: 157). Although such formal stylisation had ceased in films before Hitchcock began directing in 1925, there is no doubt that he was extremely sensitive to the nuances of gesture, and it could be argued that his formative years as an avid theatre-goer served to familiarise him with the conventions, and that his own expressive use of hands had its roots in such conventions. Hitchcock was also influenced by the German Weimar cinema of the late 1910s and early 1920s: acting as well as imagery in these films was frequently highly stylised; again, we would expect elements of this stylisation to find their way into Hitchcock's work, particularly his early films. For example, before the Lodger orders bread and butter and milk, his whole person registers his irritation at Mrs Bunting's chatter by stiffening, whilst his hands extend in front of him, flexed like claws. It is an animal-like reflex, but its enactment by Ivor Novello suggests, rather, that the Lodger is a supersensitive soul who has had a rather tiring day and he would like, now, to be left in peace. In fact, Novello treats us to a whole repertoire of exquisite hand gestures during the movie, and one senses a degree of sadism on Hitchcock's part when he finally has his star handcuffed, thus preventing him from continuing the practice (➤ HANDCUFFS AND BONDAGE).

Novello's highly stylised, self-conscious use of gesture I would term Expressionist in the sense that it evokes the aesthetics of the German Expressionist cinema. In later Hitchcock films we only find such extreme Expressionist stylisation occasionally, as in the scene of Miriam's murder in STRANGERS ON A TRAIN. As Bruno strangles her, Hitchcock shows the murder through one of the lenses of Miriam's spectacles, which have fallen off: 'The shot is one of the cinema's most powerful images of perverted sexuality… It ends with Bruno's hands enormous in the lens as he moves back from the body' (Wood 1989: 90). It is this overt visual distortion of Bruno's gloved hands in particular which shows the German Expressionist influence, recalling as it does the famous image from NOSFERATU (F.W. Murnau, 1922), where we see the elongated shadow of

Nosferatu's hand as he mounts the stairs to the heroine's bedroom. The sickness in Bruno, in other words, is fleetingly associated with that in Nosferatu: see LIGHT(S) for further links between the characters.

However, examples which evoke the more general meaning of expressionism – external elements serving to express the inner feelings of a character – occur across Hitchcock's work. In *The Melodramatic Imagination*, Peter Brooks argues that: 'In psychic, in ethical, in formal terms, [melodrama] may best be characterised as an expressionistic genre' (Brooks 1976: 55). In other words, melodrama is *inherently* expressionist. This, I would argue, is what is at the heart of Hitchcock's use of hands. It is, in particular, when the hands are filmed in close-up that the stylisation and emotional intensity appropriate to expressionism can be seen. After the traumatic scene in which she shoots her beloved horse Forio, Marnie goes to steal from the Rutland safe. We see her gloved hand approaching the camera as she reaches for the money, but at this point it seems to freeze, and her face in the background registers shock that it won't move any further. In his comments about Hitchcock's hands, Demonsablon refers to their 'autonomous will' (Demonsablon 1956: 26). This scene is a good example: as Marnie looks at her hand, and as Hitchcock isolates it in close-up, it seems to take on a life of its own. To dramatise the tension in Marnie – she wants to steal, but she cannot – in a reverse angle shot, Hitchcock zooms in and out on the money. By now, Marnie's face is sweating with the effort of trying to force her hand into the safe: she gives up, leans against the safe, and Mark's voice in the background announces his arrival. Here the use of the hand is expressionist in the sense that its refusal to take the money dramatises the conflict in Marnie's psyche.

Richard Dyer suggests that there is also a moral dimension to gesture in melodrama:

> Melodramatic performance may be defined as the use of gestures principally in terms of their intense and immediate expressive, affective signification. In melodrama these emotions are also moral categories.
>
> (Dyer 1979: 156)

The refusal of Marnie's hand to take the money also signals a moral change: she no longer sees Mark as someone from whom she can steal. As a result of this change, the way is prepared for the climactic events of the film's final scene. For further examples of the 'moral dimension' to Hitchcock's use of hands, see HANDS, especially the subcategory *Male hands/female hands*.

From such hand gestures, we can readily infer a character's feelings and impulses. Similarly, other motifs which are typically shown in close-up – e.g. KEYS, HANDBAGS, JEWELLERY, PORTRAITS and CORPSES – would usually be integrated into an editing plan which serves much the same function as

Hitchcock's use of hands: to express the inner world of his characters. The meal
scene from Sabotage, with its play around looks, gestures and objects such as
the knives, is an excellent example of this aspect of his films, and one would
probably say much the same of the way he deploys 'symbolically charged objects' in general. It is to a large extent because Hitchcock uses highly sophisticated editing plans to assemble his individual scenes that the motifs become
woven into the fabric of his films in a distinctively expressive manner.

At the same time, the motifs also serve to indicate Hitchcock's own auteurist
position, and in some cases this inflection may be dominant: e.g. BED SCENE,
BLONDES AND BRUNETTES, MOTHERS AND HOUSES and STAIRCASES.
Nevertheless, this perspective does not necessarily exclude the sense of a motif
as revelatory of character – as the example of the Bed Scene in Rebecca makes
clear. Accordingly, with many of the motifs it would be more accurate to say
that there is a double operation: Hitchcock is revealing both the inner worlds of
his characters and his own (usually dark and pessimistic) point of view.
HEIGHTS AND FALLING is an excellent example. The full range of ways in
which the motifs function across his work is discussed in Part II.

Diagrammatic representations

A crucial feature of Hitchcock's motifs is that, collectively, they serve to say a
great deal about the 'world' Hitchcock creates through his films; in some cases
illuminating areas which one feels would have surprised him. They may appear
fragmentary, but they are, rather, part of a complex, a network of associations
which only really emerges when the motifs are considered across the whole of
Hitchcock's work. Although it would not be possible to illustrate diagrammati-
cally all of the ways in which the motifs interrelate with one another, the two
figures are intended to indicate the dominant patterning of the individual motifs across two basic grids: one dealing with locations; the other with characters.

The locations grid merely groups the motifs according to the sites where they
are concentrated. Lowercase letters indicate that the motif also occurs at these
places, but less frequently.

The characters grid attempts something more complicated: to indicate the
ways in which (most of) the motifs serve to connect the key figures of hero,
heroine, villain and the police in a variety of ways. Thus the police typically
bring the hero and heroine together under ENDINGS AND THE POLICE. Under CONFINED SPACES there is a quite different dynamic around these three
figures, but all three are nevertheless frequently involved in the workings of the
motif. By contrast, the BED SCENE usually connects the characters of hero,

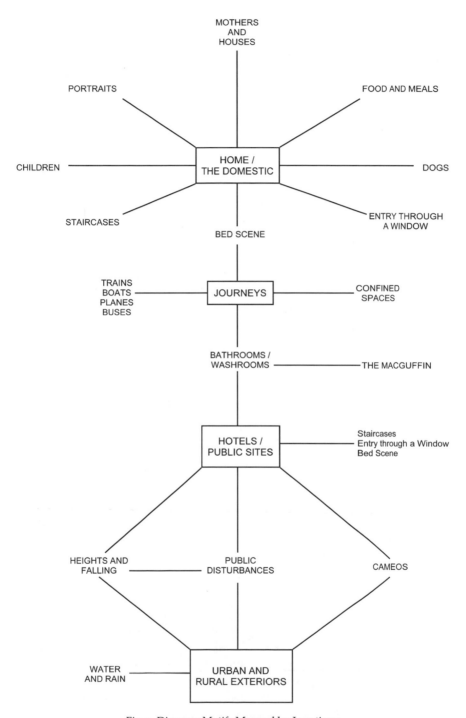

Fig. 1. Diagram: Motifs Mapped by Locations

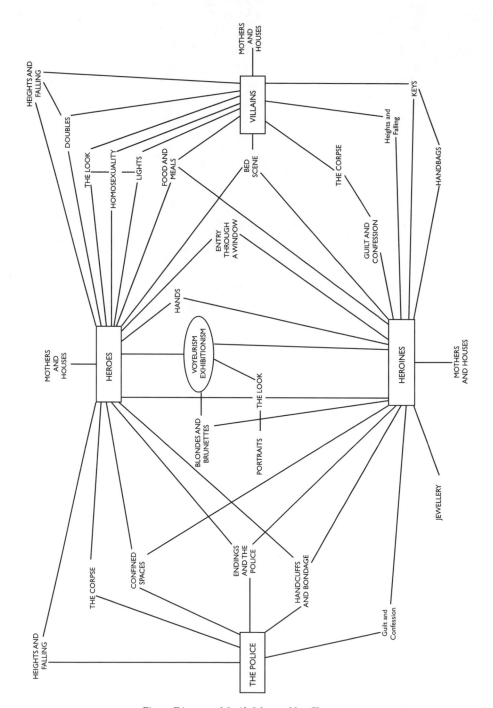

Fig. 2. Diagram: Motifs Mapped by Characters

heroine and villain in separate pairings, so the diagram should be read slightly differently: hero and heroine, hero and villain and heroine and villain are brought together under the motif. FOOD AND MEALS likewise involves all three of these key characters in a variety of combinations.

With other motifs, two of the key figures are privileged. Thus in ENTRY THROUGH A WINDOW, the hero is usually going into the heroine's bedroom. The HANDS motif is used to connect the hero and heroine much more than any other characters. VOYEURISM AND EXHIBITIONISM connect hero and heroine in a frequently complementary manner; Hitchcock's BLONDES in particular are a powerful source of attraction for the hero. KEYS serve to connect the heroine and the villain (villainess in Under Capricorn) more often than not.

Where the motif is listed more than once, as with THE CORPSE, this is to indicate a different sort of link for the relevant figures. For the heroines, the dominant link is with the villains, and an additional feature is shown here: that the heroine's relationship to a corpse is typically mediated by GUILT. With the heroes, the police provide the dominant connection, since the hero is usually falsely accused of the murder and is in flight from corpse and police. Guilt is not usually involved. With HEIGHTS AND FALLING, the villain typically seeks to make the hero fall; the police, by contrast, are usually concerned witnesses to the fall, and may even actively intervene, as in Rear Window. For the heroines, this motif is not so strongly linked to another of the key figures, but a lower-case link to the villains indicates that there is, nevertheless, such a connection on some occasions.

Connections between the motifs indicate another sort of link. That shown between HEIGHTS AND FALLING and DOUBLES for the hero and villain refers to the fact that Hitchcock's preferred method of 'dealing with' the double is through a death fall in the presence of the hero (on one occasion, the heroine). That between HOMOSEXUALITY and LIGHTS and these two characters is to stress the very strong connection between these two motifs, especially when the hero and the villain are involved. THE LOOK is privileged in that it is shown twice and is connected to another motif on both occasions. Between the heroes and the heroines, the look is directed overwhelmingly from the former to the latter. In addition, for both these figures, PORTRAITS are mobilised through the look. With the heroes and villains, THE LOOK is connected to HOMO-SEXUALITY, a further reflection of the sexualisation of the look in Hitchcock (➢ *Espionage and the look* under HOMOSEXUALITY for details). I have drawn relatively few of these interconnections, but that is only because there are so many individual links that the diagram would become unhelpfully cluttered. I have concentrated on those links which occur across a significant number of films. Links between the motifs may also be gleaned from the subheadings under some of the motifs, e.g. *Food and guilt*.

I have included two more or less autonomous links for the heroines: JEWEL-
LERY and HANDBAGS. Handbags in particular are something the heroines
seek to keep private, although men have a nasty habit of putting their hands in
them. Jewellery is rather more complicated: since the jewellery may well be a
gift, the heroine's control over it may well be unstable. Nevertheless, there is
not a dominant interconnection between the heroine's jewellery and another of
the key figures.

Finally, the absence of a motif on this diagram does not mean that it is not
important to any of the figures. It simply means that there isn't a recurring link
between the motif and two of the figures. STAIRCASES is a major Hitchcock
motif, but it does not function in such a way as to fit the Characters diagram.
Similarly with PUBLIC DISTURBANCES. Although the hero and/or heroine
and/or villain is almost invariably present for this motif, it is essentially a social
rather than a personal motif and so I have not included it on the diagram.

Overview of the key motifs

My general argument is that a psychoanalytical reading of Hitchcock's motifs
helps reveal the resonances, undercurrents and associations. In a number of examples, the motif is sexualised: ENTRY THROUGH A WINDOW, EXHIBI-
TIONISM / VOYEURISM / THE LOOK, HANDCUFFS AND BONDAGE,
KEYS AND HANDBAGS. One could even say the same of THE MACGUFFIN:
when it is an object, it frequently hints at a sexual meaning. The sexualisation of
(elements of) Hitchcock's cinema is well-known, but it almost always has a disturbing edge or forbidden undercurrents to it. On the one hand, this is a reflection of the general sense in Hitchcock that sex is fraught with difficulties, or
displaced into other actions (notoriously, violence); on the other, the coding necessary to 'smuggle in' a sexual subtext allows the director to allude to areas
which would otherwise be impossible because of censorship considerations.

The sense that Hitchcock's films, like dreams, deal (in Wollen's phrase) in 'the
rhetoric of the unconscious' is also relevant to those motifs which touch on the
unconscious and the repressed: DOUBLES, LIGHT(S), WATER AND RAIN.
Other sites for 'the return of the repressed' include BED SCENES and *Bathrooms*
(under CONFINED SPACES). 'The repressed' in these examples relates both to
the individual characters – e.g. the sense that the double is enacting the unconscious wishes of the protagonist – and to the culture generally: e.g. the notion
that the chaos world lies just underneath the surface of the everyday world.
PUBLIC DISTURBANCES are another sort of example. They function in a social

sense like the return of the *suppressed*: the veneer of politeness and decorum cracks, and chaos ensues.

One motif in particular – THE CORPSE – frequently marks the entrance of a protagonist into the chaos world. HEIGHTS AND FALLING often suggest the sense of the abyss: another metaphor for the chaos world. Other motifs which are linked to the dangers of the chaos world include STAIRCASES (which regularly lead to a 'sinister domain'), VOYEURISM (looking into the chaos world) and houses with hostile mothers or mother figures in them (➤ MOTHERS AND HOUSES). TRAINS are used to condense the chaos world into a specific set of threats, such as murder attempts, or the dangers of espionage activities. BOATS are frequently associated with physical distress: sickness, deprivation, the threat of being drowned.

Embodiments of a forbidding cultural superego, the police are often implicated in creating the chaos world. They are cited as threatening superego figures under a number of motifs, especially CONFINED SPACES. Nevertheless, ENDINGS AND THE POLICE also notes their role on occasions as gatekeepers out of the chaos world.

Hitchcock's evocation of childhood fears is discussed under CONFINED SPACES, HEIGHTS AND FALLING and STAIRCASES. These fears lead to a consideration of the role of parent figures in his work: such figures enter into the films both in an Oedipal sense and as (frequently forbidding) figures of authority. Their power can indeed be formidable, and is also discussed under MOTHERS AND HOUSES, STAIRCASES and PORTRAITS. Oedipal overtones in Hitchcock occur across his work: further instances are cited under e.g. THE CORPSE and THE MACGUFFIN.

Truffaut makes a connection between the fears in Hitchcock's work, the unconscious and fairy tales (Truffaut 1968: 218-19). There are indeed features in Hitchcock which suggest the world of the fairy tale: the blonde princess (➤ BLONDES AND BRUNETTES); the wicked witch (➤ MOTHERS AND HOUSES); the hero's quest; the role of (often working-class) helpers (➤ ENTRY THROUGH A WINDOW). But a magical agent such as THE MACGUFFIN, far from bestowing power to those who possess it, seems in Hitchcock more like a curse. Typically, he introduces a darker than usual inflection of familiar elements.

Other motifs which can be traced in origin back to Hitchcock's childhood are GUILT AND CONFESSION (his Catholic upbringing) and TRAINS AND BOATS (a childhood interest). I would not wish be too biographical about this: the correlation between an artist's life and his work is a complex one, with layers of mediation on the one hand and the general influence of the culture on the other also needing to be taken into account. Nevertheless, guilt is a major Hitchcock preoccupation. It is referred to under several motifs, e.g. THE

CORPSE and HANDS, and there is a *Food and guilt* subsection under FOOD
AND MEALS.

Some motifs are discussed at least in part from the perspective of gender politics. Sexual politics is relevant to HANDS, BLONDES AND BRUNETTES, THE
CORPSE, EXHIBITIONISM / VOYEURISM / THE LOOK and SPECTACLES.
These motifs illustrate both the positive and the negative aspects to Hitchcock's
male/female relationships, but again there are wider cultural features in play.
Homosexual undercurrents are one of the most persistent and significant fea-
tures to Hitchcock's films. They are discussed to a substantial extent not only
under HOMOSEXUALITY, but also under LIGHT(S) (which has a subsection
Murder and homosexuality) and throughout several of the TV episodes in AP-
PENDIX I. They are also alluded to more briefly under a number of motifs,
including the BED SCENE, ENTRY THROUGH A WINDOW and HEIGHTS
AND FALLING.

Above all, Hitchcock's motifs reveal a much bleaker world than is usual in
mainstream culture. The STAIRCASES motif is common in both other films
and other art forms, but the traditional associations – of ascents as positive and
descents as negative – do not hold sway in Hitchcock, where the motif consistently hints at the sinister. The sense of Hitchcock's films depicting a darker
world than the norm even extends to motifs such as LIGHT(S) and WATER,
the connotations of which are overwhelmingly positive in the culture – but not
in Hitchcock. The BED SCENE in his films is associated primarily with pain and
suffering, and very rarely indeed with pleasure.

Hitchcock's inflection of STAIRCASES and the BED SCENE also reflects on
the representation of the domestic in his films, which is at best troubled, at
worst traumatic. Just as his view of married life is 'bleak and skeptical' (Wood
1989: 246), so the associations of those motifs which enter into the domestic
sphere tend to be negative. MOTHERS and mother figures are usually hostile,
threatening figures, and the houses they occupy are to a greater or lesser extent
infected by this hostility. The representations of CHILDREN vary, but few are
entirely positive. Even FOOD is rarely simply enjoyed, but used, rather, metaphorically, e.g. to express the tensions in a marriage or other relationship, or to
suggest macabre undertones to a scene. Similarly, MEALS sometimes become
settings for the return of the suppressed: when someone comes out with
'bottled up' feelings in a vehement fashion. Perhaps DOGS emerge most positively here, a strong indication of Hitchcock's personal feelings.

There are two contrasts in the motifs which underscore Hitchcock's problems
with the domestic. First, the difference between the treatment of bathrooms and
washrooms in domestic and non-domestic spaces; second, the contrasting overtones to the parallel acts of ENTRY THROUGH A WINDOW and ascending
STAIRCASES. There are a couple of exceptions in Hitchcock's early films, but

otherwise scenes actually set in a bathroom or washroom only occur away from home. The domestic bathroom, it would seem, has little interest for him; by contrast, in hotels and other non-domestic settings, a voyeuristic fascination with the bathroom comes into play. Equally, just as entrances through a window – surreptitious entries into a house – are overwhelmingly sexual in import, ascents of staircases within a house are not: except on a very few occasions and then usually in a compromised sense.

Finally, in some cases the positioning of the motif is significant: CAMEO APPEARANCES; some of the journeys under TRAINS AND BOATS / PLANES AND BUSES. The structural patterns to Hitchcock's narratives is nevertheless another project: I only touch on it here. However, I have already discussed the close structural similarities between two Hitchcock films in 'The Stolen Raincoat and the Bloodstained Dress: YOUNG AND INNOCENT and STAGE FRIGHT' (Walker M. 1999: 187-194).

Part II

The Key Motifs

I have not attempted to mention every example of a particular motif, but have sought (a) to include all the important instances and (b) to consider the full range of inflections of the motif. Most of the entries also have a note at the end on the motif and the police. Hitchcock's police are famous for their knack of getting things wrong, but the notes nevertheless cover the full range of police representations in his films, including their occasionally more helpful efforts.

BED SCENE

Fig. 3. Still: THE 39 STEPS: Bed scene and corpse. Hannay (Robert Donat) is woken by Annabella Smith (Lucie Mannheim) who warns him and then dies on top of him.

The first bed scene in Hitchcock is when Jill shares Patsy's bed in THE PLEASURE GARDEN. As Truffaut has suggested, with Patsy wearing pyjamas and Jill a night-dress, there are perhaps suppressed sexual undercurrents to the scene

(Truffaut 1968: 33). But the rather playful tone of the scene is less typical of Hitchcock than the film's subsequent, more troubled, bed scenes. When Patsy marries Levet, the ensuing extended honeymoon sequence includes a scene of her waking after her wedding night and being tended by him. Levet seems considerate, but the honeymoon sequence overall serves, rather, to emphasise his moral corruption: in fact, he has little time for Patsy's feelings – all he is interested in is sex. Even at this point in his career, Hitchcock was not only critical of male sexuality but quite prepared to show a honeymoon, that most privileged of romantic experiences, in a negative light.

Later bed scenes are darker. Levet leaves Patsy to return to his work in a West African colonial outpost; Patsy follows him and finds him in a drunken, dissolute state living with a 'native woman'. She recoils from him; Levet murders the native woman (➤ WATER). As this occurs, Patsy is nursing the bed-ridden Hugh, Jill's ex-fiancé, and Hitchcock effects a brilliant juxtaposition between Levet's murderous hands and Patsy's caring ones (➤ HANDS). This also leads to juxtaposed bed scenes. As Patsy nurses Hugh, the latter in his fever thinks that she is Jill. This is cross-cut with Levet hallucinating that the native woman is coming back to haunt him, and she first appears, ghost-like, over his bed. Levet then comes to reclaim Patsy from Hugh, arriving just as Patsy – acting 'as' Jill – responds to Hugh's request and kisses him. The kiss makes Hugh realise who Patsy is, but provokes Levet into threats of violence: Patsy is obliged to return home with him. We next see Levet back in his own bed; Patsy lights a lamp. This wakes him, and he now hallucinates the native woman emerging from the bed to point at some swords on the wall, which he takes as a sign that he should murder Patsy.

Although Levet is the villain and the native woman his victim, there is, nevertheless, a rather suspect ideological undertow to this sequence: the notion that a white man in the colonies is prone to drunken and sexual dissolution – or, in Hugh's case, a disabling fever. Even so, it is striking that Hitchcock should focus both Levet's decline into 'madness' and Hugh's suffering around bed scenes. For each, the bed is a site of torment. In fact, the outcome for Hugh is positive: his fantasy that the faithless Jill has returned to him is replaced by the reality of the caring Patsy. But the outcome for Levet is death: Patsy is only saved from his murderous attack when another white man arrives and shoots him. At this point, improbably, Hugh is brought on his sick bed to reunite with Patsy. Her kiss did the trick: he now seems on the way to recovery.

The negative associations to the bed scenes are no less in evidence in THE LODGER. Here there are three such scenes: one for each mother, one for the Lodger. Chronologically the first is when the Lodger's mother, dying from the shock of her daughter's murder, imparts to him her deathbed wish: to find the murderer. Shown in flashback, this is the imperative which lies behind the

Lodger's activities in the present; in effect, it generates much of the narrative. Daisy's mother's scene concerns her growing anxieties about the Lodger: alone in her bed (her husband is out working) she wakes when she hears the Lodger go out, creeps downstairs, searches his room, and returns to bed as he comes home. This is cross-cut with the murder of another golden-haired girl: like a projection of Mrs Bunting's fears about the Lodger. One mother asks him to find the Avenger; the other thinks he is the Avenger: these bed scenes thus provide two nodal points, summarising the action. But what the mothers actually experience in the bed is death and acute anxiety. Similarly with the third bed scene: in the film's penultimate scene, the Lodger is in a hospital bed, suffering from 'severe nervous strain'.

Both these sets of examples are entirely typical. Almost every Hitchcock film has at least one bed scene and, throughout his career, the bed is a 'site of disturbance', associated, more often than not, with pain, suffering and death. Of course, censorship considerations meant that, in most of his films, Hitchcock could not associate the bed with sexual pleasure. Nevertheless, scenes in which we see the bed used 'innocently', as in countless examples in the cinema – e.g. simply to sleep in, or sit on – are rare. There is almost invariably something else going on and, more often than not, this is painful or otherwise distressing for the individuals concerned.

The British films do, however, have a number of comic bed scenes. The deathbed wish imparted to the housekeeper Minta in THE FARMER'S WIFE is, 'Don't forget to air your master's pants.' In CHAMPAGNE, whilst her father in pyjamas does press-ups, the Girl decides to make the bed, including turning the mattress, so that he is buried under bedding. Sir John's cup of tea in bed in MURDER! is interrupted by the noisy activities of one landlady, five children and a kitten (➤ CHILDREN). In WALTZES FROM VIENNA, the Prince thrashes around in bed, acting out his dream of fighting a sword duel. At the Balkan inn where English tourists Caldicott and Charters find themselves obliged to stay in THE LADY VANISHES, they have to share both a double bed and a single pair of pyjamas, and to cope with the uninhibited intrusions of the non-English speaking maid. Hitchcock then cuts to another bed scene: the meeting of hero and heroine. Displaced from his own room by Iris's complaints about the noise of the peasant dance he was conducting, Gilbert wakes her and, by way of revenge, shows every intention of sharing her bed with her. Similarly, in THE 39 STEPS, Hannay and Pamela, handcuffed together, are forced at an inn to occupy the same double bed despite her objections (➤ HANDCUFFS AND BONDAGE). It is perhaps not surprising that Hitchcock's feuding couples should find themselves feuding on or around a bed. These are not however the dominant examples of the motif.

Other examples in the British movies are not so light-hearted. In both CHAMPAGNE and RICH AND STRANGE, the male protagonist is seasick, which may ap-

pear amusing, but it associates the bed, once again, with pain. This is taken
further towards the end of DOWNHILL, where Roddy lies on a ship's bunk, feverish and hallucinating. And twice in the British movies the motif is associated
with killing. Early in THE 39 STEPS, Hannay, sleeping on the couch, is woken by
Annabella Smith staggering from the bedroom with a knife in her back, telling
him to flee or they'll get him next: she then dies, collapsing on top of him. In
BLACKMAIL, Crewe tries to rape Alice on his bed, a scene which culminates in
her knifing and killing him.

The ways in which the last two scenes convert (potential) sex into a violent
killing is an extreme illustration of the dangers associated with the bed in
Hitchcock (➤ THE CORPSE for a discussion of the impact of the corpse on each
protagonist). But the example I would like to consider here is DOWNHILL. In the
Bed Scene in Part I, I suggest that the bed scenes in REBECCA and MARNIE help
dramatise the troubled inner worlds of each heroine. Roddy's hallucinations in
DOWNHILL are similar. The hallucinations – mixed with fragmented memories
of his encounters with women – are of two kinds. In one example, he fantasises
that the women – and his sexual rival Archie – are grouped together round a
table, dividing up his money and mocking him (the disturbing ideological overtones here are discussed under HOMOSEXUALITY). The other type of hallucination occurs twice: he sees a man in front of him assume the forbidding face of
his father. At the start of his 'five days and nights in a world of delirium', the
man is a sailor with a knife, from whom Roddy cowers in terror; at the end,
when the ship arrives in London, he is a policeman standing on the dock. Collectively, these images express Roddy's fears: of devouring, voracious women;
of his castrating, punishing father. Here, too, the bed is the site for registering
the terrors of the inner world of the protagonist.

In the Hollywood films, there is an even greater range of traumatic examples
of the motif. In FOREIGN CORRESPONDENT, the bed is the place where the statesman Van Meer is tortured by the Nazis; in NOTORIOUS, where Alicia is confined
after being poisoned by her Nazi husband and his mother. In UNDER CAPRI-
CORN, Hattie shares her bed with a shrunken head; in PSYCHO, as Lila searches
the Bates house, she looks at the puzzling indentation in Mrs Bates's bed and
gingerly feels it. We later realise that this, too, relates to a dead body: Mrs
Bates's skeleton. In REAR WINDOW, the important bed scenes are located in the
other apartments – so that we do not see the key events – but the comedy of the
insatiable bride is answered by the murder of Mrs Thorwald. In VERTIGO, the
first (unseen) bed scene is where Scottie undresses 'Madeleine': 'One of the cinema's most perverse (and most "romantic") love scenes' (Wood 1989: 385). But
the second bed scene is when Scottie has his nightmare and breakdown.

Nazi sadism, mummified dead bodies, murder and breakdown – these are
negative associations indeed. To these examples, one should add those from

the British films which bring in additional traumatic associations: terrifying hallucinations, sickness, dying and sexual assault. In all these darker examples of the motif, it's as if what happens in the bed serves as a metaphor for the terror and darkness in the films; it is in the bed that a character's suffering and pain is focused.

UNDER CAPRICORN provides a specific illustration of the nature of this suffering. Our first sight of the shrunken head in Hattie's bed is a moment of revelation, showing us that Hattie has not been experiencing DTs, as everyone, including her husband Sam, had assumed, but that someone – the housekeeper Milly, we soon learn – has been victimising her. However, the head also functions metaphorically: like a hideous substitute for the child the couple never had, it symbolises the infertility of the marriage. Here the grotesque image takes us to the heart of the Gothic thread that runs through the film. As with the examples of REBECCA and MARNIE, the bed scenes in this film – and others – could be used as a starting point to explore the undercurrents in the films, an exploration which would inevitably reveal further dimensions to the sense of sexual disturbance in Hitchcock's work.

Even mundane bed scenes in Hitchcock tend to have negative associations. In YOUNG AND INNOCENT, Erica lies on her bed and cries herself to sleep, because – as things stand – her chief constable father will be forced to resign his job because of her. The matching introductions of Uncle Charlie and Charlie in SHADOW OF A DOUBT, each lying on a bed, may appear innocent enough, but they in fact serve to introduce the film's incest theme, discussed, for example, by Robin Wood (1989: 297-300). And the scene when Uncle Charlie has breakfast in bed is remarkable for the shots in which Hitchcock frames him against the headboard, so that he seems to have sprouted black angel's wings. As Robin Wood almost but never quite says, Uncle Charlie is the film's dark angel, the structural opposite to Clarence in IT's A WONDERFUL LIFE (Frank Capra, 1946). Even THE WRONG MAN includes a bed scene associated with pain: when Manny gets home in the early hours, he finds that his wife Rose has been unable to sleep because of toothache.

Annabella slumping across Hannay with a knife sticking out of her back is a blunt example of another fear which plays through Hitchcock's bed scenes: that to wake up is to be plunged *into* a nightmare, a nightmare which frequently concerns fears or threats of murder. In SUSPICION, Lina wakes to find that her husband Johnnie has left – she thinks to commit murder. In SPELLBOUND, J.B. wakes to discover that he has lost his memory, and that he has been impersonating Dr Edwardes – this convinces him that he himself must have murdered Edwardes. In I CONFESS, Ruth is roused by her husband to learn that the evidence she gave to the police did not, as she had hoped, help clear Father Logan of the suspicion of murder but, on the contrary, provided them with a motive

(➤ GUILT AND CONFESSION). In Dial M for Murder, the ringing phone which wakes Margot is part of her husband's plan to get her out of bed so that she can be murdered. Those rare characters who do sleep peacefully in Hitchcock's films are almost always either shown to be under threat (Margot's sleeping is cross-cut with Swann, her prospective murderer, entering her flat) or are woken to be confronted with a frightening situation.

With Hitchcock's villains, however, there is a variation of this version of the motif. When Sebastian wakes his mother in Notorious to inform her that he is married to an American spy, Mme Sebastian is secretly delighted with the news: it confirms her suspicion that Alicia is not 'one of them' and she swiftly moves on to plan Alicia's murder. As she savours her triumph, she even smokes, so that the scene borders on the incestuous: she can now reclaim her son (➤ MOTHERS AND HOUSES). Another richly suggestive variation occurs in Strangers on a Train. Guy enters Mr Antony's bedroom apparently to kill him, but in fact intending to talk to him about Bruno, who planned the crime. However, the light is switched on to reveal Bruno, not his father, in the bed. Here, too, the motif is turned back in a sexual direction. Although Bruno is still dressed in his dinner jacket, the gay subtext is plain enough: the map Bruno provided has served to guide Guy, Bruno's object of desire, to Bruno himself, waiting in bed.

In such examples, the bed functions as a site of disturbance in a slightly different sense: along with a number of features in Hitchcock's films, it marks a point of transition either into the chaos world or to a state of heightened threat within that world. A bed scene like the ending of Sunrise (F.W. Murnau, 1927) – where the arrival of dawn marks the reunion of the family – is absolutely unthinkable in Hitchcock. Despite the occasional comic bed scenes, this is one of his motifs which has the fewest number of positive examples. The best one can come up with are scenes which are hopeful: the outcome of Erica's bed scene when Robert comes in through the window (➤ ENTRY THROUGH A WINDOW), a later bed scene in The Wrong Man, when Manny's son comes in to tell him what a great father he is and, finally, the scene in The Birds when Melanie brings Lydia tea in bed after the latter's traumatic encounter with Dan Fawcett's corpse. Despite Lydia's heightened state of anxiety, both women in this scene take crucial steps towards getting to know one another better (➤ MOTHERS AND HOUSES).

Couples and beds

The murderousness (or feared murderousness) of the husbands in Notorious, Dial M for Murder and Suspicion is registered in the bed scenes cited, and the motif is also used to comment on Hitchcock's other married couples. In Sabotage, the motif is associated with Verloc's deceptiveness towards his wife: he lies on the marital bed in the blackout his sabotage has created and denies to her that he has been out. Mr and Mrs Smith offers a screwball example: it begins with Ann Smith in bed, but she has been there for three days in a hostile sulk; in the meantime, a frustrated, unshaven David Smith plays solitaire on the bedroom floor. At the end of the film, the situation is reversed. Now David is the one using the bed as weapon in a marital game: he is pretending to have a fever, whilst Ann is the one running around in response to his ridiculous demands. In the scene in The Man Who Knew Too Much (1955) where Ben tells Jo that their young son has been kidnapped, he first sedates her and then holds her down on the bed in order to control her hysterical reaction (➤ HANDS). The implicit sexual dominance here becomes explicit in Marnie, when Mark rapes Marnie on the honeymoon bed. In The Paradine Case, two successive bed scenes link the two women in Tony Keane's life: Mrs Paradine, with whom he is in love, and Gay, his wife. The first scene also comments on the oppressive lack of privacy in prison: Mrs Paradine lies awake, a female guard sitting only feet away. Hitchcock then cuts to Gay in bed, also awake. But, as she hears Tony approaching, she closes her eyes so that he won't come to bed with her. She is punishing him for his growing obsession with Mrs Paradine.

Lying behind these little scenes is the sense that married life in Hitchcock is constantly in a state of tension and conflict, and – contrary to Mark's comments on the honeymoon in Marnie – it is indeed in the bedroom that the battle lines are drawn. Apart from Rebecca (➤ Bed Scene in Part I), there is, I think, no Hitchcock film with a significant married couple which does not have a bedroom scene between them of some kind, varying from the parodic (the drunken misunderstanding over praying at the bedside in Rich and Strange) to the Gothic (the climactic struggle in Hattie's bedroom in Under Capricorn: ➤ KEYS). But it is extremely difficult to find even one such scene which is genuinely happy and free from tension. The first scene between Tony and Gay may well be the best example (➤ Couples and staircases).

Even Hitchcock's honeymoons are, at best, deceptively happy, as in The Pleasure Garden. In fact, Hitchcock's usual pattern is to elide the honeymoon, and move on to a post-honeymoon scene which shows things beginning to go wrong, as in Downhill, Easy Virtue and Suspicion. Rebecca represents the most sophisticated variation here: we only see the honeymoon through the chaste mediation of the home movie, but it is explicit that the happiness apparent in it has since faded (➤ *Home Movies* in Part I). The two other significant honeymoons in Hitchcock's films are more brutally represented. The 'bloody honeymoon cruise' (Mark's words) in MARNIE is discussed under the *Bed Scene* in Part I. Hattie herself tells the story of her honeymoon in UNDER CAPRICORN, describing how it was violently interrupted by the arrival of her brother, who attempted to shoot her. In self-defence, she shot and killed him, which caused her to have a nervous breakdown. By the time she had recovered, her husband Sam, who took the blame for the killing, had been convicted and was en route to the penal colony in Australia. Here the honeymoon turned into such a nightmare that the marriage never recovered; at least, not until the end of the film, many years later.

The pretend honeymoon at Dr Brulov's house in SPELLBOUND merits a separate mention. Here, where sex could not occur, the sexuality is displaced into substitutions. With Constance asleep in the bed, J.B. gets up from the couch and goes into the bathroom. As he starts to shave, he is subjected to a barrage of sexual symbols, beginning with the foam on his shaving-brush (➤ CONFINED SPACES). Driven from the bathroom by the force of these, he returns to the bedroom. Clutching his razor in an overtly phallic way, he looks intently at Constance, the lines on the bedcover directing his gaze to her face. This is an emblematic Hitchcock bed scene: the heroine is indeed peacefully asleep, but the hero's gaze at her is ambiguously both desiring and murderous, the latter emphasised by the substitution of razor for phallus.

The relaxation of censorship in the 1960s allowed Hitchcock to show a couple in or on a bed either during or after sex, but the darker overtones are still rarely far away. PSYCHO, TORN CURTAIN, TOPAZ and FRENZY all have such scenes, but in three of the films the woman is subsequently murdered: only Sarah in TORN CURTAIN escapes this fate. To state the link in such terms is to raise the difficult issue of Hitchcock and misogyny: why is it only his women who are killed after sex? Each of these deaths arises out of a specific set of circumstances, and with a specific type of killer; each is also very powerful and moving: there is no sense in which we are invited to derive secret satisfaction from the killing. Nevertheless, it still seems to be the case that Hitchcock expects his heroines to carry more of the burden of guilt for sex. The distinctive relationship between sex, guilt and murder in Hitchcock is discussed further under THE CORPSE.

Overall, women also suffer more in the actual bed scenes themselves, but the imbalance between the sexes is not as great here as one might have anticipated. In general, men are more likely to experience inner physical pain such as seasickness or illness; women are more likely to be victims of the violence of others. But both suffer from nightmares, and both experience the shock of the traumatic awakening. The sense of the bed as a site of disturbance is also registered in the

Fig. 4. Still: SPELLBOUND: Bed scene and trauma. In a trance, holding a razor,
J.B. (Gregory Peck) gazes at the sleeping Constance (Ingrid Bergman).

examples where it is the setting for the return of the repressed, from Levet's
hallucinations of the native woman to Marnie's nightmares.

Finally, as if to emphasise the importance of the motif, three of Hitchcock's
later films include a bed scene at the end. In NORTH BY NORTHWEST, Roger
hauls Eve up to the top sleeping bunk on a train: it is their honeymoon, and
Hitchcock celebrates by showing the train enter a tunnel, an image which he
has famously admitted is 'phallic' (Hitchcock 1959: 24; quotation cited in Wood
1989: 131). This is indeed a genuinely happy ending and a genuinely happy bed
scene, but it only lasts a matter of seconds.

In FRENZY, the scene is traumatic. Framed by Rusk for the 'necktie murders',
Blaney escapes from jail to take revenge. He enters Rusk's flat and, thinking the

figure in the bed is Rusk himself, bludgeons it with a car starting-handle. He then finds that the figure is in fact the naked body of Rusk's latest female victim; at that moment, Chief Inspector Oxford bursts in. Blaney's crisis is short-lived – Rusk turns up, moments later, to be incriminated – but the shock of being caught by the police next to a dead body and clutching a murder weapon is undeniable, and Hitchcock does not entirely let Blaney off the hook (➤ THE CORPSE).

The basic material of the bed scene at the end of FRENZY is then reworked for the equivalent scene at the end of FAMILY PLOT. In this case, the climactic scene is preceded by a brief but crucial bed scene: the reunion of hero and heroine. Blanche has been kidnapped and drugged by the villains, Adamson and Fran, and she lies, apparently unconscious, on the bed in their secret room. But, when George finds his way to her, he discovers that she is fully alert.

Feigning unconsciousness, Blanche stays on the bed whilst George hides outside the room. And so, here it is the heroine who lies on the bed, and the villains who enter the room, intending to take her off to be murdered. As Adamson and Fran try and fail to lift Blanche off the bed – she is surreptitiously gripping the bed frame – she suddenly leaps up with such wild abandon that they are shocked into letting her escape through the door, which George immediately locks. The kidnappers are thus trapped in their own secret room.

Here, as in FRENZY, we have the body on/in the bed, the murderous advance, the sudden shock, and the crucial intervention of a figure from outside who seals the villain(s)' fate. Such reworking of material occurs again and again across Hitchcock's work, not just indicating the depth of his engagement with his material, but setting up highly suggestive resonances. One effect of the parallels here is to emphasise how like a villain Blaney is. So far as the bed motif is concerned, however, it is the inversion which is so striking: the corpse yielded up by the bed in FRENZY transformed into Blanche's wonderfully manic eruption into life. It is very cheering that, after so many negative examples, Hitchcock's final bed scene should be so liberating.

There are two striking points about all these examples: (a) the fact that so few of them are positive (either romantic, or therapeutic, or peaceful) and (b) their prevalence: there are very few Hitchcock films without a bed scene. It's as if Hitchcock gravitates to such scenes because he is fascinated with the sexual, but the sexual, for him, is almost invariably fraught with difficulties. There are bed scenes which are more comic, where harmony is disturbed by such temporary inconveniences as seasickness, or emotional games-playing, but there are many more examples in which the bed becomes associated with physical pain, or nightmare and hallucination, or even with the threat or realisation of murder. The scenes provide a very clear insight into the overall sense of Hitchcock's

Fig. 5. Still: FAMILY PLOT: Bed scene reunion. George (Bruce Dern) finds the kidnapped Blanche (Barbara Harris) feigning unconsciousness on the bed in the villains' secret room. The reunion which sets up Hitchcock's final bed scene.

world as marked, not simply by external threats (the chaos world), but also by the personal sufferings – both physical and psychological – of his characters.

See also APPENDIX I.

Beds and the police

In the opening sequence of BLACKMAIL, Frank and his colleague go to a work-ing-class area of London and arrest a man who is sitting in bed reading a news-paper. As the man starts to dress, a stone is thrown through the window at Frank, narrowly missing him. The stone has evidently come from a crowd of locals outside the house who resent the intrusion of the police. The man grins.

During the climactic siege in THE MAN WHO KNEW TOO MUCH (1934) – again, in a working-class area of London – the police move inhabitants from nearby houses. Two PCs go into a young woman's bedroom, displacing its occupant, and one makes jocular comments about the bed she has just vacated: 'I could do with a bit of a sleep on that meself' (feels the bed) 'Still warm, too.' His colleague recognises the sexual intimations: 'Gertcha – tell your missus about you.' They then drag the mattress over to the window for cover. But the blind flies up unexpectedly, prompting a burst of fire into the room. The PC who was so interested in the young woman's bed is shot dead.

The link between these two moments is undeniable. Although the bed connection may be coincidence, the hostility towards the police is not. The fact that an ordinary citizen threw the stone and a group of assassins fired the shots is secondary. The police were the targets.

Nevertheless, the later scene also shows the police as victims. In the light of the PCs' conversation, it's as if, out there in the darkness, a monstrous superego is just waiting to punish even the most light-hearted and harmless suggestions of sexual transgression.

BLONDES AND BRUNETTES

Fig. 6. Still: DIAL M FOR MURDER: the Hitchcock blonde under threat.
Swann (Anthony Dawson) about to try and strangle Margot (Grace Kelly).

Although Hitchcock's preference for sophisticated blonde heroines did not really dominate the casting of his films before Grace Kelly in the mid-1950s, it has nevertheless tended to dominate the relevant discussions of his films. To my knowledge, only Molly Haskell in *From Reverence to Rape* makes a point of considering Hitchcock's brunettes alongside his blondes (Haskell 1974: 349-354). I shall follow her example, and indeed look at the full range of Hitchcock's heroines, albeit from the rather selective point of view of the implications of their hair colour. Feminist studies such as Tania Modleski's (1988) have explored in detail the characterisations of Hitchcock's heroines and the complexity of his own attitude towards them; my concern here is with his types of heroine, a set

of classifications in which hair colour is crucial. My argument will be that
although there is no question that the blondes are the most important figures
overall, (a) there are different types of blondes and (b) the blondes themselves
come into sharper focus when set against the brunettes, particularly in those
films where Hitchcock includes both, as he does in all his late works. Equally,
the brunettes themselves cover a wide range of different colours, and the variation there, too, can often be significant. Finally, there are even a few scattered
redheads.

Blondes versus brunettes

Hitchcock's evolving attitude towards his preferred type of heroine may be
traced in three articles reprinted in *Hitchcock on Hitchcock* (Gottlieb 1995), all
dating from the English period. In 'How I Choose My Heroines' (1931),
Hitchcock states that the heroine must appeal primarily to the female members
of the audience. He argues against those 'who assert that sex appeal is the most
important quality' of a screen actress in favour of actresses such as Mary Pick-
ford, Lillian Gish, Betty Balfour, Pauline Frederick and Norma Talmadge,
whose success relies not on sex appeal but on 'the fact that they ... appear in
roles which ... appeal to the best in human nature' (Hitchcock 1931/1995: 73).
In the second article, 'Alfred Hitchcock Tells a Woman that Women Are a Nuisance' (1935), Hitchcock is interviewed accusingly by Barbara J. Buchanan, who
went to see him 'to get to the bottom of (his) brutal disregard for glamour, love-
interest, sex-appeal, and all the other feminine attributes which the American
director considers indispensable'. Thus we hear that in THE 39 STEPS Hitchcock
'deliberately deprived Madeleine Carroll ... of her dignity and glamour' and
Buchanan adds 'He is quite unrepentant and fully intends to do the same with
Madeleine in her next film for him, SECRET AGENT' (Buchanan 1935/1995: 79).
However, Buchanan also allows Hitchcock himself to speak. In particular, he
makes two observations which he also echoes in the third article, 'What I'd Do
to the Stars' (1939): he expresses dissatisfaction with the tendency of English
actresses to want to appear ladylike at all times (Buchanan 1935/1995: 80-81;
Hitchcock 1939/1995: 92) and he elaborates a fantasy of directing Claudette Colbert so as to reveal the sluttishness underneath the glamour of her public persona (Buchanan 1935/1995: 80; Hitchcock 1939/1995: 92).

Hitchcock's dislike of actresses with overt sex appeal would remain a constant. Equally, that it is Madeleine Carroll whom he is depriving of her dignity
and that, in his second Claudette Colbert fantasy, he wants to put her into a
blond wig (Hitchcock 1939/1995: 92) foregrounds the 'blond issue'. One can

readily extrapolate from Hitchcock's observations in these articles to the more familiar views he would express later about his preference for 'the sophisticated blonde' who becomes a 'whore in the bedroom' or who 'looking like a school-teacher, is apt to get into a cab with you and … pull a man's pants open' (Truffaut 1968: 189). In the 1930s it is already the blonde who excites him into seeking to break down the glamour and reserve. By the time of the Truffaut interview, the fantasy has been elaborated: now it is the woman who herself breaks through the glamour and reserve to reveal the 'whore within'.

At the same time, the heroines who through their characterisations appeal strongly to women are another important thread to his films. Whatever the heroine's hair colour, she is usually sympathetic. There is thus a tension in Hitchcock's attitude to his heroines: on the one hand, most of them are figures with whom we can identify; on the other, Hitchcock is clearly troubled by 'the ladylike' and wants to see such women taken down a peg. Here one senses the petty-bourgeois thinking of Hitchcock's class origins, which Colin McArthur – referring en passant to Hitchcock's blondes (McArthur 2000: 24) – has traced in certain attitudes underlying the director's work. It is the blonde in particular who focuses such tensions: the young women in his films who do seem less sympathetic are most often blondes of a particular kind, those who convey a sort of class aloofness.

This can be seen in the contrasting characters played by Isabel Jeans in DOWNHILL and in EASY VIRTUE. In both films she is blonde, but whereas in DOWNHILL her character Julia – a stage star – is calculating and manipulative, in EASY VIRTUE she plays the entirely sympathetic Larita, trying to cope with a succession of unsatisfactory men. Under HOMOSEXUALITY, I suggest that her characterisation in the earlier film is more down to Ivor Novello as star and co-writer than to Hitchcock, but it is nevertheless the case that, in retrospect, Julia is an intriguing prototype of the haughty Hitchcock blonde. In the trilogy THE RAT (1925), THE TRIUMPH OF THE RAT (1926) and THE RETURN OF THE RAT (1929), all directed by Graham Cutts, starring Novello and Jeans and co-written by Novello, Isabel Jeans plays an aristocratic femme fatale, using her sexuality to get what she wants: The Rat/Novello is repeatedly her victim. Conforming to stereotype, there however she is a brunette, her natural colour. Since DOWNHILL came after the first two of these films, making her a blonde in it is clearly significant.

In fact, Isabel Jeans was not the first Hitchcock blonde, Daisy in THE LODGER preceded her. Although Daisy is a model, a glamorous profession, she is redeemed from seeming snooty by her class origins, which are, like Hitchcock's, petty bourgeois. Daisy is both elegant and easy-going, self-assured and sexy, a set of combinations untypical of Hitchcock's blondes – at least until Grace Kelly. At the same time, the film's serial killer targets golden-haired young women.

Although he is only a shadowy figure, barely glimpsed in the narrative, he is an unusually distinctive embodiment of the dark forces which threaten Hitchcock's characters and create the chaos world. On the one hand he is like the repressed alter ego of The Lodger (➤ GUILT AND CONFESSION); on the other, calling himself The Avenger, as if his murderousness is in response to some perceived wrong or humiliation, he is like a condensed, perverted version of the male Id, prowling the streets of London.

Anny Ondra in THE MANXMAN and BLACKMAIL plays a different sort of petty-bourgeois Hitchcock blonde. Like Daisy, she is both sympathetic and sexy, but she is also naïve and vulnerable, lacking Daisy's style and self-possession. She seems 'innocently' sexy – more Clara Bow than Jean Harlow – which conforms to Hitchcock's requirement that his actresses are not overtly sexual, but which also leads her into tricky situations. Indeed, Ondra's sensuality generates a charge absent from other Hitchcock films of the era. If she is compared with the other main Hitchcock blonde of the English period, Madeleine Carroll, one can see two general types emerging: Ondra warm, sexy, open, vulnerable and rather reckless; Carroll the more familiar type: cool, sophisticated, aloof. Daisy is somewhere in between.

Beginning her consideration of Hitchcock's blondes with Carroll, Molly Haskell suggests that the director's 'moral coordinates' are:

> blonde: conceited; aloof; brunette: warm, responsive, ... a fascinating switch of the traditional signals. The sexual connotations of the old iconography remain – blonde: virgin; brunette: whore – but the values are reversed, so that it is the voluptuous brunette who is 'good' and the icy blonde who is 'bad'. For Hitchcock ... the blonde is reprehensible not because of what she does but because of what she withholds: love, sex, trust. She must be punished, her complacency shattered; and so he submits his heroines to excruciating ordeals, long trips through terror in which they may be raped, violated by birds, killed. The plot itself becomes a mechanism for destroying their icy self-possession, their emotional detachment.
>
> (Haskell 1974: 349)

In fact, most of Hitchcock's more famous blondes are not virgins, most of his brunettes are not more sexual than the blondes, and very few indeed could even be termed promiscuous, let alone whores. Moreover, Haskell's characterisation of the blondes only covers the 'cool, aloof' figures; she ignores the 'warm' blondes. In the Hollywood films, the latter include Constance in SPELLBOUND, the Grace Kelly heroines in DIAL M FOR MURDER, REAR WINDOW and TO CATCH A THIEF, Marion in PSYCHO and Blanche in FAMILY PLOT. Of these figures, only Constance is virginal, none of them withholds love (or sex) and only Francie in TO CATCH A THIEF (briefly) withholds trust. It is also true that Margot in DIAL M

FOR MURDER has been unfaithful, but this is in the past and all the signs are that she is now perfectly loving with her husband Tony.

These women may all be seen as rather more developed (intelligent, mature) versions of the Ondra blondes. It is with these figures – the Grace Kelly heroines especially – that one senses the passionate undertow to the elegance and poise. They may be middle or even upper-middle class, but they are not discredited because of a temperamental withholding of affection. They should be contrasted with the cool blondes, successors to the Carroll heroines: Pat in SABOTEUR, Charlotte in STAGE FRIGHT, 'Madeleine' in VERTIGO, Eve in NORTH BY NORTHWEST and, up to a point, the Tippi Hedren heroines in THE BIRDS and MARNIE. These are women who do hold back from emotional commitment, or who trouble the hero with their elusiveness.

However, this distinction, too, should be further qualified. Pamela in THE 39 STEPS and Pat in SABOTEUR are indeed at first irritatingly haughty, as they align themselves with the pursuing police at the expense of the falsely accused heroes, but Elsa in SECRET AGENT is more complicated. She has the demeanour of the aloof blonde, but her actions frequently belie this; for example, after she has decided, rather precipitously, that she is in love with Ashenden, her behaviour becomes increasingly reckless. There are other exceptions. Dietrich's Charlotte in STAGE FRIGHT is a special case: she is a glamorous singing star, who carves out her own destiny. No man in the film is worthy of her love; she is perfectly right to withhold it. 'Madeleine' and Eve are each playing a role, the former controlled by a charismatic villain, the latter by the Cold War demands of her country. Indeed, both have the quality of fairy-tale princesses under a spell. I suggest under *Sinister staircases* that Elster's power seems quasi-supernatural; this also applies to the way in which he manipulates Judy as 'Madeleine', who often seems like a sleepwalker. Eve in turn seems under an ideological spell, surrendering her life to the 'higher cause' of espionage. In VERTIGO, the spell is too powerful and Scottie cannot save Judy; in NORTH BY NORTHWEST, a typical fairy-tale outcome is supplied: the hero rescues and marries the princess.

The Hedren heroines are also more complicated than Haskell's summary suggests. Melanie in THE BIRDS is certainly rich and spoilt, but she has already begun to tire of her playgirl persona. Certainly, she sweeps through the early scenes of the film with the style of a woman used to getting her way, but equally she is fully prepared to commit herself to doing what she can when the call comes. And Marnie is psychologically damaged: the whole thrust of the film is therapeutic, seeking a way to account for and cure her hostile frigidity.

In short, the characteristics Haskell ascribes to the Hitchcock blonde – superiority, haughtiness, sexual detachment, emotional coldness – are simply too limited. At best they may be described as a tendency in some of his blondes, a tendency which is only followed up to a point, and even then usually because of extenuating circumstances. As heroines, most of these young women are in fact sympathetic, and even when the persona of the haughty blonde seems to apply, it is usually revealed to be only on the surface: there is a more loving, vulnerable woman underneath.

To complicate matters further, there is yet a third category of Hitchcock blonde: if the hero has a wife at the beginning of the film, she is almost invariably blonde. Examples range from Emily in RICH AND STRANGE and Jill in THE MAN WHO KNEW TOO MUCH (1934) in the English films, to Ann in MR AND MRS SMITH, Gay in THE PARADINE CASE, Jo in THE MAN WHO KNEW TOO MUCH (1955), Nicole in TOPAZ and Brenda in FRENZY (an ex-wife). Although in some of these cases the star persona of the actress includes her blondness (Carole Lombard as Ann, Ann Todd as Gay and Doris Day as Jo are the most obvious examples), the pattern is surely too dominant to be coincidence: most of these actresses would have been cast by Hitchcock, none of them appears in his other films. The only exception to the blonde wife rule is Hattie in UNDER CAPRICORN, where Hitchcock evidently felt the need to signal her Irish ancestry in her hair colour and so he has made Ingrid Bergman a redhead.

None of these wives really fits the already-established types for blondes. Ann is another special case: for Hitchcock, MR AND MRS SMITH was a one-off screwball comedy, and Carole Lombard's star image as the wild and wacky screwball heroine is paramount here; in no sense is she a *Hitchcock* blonde. Although Emily, Jill and Jo anticipate certain characteristics of Hitchcock's late blondes in particular – they are all peripatetic, and the misfortunes which happen to them occur away from home – each, nevertheless, is of a quite different temperament. Nicole and Brenda are both somewhat prim and are contrasted with 'warmer' brunette mistresses – Juanita in TOPAZ; Babs in FRENZY – but the nature of their reserve is different from that of the other blondes. Finally, THE PARADINE CASE is the great exception in Hitchcock's work, in that the blonde and the brunette are both cast the 'wrong' way round. This will become clearer if we look at the brunettes and redheads.

Molly Haskell comments: 'The brunette – Kim Novak (as the "real" Judy in VERTIGO), Diane Baker (MARNIE), Suzanne Pleshette (THE BIRDS), and Karin Dor (TOPAZ) – is "good", that is, down to earth, unaffected, adoring, willing to swallow her pride, even maternal' (Haskell 1974: 349). Apart from Annie in THE BIRDS, I'd question maternal, but otherwise these observations are easier to agree with than those about the blondes. Nevertheless, all these are relatively late in Hitchcock's career and all are in films in which there is also a blonde. What about Hitchcock's brunettes in general?

In fact, there is an English film, WALTZES FROM VIENNA, in which the hero is between a blonde and a brunette, and the contrast between them is quite unlike the later examples. As character types they are typical – sophisticated, aristocratic blonde; simple, unworldly brunette – but the moral values are trans-formed from the Haskell paradigm. Here it is the heroine, Rasi, who is the brun-ette, but she is the selfish, demanding figure, and it is the glamorous blonde Countess who has the hero's best interests at heart. For once in Hitchcock, the heroine is undermined: Rasi spends most of the film using the fact that Schani loves her to try and divert him from a musical career – his real name is Johann Strauss Jr. – to become a baker so that, when he marries her, he will carry on her father's family business. It is only because the Countess contrives to set up a situation in which Schani is a success with a public performance of his composi-tion 'The Blue Danube' that he escapes the petty-bourgeois future Rasi has mapped out for him. Here the sexually seductive blonde is structurally the 'other woman', but it is she who makes the heroine see the error of her ways and accept the hero's true destiny as a gifted musical composer.

Overall, however, the English brunettes do not seem as distinctive a group as the English blondes, even in the late films. For example, the most sophisticated (rich, upper-middle class) heroine in the English films is probably Iris in THE LADY VANISHES, and Hitchcock was obviously happy to leave her as a dark brunette. Although I shall include Iris as a marker of the English period, I shall otherwise restrict discussion of the brunettes to the Hollywood films.

Joan Fontaine in REBECCA plays one of Hitchcock's meekest heroines, and her hair colour and styling fit this: her hair is light brown and is often unkempt and easily bedraggled – as when she arrives at Manderley. She becomes more self-conscious about it as the film progresses, but her attempts to make it more sty-lish are not a success. When she makes herself up to look like Caroline de Winter in a family portrait (➤ PORTRAITS), she wears a black wig in the period style of the portrait. But she suffers acute humiliation in this costume (➤ EXHIBITIONISM / VOYEURISM). Since Rebecca herself was black-haired, the heroine's failure could be seen as symptomatic: as if black were simply too striking a hair colour for her.

This suggests an ideological coding: for the brunettes, the blacker the hair, the stronger the personality. Many dark-haired Hitchcock heroines, including Rasi and Iris, fit this. Carol in FOREIGN CORRESPONDENT, Charlie in SHADOW OF A DOUBT and Juanita in TOPAZ are all relatively strong willed. Likewise Lil in MARNIE, who seems to me a lot tougher than in Haskell's characterisation: she offers herself to Mark at one point as a 'guerrilla fighter', which suits her. In-deed, in perhaps Hitchcock's most overt example of a brunette seeking to dis-comfort her blonde rival, Lil sets up a confrontation at a reception between Marnie and Strutt, Marnie's late employer (➤ EXHIBITIONISM / VOYEUR-ISM).

Equally, other brown-haired heroines – e.g. Lina in SUSPICION, Rose in THE WRONG MAN, Judy in VERTIGO – tend to be quiet and introverted. There are

Fig. 7. Still: MARNIE: Blonde and brunette. Lil (Diane Baker) on the right sets up a charged re-
meeting between Marnie (Tippi Hedren) on the left and Strutt (Martin Gabel). Mark (Sean Connery)
supports Marnie; Mrs Strutt (Louise Lorimer) in the middle.

occasional exceptions – the black-haired Annie in THE BIRDS is relatively self-
effacing; the seemingly brown-haired Connie in LIFEBOAT is undeniably forceful
– but otherwise the coding marks a strong tendency in Hitchcock's films.

Moreover, with the obvious exception of Rebecca – and with certain qualifica-
tions for Rasi – all these women are warm-hearted and generous, which does
indeed seem to be a feature of most Hitchcock brunettes. It is the same with his
redheads: Mary in JAMAICA INN; Jennifer in THE TROUBLE WITH HARRY and Hattie. In general the brunettes and redheads tend to be associated more with domestic settings, particularly in the late films, where they are contrasted with
blondes. Whereas the blondes tend to be glamorous, peripatetic figures, the
brunettes and redheads tend to be located at home, or in the neighbourhood,
which contributes to the sense of availability that they typically convey. Again,
there are exceptions, like Iris, but again we could speak of a marked tendency.
One feels that someone like Charlie in SHADOW OF A DOUBT needs to be brunette; blondness would make her a little too exotic for the role of the typical
small-town girl. It is perhaps for similar reasons that, in the two main Hitchcock

movies which deal (subtextually) with a gay male relationship, ROPE and STRANGERS ON A TRAIN, there is no blonde: she would be too much of a distraction from the relationship between the two men. Instead, in ROPE, it is the male murder victim who is blond.

THE PARADINE CASE reverses the usual pattern: the blonde wife Gay is the loving, stay-at-home figure; the dark-haired Mrs Paradine is the cold, glamorous, manipulative figure. The hero is between the two, but here it is the icy brunette who transfixes him, and the warm blonde wife whom he ignores. A result of Selznick's casting, the reversal is even more remarkable because the novel conforms to the Hitchcock paradigm: Mrs Paradine is a striking Swedish blonde with 'marvellous hair, pale, very pale, yellow with gold lights in it here and there' (Hichens 1933/1958: 31), and Gay's hair is brown. Nevertheless, the very fact that the two women are the opposite way round from the rest of Hitchcock sets up interesting tensions.

Blond allure / blond iconography

Although THE PARADINE CASE is the only example where the casting dramatically violates the norms of the hair colour motif in Hitchcock, there is also a point which has already been touched on: that sometimes a particular colour simply comes with the preferred actress. However, one feels sure that, whenever he had the power to do so, Hitchcock would change any hair colour with which he was unhappy, as with Bergman in UNDER CAPRICORN.

There is even a subtle difference of hair colour between Bergman's other two Hitchcock roles. Although the actress is fair-haired rather than blonde, I have included Constance in SPELLBOUND with the blondes. This is because blond highlights in her hair and Hitchcock's lighting throughout the film make her *seem* blonde. In particular, there is an early scene on a hilltop where close-ups of Constance draw attention both to the highlights and to the fetchingly dishevelled state of her hair. During the scene, she comments: 'People fall in love ... because they respond to a certain hair colour or vocal tones or mannerisms that remind them of their parents.' More romantic, J.B. responds: 'Sometimes for no reason at all.' Then, that evening, she and J.B. admit that they are in love. Not only do Constance's comments thus have a self-reflexive quality, I feel that it is the 'blond allure' of her hair which they foreground. When the couple fall in love, it's as if the blondness has worked its magic.

In NOTORIOUS, by contrast, Bergman's hair looks darker: no blond highlights and a lighting scheme which frequently subdues its natural fairness. Here, too, there is a scene on a hilltop at a similar point in the narrative, but it has little of the romanticism of its equivalent in the earlier movie. The scene terminates with a kiss, but it is a crude kiss, precipitated by Devlin wanting to stop Alicia continuing her bitter comments about his feelings for her. In contrast to SPELL-BOUND, 'blond allure' is denied.

It is entirely possible that the suppression of blondness in Alicia is ideological: in a film about exposing Nazis she needs to be distinguished from the light blondes of Nazi ideology. The sensitivity of reviewers to such blondes at the time is epitomised by critical comments about L'ETERNEL RETOUR (Jean Delannoy, 1943), released in Britain in 1946. The film is based on the legend of Tristan and Iseult and both its stars, Jean Marais and Madeleine Sologne, are strikingly blond, which prompted hostile comments from British newspaper reviewers on its release about 'Nazi types' (see Paris 1983: 100). The film was not released in the USA until early 1948.

Priscilla Lane is another actress who is fair-haired rather than blonde but, like Constance, I have included Pat in SABOTEUR with the blondes. The main reason is structural: Pat is closely based on Pamela in THE 39 STEPS and so she fits the prototype of the cool Hitchcock blonde. In SABOTEUR, however, there is also a genuine blonde in the film. The film is an anti-fascist wartime production, and its whole narrative is set in motion by a blonde factory worker, who gives Barry's friend Ken the eye and distracts him, thereby causing him and Fry, the saboteur, to get entangled with one another and fall over. As a result of the men's tumble, Barry learns who Fry is, and has an address to pursue him to; the address is that of the master saboteur Tobin, and Barry's pursuit will result, ultimately, in the unmasking of him and his fifth columnists.

The blonde's role in all this is intriguing. On the one hand, she causes a disturbance: when the men fall over one another, Barry jokes 'Bottleneck: Mr Roosevelt should hear about this.' Then, as Fry stalks off, he shouts after him: 'Just goes to show you what a little blonde can do to hold up national defence.' Although this, too, is a joke, the stress on the factory production line is vital to the film's message, and it will soon become apparent that it is Fry himself who is sabotaging the defence effort. Inadvertently, the blonde here has helped to finger him. Her importance to the narrative is reiterated in the Statue of Liberty just before the film's climax. Pat explains how she knows who Fry is by telling him: 'It all started with an unknown blonde, an aircraft worker in a factory in Glendale, California…' Fry's response, referring to Pat, is: 'I get it – little Miss Liberty, carrying the torch' (Pat has just read Fry part of Emma Lazarus's poem inscribed on the statue). The film would seem to be making a connection from the blonde, through Pat, to the ideals embodied in the Statue of Liberty herself.

The 'unknown blonde' thus has a certain iconic force. Validated by Pat's citing her at the end, she represents the ordinary factory worker, doing her bit for her country in its time of need. She is thus the epitome of the working-class

American blonde. Pat, who begins by acting like a cool blonde but then shows her mettle by pursuing the saboteurs, helps 'carry the torch' all the way to the Statue of Liberty. The billboards with Pat as model on them which punctuate Barry's journey east help symbolise this: her uncle says that, placed end to end, they would 'reach across the continent'. On these billboards, Pat's hair looks darker. Blondness in the negative sense is then displaced on to the fascist saboteurs, and registered above all in the characterisation of Freeman, who is eager to tell Barry about the 'long golden curls' he had as a child and his reluctance to have his own son's hair cut. It is much the same in NOTORIOUS, where it is Mme Sebastian, the Nazi mother, who looks blonde, as is apparent when she and Alicia first meet. In other words, when linked to Nazis and other fascists, blondness becomes sinister.

The overvaluation of the blonde in popular consciousness is deeply rooted, going back both to fairy tales and to Christian iconography, and reinforced in modern times by blond iconography in advertisements and the movies. Marina Warner discusses the phenomenon in *From the Beast to the Blonde* (1995). Commenting that in fairy tales 'Golden hair tumbles through the stories in impossible quantities', she also points out that 'Among the heroines of fairy tale only Snow White is dark' (Warner 1995: 365). Indeed, blondness attracted so many positive associations that they could become contradictory: 'Although blondeness's most enduring associations are with beauty, with love and nubility, with erotic attraction, with value and fertility, its luminosity made it also the traditional colour of virgins' hair' (Warner 1995: 367). It also had connotations of wealth:

> [On occasions] hair's connotation with luxuriance and fertility becomes material wealth, literal gold and jewels and riches... Blondeness ... with its much noticed sensuous associations with wholesome sunshine, with the light rather than the dark, evoked untarnishable and enduring gold; all hair promised growth, golden hair promised riches. The fairytale heroine's riches, her goodness and her fertility, her foison, are symbolised by her hair.
>
> (Warner 1995: 378)

In fairy tales such hair is golden, but with the arrival of hair dyes, silver and platinum also became options, both still connoting wealth. In that fairy-tale heroines are often princesses or are destined to become princesses, their blondness also carries upper-class connotations. These notions, too, feed into the popular associations of blondness, and complicate the wealth of associations of the Hitchcock blonde.

Destined to become a princess, Grace Kelly is the archetypal Hitchcock blonde. On the one hand, she is beautiful, elegant, graceful and poised; on the other, there is no doubting the passion underneath the sophistication and glamour. When, after a ladylike walk down a hotel corridor with Robie in To CATCH A THIEF, Francie turns to kiss him as she enters her room, she signals her desire in the closest one could achieve under the Production Code to Hitchcock's 'back of a taxi' fantasy. Kelly also typifies the 'allure' of the Hitchcock blonde in other ways. First, although a natural blonde, she lightened her hair. Most of Hitchcock's famous blondes enhanced their blondness through the use of hair dyes, thereby bringing them closer to the blondes of popular mythology. Second, Kelly strengthens the association of blondness and class privilege. In DIAL M FOR MURDER, Tony married Margot for her money; in REAR WINDOW, Lisa's profession leads her to mix with society; in To CATCH A THIEF, Francie is an oil heiress. Such class/wealth associations do not apply to all the late Hitchcock blondes, but they are also important to the glamour of the blonde in VERTIGO, NORTH BY NORTHWEST and THE BIRDS. Finally, Kelly has a 'naturalness' which has also contributed to her star image (see Bruzzi 2000: 206-207) and which enables her, in REAR WINDOW, to move effortlessly from her role as fashion consultant to Girl Friday, shinning up the fire escape in a dress to climb in through the window of Thorwald's apartment. (Producer Herbert Coleman notes in his autobiography that Kelly eschewed the stunt double he had hired and insisted on doing the action herself: see Coleman 2003: 180.) In DIAL M FOR MURDER, Hitchcock cast Kelly, rather conventionally, in a 'blonde as victim' role, but in REAR WINDOW and To CATCH A THIEF he allows her the space to display her considerable talents. She does so with style.

By contrast, Tippi Hedren, Kelly's successor, is cooler and less 'natural'. Referring to the scene in THE BIRDS where Melanie applies peroxide to the wound from the first bird attack, Camille Paglia comments:

> As a bottle blonde herself, she seems to gain strength from the peroxide, which operates on her like a transfusion of plasma. The dye theme appears in Hitchcock as early as THE LODGER, where a serial murderer is stalking blondes: a young woman exclaims... 'No more peroxide for yours truly!' Hitchcock treats blonde as a beautiful, false colour, symbolising women's lack of fidelity and trustworthiness.
>
> (Paglia 1998: 40)

The final comment seems appropriate for Hedren, but not for Kelly. Nevertheless, the greater sense of artificiality of the Hedren blonde in no way diminishes her 'blond allure' for Hitchcock and his heroes. It is this which needs further exploration.

The Hitchcock heroine who expresses blond allure most potently is probably 'Madeleine' in VERTIGO. VERTIGO is also the best film to focus the interplay of blonde and brunette in Hitchcock, since both are in fact the same woman. As John Russell Taylor was one of the first to point out, VERTIGO was extremely personal to Hitchcock, and the operation of blondness in the film is a part of this. Hitchcock has transformed 'Madeleine', a brunette in the novel, into a blonde, and in the later stages of the film what Scottie does to Judy – converting her from brunette back to the blonde 'Madeleine' – is 'what Hitch has done over and over again to his leading ladies' (Taylor 1978: 243).

Mesmerised by 'Madeleine', Scottie ignores Midge, who is also in a fact a blonde. But Midge's blondness seems natural, whereas 'Madeleine' is a platinum blonde, reinforcing the potency of the artificial blonde. Moreover, Scottie thinks that 'Madeleine' is upper class and rich: Elster tells him that he married into the ship-building business. However, this only applies to the real Madeleine Elster; Judy's 'Madeleine' creates an *illusion* of sophistication, wealth, privilege. Indeed, one could argue that Judy as 'Madeleine' also only achieves an illusion of the 'cool blonde'; in the more intimate scenes, where her role-playing becomes complicated by her feelings for Scottie, one senses a reserve which suggests vulnerability rather than poise.

Scottie loses 'Madeleine' twice: first, when he thinks that she commits suicide; second, when the Judy he has transformed back into 'Madeleine' really is killed. His failure is symptomatic. 'Madeleine' is the Hitchcock blonde at her most illusory and elusive; she never shakes off her ghost-like nature. Richard Lippe has argued that VERTIGO makes remarkable use of Kim Novak's star persona: 'Its entire structure depends on a splitting of the identity of the lead female character and the two aspects of that identity correspond closely to the contradictory aspects of Novak's persona', the upper-class socialite of THE EDDY DUCHIN STORY (1956) and the vulnerable girl next door of PICNIC (1955) (Lippe 1986: 10-11). It is nevertheless the case that the 'Madeleine' half of the split is much more closely aligned with the *dominant* Novak star image from PUSHOVER (1954) to PAL JOEY (1957): the seductive, reserved blonde. In effect, 'Madeleine' enhances certain tendencies in that image – mystery; elusiveness – to the point where they create a movie star aura of otherness. 'Madeleine' is Novak as glamorous movie star, and the very fact that the film foregrounds the process of construction in building up her image is also a comment on the operation of the star system: the manufacturing of the female star to satisfy male fantasies. It is only to be expected that 'Madeleine' remains ungraspable, elusive.

The final stage of Scottie's transformation of Judy back into 'Madeleine' is when he insists on her hair being pinned back in a tight coil on the back of her head. This is one of the most resonant hair images in Hitchcock. It is these formally coiffured hairstyles which Hitchcock fetishises with lingering shots of the back of the head, often emphasised through a slow track in. Grace Kelly and Tippi Hedren in particular are favoured with such shots, which are reserved almost exclusively for blondes. It is when Hitchcock introduces Mrs Paradine with a track in to her elaborately coiffured hair as she plays the piano that one is alerted to the aberration of the blonde/brunette motif in this movie.

One of the connotations of such styling is glamour. When a prison guard unpins Mrs Paradine's hair, this is like a defilement: she is being stripped of her bourgeois refinement preparatory to incarceration. Equally, the elegantly coiffured hairstyle may also connote a certain bourgeois self-restraint, so that the unpinned hair is then associated with release. When Marnie rides Forio, her otherwise tightly controlled hair is let down and blows freely in the wind. But when, on her honeymoon, she lets her hair down for bed, this does not connote the sexual release which applies elsewhere in both Hitchcock and the culture generally on such intimate occasions. However, after the riding accident which climaxes with her shooting Forio, Marnie's hair remains down for the rest of the movie. Symbolically, this suggests a lowering of defences: she is thus in a more receptive state to remember her traumatic event.

In VERTIGO, the connotations are different again. Here the fetishistic aspect is very strong, as Scottie goes through all the stages – clothes, make-up, hair colour – of transforming Judy into 'Madeleine' and is still not satisfied until her hair, too, is pinned exactly like 'Madeleine's'. Hitchcock reinforces the fetishisation in his comment to Truffaut that in dressing Judy this way, Scottie is metaphorically undressing her, and her refusal at first to have her hair pinned back is like refusing to take her knickers off (Truffaut 1968: 206). The fetishisation is also implicit in the first close-up of the coil in 'Madeleine's' hair – in the Art Gallery – when it looks both formally forbidding – tightly bound hair connoting non-availability – and vaginal. Scottie dresses Judy as 'Madeleine' in order then to undress her for sex.

So far as the blonde/brunette split works, however, it is explicit that in VERTIGO the brunette is the 'authentic' woman; the bottle blonde the male fantasy construct. The 'Madeleine' that Scottie recreates turns out to have been a fabrication all along. The greater authenticity of the less charismatic figure of the brunette is echoed in later Hitchcock films – e.g. THE BIRDS, MARNIE, even PSYCHO, where Janet Leigh as Marion is simply more glamorous than Vera Miles as her sister Lila. The lure of the artificial blonde – for both Hitchcock and his heroes – is nevertheless almost always paramount. And in VERTIGO, the outcome of Scottie's obsession with the romanticised ideal of the manufactured blonde is tragic.

The blonde/brunette opposition works rather differently in Hitchcock's last three films. In both TOPAZ and FRENZY, as noted, it is the wife/ex-wife who is blonde, but she is not a glamorous blonde: both actresses seem to be wearing ash-blond wigs, which means that their hair stays the same under virtually all circumstances, which takes away its life and lustre. It would seem that Hitchcock wanted to distinguish them both from the warm, brunette mistresses in each film but also from his other blondes. Unlike the famous Hitchcock blondes, and even most of the earlier wives, Nicole and Brenda lack blond allure. They are not unsympathetic figures, but they are self-consciously middle class, seeking to keep up appearances: the ladylike notion again. On the other hand, they also have to deal with either unfaithful (TOPAZ) or spectacularly bad-tempered (FRENZY) (ex-)husbands, which distinctly strains their equanimity. Nicole survives for a happy ending of sorts with the hero, but Brenda is horribly assaulted and murdered, and the pathos of her suffering undoubtedly contributes to our sympathy for her. Overall, however, the blonde/brunette opposition in these two films is essentially gestural, lacking the resonances of the earlier works.

In FAMILY PLOT, Blanche is a blonde; Fran a dark brunette. However, in her role as the super-cool kidnapper (so cool, she does not even speak), Fran wears a long blond wig, which she stashes in the refrigerator when she gets home. It's as if, through this act, Hitchcock is signalling that the 'cool, aloof' blonde is now relegated to cold storage, and it is the warm blonde, Blanche, who has his sympathy and interest. Although Blanche is hardly sophisticated, she still dresses with style and carries off her role as (phoney) clairvoyant with self-assurance, and Hitchcock even allows her a privilege unique in his films: a final wink at the camera (➤ EXHIBITIONISM / VOYEURISM). I also suspect that a part of Barbara Harris's charm for Hitchcock was that she is left-handed. From VERTIGO onwards, all the main Hitchcock blondes apart from Janet Leigh are left-handed: Kim Novak; Eva Marie Saint; Tippi Hedren; Barbara Harris.

In FAMILY PLOT, reverting to stereotype – and explicitly contradicting Molly Haskell – it is the brunette who is 'bad'; the blonde who is 'good'. Although Hitchcock still shows concern for Fran – she was seduced into becoming a criminal by the psychopathic Adamson; she becomes most upset when the latter indicates that he intends to murder Blanche – she does not really redeem herself, and so she is obliged to share in the villain's punishment: locked with him in the secret kidnap room. Only at the very end of his career does Hitchcock play out the blonde/brunette opposition in archetypal terms: the 'bad' brunette locked away below; the 'good' blonde floating up the stairs – accompanied by an angelic choir, no less – to a happy ending (➤ STAIRCASES).

Blondes, brunettes and violence

Molly Haskell's other major point about the blondes is that they are 'punished' more than the brunettes, which certainly does seem to be the case. From the attempted rape of Alice in BLACKMAIL to the murder of Brenda in FRENZY blondes have been Hitchcock's most regular victims. As censorship restrictions relaxed, so these scenes of violence become more explicit, more violent, more prolonged. In such cases, it is not so much Hitchcock as director seeking to break down the glamour and reserve as subjecting his heroines and other young women to a series of brutal violations. Perhaps this is why Hitchcock wanted the heroine in each version of THE MAN WHO KNEW TOO MUCH to be blonde: in the drawn-out suspense of the Albert Hall climax, the focus would then be on a blonde in a state of excruciating agitation.

Such thinking is not just confined to Hitchcock. Because of the overvaluation of the blonde in popular mythology, it would seem that there is more of a frisson in putting a blonde in danger. In the famous monster films of the early 1930s, for example, the heroine is usually blonde: Helen Chandler (DRACULA, 1931); Mae Clarke (FRANKENSTEIN, 1931); Miriam Hopkins (DR JEKYLL AND MR HYDE, 1931); Fay Wray (KING KONG, 1933). Nevertheless, this does not account for the specifics of the threats to Hitchcock's blondes.

Brunettes suffer as well in Hitchcock, but the examples we see are less frequent and generally less extreme. Apart from Miriam's murder in STRANGERS ON A TRAIN – an exception, since she is a rare example of an unsympathetic young woman in Hitchcock – those I would include are Lina's cliff-top drive in SUSPICION (➢ HEIGHTS AND FALLING), Charlie being manhandled by her uncle as he prepares to throw her off the train in SHADOW OF A DOUBT and Juanita's murder by Rico Parra in TOPAZ (for both these ➢ *Held wrists* under HANDS). On the other hand, each of these last three attacks – unlike the blonde examples – is enacted by a man who is emotionally close to the heroine (husband; uncle; lover), so that her fear is compounded by the violation of the emotional trust. This is a consequence of the 'domestication' of the brunettes: when something terrible does happen, it is usually very close to home.

For both the blondes and the brunettes, most of these ordeals are sexualised. Even when the assault does not actually involve rape, it is often filmed to evoke rape: the attempted murder of Margot, the actual murder of Marion and the birds' assault on Melanie are obvious examples. Juanita's shooting, too, is highly sexualised. The sexualisation of violence in Hitchcock is undeniable, but it is outside my concern here. However, a few comments on Haskell's reasons for the 'punishment' of the blondes are in order.

Although I consider Haskell's explanation inadequate, there is a sense in which the attractiveness of the blonde is a disturbing force in Hitchcock, and his films show a whole series of inadequate – or even insane – men reacting with violence to that disturbance. Crewe trying to rape Alice; Sebastian and his mother poisoning Alicia (Alicia *suffers* like a Hitchcock blonde); Tony setting up the murder of Margot; Scottie dragging Judy up the bell tower; Rusk failing to rape Brenda and then strangling her – in each case, the violence of the attack is exacerbated by the blame (or, in Crewe's case, the willingness) which the attacker has projected on to his victim. Two examples which fit more obliquely are

Thorwald assaulting Lisa in REAR WINDOW and 'Mrs Bates' murdering Marion. Yet there, too, a man disturbed by the attractiveness of the heroine is behind the violence: Thorwald's assault is an unconscious projection of Jeff's hostility towards Lisa (➤ DOUBLES), and the hysterical fury of 'Mrs Bates's' attack is a reflection of Norman's psychosis (➤ MOTHERS AND HOUSES). The only violent attack on a woman in Hitchcock which seems to be – metaphorically, at least – the result of female rather than male aggression is the birds assaulting Melanie (➤ CHILDREN).

It is perhaps significant that the only brunette to suffer in quite this way is Rebecca. Rico's murder of Juanita is almost tender: he shoots her because he cannot bear the thought of her being tortured. But the black-haired Rebecca, with her 'breeding, brains and beauty', suffered a very different fate. Rebecca's power went beyond that of even the most charismatic Hitchcock blonde, and the challenge to patriarchy which it embodied finally provoked her husband Maxim into violently assaulting and killing her.

The example of Rebecca illuminates the nature of the problem of the haughty blonde in Hitchcock. On the one hand, she carries the burden of male fantasies about beautiful, glamorous women, and the violence she suffers arises from the shattering of such fantasies – for which she is of course blamed. On the other, her cool sophistication, with its implicit corollary of emotional and financial independence, is perceived as a threat to patriarchy: again, violence at such a threat often follows. Perhaps the most unpleasant attack on a woman in Hitchcock is Rusk's 'rape' and murder of Brenda, and just as Rusk himself fits the profile of the fantasising figure who blames the woman both for arousing him and for his subsequent sexual failure, so Blaney hates Brenda for her business success when he himself is such a miserable failure (➤ *Damaged hands*). Since Rusk also functions in the film as Blaney's psychopathic alter ego (➤ THE CORPSE), one can see that Brenda is in effect a victim of the virulent hostility of both men: it is no wonder that she is subjected to such brutality.

By contrast, the warm blondes and the brunettes are more approachable and less ambitious, and thus less of a threat on either of these counts. Barring encounters with would-be rapists like Crewe or insane young men like Norman, they are unlikely to suffer such violence. However, occasionally such women inadvertently discover something about the violent male psyche – Charlie about her uncle; Blanche about Adamson's kidnapping activities – which does then unleash on her the sort of aggression suffered by the sophisticated blondes. In Hitchcock, it is dangerous even for nice women to find out too much.

Blondes, brunettes and the police

In most cases, Hitchcock's policemen play it safe: if they do fall for a heroine, they stick to the warmer brunettes/redheads: NUMBER SEVENTEEN, SABOTAGE, JAMAICA INN, SHADOW OF A DOUBT, STAGE FRIGHT. Alicia in NOTORIOUS probably belongs here, too. The policemen who are foolish enough to fall for a blonde are Joe in THE LODGER, Frank in BLACKMAIL and Scottie in VERTIGO. They do not have happy endings: Joe loses Daisy to the Lodger; Frank and Alice cover up her involvement in a killing; Scottie loses Judy and 'Madeleine'. The moral for cops is clear: stick to brunettes.

CAMEO APPEARANCES

Fig. 8. Production still: YOUNG AND INNOCENT: Hitchcock in position for his cameo outside the courthouse. The sergeant (H.F. Maltby) seems to be already holding forth.

A full listing of Hitchcock's cameo appearances in his films will be found in the filmography. Despite the familiarity of the cameos as a phenomenon, there have been relatively few attempts to look at them analytically. Two contrasting discussions date from 1977. In 'Hitchcock, The Enunciator', Raymond Bellour considers some of the cameos from a psychoanalytical point of view, suggesting that the 'appearances occur, more and more frequently, at that point in the chain of events where what could be called the film-wish is condensed' (Bellour 1977/ 2000: 224). Bellour's argument is that, through his cameos, 'Hitchcock inscribe [s] himself in the chain of the fantasy' (228). Although, insofar as I understand him, I feel that Bellour is forcing his argument in many of his examples, it remains suggestive for some, and I will return to it. A more comprehensive discussion is by Maurice Yacowar in *Hitchcock's British Films* (Yacowar 1977: 270-78). Yacowar's approach seems to me rather quirky: there is a lot of speculation about the symbolism of details. But the general thrust of his argument – that Hitchcock's cameos tend to cast him in the same sort of role as the painting of the jester in BLACKMAIL, ironically commenting on the 'fictions and follies' of his characters (278) – is, again, suggestive.

In *Find the Director and Other Hitchcock Games*, Thomas Leitch discusses the epistemological status of the cameos, suggesting that they are a prime illustration of Hitchcock's 'ludic approach to storytelling', a feature of his films' 'self-advertising style' (Leitch 1991: 10), 'reminding the audience of the … film's status as an artifact, an artful discourse rather than a transparent story' (6). Equally, however, he argues that the cameos do not, as one might expect, 'disturb (the) sense of the film's coherence' but 'intensify the audience's pleasure' (21). We enjoy the artifice and the game of 'find the director' (8) that Hitchcock is playing with us through his cameo appearances. I have no quarrel with Leitch's argument, but feel, nevertheless, that there is more to be said.

It would be useful to begin by positioning the cameos. First, where and how do they tend to occur? Hitchcock's first appearance, in THE LODGER, was not planned as a cameo, but as a way of filling a space on the screen. His first cameo proper is in EASY VIRTUE, where he is a chubby gentleman – wearing spats and sporting a cane – who walks past Larita out of a tennis court in the South of France. Although this is not widely recognised as a Hitchcock cameo – it is not cited in Charles Barr's *English Hitchcock* (1999), for example – I believe that it is one. It is entirely typical: the brief, jaunty appearance in conjunction with the heroine, who merely glances at him. Presumably he is supposed to be another hotel guest, but essentially he's just a passer-by. The timing also fits later examples: it immediately precedes the moment when Larita is struck by a tennis ball, which leads to her meeting the young man whom she will subsequently marry. I shall take it as the first true Hitchcock cameo.

In his next appearance, in BLACKMAIL, he elaborates a little scene around himself: he is a passenger on a London Underground train who, as Alice and Frank sit impassively, is harassed by a small boy. Together with his appearance in YOUNG AND INNOCENT, this is his longest cameo. In MURDER!, he returns to the more self-effacing role of a casual passer-by, walking past the camera – with a female companion – as it records a conversation between Sir John and the Markhams on the other side of the road. These first three examples collectively establish the pattern. Most of the cameos are set in places – such as hotels, public transport or the street – where Hitchcock can appear as a (usually unobserved) guest, fellow traveller or casual passer-by. The only significant additions to this list of public places where he appears are railway stations (first example,

THE LADY VANISHES) and, in one instance (TOPAZ), an airport. More than two thirds of all the cameos occur at one or other of these sites.

Second, when do they occur? Again they are clustered: setting aside the special case of THE WRONG MAN (where Hitchcock is outside the diegesis), there are five in the first few minutes, but most are just after the introduction, which may be one developed sequence (e.g. Hannay in the Music Hall in THE 39 STEPS; Bruno and Guy on the train in STRANGERS ON A TRAIN; Marion and Sam in the hotel in PSYCHO), or several shorter ones (e.g. BLACKMAIL; VERTIGO; SHADOW OF A DOUBT). In each case the appearance also marks a point of transition: Hannay and Annabella Smith catch the bus back to his flat; Guy gets off the train in Metcalf; Marion arrives back at her office; Alice and Frank are going for supper at a Lyons Corner House; Scottie is going to see Elster; Uncle Charlie is travelling by train to Santa Rosa. It is this which is crucial. As the cameos move further into the first act, and even into the second act, most of them signal a geographical – or narrative – shift, e.g. when the action moves to Copenhagen in TORN CURTAIN, or to New York in TOPAZ, SPELLBOUND and (at a relatively late stage) SABOTEUR. Similarly, Hitchcock appears when Eve is en route to meet Charlotte in STAGE FRIGHT, or when the falsely accused hero goes on the run from the police in YOUNG AND INNOCENT and TO CATCH A THIEF. At the time of the Truffaut interviews, Hitchcock said that the cameos had become 'a rather troublesome gag, and I'm very careful to show up in the first five minutes so as to let people look at the rest of the movie with no further distraction' (Truffaut 1968: 42). But even when, as in all the films from VERTIGO to TORN CURTAIN, Hitchcock does ensure that his cameo is close to the beginning, its positioning is still carefully considered.

Another feature of the cameo in BLACKMAIL is that, as Susan Smith has pointed out, it makes Hitchcock himself – failing to control the unruly boy – 'the butt of the humour' (Smith 2000: 70). This applies to a number of the cameos. In YOUNG AND INNOCENT, Hitchcock's frustrated attempts to take a photograph amidst the confusion caused by the hero's escape from police custody are very funny indeed. As Susan Smith also notes, the contrasting photographs of Hitchcock in the Reduco advertisement in LIFEBOAT contradict the message: it is the heavier Hitchcock 'which strikes the more positive, energetic pose'; the slimmer Hitchcock looks 'downcast' (102). The joke is very personal: Hitchcock has had to give up his beloved food to achieve his slimmed-down state. Other instances of Hitchcock joking at his own expense are his missing the bus in NORTH BY NORTHWEST, being urinated on by a baby in the hotel lobby in TORN CURTAIN and his silhouette gesturing rather rudely behind the glass of the 'Registrar of Births and Deaths' office door in FAMILY PLOT. In other examples, the cameo has a joking flavour through its nature and timing: Hitchcock holding an unbeatable bridge hand (all the spades) on the train in

SHADOW OF A DOUBT (which elicits a comment that he doesn't look very well); carrying a huge double bass on to the train in STRANGERS ON A TRAIN; leaping out of a wheelchair at the airport in TOPAZ; gazing intently at the corpse in the Thames in FRENZY. All these examples help illustrate Leitch's point about the ludic nature of the cameos.

Some of the cameos are also linked to a motif. Already noted: one *corpse*; two falsely accused heroes (Wood 1989: 241-42) and a number of transport examples, including four *trains*/railway stations. In I CONFESS, Hitchcock walks across the top of a *staircase*; in THE BIRDS, he exits from a pet shop accompanied by his *dogs*. There are several *food* or drink examples: in REAR WINDOW, he appears in the composer's apartment as Lisa brings out the lobster dinner for Jeff; in LIFEBOAT, the slimming advertisement is an ironic comment on the lack of food in the lifeboat; in NOTORIOUS, he increases the suspense at the Sebastian party by helping to consume the champagne. Although some of these examples are no more than a glancing reference to a given motif, others – such as the corpse in FRENZY – are crucial to the plot.

More rarely, Hitchcock's cameo relates to a motif in a deeper sense. Bellour's main example is his appearance in MARNIE, which highlights 'the look'. In the second scene of the film, Strutt and Mark discuss Marnie. The scene ends with a track into Mark's contemplative face, so that the next shot, accompanied by wistful music, seems like his daydream. We see Marnie, attended by a heavily laden bellboy, walking away from the camera down a hotel corridor. As she does this, Hitchcock appears out of a room and observes her from behind, then turns and glances at the camera.

Bellour suggests that, by appearing at this point, Hitchcock inscribes 'himself in the chain of the look' so as to 'determine the structuring principle of the film' (Bellour 1977/2000: 223). By observing Marnie, 'Hitchcock becomes a kind of double of Mark and Strutt', his look reinforcing 'the desire of the camera, whose chosen image here is the woman'. We still have not seen Marnie's face – and she is still in disguise as the brunette Marion Holland – but it's as if Hitchcock steps out to relay Mark's imagined look towards Marnie, 'who is both object of desire and enigma' (224). The argument is ingenious, but Hitchcock's glance at the camera – unprecedented in his cameos – complicates matters. Bellour seems to imply that, in drawing attention to the camera, the glance is a feature of the self-reflexivity of this cameo. But it also suggests that the camera has caught Hitchcock looking at Marnie, and he turns away so quickly because this has revealed something about himself. There is also an unusually self-revelatory aspect to the cameo.

Bellour discusses another of his major examples – the cameo in STRANGERS ON A TRAIN – in an interview with Guy Rosolato in E. Ann Kaplan (ed.): *Psychoanalysis and Cinema*.

> [Hitchcock] gets on a train with a cello (sic) in his hand. What you have here is con-
> densation: the young woman who will be the victim of the murder works in a music
> store, and the exchange of murders between the two heroes takes place on the train.
> Hitchcock puts himself at the heart of the metaphorical circuit between the sexes.
>
> (Bellour and Rosolato 1990: 201)

If Bellour had remembered, as he does elsewhere (Bellour 1977/2000: 225), that the musical instrument was a double bass, he could have added – as critics have observed – that, in this film about the hero and his double (➤ DOUBLES), the instrument is also a visual double of the director. This is indeed one of Hitchcock's more significant cameos, but I would like to focus instead on its timing, which is typical of a number of the cameos.

Guy is on his way to see Miriam to talk about the arrangements for their divorce. Miriam leads Guy on, and then says she is not going through with the divorce. Pregnant with another man's child, she'll claim that the child is Guy's. Guy loses his temper with her and later, on the phone to Anne, his new girl-friend, says that he could strangle Miriam. Bruno, symbolically Guy's double, then proceeds to carry out the crime.

The point about the scenes with Guy in Metcalf is that they mark a turning point. Guy's frustration and anger symbolically 'activates' Bruno, whose mur-der of Miriam precipitates Guy into the chaos world. I would maintain that this is typical of what happens in many of the scenes which follow a cameo at a point of transition, especially if this is early in the film: the cameo marks the moment when the protagonist goes to the location where he/she will make the fateful decision which leads him/her into the chaos world.

Thus, it is at the Lyons Corner House that Alice meets Crewe who, later that evening, will tempt her into his studio and try to rape her. It is when Hannay escorts Annabella Smith back to his flat that he takes the step which will plunge him into the dangerous world of the spies. Both these journeys end with the protagonist confronted with a corpse on a bed (➤ THE CORPSE), which results in a potential or actual accusation of murder. What happens in STRANGERS ON A TRAIN is essentially a more elaborate version of the same idea. Similarly, it is when Scottie visits Elster that he makes the decision which will lead to his being enmeshed in the latter's murder plot; it is when Marion returns to her office after her extended lunch hour that she is tempted by the $40,000 waved in front of her by Cassidy; it is in the pet shop that Melanie meets Mitch, and his practi-cal joke on her goads her into deciding to reciprocate, which takes her to Bodega Bay. In all these examples, the protagonist is crossing a threshold, and Hitchcock's cameo is like a coded signal: what is about to occur is a certain sort of scene. It may begin innocently or even seem innocent throughout, but in fact it marks a – distinctly Hitchcockian – turning point. As a result of this scene, the protagonist will be precipitated into the chaos world. The literal intrusion of the director into the diegesis could thus be seen as a mark of Hitchcock's self-conscious control over the narrative.

More specifically, the scene which follows the cameo usually involves the protagonist being in some sense tested. Guy fails the test in that he becomes violent with Miriam: Bruno as killer emerges 'out of' his murderous rage (➢ DOUBLES). Alice and Marion fail by succumbing to temptation, which leads to disaster. In VERTIGO, we realise in retrospect that Elster as villain is testing Scottie for *weakness* – acrophobia; gullibility; susceptibility to a mysterious woman – which Scottie confirms, revealing him as a suitable dupe for Elster's plot. It is this failure of moral character which serves to set the protagonist on the path into the chaos world. Hannay also succumbs to temptation, and although he behaves perfectly honourably with Annabella, there is still a sense that he is being punished for taking a mysterious woman to his flat for the night. Even in Melanie's case, there is a structural link between the chaos created by her releasing the canary in the shop – a consequence of Mitch's practical joke – and the future chaos world created by the birds in Bodega Bay. The sense of Melanie being 'tested' is certainly attenuated, but the scene still has elements which anticipate those of the chaos world to come.

The cameo in EASY VIRTUE, too, fits this argument. Larita has just escaped from one domestic chaos world (a vicious husband, a compromising suicide and a messy divorce) and is about to meet the man who will take her into another (a hostile mother-in-law and a weak husband) (➢ MOTHERS AND HOUSES). And she, too, fails a test: she does not tell her ardent suitor about her scandalous divorce, and so leaves herself open to the consequences of its subsequent discovery (➢ GUILT AND CONFESSION).

A similar argument – in terms of the cameo preceding a test of the protagonist's character – could be made for other examples. The hotel lobby cameos in SPELLBOUND and TORN CURTAIN, and the airport one in TOPAZ all precede a scene in a hotel room involving a couple and an outside threat. Here, it is as if the couple's relationship is being tested. In SPELLBOUND, where the outside threat is the pursuing police, the characters pass the test: the scene is therapeutic – Constance begins to help cure J.B's amnesia. The outcome in the two movies where the outside threat is espionage is not so positive. In TORN CURTAIN, the scene – which ends with Sarah going off to collect the book containing the espionage message – shows that Michael has not confided in her about his plans. In TOPAZ, André does what the American CIA agent Nordstrom asks, and gives up his family reunion evening to go on a spy mission. Each hero thus puts espionage before romance or family, a telling indication of his priorities.

All these examples show that the positioning of the cameos can be highly significant. The ways in which Hitchcock stages his appearances is where the 'ludic' elements mainly reside – most are amusing – but the positioning belongs to another order of complexity. There is no doubt that Hitchcock's narratives are usually highly patterned in their structure; the sophistication of the location of the cameos is yet another example of this. It would not be difficult to add to these instances where the cameo marks a crucial moral or strategic turning point in the protagonist's journey.

I would like, finally, to look at a small number of examples where the cameo has its own built-in charge, along the lines of Bellour's notion of the 'film-wish'. James Vest has already explored in detail the cameos in TORN CURTAIN and VERTIGO for their potential meanings (Vest 1998-99: 3-19; Vest 1999-2000: 84-92). Although Vest does make reference to the significance of the positioning of the cameos, I'm afraid I often find his arguments fanciful – like Yacowar, he, too, is prone to get carried away by small details.

By contrast, I am fully in accord with John Fawell's analysis of Hitchcock's cameo in REAR WINDOW (Fawell 2001: 99-101). Hitchcock appears in the composer's apartment, winding a clock, as the composer plays the song he is currently writing on the piano. Fawell draws a parallel between the role of the composer and that of Hitchcock the director. First, the song is being composed throughout the film, and Hitchcock wanted it to be completed – in the sense of finished and recorded – only at the end, paralleling the film itself. Second, when Lisa says of the song, 'It's almost as if it were being written especially for us', she is right: this is the film's love song and her remark is self-reflexive, a comment on the song's function within the film. Third, Fawell has asked lip-readers to read what Hitchcock is saying to the composer, and they agree that it is 'B, B flat', i.e. he is advising the composer about the song's composition. He thus makes his cameo appearance here assisting in the creation of the film itself, another self-reflexive detail in what is, surely, his most self-reflexive film.

In SUSPICION, Hitchcock appears posting a letter in the background behind Lina in the village. The cameo occurs immediately after Johnnie's friend Beaky has had a violent attack from drinking some brandy and Johnnie, knowing how dangerous brandy is for him, has commented: 'One of these days, it will kill him.' It is this positioning which is crucial. We know that Hitchcock wanted to end the film with Johnnie posting a letter which would incriminate him for Lina's murder (➤ Milk in Part I). Unable to have this ending, Hitchcock seemingly refers to it by himself posting a letter at this precise point, thereby alerting us to the prophetic import of Johnnie's words: he will be the man responsible for Beaky's fatal attack after drinking brandy in Paris. In other words, the nature and timing of the cameo is such that Hitchcock seems to be introducing an oblique comment on how we should read the film's ambiguous hero.

In NOTORIOUS, the 'film-wish' is more straightforward: Hitchcock is helping to consume the champagne because he wants it to run out, so that he can ratchet up the suspense for Alicia and Devlin's trip to the wine cellar. Equally, he is doing what the audience expects of him: we would be disappointed if he did not make the cellar sequence suspenseful. Moreover, he has an ally. The second that he steps out of the shot, Señora Ortiza steps in, and prises Devlin away from Alicia, so that the couple's trip to the cellar is necessarily further delayed. It looks as though Hitchcock the party guest planned the little manoeuvre on behalf of Hitchcock the director. This is one of the cameos where he appears in his film as his own alter ego, craftily manipulating the events to forward the plot.

In THE MAN WHO KNEW TOO MUCH (1955), Hitchcock appears in Marrakech at the back of a crowd watching a troupe of acrobats. Ben and Jo are already watching, and when Hitchcock comes into the shot and stands on the left, a man in a white robe is neatly positioned between him and his protagonists on the right. All four are shown from behind. The film then cuts to another white-robed man squatting on the ground; we are now inside a crowd of spectators, who are in the background. The man is positioned in the frame exactly where Hitchcock was in the previous shot and is likewise shown from behind. This is in fact another 'attraction' and another crowd: among it are Hank and Mrs Drayton. A closer shot of them follows, then their point of view of the man, then Mrs Drayton explains to Hank that the man is a 'teller of tales'.

This is highly compressed filmmaking. The sudden cut to a new location is startling: it looks so similar to the previous one – a crowd of people, mostly Arabs, around a central attraction – that we are momentarily disorientated. Yet once again the cameo could be seen as alerting us: Hank has already been separated from his parents, and is in fact with the woman who will shortly kidnap him (➤ CHILDREN). The two white-robed men anticipate Louis Bernard in his disguise as an Arab – in all three cases, the robes are identical and the man is (first) shown from behind. In addition, Mrs Drayton's comment suggests that the second of these men, the story-teller, can also be seen as a Hitchcock surrogate in the film. It's as if Hitchcock steps into the frame to initiate a mysterious chain of white-robed 'Arab' figures, a chain which should also include a (similarly white-robed) woman carrying a baby whom Jo sees just before Louis's pursuit and murder (which prompts her remark to Ben about having another child), and the man who stabs Louis, who is like Louis's double.

The chain is in fact circular: from spectator, to story-teller, to mother and child, to fugitive spy, to assassin, to the spy returning to the hero, communicating his own cryptic story and dying. Hitchcock is only linked directly to the first two figures – the spectator and the story-teller – but the others are all linked, in one way or another, to the heroine and hero. The mother and child can be seen as a projection of Jo's wish, and I argue under DOUBLES that the killing of Louis may be read as Ben's unconscious 'answer' to Jo's wish, since Louis's dying message leads to the kidnapping of Hank, and so deflects their concerns away from any thoughts of another child. Moreover, at the point when Jo and Ben leave the back of the crowd watching the acrobats, their place is taken by Drayton, so that he and the white-robed figure are now standing side by side. In that Drayton, too, is dressed in white (suit and hat) and that his role in ordering Hank's kidnapping makes him seem like Ben's double (➤ DOUBLES), he too has a place in this highly patterned sequence.

This chain would seem to be where the 'film-wish' resides: it summarises the events which precipitate Jo and Ben into the chaos world. The narrative trajectory is similar to that which follows the cameos in BLACKMAIL, THE 39 STEPS and STRANGERS ON A TRAIN. It likewise shares with this last a (here more compact) circular structure, with the trajectory looping back to the hero and emphasising his own symbolic implication in the post-cameo murder by introducing a 'polluting' element from the corpse (➤ THE CORPSE).

Finally, TO CATCH A THIEF, which is unique amongst the cameos in that the protagonist really stares at Hitchcock, and so draws attention to the latter's presence in a most uncharacteristic way. When Robie first escapes from the police, he boards a bus and sits on the back seat. He smiles at the sight of the police driving the other way, and is then distracted by two birds cheeping in a cage on his right. He looks at the middle-aged woman who owns the birds, and she reacts by looking affectionately at them. This leaves him slightly nonplussed, as if there is something odd about being on a bus with a cage of birds; he then turns to stare at the figure on his left, who is Hitchcock, poker-faced and looking ahead. An effect of the stare – which is deliberately expressionless, inviting different interpretations – is that Cary Grant seems at this moment to step out of character and become himself; his stare thus seems directed at Hitchcock as director. In addition, according to Steven DeRosa, Hitchcock made a point here of being filmed with only half his face visible in the VistaVision frame (DeRosa 2001: 119). All these details suggest that there is something peculiarly enigmatic about this cameo.

Reference to David Dodge's novel *To Catch a Thief* (1953) is instructive. The only other person on the bus with Robie at this point in the novel is Francie (albeit yet unidentified). If Cary Grant had read the novel, his stare could perhaps be accusatory – I was supposed to find myself next to Grace Kelly at this point, not a middle-aged woman and some birds. Hitchcock pointedly ignoring the stare but also 'hiding' half his face could then be seen as a comic attempt to disregard such censure, and the cameo itself as another self-reflexive example, drawing attention to Hitchcock's manipulation of the narrative. But perhaps Hitchcock himself wanted to 'stand in for' Grace Kelly? If so, the middle-aged woman, the birds and only half his face being visible could be seen as camouflage/disavowal. In that case, Cary Grant's face is surely expressionless because

he is a gentleman. He has perhaps recognised his director's secret wish, but his
lips are sealed.

Cameos and the police

Fig. 9. Still: REBECCA: Hitchcock's cut cameo outside the phone booth under the eye of the law.
Favell (George Sanders) in the booth.

From the stories Hitchcock has told over the years about his fears of the police,
we would expect him to do his best to avoid them in his cameos. In general, he
is successful. In MURDER!, Markham is talking about going to the police as
Hitchcock walks past, but the latter, in conversation with his companion, pointedly does not notice. In FRENZY, he watches the police attending to the corpse
fished out of the Thames, but it is the corpse that they are interested in, not
Hitchcock. In the still of the cameo from REBECCA (Hitchcock outside a telephone booth waiting for Favell to finish his call), a policeman looks on suspiciously, but Selznick cut the scene; perhaps, in this instance, doing Hitchcock a

favour by removing the law's intimidating gaze. Nevertheless, the fact that the policeman is also looking towards Favell in the booth literalises the sense of the 'threat of the law' outside Hitchcock's booths (➤ CONFINED SPACES), so that it would have been instructive to have seen the cameo as filmed.

Only in YOUNG AND INNOCENT – where Hitchcock has unfortunately placed himself outside the courthouse as the hero goes on the run – do we see the police get too close for comfort. As a sergeant comes out and barks orders, Hitchcock grimaces with disgust at this officiousness, but he still seems bent on taking his photograph despite the chaos, which leads to a little pantomime of frustration. He clearly blames the police for all this, and at the point when the film cuts to follow the hero's escape, Hitchcock is still giving the sergeant a baleful look. However, he is not intimidated: he stands his ground. I take that as a distinctly positive sign.

CHILDREN

Fig. 10. Still: STAGE FRIGHT: the disruptive child. The cub scout spooks Charlotte (Marlene Dietrich) on stage by holding up a doll with a bloody dress. On the right, Freddie Williams (Hector MacGregor), Charlotte's manager.

Children's cameos

At first glance, children may not seem to be a major feature of Hitchcock's work. They have substantial roles in relatively few of his films, and even in these they are seen primarily in relation to the adults: Hitchcock does not enter into the child's world in the manner of, say, Robert Mulligan. The TV episode 'Bang! You're Dead' is the furthest he has gone in that direction (➤ APPENDIX I). On the other hand, children do in fact make some sort of an appearance in a surprisingly large number of his films and, even though their parts may be small, they are usually vivid. At the most basic level are little scenes in which children turn up as mischief makers, usually at the expense of the adults. Examples include the upper-middle class boys who fight each other and later disrupt the school dinner in DOWNHILL and their lower-class equivalents who, later in the first act, prompt Roddy into behaving foolishly in the Bunne Shoppe; the landlady's children who surround Sir John's bed and create chaos in MURDER!; the cousins who make off with Johnny's bowler hat during the family farewell in FOREIGN CORRESPONDENT and the street urchins who, when Mr and Mrs Smith decide to dine alfresco at Momma Lucy's, appear looking hungry at their table and drive them indoors.

In all these scenes, the children disrupt the adults' world with their insistent presence. The disruption is particularly in evidence when there is a class difference between adults and children. In DOWNHILL, Roddy gives the boy in the shop an expensive box of sweets for a half-penny, but then rings up £1 on the till, which obliges him to pay Mabel, the shopgirl, £1 in compensation. Mabel later exploits this payment in her story that he is the young man who got her pregnant. In MR AND MRS SMITH, David and Ann try and outstare the children, but are themselves outstared; here the children are like guilt images, drawing attention to the couple's wealth and their own deprivation. Only Sir John handles the children's intrusion with relative equanimity, coping with the incessant noise of a crying baby, a small boy who shakes the bed as he holds his cup of tea and a small girl who releases a kitten under his blankets and then cries out that he's got her pussy. After the kitten has been rescued, the girl then climbs on to the bed and affectionately hugs him. Meanwhile, Sir John is trying to concentrate on information the landlady is communicating relevant to the case he is investigating.

On an analogy with Hitchcock's own cameos, these scenes could be seen as children's cameo appearances. Whereas Hitchcock enters the narrative surreptitiously, and is usually quickly gone, children have a habit of entering it rather more forcefully, making their presence felt through a variety of anarchic or otherwise unsettling activities. In BLACKMAIL Hitchcock illustrates the difference between his own undemonstrative cameos and a typical children's one by combining them, and showing himself – a peaceful passenger on a London tube innocently reading a book – as a victim of harassment by an unruly small boy. And in TORN CURTAIN, he makes his appearance with a junior member of the tribe: a peeing baby.

At the next stage up in terms of complexity are those children who serve to provide a commentary on the world of the hero or heroine, or who are integrated into the narrative in a more developed sense. These would include Erica's brothers in YOUNG AND INNOCENT, who appear at two mealtimes: at

lunch to make her realise, through their lurid conversation, the predicament she
has left Robert in, and the next day at dinner to offer their silent support for the
predicament she finds herself in. The first scene captures very acutely the way
English boys of that sort of background interact with one another (➤ *Food and
guilt*); the second shows a completely different side to them, with their earlier
ebullience transformed into an unexpected sensitivity. Another example is the
cub scout who spooks Charlotte during her performance at the garden party in
STAGE FRIGHT by walking on to the stage and holding up a doll with a bloody
dress (➤ EXHIBITIONISM / VOYEURISM). In my essay on YOUNG AND INNO-
CENT and STAGE FRIGHT, I suggest that the scout is in fact quite a complex image, threatening Charlotte with exposure (embodying her guilt) even as the doll
itself hints at her own past violation at the hands of a brutal husband (embodying her suffering) (Walker M. 1999: 200-201).

The children in the fairground in STRANGERS ON A TRAIN are further examples. When Bruno is pursuing Miriam, he is suddenly accosted by a small boy
dressed as a cowboy and carrying a balloon who points a gun at his head and
says 'Bang! Bang!' Bruno's reaction is to burst the balloon with his cigarette.
Then, during the fight between Bruno and Guy on the runaway merry-go-
round at the climax, there are children on a number of the carousel's rides. In-
stinctively identifying Bruno as the villain, a small boy on a wooden horse starts
to hit him, whereupon Bruno knocks him off the horse, and the boy would have
been swept off the merry-go-round had Guy not saved him. In *The Strange Case
of Alfred Hitchcock*, Raymond Durgnat mentions the two boys, suggesting that
the former's act is 'another form of innocent-guilty complicity in the idea of
murder' and that saving the latter 'presumably enables Guy to expiate his le-
gal-moral guilt' (Durgnat 1974: 220).

Sabrina Barton makes another point about the small boys in the film. The
cowboy outfit worn by the first one is elaborated into a whole series of Western
elements in the merry-go-round climax: 'good guys and bad guys, guns, horses,
a chase, a fistfight, screaming women, the law, a mother and her son'. These in
turn comment on the little boy's attack on Bruno: 'Cultural representations supply the tropes through which male identity gets constituted' (Barton 1995: 232).
One could go further. Hitchcock uses the iconography of the Western here to
comment not just on the little boy, but on the 'trigger-happy' cop (➤ *Public disturbances and the police*) and on the sharp contrast between the responses of the
males and females in the scene. The anxiety of the mother who calls out for 'My
little boy!' is comically counterpointed by the evident enjoyment of the boy himself on his speeded-up carousel horse, but supported by the terror of the girls on
theirs. As the men shoot and fight, and the little boy joins in 'the fun', the women and girls are quite properly terrified.

It is also significant that Hitchcock has chosen small boys to finger Bruno: the former alluding to the crime Bruno is about to commit; the latter to his role as villain. Because Bruno is a psychopath who feels no guilt, the first boy, unlike the one in STAGE FRIGHT, does *not* disturb him as a guilt image, and he seems to have no qualms about swatting the second one as one would a fly. Nevertheless, the boys fit into another pattern within the film. The first one stares straight at Bruno before Miriam's murder and – in effect – illustrates his murderous thoughts. After Bruno has strangled Miriam, it is her look which then haunts him, as is shown by his reactions to the sight of Barbara, reactions which suggest the return of his repressed guilt (➤ SPECTACLES). Moreover, immediately after the murder, Bruno helps a blind old man across the road, an act which Robin Wood has suggested is 'unconscious atonement' (Wood 1989: 90). I think it is more a question of disavowal, as if Bruno has already been disturbed by the looks which have been directed at him and is unconsciously seeking solace with someone who cannot see. The small boys thus complement Barbara: like young versions of Bruno accusing him, they allude to the 'bad thoughts' which he has to deny. Hence he has to quickly resist them, brush them aside: he bursts the balloon; he swipes the boy off the horse.

A child who functions in a very different sense as a younger version of the protagonist is Jessie Cotten in MARNIE. When Marnie first visits her mother, Jessie – aged about six – opens the door, and throughout the visit she is constantly in the background: either as a nagging physical presence, or – after she has left – as a topic of conversation. It is apparent that, whereas Mrs Edgar is quick to criticise Marnie, she is kind and indulgent towards Jessie. This makes Marnie jealous, which Jessie, noticing, triumphantly exacerbates: the incident in which Mrs Edgar brushes Jessie's hair is mentioned in the *Bed Scene* in Part I. Although I criticise Mrs Edgar there for her coldness and insensitivity towards Marnie's feelings, one can nevertheless understand her wish to pamper Jessie in a way that she felt she couldn't Marnie when she was little. Jessie thus serves to focus the tensions between Mrs Edgar and Marnie: the former seeking to use her to create an idealised mother-daughter relationship; the latter seeing only that she has been replaced in her mother's affections by a little girl.

It is thus important that, unlike the boys in STRANGERS ON A TRAIN, Jessie only appears in this one scene. In the matching scene in Mrs Edgar's house at the end, she is replaced, structurally, by Marnie herself as a little girl in the flashbacks to the childhood trauma. This contrast between the two films is significant. Unlike Bruno, Marnie changes, a change signalled by her remembering what happened to her as a little girl. The memory is undoubtedly traumatic, but it is also therapeutic. The later film's use of the Children motif is more dynamic.

A film in which the absence of children is symbolically significant is REAR WINDOW. In the apartments across from Jeff's, we catch only fleeting glimpses of a child – a little girl with her parents on a balcony – and although children play in the street at the end of the side alley, again we only see them in glimpses. Since events in the 'dream screen' across the courtyard may be read as a distorted reflection of Jeff's own inner world (➤ DOUBLES; RAIN), the marginalisation of children is symptomatic. Because of Jeff's animus towards marriage and domesticity, children are strictly a background presence in his psychic world.

Family members

Children become more important to Hitchcock's plots when they are part of the hero and/or heroine's family. In the British films, there are two major examples: the kidnapped fourteen-year-old Betty in THE MAN WHO KNEW TOO MUCH (1934) and Stevie, Mrs Verloc's teenage brother, in SABOTAGE. In the Hollywood films, there are Charlie's young siblings, Ann and Roger Newton, in SHADOW OF A DOUBT; boys in three successive films in the mid-1950s – Jennifer's son Arnie in THE TROUBLE WITH HARRY, the kidnapped Hank in the remake of THE MAN WHO KNEW TOO MUCH (1955), and the two young Balestrero sons in THE WRONG MAN – and finally Mitch's eleven-year-old sister Cathy in THE BIRDS.

Inevitably, some of these children are more important than others. The Balestrero boys are essentially just a part of the family, serving to show that Manny is a calm father who can successfully mediate when the two have a dispute. In SHADOW OF A DOUBT, there is an imbalance between Roger, whom everybody ignores, and Ann, who is observant and caustic: she senses that there is something odd about Uncle Charlie; she comments on both her father's lowbrow taste in literature and her mother's failure to understand that she does not need to shout when she is on the telephone. Although she, too, is ironised – 'I never make anything up. I get everything from books. They're all true' – she is an early, children's version of a figure more developed in two films of the 1950s: Anne's sister Barbara in STRANGERS ON A TRAIN and the nurse Stella in REAR WINDOW. These are characters who stand to one side of the main thrust of the plot and make incisive comments about what is going on, saying the sort of things the other characters may think but are too refined to express. In some respects, they are like surrogates of the Hitchcock persona familiar from his TV episodes, where he appears outside the diegesis and makes, on occasions, the same sort of comments about the events depicted.

Although Ann does little to further the plot of SHADOW OF A DOUBT, she is different from the other children so far discussed in that she is not shown just in relation to the other characters. She has her own interests – mainly reading – and operates within her own space. There are few of the more important children who are not given a hobby or passion, such as Stevie's model yacht-building, or the Balestrero boys' talent for music. Hitchcock may only allude briefly to the child's world, but he is aware of its importance.

Since the two versions of THE MAN WHO KNEW TOO MUCH are quite close structurally, with the child's scenes concentrated in each at the beginning and the end, Betty and Hank may be considered together. Typically of Hitchcock's children, both begin by creating a disturbance in the adults' world. Indeed, Betty is directly or indirectly responsible for two successive disturbances, both leading to sporting failures. First she lets a dog slip from her grasp during a ski jump competition and, running after it onto the course, causes a competitor to fall. The competitor is Louis Bernard, who admonishes her, 'It's your fault, terrible woman'. Betty blames the dog, but it was in her charge. She promptly moves on to distract her mother Jill during the clay-pigeon shooting finals, interrupting her just as she is about to fire her deciding shot. Jill then makes matters worse by giving Betty a brooch: this so excites her that she has to be shushed twice by the crowd. Finally, as Jill is actually firing, Abbott's chiming watch adds yet another distraction, but it is clear that Betty has contributed to Jill's lack of concentration. After she has missed, she comments ruefully to her rival Ramon – who goes on to win – 'Let that be a lesson to you: never have any children', and Betty is once again admonished, on this occasion by her father Bob: 'It's your fault, fathead.'

In *English Hitchcock*, Charles Barr suggests that the first of Betty's disturbances may be prompted by her mother's relationship with Louis:

> Louis and Jill's relationship is one of weirdly exaggerated flirtation, at which Bob, with equal exaggeration, connives. Perhaps Betty's causing Louis to fall … is subconsciously motivated by his threat to the stability of her family. It could, conversely, be motivated by her wish to promote his romance with her mother, so that she can have her father to herself. Louis's accident will bring Jill to comfort him, as Betty has foreseen; her first words to him are 'Mum will cry her eyes out… She adores you'.

(Barr 1999: 135-36)

But with the second disturbance, Bob, too, is implicated: the moment when he 'allows' Betty to run forward and distract Jill echoes the moment when Betty lets the dog slip and run forward, and the effect on the competitor is the same. Alongside the jokily registered Bob-Jill-Louis triangle, there is also an Oedipal triangle. Indeed, Jill – likewise exaggeratedly – plays along with this: she declares to Bob that she is going off with Louis, then adds, 'You go to bed early –

with Betty.' Both Louis's murder *and* Betty's kidnapping thus seem to arise out of the tensions between the adults: the former Bob's unconscious wish; the latter Jill's (➤ DOUBLES).

The disturbance Hank causes is of a different nature: as the family travel on a bus to Marrakech, he is jerked by a sudden movement of the bus and accidentally pulls the veil off an Arab woman. The woman's male escort gets very excited, and Louis Bernard makes his entrance on this occasion as a fellow passenger who calms matters down. This is much more obviously just an accident, but Louis points out to the McKennas that 'The Muslim religion allows for few accidents.' The sexual and Oedipal triangles of the first version have been replaced here by a sense of racial and religious otherness, which can be upsetting (➤ *Food and marriage*), but which is by no means as potentially harmful to the marriage. Nevertheless, I argue under DOUBLES that the sequence of events which leads to Hank's kidnapping – the pursuit and murder of Louis; the message he passes on to Ben – may be read as arising out of Ben's hostility to Jo's sudden request for another child. Hank is an entirely innocent figure in this but, again, it's as if marital tensions serve to generate a crisis around the couple's child.

Betty and Hank are kidnapped to stop their parents from informing the authorities about a planned assassination. The tension this creates for the mother, who at each film's climax can only prevent the assassination by risking her child's life, is detailed under PUBLIC DISTURBANCES. Only after the assassination has been foiled are the authorities mobilised to rescue the kidnapped child, but in both films it is in fact the parents who are the prime agents in effecting the rescue. It would seem that the guilt they feel for the way in which they 'allowed' their child to be kidnapped can only be assuaged if they themselves save her/him. However, in the first version at least, this leads to the return of some of the troubling undercurrents of the early scenes.

By this stage in the 1934 film, Bob, too, has been taken prisoner by the assassins. As a siege between the assassins and the police then takes place, the Oedipal material of the early scenes returns, but in a nightmare form. Bob tries to escape from the besieged building with Betty – who is wearing only her pyjamas – when Ramon stops them and shoots and wounds him. Betty is then pursued on to the roof by Ramon but saved by Jill in the street below, who coolly shoots him. If, in the opening scenes, it's as if Ramon murders Louis in response to Bob's unconscious wish to eliminate a rival, here his shooting Bob suggests that he is acting as Jill's dark alter ego, blocking the father-daughter Oedipal relationship not by removing Betty (as at the beginning) but by disabling Bob. It is thus imperative that Jill herself kills Ramon; only then can family harmony be restored. Even so, the final family reunion – as a sobbing Betty is lowered by policemen into the arms of her anxious parents – is somewhat tentative. Hitchcock has commented on the effect he wanted: 'I made her so terrified by the ordeal that she had been through that she shrank from them' (Hitchcock 1938/1995: 83).

The remake lacks such tensions. Jo and Hank do sing a duet of 'Que Sera Sera' and dance together on the evening before his kidnapping, but this has little of the Oedipal suggestiveness of the early exchanges between Bob and Betty. Nevertheless, the sense that the Draytons, who kidnap Hank, are in some sense doubles of Ben and Jo, does raise the issue of parental ambivalence towards having a child. This is especially relevant in Ben's case – just as the kidnapping itself seems to arise out of his unconscious, so Drayton repeatedly thwarts his attempts to rescue Hank. Even when Mrs Drayton has enabled Ben to find where Hank is imprisoned (➤ *Couples and staircases*), her husband turns up and holds Hank at gunpoint. But the subtextual tensions around the kidnapping of Hank have nothing of the sexual intimations of those around Betty.

It is not difficult to account for this difference between the two versions: Betty is a teenager; Hank is about eleven. Any story about a kidnapped teenage girl is extremely likely to include some sort of sexual threat, although I do not think that the threat was actually fulfilled in a film until THE SEARCHERS (John Ford, 1956). However, the first version of THE MAN WHO KNEW TOO MUCH clearly registers such a threat. On the one hand Bob is presumably taken prisoner to help defuse intimations of any such a threat from the kidnappers; on the other, the threat returns through the already-sexualised father-daughter relationship. The equivalent scenes in the 1955 film are contained within a maternal kidnapper-victim relationship, and it is not even necessary for one of the parents to kill the murderous kidnapper: he is killed by his own gun as Ben knocks him downstairs.

The contrast between the roles of the kidnapped child in each version of THE MAN WHO KNEW TOO MUCH says a lot about the difference between Hitchcock's two periods. Ina Rae Hark argues that the reason Hitchcock remade the film was to correct the patriarchal imbalance of giving 'too much power' to Jill in the British version (Hark 1991: 209-222). But he also eliminated the profound sexual disturbance to the family unit which can be caused by a teenage daughter – a subject which he avoided throughout his Hollywood movies. As a result, the family reunion at the end of the remake seems genuinely happy, lacking the unease of the ending of the British version.

Children and violence

Although Betty and Hank are kidnapped, this is done with the minimum of force and the kidnappers only resort to threatened violence in the last few min-

utes of each film. Stevie is a very different matter: he is actually killed. Moreover, this occurs at the end of a long, suspenseful sequence, as we watch Stevie
unknowingly delivering a bomb – which is primed to go off at a certain time –
for his brother-in-law Verloc. The issue of Stevie's death has occasioned much
debate over the years, with Hitchcock suffering such an extreme attack from
critics at the time – Charles Barr cites C.A. Lejeune as the main offender (Barr
1999: 172) – that he subsequently said on a number of occasions that he re-
gretted having killed him in this manner (e.g. Hitchcock 1949/1995: 120-21). Indeed, to Truffaut he goes further, and agrees with him that he shouldn't have
killed Stevie at all (Truffaut 1968: 87).

Susan Smith offers a much more sophisticated reading of the film, in which
she suggests that Hitchcock's role in SABOTAGE is *like* that of a saboteur, breaking the rules of the implicit filmmaking contract (Smith 1999: 45-57). In other
words, the killing of Stevie fits a reading in which the film itself is like an act of
sabotage. She also questions the conventional reading of Stevie as 'an innocent',
pointing out that he has watched the film that he carries with the bomb,
BARTHOLOMEW THE STRANGLER, fourteen times, and that both the policeman
Ted and the bus conductor jokingly call him 'Bartholomew'. Furthermore:

> The fact that it is the conductor's playful recognition of Stevie as the strangler figure
> that sways him to relax his rules and allow the boy onto the bus is particularly crucial
> as it points to Stevie's association with such male violence as the underlying cause of
> his death.

> (Smith 1999: 54)

I take Smith's point, but I think that the film does present Stevie as, essentially,
an innocent; there is nothing about him of the sharpness of Erica's brothers, or
even the perceptiveness of the much younger Ann Newton. He is introduced
bumbling about in the kitchen, where his clumsiness leads to his breaking a
plate which he hides in a drawer, just as the similarly clumsy – and innocent –
heroine in REBECCA hides a china cupid she breaks in a drawer. He is eager to
please and easily distracted, or he wouldn't have been fatally delayed in his
journey into the West End with the bomb. For all that he has repeatedly
watched BARTHOLOMEW THE STRANGLER, there seems to be absolutely nothing
malicious about him. Finally, as he sits on the bus as the minutes tick towards
the moment when the bomb will explode, he plays with a puppy, a classic depiction of childhood innocence.

This is important to the shocking impact of his death; both for the audience
and for Mrs Verloc. So far as the audience is concerned, 'the efficacy of future
suspense sequences could only be enhanced by the demonstration that a happy
ending was not inevitable' (Barr 1999: 172). As for Mrs Verloc, she is so traumatised that, later that day, she murders Verloc (➤ *Food and murder*). But because

we have shared her shock, we empathise. Stevie's death is emblematic of the darkness of Hitchcock's vision: even a child is not necessarily safe from the unpredictable violence of the world. In 1930s Britain, no other filmmaker surely went so far.

Arnie in THE TROUBLE WITH HARRY provides an obvious contrast with Stevie. The film begins with Arnie, armed with toy weaponry, roaming the woods near his home. Hearing shots, he dives for cover. Then, shortly afterwards, he discovers Harry's body. But the intrusion of death into the Vermont countryside is handled throughout in a comic vein, and neither Arnie nor any of the other characters – even those who think that they killed Harry – come to any harm. Arnie's main role is to keep the plot moving. First, he informs his mother Jennifer about the corpse, and since Harry is her unlamented husband, she is now free for romance with Sam, the film's hero. Sam and Arnie enjoy an easy-going relationship, so out of that romance Arnie himself will gain a non-repressive father. At one point Arnie takes Captain Wiles a rabbit that the latter shot; this makes the Captain realise that he did not, as he had assumed, shoot Harry. In other words, Arnie helps clear the Captain's conscience. Finally, Arnie is vital to the happy ending. After Harry has been interred and disinterred throughout the day (➤ THE CORPSE), he is cleaned up and placed back on the hillside so that Arnie can rediscover him the next day. Since Arnie is confused over the meaning of the words yesterday, today and tomorrow, his report about this should likewise confuse Deputy Sheriff Wiggs and thus keep the law in ignorance about what has been going on.

The opening sequence of Arnie playing in the woods sets the tone: the film overall is ludic and, although its 'trouble' is a recent corpse, this somehow fails to disrupt the living in the usual manner of corpses. In effect, a child's 'world of innocence' is here distributed across the narrative. At the same time, in diving for cover Arnie is showing a proper sense of self-preservation in an adults' world in which an old man is liable to shoot at anything that moves in the hope that it is a rabbit. In SABOTAGE, the destructive violence of the adults' world bursts into the innocence of the child's; in THE TROUBLE WITH HARRY, the innocence of the child's world triumphs.

Cathy is almost another child victim, and she is linked to Stevie through the motif of two caged birds which are brought to her by Melanie in the latter's pursuit of Mitch. In Susan Smith's words:

> Verloc's gesture of giving Stevie the cage of canaries that had earlier been used to transport the bomb is mirrored in complex form by Melanie's action of bringing a pair of caged lovebirds to Bodega Bay as a birthday gift for … Cathy, the delivery of which seems to serve on this occasion as the trigger for unleashing a whole spate of actual bird violence on the town, the family and herself.
>
> (Smith 2000: 125)

In both cases, then, the caged-bird gift to a child serves as both a mask and conduit for another person's private agenda, and although the bird attacks cannot be attributed to Melanie in the direct way that the bomb explosion can to Verloc, the link is suggestive. Susan Smith does in fact go on to argue that a number of the attacks make sense as an expression of Melanie's anger and resentment at being abandoned aged eleven by her mother. On this scenario, Cathy is a stand-in for Melanie as a girl.

Another link between Stevie and Cathy is the place of each in an unusual Oedipal triangle. Stevie seems more like Mrs Verloc's son than her brother, and his 'murder' at the hands of Verloc has the structure of an Oedipal crime, which Mrs Verloc avenges (➤ HEIGHTS AND FALLING). Similarly, Cathy seems more like the daughter of Lydia and Mitch than the latter's sister: this is implicitly Lydia's fantasy, a fantasy which Melanie's arrival in pursuit of Mitch threatens. Hence Margaret Horwitz's reading of the film, in which the birds 'function as a malevolent female superego, an indirect revelation of Lydia's character' (Horwitz 1986: 281), and where the final attack on Melanie 'can be seen as an expression of Lydia's jealousy' (285). As a result of the attack, Melanie is infantilised, and becomes a submissive daughter figure to Lydia rather than a sexual threat. On this reading, the Oedipal fantasy survives at the heroine's expense.

In both Horwitz's and Smith's readings, Cathy is significant primarily for her role in another woman's psychodrama; she lacks her own space and development. Although she is very welcoming towards Melanie, there is only one scene where, making cracks about Mitch's clients in San Francisco, she shows the independence of thought of someone like Ann Newton. It would seem that Cathy's main role – like Jessie Cotten's – is to focus the tensions between the female adults. In THE BIRDS, such a view may also be extended to the other children who appear in the film. Twice a group of children is subjected to attacks by the birds, and on both occasions they are shown, simply, as children, with virtually no attempts to individualise them.

The first of these scenes – Cathy's birthday party – may be contrasted with Felicity's birthday party in YOUNG AND INNOCENT: on both occasions, the children play blind man's bluff. Although Felicity's party is essentially a comic setting for Erica and Robert's attempts to elude the probing questions of Erica's rather formidable Aunt Margaret, some of the children are nevertheless depicted in the typically vivid manner of those in Hitchcock's English films. During Cathy's outdoor party there is no attempt to individualise the children: as soon as Mitch and Melanie come down to join them, the gulls attack. The attack does lead to some rather harrowing shots of children being pecked, but essentially the latter are shown simply as victims who have to be rescued and herded into the safety of the house by Annie, Melanie and Mitch.

Fig. 11. Still: THE BIRDS: children under attack. The birds attack during Cathy's birthday party. Cathy (Veronica Cartwright) is blindfolded; Annie (Suzanne Pleshette) runs to help her.

It is much the same with the crows' attack on the schoolchildren the next day. In class, the children do everything in unison: sing a repetitive song; chorus their amazement that Miss Hayworth is suddenly giving them a 'fire drill'. Out-side, as they flee from the crows, again Hitchcock shows some of them indivi-dually being attacked, but again they are essentially just frightened victims whom Annie and Melanie are hurrying to safety.

Horwitz's argument that the birds' aggression derives metaphorically from adult female hostility and jealousy is highly suggestive here. (A particularly tell-ing image is the way that the crows mass on the jungle gym behind an utterly oblivious Melanie, suggesting that they are being symbolically produced out of her unconscious.) Although none of the children dies, they are the only figures, apart from Melanie, to suffer more than one attack. This suggests an unresolved hostility towards the children themselves: in effect, the second bird attack drives all the local children but Cathy out of the narrative. The two children with an anxious mother in the Tides Restaurant do then contribute another little cameo, but it is one in which the mother's own fears induce anxiety in her children. Overall, this suggests an ambivalence on the part of the adults towards the chil-dren. This ambivalence may be taken as summarising the way in which children function in Hitchcock's films. On the one hand, children can be cheeky, amusing and sharply observant – like Hitchcock himself – and one senses that he half recognises that they are in certain respects like alter egos, puncturing the pomposity of adults. On the other, they can equally be difficult and troublesome, and they may well generate a fair degree of adult hostility. Refusing to sentimentalise them, Hitchcock registers both points of view across his films.

It should also be noted that, in Hitchcock's last few films, not only are children's appearances rare, but those who do appear – Dr Koska's violin-playing daughter in TORN CURTAIN; the Sunday school kids having Cokes with the priest in FAMILY PLOT – are quite remarkably polite. When the priest's secret date, a lady in red, enters the café, all four children stand up until she is seated. It would seem that Hitchcock in his old age was reluctant to permit the anarchic behaviour of the children in his earlier films.

Children and the police

What happens when children's mischief is witnessed by Hitchcock's police: do the latter promptly restore order? Not necessarily. When naughty schoolboys in THE RING hurl eggs instead of the official missiles at a black man in a fairground sideshow (➤ FOOD AND MEALS), a policeman in the crowd is most amused. It is only when the sideshow's owner comes over and protests that he does his duty and chases the boys away.

There is also one Hitchcock policeman who befriends a child: Ted in SABOTAGE. Although he does this in the exercise of his duty, he seems genuinely fond of Stevie. It is true that, to a modern, more cynical eye, Ted might appear to be a little too friendly towards Stevie (➤ *Entry through a window and the police*), but I do not think it would have seemed that way at the time. If an ulterior motive to the friendship was suspected, it would have been the safe one that Ted was naturally anxious to get close to the highly attractive Mrs Verloc.

CONFINED SPACES

Fig. 12. Still: NORTH BY NORTHWEST: Confined space – Roger (Cary Grant) under the oil tanker.

Confined spaces is a loose term. I wanted a designation which covered two
sorts of setting in Hitchcock: on the one hand, small private rooms such as bathrooms and toilets; on the other, a variety of public spaces, from jails to telephone
booths, which enclose the characters in more or less claustrophobic ways. There
are also more elaborate examples: the action of LIFEBOAT is entirely confined to
the lifeboat itself; that of ROPE to the increasingly claustrophobic apartment of
the two killers. But my concern here is with small rooms and with 'boxed-in'
spaces such as booths, bunks and trunks, where the sense of confinement functions in two broadly contrasting ways: either as a retreat/hiding place from the
world or as an imprisoning cage. Although there may seem to be little connec-

tion between a bathroom and a telephone booth, my argument will be that, if we look at how they are used across the films, a pattern emerges.

Bathrooms and washrooms

Only occasionally are bathrooms and washrooms in Hitchcock's films used purely for conventional purposes, such as taking a bath (as in THE LODGER). More often, something else is going on. In particular, they occur repeatedly in the spy movies. In THE MAN WHO KNEW TOO MUCH (1934), there is a minor example: Bob finds the MacGuffin hidden in a shaving-brush in Louis Bernard's hotel bathroom. In SECRET AGENT, the bathroom scene is much more significant. Shortly after Ashenden and Elsa have first met, Hitchcock stages a long scene between them in their hotel bathroom, in which Ashenden reads Elsa a decoded message and they discuss both the terms of their fake marriage and their forthcoming mission. The General enters during this, and he becomes so upset that Ashenden has been 'issued with' a wife and he has not that he assaults a toilet roll, an act which Hitchcock must have been delighted to have got past the censors. Throughout the scene Elsa has been putting on her makeup, but when she presents her beautified face for Ashenden's approval, he is so rude that she slaps him, prompting him to slap her. 'Married life has begun,' she comments, tartly.

Marty Roth uses SECRET AGENT to suggest that 'the espionage thriller (is) a genre that is always on the verge of a homosexual subtext' (Roth 1992: 37). The bathroom scene is crucial to such a reading: it suggests Ashenden's distaste at finding himself saddled with a 'wife', and his rudeness to Elsa may be contrasted with the way he seeks to placate the General: 'This girl's been issued to me as part of my disguise' (read, as a heterosexual) (40). In addition, although the General is ostensibly a womaniser, he 'comes across as a dandy and a sissy', prefiguring Peter Lorre's performance as Joel Cairo in THE MALTESE FALCON (John Huston, 1941) (41). I discuss the gay subtext to SECRET AGENT further under HOMOSEXUALITY.

The bathroom scene in SECRET AGENT also links with that in THE MAN WHO KNEW TOO MUCH (1934) in that each refers to the world of espionage: the MacGuffin; the decoded message. Similarly in other spy movies. In NORTH BY NORTHWEST, Roger hides in Eve's washroom on the train when, unseen by him, she sends Vandamm the message which first reveals to us that she is connected with the spies. Later, in her Chicago hotel room, Roger pretends to have a shower whilst spying on her through the door. After she has left, he then 'decodes' the imprint of the address she wrote on a notepad, and follows her to

Vandamm, who in this same scene acquires the MacGuffin. In Torn Curtain, the two settings of washroom and shower, and the hero's actions within them, are reversed. Both are in the Copenhagen hotel, but in the shower scene Michael misses the important action – Sarah going off to fetch a book with a hidden message – whereas in the washroom scene he goes into a toilet cubicle to decode the book's message, which relates to a secret organisation called pi. In pursuit of the first MacGuffin in Topaz, DuBois and Uribe first meet inside the Hotel Theresa in Uribe's bathroom. Then, on the plane out of Cuba, André goes into a toilet to discover the second MacGuffin: a microfilm hidden in a book Juanita gave him.

Bathrooms and toilets in the spy movies would thus seem to function in a metaphorical sense, as private spaces in which the secrets of the espionage world are referred to in a coded form. First, there is a link with the notion of voyeurism: as if Hitchcock keeps placing his professional voyeurs in these rooms because he associates the rooms themselves with voyeurism, an association finally made explicit when Norman spies on Marion in Psycho. Second, the typically furtive use of the rooms also suggests that the spies' activities within them are in some sense a displaced expression of their concerns. Third, the emphasis on such settings would also seem to be a feature of the general sexualisation of the espionage world (➤ HOMOSEXUALITY).

There is often also a sense, albeit coded, that the bathroom is a site for the return of the repressed (or, at least, suppressed): characters enter a bathroom and 'buried truths' emerge, such as Ashenden's real feelings about being issued with a wife. In Torn Curtain, Michael had tried to keep the book that Sarah goes to fetch a secret from her. In North by Northwest, Roger is much more on the ball: he watches Eve slip out to her rendezvous. In both these cases, the deception by one partner of a romantic couple is to do with the quest for the MacGuffin, again illustrating the ways in which this quest damages personal relationships. In Topaz, the repressed is the MacGuffin itself: André peels back the book's cover to reveal the microfilm. Juanita has inscribed the book with love, but the MacGuffin is her secret gift, for which she has already been killed. Since we will shortly learn that the Americans have already obtained evidence of the missiles on Cuba (➤ THE MACGUFFIN), this in fact an extremely poignant scene: Juanita and her colleagues have died obtaining redundant information.

The bathroom and the airline toilet in Topaz mark the beginning and the end of the quest for the film's two linked MacGuffins, but there is a third confined space which mediates between them: Juanita's darkroom at the back of her pantry. The darkroom echoes Uribe's bathroom in that both rooms are illuminated by a naked light bulb, but it is also linked narratively into the functioning of the motif in that it is where the microfilm MacGuffin is prepared. Moreover, just as

Rico Parra bursts into Uribe's room and exposes him as a spy, so Rico's troops break into Juanita's darkroom and expose her as a spy, which leads directly to her murder. This emphasises the sense that, in the spy movies, the bathrooms and toilets function as displaced versions of the spy's secret rooms.

A very different bathroom scene occurs in SPELLBOUND. Constance and J.B. are staying at Dr Brulov's house, having pretended to him that they are on their honeymoon. With Constance asleep in the bed, J.B. gets up from the couch and goes, as if in a trance, into the bathroom. He begins to shave, whereupon he is confronted with the symbolic expression of his forbidden sexual desires in the form of the foam on his shaving-brush. He recoils in horror from this, and then turns and looks at objects and fittings around the room. Each of these – shown in a series of point-of-view shots – causes him to react with shock. On the surface, he is reacting in this manner because everything he sees is white, but some of the fittings are also readable as sexual symbols: for example, there are some ingenious arrangements of water taps. Here the return of the repressed takes the form of an explosion of Freudian sexual symbolism, dramatising just what is being 'repressed' on this pretend honeymoon. This is indeed one of Hitchcock's emblematic bathroom scenes, conveying – albeit again in a coded form – the sexual undercurrents so often implicit in such scenes. We can now see why Louis Bernard's MacGuffin should be hidden in his shaving brush: he was Bob's sexual rival, and the shaving brush is like a comic reminder of this.

In the later examples of such scenes, it is obvious that Hitchcock is taking advantage of the fact that, since PSYCHO, it is possible in a mainstream film to acknowledge the existence of toilets (the offending appliance is hidden under a record player in SECRET AGENT), something which he had clearly long wished to do. But a general point about the scenes is more surprising. Virtually all Hitchcock's bathroom and washroom scenes are set in hotels, workplaces (Scotland Yard in BLACKMAIL, a garage in PSYCHO, the office in MARNIE), on public transport or at stations (Chicago in NORTH BY NORTHWEST). Indeed, since MURDER!, Hitchcock has not staged a single bathroom scene in the home of either the hero or heroine. There are scenes in which the protagonists in their own homes go to the bathroom, and occasions when we see through the bathroom door – e. g. to see Harry's body in Jennifer's bath in THE TROUBLE WITH HARRY – but we do not go into the rooms. Given that we do go into the bathrooms etc. in hotels and other non-domestic settings, this would seem to mark a curious point about Hitchcock's films, suggesting a prurience about the domestic bathroom which becomes a voyeuristic fascination with those in less private settings.

Confinement and concealment

The bathrooms and toilets in Hitchcock are typically used to hide, or to do something in private. At the other extreme are confined spaces in which someone is imprisoned. Only occasionally is this the work of the villain, as when Uncle Charlie in SHADOW OF A DOUBT traps Charlie in the garage in order to kill her with carbon monoxide poisoning. More usually, it is the police who imprison people in Hitchcock's films. The intensity of these scenes is commonly attributed to Hitchcock's well-known fear of the police, which he traces to a childhood incident in which he was briefly locked, as a punishment, in a police cell (see Truffaut 1968: 22). Hitchcock's jailed heroes are invariably innocent, and he conveys the trauma of false imprisonment through some powerful expressionistic devices, e.g. the circling camera shots suggesting Manny's mental crisis when he is first locked up in THE WRONG MAN or the overhead shot of Blaney shut in his cell in FRENZY. Here, clearly, the cage metaphor applies. Such scenes may be contrasted with those in MURDER! and THE PARADINE CASE showing the heroine in jail. Both are much more extended than the scenes for the heroes, dealing with long periods of imprisonment and with debilitating and degrading prison routines, focusing in particular on the lack of privacy due to the ubiquitous presence of female guards. With the heroes, Hitchcock conveys the trauma primarily as shock and a dizzying loss of personal agency; with the heroines it is more the steady accumulation of oppressive details which wear away at the sense of self.

Seeking to avoid capture by the police, Hitchcock's heroes, like most pursued figures, try to hide. But there is a particular manner of their hiding which occurs across a number of films and which is very suggestive. In three closely connected instances, the hero is with a young woman, but only he is hidden: in SABOTEUR, when the police stop the circus caravan and Barry hides on an upper rack whilst Pat sits below with the other members of the circus troupe; in To CATCH A THIEF, when Danielle hides Robie under the foredeck of her motor boat, and when Eve hides Roger behind the closed upper bunk of her train compartment. The first and the last examples are particularly close: each heroine is sitting just beneath the hiding hero and the police question her about him. In To CATCH A THIEF, the police are in a small plane flying over Danielle's boat and she waves to them.

Concealing the hero in this manner makes it seem as though he is metaphorically hidden behind a young woman (in two cases, the heroine), as if he were her guilty secret. The examples also suggest a variation of the childhood game of hide and seek. In his analysis of children's games in *Playing and Reality*, D.W. Winnicott identifies the strategic role of the mother in the early years of childhood in creating a safe space within which a child can play (Winnicott 1970: 47-52). The fear implied by these little scenes is that the hero has not been safely hidden, and that the woman who knows where he is will reveal his presence to the police. The woman who hides the hero thus symbolises the protective mother, and the police the hostile, searching father. Once again, the overtones are Oedipal.

This is illustrated most comprehensively in NORTH BY NORTHWEST. The last scene between Roger and his mother takes place in a crowded hotel lift, which erupts with laughter at Mrs Thornhill's question to the pursuing spies: 'You two gentlemen aren't *really* trying to kill my son are you?' As soon as the lift stops in the lobby, Roger flees – in effect, from his mother. The last time he speaks to her is when he then calls her from a phone booth on Grand Central Station. Both confined spaces (lift and phone booth) symbolise Roger's claustrophobic relationship with his mother, which symbolically ends with the phone call: she is not heard from again. The moment when Eve releases Roger from the confinement of the upper bunk is thus, structurally, a rebirth, with Eve herself as the symbolic mother – a point made by Stanley Cavell (Cavell 1986: 255).

The confined spaces where the hero hides are at the opposite extreme from those where he is locked up. But the childhood overtones indicate the way in which the opposition works in the Hitchcockian unconscious: jail is where the father sends 'naughty boys' (Truffaut 1968: 22); the mother's role is to protect the hero from such a terrible fate by hiding him.

This implicit paradigm enables the variations of the hiding scene to be analysed. In THE LADY VANISHES, the scene is anticipated by a comic variant and its basic structure is then inverted. As Iris and Gilbert search the train's luggage wagon for the missing Miss Froy, they look in various trunks and other containers, but the tone is ludic: each disappears in turn into Signor Doppo's Vanishing Lady cabinet, and Signor Doppo himself escapes from confinement in a trunk by using its false side. Without the threat of the police, comedy is possible: the overtones are of children playing. Then, after the couple have found and rescued Miss Froy, it she who is hidden in a closet in a train compartment and it is Gilbert and Iris who are scrutinised (they are pretending to be unconscious) by Dr Hartz, the equivalent of the police.

This is I think the earliest example of the hiding scene in Hitchcock. Since Miss Froy is explicitly a mother figure to Iris, the fact that she is the concealed figure on this occasion suggests that the elements are there, but they have not yet jelled into the dominant form of the scene one finds in the Hollywood movies. Here the children gallantly hide the English mother figure from the murderous foreign father figure. Oedipal overtones are suppressed in the light of the eve of war tensions in 1938 Europe.

Similarly in TORN CURTAIN, where Cold War tensions dictate the articulation of the motif. Michael and Sarah are hidden in separate costume baskets on a ship making the journey from East Germany to Sweden. As the ship docks and the baskets are unloaded, a suspicious Russian ballerina shouts out that they contain 'amerikanische Spione', prompting an East German policeman to machine-gun them. He shoots the wrong baskets, but it is nevertheless clear that the ballerina functions symbolically as the dangerous communist mother who threatens the children of the capitalist West with death.

STAGE FRIGHT offers another variation. At the climax, Eve hides Jonathan from the police in a theatrical coach under a stage. It is only now that she learns that, far from being falsely accused, Jonathan really is a murderer. And she learns this from her father, who is with the hunting police and who calls out to her. This turns everything round. Now it is the heroine who is threatened, the man she is hiding who is the threat, and the police and her father who are her potential saviours (➤ HANDS).

The persistence of the hiding scene in Hitchcock, and the way in which the basic ingredients are reworked in different forms to suit different agendas indicate just how patterned his films often are. Perhaps the most remarkable common aspect is that each hiding place is on a mode of transport, albeit stationary at the point when the police intervene in SABOTEUR and a purely theatrical version in STAGE FRIGHT. In 'ROPE: Three Hypotheses', Peter Wollen mentions that he once asked Farley Granger why Hitchcock was so interested in trains. Granger replied: 'The mixture of claustrophobia with movement' (Wollen 1999: 82). These scenes go a stage further, dealing with a claustrophobic enclosure within the means of transport itself. Consistent with Granger's comment, most of the hiding places represent a safe space to hide: like symbolisations of the womb where the hero can feel safe under the protection of the heroine as mother figure. This emphasises the ideological violation in TORN CURTAIN, but also that, when a villain seeks to hide in this manner, as in STAGE FRIGHT, the space is no longer safe.

In FRENZY there is a sequence which seems like a perversion of the hiding scene: when Rusk wrestles with Babs's corpse in a sack of potatoes on the back of a moving lorry. The confined space, here, is like a grave: it's as if Rusk has crawled into the grave to retrieve something from the corpse, and he is punished for this violation by the sheer intransigence of the woman's dead body (➤ THE CORPSE). Yet once again it is fear of exposure to the police which has prompted Rusk to take this desperate measure, and when he leaves the body in effect disinterred and out of its grave (the sack), it is the police who immediately spot it.

There is also a subsequent twist to the hiding scene in NORTH BY NORTHWEST. Although Eve protects Roger from the police, she betrays him to the spies. This leads to the famous pursuit by the crop-dusting plane ($\blacktriangleright$ TRAINS and PLANES). To escape from the plane, Roger flags down an oil tanker, which only just stops in time. He ends up supine under the tanker; the plane crashes into it. Roger's position here echoes the boxed-in space of the bunk bed, but now the space is highly dangerous: the plane immediately catches fire and the tanker will blow up at any moment. The association of the two spaces serves to undermine the apparent security of the bunk bed; in effect, Roger under the tanker reveals the mother figure's duplicitousness: this is where she has really sent him. Roger has to clamber out and flee for his life.

Cages and bars: fears of imprisonment

In contrast to the generally successful hiding places on the various means of transport, there is another set of examples in Hitchcock's films where the characters are within a confined space but are also highly exposed: when they are in a glass booth. In BLACKMAIL, Frank invites Alice into the phone booth of the shop where she works and produces her glove, which he found in Crewe's studio whilst investigating his 'murder'. This cues the entrance of Tracy, the future blackmailer, who has been watching them. He knows the significance of the glove (he found the other one); as he comments later: 'Detectives in glass houses shouldn't wave clues.' In STRANGERS ON A TRAIN, Guy and Miriam go into a soundproof record booth in the shop where she works. As if confirming the metaphorical associations of the space, Miriam now traps Guy (in a legal sense) by declaring that she is not, after all, going to divorce him. Moreover, as she outlines her intentions – to pretend that the child she is carrying is Guy's; to join him in Washington as his wife – he becomes so enraged that he shakes her, an act observed by those in the shop, including the proprietor. Here, as in BLACKMAIL, having witnesses to the private scene makes it especially dangerous: the secrets of the couple are threatened with exposure.

Obviously, in a world in which looking is so important, and, indeed, often so threatening, to be in a glass booth is to be exposed. Yet once again it is exposure to the police which is the real threat. This is made explicit in BLACKMAIL, where Tracy says to the couple in the booth that he wants to phone Scotland Yard. It is also implicit in STRANGERS ON A TRAIN after Miriam has been murdered: there are witnesses to Guy's violence towards his wife shortly before her murder. Later in the film, Hitchcock actually frames Guy and Bruno together behind some railings as Guy hides from the police, so that the fear of the police (and imprisonment) is there expressed directly by the cage imagery.

A parallel example is the scene in I CONFESS when Logan and Ruth are caught in the summerhouse by Vilette. The summerhouse is open to observation in a similar way to the glass booths, and Vilette's recognition of Ruth as 'Madame Grandfort' provides him with the material with which to blackmail her. Here the police only become involved after Vilette's murder, but what happened in and just outside the summerhouse becomes the basis of their whole case against Logan, so that here, too, it is exposure to the police which emerges as the ultimate threat behind this little scene.

The birds' attack on Melanie in the phone booth in THE BIRDS is obviously a more literal threat. As with Blaney's imprisonment in FRENZY, Hitchcock emphasises the cage metaphor by including an overhead shot of Melanie as she turns from side to side in her terror. This scene, too, may be connected metaphorically with the fears implicit in the other examples. The police may be seen as social embodiments of the superego, judging and punishing (mis)behaviour. And Margaret Horwitz has argued that in THE BIRDS 'The wild birds function as a kind of malevolent female superego' (Horwitz 1986: 281) (➢ CHILDREN). The sense of a 'malevolent superego' out there could be seen as broadly complementary to Bill Nichols's reading of the way in which the motif of 'at the window' functions in THE BIRDS: 'assault at the window only serves to confirm the fundamentally paranoid constitution of the subject (or ego)' (Nichols 1981: 159). The bird attacks are an extreme expression of such paranoia. More generally in Hitchcock, it is in the threat embodied by the police that the paranoia so often apparent in the narratives resides.

Both the images of imprisonment in a glass cage and the examples where the hero (especially) hides from the police are indicative of specific fears in Hitchcock's films where, again and again, the police create the chaos world into which the characters are plunged. As soon as Roger exits from the phone booth into the crowds on Grand Central Station, he becomes a man hunted: police are everywhere. He goes to a ticket office window, the clerk recognises him, alerts the police and Roger is once more on the run.

Moreover, this scene is in turn a reworking of its equivalent in SPELLBOUND, when Constance and J.B., on the run from the police, go to buy a train ticket at Pennsylvania Station. In this case, the ticket clerk is behind bars, and Hitchcock incorporates the imprisonment imagery into the dynamics of the scene. As J.B. – who is amnesiac – approaches the ticket window, he is trying to remember a past destination; as he reaches the window, the shadows of the bars are then cast on his own face. The stress of trying to remember seems compounded by the sight of the man behind bars, and the 'cage motif' then transfers to the hero: J.B. collapses on the counter, and Constance has to lead him away. But this little scene has drawn the attention of a policeman, who comes over and offers assistance.

Fig. 13. Still: SPELLBOUND: Confined space – the caged ticket seller (George Meader) at the station. J.B. (Gregory Peck)'s breakdown draws the attention of a policeman (Matt Moore); Constance (Ingrid Bergman) seeks to protect him.

It's as if the sense of a trap implicit in the bar imagery *produces* the policeman, like a pre-echo of the hero's eventual imprisonment in jail, where the cage imagery returns as Constance addresses an unseen J.B. through prison bars.

In short, the fear of the police which haunts Hitchcock's films manifests itself in any number of ways: not just in the scenes of incarceration, but in the hiding scenes, in the cage metaphor, in the recurring imagery of bars. The confined space motif serves to condense these fears into concrete little scenes, scenes where the ways in which the characters are visualised (in prison; in a glass booth; behind bars) is as important as their actions.

Paranoia about the police is not the only feature of this motif which could be said to have roots in Hitchcock's childhood. Recalling Hitchcock's Catholic upbringing, some of the confined spaces involving two people also evoke the confessional. In the phone booth in BLACKMAIL, Frank wants Alice to 'confess', but she is too upset to speak. In the theatrical coach in STAGE FRIGHT, Jonathan really does confess. The record booth scene in STRANGERS ON A TRAIN is also like a confession: Guy learns what Miriam's real intentions are; Miriam learns that Guy is 'serious' about Anne. When, later, Bruno tells Guy that he has murdered Miriam, Hitchcock films the scene so that the railings Bruno is behind pointedly evoke the grille in a church confessional. I Confess contains a genuine confession in a real confessional, and the subject of the confession – Keller's to the murder of Vilette – is not only the equivalent of this scene in Strangers on a Train, but it also has the same underlying fear as all these other examples: that the police will find out. The most painful confession scene is, nevertheless, in the bell tower at the climax of Vertigo. The top of the tower is a confined space which is exposed in the sense that it has open archways, and this serves to make it *physically* dangerous. After Scottie has forced a confession from Judy, the 'superego intrusion' which then occurs is devastating: a nun appears as if from nowhere, an apparition which so frightens Judy that she steps through an open archway and plunges to her death (➢ GUILT AND CONFESSION). All these examples may in turn be related to the broader theme of confession in Hitchcock's work.

Finally, the most famous bathroom scene in all cinema. In Hitchcock's work in general, the bathroom is a place of refuge. It may turn out to be threatening, as in Spellbound, but even there it is not really a trap; albeit somewhat traumatised, the hero walks out of it. Psycho breaks the rule. Marion treats the bathroom as her private space, and she begins her shower with a voluptuous surrender to the water. 'Mrs Bates's' attack violates this space: Marion is trapped and savagely murdered. The shattering impact of the scene has prompted many excellent analyses, but the point I wish to make here is in terms of Hitchcock's motifs. First, the return of the repressed takes the form here of a murderous 'mother': an extension of the negative representations of mothers in Hitchcock (➢ MOTHERS AND HOUSES) into a veritable monster. Second, a confined space which has hitherto functioned as a place of retreat from the chaos world is suddenly and violently transformed into the chaos world. In effect, the 'malevolent superego out there' bursts into the confined space, with annihilating force. The bathroom has become like the phone booth in The Birds, but with an even more devastating outcome: the attacking intruder not only traps the heroine, but brutally murders her.

In his references to the cage imagery in Hitchcock's films, Hartmut W. Redottée concentrates primarily on the sense of a trap implicit in the motif (Redottée 2000: 34-36). My argument throughout this discussion has been that there are as many examples in which a confined space functions as a hiding place or refuge. However, hiding places can be precarious, so that it would be more accurate to say that there is often a dialectic in play: a confined space which seems to be a refuge could also be a trap, and the two contrasting functions may well be in tension. Nevertheless, Marion's murder is quite exceptional. Although Hitchcock repeats the brutal attack on the heroine in the attic bedroom assault on Melanie in THE BIRDS, the shower-bath murder is the *locus classicus* of such scenes. Apart from the brilliance of the realisation of the scene, and the fact that it is the film's heroine who is being slaughtered, another reason is surely the shock of the violation of the hitherto safe space of the bathroom. Indeed, it is partly because of this violation that I have grouped together, under one motif, otherwise diverse spaces such as bathrooms and phone booths. I mention at the beginning that the motif functions in two broadly contrasting ways. In this scene, the contrasting ways are collapsed.

See also APPENDIX I.

Washrooms and the police

The involvement of the police in this motif has been as threatening figures: looking for people who are hidden; locking people up. I would like therefore to mention two contrasting examples: the washroom scene in Scotland Yard in BLACKMAIL, and that on the Chicago station in NORTH BY NORTHWEST. In the former, Frank and his colleague join other policemen at the end of the day's shift, and the men's room camaraderie of the scene is most unusual for Hitchcock, especially for Hitchcock's policemen. Here, for once, we see the police as a community, enjoying one another's company: all are chatting and joking; one is using his handcuffs to open a tin of tuna. This is really quite a relaxed little scene, indicating that, even in Hitchcock, the police – albeit when off-duty – are allowed their moments of cheerful spontaneity.

Unfortunately, in the second scene, the police are back in their more familiar role of looking at someone they are pursuing and not recognising him. As Roger, his face covered in shaving cream, prepares to shave, the two detectives from the train burst into the washroom and look wildly around. Since they do look (briefly) at Roger, his disguise is clearly a good one. Off-screen, we then hear the rhythmic crash of them opening the toilet cubicles; they then leave. In fact, what perhaps saves Roger is that he is not the only man shaving, and the other man also has a face covered in shaving cream. It could be that the detectives are still looking for Roger in his redcap disguise. It could equally be that the sight of two shaving men simply fooled them.

THE CORPSE

Fig. 14. Still: MURDER!: the traumatising corpse. Diana (Norah Baring) sits in an amnesiac fugue in front of the body of Edna Druce (visible in the mirror). On either side of Diana are Doucie (Phyllis Konstam) and Ted Markham (Edward Chapman); kneeling by the body is Edna's husband, Gordon Druce (Miles Mander).

Just as most Hitchcock films include at least one murder (or other violent killing) which in some sense involves the hero and/or heroine, so most of them include at least one corpse. This applies, of course, to many films, but Hitchcock's corpses are sufficiently important to the narrative to function as a motif: they are related to the characters and to the internal dynamics of the films in a patterned way. The importance of the corpse in Hitchcock may be gauged from its place in the repressed childhood traumas of the hero in SPELLBOUND and the heroine in MARNIE: when the incident is finally recalled, the dead body is the climactic image, a testament to the nature of the trauma. Yet even without the sense of such a founding trauma, an encounter with a corpse in Hitchcock is usually highly disturbing. The associations are however significantly different for the three principal figures: heroine, hero and villain. I will, accordingly, look at the functioning of the motif for each of these figures in turn.

The heroines

My main concern here – as with the heroes and villains – is with the impact of a corpse *on* a heroine. However, the fact that Hitchcock's work also includes some shocking corpses *of* a heroine should also be noted. These fall into a different category from the main examples on those occasions when the image of the corpse is shown to us without the mediation of a third party. There are three main examples: Marion's corpse in PSYCHO, Juanita's in TOPAZ and Brenda's in FRENZY. We see their murders, but then Hitchcock films each corpse so we experience its force directly, rather than through the eyes of the killer, even when, as in TOPAZ, he is clearly disturbed by it.

In PSYCHO, as Hitchcock's camera spirals out from Marion's dead eye, we are still numbed by the shock of her murder. Our reaction is very different from Norman's, who is upset less by Marion's fate than by the revelation of what his 'mother' has done. Nevertheless, as Norman cleans up, he treats the corpse respectfully, and the shot of him carrying it wrapped in the shower curtain out of the cabin has a definite charge. In *A Long Hard Look at 'Psycho'*, Raymond Durgnat notes that the curtain 'makes a shroud, but also evokes a wedding dress (carried over a threshold – the wrong way)' (Durgnat 2002: 134). This Gothic-romantic image is our last view of Marion, and it is both poignant and haunting.

Juanita's death is TOPAZ's most memorable image: Hitchcock films the moment when Rico Parra shoots her in an overhead shot in which her purple dress billows out under her body. This is a moving, poetic death: Rico has killed the woman he loves (➤ HANDS). By contrast, Brenda's body in death is grotesque: eyes bulging, tongue lolling out of her mouth. Tania Modleski discusses the problem of the 'repellent' images of women in FRENZY, suggesting an ambivalence on Hitchcock's part: 'the film ... veers between disgust at the "lusts of men" and loathing of the female body itself' (Modleski 1988: 113). But Hitchcock repeats the image of the grotesque female corpse later in the film: when Babs's naked corpse falls from the lorry on to the road and we see her face, and with the anonymous victim at the end. We take it that this is the way Hitchcock prefers to show his murdered women, and it seems to me that a sense of revulsion is uppermost. The relaxation of censorship exposes a disturbing misogyny, a far cry from the earlier, eloquent images.

Corpses have a different sort of impact on Hitchcock's heroines depending on whether they are male or female. Where the corpse is male, the childhood killing in MARNIE does indeed provide the core material. In a fight with one of her clients, Marnie's prostitute mother fell and broke her leg; summoned by her cries for help, the five-year-old Marnie beat the sailor to death. During the fight, the primal scene was evoked in a shot of legs twisted together; Marnie was thus responsible for killing the father figure in a manner which stressed the brutal suppression of sex (➤ *Bed Scene* in Part I). In other examples where the heroine does the killing, a similar notion applies. In BLACKMAIL, Alice kills Crewe as he tries to rape her. In DIAL M FOR MURDER, Margot kills Swann as he tries to strangle her – an assault which Hitchcock films very much like an attempted rape. Even in SABOTAGE, Mrs Verloc kills her husband shortly after he has suggested that they should make up for her brother Stevie's death (for which he is responsible) by having a child of their own. Although Alice and Margot are acting in self-defence, and Marnie to help her mother, the sexual overtones are important to the charge the corpse carries. It's as if – directly or symbolically – killing has replaced sex: the corpse's potency is increased by its association with a sexual threat which has been violently repressed.

The power of the corpse in these examples is registered in its insistent presence, which takes different forms. In MARNIE and BLACKMAIL, the heroine is haunted by what are, in effect, guilt images of it: the moments when Marnie reacts to the colour red; Crewe's dead arm which Alice keeps 'seeing' in other men's arms (➤ HANDS). Marnie's memory of the childhood killing has been repressed, but her fraught responses to red – the threatened return of the repressed memory of the sailor's blood – in effect signify unconscious guilt. She has internalised the disturbing power of the corpse, but these moments bear testament to its force. Alice is similar: although she has not repressed the memory of the killing, her reactions to other men's arms – and later to the word 'knife' – are involuntary, like Marnie's. She also hallucinates a neon sign of animated cocktail shakers transforming into two knives, one of which stabs energetically at the 'cock' in the word 'cocktails'. Together with the (phallic) dead arm and the knife, this stabbing emphasises the disturbing power of both the killing and the corpse, as if Alice is compulsively re-enacting the trauma in her imagination.

In SABOTAGE and DIAL M FOR MURDER, the body itself serves the function of a guilt image: it lies on the floor of the marital home, contaminating the household with its insistent presence, and the heroine seems unable to get away from it. Margot also gets almost hysterical about Swann's 'staring eyes', which is

another guilt image (as if the eyes were accusing her) but also an echo of
Swann's murderous attack on her (the hard stare of the killer/rapist).

Even where the heroine – or another woman – is innocent of the killing, a
male corpse linked to her tends to have a 'repressed' sexual charge. In THE
MAN WHO KNEW TOO MUCH (1934), Louis Bernard says that the jumper Jill is
knitting for him is 'to wear over my beating heart'. Moments later, he is shot
over the heart. Given that Jill seems to have been spending most of her family
holiday flirting with him, and that he is killed whilst they are dancing together,
this fatal wound is like a 'mark of repression', punishing him for his Gallic se-
ductiveness and her for her adulterous desire. Even Lydia's shocking encounter
with Dan Fawcett's dead body in THE BIRDS seems sexualised, as if she is being
punished for intruding into a man's bedroom by being presented with the man,
in pyjamas, as a bloody corpse, with the mark of repression figured here in his
eyes, pecked out as a displacement for castration.

I am using the notion of a mark of repression to refer to a physical detail,
usually a wound, which, by its nature, stresses that the corpse carries a repressed sexual charge. Dan's pecked-out eyes, emphasised through two abrupt
cut-ins, are a particularly brutal example. The concept may also be applied to
MARNIE. The climactic image of the flashbacks to the childhood trauma is not
just of the sailor's body, but of the blood on the body, which fills the screen. The
bloodiness may be seen as the mark of repression on the body at the moment of
killing. Here the power of the corpse has been condensed into this image, and it
is this which functions as the return of the repressed for the adult Marnie.

The corpse as a (sexualised) guilt image; its insistent presence; a mark of repression on it: such elements indicate ways in which Hitchcock's corpses have a
specific, disturbing charge for these heroines. However, not all Hitchcock's famous corpses are traumatising. Harry in THE TROUBLE WITH HARRY is certainly
the director's most persistent corpse: the whole film revolves around the problem of his disposal. But here the film's humorous tone significantly reinflects
the material. First, although the notion of sexual repression still applies, this is
presented in comic terms. Harry died after two women responded to his sexual
overtures by conking him on the head: Jennifer with a milk bottle, Miss Gravely
with her robust hiking shoe. Second, although he was Jennifer's husband, she is
absolutely delighted to see him dead. Neither she nor Miss Gravely feels guilt at
the possibility that either may have dealt the fatal blow. Even the mark of repression – the blow on Harry's head – is scarcely an issue; Sam and Captain
Wiles discuss it as a sign that he was murdered, but again the tone is essentially
comic. Nevertheless, Harry's body is still a very insistent presence, and its multiple interments and disinterments bear witness to the disturbance it creates.

Where the heroine is linked to a woman's corpse, there is a different inflection
of the motif. In MURDER!, Diana is found – in an amnesiac fugue – next to the

corpse of Edna Druce, another member of her acting troupe. Although she is innocent, her proximity to the body and to the murder weapon results in her being arrested, tried and convicted for the murder – she becomes, like Margot, one of Hitchcock's rare falsely accused women. It is only much later in the film that the circumstances of the murder are worked out, and the real murderer and his motive identified (➤ ENTRY THROUGH A WINDOW). But the way Diana sits, in a daze, with Edna's body in front of her, together with her inability to remember what happened, shows that something has psychically traumatised her. It's as though the murderer has carried out Diana's own unconscious wish: to eliminate a woman who, for whatever reason, she actively disliked and who was on the point of saying something 'unspeakable' about Fane, the troupe's leading man. That it was Fane who actually carried out the murder – wanting, like Diana, to silence Edna – adds to the sense that he acted as Diana's agent. The power of the corpse here derives from the heroine's confused sense that she herself must have committed the murder: at her trial she does not deny the killing, but says, rather: 'Whatever I did must have happened when I was not conscious of myself.'

In VERTIGO, the heroine actually was an accomplice in another woman's murder: Judy assisted Elster in his plan to murder his wife – the real Madeleine. This is revealed, after Scottie has first met her as Judy, through a flashback and a letter Judy writes, both of which also disclose that she had impersonated Madeleine, and that it was this impersonation, 'Madeleine', Scottie fell in love with. In showing us for the first time what really happened in the bell tower when Madeleine fell, the flashback and letter also reveal Judy's own feelings. When Scottie saw the body fall, he heard a scream: the scream, he assumed, of a woman committing suicide. The flashback is shown silent, but we now see that Elster had already killed Madeleine by the time Judy clambered up through the trapdoor at the top of the tower; it was Judy who screamed, as if she were the victim, as Elster threw the body down. Judy says to Scottie at the end that she rushed up the tower still hoping to prevent Madeleine's murder; her scream thus also signalled her failure. Judy's frightened reaction caused Elster to put his hand over her mouth, and so she watched Madeleine fall – shown from her point of view – whilst being held over the drop by Elster in a manner similar to the way he had just held Madeleine herself. But it was not just the falling body which traumatised Judy: with Elster's hand still muzzling her, she turned to look at the trapdoor, fearing (hoping?) that Scottie might appear. This alerts us to the fact that Judy's trauma was compounded: also, at this moment she lost Scottie, whom, as the letter confirms, she loved.

Although Madeleine's corpse was only a part of Judy's trauma, we can see from the subsequent events that it must, nevertheless, be functioning as a powerful guilt image. First, the moment when Elster threw Madeleine from the tower was necessarily also the point at which Judy's impersonation abruptly ceased, so that Judy in effect witnessed Madeleine die in her place. In a way, her scream marked the psychic connection: as 'Madeleine' she screamed on behalf of Madeleine. And now, as Scottie obsessively refashions her into 'Madeleine', she becomes more and more fraught. She is being transformed back into a role which has terrible associations: 'Madeleine' was an accomplice in a murder; Madeleine, her double, was the victim. From Judy's point of view, Scottie is forcing her back into both these roles; they can no longer be coherently distinguished. The sense of a psychic link between corpse and heroine is here fully elaborated, through to the heroine herself dying at the end of the film in a manner which precisely echoes her last sight of the falling body (➢ STAIRCASES).

In MURDER! and VERTIGO, the corpse lacks a sexual charge for the heroine, but it still traumatises her with guilt, even though we are only able to understand this in retrospect. But these examples are exceptional. Because each film pivots around 'what happened' when the woman was killed, the murders are 'over-determined' moments. The heroine feels such guilt because of the nature of her relationship to the woman and to the murder. This is not however the case in my final example: when Mitch and Melanie in THE BIRDS find Annie's body, a victim of the bird attacks, outside her house.

Although both Mitch and Melanie are upset by Annie's corpse, circumstances force them to take action: to rescue Cathy from the house, to get away. It is Melanie who is the guiding intelligence here: who first thinks of Cathy, who stops Mitch from angrily throwing a stone at the crows, who tells him not to leave Annie's body outside. Melanie's ability to keep functioning sensibly even though she is very upset contrasts sharply with Lydia's reaction to Dan's body. This suggests that Melanie's psychic experience of the corpse is of a different order from the earlier examples. Susan Smith argues that it is, in fact, potentially therapeutic: 'Annie's death can be seen to function from Melanie's point of view as a redemptive act of atonement for her mother's abandonment of her as a child', with Cathy representing Melanie herself as a child (Smith 2000: 139). In other words, here the disturbing sight of the corpse – expressed, for instance, in Melanie's turning away from it – is mitigated by its deeper psychic resonances for the heroine.

For women in general, the experience of a corpse in Hitchcock is almost always to a greater or lesser extent traumatic. Amongst these examples, only Jennifer in THE TROUBLE WITH HARRY seems entirely unfazed by the encounter. The fact that a male corpse is usually more disturbing than a female suggests one reason: that the corpse often possesses a sexual charge. But this is by no means the whole story. In particular, the guilt that the heroines so often feel in the presence of a dead body clearly merits further discussion. First however I would like to look at what typically happens in the case of a hero.

The heroes

The main examples where the hero is linked to the corpse of a woman divide neatly into three groups: two 1930s English films (THE 39 STEPS and YOUNG AND INNOCENT), two Hollywood films (REBECCA and VERTIGO) and FRENZY. In THE 39 STEPS and YOUNG AND INNOCENT, the hero is confronted with a corpse early in the film, and is then pursued by the police for the woman's murder. But not only is he innocent of the murder, he also seems to be free of the guilt feelings which afflict Hitchcock's heroines under similar circumstances. In THE 39 STEPS, Annabella's going with Hannay back to his apartment clearly possesses sexual overtones, but Hannay ensures that they retire to separate beds. And so, when she falls across him in bed with a knife in her back (➢ BED SCENE), it's as if her anonymous killers have acted on his behalf, and eliminated her sexual threat – with the knife wound as the mark of repression. The use of the knife is in itself significant: the previous evening, when Hannay went to check Annabella's story that two men – the presumed killers – were following her, he rather oddly took the knife with him. The film would seem to be making a point of linking him to the killers.

In YOUNG AND INNOCENT, when Robert finds Christine's corpse on the beach, we see at once that he knew her. Here the murder weapon – a raincoat belt – is lying next to the body and, at the end of the film, we learn that it is in fact Robert's belt. Moreover, Christine's ex-husband strangled her partly out of jealousy over her relationship with Robert, a relationship he assumes was sexual. Robert himself denies this, but the denial connects him with Hannay: here, too, the hero is linked to the body through the murder weapon in a manner which hints that he may have unconsciously desired the woman's murder. In both films, the murdered woman is coded as sexual, but the hero ignores (resists?) this: could the murder be seen an expression of his desire to be rid of her threat?

Although this possibility is implicit, Hitchcock seems to hold it in check. Unlike most of the heroines, these two heroes seem to be genuine sexual innocents, a status which protects them from guilt: as if sexual innocence guarantees moral innocence. In contrast to the typical experience of a heroine confronted with a male corpse, Annabella's and Christine's corpses apparently lack a sexual charge for the hero, and so he does not feel guilt. That sexual desire in Hitchcock is haunted by guilt is well-known, and the mark of repression on so many of his corpses bears testament to its disturbing force. Nevertheless, the knife in Annabella's back notwithstanding, after her death Hannay remembers not her allure, but the moments when she referred, cryptically, to her mission. And even this is presented by Hitchcock in desexualised terms: we see faded superimpositions of Annabella repeating words she said earlier, but in a disembodied voice – like a ghost. As for Robert, he only ever speaks of Christine as someone with whom he had business dealings; one senses no spark of suppressed sexual feeling.

However, REBECCA and VERTIGO depict a very different impact of a female corpse on the hero. In REBECCA, the hero himself is the killer. His crime parallels the villain's in YOUNG AND INNOCENT: just as Guy resents Christine's sexual independence (she has obtained a 'Reno divorce'), so Maxim struck Rebecca – and accidentally killed her – when she said she was going to have someone else's child but raise it as his. Here, too, the row which led to the killing took place in a building on the seashore, and the husband then disposed of the body at sea. And, although we never see Rebecca's body, it is central to the film's plot: in a spectacular example of the return of the repressed, it resurfaces from its grave on the seabed to confront Maxim with his crime, forcing him into a confession. VERTIGO is even darker. After Scottie has witnessed Madeleine's fall from the tower, he begins to identify with the 'Madeleine' he thinks is dead, which culminates in his nightmare (in which he imagines falling into her grave) and nervous breakdown. It's as if he is seeking, psychically, to join 'Madeleine' in death.

The difference between these two examples and those in THE 39 STEPS and YOUNG AND INNOCENT lies in a number of factors, but a crucial feature is the two kinds of hero involved. Hannay and Robert are not just (implicit) sexual innocents, but are also largely free from the neuroses and inner torments of Maxim and Scottie; it is only to be expected that the latter suffer more. Maxim's suffering betrays the guilt he tries to disavow for Rebecca's death: the killing was crucially motivated by sexual repression. As Tania Modleski has pointed out, Scottie's suffering is enhanced because it is 'feminised': he is 'plunged into the "feminine" world of psychic disintegration, madness, and death' (Modleski 1988: 95). There are many examples in both literature (Flaubert's *Madame Bovary*, 1857; Cornell Woolrich's *Phantom Lady*, 1942) and cinema (FURY, Fritz Lang, 1936; HIROSHIMA MON AMOUR, Alain Resnais, 1959) of a woman reacting to the loss of her lover with a nervous breakdown or a psychosomatic illness. However, for a man to react this way, as Scottie does, is quite exceptional.

Where the hero is (or seems to be) implicated in a man's death, there are different inflections of the motif, depending on the circumstances. If the man is older than the hero, the association is predictably Oedipal. Here the childhood trauma in SPELLBOUND *is* relevant, but at one remove: it is the death of Dr Edwardes, a father figure, that the hero feels immediate guilt for (➢ DOUBLES); this guilt masks the repressed guilt for the childhood killing.

Raymond Bellour has discussed the Oedipal overtones to the killing of Townsend in NORTH BY NORTHWEST (Bellour 1975/2000: 85-88). These overtones are
linked to a more general notion in the film: that of the hero as a child. When
Roger plucks the knife out of Townsend's back – and so seems to be his murderer – this looks like unconscious exhibitionism: he even has his photograph
taken holding the knife. Whilst the narrative premise is to project Roger into the
familiar 'falsely accused-man' plot, the subtext (as in many examples in the
film) presents Roger as a child figure forever getting into scrapes and then running away from adult wrath.

TORN CURTAIN takes this further, in that the hero really does kill a man.
Michael kills Gromek, his Communist minder, and the presence of an older woman as his accomplice enhances the Oedipal sense of killing a physically powerful father figure. After the murder, as if Michael were a child, the woman takes
off his coat and leads him to the sink to wash his bloody hands. Recalling the
childhood traumas in SPELLBOUND and MARNIE, he has been infantilised by the
experience.

Other examples include one aspect of Judy's trauma in VERTIGO: someone
else dies in the hero's place. In SABOTEUR, as Barry goes to combat the opening
act of sabotage, his co-worker Ken Mason takes the booby-trapped fire extin-
guisher from his hands so that he, not Barry, goes up in flames. In TO CATCH A
THIEF, when the villains try and kill Robie, they accidentally kill Foussard, one
of their own. But in neither case does the killing have the sort of impact on the
hero that is typical of the heroines. Even though Barry sees his best friend incin-
erated, there is no sense that he registers Ken's death as a guilt image. Robie
does not learn who was killed in his place until later, and although the police
identify Foussard as the 'cat', Robie's sobriquet, as if he was Robie's double, the
association fails to work dramatically. Even as a corpse, Foussard lacks dramatic
interest.

Equally, sometimes a corpse is just a corpse. In SECRET AGENT, Ashenden and
the General are to rendezvous with the organist in a Swiss church. When they
enter, the man is immobile, playing a single chord, and they soon learn why: he
has been murdered. But even though his body slumps dramatically, there is
nothing traumatic about its discovery: indeed, the General comments approv-
ingly on the skill of the killer. Nevertheless, this example is untypical: a corpse
in Hitchcock's films nearly always carries some sort of charge.

A final example of the linkage of hero and a male corpse shows that sometimes this charge, although implicit, can be difficult to grasp. In the remake of
THE MAN WHO KNEW TOO MUCH, Louis Bernard dies, with a knife in his back,
as he passes on a vital message to Ben; the scene duplicates Annabella's equivalent death, where she passes on the map which sends Hannay to the Scottish
Highlands. Here, however, Hitchcock takes things further: Louis was disguised

Fig. 15. Still: THE MAN WHO KNEW TOO MUCH (1955): the contaminating corpse. Disguised as an Arab, Louis Bernard (Daniel Gélin) tells Ben (James Stewart) about a planned assassination before he dies. The streaks show where his facial makeup has been transferred to Ben's hands.

as an Arab, and his facial makeup comes off on Ben's hands. That this is signifi-cant is suggested by Ben's reaction: as he looks at his stained hands he says, 'I feel kinda funny'; then, as he wipes the makeup off, he wonders, 'Why should he pick me out to tell?' Ben would seem to feel singled out, for some unknown reason, as Louis's successor, and the stain on his hands is like a sign of this. But the stain still lingers on as something of a mystery, especially since Louis's own hands were stained, at the moment of his death, with a blue dye spilt on him in his flight from his pursuers.

It can be seen that the four sexual permutations of protagonist and corpse produce rather more than four sets of associations, but there are nevertheless certain patterns. With the heroines, the corpse is usually in some sense a guilt image. For a male corpse, this is often compounded by overtones of sexual repression; for a female corpse, the heroine's reaction depends more on the circumstances. Diana and Judy are overwhelmed by guilt, but Melanie is more controlled and practical (here it is Cathy, saved by Annie, who suffers the burden of guilt). With the heroes, the associations are more diverse. Where the corpse is male, there is usually an underlying Oedipal scenario, testifying, once again, to the Freudian nature of Hitchcock's narratives. But, where the corpse is female, even though the circumstances surrounding the killing might seem to be sexually charged, the guilt so prevalent with the heroines is generally much less in evidence. Hannay and Robert are only superficially disturbed by the corpse; Maxim seeks to locate the moral blame for Rebecca's death with her. Only Scottie is genuinely haunted by guilt.

This difference between the heroes and heroines can be explored further by looking at the films' narratives. For the heroes, THE 39 STEPS and YOUNG AND INNOCENT establish the paradigm: the hero is hunted for the murder of the woman whose corpse he is linked to, a chase which leads him to the heroine. The corpse, in other words, obliges him to go on a journey which eventually has a romantic happy ending. Although dealing with male corpses, SABOTEUR, SPELL-BOUND and NORTH BY NORTHWEST are all very similar. In each of these five films, we have the familiar quest of the falsely accused hero: he needs to prove to the authorities that he is innocent, which requires that he pursue his own investigation.

However, Hitchcock denies such an option to his heroines, even the similarly falsely accused Diana and Margot. One might feel that this could be taken as further support for the proposition that Hitchcock tends to see his heroines as guilty. But an important point about the corpse is that it embodies a silent accusation: someone has caused the death. The heroines, trapped within an oppressive patriarchal system, tend to feel themselves guilty; the heroes – with the crucial exception of the 'feminised' Scottie – tend to disavow such guilt. Hence the way in which the corpse is shown to mesmerise most of the heroines: as if it represents some kind of judgement on her which renders her incapable of clear thought. Jennifer and Melanie are exceptions, but only Jill manages to keep her cool as someone is actually killed in front of her, enabling her – uniquely amongst these heroines – to share the hero's quest to track down the villains.

Hitchcock's final corpse occurs, very dramatically, at the end of FRENZY. Under the BED SCENE, I mention the key points: seeking revenge, Blaney bludgeons the shape in Rusk's bed, only to discover that he has been hitting the naked body of Rusk's latest victim. Chief Inspector Oxford's arrival at that moment makes it seem as though Blaney is about to be projected back into the falsely accused man role, but Rusk himself then reappears, letting Blaney off the hook. More, however, is going on. The moment when the corpse is revealed to be a woman is unique in Hitchcock's work: so far as Blaney is concerned, the corpse changes sex – it should have been Rusk. Here, as in a number of the earlier examples of the motif, we are dealing with an 'overdetermined' moment, a condensation of elements implicit in the film. Blaney's shock when he first sees the corpse and the fact that he *looks* so guilty suggest that the corpse is a genuine guilt image, confronting him with his own inner violence towards women. Moreover, the shot which alerts us to the corpse's gender is a very precise echo of Crewe's death in BLACKMAIL: the woman's lower arm suddenly slumps into view from under the covers. On the principle that all Hitchcock's films interconnect with one another, so that visual echoes from one film to another are always significant, this suggests that we should read this scene in the light of its equivalent in BLACKMAIL. Alice was fighting off a sexual threat: this implies that Blaney's hostility towards women – without the justification which applies in Alice's case – is based on sexual fears. But such a pathology – a hatred of women stemming from a sense of sexual inadequacy – characterises Rusk. Accordingly, the sense that Rusk is Blaney's alter ego is here given strong reinforcement. Not for the first time in Hitchcock's work, the villain is indeed the hero's dark double, brutally enacting the latter's own inner violence.

This is the last corpse in Hitchcock's work, and it has an emblematic force. It summarises the significance of the motif: at least, so far as a female corpse and male characters are concerned. Hence the power of the film's penultimate shot. In it, Hitchcock frames the three men together with the woman's corpse on the bed in the background. Implicitly, this indicts all of them: Rusk for her murder; Oxford for the miscarriage of justice which left Rusk free to murder again; Blaney for the violence of his misogyny and his murderousness towards Rusk.

The villains

In general, Hitchcock's heroines and heroes kill only in self-defence, or accidentally, whereas his villains are often genuine murderers. A different dynamic thus exists between the villains and the various corpses for which they are responsible. The absence of guilt in most of Hitchcock's villains is discussed under GUILT AND CONFESSION, but I also note certain cases where the murder victim – or someone who stands in for the victim – 'returns' in some form to haunt the killer, like the return of the repressed: THE PLEASURE GARDEN, JUNO AND THE PAYCOCK and STRANGERS ON A TRAIN. Such images suggest the return of the killer's disavowed or repressed guilt. Except for the special case of Marnie, this is rather different from the guilt which afflicts those Hitchcock heroines confronted with a corpse. Nevertheless, there are other examples in which the relationship between villain and corpse is rather similar to that found with the heroines, in that the killing seems to be motivated by the repression of sexual desire and the corpse possesses what I call an insistent presence.

ROPE is a good example. It is generally agreed that the opening strangling of David is filmed like the climax of a sex scene, with the two gay killers panting with exertion, Phillip not wanting the lamp switched on just yet, Brandon lighting a cigarette and, a little later, the equivalent of 'how was it for you?' (See, for example, Wood 1989: 353). It's as if the murder has served both to repress the desire the two killers implicitly felt for David and to bind them together through their sharing the highly charged experience of a sexualised murder. David's corpse in the trunk throughout the rest of the film thus functions symbolically as their guilty secret, both their murderousness and their homosexuality. But there is also a tension between the two killers over the 'insistent presence' of the corpse. Whereas Phillip repeatedly shows signs of guilt for the murder, Brandon does not, and he even sets up a monstrous 'practical joke' on David's relatives and friends as he arranges for them to eat food off his 'tomb' (➤ *Food and murder*).

The contrasting responses of the two killers seems to me symptomatic. Phillip (the passive partner) is reacting like a heroine; Brandon (the dominant one) like a villain. Hitchcock's villains – like melodrama villains in general – may be sexual figures, but they tend to have a rather more perverse relationship to the corpses they are responsible for than the heroines. REAR WINDOW and FRENZY provide further illustrations of the distinction. In REAR WINDOW, we see neither the murder nor the corpse, but the former presumably took place in Mrs Thorwald's bed and the latter certainly proved a problem for Thorwald: he dismembered his wife and distributed the various parts of her body around the neighbourhood. But we could hardly characterise the murder as repression of desire: Thorwald was getting rid of an unwanted wife; the bed only became the (presumed) site for the murder because she was an invalid. In his series of 'necktie murders' in FRENZY, Rusk first 'rapes', then strangles his victims. Here we could perhaps characterise the murders as stemming from the repression of desire, but this is enacted in a highly perverse manner: Rusk is projecting on to the women blame not just for his own rapacious impulses, but also for his failure to complete the sex act (Modleski 1988: 113).

The 'insistent presence' of the corpses in these two films is also of a different order to that found with the heroines. In REAR WINDOW, it is Mrs Thorwald's head which refuses to stay put: first buried in the garden, then dug up when a neighbour's dog smells it, it ends in a hatbox in Thorwald's apartment. In

FRENZY, it is Babs's body which presents Rusk with an equivalent problem. He is obliged to return to it in order to retrieve his tie pin, and his struggle to achieve this occurs with the body in a sack of potatoes on the back of a moving lorry, so that villain, corpse and potatoes are hurled around in a grotesque danse macabre. In both these films, the corpse seems to possess a mysterious power over the killer, forcing him to return to it and eventually causing him to incriminate himself: Thorwald through his murder of the dog that 'knew too much'; Rusk through the potato dust on his clothes.

Even more than with a heroine, a corpse seems to exert power over a villain: either the killer hallucinates its return as a 'ghost', or it draws the killer back to it, or – as in ROPE – it simply stays put until the killers betray its presence. There are exceptions: Rusk walks away undetected from Brenda's corpse; Rico unchallenged from Juanita's in TOPAZ. However, if the police had been doing their job properly, they would have tracked Rusk back to Brenda much earlier: his file – under the Dr Crippen pseudonym of Robinson – is actually in the same room as her body. And Rico's case is exceptional: because he kills the woman he loves, it is the murder itself which is traumatic. Significantly, after he has walked away from Juanita's corpse, we never see him again.

In both STAGE FRIGHT and I CONFESS, the murderer returns to the scene of the crime, hoping to cover his tracks, but his presence there endangers him: Jonathan is observed by a witness; Keller is obliged to report the 'discovery' of Vilette's body to the police. In STAGE FRIGHT, since we only have Jonathan's duplicitous account (the famous 'lying flashback') of his return to Charlotte's house – where her husband lies murdered – it is not apparent that he is, in fact, the murderer. However, as he goes round trying to make it seem as if a burglar was responsible, he looks like the guilty man he really is. In this film, too, the pseudonym Robinson is bestowed on Jonathan, and Commodore Gill even cues us to make the connection by mistakenly referring to him at one point as 'Crippen'. In I CONFESS, we see Keller at Vilette's house after he has called the police. He is acting in a very agitated manner, and but for the distracting effect of Logan's behaviour (➤ *Corpses and the police*), would probably have given himself away. In both cases, the power of the corpse in drawing the murderer back serves – or should have served – to help incriminate him.

PSYCHO is the most important example of the corpse motif for the villains. The nature of Marion's murder – brutal, sexualised killing; a long sequence in which Norman cleans up and disposes of the corpse – locates Norman as a villain. He thinks he is cleaning up to protect his mother, just as Jonathan says he tampered with evidence to protect Charlotte. Although in both cases this is partly true, the two scenes are more strongly linked in that the man himself is the real murderer. And in PSYCHO the background presence of the long dead corpse of Mrs Bates – Norman's guilty secret, which he hides in the cellar – adds another dimension. In effect, Norman is in a psychotic Oedipal relationship, possessed by the corpse of the mother he killed: the psychic connection between corpse and protagonist goes even further than with Judy in VERTIGO, right through to the merging of the two in the penultimate shot. As this happens, Hitchcock dissolves to the car containing Marion's corpse being hauled out of the swamp: Norman, Mrs Bates and Marion in the car trunk are thus all connected in the film's astonishing ending.

Tania Modleski discusses the function of the corpses in PSYCHO and FRENZY in terms of Julia Kristeva's concept of 'the abject', arguing that the female corpse threatens the male order with pollution (Modleski 1988: 107-109). Hence Norman's meticulous cleaning up after Marion's murder, or the way the first corpse in FRENZY interrupts the politician's speech about cleaning up the Thames by appearing in the river itself, like a mocking example of the pollution he is referring to. To extend Kristeva's concept to other Hitchcock corpses would be helpful, I feel, in certain cases. The corpse (female and male) is one of Kristeva's main examples of the abject. Glossing her ideas, Elizabeth Grosz writes:

> Corporeal waste is Kristeva's second category of abjection. Bodily fluids, waste products, refuse – faeces, spit, sperm etc. – provoke cultural and individual horror and disgust, symptomatic of our cultural inability to accept the body's materiality, its limits, its 'natural' cycles and its mortality... For Kristeva, the most horrifying example of waste is the corpse, which is almost universally surrounded by taboos and rituals to prevent 'contamination' of the living... The corpse is intolerable; it exists at the very borders of life... It poses a danger to the ego in so far as it questions its stability and its tangible grasp on and control over itself.
>
> (Grosz 1990: 91-92)

These ideas help account for the mixture of horror and fascination with which the main characters often respond to Hitchcock's corpses. In addition, the notion of a corpse 'polluting' is not confined to female corpses and could be applied to a number of films. For example, perhaps Ben's hands are stained by Louis Bernard's corpse as a mark of guilt: the previous night Jo had worked him into a rage against Louis for standing them up. Louis's murder may also be seen as one element in a series of events 'prompted by' Ben's hostility to Jo's suggestion here that they have another child (➤ DOUBLES). On this reading, the murder arises out of Ben's unconscious; another reason for his hands being stained with guilt. This links with the moment in STRANGERS ON A TRAIN when Bruno hands Guy Miriam's cracked spectacles. Bruno carried out Miriam's murder for Guy, and now his gesture signals Guy's own responsibility in Miriam's death. Guy's hands, too, are symbolically 'stained' by association with a corpse.

Fig. 16. Still: THE TROUBLE WITH HARRY: the concealed corpse, the curious child and the baffled
policeman. Jennifer (Shirley MacLaine) seeks to prevent Arnie (Jerry Mathers) from revealing
to Deputy Sheriff Wiggs (Royal Dano) that Harry's body is hidden in the bath.

In other films, the sense of the corpse as polluting is conveyed, as in PSYCHO,
by the excessive care with which any traces of pollution are removed. Before
Harry's body is restored to its original position on the hillside, all four of those
involved in the multiple burials and disinterments work hard to clean it up;
here the scrupulous cleaning of the corpse suggests, by projection, that the characters are symbolically cleansing themselves of having tampered with it. At the
end of REAR WINDOW, Thorwald's apartment is being redecorated, as if to remove any trace of the corpse's polluting presence. DIAL M FOR MURDER includes a perverse version: after Margot has been convicted of Swann's murder,
Tony moves his bed to sleep next to the place where the corpse lay. Mark's conclusion – that Tony feels too guilty about Margot's fate to sleep in the bedroom
– merely accounts for moving the bed; it does not account for its new position,
which suggests that Tony is identifying himself psychically with the corpse itself. Although Kristeva's theories do not cover all the ways in which the corpse
motif functions in Hitchcock, these examples indicate that the theories are,
nevertheless, frequently suggestive.

In conclusion, I would like to look further at the three films which depict what are perhaps the strongest examples of the motif: REBECCA (for the hero), VERTIGO (for the heroine and hero) and PSYCHO (for the villain). Here, a particular inflection of Kristeva's ideas seems to be in play: these four characters are haunted by the corpses in the films to the point of threatened or actual dissolution of the ego – a terrifying loss of self. Indeed, I would go further: the corpse would seem to trigger the return of the repressed death drive for these characters. When Rebecca's body is found, Maxim's fatalistic 'I've always known that Rebecca would win in the end' signals his submission to the fate she had planned for him: execution for her 'murder'. With Judy, we sense that, all along, she has carried a punishing guilt for Madeleine's murder, so that the eerie appearance of the nun which she interprets (we assume) as Madeleine's ghost in effect shocks her into stepping off the tower to fall to her own death (➤ GUILT AND CONFESSION). With Scottie, his nervous breakdown – acute melancholia – is a clinical expression of the devastating force of the death instincts. With Norman, who is genuinely psychotic, it is as if his guilt for matricide which has prompted him to keep his mother alive in fantasy is actually masking his deeper wish to join her in death. At the end of the film, when Norman is completely possessed by the personality of his mother, the deeper wish, in effect, triumphs. However, when we consider the fates of these characters, we can clearly see the psychic differences for the three principal figures: the heroine dies, the heroes are saved, the villain is insane.

See also APPENDIX I.

Corpses and the police

Given all the corpses in Hitchcock's movies, there are inevitably scenes where we see the police with a body, at the start of their investigation. Indeed, Hitchcock will often keep the police at the site – or return them to it – in order to focus on their thinking with respect to the body. THE LODGER establishes the pattern. Joe has returned to the place where the Avenger's most recent victim was discovered, and he sits on a park bench, looking down at the ground where the body lay. A series of images superimposed on a footprint illustrate his thoughts, and tell us that he is concluding – wrongly, we later learn – that the Lodger is the Avenger.

This is the familiar paradigm for Hitchcock's police: their conclusions lead them, with remarkable regularity, to the wrong suspect. Indeed, one senses that their preferred scenario is to find someone conveniently to hand beside the corpse: they then do not have to look any further. MURDER! and YOUNG AND

INNOCENT both illustrate this: the police discover both the murder weapon and a suspect beside the body, so they arrest the (innocent) suspect.

I CONFESS and DIAL M FOR MURDER are more complex. First, the corpse in these two films is given unusual prominence. In I CONFESS, it is introduced, dramatically, at the beginning: Hitchcock's camera goes through a window to show Vilette's body on the floor. This is a peculiarly troubling corpse, in that it ties together villain, hero and heroine in a whole series of unfolding events. In DIAL M FOR MURDER, the corpse is a marker of the husband's murderousness – it is powerful partly because it carries a 'message' which no-one at first decodes.

Second, the activities of the police at the scene of the killing extend the baleful effect of the corpse. Here the murderer (I CONFESS) or attempted murderer (DIAL M FOR MURDER) and the figure who is about to be falsely accused are in fact both present with the police at the site where the body still lies (I CONFESS) or where it recently lay (DIAL M FOR MURDER). But the policeman in charge looks past the villain at the innocent person whom he will shortly arrest. In I CONFESS, Hitchcock presents this notion literally: in a famous shot, Inspector Larrue's eye appears from behind Keller's head as he looks out of the window at Father Logan, who, having left the murder site, is now pacing up and down on the pavement outside. In DIAL M FOR MURDER, the idea is structured into the way the whole scene is filmed: it is obvious, from Chief Inspector Hubbard's approach, that it is Margot whom he suspects. But there is a moment in this scene when Hitchcock stages a very similar effect to Larrue's suspicious eye: as Hubbard questions Margot, we see – from her point of view – Tony looking intently at her as he walks just behind Hubbard. Here we have the same three key figures as I CONFESS, but repositioned, and now it is the villain's gaze which is emphasised, and the innocent person is not only aware of the gaze but acts under its direction: Margot tells Hubbard the lie that Tony had asked of her. Significantly, at this moment, Tony is pacing over the exact position where Swann's body lay, another intimation that he is somehow linked with the corpse. Indeed, Margot's answers to Hubbard unconsciously connect the two men: less than a minute after she has been subjected to Tony's intimidating stare she becomes distraught at the memory of Swann's 'staring eyes'.

In context, Larrue's observant stare signals his alertness: Logan, waiting for and then meeting Ruth, is behaving a little oddly for a priest. Here it is essentially ironic that, as Larrue looks at Logan, he is distracted from the real murderer in front of him. By contrast, Hubbard simply fails to see what is going on: the focus on Tony's gaze emphasises that it is he who is in charge, guiding the investigation the way he wants. Each of Tony's lies in this scene contributes to his framing of Margot, and Hubbard swallows them all.

In BLACKMAIL, the scene with the police at the corpse swings in a completely different direction. On this occasion, the heroine Alice is responsible for the killing, albeit in self-defence, and the policeman Frank is her boyfriend. When Frank recognises the corpse as that of the man Alice left with the previous night, he conceals evidence – her glove – which would have incriminated her. This is the reverse of DIAL M FOR MURDER, where Tony plants Margot's stockings in order to incriminate her. Nevertheless, although Frank's tampering with the evidence is honourably motivated, its outcome is the same as in the other films: shortly afterwards, the police hotly pursue someone who is innocent of the killing.

DOGS AND CATS

Fig. 17. Still: THE BIRDS: Dogs. Hitchcock being led by his West Highland terriers out of the pet shop. Although in the film itself the dogs and Hitchcock exit to the left of Melanie (Tippi Hedren), this still is not the wrong way round. On this take the dogs must have decided to go to the right. Tippi Hedren's skilful swerve registers the dogs' change of direction.

On the evidence of his films, Hitchcock did not think much of cats. They appear quite often in the British films, and occasionally in the Hollywood ones, but usually a bit sneakily. They turn up on dinner tables (RICH AND STRANGE, MR AND MRS SMITH); their propensity to flee from danger is used to signal murders (THE LODGER, MURDER!) or to add a sense of farce to a panicking crowd (JUNO

AND THE PAYCOCK: ➤ PUBLIC DISTURBANCES). They tend to be metaphorically associated with suspicious behaviour: when the Lodger sneaks out late at night, the shadow of a prowling cat behind Mrs Bunting illustrates her thoughts about the manner of his exit; when Verloc in SABOTAGE manicures himself after his successful act of sabotage, a cat in the foreground washes itself; a cat is used to signal the surreptitious roof-top manoeuvres of the cat burglar in To CATCH A THIEF. In RICH AND STRANGE, when Fred and Emily are rescued from their sinking ship by a Chinese junk, Emily also saves the ship's cat. Later, the Chinese give them a rice and meat meal which they find delicious. Then one of the crew pins the cat's hide on a wall and the couple realise what they have eaten. They are promptly sick.

Dogs are a very different matter. It is well known that Hitchcock liked them: not only did he personally own a number of dogs during his life, but his production company for MARNIE was named Geoffrey Stanley Inc., after his two Highland terriers. In *English Hitchcock*, Charles Barr includes a section 'Hitchcock and Dogs' in which he discusses dog appearances in, mainly, the British movies (Barr 1999: 186-9). His overall argument is that the dogs, almost always family pets, tend to operate in these films as a 'moral touchstone' (189), as in THE PLEASURE GARDEN, where the dog identifies Levet as a villain from the latter's first appearance, and is duly rewarded at the end with the heroine's recognition of his talents: 'How do you like that? Cuddles knew all the time.' Given Charles Barr's detailed coverage of the British movies, I will concentrate here on the Hollywood examples.

First, the continuity of roles for dogs in the early Hollywood films set in England – REBECCA, FOREIGN CORRESPONDENT and SUSPICION – suggests that 'Possibly Hitchcock saw the attachment to dogs as something particularly English' (Barr 1999: 189). In the early 1940s films, only SABOTEUR has a dog in an American setting, and this is a rather special case in that it is a blind man's (Philip Martin's German shepherd). After these early Hollywood films, dog roles become markedly more scarce: only STRANGERS ON A TRAIN and REAR WINDOW contain significant examples, with Geoffrey and Stanley's guest appearance in THE BIRDS – leading their master out of the pet shop as Melanie enters – as like a coda.

Dogs in Hitchcock divide into two broad categories: small domestic pets and large guard dogs. In the British movies, only the three barking German shepherds in the baggage car in THE 39 STEPS are of the latter category, although they still serve to assist the hero in that they prompt him to get off the train, thus enabling him to elude the police who are pursuing him. In the Hollywood movies, the two kinds divide more evenly. Here Philip Martin's German shepherd is again a special case: it is watchful – barking at the window when Barry first arrives at the isolated house; then, later, when police are outside talking to

Pat – but it does not seem to be hostile; certainly not to Barry. Just as Philip (the familiar figure of the blind seer) intuits Barry's innocence, so one feels the dog does, too.

In FOREIGN CORRESPONDENT and STRANGERS ON A TRAIN, a Great Dane is associated with the film's villain. The earlier, linked to the closet Nazi Fisher, is presented ambiguously. As Fisher and his henchman Krug discuss what to do about getting rid of the hero, the dog barks at strategic points, but it is difficult to tell whether it is signalling approval of their nefarious plan or registering alarm. The Great Dane in STRANGERS ON A TRAIN, however, is more show than substance. As it stands, imposingly, at the top of the stairs in Bruno's house, it presents an apparently formidable obstacle to Guy. But when he reaches it, it benignly licks his hand, presumably recognising that Guy is not really danger-ous, despite his apparent mission (➤ BED SCENE).

In REBECCA, Jasper used to be Rebecca's dog, and at first he is something of a problem for the heroine. He leads her to the boathouse, causing Maxim to have one of his tantrums, and he rather recklessly greets Rebecca's ex-lover Favell when the latter takes advantage of Maxim being away from Manderley to pay a visit. Nevertheless, as a spaniel, he is inevitably going to turn out to be a good dog, which is demonstrated when he discerns Mrs Danvers's sinister plan to burn down Manderley and saves the heroine's life.

In REAR WINDOW, the middle-aged couple who live above the Thorwalds own a terrier, which the wife lowers in a basket so that it can run around in the courtyard. Towards the end of the third act (of four), the dog is killed. This prompts an impassioned speech from its owner, denouncing the other local re-sidents for their lack of neighbourliness: Hitchcock signals his sympathy for her trauma by taking the camera, for the first time, out of Jeff's apartment. The scene also marks a decisive turning point. Shortly before it, Lt. Doyle had finally convinced Jeff and Lisa that they were wrong about Thorwald being a mur-derer. But whereas everyone else is brought to their windows or balconies by the wife's outburst, Thorwald ignores it. Jeff is quick to realise the implication: that Thorwald himself killed the dog. This reawakens his suspicions, and he and Lisa move on to the decisive stage of their investigation. In short, it is dog murder that brings about the villain's downfall. And one is pleased to note that, in the film's coda, the wife is training a new dog to use the basket descent.

The dog in SUSPICION functions in a more subtle way. My position on the film is that Johnnie is a thoroughly nasty piece of work, quite clearly plotting to kill his wife (➤ *Food and marriage*; HEIGHTS AND FALLING; LIGHTS), but it is he who buys the dog, saying that it is for himself, and it is moreover a Highland terrier. I take it that Hitchcock is indicating just how sneaky Johnnie is: he'll stoop so low as to come home with a dog to make himself seem lovable. In fact, his true colours do subsequently shine through: he has nothing more to do with the dog, so buying it was just a gesture.

Another illustration of the concern for dogs in Hitchcock occurs in THE PARA-DINE CASE. When Tony cross-examines the valet Latour, he reminds him of an incident in which he put down one of Col. Paradine's hunting dogs when it became sick. As he takes Latour back over the process of obtaining and administering the poison, the court-room suddenly becomes very quiet; for the first time in the whole court-room sequence, there is a palpable tension. Now this could be attributed to the direction in which Tony is leading Latour: to insinuate that he poisoned his master. But that wouldn't necessarily account for the way in which the film becomes intense the moment the poisoning of the dog is mentioned. I think the intensity stems in the first instance from the events being recalled. Latour is being reminded of something which was genuinely distressing: the mercy killing of a beloved dog.

The absence of dogs in Hitchcock's films after REAR WINDOW goes along with the sense that, as he grew older, so his vision became darker. A close look at the scene in the pet shop at the beginning of THE BIRDS reveals that, on the ground floor, there are also dogs in cages, so that Mitch's reference to the 'poor little innocent creatures [that are] caged up' applies equally to them. Accordingly, Hitchcock's cameo appearance also has the diegetic status of a rescue mission; as if he has liberated the two terriers.

Dogs and the police

There is in fact a late example of a dog appearance: in FRENZY, a German shepherd accompanies the police who burst into Rusk's flat to arrest Blaney. However, whilst the police are doing their usual number in arresting the wrong man, the dog clearly cannot in any way be blamed.

DOUBLES

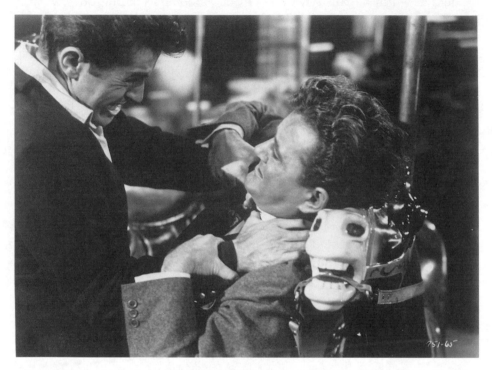

Fig. 18. Still: STRANGERS ON A TRAIN: Doubles. Guy (Farley Granger) and Bruno (Robert Walker)
fight on the merry-go-round at the climax.

One of the more familiar of the director's motifs, the double has received a fair amount of attention in the Hitchcock literature. Its prominence in Hitchcock's work is not surprising: not only was it a feature of some of the writers whom he admired – Edgar Allan Poe; E.T.A. Hoffmann – it was also found extensively in the German Expressionist cinema of the 1910s and 1920s which influenced him so strongly. Both these traditions are examined in Otto Rank's seminal psychoanalytical study of the double *Der Doppelgänger* (1914), and Rank's discussion in turn influenced Freud. (See Rank 1971, which includes a publication history of Rank's German articles on the subject; Freud's incorporation of Rank's ideas are in his essay 'The Uncanny', Freud 1919/1985: 356-58.) Although the range of doubles in Hitchcock is rather wider than those Rank considers, the latter's analysis is nevertheless extremely useful.

Rank begins his study with a detailed examination of DER STUDENT VON
PRAG (Stellan Rye, 1913). In this film, and in Rank's main literary example,
Dostoyevsky's *The Double* (1846), the double looks exactly like the hero but has
an independent identity. Apart from the TV episode 'The Case of Mr Pelham'
(1955), which is clearly modelled on Dostoyevsky's novella (➤ APPENDIX I),
Hitchcock's doubles do not possess this uncanny resemblance to the protagonist
and may even be of a different gender. Nevertheless, as in Rank's main examples, the connection between protagonist and double is usually psychological,
with the double functioning as a sort of alter ego who typically carries out the
protagonist's repressed or disavowed desires (in Jungian terms, his/her shadow).

In the British films, the motif of the double is in fact relatively rare. It applies
to THE LODGER, in that the Avenger may be seen as the Lodger's murderous
alter ego (➤ GUILT AND CONFESSION). It might have been present in DOWN-
HILL, in that the offence for which the public school hero is blamed (getting a
local girl pregnant) is committed by his best friend with the hero's connivance:
the hero could have secretly wanted the sex. However, the Novello subtext (the
registering, in his films, of his gayness) quite spectacularly undermines this
(➤ HOMOSEXUALITY). Otherwise, the only other significant examples in the
British movies would seem to be in THE MAN WHO KNEW TOO MUCH (1934). In
English Hitchcock, Charles Barr discusses one of these: Abbott as the hero Bob's
double. It is Abbott who orders the murder of Louis Bernard, with whom Bob's
wife Jill has been openly flirting: he thus seems like Bob's dark alter ego, eliminating this sexual rival (Barr 1999: 137). I believe that the assassin Ramon may
equally be seen as Jill's double. As Barr does in fact point out, there are two
triangles at the beginning of the film: just as Louis is Bob's rival in an adulterous
triangle, so Bob and Jill's daughter Betty is Jill's rival in an Oedipal triangle
(135-36). And it is Ramon we see making off with Betty when she is kidnapped. Although it was also Ramon who shot Louis, we do not see this: there
the focus is on Abbott who ordered the shooting. Here the focus is on Ramon
– like Jill, a crack shot – who in kidnapping Betty thus seems like Jill's dark
alter ego, eliminating *her* rival. The implications of this are developed further
at the film's climax (➤ CHILDREN).

The kidnapping of Hank in the remake of THE MAN WHO KNEW TOO MUCH
may be read in similar terms, although the doubling of Hank's parents in the
Draytons, the couple who do the kidnapping, works differently from the first
version. First, the events which prompt the kidnapping – Louis Bernard's pursuit and stabbing; his dying words to Ben (the MacGuffin) – occur almost immediately after Jo has suddenly asked Ben, 'When are we going to have another
baby?' Since Hank's kidnapping is designed to stop Ben passing on the
MacGuffin, it's as if Ben is so disturbed by Jo's request that his unconscious

conjures up a crisis around their existing child. And so Drayton, who presumably orders the murder and definitely orders the kidnapping, is here like Ben's dark alter ego. At this stage, Mrs Drayton likewise seems a dark double of Jo: she appears maternal, but she is nevertheless an accomplice in the kidnapping. By the end of the film, she has however reformed, and when she helps reunite Hank with his mother, she redeems herself (➤ *Couples and staircases*). By contrast, Drayton remains malevolent until the very end, and the manner of his sudden appearance during the Embassy climax (pointing a gun at Hank's head in front of Ben's eyes) re-emphasises his role as Ben's dark double. Likewise the manner of his subsequent death, shooting himself with his own gun as he falls downstairs: death by falling is Hitchcock's preferred method of killing off the double (➤ HEIGHTS AND FALLING).

In the Hollywood films, the alter ego figure is found particularly where the hero is falsely accused of a crime, usually a murder. In most of these cases, the hero is in some sense morally implicated. Either the murder was unconsciously or secretly desired (the Lodger's sister in THE LODGER, Miriam in STRANGERS ON A TRAIN, Brenda in FRENZY), or it conveniently solved the hero's problem (Vilette in I CONFESS). In TO CATCH A THIEF, where the hero is accused of a series of jewel thefts, this is a crime the hero used to commit. The person who carries out the murder or other crime is thus like the hero's alter ego, and the hero's pursuit of this figure is symbolically a quest after the dark side of himself. This is discussed further for Blaney in FRENZY under THE CORPSE. Films where the falsely accused hero is completely innocent – as in SABOTEUR and THE WRONG MAN – are less common. Even though the latter is Hitchcock's one film based on a real-life case, with the hero arrested purely because of his visual resemblance to his double, the director's more characteristic position is that the falsely accused hero is usually in some sense guilty.

STRANGERS ON A TRAIN and REAR WINDOW illustrate typical ways in which the alter ego double functions. In both films, the double may be seen as enacting the hero's wish to get rid of a woman. In STRANGERS ON A TRAIN, this is enacted literally: Bruno murders Guy's troublesome wife Miriam. In REAR WINDOW, Thorwald's murder of his own wife may be seen as a displaced version of Jeff's hostility towards Lisa. Both films also accord with Rank's analysis of the double:

> The most prominent symptom of the forms which the double takes is a powerful consciousness of guilt which forces the hero no longer to accept the responsibility for certain actions of his ego, but to place it upon another ego, a double … [the] detached personification of instincts and desires which were once felt to be unacceptable, but which can be satisfied without responsibility in this indirect way.
>
> (Rank 1971: 76)

In other words, the narratives work by projecting the hero's murderousness on to his double, so that he himself can feel innocent. In a phone booth on Metcalf station, frustrated that Miriam won't now give him a divorce, Guy shouts down the phone to Anne: 'I said I could strangle her.' Hitchcock's dissolve to Bruno's hands makes the point: Bruno will do this for him. In a discussion of the doubles motif in the film, Barbara M. Bannon points out that when Bruno arrives at Metcalf he goes into the same phone booth in order to look up Miriam's address so that he can stalk and kill her (Bannon 1985: 62). At the end of the murder sequence, Bruno looks at his watch. Cut to Guy on the train looking at his watch. It's as if Bruno has executed Guy's plan, and both men are noting the time of completion. In DIAL M FOR MURDER, Hitchcock reuses the device of two men in different locations checking their watches at the same time, and there this is explicitly in connection with a murder plan in which one of the men has been hired to kill the other's wife.

However, Guy's response to the discovery that Bruno has killed Miriam for him is outraged innocence. Hitchcock may insist on Guy's moral culpability (➤ Cigarette case/lighter in Part I), but Guy himself shows no awareness whatever of this. This is the crucial point in the Rank quote: the double is disavowed as 'other'. REAR WINDOW operates on the same premise. It would, perhaps, be stretching a point to say that Jeff unconsciously wants to kill Lisa, but he certainly wishes to get rid of the threat posed by her desire to domesticate him: to turn him into someone like Thorwald. It is Thorwald and his wife whom he is watching when he imagines to his boss what would happen to him if he married: 'Can't you just see me rushing home to a hot apartment to listen to the automatic laundry and the electric dishwasher and the garbage disposal and a nagging wife?' It is also the night after Jeff and Lisa's row over their incompatible lifestyles that Thorwald murders his wife: like the projection of Jeff's hostility. In Jeff's subsequent investigation of Thorwald, we can see the same sort of disavowal of his own guilt as with Guy: I'm not the one that wanted to get rid of a nagging partner, he is.

In the oneiric logic of these and other Hitchcock films, the function of the double as the hero's alter ego is to subject the hero's deeper desires to critical analysis. REAR WINDOW is perhaps the most complex example of this because of the way in which the 'dream screen' across the courtyard seems like a projection of Jeff's inner world. Not only is Thorwald like a domesticated version of Jeff himself – the worldwide travelling photographer reduced to a city-based travelling salesman – but the other characters with apartments overlooking the courtyard could be seen as summarising, in a distorted form, various possibilities for Jeff and/or Lisa. The composer and Miss Torso are discussed briefly from this point of view under RAIN: they are more like part-projections of Jeff and Lisa as they are now. By contrast, the other residents suggest possible future outcomes to their relationship. Miss Lonelyhearts – linked to Lisa through her green dress and to Jeff through her age – illustrates the loneliness of the single person in the city. The honeymoon couple (after all the sex, the bride discovers that the groom has lost his job) and the middle-aged couple who sleep chastely head to toe suggest equally unsatisfactory futures in marriage.

The sense that the 'dream screen' represents Jeff's inner world finds its most direct expression when Lisa breaks into Thorwald's apartment to look for evidence against him. She finds it (➤ JEWELLERY), but Thorwald catches her and starts to assault her. Helpless to do anything, Jeff is forced to witness this. For once, a Hitchcock hero is directly confronted with a scene which is like a projection of his repressed violent impulses. It is no wonder that Jeff can barely watch (➤ EXHIBITIONISM / VOYEURISM).

In their conceptualisation of one form of projection, Laplanche and Pontalis actually use a cinematic metaphor:

> A sense [of projection] comparable to the cinematographic one: the subject sends out into the external world an image of something that exists in him in an unconscious way. Projection is defined here as a *refusal to recognise (méconnaissance)* which has as its counterpart the subject's ability to recognise in others precisely what he refuses to acknowledge in himself.
>
> (Laplanche and Pontalis 1973: 354)

Given that REAR WINDOW also permits a reading in which the 'dream screen' may equally be seen as an analogue for the cinema screen (see Stam and Pearson 1986: 193-206), this suggestively links the two ways of understanding the film's metaphorical construction.

In STRANGERS ON A TRAIN and I CONFESS, and at the climax of REAR WINDOW (when Thorwald enters Jeff's apartment and attacks him), the hero is persecuted by his double. This is a familiar feature of the examples Rank discusses, and he suggests that such a paranoid structure has at its root a sublimation of homosexuality, which is disavowed by projection, but which returns in the form of the narcissistic image of the persecuting double (Rank 1971: 74). This is discussed further for I CONFESS under LIGHT(S) and for REAR WINDOW under HOMOSEXUALITY, but a few comments about STRANGERS ON A TRAIN are in order. Critics have discussed at length the film's homosexual subtext: that Bruno is coded as gay, that he seems to pick Guy up, that he kills Miriam 'for' Guy, thus fulfilling Barbara's comment to Anne and Guy: 'I still think it would be wonderful to have a man love you so much he'd kill for you.' Under *Cigarette case/lighter* in Part I, BED SCENE and LIGHT(S), I mention details in the film which support such a reading. But the fact that the nature of Bruno's persecution also includes turning up – as in DER STUDENT VON PRAG – to interrupt or otherwise disturb the hero's scenes with his fiancée, suggests that we should also apply Rank's analysis to Guy himself: he is the figure who has 'conjured up' this seductive man; he is the repressed homosexual.

In Spellbound and North by Northwest, the notion of the alter ego as double is inflected differently. Although each hero, like Guy, is falsely accused of murder, it is not his alter ego who carries out the crime. In Spellbound, the hero suffers from amnesia, and the alter ego he is searching for is himself – his own true identity. In North by Northwest, the alter ego is a fictitious government agent, George Kaplan. The films are nevertheless linked in that each alter ego possesses the secret which the hero must learn before he can escape the chaos world – and, in Spellbound, free himself from his feelings of guilt for the murder. Moreover, the man whose murder is blamed on the hero is structurally a father figure, and the films can be seen to have an implicit Oedipal narrative, with the murder serving to bring the hero and heroine together. Here, too, the alter ego is invoked in a drama of false accusation which relates dynamically to the inner world of the hero.

Shadow of a Doubt develops the idea of the double in two senses. First, in relation to the heroine, who sees herself and her Uncle Charlie as 'like twins', a parallel reinforced by the equivalent introductions of each of them lying on a bed. Second, in relation to Uncle Charlie as the Merry Widow murderer, who has his own alter ego: a man with his initials whom the police are hunting as a suspect in the east of the USA whilst he is hunted in the west. The first of these ideas is developed, again, in an Oedipal sense: it is not as a twin that Charlie is attracted to her uncle, but as a potential lover, and her rival – in the film's remarkable 'double incest theme' (Wood 1989: 300) – is her mother. (James McLaughlin discusses the ways in which Uncle Charlie overshadows the husband/father for both women: McLaughlin 1986: 144-45.) Accordingly, if the film is seen as Charlie's fantasy, her uncle's murdering middle-aged widows is like a displacement of the Oedipal material: they are stand-ins for her mother. As with the alter ego figures who carry out the (repressed) desires of the heroes, Uncle Charlie enacts – by displacement – Charlie's similarly repressed desire. The second example of the doubles motif is, however, underdeveloped. In another Hitchcock film, the presumably innocent other suspect would be the falsely accused hero; as it is, he seems uncharacteristically redundant to the plot, and is summarily disposed of.

In Rank's examples, the death of the double leads immediately to the death of the hero, confirming that they are, in effect, the same person split into two. This does not generally apply in Hitchcock: although the double does usually die, his death is, rather, beneficial for the protagonist and is frequently visualised as like the shedding of a burden (➤ HEIGHTS AND FALLING). There are, however, exceptions. In Shadow of a Doubt, the nature of Uncle Charlie's death (hit by a train) echoes the death of his double back East (cut to pieces by an aircraft's propeller), so that a link is nevertheless forged between them.

Impersonations also frequently lead to linked deaths. Although Rank's examples do not cover impersonations, these may be seen as another version of the double. In VERTIGO, Judy impersonates Elster's unseen wife Madeleine up to the point where the latter is murdered, and is subsequently forced by Scottie to recreate this impersonation – which leads to Judy's own death (➤ THE CORPSE). The sense that the impersonator is herself doomed to die, like her predecessor, is however not just a Hitchcock motif. It applies to many impersonations in the cinema, in the case of men stretching back to THE WHISPERING CHORUS (Cecil B DeMille, 1918) and forward to SOMMERSBY (Jon Amiel, 1993). It is rarer for women, but THE LEGEND OF LYLAH CLARE (Robert Aldrich, 1968) and FEDORA (Billy Wilder, 1978) furnish two additional examples. In all these cases – and VERTIGO is certainly one of the most poignant – it would seem that to impersonate another is to invite death, even when, as in FEDORA, the impersonated person is not already dead. The death may even occur in the same manner as that of the impersonated person, as in VERTIGO and THE LEGEND OF LYLAH CLARE.

In PSYCHO the 'impersonation' is rather different in that it is unconscious. It would be more accurate to describe the Norman/'mother' relationship as a reworking of the material in another famous nineteenth-century literary example of the double, Robert Louis Stevenson's *Dr Jekyll and Mr Hyde* (1886), mentioned only in passing by Rank. A major difference between Stevenson's novella and PSYCHO is that the monster within Norman is a superego figure (➤ MOTHERS AND HOUSES), very different from the rampant Id figure of Mr Hyde. Nevertheless, in both stories the double represents the hero's repressed side, and he/she gradually assumes dominance over the former's life – as in Rank's examples. The novella ends before the death of Jekyll/Hyde, but film versions typically end with the death of Hyde who then turns into Jekyll, so that what we actually see is the death of the double 'resulting in' the death of the hero. At the end of PSYCHO, Norman, too, has been completely taken over by his double, and although this does not lead to his actual death, it results in a living death. The elements are all there.

SPELLBOUND and NORTH BY NORTHWEST also involve impersonations, but with a positive outcome. In the former, J.B.'s amnesiac state is provoked by his witnessing the death of Dr Edwardes: he himself feels guilty for the death (which turns out to be murder) and he unconsciously impersonates Dr Edwardes as a way of seeking to erase the guilt. In the latter, Roger is asked by the CIA's Professor to impersonate Kaplan in a meeting with Vandamm and Eve in the later stages of the film: the cafeteria scene. J.B. only recovers his memory when he recreates the circumstances under which Dr Edwardes died, skiing to the edge of a precipice. In other words, he almost suffers the fate of the man he impersonated. This is also the moment when his alter ego is finally revealed: symbolically, hero and double merge, and the anonymous J.B. becomes John Ballyntine (➤ HEIGHTS AND FALLING). Roger's impersonation is abruptly terminated when Eve shoots him with blanks: an act which, in effect, 'kills' Kaplan, his alter ego (➤ PUBLIC DISTURBANCES). In these two films, the elimination of the double is therapeutic, a crucial step towards providing the hero and heroine with a happy ending.

Again and again, harmony can only be restored when the double dies. We would expect this if the double has committed a serious crime, but it is striking how many of these figures die in the presence of the hero/heroine, as if it were crucial that the hero/heroine witness the death. Two final examples illustrate the archetypal fate of the double. First, the original ending of TOPAZ, which was rejected by the preview audience. In it, André, the hero, and Granville, André's double in the espionage sense (spying for the East as André spies for the West) face each other dressed in identical black outfits to fight a duel. Whilst it would not have been possible, ideologically, for either to kill the other, the matter is still resolved in the manner appropriate to the doubles motif: Granville is shot by a Soviet sniper as he levels his pistol at André. Second, in FOREIGN CORRESPON-DENT, the statesman Van Meer is kidnapped and his place taken by a man who is his perfect double (i.e. played by the same actor). The impersonator only lasts up to his first public appearance before he is shot.

Doubles and the police

This is a motif in which the police can be positively dangerous, since their con-viction that it is the hero, not his double, who is guilty can lead to some hair-raising climaxes. When the hero goes after his double on the merry-go-round at the climax of STRANGERS ON A TRAIN (➤ *Homosexuality and the police*) or on the roof at the climax of TO CATCH A THIEF (➤ *Lights and the police*), it is the hero whom the police are shooting at.

A more general problem here is that the police tend be confused when they see two people looking very much alike (➤ *Washrooms and the police*). Accord-ingly, it is to the credit of Det. Matthews in THE WRONG MAN that, when he sees Manny's double, he is quick to recognise the man's similarity to Manny, and to set up an identification parade which exposes the miscarriage of justice. Equally, at the end of I CONFESS, when Logan goes to confront Keller, structurally his 'double', the police could not possibly be confused: Logan is a priest and is dressed as such. On this occasion it is indeed the double whom they shoot.

ENDINGS AND THE POLICE

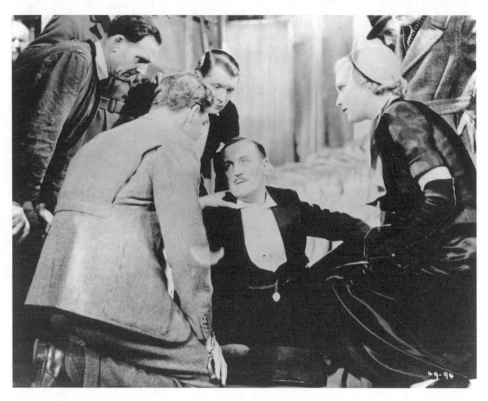

Fig. 19. Still: THE 39 STEPS: Endings and the police. As the dying Mr Memory (Wylie Watson) recites what he remembers of the MacGuffin, Hannay (Robert Donat) and Pamela (Madeleine Carroll) look on sympathetically. Behind Pamela are two policemen. In the concluding shot of the film, their colleague joins the group to register that Hannay has been telling the truth, which frees the latter for his concluding hand-clasp with Pamela.

In *The Hitchcock Romance: Love and Irony in Hitchcock's Films*, Lesley Brill points to the similarity in the endings of THE 39 STEPS, YOUNG AND INNOCENT, SABO-TEUR and TO CATCH A THIEF. The police do not simply get the 'right man' (wo-man in TO CATCH A THIEF), and so free the falsely accused hero for his reunion with the heroine. Their role goes further: it's as if they supervise the happy end-ing: e.g. in SABOTEUR a policeman helps Barry to safety on the Statue of Liberty and into Pat's arms; in TO CATCH A THIEF the police drive Francie up to John Robie's villa for their reunion (Brill 1988: 26-28).

Brill's argument could be extended to those Hitchcock films – falsely accused man and otherwise – where, in the penultimate scene (usually), the police or their equivalents set up the final scene reunion of hero and heroine. In THE LODGER, the detective Joe, Daisy's previous boyfriend, helps save the Lodger from a lynching. In REBECCA, Col. Julyan clears (the in fact guilty) Maxim of responsibility for Rebecca's death. In STRANGERS ON A TRAIN, the police identify Bruno as Miriam's murderer and clear Guy. In REAR WINDOW, the police catch Jeff as he falls from his apartment window and arrest Thorwald. In NORTH BY NORTHWEST, the state troopers (supervised by the CIA's Professor) save Roger and Eve on Mount Rushmore and arrest Vandamm, Eve's former lover. In TORN CURTAIN, the Swedish immigration authorities play an equivalent role, welcoming Michael and Sarah into the safety of the 'free world'. THE MAN WHO KNEW TOO MUCH (1934) shows a family example: in the last shot, the police gently lower a sobbing Betty down through the skylight to reunite her with her parents.

Policemen who have played a major role during the film may even be present at the end. In DIAL M FOR MURDER, Chief Inspector Hubbard – who set up the plan to expose Tony as a murderous husband – is the subject of the shot which winds up the narrative. In I CONFESS, Inspector Larrue witnesses both the establishment of Father Logan's innocence and his return to his ministrations as a priest. In FRENZY, Inspector Oxford arrives not just to surprise Blaney with Rusk's murder victim (➤ BED SCENE), but also to catch Rusk himself out.

As in Brill's examples, these endings would seem to extend the typical role of the police. We are entirely familiar with crime narrative endings in which the wrong-doers are identified and arrested or killed and those who are innocent are allowed a more or less happy ending. This familiar pattern is an example of one of the ways in which 'the law' *processes* a certain sort of narrative, guiding it along a particular path until closure can be achieved with the correct answer to the question of guilt and an appropriate apportioning of 'just desserts'. Hitchcock's police go further. In some cases, their previous misapprehensions perhaps provide a rationale: they are brought on at the end in order to make amends at the personal as well as the legal level. Even when they have not previously been a party to false accusations against the protagonist(s) – e.g. in THE MAN WHO KNEW TOO MUCH (1934) or TORN CURTAIN – the police may still serve to mark a 'zone of safety' which the hero and heroine (and, in the former film, their daughter) can now occupy: they are gatekeepers out of the chaos world.

This notion applies even when there is no heroine available for the hero, so that the question of a final scene reuniting the lovers does not arise, as in I CONFESS and FRENZY. Two darker films also present variations. In THE WRONG MAN, although the penultimate scene depicts the police getting the right man and freeing Manny, his reunion with Rose is clouded by her mental breakdown. In

PSYCHO, although Norman is now in jail, Marion is dead, and Sam and Lila do not have the status for a happy ending together. Nevertheless, in all these films, it's as if the characters we care about require, in some sense, the blessing of the police before their traumas can be put to rest.

All these examples recast the police, ultimately, as positive, paving the way for the 'happy ending'. However, where the 'hero' is himself a policeman (or equivalent figure), this notion is rendered distinctly problematic. The relevant films are BLACKMAIL, NUMBER SEVENTEEN, SABOTAGE, JAMAICA INN, SHADOW OF A DOUBT, NOTORIOUS, STAGE FRIGHT and VERTIGO (where Scottie is an ex-policeman). Whilst few Hitchcock endings are unequivocally happy, in this group they are peculiarly troubled. Part of the problem lies in Hitchcock's tendency to desexualise his policemen: in a number of these films, it is the villain who is the sexual figure; the policeman, by contrast, is dull and unromantic. There is also the question of the presumed narrative motivation for making the hero a policeman – either the heroine has herself been transgressive, or she has been involved, to a greater or lesser extent, with the villain(s). In such cases, it would seem, a policeman is considered to be an appropriate figure to 'save' her: the familiar situation of the heroine being recuperated into the arms of the law. I have already discussed this feature in Hitchcock, suggesting that the problem with endings in which the heroine 'goes off with' a policeman stems from the latter's 'moral superiority' over her: 'either the heroine herself has killed someone (BLACKMAIL and SABOTAGE) or he himself has been proved right about the guilt of the charismatic villain who has just been killed' (SHADOW OF A DOUBT and STAGE FRIGHT) (Walker M. 1999: 196). Indeed, in these four cases, the heroine was originally either strongly attracted to the villain or (SABOTAGE) married to him, which compounds her 'guilt by association'. I except NOTORIOUS from this critique, since there the policeman hero learns at the end that he has been mistaken (not about the villain, but about the heroine) and he is, accordingly, chastened. In addition, Cary Grant's Devlin is undoubtedly a more sexual figure than Claude Rains's Sebastian. Nevertheless, one could still argue that the film's ending is made uneasy by the abominable way Devlin has treated Alicia. Even JAMAICA INN, in which the heroine has firmly resisted any involvement with the villains, has the charismatic villain/dull policeman hero structure of BLACKMAIL and SHADOW OF A DOUBT.

The sense of the policeman's moral superiority over the heroine is perhaps the crucial feature which disturbs the endings. Particularly where the heroine has been transgressive – and this includes NUMBER SEVENTEEN – there is a sense that she is being arrested into marriage. BLACKMAIL is especially uneasy in this regard. At the end, Alice is in the entrance lobby to New Scotland Yard and, whilst her policeman boyfriend and the desk sergeant share a joke about women police officers, she sees a painting of a jester (and a sketch) belonging to the man she killed carried past her into the building. Still inside police head-quarters, positioned between the two laughing policemen and the two poten-tially incriminating paintings (the jester, too, seems to be laughing at her), Alice is in a state of suspension. As I argue under PAINTERS, this is a remarkable ending, refusing the closure normally so crucial to mainstream cinema. The ending of VERTIGO is even darker. Here, Judy was both involved romantically with the villain and implicated in murder and, when Scottie realises this, he unleashes such a virulent condemnation of her that he drives her – in effect – to her death.

Overall, the motif registers Hitchcock's deep ambivalence about the police. On the one hand, they are necessary to the restoration of order: without them, the chaos world would still reign. On the other, they are frequently the figures responsible for the chaos world: especially in the falsely accused man films. In effect, they function as superego figures who must be appeased: as if the hero and heroine cannot be allowed a happy ending without the police in some sense sanctioning it. This also helps account for the unsuitability of a policeman as a romantic figure: he embodies too great a power of judgement over the heroine, especially where she has been transgressive. We could, accordingly, see MARNIE as an attempt to work through the problem of the transgressive heroine without involving the police. It is perhaps important that here the police make only one, brief, appearance – at the very beginning of the film.

See also APPENDIX I.

ENTRY THROUGH A WINDOW

Fig. 20. Still: REAR WINDOW: Entry through a window. Lisa (Grace Kelly) enters Thorwald's apartment to look for his wife's jewellery.

There is nothing very interesting about most of the *exits* through a window in Hitchcock's films: someone is usually escaping. The motif of someone entering through a window is very different, because almost all the examples are sexualised. (The stress, here, is on *someone* entering. I exclude examples in which the camera alone enters, which may – the beginning of PSYCHO – or may not – the beginning of I CONFESS – be sexualised.) In the British films, the motif receives a number of different inflections. In THE MANXMAN, before Pete goes abroad, he tries to get Kate to say that she'll wait for him, a scene which involves him standing on Philip's shoulders in order to reach Kate's bedroom window. Although Pete does not enter the room, this is an embryonic version of the motif: Kate teases him with conflicting responses to his request, but finally gives in and kisses him. Almost immediately, she has second thoughts, but Pete has left, now considering himself engaged. Here the undercurrents to the motif are troubled: Philip's enforced impotence, Pete's insistent pleading, Kate's misleading flirtatiousness.

YOUNG AND INNOCENT provides a different sort of example. After Erica has cried herself to sleep (≻ BED SCENE), Robert lifts the bedroom window and climbs in: exactly as if she has dreamt him up. They embrace, but all seems lost: he says that he is going to turn himself in to the police. However, she has information which gives him fresh hope, and their quest to track down the real murderer recommences. Here the entry through a window leads to a scene which is touching and quietly romantic, in keeping with the tone of the film.

The other major examples in the British films are more elaborate. In WALTZES FROM VIENNA, we are introduced to Schani and Rasi – hero and heroine – as they sing together at the piano. Without their realising, the building has caught fire, and Leopold – Schani's rival for Rasi's affections – climbs up a ladder to the window to inform them. The fire is not serious, but Leopold resists Rasi's suggestion that they walk downstairs and insists that she be rescued. This starts a squabble between the men over who should rescue her, and Rasi is ignominiously pulled to and fro as they argue over the matter. The conflict is only resolved when she submits to Leopold's demand and allows him to carry her down the ladder. The indignity of this – she protests that it would be safer if she climbed down – is then compounded when her skirt catches on the ladder and is torn off. Again in keeping with the tone of the film, the scene is entirely comic, with the sexual elements displaced into farce: Rasi being manhandled by the men, her loss of her skirt.

MURDER! provides another contrasting example, since the entry resulted in murder. As Sir John investigates Edna Druce's murder (≻ THE CORPSE), he deduces that the killer, Fane, must have entered unheard through the window, picked up a poker, advanced on Diana and Edna – who were arguing about him – and struck Edna before she could reveal his, Fane's, secret: that he was a 'half-caste'. We do not see this, but we do see the scene as restaged by Sir John in an attempt to trick Fane – manoeuvred into playing himself – into giving himself away by revealing a knowledge of the climactic revelation. In this restaging, Fane knows perfectly well what is going on, and he betrays his unease by going unprompted to the window to make his entrance.

The scene has been analysed in detail by William Rothman (1982: 85-88), and all I seek to do here is highlight the way in which the cat-and-mouse game between Sir John and Fane generates a tension which is also sexualised. Fane asks for a poker, Sir John offers a pencil, Fane declines it. In the original scene, Fane held the poker as he came up behind Diana – whom he 'dared to love' – so that there are clear Freudian overtones to this exchange: Sir John denies Fane his phallic weapon; in effect, he 'unmans' him. Since Fane's sexuality is ambiguous (➤ HEIGHTS AND FALLING), we could see the cat-and-mouse game as a translation of the original scene, with its own sexual tensions, into a sadistic homoerotic variation. Sir John obliges Fane to rehearse the scene with an imaginary poker, but he still wants him to ejaculate the forbidden word. At the same time, as Fane sweats under the stress and anticipation of this climax, Hitchcock alludes to the original scene, where the climax had been murder: we can now see that murderous and sexual impulses in Fane had been combined. But here it is the sexual element which dominates. At the climax, showing great control, Fane does not utter the forbidden word. Then, after he has regained his composure, he comments: 'What a pity, Sir John, the scene isn't finished; I was getting quite worked up to it.' The abruptly truncated climax now seems like coitus interruptus.

After Fane has left the room, the stage manager Markham then comes through the window, brandishing a poker. It is a very bizarre moment: the only logical explanation would seem to be that he was arriving, armed, in case Fane tried to make a sudden getaway. But his arrival has the effect of dramatically restating the motif, as if to say: this scene really is premised on an entrance through a window. In addition, Markham is the hero's working-class helper, a figure who occurs in a number of Hitchcock movies, but on the other occasions where the figure is present for this motif, he (Old Will in YOUNG AND INNOCENT) or she (Stella in REAR WINDOW) is left at the bottom of the ladder. Markham is thus (a) privileged with access to the hero's rooms and (b) shown arriving with his poker at the ready – further intimations of a gay subtext.

In the British films, the motif can be seen to operate in a variety of ways, but the sexual overtones function mainly in a displaced or embryonic form. In the Hollywood films, the motif becomes more common, and the sexual overtones more overt. There is also one Hollywood example which follows MURDER! in its strong suggestion of a gay subtext. In THE PARADINE CASE, when Tony is staying in a Lake District inn, Latour, Col. Paradine's valet, comes to see him, entering through a back door. But Hitchcock includes an elaborate preamble to the entry which makes it seem, until the last moment, that Latour is in fact seeking entrance through a window. The scene between the men is then charged with suppressed sexual tensions (➤ HOMOSEXUALITY), and Latour's clandestine entrance would seem to be a part of this.

In FOREIGN CORRESPONDENT and NORTH BY NORTHWEST, the hero escapes from deceptive authority figures (Nazis disguised as Dutch police; the CIA's Professor disguised as benevolent) by going out a window, along the outside of the building and in through another window. Predictably, he enters into a woman's room: in the earlier film, the heroine's bathroom; in the later, an anonymous female hospital patient's bedroom. The reception he gets varies. Whereas the hospital patient is delighted to discover that her intruder is Cary Grant (➤ SPECTACLES), Johnny in FOREIGN CORRESPONDENT is then caught stealing into Carol's bedroom by Mrs Appleby, who naturally interprets this as the sign of an illicit liaison. This embarrasses Carol, and she is most annoyed with Johnny, who is only wearing a dressing-gown over his underwear. Her annoyance is echoed in an ensuing scene in NORTH BY NORTHWEST. Roger repeats his skilful entry through a window by climbing up to Eve's bedroom, but she is not pleased to see him: 'What are you doing here, Roger? You'll ruin everything.' In both these films, the tone is essentially comic, as the women interpret the hero's unexpected entrance as indicating sexual ardour and the hero has to navigate the ensuing complications.

In REBECCA, Favell signals his persona as lover figure by leaping through the window to shake the young heroine's hand. The presence of Mrs Danvers inhibits the intrusion from going too far, but Favell's insinuating manner leaves no doubt about his character. In UNDER CAPRICORN, Charles shins up to Hattie's bedroom window and enters to find her drunk in bed. In the ensuing scene, he suddenly kisses her passionately, but he is outraged when the housekeeper Milly, having found the bedroom door locked, later implies that something had gone on between him and Hattie. Charles's behaviour here seems even more suspect than Favell's, and the presence of the hostile but observant housekeeper serves, in this case, to expose his hypocrisy. In addition, when Charles climbs up to the window, he leaves below Hattie's (working-class) husband Sam. Linking Sam with the working-class helpers in the other films emphasises the snub: Charles is putting Sam in his place.

Freud has mentioned that a house was often a dream symbol for a body, and that 'windows, doors and gates stood for openings in the body' (Freud 1916/ 1973: 193). But if this helps account for the general sense in Hitchcock that entry through a window (penetration) is sexualised, this logically only applies to men. What happens when a woman enters?

This occurs in two films, and Hitchcock handles each quite differently. In REAR WINDOW, Lisa climbs through Thorwald's apartment window to search for his wife's jewellery, and she does indeed succeed (➤ JEWELLERY). But a hostile confrontation with Thorwald ensues, which culminates with him attacking her. Now, his attack – for which he turns out the light – could be seen as like a displaced rape, but it could equally be seen as the murderous violence of a wife-killer. The dominant impression is that Lisa is being brutally punished for her entry, a punishment which is extended vicariously to Jeff, who is forced to watch. In other words, this particular entry results in quite disturbing violence, and the hero is only able to stop it by summoning the police. Here the motif seems less significant on its own than as an aspect of the film's deeper concern

of using the events across from Jeff's apartment as a comment on his psyche
(➤ EXHIBITIONISM / VOYEURISM and DOUBLES).

To Catch a Thief provides a contrasting view. Although the film deals with
cat burglaries, not a single entry through a window is shown. It would seem
that, from Hitchcock's point of view, the burglaries – committed against older
women by a young woman disguised as a man – lack sexual overtones. Nevertheless, it is intriguing that the only occasions in Hitchcock in which a woman
enters through a window she is searching for another woman's jewels, jewels
themselves being a familiar Freudian symbol of female sexuality.

The Freudian significance of the window in Hitchcock is also illustrated by a
very different sort of example: in The Birds the sexualisation of the bird attacks
is stressed through their attacks on windows. A striking series of shots occurs
when Melanie is in the phone booth. First, the booth is drenched from water
from a thrashing phallic hose; then, the moment that Mitch starts to run towards Melanie, a gull hits the glass; she turns away, and another hits the glass
on the opposite side. The Freudian overtones are unmistakable. Even the tree
crashing through the window of Mark's office in Marnie seems linked to sexuality (➤ RAIN).

There are examples in which entry through a window does not seem to be
sexualised: in Saboteur, when Barry and Pat climb into the saboteurs' hideout
in the ghost town, and in Family Plot, when George climbs into Adamson's
garage to look for Blanche. Yet even here there are Freudian traces of the sexualisation of the motif: in the former, through the way the couple set about getting
a telescope out of its box and up on a tripod, ready for action (Pat is particularly
eager here); in the latter, through the fulfilment of George's search, when he
finds Blanche on a bed. Overall, this is one of Hitchcock's major Freudian motifs, with a range of different inflections: from the farce of Waltzes from
Vienna to the trauma of The Birds and Marnie, in which the broken windows
are like displacements of Hitchcock's cinematic sexual assaults on Tippi Hedren.

Entry through a window and the police

There are three linked examples in which the police are involved in an entry
through a window; linked in the sense that the window is either a skylight
(Number Seventeen, The Man Who Knew Too Much, 1934) or a fanlight (Sabotage) and so the entry is down. However, none of the examples is remotely
sexualised. In Number Seventeen, when Rose – looking for her policeman
father – crashes through a skylight into the eponymous derelict house, she falls

into the arms of the hero, Barton, an undercover cop. But any erotic potential is defused in the clumsy jokiness of the encounter, just as it is in the subsequent scene when the two are tied up together (➤ HANDCUFFS AND BONDAGE). In THE MAN WHO KNEW TOO MUCH (1934), the police are just being helpful: guiding the teenage Betty down through a skylight to reunite with her parents (➤ CHILDREN). SABOTAGE, by contrast, shows police incompetence: under-cover cop Ted, caught by the saboteurs eavesdropping through the fanlight, is unceremoniously hauled down into the room by one of them. Here the inno-cence of the boy Stevie – who pops his head through the fanlight and says he was just showing Ted the back of the cinema screen – conveniently provides Ted with an explanation for his behaviour, but his cover is blown: another of the plotters recognises him.

We have here a range of representations of Hitchcock's police: bemused, ben-evolent and blundering. The absence of eroticism is only to be expected in the family-centred ending of THE MAN WHO KNEW TOO MUCH, but the other two examples are potentially more risqué. Normally, when a young woman falls into the hero's arms, this is a prelude to each finding the other sexually attrac-tive. Equally, a suspicious person might well wonder what Ted was up to at the back of the cinema screen with the schoolboy Stevie. But the fact that each of these heroes is an undercover policeman seems to check any sexual intimations. In Hitchcock's films, policemen are simply not very sexy. Thus, even when they are put into situations which potentially have an erotic charge, this is dissi-pated.

EXHIBITIONISM / VOYEURISM / THE LOOK

Fig. 21. Still: STAGE FRIGHT: Exhibitionism and Freudian set design. Charlotte (Marlene Dietrich) sings on stage in the West End.

EXHIBITIONISM / VOYEURISM

'Voyeurism has become identified with masculinity, and exhibitionism with femininity' (Grosz 1992: 448). Hitchcock's films conform quite strongly to the first half of this statement, but more loosely to the second. The fact that Hitchcock's voyeurs are generally male is well known. In her seminal article 'Visual Pleasure and Narrative Cinema', Laura Mulvey uses Hitchcock to sup-

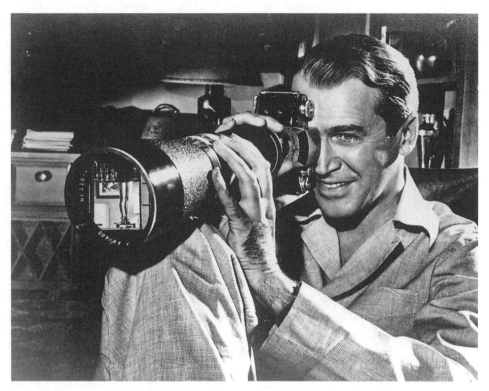

Fig. 22. Publicity still: REAR WINDOW: Voyeurism and its object. Jeff (James Stewart) posing with his telephoto lens and reacting to Miss Torso (Georgine Darcy) in a pose we do not in fact see in the film.

port her theoretical discussion about the function of 'the male look' in identification processes in the cinema (Mulvey 1975: 6-18), and numerous feminist critics have followed suit.

In *Hitchcock's Films Revisited*, Robin Wood challenges Laura Mulvey's model of identification, noting in particular its failure to account for our identification with (Hitchcock's) heroines (Wood 1989: 303-310). I am in sympathy with Wood's critique, but a consideration of the play of exhibitionism and voyeurism in Hitchcock's films necessarily brings in gender politics, and I want to take account of this. My comments on the look occur later, when I also consider the implications of the scarcity of female voyeurs in Hitchcock.

Hitchcock's exhibitionists may be mainly women, but there are occasional male examples. For instance, the startling last shot of NUMBER SEVENTEEN, when the working-class Ben whips open his raincoat like a flasher to exhibit himself in his long johns wearing the missing necklace. Or the chilling moment in THE 39 STEPS when Professor Jordan dramatically displays his amputated finger and so reveals himself to Hannay as the master spy. In ROPE, the party itself is designed as an exhibition of Brandon and Phillip's 'cleverness', which helps explain why they keep behaving in a manner which threatens to give themselves away: Brandon, at least, secretly wants the cleverness to be recognised (➤ *Food and murder*). Bruno in STRANGERS ON A TRAIN and Roger in NORTH BY NORTHWEST are each given a number of exhibitionist set-pieces, e.g. Bruno with the 'Test your strength' machine (artfully edited by Hitchcock so that his power to get it up becomes the focus of Miriam's admiration); Roger as Kaplan pretending to be shot by Eve in the cafeteria; later he comments to her on how graceful he was.

I am using exhibitionism here in the colloquial sense of 'showing off', but behind these ostentatious displays the male exhibitionist is also demonstrating his power to his audience. William Rothman suggests that Jordan's grin as he watches Hannay's reaction to his gesture is 'that of a hunter in the face of its prey' (Rothman 1986: 144). Bruno's demonstration of his strength is equally sinister: before performing, he actually admires his hands, which will shortly be used to strangle Miriam. Even Sir Humphrey's suicide from the ship's yard-arm in JAMAICA INN is enacted like a display of power, as he shouts down to the onlookers that his death fall will not only be a 'spectacle', but the moment when 'the great age ended'.

With the women, by contrast, the conventional view is that, because they are displaying themselves for the male look, it is the man who has the real power. Now, this is certainly true for many examples in Hitchcock, but there is a striking exception at the beginning of his career. In the first scene of his first film, THE PLEASURE GARDEN, skimpily dressed chorus girls cavort on a stage and an elderly man in the front row singles out the heroine, Patsy, for inspection. Through his opera glasses, we see a point-of-view shot which tilts up from her legs to her face. When she notices the man's interest, she returns his gaze with a look that is challenging rather than flirtatious, and when the man contrives to be introduced to her at the end of her number, he is so uncomfortable that she has little difficulty in mocking him. The sequence is remarkably sophisticated: it shows (a) that voyeurism and exhibitionism can be complementary, (b) the undermining of the voyeur's sense of power by the exhibitionist's uninhibited élan and forthright returning of the look, and (c) the voyeur's awkwardness when the distance between him and his object of desire is removed.

Hitchcock repeats the point of view introduction of the heroine in EASY VIRTUE, but here she is in court being sued for divorce and the observing figure is the judge. This is a very different matter: Larita did not choose to be 'on exhibition' and the judge has genuine power over her. There is then a scene late in the film where Larita reverses this power structure and puts herself on exhibition. In order to scandalise the stuffy bourgeois society of her prudish in-laws, she comes downstairs at a party in a low-cut dress. However, although her entrance does indeed have the impact she desires, her triumph is short-lived: she knows that her in-laws are about to expel her for her 'scandalous' past. The film then ends with Larita once more humiliatingly on display, photographed by the press as she comes out of the law court after her second divorce. In a line which Hitchcock would retrospectively call 'the worst line I've ever written' (Truffaut 1968: 44), she responds masochistically: 'Shoot, there's nothing left to kill!'

EASY VIRTUE sketches out the general pattern of female exhibitionism in Hitchcock's films: moments of humiliation when the heroine is forced against her will to be 'on exhibition'; a short-lived moment of triumph when she succeeds in displaying herself on her own terms. The pattern is repeated, for example, in UNDER CAPRICORN. Much of the film is concerned with Charles seeking to restore Hattie's social self-confidence, so that she will be able to take her place in the society which spurns her for her alcoholism. Again, a staircase descent – with Hattie wearing her ball dress – marks the heroine's moment of triumph in her personal journey (➤ STAIRCASES), and in Hattie's case the triumph extends to her impact at the ball. Again, however, her triumph is short-lived: prompted by the housekeeper Milly's insinuations about Hattie and Charles, Hattie's husband Sam arrives at the ball, creates a scene and forces a mortified Hattie to flee.

In REBECCA, even the staircase descent ends in humiliating failure. Prompted by Mrs Danvers, the heroine has copied her ball dress from that in a family portrait (➤ PORTRAITS), but she has kept this a secret. As she comes down the stairs for the ball, Maxim and his sister Beatrice are turned away from her. Her expression tells us her feelings: her anticipation of Maxim's praise for such a glamorous and original costume. Instead, he reacts with fury, and Beatrice's shocked comment 'Rebecca!' tells us why: she is wearing an exact copy of the dress Rebecca wore for an equivalent ball. The whole scene has in effect been staged by Mrs Danvers with the specific intention of humiliating the heroine (➤ BED SCENE in Part I). An equivalent humiliation occurs in MARNIE. In making the arrangements for a party at Wykwyn, Lil, Mark's sister-in-law, invites Strutt, because she knows that there is something shady to do with him in Marnie's past. At the party, Marnie is coping very well with being on display for the Philadelphia bourgeoisie ('I'm not a bit nervous, Mark') and on this occasion her husband is entirely supportive: 'You've no reason to be. You're unquestionably the best-looking woman here, the best-dressed, the most intelligent, and you're with me.' But Marnie then sees Strutt (the employer from whom she stole at the beginning of the film) and her self-confidence evaporates: like the heroine in REBECCA, she now wants desperately to flee.

In these last three examples, Hitchcock emphasises the vulnerability of a woman in a social world where envious women and bullying men dictate the terms of her success. Although, as with the male examples, I am using

exhibitionism here more colloquially – to refer to those occasions when a woman sets out to make an impact at a social gathering through her beauty and/or
style and/or glamour – the heroine has a great deal of emotional investment in
her success. It is extremely important to her to be able to shine in the social
world of the film; hence the humiliation of her failure. That both women and
men are responsible for undermining her is a comment on her innocence as
well as her emotional vulnerability: the women are the scheming figures who
plot her downfall; the men are doing little more than dance to their tune (➤ *Bed
Scene* in Part I).

This illustrates the terms under which women may be successful exhibitionists. Their success necessarily lies in the response of others, and there is usually
too much resentment (from other women) or too much of a sense of insecurity
(from the men who should be supporting her) for them to succeed unequivocally. Mark is not insecure, but his final comment ('and you're with me') still
serves to qualify Marnie's triumph. It has a double meaning: not just that
Marnie's glamour is enhanced by Mark's own status, but that it also contributes
to Mark's status: she is a suitably distinguished wife for a powerful and wealthy
man. This points to another unwritten rule: in displaying themselves, women
are expected to soothe and flatter male vanity, not to disturb it. The tantrums of
Maxim and Sam bear witness to the upsetting consequences of the heroines'
(quite unwitting) failure to observe the rule.

In general, men tend to feel threatened by women exhibiting themselves 'too
freely', and so hasten to suppress this. In THE LODGER, Daisy is a model, but
when the Lodger buys a dress that she models and has it delivered to her, her
father is outraged and insists on returning it. He has been made aware of the
effect of her profession on male customers, and he is shocked by the implications. In CHAMPAGNE, the Girl's father pretends to be bankrupt, and so, to earn
money, she goes to work as a flower girl in a cabaret. Finding her in such an
environment shocks her boyfriend, who fetches her father: both men then turn
on her for her choice of job. Later examples would include David in MR AND
MRS SMITH bursting into the department store where his wife works and creating a scene, or the way both Jeff in REAR WINDOW and Ben in THE MAN WHO
KNEW TOO MUCH (1955) are uneasy about the professional success of each film's
heroine and so seek to belittle or curtail it. Nevertheless, both these later films
climax with the triumph of the heroine's exhibitionism: Lisa's entry into
Thorwald's apartment and discovery of the murder evidence against him
(➤ JEWELLERY), and Jo belting out 'Que Sera Sera' at an embassy reception to
communicate with her kidnapped son, which enables Ben to rescue him
(➤ *Couples and staircases*).

Relevant to Jo's success here is that she is using her professional talents as a
singer, just as Patsy had been able to use her skills as a stage performer to

handle the elderly gentleman's unwarranted attentions. Professional performers are one group of women in Hitchcock who usually do possess the poise and self-sufficiency to triumph as exhibitionists. Another example is Charlotte in STAGE FRIGHT, who – brilliantly played by Dietrich – is perhaps Hitchcock's most untrammelled and entertaining female exhibitionist. Yet even she is threatened during her stage performances by interruptions from men with their own agendas. On the West End stage singing 'The Laziest Gal in Town', she is able to control her reaction to the interruption: the appearance in the audience of Jonathan, her husband's murderer. However, when she sings 'La Vie en Rose' at a garden party, she is confronted with a cub scout holding up a doll with a bloody dress, which so disturbs her that she stops singing. Here, the interruption has been contrived by Commodore Gill, whose agenda is to seek to demonstrate that Charlotte is herself her husband's murderer. Once again, a bullying male chokes off a woman's triumphant display.

Very occasionally, a female performer successfully threatens the hero. In TORN CURTAIN, a ballerina dancing on stage recognises Michael in the audience (shown in a series of freeze shots of her face, looking at him); her power is then confirmed when she goes off-stage to look through a peep-hole and point him out to the stage manager. It is her eye we see gazing through the peep-hole; in effect, she becomes one of Hitchcock's rare female voyeurs. Under STAIRCASES, I note that in the scenes set in communist countries, a dominant Hitchcock structure is inverted. The notion could also be applied here: in East Germany – and later on a communist ship – a woman can be a voyeur. However, if the ballerina is successful in that she forces Michael and Sarah to flee, her success is at the expense of her performance, which is disastrously interrupted (➤ PUBLIC DISTURBANCES). Her triumph, too, is short-lived.

FAMILY PLOT begins and ends with female exhibitionism. Blanche makes her living as a 'spiritualist', and the film opens with her session with Julia Rainbird, whose wish to track down her sister's lost son initiates one thread of the narrative. We are made aware from this first scene that, when Blanche is with a client, she self-consciously puts on a performance, including the use of a deep masculine voice when she wishes to signal that one of her spirits is 'possessing' her. At one point in the film, George does what men so often do when women are performing: he interrupts (to borrow Blanche's car: ➤ KEYS AND HANDBAGS) and Blanche is obliged to integrate the interruption into the performance. But at the end, as she first escapes from the villains and then leads George to where the ransom diamond is hidden, her performance moves to a different level. I discuss her wonderfully manic bamboozling of the villains under BED SCENE, and her equally successful duping of George under STAIRCASES. Unlike the villains, George does not even realise that Blanche is indeed performing: he tells her that she really is psychic, and not a fake. The penultimate shot, of Blanche winking at the audience, is like her final bow. Female exhibitionism may only triumph on occasions in Hitchcock but, as with the linked example of STAIR-CASES, the fact that his directorial career is framed by instances of such triumph is in itself significant. Against the odds, he has succeeded in giving a woman metaphorically the first and the last word on the subject.

In 'Hitchcock's Vision', Peter Wollen discusses exhibitionism and voyeurism (scopophilia) in the director's films and writes 'The act of watching dominates his films, both in the narration and in the narrative, in his style as director and in the relations between the dramatis personae. Hitchcock's look is not the "neutral" look of simple sight: it is charged with meaning' (Wollen 1969: 2). There are two distinct ideas here. In Hitchcock's films we repeatedly see events through the eyes of individual characters. Effected through the use of point-of-view editing, this is one of the most distinctive features of his work and it has provided a starting point for numerous discussions of his 'audience-identification techniques' and their implications. The notion that Hitchcock as auteur is 'like' a voyeur, that a sense of voyeurism is infused into the fabric of his films, is however more problematic. One may sense it intuitively, but it is difficult to pin down. There are of course key films, notably REAR WINDOW and VERTIGO, which could be said to illustrate the notion. But the voyeurism in these films still works through an individual: we are seeing events from the voyeuristic hero's point of view.

In Freudian terms, the primal scene may be seen as a founding moment of scopophilia. In REAR WINDOW, perhaps the cinema's most profound film *about* voyeurism, most of the apartments into which Jeff looks have scenes which may be read as versions of the primal scene. At first, the film preserves decorum: all the examples he sees (the childless couple sleeping head to toe; Miss Torso and Miss Lonelyhearts rejecting amorous suitors) show denial of sex; those closer to the material of the primal scene, notably the honeymoon couple, are discreetly hidden from view. A more significant example is the Thorwalds, where the child's perception that the father in the primal scene is hurting the mother is translated into murder and dismemberment. As so often in his films, Hitchcock shifts from sex to murder, the displacement here a reflection of the hero's neurotic psyche. But again the violence is hidden from view, and Jeff seems relatively detached about it. However, when Thorwald – this time in full view of Jeff's gaze – attacks Lisa, Jeff becomes overwrought, scarcely able to look, his distress mirroring that of a child witnessing the perceived violence of the primal scene. This is also the point when Lisa's exhibitionism – in breaking into Thorwald's apartment, she has been showing off her 'Girl Friday' skills to Jeff – comes viciously under attack. As I note under DOUBLES, it's as if Jeff is seeing his own repressed violence against Lisa unleashed through Thorwald. His distress is thus doubly motivated.

In PSYCHO, Norman's voyeurism is more conventional: he spies on Marion undressing. Again, however, the outcome is a displacement from (potential) sex to murder, as Marion is stabbed to death in the shower in a manner which suggests, inter alia, a hideous parody of rape. VERTIGO returns to the notion of voyeurism and exhibitionism as complementary. For all that we experience the first third of the film from the point of view of Scottie as voyeur, in retrospect we realise that Judy as 'Madeleine' was in effect an exhibitionist. She knew that Scottie was following and observing her; she ensured that he always kept up with her and had a good view. But if this suggests that 'Madeleine' was the figure in control, leading Scottie, it should be qualified: 'Madeleine' was herself being controlled by the future murderer, Elster.

Each of these three films offers a different slant on voyeurism. In REAR WIN-DOW, there are two different but interlocking ways of reading Jeff's voyeurism. On the one hand, what he sees is a reflection of his inner world: the characters and situations he observes are like projections of (a) his fears and fantasies and (b) the tensions between him and Lisa (➤ DOUBLES; RAIN). On the other hand, the film also draws a highly sophisticated self-reflexive analogy between voyeurism and the experience of watching a film: see Stam and Pearson 1986: 193-206. (See also Belton 2000 and Fawell 2001 for further discussion of these matters.) In PSYCHO, Norman's voyeurism becomes retrospectively complex through the additional features we learn about him: his impotence, his psychosis, the sense that, even as he spies on Marion, his 'mother' spies with him and is aroused in a very different sense. In VERTIGO, Scottie's voyeurism is like an entrancement: as voyeur, he is being visually seduced by 'Madeleine's' beauty and mystery.

For all that we share the point of view of the male voyeur in these famous examples, he is also viewed critically. Jeff's voyeurism is certainly not all bad – it serves to uncover a murder – but Hitchcock nevertheless suggests that there is something unhealthy about it: it is a little too obsessive. In PSYCHO, we subsequently learn that we have spied on the heroine through the eyes of a psychotic. In VERTIGO, it is evident that Scottie's fascination with 'Madeleine' reflects a disturbed psyche; that of a stalker, to use a modern term. Hitchcock certainly uses the point-of-view editing in these films to involve us with the hero, but it is to a greater or lesser extent a troubled involvement.

SPY FILMS / THE LOOK

Wollen includes Hitchcock's spy films as further instances of his voyeuristic impulses: 'The spy, who strives to see what is forbidden, and fears that others are watching him, invites Freudian analysis' (Wollen 1969: 2). One insight deriving from Freud relates to his argument in 'Three Essays on the Theory of Sexuality' that scopophilia and exhibitionism are the active and passive forms of a pair of instincts, and that 'Every active perversion is … accompanied by its passive counterpart: anyone who is an exhibitionist in his unconscious is at the same time a voyeur' (Freud 1905/1977: 81). This would suggest that spies (professional voyeurs) are also repressed exhibitionists. One senses this repeatedly in Hitchcock, from Jordan displaying his amputated finger to André's insistence, in TOPAZ, in placing himself amongst a crowd at a Cuban function in two different countries, with the result that his presence is noticed and so seems suspicious. Like Brandon in ROPE, the spies – albeit unconsciously – seem to want to be exposed, because then their skill and daring will be recognised.

A particularly sinister version of this occurs in NOTORIOUS, when Devlin forces Alicia to kiss him in view of her husband Alex. His rationale is that this will conceal the real purpose of their visit downstairs, which has been to spy (➤ THE MACGUFFIN). His kissing Alicia is in itself an exhibitionist display, asserting his power as lover, but it also has the effect of revealing its deeper, repressed aspect: to show off to the enemy Devlin's skills as a spy. Moreover, this in turn betrays Alicia as a spy to her Nazi husband, and so reveals yet another masked (repressed) wish: to punish Alicia. André's recklessness has a very similar outcome: Rico Parra's realisation that he is a spy causes suspicion to fall on Juanita, the lover of both men. It would seem that the unconscious exhibitionism of some, at least, of Hitchcock's spies may reveal distinctly disturbing undercurrents.

In the introduction to *Alfred Hitchcock's Sinister Spies*, there is a comment: 'Women, with their eye for detail and their acting ability, make excellent spies' (quoted in Atkins 1984: 9). Now it is possible that Hitchcock did not in fact write this. Martin Grams Jr. notes that 'the majority of these titles [in the Hitchcock anthologies] were compiled and edited by in-house publishing staff, who even wrote the introductions' (Grams Jr. 1999: 174). However, I take the fact that the introductions were signed by Hitchcock as indicating his approval of their contents. But there is a significant difference between the quoted comment and what is actually found in the majority of spy films, including Hitchcock's. The acting ability of the female spies is certainly in evidence, but their eye for detail is hidden: we hardly ever see them actually spying. It is the sexual liaisons which complicate the life of the female spy which have primarily interested filmmakers over the years. It is the same with Hitchcock: his spy films repeatedly include sexual triangles – a beautiful female spy between two men – but we rarely see these heroines spying. Alicia requires Devlin's assistance to search the cellar and find the MacGuffin. We do not see Eve in NORTH BY NORTHWEST do any spying at all; again it is the hero who uncovers the MacGuffin

(➤ HOMOSEXUALITY). Juanita in TOPAZ runs an espionage network on Cuba, but it is her agents who do the field work. And even though one of them is a woman, in the scene in which Mrs Mendoza spies, (a) she is with her husband, (b) they are careless about the food from the picnic basket – which attracts gulls – and are spotted and (c) Mrs Mendoza is shot in the arm as they flee, and this serves to identify them to the pursuing troops. They are captured, tortured and presumably executed. Under torture, they reveal Juanita's name, which leads to her likewise being killed. In other words, when we do see a woman actually spying, things go seriously wrong.

There is a similar problem with any woman who investigates. Either (a) she does this more by eavesdropping than looking (e.g. Mary overhearing a crucial conversation between Sir Humphrey and Jem Trehearne in JAMAICA INN, or Lil overhearing Marnie on the phone to her mother), or (b) her quest takes place in the absence of people and is focused on texts (letters, newspapers) or objects – as in SUSPICION, SHADOW OF A DOUBT or when Lila searches the Bates house in PSYCHO. Even Hitchcock's most assiduous female investigator, Eve in STAGE FRIGHT, learns most of her information by eavesdropping. The problem of the 'woman's look' is discussed under SPECTACLES, where I argue that its suppression in his films is an example of Hitchcock conforming to the (reactionary) thinking of his culture and period.

All these examples indicate that Hitchcock, like other male filmmakers, feels uncomfortable with the idea of women actually doing any sort of spying. Once again, we encounter the problem of the woman's look. The events in NOTORIOUS and in the Cuban section of TOPAZ also conform to another feature of the spy genre: that undercover work is more dangerous for female than for male agents. From DISHONORED (Josef von Sternberg, 1931) to LE SANG DES AUTRES (Claude Chabrol, 1984), a female undercover agent is much more likely than her male counterpart(s) to be killed in the service of her country. This is brutally emphasised in THE COUNTERFEIT TRAITOR (George Seaton, 1961), where the hero is forced to watch the heroine's execution by a firing squad. That Alicia is almost poisoned to death, and that Juanita and her agents are shot, whereas the heroes remain unscathed, is thus typical. One reason why women spies are more vulnerable than men in these films is that their emotions are more likely to compromise their work. It is because of their love for the hero that Alicia and Juanita enact the espionage which leads to their exposure. Eve in NORTH BY NORTHWEST only becomes the subject of Vandamm's suspicions after Roger has entered her life. But perhaps there is a deeper problem with women being spies: implicitly, it lends them the power of the look, and this is sufficiently disturbing for the ideology that they are repeatedly and savagely punished.

With a hero in a Hitchcock spy movie, key moments of revelation may well be linked to his look (➤ *Espionage and the look* under HOMOSEXUALITY).

Fig. 23. Still: MARNIE: the anxious look. Having burgled the Rutland safe, Marnie (Tippi Hedren)
discovers that she is not alone. Rita (Edith Evanson) cleaning on the left.

Nevertheless, with the exception of TOPAZ, actual espionage in the movies is
more often subordinated to the fear of exposure or being caught. Indeed, this
anxiety frequently plays through Hitchcock's films in general, especially when
someone is guilty. On such occasions, the look is an anxious one, concerned
with avoiding observation or suspicion. Famous examples from the non-spy
movies include Guy's twitching eye at the climax of YOUNG AND INNOCENT
(➢ GUILT AND CONFESSION), Melanie delivering the love birds across
Bodega Bay in THE BIRDS (discussed later) and Marnie seeking to avoid the
gaze of the cleaner as she sneaks out of the Rutland office with the stolen
money. In this last scene, the cleaner is similar in appearance to Marnie's mother
– age, cardigan, hairstyle, class – so that, metaphorically, it is her mother's accusing gaze Marnie is seeking to avoid. Mrs Edgar does not know that Marnie
obtains her money by stealing.

  Paralleling such cases, the look may well unsettle someone who is aware of
being observed. This, too, occurs repeatedly in Hitchcock, and both sexes experience it. In CHAMPAGNE, the Man's hypnotic stare at the Girl exerts such

power that, in a sequence in the cabaret, it causes her to fantasise that he takes her to a private booth and sexually assaults her. But the only example of genuine hypnotism in Hitchcock is in THE MAN WHO KNEW TOO MUCH (1934), where a woman hypnotises a man. In FOREIGN CORRESPONDENT, Johnny's staring at Carol during her speech is sufficient to cause her to become muddled and dry up, but in STRANGERS ON A TRAIN it is Guy who is unnerved when he becomes the object of Bruno's look. Also in this film is a rare example of a woman and a man being simultaneously disturbed by the other's look: the two scenes when Bruno and Barbara stare at each other (➤ SPECTACLES). In PSYCHO, women are disturbed by the look: Marion by the traffic cop; Norman as 'mother' at the end, imagining herself the object of scrutiny: 'They're probably watching me.' But in TORN CURTAIN, it is Michael who is constantly unsettled by the looks of others, first Sarah, then Gromek. And Hitchcock's most famous example of someone being disturbed by the look is surely the moment in REAR WINDOW when Thorwald, finally, returns Jeff's look.

There are two main types of look involved in these examples: those which disturb primarily because of their sexual overtones (both heterosexual and homosexual) and those which disturb because the protagonist feels guilty about something. However, Colin McArthur has suggested that there is another type of look in Hitchcock, which relates 'primarily to class' (McArthur 2000: 24). Discussed further under PUBLIC DISTURBANCES, this too can prompt unease in someone subjected to its accusatory power. The judge's look at Larita in EASY VIRTUE is echoed in the hostility with which the haughty Mrs Whittaker views her after her marriage to the latter's son (➤ MOTHER AND HOUSES). In YOUNG AND INNOCENT, just as the middle-class Erica is viewed with suspicion when she asks questions in a lorry-drivers' café, so the working-class Will is viewed with suspicion when he hires a dress suit to go into a posh hotel. Hitchcock's British films frequently register class tensions, and it is only to be expected that the look will, on occasions, serve to express these.

Yet another type of look which is articulated across Hitchcock's films is the jealous look of a woman at her rival. An additional feature here is that the jealous woman is repeatedly shown to look down at the more glamorous rival. When Gay arrives in the balcony at the Old Bailey in THE PARADINE CASE, Hitchcock emphasises her first sight of Mrs Paradine in the dock by a crane down to the latter along the axis of Gay's look. The one time Midge sees 'Madeleine' in VERTIGO, she is in her car higher up the hill as the latter comes out of Scottie's apartment. In THE BIRDS, Annie and Lydia in turn look down on a seated Melanie as each shows her understanding of the significance of the gift of the love birds: 'I see.' In the first scene between the 'rivals' in WALTZES FROM VIENNA, STAGE FRIGHT and TO CATCH A THIEF the feature is also present with only a slight modification. The axis of the look may suggest to the jealous woman that she is 'looking down' on her rival, but her sense of moral superiority is misplaced: it is the glamorous woman whom the hero is – or soon will be – in thrall to. This emphasises the exception of the first look exchanged between Lil and Marnie, contributing further to the hint of a suppressed sexual attraction between them (➤ HOMOSEXUALITY).

A sequence which uses the look to capture the underlying tensions of the gender politics in Hitchcock occurs when Melanie delivers the love birds. The sequence has in fact been analysed shot by shot by Raymond Bellour (Bellour 1969/2000: 28-67). I merely wish to focus – in the context of the overall sequence – on the two moments when Mitch and Melanie look at each other. As Melanie makes her way by boat across Bodega Bay and delivers the birds, Hitchcock uses point-of-view editing from her position. But her concern, as noted, is to avoid being seen; although, for example, we watch the Brenners leave the house through her eyes, she is not really spying, but waiting for a moment when she can act unobserved.

After Melanie has delivered the birds and returned to her boat, she moves offshore and watches as Mitch re-enters the house and then comes running out, looking for whoever has brought the birds. Noticing the boat, he goes back indoors, cueing Melanie to sit up to try and restart the outboard motor. As Mitch comes out again, gulls fly ominously into the shot (we are still waiting for the first bird attack). This shot of him, like all the others thus far in the sequence, is from Melanie's point of view, but now Hitchcock cuts to a close shot of Mitch as he raises a pair of binoculars. Through the binoculars, we now see his point of view of Melanie, who finally manages to start the outboard motor and looks back at him. Mitch smiles, and lowers the binoculars. All of this is a game, but now he understands the rules, and as Melanie sets off back across the bay, he jumps into his car and races round the bay to arrive at the quayside before she docks. As she approaches the dock, she cocks her head flirtatiously at him, and the first bird attack occurs: a gull flies down and strikes her head.

Mitch's smile is of recognition, but Hitchcock structures it as also one of power: he has the woman in his sights and she is not going to get away. At the moment when the point of view reverses, and the man's look is privileged, the power relations change. Although we assume that, now that her scheme has succeeded, Melanie wants Mitch to see her, something else is unleashed. The milling gulls translate the tension of looks into something more sinister; it's as if Mitch's eagerness to see Melanie produces the gulls, one of which will indeed shortly attack her. Moreover, the attack occurs when their looks meet again at the quayside, and Melanie's coquettish (exhibitionist) gesture signals her pleasure that her little game has had the effect she desired. Even as hero and heroine play out a courtship ritual with good-humoured ease, Hitchcock charges their looks with undercurrents of violence. When, much later, Melanie is trapped in a phone booth by the bird attacks, the violence is much more sexualised (➤ ENTRY THROUGH A WINDOW). These moments qualify Margaret Horwitz's reading of the reason for the bird attacks in the film, which she relates primarily to the jealousy of Lydia (Horwitz 1986: 279-287) (➤ CHILDREN).

All these examples suggest that there is a dynamic around exhibitionism, voyeurism and the look in Hitchcock's films: that the films are frequently mobilised by the interplay of these elements. The look is the master feature here – in many respects, it is like the cement that ties Hitchcock's narratives together. The multiplicity of examples in which we share somebody's point of view, the voyeuristic drive within certain key films, threatening gazes, emotionally charged looks, the sensitivity of characters to being observed and even the theatrical élan with which some of his characters show off their talents – all are dependent on Hitchcock's deployment of the look as a crucial structuring feature in his films. Equally, it is the way in which Hitchcock articulates the look which helps determine the close identification he establishes between the spectator and his characters. In short, we are dealing here with a highly significant feature of his films.

See also *Espionage and the look* under HOMOSEXUALITY.

Exhibitionism, voyeurism and the police

Hitchcock's police are not really exhibitionists. Their role is to observe, not to show off. There are two policemen who do seem rather pleased with themselves – Joe in The Lodger and Chief Inspector Hubbard in Dial M for Murder – but, apart from Joe's performance with the handcuffs (➤ HANDCUFFS AND BONDAGE), this does not really translate into exhibitionism. More unexpectedly, we do not encounter many policemen voyeurs. Although there are films in which the police are watching somebody, this is rarely presented in terms of 'voyeuristic observation'. The most common structure is for them to be watching a man who is a relative of the heroine (Sabotage, Jamaica Inn, Shadow of a Doubt), and it is predominantly her point of view which we share. Only in the special case of Vertigo, where Scottie is an ex-policeman, does the full voyeuristic structure come into play.

Nevertheless, there are films in which the gaze of the police is indeed significant. Here we are on familiar Hitchcock territory: the police look, but they do not see. Examples from Saboteur and To Catch a Thief are mentioned under *Lights and the police*. As Bruno and Guy fight on the runaway merry-go-round at the climax of Strangers on a Train, the boat attendant tells the police that 'he's the one who killed her'. The police assume he means Guy. Doyle in Rear

WINDOW spends most of his time refuting Jeff's story of what has happened to Mrs Thorwald. Scottie spends the first half of VERTIGO mesmerised by 'Madeleine', but unable to fathom what is going on and who she really is. In such a context, a moment in FRENZY deserves mention. After Blaney's conviction for the necktie murders, Chief Inspector Oxford begins to believe his story – that he was framed by Rusk – and he takes a photographer to get the latter's photograph. As he points Rusk out to the photographer from a moving taxi, we actually see Rusk in a point-of-view shot from the taxi. Here the police are indeed like voyeurs, watching their man unobserved. And on this occasion they've finally got the guilty man.

FOOD AND MEALS

Fig. 24. Still: YOUNG AND INNOCENT: the disrupted meal and the disrupting child. During the family lunch, Chris shows his sister Erica (Nova Pilbeam) a rat he has shot.

In *The Alfred Hitchcock Quote Book*, Laurent Bouzereau includes a chapter on Hitchcock and food, beginning with a bold statement:

> Hitchcock's greatest preoccupation was not sex, women or crime. It was food. While it had a place of honor in his everyday life, it quickly became an important theme in his films; food is linked to (or is the substitute for) marriage, sex and murder.
>
> (Bouzereau 1993: 128)

Although Bouzereau merely cites quotations from the films – there is no discussion – he at least provides a start. Because of the number and range of examples, food is a tricky motif to analyse in Hitchcock: there is probably not one of his films in which food (and/or meals) is not an issue at some point. I would like to begin by considering Bouzereau's three main categories – food and marriage, food and sex, food and murder – taking into account both the examples he cites and others. I shall also refer to the very useful ideas in Susan Smith's PhD thesis, *Cinematic Point of View in the Films of Hitchcock* (1997). Smith includes a section on the food motif in Hitchcock, and although she concentrates mainly on SABOTAGE, she also discusses Hitchcock's use of the motif elsewhere. I have also included meals, because on occasions the food is less important than the eating occasion itself. In the headings which follow, then, and in references to 'the food motif', food is an inclusive term: it also implies meals.

Food and marriage

With the striking and symptomatic exception of Miss Lonelyhearts in REAR WINDOW, characters in Hitchcock do not eat alone – they always have company. Hitchcock thereby uses meals to probe relationships – and this is especially true of his married couples. Sometimes the meal is simply a suitable setting to register general marital tensions: the patronising contempt Lord Horsfield directs at his wife in THE PARADINE CASE; the reconciliation breakfast which turns tense when Ann asks charged questions in MR AND MRS SMITH. However, sometimes the food itself plays a part: where the marriage is uneasy, the husband's dissatisfaction may well be expressed in complaints about the food. Fred moans about the regular evening meal of steak and kidney pudding in RICH AND STRANGE, as does Verloc about the greens in SABOTAGE. In FRENZY, by contrast, we can see that Chief Inspector Oxford is doing his best not to complain about the *cordon bleu* cooking his wife is inflicting on him: he is carefully preserving a veneer of civility.

On the other hand, food and marriage may be imagined, by those who are unmarried, as entirely harmonious. In NOTORIOUS, when Alicia carries out the chicken she has cooked for herself and Devlin, she says, 'Marriage must be wonderful with this sort of thing going on every day.' In REAR WINDOW, Jeff compliments Stella on the breakfast she has just cooked him: 'I can't tell you what a welcome sight this is. No wonder your husband still loves you.' But the eating of both the ensuing meals is then spoiled, like a comment on the sentiments expressed. In THE BIRDS, Lydia tells Melanie about her sense of loss at her husband's death: 'Sometimes, even now, I wake up in the morning and I think "I must get Frank's breakfast"… There's a very good reason for getting out of bed – until, of course, I remember.' It is entirely typical of Hitchcock that a widow's loss should be expressed in terms of no longer needing to prepare food for her husband. But the point is also that her sense of marital happiness is, now, only a memory.

Fig. 25. Still: REAR WINDOW: the lonely meal. Miss Lonelyhearts (Judith Evelyn) pours the wine for an imaginary dinner guest.

Bouzereau quotes one example in which food is referred to within a marriage in a nurturing context. When Manny comes out of jail in THE WRONG MAN, he is weak and faint, and Rose reassures him: 'Manny, we're going home now. I've got some coffee and lasagne. Manny, you'll be all right.' To the best of my knowledge, this is the only such example in Hitchcock, and it is very fleeting. Nurturing is not a feature of Hitchcock's marriages, and – so far as we see – not even food is enjoyed unproblematically by his married couples.

Susan Smith discusses some of these examples, arguing that when the husband complains about the food, this may be seen as an expression of more specific fears, notably of female sexuality. Fred's seasickness in RICH AND STRANGE is a case in point. It first occurs when he is trying to take a photograph of his wife Emily on a moving ship's deck. Smith suggests that:

> the translation of [Fred's] revulsion towards his wife into a loss of appetite for food [is] effected by a transition from a medium shot of Emily circled by revolving white spots of light to a montage of soup bowls... Whilst Fred construes his waning interest in his wife (expressed through a loss of appetite for her regular evening meals of 'steak and kidney pudding') as motivated by a desire for a more exciting, sexualised

female ('Water is a good drink, but champagne is better…'), the film's depiction of his unsteady, but rather glamorous, romanticised view of his wife through the camera viewfinder suggests that it is in fact triggered by his uneasiness at beginning to see her in a different, more sexualised way.

(Smith 1997: 270)

In short, Fred's boredom with Emily's cooking is a symptom of his jaded view of the marriage, but behind that view lies a deeper fear of sexual inadequacy. I fully agree with this argument, which is supported by other details. In the couple's first scene, Emily is working at her sewing machine when Fred arrives home from work. As she comments: 'I think you'll like me in this dress when it's done', his umbrella – which has been giving him trouble all the way home – collapses. It is not difficult to see the umbrella as a phallic symbol, collapsing to express Fred's unease at the idea of a newly attractive Emily. It is then that Emily mentions the steak and kidney pudding that she has cooked, and makes suggestions for their evening together. Fred promptly launches into a bitter tirade about the life they lead, going so far as to suggest that 'The best place for us is a gas oven'. At this point, a letter from his uncle arrives, offering them money to experience life by travelling. However, far from improving Fred's temper, this simply reinflects it: under the pretext that Emily can now have some 'real clothes', he sadistically tears the dress she is working on from the machine, and looks triumphant when she protests. The last shot of the scene is of Emily's cooking on the stove: the steak and kidney pudding boils over. It's as if Fred's resentment and bitterness is displaced on to the cooking, which erupts to signal that, despite the change in their fortunes, he is just as bad-tempered as ever.

In SABOTAGE, Verloc complains twice about the greens, on both occasions after an act of sabotage. The first time, the complaint is staged: he has just been manicuring his nails, but he quickly hides this from Mrs Verloc when she and her young brother Stevie enter the room with the food. His comment about the unsatisfactory state of the greens would thus seem to be his way of trying to hide that he is pleased with himself by reverting to what we deduce is his normal behaviour. But that in turn suggests a similar dissatisfaction with the state of his marriage to Fred's. In each case, the husband's complaints about the food functions as a displacement from his deeper resentments.

When Verloc complains a second time, there are different overtones:

In following on from his 'accidental' killing of Stevie and Mrs Verloc's outright rejection of his request for a child, Verloc's second complaint about the food serves quite clearly as a defence for deflecting attention away from his own sense of guilt and heightened sexual anxieties.

(Smith 1997: 178)

It is made clear, elsewhere in the film, that Mrs Verloc married her husband not for love but because he was 'kind' to Stevie. Now his secret activities as a sabo-teur have resulted in Stevie's death. But Verloc, with astonishing insensitivity, is still moaning about the greens. It is surely no accident that this is the last thing that he says; that the remark serves, in effect, to prompt his wife to 'murder' him. In this film, the meal scenes are not only pointers to the state of the mar-riage, but are charged underneath with the violence of the husband's saboteur work. The violence enters the domestic space and results, ultimately, in a killing.

In both these films, it is the husband's sexual and emotional inadequacies which emerge when one looks at his comments about – and reactions to – the food in the context of other elements. It is this sense of the food as a metaphor which is relevant to the wider functioning of the motif in Hitchcock. The impli-cit meanings may vary, but food is rarely simply a means of nourishment, and meals are rarely simply an occasion for eating. The problems in Hitchcock's marriages emerge during meals no less than in the bedroom, it is just that the forms in which these are expressed are different. FRENZY supplies another sort of example. Tania Modleski argues that Mrs Oxford's cuisine may be seen as her 'wreaking revenge on her husband because of his lack of sexual inclination' (Modleski 1988: 109). Here, where the dinner-table topic of conversation is in-variably about the progress of Oxford's current case – i.e. the serial killer story narrated in the rest of the film – the murderous violence seemingly only enters the home in the form of discussion. But it also seems as if violence has been sublimated into the food, with the wife deliberately preparing meals which she knows her husband will find unpalatable.

In all these examples, the general inability of Hitchcock's married couples to enjoy a meal together is symptomatic. Discussing Hitchcock's 'stories about a marriage', Robin Wood comments: 'From RICH AND STRANGE through to FREN-ZY, the attitude to marriage is remarkably (given the very high value placed on that institution within patriarchal ideology…) bleak and skeptical' (Wood 1989: 246). Even the meals Hitchcock's married couples eat away from home tend to be filled with tension. When David and Ann Smith return to Momma Lucy's, the favourite restaurant of their courtship, the intended celebration is rendered distinctly uncomfortable by the run-down state of the place, the third-rate food and Ann's anxiety about whether David is going to come clean with her about the fact that they are not legally married. When Ben and Jo go to a restaurant in Marrakech in THE MAN WHO KNEW TOO MUCH (1955), first he has a terrible time with the Arab technique for eating a roast chicken, then Jo works him into a rage over the presence at another table of Louis Bernard, who had invited them to dine with him and then changed his mind. What began as a traditional tourists' evening out ends in tension and frustration. SUSPICION includes per-haps the most sinister example. When Johnnie and Lina dine at the novelist

Isobel Sedbusk's, he spends most of the meal pumping Isobel and her brother Bertram, a Home Office pathologist, for details of an untraceable poison. The implication, clearly expressed through the way Hitchcock stages and edits the scene, is that Johnnie wants the poison to murder Lina. He does not succeed in obtaining the information he wants in this scene, but he does later, and the poison, I am convinced, ends up in Lina's bedtime milk (➤ *Milk* in Part I; LIGHTS).

Overall, then, meals are something of a battleground for Hitchcock's married couples. Whereas in the films of Claude Chabrol, another well-known gourmet film-maker, the meals can still be enjoyed even when the marriage is in difficulties (e.g. in La Femme Infidèle, 1968, and Les Noces Rouges, 1973), in Hitchcock this is rarely the case. In Chabrol, the food tends to relieve the tensions; in Hitchcock it is more likely to focus them.

Food and sex

In To Catch a Thief, Francie asks Robie, ostensibly referring to the picnic chicken: 'You want a leg or a breast?' This may seem to be no more than a somewhat adolescent sexual innuendo, but Francie is clearly flirting with Robie, just as she is when, later, she uses her necklace as bait (➤ JEWELLERY). Thus a more important point here is the way in which food is used as a mechanism to express a woman's arousal. This notion occurs across Hitchcock's work. Early in Suspicion, Lina comes in to Sunday lunch after passionately kissing Johnnie and asks the butler – referring to the roast beef – 'Could I have some well done, please?' In Vertigo, after she and Scottie have finally made love, Judy declares: 'I'm suddenly hungry… I'm gonna have one of those big beautiful steaks.' Strangers on a Train provides perhaps the most pointed example. In the fairground, when Miriam gets an ice cream, she wonders whether she should have a hotdog first: it might satisfy her craving better. One of her escorts asks, sarcastically, 'Craving for what?' At this point, licking the ice cream lasciviously, Miriam turns round – and notices Bruno.

Hitchcock may even relate a woman's lack of appetite to her lack of sex. In Rebecca, there are references both before and after the marriage to the heroine not being hungry, but when she faints during the inquest, Maxim is quick to diagnose: 'I told you should have had some breakfast. You're hungry – that's what's the matter with you.' Since the inquest follows immediately after the first scene of passion between Maxim and the heroine, the implication here is that she now needs to eat properly. Such overtones, however, are given a rather unpleasant twist in Frenzy. In the context of Hitchcock's cinema, Brenda's 'frugal lunch' of an apple and milk implies a sexually abstemious life. But it is Rusk who interrupts the lunch and comments on the frugality, and he then goes on to savagely 'rape' and murder her.

In none of the examples so far in this category is food implicitly substituting for sex; an argument which applies at one level to Mrs Oxford's cuisine. Instead, the examples suggest a more or less direct correlation between a woman's sexual and dietary appetites. Sex may interfere with eating, as in the openings of PSYCHO (where Sam comments that Marion hasn't eaten her lunch) and TORN CURTAIN (where Michael and Sarah have stayed in bed and missed breakfast). This does not, however, detract from the more general point: a sexually active woman is a hungry woman. When, in FAMILY PLOT, Blanche asks a reluctant George to cook her another hamburger, she is also referring to a matter alluded to elsewhere in the film: that her sexual desires exceed his.

A more sinister example in this category is the conflation of sex and food, as in 'Mrs Bates's' admonition to Norman: 'Go tell her she'll not be appeasing her ugly appetite with my food, or my son.' There is a similar notion in play when Rusk says to Brenda before assaulting her that in his trade (greengrocer) they have a saying: '"Don't squeeze the goods until they're yours"... I would never do that.' But the figures who deliver these lines are mentally disturbed, so that the conflation of the two elements is the product of a disordered mind. Both go on to kill the woman to whom they are referring.

Food and sex have often been linked in the cinema, but normally in a celebratory, erotic sense: see the gangster story in TAMPOPO (Juzo Itami, 1986) for a particularly explicit example. Not so in Hitchcock. The two elements never really work together, and the outcome may indeed be brutal: both Judy and Miriam die before their hunger is satisfied. In addition, as in the married couple examples, a man's fear of a woman's sexuality may be expressed in his reaction to the food which she has prepared. In REAR WINDOW, Lisa takes great trouble to order and transport a lobster dinner from the 21 Club to Jeff's apartment, but he is unable to respond enthusiastically. Susan Smith comments:

> That it is Lisa's active, threatening sexuality which Jeffries is rejecting via the food is indicated by the redness of the cooked lobster which she serves up to him and by its associations with pincers and claws (as sharp 'female' implements that precede those used by Thorwald to cut up his wife).
>
> (Smith 1997: 183)

Jeff's unease is entirely typical. Apart from the occasional successful flirtation – e.g. Roger and Eve on the train in NORTH BY NORTHWEST – food and sex are linked in Hitchcock in a manner typical of his films: to suggest tensions, hostility, fears of inadequacy. His hungry women tend to remain hungry, his neurotic men to find fault. Blanche does not get her extra hamburger.

SPELLBOUND includes a number of examples which summarise the range of associations in this category. When J.B. joins the other doctors at Green Manors for dinner, Constance enthusiastically draws an outline of a planned swimming pool with her fork on the table-cloth. The design is clearly vaginal (or, more properly, vulval), and J.B. reacts badly: 'I take it that the supply of linen at this institution is inexhaustible.' His use of the word linen betrays the unconscious thought processes, linking the table-cloth to bed linen. As in REAR WINDOW, it is the heroine's threatening sexuality that the hero is really reacting against: what is unconsciously disturbing him is the thought of bed linen, bloodied by defloration. Hitchcock cheekily underscores this by a juxtaposition at the end of the scene. As J.B. rubs out Constance's design with his knife – i.e., symbolically, both repudiates *and* accepts her unconscious sexual offer – the story she is telling about Dr Brulov's equivalent neurotic symptoms ends with the word 'ketchup', a sauce popularly associated with the simulation of (unconvincing) film blood.

J.B.'s fear is then restated in different forms throughout the film: 'the series of hysterical breakdowns which he suffers … are all associated with moments of extreme sexual tension' (Britton 1986: 80). The final example returns to the food motif. Constance is eating a meal on a train, and notices that J.B. is disturbed by her cutting the meat. Tactfully, she lays the knife aside. Even so, J.B.'s fraught reaction continues through the climactic ski run (➢ HEIGHTS AND FALLING). Andrew Britton discusses the meal scene, commenting on the castration fear which underlies it, a fear heightened by Constance's topic of conversation, which is about her newfound desire to wear 'feminine clothes' (Britton 1986: 82). In other words, the thought of Constance becoming more sexually attractive is compounding the hero's castration anxieties. As in RICH AND STRANGE, food is located within the dynamic of the scene as a focus for the anxiety. But, in line with the earlier comments about hungry women, from Constance's point of view she is 'innocently' expressing her sexual arousal. The scene thus summarises the Hitchcock food and sex thematic: aroused, hungry woman; neurotic, hostile man.

In the dinner scene at Green Manors, Constance tells her story about Dr Brulov, her old mentor, as a way of making light of J.B.'s sudden outburst. The story implies a parallel fear for Dr Brulov, who 'could never stand a sauce bottle on the table, or even a salt shaker. They took his appetite away.' Given that these, and the bottles of ketchup which also once intimidated him, are offered by Constance as equivalents to the design which has so disturbed J.B., we are prompted to see them as phallic symbols. Accordingly, it would seem that Dr Brulov's (unconscious?) fear is of male sexuality. This implies a revisionist reading of the later drugged milk scene at Dr Brulov's house. J.B., still in a trance after the BED SCENE, descends the stairs with the razor still sticking out in a pointedly phallic way. Dr Brulov, waiting for him, sees that he is dangerous and prepares some drugged milk. But the drug he uses to knock J.B. out is bromide, familiar from its use at the time to reduce the sex drive of male service personnel.

The negative references to milk in Hitchcock's films are discussed in Part I. The SPELLBOUND example is, nevertheless, one of the most pointed: unmanning the hero under the cover of giving him milk. Nor does Dr Brulov stint the dose: 'Enough to knock out three horses.' The traditional reading here (supported, for example, by Andrew Britton) is that the relationship between Constance and Dr Brulov is Oedipal, so that J.B. is the older man's sexual rival for the heroine. This would certainly account for the bromide. But I think that the food motif suggests another interpretation: Dr Brulov unmans the hero because he himself fears his sexual attractiveness.

Food and murder

The most frequent way in which Hitchcock juxtaposes food and murder is through conversation during a meal. Sometimes, as in Isobel's dinner in SUSPICION, this is sinister; more frequently it is done humorously. What spoils Jeff's appreciation of Stella's breakfast is her own speculations about what Thorwald did with his wife's corpse: 'Just where do you suppose he cut her up? Of course, the bath tub. That's the only place where he could have washed away the blood.' Her comments are precisely timed to catch Jeff as he is about to eat some bacon. Similarly in FRENZY. As Chief Inspector Oxford wrestles with a pig's trotter, he mentions to his wife that, whilst Babs's corpse was on the potato lorry, someone tried to take something from it: 'The corpse was deep in rigor mortis. He had to break the fingers of the right hand to retrieve what they held.' At this point, his wife absent-mindedly snaps a bread-stick. In both these cases, Hitchcock is enjoying the effect of introducing the topic of murder into a conversation in such a way as to unsettle the appetite. But these are really no more than typical examples of his black humour.

To CATCH A THIEF goes further. Twice characters connect preparing food with the violent activities of the French underground during the war. One example is, again, typical Hitchcock black humour. As Hughson savours the quiche Lorraine Robie's cook Germaine has just made, Robie makes a point of telling him about her 'sensitive hands' and 'light touch': 'She strangled a German general once – without a sound.' The other example is more macabre. When Robie first goes to Bertani's restaurant, the latter asks him: 'What do think of my kitchen? Works like a machine, yes? Just like our little band in the underground dur-

ing the war: cutting, slicing, just like the old days.' Although the reference to
cutting and slicing is perhaps ambiguous – Bertani could mean sabotage activities – one feels that he is in fact referring to bodies, like the German general's. In
other words, he is likening the cutting up of food in his kitchen to the cutting up
of the enemy in the war. This association is then reinforced when one of the
kitchen staff signals his hostility to Robie by aggressively strangling a bunch of
carrots.

SABOTAGE and ROPE go further still: here Hitchcock juxtaposes food and an
actual murder. In SABOTAGE, revolted by her husband's suggestion that they
make up for Stevie's death by having a child of their own, Mrs Verloc leaves
the room and goes into the cinema. After seeing a clip from WHO KILLED COCK
ROBIN? (➤ HEIGHTS AND FALLING), she returns and starts serving the dinner. As she does this, she notices the carving knife and fork in her hand and
quickly puts them down, using a table knife and fork instead. It is then that
Verloc complains about the greens, asking if they could send next door for
some cabbage. This reminds Mrs Verloc of Stevie, who used to perform this
errand: she looks towards Stevie's empty place. She continues serving, but then
notices that, once more, she is holding the carving knife and fork. She puts them
down again, and looks at Verloc. Suddenly, he notices her preoccupation with
the knife and gets up and walks round to her. Both reach for the carving knife at
the same time, but she is quicker – and she stabs him. Constructed almost entirely through editing and the characters' looks (only Verloc speaks), this is brilliant example of Hitchcock's filmmaking art. (Truffaut includes a series of 24
frame stills from this sequence – Truffaut 1968: 90-91 – but their order is badly
muddled. The error is not corrected in the 1984 revised edition.) Mrs Verloc's
handling of the carving knife dramatises her thoughts: the conflict between
wanting to kill her husband and trying to suppress any such idea. The scene
shows how Hitchcock can charge as familiar a routine as a wife serving her
husband's meal with tensions which build up to 'murder'.

In ROPE, Brandon and Phillip set up their party buffet on the actual chest in
which they have hidden the corpse of David, their murder victim. Brandon
even says to Mrs Wilson, the maid, referring to the candles on the chest: 'I think
they suggest a ceremonial altar, which you can heap with the foods for our
sacrificial feast.' But Brandon's excitement at the association between food and
murder also belongs with the perverted reasoning of 'Mrs Bates' and Rusk: he is
another of Hitchcock's psychopaths. Phillip, by contrast, is in a constant state of
agitation at the games Brandon plays, and his reaction to the food on the chest
is very different: ➤ *Food and guilt.*

The placing of the buffet over the corpse invites a suggestive link with 'the
totem festivals of savages (sic) ... which unconsciously [mean] the idea of eating
the dead person' (Fenichel 1946: 394). Otto Fenichel is referring here to feasts in

which animals are eaten in place of the more archaic practice of eating the slain enemy. Nevertheless, the principle is the same: in J.G. Frazer's words 'the flesh and blood of dead men are commonly eaten and drunk to inspire bravery, wisdom, or other qualities for which the men themselves were remarkable' (Frazer 1957: 652). Freud makes a similar point in 'Totem and Taboo' (Freud 1913/1985: 139). Eating food which by virtue of its properties, preparation or consumption is associated with a dead man serves the same magical purpose. One feels that Brandon would be slightly miffed to learn that a psychoanalyst would relate his self-described 'masterpiece' to a traditional practice of 'savages'. But the association is apt: Brandon is like a cannibal, seeking to gain (magical) power from the execution and celebration of David's murder. Hence he kills the clever and able David rather than the more intellectually plodding Kenneth. In addition, throughout the party, David's body lies *under* the food, like 'the repressed'. Indeed, when Mrs Wilson is clearing the chest of the dishes and left-overs, she is on the point of discovering it. The body is also Brandon and Phillip's guilty secret (➤ THE CORPSE), and the food is like an elaborate way of hiding it.

FRENZY provides an even more brutal link between food and murder. After Rusk has delivered his line about not squeezing the goods, he takes a bite of Brenda's apple. Then, after killing her, he takes another bite and, as he leaves, picks up the apple and pockets it. There is a quite horrible sense here that assaulting and murdering Brenda is a part of Rusk's lunch. Eating has been displaced into murder. In her discussion of FRENZY, Tania Modleski suggests that this scene is then echoed in the Oxfords' dinner scenes:

> Rusk sexually attacks a woman he likens to food; unable to achieve orgasm, he explodes in a murderous rage and strangles her. In the later scenes, the inspector eats food that is likened to a woman; and though he experiences great difficulty consummating *his* meals, he remains civil to his wife.

> (Modleski 1988: 109)

Modleski, too, goes on to invoke cannibalism, suggesting that the dinner-table meals 'flirt with connotations of cannibalism' through 'the idea of feeding off the "carcass" of the dead woman' (109). The argument is perhaps a little stretched, but Rusk did try and bury Babs in food, and, following the discussion about what happened to her body on the potato truck, Oxford spits out the unpalatable pig's trotter, as if in response to the subject-matter of the conversation. This may be tied in with Modleski's use of Julia Kristeva's concept of abjection (➤ THE CORPSE) in relation to food. In Elizabeth Grosz's words:

> Oral disgust is the most archaic form of abjection... The expulsion of food and the refusal to accept and incorporate it is a refusal of the very stuff, the very substance, of maternal and parental love.

> (Grosz 1990: 90)

But if Modleski's argument is valid, the food has become contaminated by (unconscious?) associations with the corpse, another of Kristeva's categories of abjection. It is not surprising that Oxford spits it out.

The oneiric displacement which associates the murdered women's bodies with food in FRENZY was in fact anticipated in REAR WINDOW. It has often been noted that Thorwald's murder of his wife may be seen as a displacement of Jeff's hostility towards Lisa (➤ DOUBLES). The association is strengthened by a detail which no-one seems to have commented on: that Thorwald's metal case (he sells costume jewellery), which he uses to transport his wife in pieces out of the apartment, echoes the metal food container in which the waiter Carl, earlier that evening, had carried the lobster dinner into Jeff's apartment. Although Carl left the apartment with an empty container, given Jeff's negative reaction to the meal, it's as if he is projecting his hostility towards Lisa on to the food, and he is – in fantasy – expelling her in its place.

There is undoubtedly something macabre about the more extreme examples in this category: the symbolic linking of food and murder. At an unconscious level, the food would seem to 'stand in for' the body, which prompts various perverse associations: the preparation of food is like murder (To CATCH A THIEF); eating it is like cannibalism (ROPE; FRENZY); eating is displaced into murder (REAR WINDOW; FRENZY). Even SABOTAGE, which does not really fit any of these associations, has its own perverse overtones. In *The Art of Alfred Hitchcock*, Donald Spoto comments on the ambiguity of Verloc's 'murder': 'he seems to walk into the knife'; it's as though 'he commits suicide' (Spoto 1979: 64). It's almost as if Verloc is seeking to expiate his sins by offering himself as a sacrificial victim in place of the food.

Bouzereau's categories are a convenient way of grouping the food motif in Hitchcock, but they are not exhaustive: Food and class (e.g. David Smith in a fancy restaurant with a working-class date), or Food and romance (nearly always an unsuccessful combination, like the Momma Lucy's scene) are other possibilities. Before discussing the more varied uses of the motif, I would like to look at one more category.

Food and guilt

In THE MANXMAN, Kate marries Pete even though she does not love him and is already pregnant by Philip. At the wedding celebration, she miscuts the cake. In BLACKMAIL, Alice is so haunted by her killing of Crewe that all she hears of a neighbour's gossip about the case is the word 'knife'. When her father asks her to cut some bread, the knife flies from her hand. These two examples are linked not only by Anny Ondra as the 'guilty' heroine, but also in the focus on the knife. In BLACKMAIL, Alice used a knife to defend herself from Crewe's rape attempt (➤ HANDS), and so her anxiety over handling one is understandable, but in both films there would also seem to be a Freudian undertow to the heroine's disturbed reaction to the knife – her guilt also has a sexual dimension. In the train scene in SPELLBOUND, it is the hero who is disturbed, but again there is a sexual dimension and again he is (unconsciously) guilty.

It is perhaps a commonplace that someone who feels guilty cannot eat. Constance eats; J.B. does not. Equally, the lack of guilt in Hitchcock's psychopathic killers is reflected in their undiminished appetites: Uncle Charlie in SHADOW OF A DOUBT; Brandon; Rusk. Likewise with the professional killer Abbott in THE MAN WHO KNEW TOO MUCH (1934). Hitchcock cross-cuts between the build-up to the assassination attempt in the Albert Hall and Abbott casually eating a meal, thereby commenting on Abbott's absence of guilt.

Occasionally however Hitchcock dramatises the connection between guilt and a loss of appetite in a highly inventive manner. During the buffet in ROPE, Phillip says that he doesn't eat chicken, and Brandon tells everyone why: Phillip was once an expert chicken-strangler, but on one occasion 'one of the subjects for our dinner table suddenly rebelled: like Lazarus, he rose from the...' At this point Phillip frantically interrupts: 'That's a lie! I never strangled a chicken in my life!', a denial which Rupert later points out was itself a lie. The cold chicken in the buffet, together with Brandon's rather pointed reference to strangling, is evidently too close a reminder of the strangled body in the chest.

The family lunch in YOUNG AND INNOCENT is another example. Erica has just helped Robert escape from the police, and now, as she sits with her father and four younger brothers, her transgression – her father is the local chief constable – is obviously bothering her. During the meal, she learns that the three shillings Robert spent on petrol for her car was all the money he had. This makes her feel guilty in another sense, a guilt exacerbated by her brothers' conversation. As Chris, the youngest, dramatically produces a rat he has shot, the brothers draw parallels between it and Robert: 'Directly he's spent those last three shillings, it looks to me as if he's caught like a rat in a trap' and 'Guns are the best things for rats... If I go and look for this chap with my gun, I could have a pot at him, couldn't I, father?' They begin to fantasise, in the lurid manner of schoolboys, about Robert fainting from hunger and dying in the fields 'with rooks pecking at his eyes'. Abandoning her own meal, Erica returns to the old mill where Robert is hiding and takes him some bread and cheese – and returns the three shillings.

Although Erica's guilt is very different from Phillip's, the rat serves a similar function to the chicken in ROPE. It acts as a (here, comic) focus for her anxieties: Chris holds the rat out directly in front of her, like a projected image of Robert's fate. In addition, just as Hitchcock delights in public violations of bourgeois propriety (➤ PUBLIC DISTURBANCES), so here he is surely enjoying the shock effect of someone producing a dead rat during lunch: it is, in Col. Burgoyne's words, 'disgusting'. Within the food motif, then, Chris's rat dramatises the nauseating effect of introducing a repellent non-food during a meal. But it does not just spoil Erica's appetite, it seems to haunt her. When she takes Robert bread and cheese – rather than the chocolate recommended for fugitives by her brothers – it would seem that, quite unconsciously, she is still thinking in terms of the rat. She even 'forgets' to bring a knife.

Guilt, conscious or unconscious, is a major Hitchcock preoccupation, and we would expect occasions when this was expressed through problems with handling or eating food. But in these key examples, Hitchcock uses objects (knives, food, a rat) to condense the tensions arising from the guilt – or, in SABOTAGE, from the heroine's suppressed murderousness. It is this which marks the distinctiveness of his approach.

The parlour scene between Marion and Norman in PSYCHO has more delicate undercurrents. Marion's guilt concerning the stolen money has already been indicated in her ambivalence about eating: when she arrives at the Bates Motel, she wants to eat; when Norman brings down the sandwiches and milk, she no longer feels hungry. At the beginning of the parlour scene, she nevertheless starts to eat. Then, as the conversation shifts to include her own actions ('What are you running away from?'), she continues to hold the bread and butter, but only nibbles at it, and finally she stops eating. This occurs after the following exchange:

> Marion: Why don't you go away?
> Norman: To a private island, like you?
> Marion: No (she puts down the bread), not like me.

The parallel that Norman has drawn between them has made Marion realise the folly of continuing her flight. When she stops eating, she signals a moral change: she has now decided to go back to Phoenix, return the stolen money and face the consequences. Before this, she felt guilty but continued to evade responsibility; now she accepts it. And the subtle shifts in her eating pattern indicate the shifts in her perceptions.

The scene is, however, made much more complex by the retrospective sense that Marion is also in conversation with 'Mrs Bates', whose peremptory interjections pop out of Norman from time to time: e.g. 'A boy's best friend is his mother' or 'A son is a poor substitute for a lover'. (It is Anthony Perkins's brilliant acting which, above all, conveys the sense that on such occasions he is repeating thoughts which 'mother' is speaking in his head.) Thus Marion is really in conversation, as she eats, with two people: a young man who, at some level, wants to violate her (the sense, in her murder, of a hideous parody of rape) and her future murderer. This means that the scene has surprisingly close links with the Rusk/Brenda scene in FRENZY, which may indeed be seen as making explicit the food-violation-murder nexus which is implicit here: the dark side of Hitchcock's preoccupation with food and murder.

These four categories are perhaps the most useful of the many which could be used to explore the food motif in Hitchcock. But there are also individual examples in which food operates in quite different ways. In one group, the motif functions in a more playful way; as with the BED SCENE, this more light-hearted inflection occurs particularly during the British period. In THE LODGER, Joe cuts out heart shapes from Mrs Bunting's pastry and uses them to signal his feelings for Daisy; when she spurns his overtures, he tears one of the hearts in two. In the bakery in WALTZES FROM VIENNA, inspired by the rhythms of the machinery and of the bakers themselves, tossing bread to and fro, Schani composes the tune for *The Blue Danube* waltz.

As Peter Conrad points out, food metaphors abound in THE FARMER'S WIFE (Conrad 2000: 85). When widower Sam Sweetland contemplates remarrying, he declares: 'There's a female or two floating around my mind like the smell of a Sunday dinner.' He imagines Louisa Windeatt, his first prospect, coming 'like a lamb to the slaughter', and to Louisa herself explains his visit to her house with: 'I come over like the foxes you're so fond of … to pick up a fat hen.' It is perhaps fortunate that Louisa does not immediately realise that she is the fat hen in question, but she still turns Sam down. Sam then accosts his next prospect as the latter is fussing with the arrangements for a tea party. Exasperated by her failure to pay attention, Sam finally shouts: 'Hang it, Thirza Tapper, I'm asking you to marry me!' Thirza's panicky response is then comically visualised through the jelly she is holding, which quivers on its plate. Still fired up with his food metaphors, Sam then insults the third woman to turn him down by accusing her of 'dressing (her) mutton lamb fashion'. In all these examples, one senses Hitchcock having fun with the elasticity of food as a metaphor: the sheer range of possible associations.

In CHAMPAGNE, his next film, Hitchcock emphasises the physicality of food. On the liner, the Boy is fighting seasickness when he sees, in quick succession, the Girl sitting with the Man (a potential sexual rival) and a dressed roast pig's head on a buffet table. He promptly retires back to bed. In Paris, the Girl's baking produces such rock-hard cookies that her father is unable to eat them. But since he is only pretending to be bankrupt, he is able to avoid hunger: we next see him in a restaurant enjoying a feast. As the Girl tries once more to master the art of baking, she covers herself with flour, which leads to her leaving floury hand-prints on the Boy when she embraces him. Comic contamination from food is then answered by cynical contamination *to* food, as Hitchcock shows the unhygienic practices of the cabaret kitchen staff – a roast chicken man-handled by grubby hands; bread rolls dropped on the floor – and then wickedly follows this with the elegant façade of serving the same food at a restaurant table. Once again, the food motif runs through the film, and here it often seems an unruly presence, not under appropriate physical or culinary control.

A more eccentric use of the motif occurs in Topaz, where an espionage cam-era is concealed in food: picnic sandwiches on the outward journey; a dead chicken on the return. Susan Smith suggests that the scene in which the maid Dolores removes the camera and its lens from the chicken is like 'mock child-birth', exemplifying her argument that, in certain films, 'food (serves as) a stand-in for the maternal body' (Smith 1997: 197). Hence, when characters, usually male, reject food, they are rejecting the maternal, nurturing function: the Kristeva notion.

Chickens and eggs

In *Alma Hitchcock: The Woman Behind the Man*, Pat Hitchcock O'Connell reports that her father's favourite dinner was roast chicken and ham (O'Connell and Bouzereau 2003: 229). The treatment of chickens in Hitchcock's movies tells a more complicated story. In The Birds, chickens are cast as innocent victims of man's voraciousness. In the Tides Restaurant, Mrs Bundy begins a speech to Melanie in defence of birds: 'Birds are not aggressive creatures, Miss. They bring beauty into the world. It is mankind...'. At this point, she is rudely inter-rupted by a waitress calling out: 'Three southern fried chicken, baked potato on all of them!' Mrs Bundy is mistaken in her defence, but the sudden reminder that mankind does indeed eat birds is salutary. Nevertheless, in Hitchcock's work overall, roast chickens tend, rather, to create problems for the characters, as in Rope and The Man Who Knew Too Much (1955). Only in Topaz is there a satisfactory outcome to a roast chicken meal. In Notorious, the imperatives of the spy plot interrupt and thereby spoil the chicken dinner before it is con-sumed. But in Topaz, the equivalent interruption – Rico Parra's arrival to order André out of Cuba (➤ THE MACGUFFIN) – only occurs after the meal. By then, the chicken has served its dual function of successfully hiding the MacGuffin and providing the hero and heroine with nourishment.

Eggs are a much simpler matter. As Hitchcock confirms in an interview with Peter Bogdanovich (Bogdanovich 1997: 551), he hated eggs, and his films unam-biguously bear this out. Jessie Stevens stubbing out her cigarette in a fried egg in To Catch a Thief is one of the director's most famous 'repellent' moments. The same sort of disgust is conveyed in Under Capricorn, when three separately cooked bacon and egg breakfasts are brought in to Hattie, Sam and Charles. Two are uneatable, but the one the camera dwells on is Charles's, which is covered in a particularly revolting uncooked runny egg. In SABOTAGE, eggs as food receive stern disapproval from Ted when he takes Mrs Verloc and Stevie to lunch at Simpson's restaurant. When she suggests a poached egg for Stevie, Ted affects outrage: 'Poached egg here at Simpson's? Why that's enough to make the roast beef turn in its gravy!' Stevie subsequently echoes Ted's sentiments when he tells Mrs Verloc how much he detests poached eggs: 'I think they're the worst things in the world.' Susan Smith connects such sentiments with Stevie's wish to grow up, to move on from 'feminising' foods such as poached eggs to a more 'manly' diet (Smith 1997: 187). But Stevie, following Ted, is also serving as Hitchcock's mouthpiece.

Hitchcock's aversion to eggs may be linked to his similar aversion to milk: both are yet another manifestation of his rejection of the maternal. Hence, it tends to be male characters who react so negatively to these foods, with the notable exception of Jessie, who is, nevertheless, a most unmaternal mother. And just as Hitchcock uses milk for nefarious purposes in SUSPICION and SPELL-BOUND, so he turns eggs into a missile in THE RING and TO CATCH A THIEF. In the opening fairground sequence of THE RING, we see a sideshow in which punters throw balls at a target in order to precipitate a black man off a platform. Two schoolboys arrive with their own missiles, eggs (no doubt rotten), which they proceed to throw at the man himself. In TO CATCH A THIEF, another of the ways in which the kitchen staff show their hostility to Robie is through one of them throwing an egg at him: it spatters on a glass partition, visually obliterating his face.

Collectively, all these examples serve to illustrate the diversity of the food motif in Hitchcock. They also suggest how rarely food is genuinely enjoyed in his films. Lesley Brill writes: 'In [Hitchcock's] romantic films, eating brings people together – even when the meals appear contaminated by anger or bad faith' (Brill 1988: 193). Unfortunately, he does not provide examples, but I cannot agree with his emphasis. Whatever the type of film, meals in Hitchcock are nearly always subject to strain. Even one of the apparent exceptions – the restaurant car scene in NORTH BY NORTHWEST – is interrupted by police boarding the train before Roger has had more than a few mouthfuls of his brook trout. Before concluding, I would like to look at two meals in which the 'contamination' takes an excessive form, because (a) someone uses the occasion to make a speech promoting murder, and (b) the speech, implicitly or explicitly, is 'fascist'.

Table talk and fascism

In 'Hitchcock and Fascism', Robin Wood discusses Uncle Charlie in SHADOW OF
A DOUBT and Brandon in ROPE as Hitchcock characters who 'make explicit the
link between fascist tendencies and Fascism' (in *Unexplored Hitchcock*, ed. Ian
Cameron, forthcoming). As evidence, he cites a key speech each makes during
a meal. Uncle Charlie's dinner speech about 'useless' middle-aged women is
cited under JEWELLERY. Brandon's equivalent speech is made as his guests
eat the buffet; in it, he maintains that murder should be the prerogative of a few
'men of such intellectual and cultural superiority that that they're above the
traditional moral concepts', and the victims 'those inferior beings whose lives
are unimportant anyway'. Wood discusses the 'fascist' implications of the two
characters' attitudes in some detail: the obsession with power and control; the
cruelty and murderousness; the contempt for a particular group of people who
'deserve' to be killed. What I am concerned with here, however, is the relationship between the speech, its reception and the meal setting.

By the time of this – the second – family dinner in SHADOW OF A DOUBT,
Charlie has found evidence which convinces her that her uncle is the Merry
Widow murderer. And so, when he expresses his abhorrence of middle-aged
widows, she is appalled, and protests vehemently: 'But they're alive! They're
human beings!' Coldly, her uncle turns to her: 'Are they, Charlie? Or are they
fat, wheezing animals? And what happens to animals when they get too fat and
too old?' Given the 1942 date of production, the Nazi overtones are unmistakable: the idea that 'useless' human beings should be 'put down'. Indeed, one of
Uncle Charlie's contemptuous phrases for the widows – 'smelling of money' – is
precisely the sort of racist rhetoric the Nazis directed at the Jews. Nevertheless,
only Charlie seems to realise just how offensive the views are. Emma does rep-
rimand her brother, but indulgently ('For Heaven's sake, don't talk about women like that in front of my club: you'll be tarred and feathered!') and her husband Joe is not shown to react at all. Then, with the arrival of Joe's friend Herb,
we have a comic echo of Uncle Charlie's speech, as the two older men discuss
ways of killing each other. Mindful that this is a meal scene, Herb suggests poisoned mushrooms and has brought a sample with him. To Charlie, their 'innocent' conversation is the last straw, and she leaps to her feet and berates them:
'What's the matter with you two? Do you always have to talk about killing
people?'

William Rothman has suggested that 'Herb's obsession with murder [is] a
displacement of a wish to commit a specific real murder he does not have the
courage even to contemplate' (Rothman 1986: 195), i.e. his mother's. One could
perhaps say the same of Joe, who is dominated by Emma in much the same way

that Herb seems to be by his mother. In other words, the preoccupation of both these men could be seen as unconsciously echoing Uncle Charlie's explicitly-stated view. But Charlie's outburst at them is clearly a displacement from the real object of her outrage. Before discussing this scene further, however, I would like to look at its equivalent in ROPE.

During the buffet, it is Rupert, not Brandon, who makes the speech which initiates the links with the dinner scene in SHADOW OF A DOUBT. And Rupert is quite open about declaring that murder is an entirely appropriate way of dealing with troublesome people: he lists not only those he considers suitable for killing – a heterogeneous group, from the unemployed and head waiters to tap dancers and small children – but also the different methods he would employ on each. Of course, the other guests assume that he is joking – certainly he amuses Mrs Atwater – but he himself insists twice that he is not. He cannot know that Brandon and Phillip have just put his theories into practice, but his speech, and the urbane, superior manner in which he delivers it, clearly indicts him. Brandon then joins in the conversation in order to endorse Rupert's sentiments. In effect, he translates Rupert's speech into an argument, since it is at this point that Mr Kentley begins to protest, a protest which becomes increasingly heated as it becomes apparent that Brandon is certainly not joking. And here the protest includes a direct reference – through the Nietzschean philosophy of the *Übermensch* – to Hitler and the Nazis.

The connections between the five main characters in this scene and the five adults in SHADOW OF A DOUBT are in themselves very striking: Susan Smith discusses a number of the links in *Hitchcock: Suspense, Humour and Tone* (Smith 2000: 52-55). In ROPE, for example, the two men who obsessively discuss murder have become the murderers, and their relationship to the figure of authority who makes the crucial speech is much more sinister. It's as if the sentiments in Uncle Charlie's speech have begun to take root: it is not just a lone psychopath who promulgates them, but a teacher, and two of his ex-pupils have already put them into practice. 'Fascist' thinking is spreading.

However, the figures who protest at the murderous sentiments seem to be very different. Charlie's protest is more personal. Her secret knowledge that her uncle is a murderer stems from her discovery that the emerald ring he gave her belonged to his most recent victim. A link is thus made between her and the murdered woman (➤ JEWELLERY), so that it is as if she is protesting on the woman's behalf. In Mr Kentley's case, he does not know that his son has already become a victim of Rupert and Brandon's *Übermensch* ideology, which means that his protest – though no less fervent – is more disinterested. (The audience, of course, is only too aware of this, which charges the protest with dramatic irony.) Nevertheless, there is also a crucial connection between these two figures: they are the characters who speak on behalf of the audience; they articulate our sense of moral outrage at the views expressed.

That each of these scenes is set during a bourgeois meal may seem to be no more than expedience: the setting provides the basic requirement of a small gathering of family and friends – a captive audience for the figures who are prompted to reveal, in Mr Kentley's words, their 'contempt for humanity'. Rather more, however, is at stake. In both scenes, a genuinely appalling attitude towards other human beings is put forward under the guise of dinner-table (or party) small talk and, in each case, only one person really protests. The setting would seem to grant a certain licence or, more sinisterly, perhaps the majority of those present are not really offended: as if such fascist sentiments have a natural place in an American bourgeois household. In addition, there is a sense of compulsiveness in two of the speeches: Uncle Charlie's is almost stream of consciousness – it seems to pour out of him – and Brandon's is characterised by a heated intensity. In both cases, it is as if the speaker is finally coming out with thoughts and feelings which have been suppressed under a veneer of 'civilized behaviour'; now he feels able to reveal what he really thinks.

That the meal setting is in itself important is suggested by the post-lunch scene on the train in STRANGERS ON A TRAIN, when Bruno proposes to Guy that they 'swap murders'. Indeed, in the so-called 'British' version of the film (➤ FILMOGRAPHY), there is an exchange, cut in the 1951 release version, in which Bruno expresses sentiments very similar to those of Uncle Charlie, Rupert and Brandon. Following Allen Eyles's practice in his 1999 NFT programme notes for the film, I will italicise the extra dialogue:

> Guy: I thought murder was against the law.
> Bruno: *My theory is that everybody is a potential murderer. Now didn't you ever feel like you wanted to kill somebody? Say, one of those useless fellows that Miriam was playing around with?*
> Guy: *You can't go around killing people just because you think they're useless.*
> Bruno: (violently) What is a life or two, Guy! Some people are better off dead!

Bruno does not elaborate on whether these people have a collective identity, but the word 'useless' clearly aligns his thinking with the sentiments of his predecessors.

It is the sense that meals are occasions when Hitchcock's characters reveal their inner desires and compulsions *despite themselves* that seems to me to be the crucial underlying feature of these and other examples. Sometimes the revelation is unconscious, as in the first meal in SPELLBOUND, which suggests the 'return of the repressed'. More generally, men in particular find themselves expressing thoughts and feelings normally kept suppressed. This would apply to a

Fig. 26. Still: STRANGERS ON A TRAIN: Table talk and fascism on a train. In elaborating his murder plot, Bruno (Robert Walker) on the right tells Guy (Farley Granger) that some people are better off dead.

number of the examples already discussed, but there are others. What spoils the chicken dinner in NOTORIOUS is Devlin's reaction to having heard about the (implicitly sexual) nature of Alicia's espionage mission: he turns on her, making a whole series of very unpleasant personal remarks. It is in a restaurant in Copenhagen that Sarah in TORN CURTAIN learns that Michael has made plans for the future which do not include her. The most unprovoked of Blaney's many outbursts in FRENZY occurs after the meal in Brenda's club: he suddenly launches into a bitter attack on her success as a career woman (➤ *Damaged hands*). In all these cases, we could speak of the 'return of the *suppressed*'; the man is finally telling the woman what he really thinks about her.

Women, too, can experience the pressure to release suppressed thoughts at meals, as SABOTAGE shows. During her blueberry muffin tea with Captain Wiles in THE TROUBLE WITH HARRY, even the benign Miss Gravely finds herself compulsively referring to having picked the blueberries 'near where you shot that unfortunate man' and to the death of her father: 'he was caught in a threshing-machine'. In general, however, women are more likely to keep their feelings bottled up: hence the translation of the tensions into the knives in THE MANX-MAN and BLACKMAIL, or into the food itself in Mrs Oxford's dinners in FRENZY.

Buried resentments; feelings of guilt; feelings of inadequacy. If one tracks each of the thoughts and feelings troubling the characters back to its source, the vast majority would relate to one or more of a small number of key areas: sex, misogyny, gender identity and a violent death, usually murder. In other words, through the food motif Hitchcock dramatises a number of his most familiar preoccupations. But he does so in an extremely complex and varied manner. Ultimately, one would have to question Bouzereau's assertion that food was a greater preoccupation for Hitchcock than sex, women or crime. On the other hand, a very strong case could be made for Food and Meals being his most elaborated motif.

Food and the police

The outcome of Chief Inspector Oxford's failure to find nourishment at home is that he eats a mixed grill breakfast at his New Scotland Yard desk. In I CONFESS, Inspector Larrue is likewise about to have lunch at his desk when Father Logan walks in to give himself up. Moreover, just as Oxford converses with his sergeant as he eats, so the timing of Logan's arrival is crucial – it means that Larrue will not eat alone. Hitchcock's policemen may be busy, but they do not stoop to the fast food consumed – usually in cars or on the street – by virtually every policeman in the modern cop movie. They like their food to be substantial: Oxford praises the provender of the lorry-driver's café; Ted orders 'Three bullocks, roasted whole!' at Simpson's. And Hitchcock ensures that even his policemen do not suffer the miserable fate of having to eat alone. Police appetites are discussed further in APPENDIX I.

GUILT AND CONFESSION

Fig. 27: Still: REBECCA: Guilt and confession. After Maxim (Laurence Olivier) has confessed to the killing of Rebecca, he and his second wife (Joan Fontaine) share a guilty embrace.

Catholic overtones

Feelings of guilt and an attendant impulse to confess haunt Hitchcock's films, a feature which led the 1950s *Cahiers du Cinéma* critics to identify a Catholic discourse in his work. The Catholic overtones are present in the narrative structure: nearly always, after the confession, a character must then face an ordeal, as if penance must be done before redemption can be achieved in the secular form of

a happy ending. In other words, confession is not just therapeutic, but also potentially redemptive, and the flawed or blocked confessions in Hitchcock's
work are to a greater or lesser extent harmful to the continuing happiness of his
characters. By tracing the ways in which the interlocked themes of guilt and
confession occur throughout Hitchcock's films, I would like to interrogate the
Cahiers position.

THE LODGER illustrates the narrative structure at an early stage, but is of major interest because the film, like the later SPELLBOUND and MARNIE, is dealing
with unconscious guilt. Indeed, when the Lodger explains to Daisy why he is
hunting the Avenger, he may not even be aware that this is a confession. But the
murder of his sister which we see in the ensuing flashback may clearly be read
as his unconscious wish. We know he has powerful feelings for her
(➢ PORTRAITS) and she was killed whilst dancing with him at her coming-out
ball: the point where she became available for other men. The Avenger in this
scene (his first murder) thus seems like the Lodger's dark alter ego, and we
could see the Lodger's pursuit of the man as, in part, an attempt to assuage his
own unconscious guilt. After his 'confession', the Lodger is pursued by an angry crowd who think that he is the Avenger, a pursuit which ends with him
hanging on some railings in a posture which evokes the crucifixion. Savagely
attacked by the crowd, he then spends some time in hospital recovering. In
both the evocation of the crucifixion and the ordeal itself, the Catholic theme is
evident. Although the notion that one must suffer before being rewarded with a
happy ending suggests a stern deity, in this case there is unexpected compensation: Daisy, another golden-haired girl, is like a romantic replacement for the
Lodger's murdered sister.

The flashback here is significant. Hitchcock uses them rarely, but when he
does they almost always concern a confession. (The 'lying flashback' in STAGE
FRIGHT is simply the reverse: Jonathan lies to avoid confessing.) Even Ruth's
extended flashback in I CONFESS is in effect a confession. She narrates the story
of her romance with Michael Logan before he became a priest, but her avowed
aim (to help clear him) is overshadowed by her deeper aim (to make public her
love for him) and what she succeeds in doing is providing the authorities with a
motive for him to have committed murder. In effect, she is confessing to adultery, and as long as she insists on her love for him (she repeats it during his
trial), she prolongs his ordeal. His ordeal – marked again by Christian imagery
(➢ HANDCUFFS AND BONDAGE) – thus stands in for her penance, and it is
only after she has accepted the impossibility of her love being returned that she
is permitted her 'happy ending'.

This basic narrative pattern – the Catholic discourse – of guilt, confession,
penance and redemption is found elsewhere in Hitchcock's work. A minor example is NUMBER SEVENTEEN, where the transgressive figure is Nora. Although

no confession is involved, she redeems herself from her involvement with the crooks by helping the hero, but is then subjected to a similar ordeal to the Lodger – suspended by her handcuffed wrists in a life-threatening situation (➢ WATER) – before being rescued for a happy ending. NORTH BY NORTHWEST includes a fully developed version of the narrative structure. Because of her involvement with the spies, Eve is guilty of setting Roger up for a murder attempt. She confesses to him in a scene in the woods, a beautifully tranquil setting, but is then snatched away and transported back into the world of the spies for her penance. Again, the climax of this involves Eve hanging in a perilous manner – in her case off the face of Mount Rushmore – before being rescued for her happy ending.

The 'hanging threat' that certain characters suffer at the climax of the films adds another Christian feature to this narrative pattern. In *The Hanging Figure: on Suspense and the Films of Alfred Hitchcock*, Christopher Morris quotes the theories of James Frazer and Michel Foucault on the significance of hanging figures in religion and mythology. In their very different ways, both these writers agree on a religious reading of such figures, Frazer stressing death and resurrection, Foucault focusing on the state's use of the potent imagery of the Christian crucifixion to infuse fear through such rituals as public hangings (Morris 2002: 55). Morris wishes to read the hanging figures differently: 'In contrast to the conclusions of Frazer or Foucault, hanging figures express no religious or political truth, only undecidability' (93). I disagree; I would align myself, in the examples thus far cited, with Frazer: what each of these hanging figures experiences symbolically is indeed like a 'death' and 'rebirth'. This also supports the sense of a Catholic theme in Hitchcock's work.

Do the films which deal with psychoanalysis have an equivalent narrative pattern? In SPELLBOUND, where the hero feels unconscious guilt for a childhood killing, the psychoanalytical process itself could be seen as standing in the place of a confession, as it moves to uncover the source of the guilt. Here both a dream sequence and a flashback to childhood are stages in the process. Nevertheless, after the flashback, the hero's ordeal is not yet over: he is arrested for murder. It's as if Hitchcock is still following the Catholic structure, and J.B. needs to suffer further before being allowed a happy ending. In MARNIE, too, the memory of the childhood trauma is shown as a (fragmented) flashback at the film's climax. Here, however, the psychoanalytical path is in itself deemed sufficient: although Marnie is by no means fully cured, there is no further ordeal for her within the narrative. It is true that Marnie has already suffered considerably from her unconscious guilt – 'I'm a cheat, and a liar, and a thief' – but when Mark responds with 'it's time to have a little compassion for yourself', this signals that Hitchcock is tacitly disavowing the Catholic requirement for penance. The therapeutic effect of uncovering the source of the unconscious guilt is in itself redemptive. There would thus seem to be a shift in Hitchcock's position between the mid-1940s and the early 1960s: as if, by the time of MARNIE, his films have moved to a more psychoanalytical understanding of confession.

There is an important distinction to be drawn in Hitchcock's work between a private and a public confession. Depending on the seriousness of the transgression and the intensity of the guilt, a private confession may not be sufficient to redeem a character, since it may simply lead to shared guilt. In BLACKMAIL and SABOTAGE, the heroine confesses to her policeman boyfriend (that she killed someone), but he stops her confessing to the authorities. This clouds the endings with the sense that the couple will, in future, live with a sense of guilt. REBECCA is similar. Maxim tells the heroine that he killed Rebecca, but she, too, stops him from confessing to the authorities. Although Maxim can convince himself that Rebecca goaded him into striking her, and that it was manslaughter, the sense of shared guilt cannot be removed: the ending is only apparently happy. These are all examples where a failure to complete all the stages of the core narrative sets up a future of guilt and unhappiness.

UNDER CAPRICORN provides an obvious contrast. Here Hattie does confess twice (to the killing of her brother): first to Charles, then to the authorities. But when she speaks to her husband Sam of the 'blessed heavenly relief' that she feels after both confessions, he turns nasty: he thinks that Charles is her lover and she is planning to follow him back to Ireland. As in SPELLBOUND, further suffering (which includes Hattie's discovery that Milly is trying to poison her and Sam's arrest for the attempted murder of Charles) again takes place after the confession. Only when all these matters have been resolved does the 'happy ending' occur.

Throughout all these examples, my point is that the Catholic discourse operates as a structuring principle. First, a character can only find genuine relief from guilt by the right sort of confession – one which brings the source of the guilt genuinely into the open. Only rarely – as in UNDER CAPRICORN – is this to the authorities, since the latter's very obtuseness disqualifies them from being able to offer even a secular form of absolution. Nevertheless, even after the confession, further sufferings ensue. The ordeals at this stage – life-threatening situations; arrest and imprisonment – take the place, in effect, of a penance. Only then can a 'happy ending' occur. But in cases such as BLACKMAIL and REBECCA, where the truth is suppressed beyond the end of the film, there is no real relief from guilt, and so no 'redemption': the corrosive effect of the guilt is destined to continue.

There are two major courtroom confessions in Hitchcock: Philip's in THE MANXMAN and Mrs Paradine's in THE PARADINE CASE. The former occurs when Kate is brought before Philip as Deemster (judge), charged with attempted suicide. Evoking the climactic scene of the Revered Dimmesdale's public confession in THE SCARLET LETTER (Victor Sjöström, 1926), Philip's confession to the court is remarkably powerful. Moved by the fact that the woman brought before him for judgement acted as she did on his account, and mindful of his deception of Pete, Kate's husband and his own best friend, Philip denounces himself and renounces his position. Again further punishment follows – Philip and Kate are banished from the community – and again there is a sense that they will henceforth live in guilt: it is Pete Hitchcock shows at the end.

In THE PARADINE CASE, where the woman on the stand is guilty of murder, the outcome is divided. Throughout her trial for her husband's murder, Mrs Paradine has maintained her innocence, but when news arrives of the suicide of her lover Latour, she breaks down and confesses. But she does so from despair, not remorse; here there is no question of redemption, and we learn in the next scene that she will hang. However, in her speech, she also attacks Tony, her lawyer, for the way he had vilified Latour, blaming him for the latter's death. This prompts Tony himself into a public admission of his own inadequacies; in effect – since his love for Mrs Paradine had blinded him to her guilt – the hero is here making his own confession, which in turn enables him to achieve a redemption of sorts. The film ends with a tentative reconciliation between him and his wife.

Philip kept his affair with Kate secret in part because he wanted to become Deemster (➢ MOTHERS AND HOUSES); his confession is thus addressed both to the people he wronged and to the society he deceived. By contrast, Mrs Paradine seems motivated primarily by a wish to hurt Tony, and her confession becomes, rather, a public attack. It is Tony's ensuing 'confession' that is closer in spirit to Philip's: he is apologising to his peers – and, by extension, his society – for his behaviour. In both films, the woman on the stand confronts the lawyer-hero with his failings, and forces him publicly to admit to them. This does indeed bring the source of the guilt into the open, and here the contrasting outcomes point to the differences between the two societies. In THE MANXMAN, it is the community which cannot forgive.

A familiar feature of melodrama and the woman's film is that it is worse for a 'woman with a past' to conceal this from a man she now loves than to confess in the first place. This is because the man will inevitably find out, and then blame her not just for the past but also for deceiving him about it. A seminal instance is Tess's failure – at first – to inform her fiancé Angel about her past in Thomas Hardy's *Tess of the d'Urbervilles* (1891). In Hitchcock this structure is found in three films, always with disastrous consequences. In EASY VIRTUE, Larita does not tell John when she marries him that she is a divorcee; his subsequent discovery of this prompts their own divorce. Here, too, we have an unforgiving

community, encapsulated in the press frenzy directed at Larita at the end
(➤ EXHIBITIONISM / VOYEURISM).

In THE SKIN GAME, Chloë has not told her husband Charles that she used to
earn her living being hired out as the 'other woman' in divorce cases. Here the
outcome is much more serious: Charles is so violent in his condemnation of her
that, overhearing, she tries to drown herself and we are not even told whether
she lives. In both these cases, the man's reaction seems to belong to an earlier,
less tolerant era: the plays on which the films were based date from the 1920s.
But VERTIGO represents a clear reworking of similar material. After Judy has re-
met Scottie, we see a flashback to 'what really happened' at the top of the bell
tower (➤ THE CORPSE); she then writes her confessional letter. But she tears
the letter up, and keeps Scottie in ignorance. Inevitably, Scottie eventually discovers the truth and here his terrible rage at this really does lead, albeit unintentionally, to the heroine's death. In these last two cases especially, Hitchcock
would seem to be hinting at a fundamental flaw in the male ego, which cannot
cope with the shattering of his own carefully nurtured fantasies about the woman he loves.

In Judy's case, her guilt concerning her past is exacerbated by her involvement in murder. This leads to a climax in which her guilt finds a powerful symbolic expression. Scottie forces her back up to the top of the bell tower as a way
of both punishing her and wresting a confession from her (➤ STAIRCASES).
After she has confessed, and told Scottie how much she loves him, their desperate kiss of reconciliation is interrupted by Judy suddenly seeing an 'apparition'
rising up through the trapdoor. Crying 'Oh no', she pulls away from Scottie,
turning as she does so. It looks as if she is so terrified that she turns to flee, and
in so doing accidentally falls from the tower. In his detailed analysis of this sequence, William Rothman speaks of Judy's vision as something which 'impels
[her] to plunge to her death' (Rothman 1988: 170). I think rather that, in her
terror, Judy forgets how dangerously exposed she is, and her death is not inten-
tional. Nevertheless, Rothman's speculation about the nature of the apparition
which so frightens her is useful:

> Surely Judy thinks she sees a ghost… Is it the ghost of the real Madeleine… seeking to
> avenge her own murder? The ghost of Carlotta Valdes, passing on her curse to Judy,
> calling on her to take her own life? Or is this Judy's own ghost, her vision of herself as
> already dead? … This ghostly apparition is 'really' a stern mother superior. Perhaps
> Judy sees this figure as exactly who she is: agent of God's law and representative of
> the world of women. In the nun's religion, Judy has not earned the happiness that
> seems within her grasp… Or is it the spectre of Gavin Elster that Judy sees?
>
> (Rothman 1988: 170-71)

The most likely of these possibilities is that Judy thinks that she sees Madeleine – as if the latter has returned to haunt her. But because the figure is in fact a nun, and it seems to surge up out of Judy's unconscious, it is highly relevant to the discussion here. It's as if Judy's guilt produces a *Catholic* 'return of the repressed', and it so disturbs her that it kills her. This is the most striking example in Hitchcock of a 'punishment' arising out of the guilt itself, and from the point of view of the Catholic discourse, it offers a sharp contrast to the climax of NORTH BY NORTHWEST.

Guilt and Hitchcock's villains

In general, Hitchcock's transgressing heroes and heroines do eventually get round to confessing. The confession may be reluctant, or too long-delayed; it may, as in Maxim's case, be steeped in self-justification, or as in Judy's, too late, but it does finally occur. This is not the case with Hitchcock's villains. Few seem to feel any guilt, and those who do confess – like Mrs Paradine – do so without genuine remorse. In *Alfred Hitchcock: A Life in Darkness and Light*, Patrick McGilligan writes: 'A death of a villain in a Hitchcock film is always confessional' (McGilligan 2003: 135). This is quite spectacularly wrong. Let's begin with the famous cases.

Uncle Charlie (SHADOW OF A DOUBT), Brandon (ROPE), Bruno (STRANGERS ON A TRAIN) and Rusk (FRENZY) are all psychopaths: they murder without feeling guilt. Only two of them actually die within the narrative, but the closest to a confession to emerge from any is Brandon's attempt to justify to Rupert the act of murdering David. Uncle Charlie knows that Charlie knows he is a murderer, but that is not the same as a confession. Indeed, his response to her knowing is to try and kill her. As Bruno is dying, he refuses Guy's plea that he confess to the police. Caught disposing of a corpse, Rusk says nothing. Other murderous villains behave in a similar fashion. At the end of DIAL M FOR MURDER, as soon as Tony walks into the room, he knows that his murder plot has been exposed. But he does not confess. Even 'Mrs Bates' does not confess: she blames Norman.

Even where a Hitchcock villain does confess, there is usually something evasive about it. In MURDER!, Fane's final letter to Sir John is a confession, but it is still indirect, recounting in the third person the missing scene from Sir John's unfinished play (➢ ENTRY THROUGH A WINDOW). When the dying Mr Memory recites what he remembers of the MacGuffin at the end of THE 39 STEPS, this serves structurally as a confession, although he is not in fact confessing: he is unintentionally showing that he is a spy by revealing that he has memorised a state secret. Verloc in SABOTAGE does not deny that he gave Stevie the bomb which killed him, and he is sorry about the death, but he blames the police: they had the house surrounded, so that he couldn't go on the mission himself. Shortly before his death in JAMAICA INN, Sir Humphrey admits to Mary that he was involved with the wreckers, justifying this as necessary to avoid penury, but I think we would agree with Mary that he is mad. Finally, at the end of STAGE FRIGHT, Jonathan does finally admit to Eve that the story he told her at the beginning was a lie and that he is in fact a murderer. But he 'confesses' only after Eve's father has called out to tell her this. And, like Uncle Charlie, Jonathan responds to the heroine's learning of his murderousness by trying to kill her (➤ HANDS).

There are similar problems with those villains who make private confessions. The heroines in BLACKMAIL and SABOTAGE show contrition and were at least intending to make a full confession to the authorities. This is not true of the villains. In I CONFESS, Keller confesses to Father Logan and to his wife that he murdered Vilette, but he shows no contrition whatever and later even frames Logan himself for the murder. Nor, to correct a common misapprehension about the film (e.g. Spoto 1976: 222), does he really confess at the end. He finally admits his guilt, but it is hardly a confession: he assumes that Logan has broken his vows as a priest and betrayed him to the police, and he even blames Logan for his wife Alma's death. When he is shot by the police, his dying words as Logan cradles him are 'Forgive me'. But a dispassionate viewer would see that for what it surely is: the terrified plea of a sinner faced with eternal damnation. In NOTORIOUS, Alex Sebastian confesses to his mother that he is married to an American spy but, like Keller, his concern is to escape punishment: he and his mother promptly begin to poison Alicia. In both these examples, the villain's 'confession' serves the opposite of a redemptive function, prompting the suffering of the hero or heroine.

Another figure I would include here is Johnnie in SUSPICION. As is well-known, Hitchcock had to film a compromise ending to the film, but I'm convinced that he nevertheless intended this to be seen as a 'false happy ending'. I believe that Johnnie is indeed a murderer who in the film's final scene on the clifftop is merely doing what he has always done: lie his way out of a difficult situation – he has just tried, and failed, to kill Lina (➤ HEIGHTS AND FALL-ING). Hence the curious nature of the 'confession': it is Lina who comes up with the idea that Johnnie was going to use the 'untraceable poison' to kill himself (and not her), and he agrees with this convenient explanation because it wins her over again. It may seem as if Johnnie is confessing, but I think he is lying, as is typical of a Hitchcock villain. Lina may hope that her sufferings are over, but it seems to me that she is still married to a murderer (➤ *Milk* in Part I).

I know of only one Hitchcock villain who confesses and then genuinely re-deems himself: Fisher in FOREIGN CORRESPONDENT, who confesses to his daughter Carol (about his Nazi crimes) and then, after the plane they are flying in crashes into the sea, sacrifices his life to further the survival chances of the others.

This is to not to say that feelings of guilt are entirely evaded by Hitchcock's villains, but it tends to be a disavowed or unconscious guilt. In two early films, a murderer hallucinates his victim coming back to haunt him: Levet in THE PLEASURE GARDEN (➤ BED SCENE); Johnny in JUNO AND THE PAYCOCK (➤ PAINTINGS). Similarly, after Bruno has strangled Miriam, the image of her 'returns' in the form of Anne's kid sister Barbara – most dramatically at Senator Morton's party (➤ SPECTACLES). Both the hallucinations and this image represent the return of the killer's imperfectly repressed guilt. YOUNG AND INNOCENT offers a variation. Christine Clay is killed at the beginning by her ex-husband Guy, who is a drummer. At the film's climax, Guy is performing with his band when he notices Will the china-mender, the one person who has crucial evidence against him. I have discussed this, too, as a guilt image (Walker M. 1999: 199-200), and its effect on Guy is traumatic: it exacerbates his facial tic, the very feature which can serve to identify him to Will, and it also prompts him to further draw attention to himself by drumming erratically and then collapsing with hysteria. When he comes to, Erica asks him what he did with the raincoat belt (the murder weapon). His response is to laugh manically: 'I twisted it round her neck and choked the life out of her!' This is indeed a confession, but one stemming less from guilt than from the fear of discovery, so that the confession functions as a wild release.

Another figure who fits here is Maxim. On the night of the ball, the heroine appears before him in the image of Rebecca, i.e. wearing an exact copy of the costume that Rebecca wore to the previous ball (➤ PORTRAITS). Then, later that night, Rebecca's body is discovered. It's as if the trauma of seeing the heroine as Rebecca's 'ghost' triggers the return of the repressed. And it is this which prompts Maxim's confession to the heroine, a confession in which, we note, he shows no contrition. As with the parallels noted under THE CORPSE between the killing of Rebecca and the murder of Christine Clay, this emphasises how like a villain Maxim really is.

Far from confessing, as McGilligan maintains, what most Hitchcock villains do is evade guilt, deny it, blame someone else, try to kill the person who knows that they are guilty. This is indeed par for the course for a villain. But their response blocks them from the redemption which is at least potentially available for the heroes and heroines. If we accept that Hitchcock's films do depict a Catholic universe, they are the damned.

Transference of guilt

A concept frequently cited in the Hitchcock literature is 'transference of guilt'. It derives from the *Cahiers du Cinéma* critics in general and Rohmer and Chabrol's *Hitchcock* in particular (Rohmer and Chabrol 1979: 92) and is given a useful gloss by Slavoj Žižek in *Looking Awry: An Introduction to Jacques Lacan through Popular Culture*:

> In Hitchcock's films, murder is never simply an affair between a murderer and his victim; murder always implies a third party… – the murderer kills *for* this third person, his act is described in the framework of a symbolic exchange with him. By means of this act, the murderer realises his [Žižek means the third person's] repressed desire. For this reason, the third person finds himself charged with guilt, although he…refuses to know anything of the way he is implicated in the affair.
>
> (Žižek 1992: 74)

The opening generalisation is simply too wild. Žižek is not talking about revenge, so who does Mrs Verloc in Sabotage kill for? Or Sir Humphrey in Jamaica Inn (who murders Mary's aunt)? Or Michael in Torn Curtain? Or Rico Parra in Topaz? Likewise, Mrs Paradine may think that she is killing her husband for Latour, but this is absolutely not Latour's repressed desire – indeed, quite the reverse (➤ HOMOSEXUALITY).

Nevertheless, the notion of a murder enacting another character's 'repressed desire' (which may be not at all repressed, as in Strangers on a Train) is productive. It applies not just to the 'great trilogy of transference of guilt' Žižek mentions – Rope, Strangers on a Train and I Confess – and to The Lodger, but to many examples.

I discuss most of these 'third party' murders elsewhere. The Man Who Knew Too Much (both versions), Strangers on a Train and Rear Window (a linked example) are under DOUBLES. Murder!, The 39 Steps and Young and Innocent are under THE CORPSE, I Confess under LIGHT(S). However, apart from Murder! (the one heroine involved here), Žižek is right that the third party in these films refuses to recognise his own guilt, even in those cases, such as Strangers on a Train, where he is directly implicated. Guy does 'confess' to Anne that he has known all along that Bruno murdered Miriam, and tells her the background to this. But he shows no personal guilt, just the desire to extricate himself from his predicament.

This raises an important issue: it means that the term 'transference of guilt' is problematic. In the original French edition of Rohmer and Chabrol, the expression was 'transfert de culpabilité' (Rohmer and Chabrol 1957: 96), which is reasonably precise. But the translation of this into 'transfer of guilt' (Rohmer and

Chabrol 1979: 92) is confusing, since guilt in English has two distinct meanings: the legal sense of culpability; the psychological sense of feeling guilty. I will take Žižek's ambiguous 'charged with guilt' as in fact meaning the former, but too many other Hitchcock commentators have implied the latter. And transference of guilt in this second sense is rare. Equally, it is a measure of the (slight) ambiguity of the original French term that when Rohmer and Chabrol discuss one example – Sam taking the blame for Hattie's past crime in UNDER CAPRICORN – they quote Jacques Rivette's different expression: 'Le transfert de la responsabilité du péché' (1957: 102) or 'The transfer of the responsibility for sin' (1979: 99).

Apart from MURDER!, I would maintain that there are only two Hitchcock films where one could argue that a 'transference of guilt' in the second sense is applicable, and even in these cases guilt is not admitted, but has to be inferred. The first is THE LODGER, where, as noted, the implication is that the Lodger feels unconscious guilt for his sister's murder. The second is ROPE, where Rupert's semi-hysterical denial of responsibility is so vehement that it betrays his feelings of guilt. There is however a further example where the hero feels unconscious guilt for a 'third party' killing which involves a quite different dynamic from that outlined by Žižek. J.B. in SPELLBOUND 'assumes guilt' for Dr Murchison's murder of Dr Edwardes – hence his unconscious impersonation of Edwardes – but his guilt here is in fact triggered by (and masks) his repressed guilt for the childhood killing of his brother. Despite the fact that Edwardes was J.B.'s psychoanalyst father figure, it would be difficult to argue that, in killing him, Murchison realised J.B.'s 'repressed desire'.

Accordingly, what is at stake in the 'transfer of guilt' in Hitchcock is overwhelmingly the law *imputing* guilt to the 'third party' who gains – or would seem to gain – from (usually) a murder. This figure is in fact legally innocent, but Hitchcock also explores the ways in which he/she is often morally implicated. But only rarely does this character actually feel any guilt.

Overall, the repeated emphasis on guilt, confession and the need for a form of penance does support the sense of a Catholic impulse in Hitchcock's work. It is worth noting that one aspect of this – that sinners must be punished – is structured into the Motion Picture Production Code, which was written by a Catholic publisher, Martin Quigley, and a Jesuit priest, Daniel A. Lord, and was for many years enforced by a Catholic, Joseph Breen. A consequence of the common Catholic background between film-maker and censors is that there is perhaps less of a sense in Hitchcock's films that the punishments meted out to the characters are excessive, crude or arbitrary – a feeling one has with many films made under the Code. In Hitchcock, the sufferings of the characters are somehow of a piece with the guilt that they feel and the threatening world in which they find themselves.

Nevertheless, as Hitchcock grew older – and the Production Code lost its force – so the Catholic impulse in his work diminished. The last film to include the narrative pattern in full is NORTH BY NORTHWEST. In particular, the later films tend to lack the Christian redemptive function. In VERTIGO, it's as though Judy's guilt actually causes her death. In PSYCHO, we know that Marion was intending to return the money and seek to atone, but none of the characters who survive the film know this. In THE BIRDS, the scriptures are quoted by a drunken Irishman who is convinced the bird attacks signal 'the end of the world'. In MARNIE, Mrs Edgar's harsh Christianity is part of Marnie's problem. In TOPAZ, Juanita's confession is immediately followed by her murder. By the time of FRENZY, when Brenda desperately recites the 91st Psalm as she is raped by Rusk and he still goes on to strangle her, we would probably conclude that Hitchcock was no longer a believer or, at least, was now a despairing believer.

As with a number of motifs, FAMILY PLOT conveniently serves to round off this theme. The narrative is initiated by the elderly Julia Rainbird's guilt at having forced her sister, forty years previously, to give up her illegitimate child. The opening 'séance' with Blanche functions as her confession about this, and she asks Blanche to find the missing heir. The search then includes a number of Christian features – a cemetery, a priest, a funeral, a cathedral service, a bishop – as if Hitchcock considered these appropriate to a story prompted by the seeking of atonement for guilt. Nevertheless, each of these features is ironised: the graveyard has been abused (as the film's poster pointed out: 'There's no body in the family plot'); the priest is secretly meeting a young woman; the funeral is for a murderer; the service is the setting for a kidnapping and the bishop is the victim. Even the use of a 'heavenly choir' as Blanche leads George to the hidden ransom diamond seems to me predominantly ironic (➤ STAIRCASES). In other words, Christian elements are cited throughout the film, but are emptied of spiritual significance. Jack Foley has argued differently (Foley 1978: 15-28), but I'm not convinced. It is true that the hero and heroine experience a couple of unlikely escapes, but so do Roger and Eve in NORTH BY NORTHWEST: the comedy-thriller form guarantees a certain sort of outcome. But for Julia Rainbird, the figure whose guilt mobilised the search, there is unlikely to be any redemption. As a result of the search, her missing heir will go to jail – one assumes for a very long sentence.

See also *Food and guilt* and BOATS.

Guilt, confession and the police

However mistaken they are, Hitchcock's policemen do not seem to feel much guilt, which means that they do not feel the need to confess. On the contrary, they consider that their business is to obtain confessions. They do not have much luck. In the cases where a policeman is involved with a guilty woman, his concern is to stop her confessing; in the cases where the police arrest an innocent person, the latter is reluctant to confess to something he or she didn't do. In fact, Hitchcock usually elides police interrogations of these innocent figures, but the exception of THE WRONG MAN illustrates the way the police think. Manny protests his innocence, but the detective is unmoved: 'You'd better think of another story, Manny, something more plausible.' When Manny insists that his story is the truth, the detective treats this as the typical evasion of a criminal: 'You want to play it that way?' In despair, Manny asks 'What can I do?' The detective tells him: 'If you come up with something else, we'll listen.'

It is quite clear that the minds of the police officers are closed: they think they've found the guilty man, and will only listen if he confirms their hypothesised version of events. Elsewhere in Hitchcock, confession is concerned with telling the truth. This is not the case with the police: confession to them is a narrative which fits the evidence that they have. Whether it is true or not is secondary.

HANDCUFFS AND BONDAGE

Fig. 28. Still: THE 39 STEPS: Handcuffs and bed scene. Handcuffed together, Hannay (Robert Donat) and Pamela (Madeleine Carroll) are obliged to share a double bed.

In THE LODGER, this motif has several inflections. (1) The detective Joe is proud of his handcuffs, telling Mr Bunting that they are 'a brand new pair of bracelets for the Avenger'. When Daisy joins the two of them, he declares cockily that when he has put a rope round the Avenger's neck – he uses the handcuffs to mime the hanging – he'll put a ring round Daisy's finger. (2) Joe then threatens to handcuff Daisy and, when she resists and flees, pursues her up the back stairs. In the front hall he catches her and carries out his threat. Daisy's scream brings the Lodger to the top of the stairs and he gazes down intently at the little drama being enacted below. Despite Daisy's distress, he does not interfere. (3) When Joe later concludes that the Lodger is the Avenger, he arrests him, putting him in handcuffs. The Lodger escapes, but his inability to use his hands gives him away, and he is pursued by a vengeful mob. As he climbs over some railings, the handcuffs get caught, and he hangs, helpless, whilst the mob attack him. Learning that he is innocent, Joe does his best to stop them, but it is in fact the prompt appearance of *The Evening Standard*, with its account of the capture of the Avenger, that serves to draw the mob away.

Here the handcuffs are used, first, to symbolise Joe's notion of marriage – as soon as he has proved himself by capturing and executing the Avenger, Daisy will become his prisoner. But the Lodger's fascination with this scene suggests something else: that he is turned on by the idea of Daisy in handcuffs? That he is seeing himself in Daisy's place? If we take it that, as with most of Ivor Novello's films, there is a gay subtext (➤ HOMOSEXUALITY) – as in Joe's earlier comment: 'I'm glad he's not keen on the girls' – we could even read this moment as suggesting that the Lodger might rather like the idea of being handcuffed by Joe.

It is therefore perhaps not surprising that, when the Lodger is arrested and handcuffed by Joe, the moment is given strong dramatic emphasis. Flanking the Lodger, Joe's colleagues force his arms up so that they stretch out in front of him: Joe's hands come into shot and effect the handcuffing. As he does this, the Lodger is transfixed, gazing at the handcuffs. It could be humiliation which produces this reaction, but it could also be that the Lodger is seeing his (repressed?) fantasy come true. The extended sequence in which he is on the run wearing the handcuffs is also unusual in tone: not at all like any of the later Hitchcock examples. Having escaped from the police, he becomes curiously passive, even childlike. Waiting on a bench for Daisy, he curls up in the foetal position. After his confession (➤ GUILT AND CONFESSION), he puts his head on Daisy's shoulder like a child seeking comfort from his mother, and she puts on his cloak as if dressing a child. In the pub, she holds a glass to his mouth for him to drink. And, as he hangs from the railings, he is again strangely passive. Before the crowd reach him, he makes only a half-hearted attempt to escape. He seems to be waiting to be punished.

What Hitchcock implies quite strongly here is the Lodger's masochism. I suggest under GUILT AND CONFESSION that he feels unconscious guilt for his sister's murder, but there may be other intimations. Has wearing the handcuffs brought out his masochism, just as brandishing them brought out Joe's sadism? (Joe seemed as keen to get Daisy in handcuffs as he was the Avenger.) The Christian overtones are a further complication: as the Lodger hangs from the railings, Hitchcock explicitly evokes the crucifixion: he admitted as much to Truffaut (Truffaut 1968: 41), and the stills on page 42 of the book show how both the crucifixion and the Pietà – with Daisy in the position of the Virgin

Mary – are suggested by the visuals of the scene. Lesley Brill has even suggested that 'the association of Christ and the Lodger is appropriate':

> In his dedication to pursuing the criminal and in his near dismemberment by the mob, [the Lodger] may be seen as a redemptive figure, one who suffers not on his own behalf but in place of the truly guilty, the society which gave rise to the Avenger and is implicated in his crimes. The fact that the Avenger is apprehended at the same time the Lodger is arrested and attacked by the mob underscores the redemptive aspect of the Lodger's sacrifice.
>
> (Brill 1986: 73)

To explore the implications of these overtones further, it is useful to look at I CONFESS, another film in which Hitchcock uses both handcuffs and the notion of Christian suffering.

As Father Logan walks the streets of Quebec, trying to decide what to do about his imminent arrest for murder, he is associated with three images/objects: a still from a film showing a man in handcuffs in police custody, a headless manikin wearing a man's suit, and a statue depicting Christ carrying the Cross on the Via Dolorosa. The third association is particularly significant in that Hitchcock also refers to Christ's passion when Logan is subsequently found innocent by the Court, but is then vilified by the crowd. In other words, Logan's suffering – like the Lodger's – is also being identified with Christ's. But in entitling their section on the film 'The temptation of martyrdom', Rohmer and Chabrol (1979: 112-19) suggest the underlying premise here: temptation. This idea is particularly relevant to the film still and the manikin since Logan reacts to them – as if he is seeing himself in them. Accordingly, just as we could see the suit as tempting Logan – conspicuous because of his priest's cassock – with the possibility of disguise, so the man in handcuffs could be seen as another image of temptation: inviting him to surrender to the punishment his calling – in its insistence that the confessional is sacrosanct – imposes on him. Again we could speak of masochism.

It may seem excessive to compare the sufferings of the Lodger and Logan with those of Christ, but the fact that Hitchcock has used handcuffs to help suggest such a link is intriguing. In THE WRONG MAN, when Manny is arrested and arraigned for a crime he didn't commit, he, too, is handcuffed. Discussing this sequence, Rohmer and Chabrol comment that 'as Balestrero comes to appreciate the futility of any protest, the idea of *redemption* is grafted on ... Fonda's face and Christ-like postures in his cell recall the iconography of the Stations of the Cross' (Rohmer and Chabrol 1979: 148). Once again, handcuffs are incorporated into what could be seen as a Christian allegory.

A throwaway line in NUMBER SEVENTEEN adds another twist. In the derelict house, undercover cop Barton and seaman Ben find an unconscious man

(Ackroyd) whose pockets contain a gun and a pair of handcuffs. Ben affects ignorance about the latter, prompting Barton's joking 'You've never seen a pair of handcuffs before?' Ben replies 'No, sir; nor worn 'em. I was brought up Baptist.' Once again, handcuffs and the Christian religion are juxtaposed; albeit here to insist on their separation. It's as if, in the Hitchcockian unconscious, being handcuffed and Christ-like suffering are somehow connected.

The suggestion of masochism also raises the question of 'bondage': a potentially erotic use of handcuffs and other forms of physical restraint. To Truffaut's 'Handcuffs are certainly the most concrete ... loss of freedom', Hitchcock replies 'There's also a sexual connotation, I think' (Truffaut 1968: 41). Clearly any such intimations could only be in the subtext, as in the hint that the Lodger may be secretly attracted to the idea of being handcuffed – and then saved – by the manly Joe. However, although there are a number of situations in Hitchcock films which might be thought similarly promising in this area, most do not really come off.

NUMBER SEVENTEEN is a good example. When Ackroyd recovers, he pretends to be one of the villains, and helps tie up Barton and Rose. Since he himself is not only Rose's father but the one who actually ties her, the situation has potential: as he fastens her to the banisters, she even gives him a conspiratorial wink. But if Hitchcock wanted to suggest that both are rather enjoying the charade, his staging fails: the moment is too fleeting to have any real charge. When Ackroyd's deception is then exposed, Barton and Rose are retied to the banisters – 'properly this time' – and left there by the villains. As they struggle to free themselves, she cheerily comments: 'Like the pictures, isn't it?' Barton's rejoinder – 'Too much for my liking' – is followed by a dramatic breaking of the banisters, leaving them suspended by their bound wrists over the stairwell: it was this image which was used on the video cover of the film in the UK. Yet the tone is strictly comic: they are soon rescued by Nora, a mystery woman who had seemed to be with the villains. At the climax of the film, the situation is reversed: Barton rescues Nora, in handcuffs, from drowning (➤ WATER). But despite the use of the handcuffs, this scene, too, lacks erotic resonances. Throughout the film, Hitchcock seems to have been more concerned with having fun at the expense of the stereotyped situations (hence Rose's comment) than in developing an erotic subtext.

THE 39 STEPS and SABOTEUR are the other two main films in which handcuffs are used: in each a handcuffed hero on the run finds himself accompanied by an unhelpful blonde. But the ways in which the handcuffs are employed in each film are quite different. In SABOTEUR, Pat takes the handcuffs Barry is wearing as a sign of his guilt, and at one point uses them to pinion him to her car's steering column. In effect, the handcuffs are little more than an inconvenience Barry has to get rid of as quickly as possible.

THE 39 STEPS is a very different matter. Here, where Hannay and Pamela are handcuffed together, Hitchcock contrives a whole range of situations: comic, violent, painful, playful, erotic. An innkeeper's wife mistakes their inseparability for romance – 'They're so terribly in love with each other' – but Pamela's continuing refusal to accept Hannay's story of his innocence leads to some quite brutal moments: at one point, he forces her handcuffed hand up her back and uses his free hand to throttle her to stop her talking. However, she does not really object too much. Only moments later, they are amicably eating sandwiches, and Hitchcock effects a charmingly erotic little scene where Hannay finds his handcuffed hand inescapably drawn to Pamela's thighs as she strips off her wet stockings; to preserve propriety, she has to give him her sandwich to hold. Later, as she sits and he lies on the double bed, he files away at the handcuffs. Here, as he invents a lurid criminal past, the tone is mainly comic, but Hitchcock nevertheless includes one shot in which Hannay's busy activity with his hand (off-screen) seems to induce a soporific bliss in Pamela. Both fall asleep. Then, when Pamela wakes and manages to pull her hand through her handcuff, Hannay promptly rolls over in his sleep and embraces her, signalling his involuntary wish to continue the closeness. That the handcuffs have served to bring them together is emphasised in the film's final shot: Hannay takes Pamela's hand, and the handcuffs – still on his wrist – are clearly visible.

A recurring image in Fritz Lang's German films is of a man or a woman tied up in ropes – or some other restraint – thrashing around trying to break free. These moments frequently have considerable erotic charge, e.g. Sonja (Gerda Maurus), bound to a chair, using her legs to join in a fight between two men at the climax of SPIONE (1928). The only Hitchcock film which has even some of this charge is JAMAICA INN. First, when Joss holds Sir Humphrey at gunpoint and then ties him to a chair, this is a charade for the benefit of the onlookers: it is only a pretence tying-up. Nevertheless, the homosexual undercurrents to their relationship (➤ LIGHTS) at least make the scene suggestive: hinting that they are enacting in public a version of what they practice in private. Then, when Sir Humphrey binds and gags Mary in order to kidnap her, there is at least a hint of eroticism: quite carried away, Raymond Durgnat invokes *Story of O* (Durgnat 1974: 165). But I do not think the comparison works: I feel, rather, that Hitchcock focuses primarily on Mary's mute distress.

Nevertheless, there is a wonderful example in Hitchcock of playful bondage: the ending of MR AND MRS SMITH. David pushes Ann, wearing skis, back into a chair, so that she ends with the skis vertical, her legs in the air. He starts to undress. She thrashes around, saying 'Get me out of these', when suddenly her left foot comes free. Quickly checking to see whether David – now behind the chair – is looking, she jams the foot back into the ski and continues to thrash around. In fact, he did see her manoeuvre – which is the giveaway – and he now advances on the chair from behind. Her hands reach up over her head to embrace him, and she murmurs, 'Oh, David'. The skis cross. It is one of Hollywood's great erotic endings.

HANDS

Fig. 29. Still: To Catch a Thief: Held wrist. Robie (Cary Grant) takes hold of Francie (Grace Kelly) in order to kiss her.

In his original *Cahiers du Cinéma* article, Philippe Demonsablon divides 'The Hand' into four subheadings: 'floating hands' (e.g. the Lodger's going down the banister rail); 'strangling gestures' (e.g. Ashenden's hands reaching out as if to strangle Marvin after the train wreck in Secret Agent); 'grasping hands' (e.g. Bruno reaching down into the drain to retrieve the cigarette lighter) and 'indicating hands' (e.g. Kate's father publicly pointing out Philip as 'her betrayer' in The Manxman). Apart from these groupings, Demonsablon makes only a few points about the overall significance of the motif: to hold something is to have it in one's power; hands tend to have an autonomous will; 'is it an accident that most of Hitchcock's killers are stranglers?' (Demonsablon 1956:

26). Altogether, he lists some thirty-five instances of the hands motif in Hitchcock, but even within the films he covers, there are many more; it is unquestionably one of the director's most significant motifs, and all I can do here is refer selectively to its usage. In Part I, I look at certain cases where the hands motif is used 'expressionistically' in Hitchcock (➤ *A melodramatic motif: hands*). Here I touch on an argument begun in Part I – that the director's use of hands is essentially 'melodramatic' – but my main concern is to use the hands motif as a means to examine key aspects of the sexual politics in Hitchcock's films.

Male hands / female hands

A moral distinction between male and female hands in Hitchcock goes back to THE PLEASURE GARDEN, his first film. In it, a naïve young woman, Patsy, marries a man, Levet, whom we know to be unworthy of her: immediately after the honeymoon, he sets off alone for a colonial outpost, where he promptly sets up house with an anonymous native woman and turns to drunken dissolution. Responding to his lie that he has had a fever (his excuse for not writing), Patsy travels out to be with him. Her arrival shocks Levet, and when an opportunity presents itself, he drowns the native woman (➤ WATER). At this moment, Patsy is tending Hugh, structurally the film's hero, who genuinely has fever. As Levet pushes the head of the native woman under the water, Hitchcock cuts to Patsy, her hand feeling Hugh's forehead. The juxtaposition – the man's hand being used to murder a woman; the woman's hand solicitously caring for a man – is simply stunning. The moral contrast could scarcely be starker, and points to a crucial aspect of Hitchcock's work. He would return repeatedly to narratives of male domination and violence, with the woman as a victim, and, by contrast – though markedly less frequently – narratives in which women, with greater or lesser success, seek to help men.

The strangling gestures Demonsablon mentions are common in Hitchcock's work, meriting the status of a sub-motif. They also signal the violence of his male characters. Twice in SHADOW OF A DOUBT Uncle Charlie's hands enact strangling gestures. In the 'Til-Two bar, without realising – until Charlie's stare alerts him – he forcefully twists a folded napkin. Later, as he contemplates killing Charlie, he looks down at his hands, which curve to evoke a strangulation grip; the gesture is like a reflex, occurring with such force that his cigar falls from his hand. Here the sense of the hands' 'autonomous will' clearly implies that Uncle Charlie cannot control his murderous impulses. In STRANGERS ON A TRAIN, Bruno's hands are repeatedly shown curved in a strangulation posture: when Hitchcock links them (through a dissolve) to Guy's angry declaration that he could murder Miriam (➤ DOUBLES); when, at the 'Test your strength' machine, he looks at his hands and then at Miriam; when he strangles her. Then, at Senator Morton's party, Bruno displays his hands as a murder weapon to the elderly Mrs Cunningham and, going into a trance, almost strangles her as well. Here, too, his hands seem to have an autonomous will: they fasten so hard around Mrs Cunningham's neck that they have to be prised off.

The effect of these gestures is to suggest that the murderousness of Uncle Charlie and Bruno is focused in their hands. As Theodore Price has pointed out, this, too, is an expressionist notion, going back to THE HANDS OF ORLAC (Robert Wiene, 1924), in which a murderer's hands are grafted on to a musician, leading the latter to fear that this will turn him into a murderer (Price 1992: 325-26). Although Price is using the link to pursue his own agenda of hunting the homosexual subtext (➤ HOMOSEXUALITY), the notion that hands can express a fundamental feature of a character's personality is highly relevant to Hitchcock's work.

In ROPE, we see a different inflection of this notion. The film begins with Brandon and Phillip strangling their 'friend' David, but the subsequent use of the hands motif only applies to Phillip. When Mrs Atwater arrives at the party the killers hold to celebrate their crime (➤ *Food and Murder*), she mistakenly identifies Kenneth, another guest, as David. This shocks Phillip, and he 'accidentally' cuts his hand by breaking his glass. This is a familiar motif in the cinema in general, and its usual meaning – discussed under *Damaged Hands* – is as a signifier of castration anxiety. Here, I would argue, it is more to do with Phillip's sense of guilt. Like Uncle Charlie and Bruno, Brandon is a psychopath and so does not feel guilt, but Phillip does. Later, Mrs Atwater looks at Phillip's hands and declares, 'These hands will bring you great fame.' She means as a concert pianist, but Phillip – as his disturbed reaction shows – inevitably interprets the comment differently. Uncle Charlie's and Bruno's hands express their murderousness; Phillip's his guilt. That hands can embody this idea is also present to a greater or lesser extent in those examples when a man washes the traces of a crime from his hands: the sabotage sand in SABOTAGE, the blood from the person he has just killed in PSYCHO and TORN CURTAIN. Whether or not the man realises this – and Norman certainly does not – he is, in effect, seeking to wash away his guilt.

In BLACKMAIL, where the character who kills and is then haunted by guilt is a woman, the motif is inflected differently again. Crewe persuades Alice to go with him up his room in order to have sex with her. She resists, so he sets out to rape her, pulling her on to his bed, which is hidden from view by a curtain. The curtain acts both as a censorship screen and as a device to dramatise the unseen struggle behind it. As Alice cries 'Let me go!' her hand comes from behind the curtain and at first seems to be thrashing around helplessly. The camera then tracks towards the bread knife on the bedside table: the movement seems to guide Alice's hand to the knife. Knife and hand then disappear back behind the curtain, which continues to twitch with the violence of the struggle. Eventually, the curtain grows still and, after a suspenseful pause, Crewe's lower arm falls into view, obviously lifeless.

This image of Crewe's arm sticking out from behind the curtain then haunts Alice. As she walks the streets of London's West End in a daze, she is reminded of the arm, first by a traffic policeman's outstretched hand, then by the lower arm of a sleeping tramp. Flashbacks to Crewe's arm emphasise its status as a guilt image. It is not the only one: Alice also imagines a neon sign of two animated cocktail shakers being transformed into an image of stabbing knives. Here the articulation of the motif is, again, expressionist – using external images to express Alice's subjective state – a notion which also applies, in the aural sense, to the ensuing scene at breakfast, when all she hears of a neighbour's gossip is the word 'knife' (➤ *Food and guilt*).

The difference between these guilt images and those examples in which a man's hands 'betray' his guilt is significant. Because the triggering image is Crewe's dead arm, its various echoes in other men's arms are like a series of silent accusations directed at Alice. With the male characters, it is their own hands which mark their guilt; this is different. When Alice emerges from behind the curtain, still clutching the knife, neither her hands nor the knife are bloody – which is strikingly 'unrealistic'. Hitchcock would seem to be concerned to keep her in some sense 'innocent'; she *feels* guilty – which is where the stabbing knives image also comes in – but we know it was self-defence, and locating the primary guilt image in men's arms (hands) could be seen as a way of signalling them as the true threat.

Alice's hand thrashing around as she is assaulted is typical of the way Hitchcock uses a woman's hands in a scene of violence. He focuses on the victim's hands in a way which captures the terror and desperation of her plight: reaching for something to defend herself with (Alice; Margot as she is being strangled in DIAL M FOR MURDER), attempting to release the strangulating grip on her throat (Mrs Cunningham; Brenda in FRENZY), warding off the attack (Melanie in the bedroom fighting off the birds) or, most poignantly, reaching for something to hold on to as she dies (Marion grasping the shower curtain in PSYCHO). There tends to be something very eloquent about these gestures: the women have usually been silenced by the nature or brutality of the attack and their hand gestures serve as a mute appeal for help. The gestures may thus be seen as 'melodramatic' in a sense advanced by Peter Brooks, who argues that the mute, gestural appeal lies at the root of the melodramatic tradition (Brooks 1976: 56-80). In TORN CURTAIN, there is then a rare (unique?) instance in Hitchcock in which a man's hands are focused on in a similar way. At the climax of the fight in the farmhouse, Gromek's hands release their grip on Michael's throat and flutter as he is gassed. The abrupt switch from a male gesture of strangling to a female one of helplessness is surprisingly powerful, and undoubtedly adds to our sympathy for the character.

Although scenes of violence are extreme examples, I would argue that the contrast between the male and female gestures in such scenes is nevertheless a powerful indication of the sexual politics in Hitchcock's films. He tends to focus on a character's hands at moments of tension, so that the gestures serve to express the tension. Since men regularly seek to dominate and control women in his films, we would expect their hand gestures to reflect this impulse. Strangling gestures are simply one extreme; there are dozens of examples in Hitchcock where a man's hands hold a woman in a powerful grip in order to impose his will on her. The hands of the female characters, by contrast, tend to suggest their vulnerability and uncertainty. Instances of their hands expressing a mute appeal are not confined to scenes of male brutality. They also occur when, for example, a woman is threatened with a dangerous fall, and reaches up for the hero to take hold of her hand: YOUNG AND INNOCENT; TO CATCH A THIEF; NORTH BY NORTHWEST. Another, particularly eloquent instance occurs in LIFEBOAT, when Mrs Higley, having lost her baby, sleeps with her hands open on her lap as if still cradling the child. In all these examples, it is the woman's distress or loss which the hands serve to convey. More often than not in Hitchcock, women are victims, and their gestures bear witness to this.

In cases where the women are not victims, the hands motif still tends – in moral terms – to favour them. When Charlie in SHADOW OF A DOUBT wears the emerald ring to pressure her uncle to leave (➢ JEWELLERY), the camera tracks in to her hand in close-up as it travels down the banister rail. In effect, her hand trumps her uncle's murderous hands. As Francie drives at speed along the corniche in TO CATCH A THIEF, Hitchcock cuts from her hands, expertly handling the steering wheel, to Robie's hands, nervously clutching his knees. In FRENZY, even as Babs is being strangled, she manages to seize hold of Rusk's tie-pin, and she holds on to it with such force that he is obliged, later, to break the fingers of her hand in order to retrieve it. Such cases may be relatively uncommon in Hitchcock, but so far as the hands motif is concerned, they assert female power in positive terms, in contrast to the way it is typically shown for the men.

Equally, the compassion expressed by Patsy's gesture in THE PLEASURE GARDEN does occur occasionally in other films. In THE RING, Mabel wipes Jack's face in one scene as if he were a little boy (➢ WATER). In RICH AND STRANGE, Emily is more preoccupied with bathing the injured Fred's head than with the fact that their ship is sinking. In SPELLBOUND, Constance strokes the head of the unconscious J.B. as she asks Dr Brulov to give her time to treat him. In VERTIGO, Midge cradles Scottie's head after he falls from the stepladder in her apartment. In all these cases, the woman is 'mothering' the hero, and the main reason for the scarcity of further examples surely lies in the sense that tenderness between couples in Hitchcock is rare: the man's desire to dominate is too strong.

Held wrists

There is a particular inflection of the hands motif, very common in Hitchcock's films, which illustrates his male characters' drive to dominate. I will call it the held-wrists motif; almost invariably it involves a man seizing a woman by one or more of her wrists in order to impose his will on her. Usually, this is with hostile intent. Twice in MRS AND MRS SMITH, David aggressively seizes and holds Ann by her wrists, whilst insisting that she is his wife (in the department store) and that she belongs to him (in the chalet at the end). When Mark finds Marnie at the office safe, unable to take his money (➤ Part I), he tries to force her to take it by holding one of her wrists with both his hands: this is a particularly violent use of the motif, with Marnie thrashing around in his strong grip. In TOPAZ, Rico grabs Juanita by the wrist in order to pull her towards him for the powerful scene which ends with him shooting her.

Again, SHADOW OF A DOUBT provides striking examples. When Charlie takes an incriminating newspaper cutting out of her uncle's jacket pocket, he angrily strides across the room and grabs her wrists with such force that she cries out that he is hurting her; it is this gesture that she remembers when the policeman Graham first raises doubts in her mind about her uncle. At the climax of the film, Uncle Charlie uses the same grip to stop Charlie getting off the train – so that he can kill her. When Charlie realises what he is doing, she actually cries out, 'Your hands!' For Charlie, her uncle's murderousness is indeed focused in his hands, and Hitchcock films their struggle at the open door of the train in terms of another stark contrast (and conflict) between male and female hands: Uncle Charlie's hands muzzling Charlie's mouth and gripping her body to manoeuvre it into position; hers reaching for something to grip to save herself.

The point about the examples in these films is that the man is using his superior strength to master the woman – to bully her into submission. He does this, typically, because he considers that he has some sort of claim on her; in two cases, he is her husband; in TOPAZ, her lover. But on two occasions his grip is also murderous, and it may well be sadistic: Mark seems to be taking pleasure in manhandling Marnie at the safe, and ends by throwing her against it. There is also a sexual charge to this assault, as there is to Uncle Charlie manhandling his niece: in both cases, Hitchcock inserts a shot of the woman's legs turning as the man grapples with her. He repeats the turning legs shot when Adamson in

FAMILY PLOT likewise manhandles Blanche in the garage in order to inject her
(➤ *Handbags and keys*). Again a man is using his grip to master a woman, and
here the assault is sexualised by the way that the needle goes into Blanche and
in her cry of response. The held-wrists sub-motif may thus also be seen as pointing to a man's desire to master a woman sexually. Even an essentially honourable hero like Hannay in THE 39 STEPS uses the technique: on the train he grabs
Pamela's wrists in order to kiss her (➤ TRAINS) and his later use of the handcuffs to force her into submission (➤ HANDCUFFS AND BONDAGE) could be
seen as an extension of his action here.

More rarely, a man is ambivalent about using force in this manner, and we see
conflicting hand gestures. In THE MAN WHO KNEW TOO MUCH (1955), Ben has
to tell his wife Jo that their son has been kidnapped. Because he is convinced
that she will become hysterical at the news, he first gives her a sedative, then
waits for it to take effect. When he finally tells her, he is so concerned to manage
her distraught reaction that he pins her down on the bed, holding her wrist to
do so. However, Ben is also genuinely upset at what he is doing; just as one of
his hands holds Jo down, so the other strokes her head: he is torn by his action,
and ends by begging her forgiveness and kissing her hand. In TOPAZ, even as
Rico restrains Juanita by gripping her hands against his chest, he shows his love
by kissing the hands. Here the erotic undertow to the scene is made absolutely
explicit: 'the closely circling camera seeming to bind the two bodies together as
Rico decides to kill her (to spare her torture); the orgasmic jerk of the woman's
body as the bullet is fired into it; the close-up of the gun in the man's hand
"going limp" as it were' (Wood 1989: 224). Although Rico's contradictory hand
gestures are only a part of the power of the scene, they nevertheless serve to
express his anguish and dividedness.

The erotic charge to the sub-motif may have a different effect on the woman:
occasionally, Hitchcock suggests that it perhaps secretly excites her. Early in
SUSPICION, a distant shot of Johnnie and Lina on a hilltop shows them engaged
in what looks like quite a violent struggle: she loses her hat, coat and handbag.
In a closer shot, Johnnie, firmly holding Lina by her wrists, mocks her panic,
wondering whether she thought he was trying to kill her or to kiss her. Richard
Allen has written of the ambiguity of this moment: on the one hand, 'Perhaps
what occurred was a romantic embrace, sharply curtailed by Lina's paranoid
fear of the ego-threatening character of her own sexuality, projected onto an
essentially innocent Johnnie.' On the other: 'from where the spectator is placed,
[the distant shot] supports the worry that Johnnie actually harbours rapacious,
murderous intentions' (Allen 1999: 225). Nor is this the only ambiguity here.
There is no doubt that Johnnie is behaving in an aggressive, patronising manner
towards Lina, but it could be that at some level she likes it; that it arouses her.
As much is suggested when the two of them return home and she responds to

an overheard remark from her parents about her spinsterishness by grabbing Johnnie and kissing him passionately. Later, missing Johnnie, she returns to the same hill. However, when Johnnie grabs hold of Lina's wrists in the film's final scene, it is the bullying overtones which are dominant. He has just rather recklessly exposed his murderousness towards her (➤ HEIGHTS AND FALLING) and he now needs to bully her into accepting a different explanation of his extraordinary behaviour.

In the early scene in SUSPICION, Hitchcock fuses the aggressive and the potentially erotic aspects of the held-wrists motif in a single example. In To CATCH A THIEF, he uses the motif throughout the film, varying its import each time it occurs. During the car picnic, Francie identifies Robie as 'the Cat' and offers herself as his companion in crime. This prompts him to grab her lower arm, and he continues to hold it throughout the ensuing conversation. Francie's remarks signal that she is attracted to him *because* he is a cat burglar, and even though he is busy denying this, he responds to her overtures; her approving comment – 'You've a very strong grip: the kind a burglar needs' – leads him to pull her down and kiss her. This, clearly, is the erotic inflection of the motif. That evening, she then seduces him (➤ JEWELLERY), but shortly afterwards bursts into his room and accuses him of stealing her mother's jewels. She even assaults him physically, and on this occasion, as he holds both her wrists to restrain her, the erotic element is suppressed by her anger. Then, at the climax of the film, Robie holds Danielle by her wrist as she hangs over a dangerous drop to the ground. This is a very different use of the motif: Robie is using his 'burglar's grip' to hold her, but also using the threat of letting go to force her to confess. Throughout the film, then, the use of the motif has modulated from playful to threatening, from erotic to bullying.

Between these last two examples of the motif there is, however, another instance, in which it is used differently again. Subsequent developments make Francie realise that Robie is innocent of the theft of her mother's jewels, and she turns up (outside the cemetery during Foussard's funeral) and apologises. She now offers to help him catch the real burglar, and when he refuses (out of concern for her safety?) grabs his arm to stop him leaving. In other words, she inverts the dominant inflection of the motif, a moment which Hitchcock seems to have felt very uneasy about: as he cuts to the close-up of her hand restraining Robie's arm, there is a bad continuity match. During this close-up, Francie says 'I'm in love with you' and then withdraws her hand. My conclusion is that the inversion was 'licensed' by the declaration of love; that only *in extremis* can a woman appropriate this gesture in order to restrain a man, and that this moment, awkwardly staged, only fleetingly allowed, gives further insight into the dynamics of Hitchcock's gender politics.

Fig. 30. Still: Spellbound: Damaged hand. Constance (Ingrid Bergman) questions J.B. (Gregory Peck) about his burnt wrist.

A general point about the held-wrists motif is that it serves to express the man's uncertainty about the woman: he holds her like this because he feels uncomfortable if she is not firmly under his control. Such a sense of insecurity frequently haunts Hitchcock's male characters: it is notable that in most of the examples quoted, it is the hero, not the villain, who grips the heroine in this manner. The first example from To Catch a Thief is particularly revealing here. The picnic occurs immediately after the hair-raising car drive, so that it's as if Robie grabs Francie's wrist in order to reassert male control after she had so stylishly usurped it with her skilful driving.

Damaged hands

Hands are a part of the body which are particularly vulnerable to injury; again, we would expect examples of this in Hitchcock to function expressively; for example by revealing something of a character's psyche, or illustrating further the differences between men's and women's hands. In SPELLBOUND, when Constance joins J.B. in the Empire State Hotel, she suddenly notices that his hand has been burned and that he has had a skin graft. She holds his arm just above the burn and tries to force him to remember the circumstances. Now clutching his hand in pain, J.B. protests that he cannot remember, but she continues to push him until he almost faints. Here the woman's grip on the man's lower arm is legitimised by Constance's role as doctor, but it is nevertheless traumatic for the man.

Andrew Britton has argued that there is an additional element to J.B.'s breakdowns in the film; that they are occasioned by Constance's presence and the sexual threat she embodies (Britton 1986: 72-83). This example, like a number of others in the film, suggests castration anxiety: in the film's oneiric system, the hand is a Freudian symbol, and the woman's focus on its 'damaged' status is almost unbearable.

It is quite common in films generally for damage to a man's hands to be linked to castration fears of some kind. Perhaps the most familiar example is when a man cuts his hand in stress or anger, usually by breaking a glass or similar object, e.g. BLOOD AND SAND (Rouben Mamoulian, 1941); SECRET BEYOND THE DOOR (Fritz Lang, 1947); NIAGARA (Henry Hathaway, 1953). In this last example, George (Joseph Cotten) cuts his hand when he breaks the record his wife Rose (Marilyn Monroe) has put on: he knows it has a romantic significance for her which does not include him. His response when the heroine Polly (Jean Peters) comes to attend to the cut is remarkable in that it makes the symbolism virtually explicit: 'I suppose she sent you to find out if I cut it off – well, I didn't!'

There is one example in Hitchcock which is similar. In a scene in FRENZY, Blaney is treated by Brenda, his ex-wife, to dinner at her club, but his gratitude (he is currently both jobless and homeless) is short-lived. Increasingly bitter about his failure with his own business enterprises and Brenda's evident success with hers, he launches into a vociferous attack on her: 'I bet you're making a fortune out of that agency, and why not? If you can't make love, sell it – the respectable kind, of course. The married kind.' His rage causes him to shatter the brandy glass in his hand. It is the context that links the moment to Blaney's castration anxiety, in that his male ego is threatened by Brenda, the other women in the club and his own sense of inadequacy. But other examples in which castration fears are expressed in a like manner are not, I believe, widespread in Hitchcock's films. Johnny in JUNO AND THE PAYCOCK – who has lost an arm – is certainly a weak, emasculated figure, but Professor Jordan in THE 39 STEPS – who has an amputated finger joint – displays his 'damaged' hand to Hannay as a sign of his power (➤ EXHIBITIONISM / VOYEURISM). The moments in STRANGERS ON A TRAIN and NORTH BY NORTHWEST in which a character who is coded as gay – Bruno and Leonard respectively – sadistically stamps on the hero's fingers could, perhaps, serve as another sort of example (see Price 1992: 87 & 193), but it is the hero's death which is the primary threat here (➤ HEIGHTS AND FALLING).

The Hitchcock film with the most extensive damage to hands is THE BIRDS. During the climactic bird attack on the Brenner house, the hands of both Mitch and Melanie are quite badly injured: Mitch's when the gulls almost break in through a window; Melanie's in the assault on her by both gulls and crows in the attic bedroom. Although, because her whole body is attacked, Melanie suffers far more than Mitch, it is probably the repeated close-ups of her hands being pecked which convey most strongly the pain of the wounding – even in her case. This emphasises the peculiar status of hands; they serve as a highly sensitive instrument to suggest what a character is feeling or suffering. But the birds' attacks on the protagonists' hands serve another function: of demonstrating just how vulnerable we are when we cannot use our hands properly. Mitch trying desperately to close the shutters; Melanie to turn the door knob behind her; Mitch to pull Melanie's prostrate body out of the bedroom – all are made excruciating to watch because of the relentless assault on their hands by the birds' pecking beaks.

The assaults on Mitch's hands are doubly significant because he is a Hitchcock hero whose gestures are generally competent and caring rather than bullying. For example, he tends Melanie's wound when she is hit by a gull in the first bird attack: a rare example of a man's hands nursing a woman. When Melanie recovers consciousness after her ordeal in the bedroom, her arms begin to flail around. Mitch takes hold of them to control them, but his gesture is calming, not threatening. The complete breakdown in the 'natural' order of things would seem to require a more balanced, less neurotic hero than the Hitchcock norm. However, after the climactic attack, Melanie's wounds are such that Mitch no longer has the skill to help her: he and Lydia administer first aid, but she will have to be taken to hospital. The hero's hands, once so capable, are no longer sufficient. The final example of the hands motif in the film is, nevertheless, positive. In the car as they are about to drive away, Melanie rests her hand on Lydia's wrist, and her trusting expression as Lydia holds her shows that she has finally found comfort in the care of a mother figure.

Occurring at the end of a film which contains so much violence, wounding and death, this image of female closeness expressed through the hands motif is surprisingly moving. In line with Susan Smith's reading of the film from Melanie's point of view as a working through of her abandonment as a child by her own mother (Smith 2000: 135-140), the moment could be seen to express the albeit tentative fulfilment of Melanie's psychic journey. But this final, soothing use of the motif also draws attention to a curious point about Hitchcock's work overall: that injuries to hands are usually improbably short-lived. There is no Hitchcock film with a hand wound remotely as painful and debilitating as, say, that of Will Lockhart (James Stewart) in THE MAN FROM LARAMIE (Anthony Mann, 1955). In STAGE FRIGHT, as part of his plan to trick Charlotte into betraying herself, Commodore Gill cuts his own hand to bloody a doll's dress. He becomes rather faint as he does this, and later a bandage covers his hand: here, at least, the wound is properly registered. Other examples tend to be more swiftly forgotten. J.B.'s war wound is not mentioned again. Guy shows no after-effects of Bruno stamping on his fingers; Roger just has a neat Band-Aid to show that Leonard did, after all, do some injury. Mitch swiftly (too swiftly in terms of the time available) bandages his pecked hand. Blaney's hand does not even seem to be cut. ROPE contains the most glaring example of this 'evasion': in one of Hitchcock's worst continuity errors, only minutes after Phillip has broken his glass, his bloody hand is miraculously 'cured'.

It will be apparent that, apart from Melanie, all these examples refer to men's hands. This, I would suggest, points to the underlying reason for Hitchcock's impulse to gloss over damaged hands. Even more than the continuity error in To CATCH A THIEF, I believe that the one in ROPE is symptomatic: a moment when Hitchcock betrays his own unease. And here the unease would seem to stem from the psychic associations of a man's damaged hand. Hence, when the next long take began, Hitchcock 'forgot' that Phillip was supposed to have a cut hand.

Holding hands

The issue of *touching* hands in Hitchcock is taken up by Joe McElhaney in the context of an excellent discussion of the hands motif in MARNIE. In an early scene in her kitchen, Mrs Edgar recoils from Marnie's touch; a moment which conveys the opposite effect to that of the final hands close-up in THE BIRDS. McElhaney argues:

> In this sequence so strongly built around close-ups of the faces of the two women and in which the activities of their hands are devoted to banal and mechanical domestic

duties (cracking pecans, pouring syrup), this close-up [of Marnie's hand touching her mother's] carries such an emotional weight because the hands are now suddenly being called upon to carry an expressive function... This expressive function is something that Mrs Edgar refuses, and she must give her hand a more precise function, slapping the accusing face of her daughter, restoring both the hand and the face to their 'proper' functions. What this sequence makes clear is that Marnie's projection of herself in the world outside of her mother's home, as an unavailable object of desire, is an unconscious response to this situation with her mother. Since her mother will not touch her, will not love her, then she will move in a world in which no one – particularly no man – will be able to touch her.

(McElhaney 1999: 94)

McElhaney is here analysing an example of the hands motif to make a highly relevant point about the heroine's psychology. I would like to conclude this section by looking at a closely allied example of the motif – holding hands – which, I believe, is similarly revealing, and revealing in particular of Hitchcock's male-female relationships. First, holding hands in the purely romantic sense is almost entirely absent from his work. Two of Hitchcock's British films end with a couple reaching to hold hands (THE SKIN GAME and THE 39 STEPS), but the former seems tentative, and the latter is ironised by the presence of the handcuffs, still attached to Hannay's wrist. There are other examples in which the hero takes the heroine's hand, but only in – or just after – a crisis: Roger and Eve fleeing across the top of Mount Rushmore in NORTH BY NORTHWEST; Mitch and Melanie after the attack which pins her in the phone booth in THE BIRDS. Towards the end of MR AND MRS SMITH, Hitchcock also includes a more unusual inflection of the motif. David is lying in bed, pretending to be suffering from nervous strain and hallucinating. As Ann shaves him, he holds out his hand for Jeff to take – Ann explains: 'He thinks he wants a manicure' – and not only does Jeff oblige, but he then has great difficulty in extracting his hand from David's grip. Despite the homosexual subtext – David has just said to Jeff: 'I'll never forget you in that little blue dress' – the use of the motif here seems to me essentially comic.

Perhaps most typical of Hitchcock, however, are those examples which look relatively sincere, but which are compromised by the circumstances under which they occur. In NOTORIOUS, just after Alicia has stolen Alex's key, he enters the room and walks towards her, hands outstretched in a kindly way, and takes hold of her hands. But she is still holding the stolen key, and as Alex starts to kiss each of her hands, she is obliged to throw her arms around him to conceal her deception. In THE PARADINE CASE, Tony becomes quite heated at one point as he asks Mrs Paradine about her relationship with the valet Latour. To block such questions, Mrs Paradine threatens to replace Tony as her counsel, and she shocks him into an apology. She was on the point of leaving the room; now she turns, and walks towards him, her hands outstretched for him to take. The moments are typical of Hitchcock in their complexity. Mrs Paradine was concerned to stop a line of questioning which was dangerous to her; now that she has succeeded, she is prepared to be generous to Tony. Her gesture is calculated in that she knows that Tony is obsessed by her; here she gives him just enough encouragement to keep him in line. Tony, in his turn, has revealed his highly unprofessional feelings for her; as a consequence, he cannot be sure what her gesture means. When he takes her hands, he signals his submission to her, but her enigmatic smile serves to preserve her sense of mystery.

The scene in NOTORIOUS has been admirably analysed by V.F. Perkins:

> [Alex] asks [Alicia] for forgiveness for his expressions of jealousy over Devlin and takes her hand to plant in its palm a formal kiss – a courteous mask on the passion that we know he feels, and, as a mask, a measure of his uncertainty. (He can never quite believe his luck in having Alicia fall for him. Poor Alex.) This gives way to Alicia's gesture of passion as she throws her arms around him in a longing embrace – and thus forestalls his discovery of the purloined key in her other hand. Alex's formality denies passion, Alicia's impulsiveness denies calculation; but we are shown (and shown that we are shown) the formality, the passion, the convincing enactment of impulse and the calculation.
>
> (Perkins 1990: 59)

On the surface, we may take these moments in NOTORIOUS and THE PARADINE CASE to be signalling a woman's duplicity, but it is much more complicated than this; the man is also highly compromised; not least, in NOTORIOUS, because he is also a Nazi. The moments capture the potential deceptiveness of the gestures which pass between Hitchcock's couples.

STAGE FRIGHT goes further, in that two key moments in Eve and Jonathan's relationship are marked by close-ups of their hands. The first occurs in Eve's car early in the film, after Jonathan has told her his story: that he didn't kill the husband of Charlotte Inwood, famous singing star, Charlotte herself did. Bearing Charlotte's bloodstained dress as his evidence against her, he has come to seek Eve's help. As Eve agrees to this, Jonathan clasps her hand in appreciation ('Good old Eve'). But Hitchcock places the close-up of their hands next to the bloodstain on the dress, so that it is as if their pact is sealed with blood. Then, at the end of the film, Eve hides out with Jonathan in a theatrical coach under a stage. Only now does she learn that Jonathan is in fact the murderer and that the story he told her earlier was untrue. The proximity of the two characters echoes their positions in the car and, as Jonathan turns murderous towards Eve, Hitchcock cuts to a close-up of their hands, almost touching because of their closeness. Jonathan's hands move, beginning to assume the strangling gesture; immediately, Eve takes hold of them, and whispers that it's quiet outside so they should escape. Through this calming gesture, Eve deflects the threatened aggression and wins Jonathan's trust; she is thereby able to lead him from the coach to a place where he can be caught. A rare inversion of the usual inflection of the motif, it is a triumph of female control over a dangerous male, captured in the way *she* takes *his* hands.

These two moments highlight Hitchcock's sophistication with motifs. First, they serve to bracket Eve and Jonathan's relationship: when he takes her hand, he is in control, imposing his corrupt will; when she takes his hands, she reverses this and escapes from his power. Second, the placing of the bloodstain next to Jonathan's hand – Eve's is almost invisible – in the first scene is a Hitchcock clue: linking Jonathan with the blood is a way of suggesting his guilt. The link is the same as in PSYCHO, when Norman washes Marion's blood from his hands; in both films, the murderer is being signalled to us long before he is officially identified. (Another revealing link between Jonathan and Norman is mentioned under THE CORPSE.) Third, the key point about the second moment is the way that it suggests mother and child: Eve is treating Jonathan like a little boy, taking him by his hand to lead him, and he – quite unconsciously, one feels – responds in kind and allows himself to be led. And these elements – a duplicitous hand clasp; blood; a woman soothing a dangerous man by mothering him – are, again, those of melodrama.

Although I have only looked at a sample of the many instances in Hitchcock of the hands motif, a significant moral pattern may be observed. On the one hand, the motif serves to illustrate the negative features of Hitchcock's male characters: their impulse to dominate; their bullying; their murderousness; the traces of their guilt. Positive examples of the motif for men are relatively rare, but they may be seen in the hero's hand rescuing the heroine in YOUNG AND INNOCENT and NORTH BY NORTHWEST, and in Mitch's nursing hands.

On the other hand, the motif tells a contrasting story for his female characters. Most frequently, it captures their plight as victims; more rarely, their gestures of concern and the occasional moments when they succeed in triumphing over male domination. Negative examples of the motif for women do occur, but they lack the threatening power of the men's gestures. They usually concern deception: a woman hides something in (or with) her hand as a corollary of hiding her feelings: Mabel concealing the snake bracelet in THE RING; Alicia the key in NOTORIOUS. In VERTIGO, the masquerade 'Madeleine' enacts for Scottie likewise extends to the hands motif: we see a close-up of her gloved hand pointing to a sequoia tree cross-section as she narrates a phoney story about a previous life. Some of the inflections of the motif are less clear-cut in terms of a moral distinction between the sexes: the scenes from NOTORIOUS and THE PARADINE CASE are good examples; there are surely others. Such examples indicate that sexual politics in Hitchcock's films is not a simple matter: there are always

Fig. 31. Still: NORTH BY NORTHWEST: the rescuing hand and the fear of falling. Roger (Cary Grant)
holds on to Eve (Eva Marie Saint) on Mount Rushmore.

exceptions, variations, complications. My basic point remains: that the hands
motif in Hitchcock serves as a pretty good guide to the gender politics of his
films.

After this section was drafted, an article by Sabrina Barton entitled
'Hitchcock's Hands' was published in *Hitchcock Annual* (Barton 2000-01: 47-72).
Following a much more selective sampling of the motif in Hitchcock, she puts
forward a different interpretation of his gender politics, along the lines that
men's hands tend to be shown as capable (Mitch's capturing the escaped canary
in the pet shop: 51; Devlin's driving the car in NOTORIOUS: 53) and women's as
incapable (the heroine's in these scenes; Marnie's at the safe: 58). But the only
film in which she discusses in detail a negative example of male hands, both
bullying and murderous, is SHADOW OF A DOUBT (62-63). She does however,
make some pertinent observations about 'involuntary' hand movements:

> involuntary or simply excessive hand-movements tend to be coded as feminine and/
> or psychotic. Western culture's conflation of femininity not only with sexuality but

also with weak cognition and control may well help to explain why so many male murderers in Hitchcock films are feminized or delicately wrapped in cinema's codified signs for male homosexuality.

(Barton 2000-01: 66)

She then goes on to look at the gestures of Phillip in ROPE, Bruno ('Bruno's hands ... flutter flirtatiously over and around the stiffly withheld body of his object of desire, Guy': 67) and Norman ('Norman's nervous hands constantly fidget and pop candy into his mouth, uncontrolled hands a bodily symptom of uncontrolled desires': 67).

At one point, Barton does qualify her overall argument: 'in Hitchcock's films, more than most, a character's gender neither wholly encompasses nor neatly predicts what her or his relation to hands and agency will be' (65). I would also agree with her general point that Hitchcock's films contain few examples of 'capable' women's hands. Otherwise, however, I feel that the hands motif in Hitchcock suggests much more criticism of the male and sympathy for the female than Barton allows.

Hands and the police

In THE WRONG MAN, when Manny is booked (➤ *Guilt, confession and the police*), he is fingerprinted. This is done in a curious manner: Det. Matthews simply takes charge of Manny's hands. First, he holds Manny's right hand and shakes it, telling him to relax. Then he efficiently goes through the procedure of fingerprinting each finger in turn. Hitchcock cuts rhythmically between close-shots of Manny and of Matthews and close-ups of the manipulated hands: Manny is passive, looking down at his hands; Matthews impassive, carrying out a practised procedure; the shots of the hands, moving to and fro, are brief, almost like flash-cuts. When his first hand has been printed, Manny stares at the stained fingers: this is a point-of-view shot, emphasising the guilt that Manny feels is being imputed to him. But the other close-ups of hands are not point-of-view: the camera is down at desk level and is much closer.

Excited by the idea of fingers being manipulated, Theodore Price incorporates this short sequence into his homosexual reading of the film (Price 1992: 86), and for once he may have something: the very brevity of the shots of what exactly Matthews is doing is oddly suggestive. The close-shots of Manny and Matthews both include a prominent overhead light just next to their faces (➤ LIGHTS for the gay overtones to this motif). But I think the sequence fits more plausibly into the overall sense of dehumanisation Manny feels throughout the long sequence in which the police take over his life. When he later ends up naked in prison (which Price also finds suggestive), this is the end product of this dehumanisation. It's as though the police are systematically taking away his identity. Now that he is a robbery suspect, Manny ceases to be the person he used to be: the police actually look at him as if he were a criminal. The fingerprinting is a key stage in this process. Manny's hands are like a synecdoche for his body and, by extension, his identity.

HEIGHTS AND FALLING

Fig. 32. Still: VERTIGO: the fear of heights. Scottie (James Stewart) suspended from the gutter in the opening scene.

The prevalence of the motif of threatened or actual falling from a height in Hitchcock's films is well known, but I am unaware of any attempt to analyse it. At a relatively basic level it refers to a fear of the abyss: another metaphor for the chaos world. Noting that we are never told how Scottie in VERTIGO is rescued from his predicament at the beginning – suspended from a roof gutter over a terrifying drop to the ground – Robin Wood suggests that: 'The effect is of having him, throughout the film, metaphorically suspended over a great abyss' (Wood 1989: 111). Although VERTIGO is perhaps the only Hitchcock film in which the Falling motif (as I'll abbreviate it) may be seen as operating throughout in such a metaphorical sense, there are plenty of moments when characters find themselves suspended over dangerous falls, and several villains – and, indeed, one heroine – die in falls. I would like to start with the villains.

One feature of the motif is the number of films in which it is Hitchcock's preferred method of 'dealing with' the double, or – whether or not he/she is a double – the person who carried out the crime blamed on the hero. Although Hitchcock said to Truffaut that it was a 'serious error' having the villain rather than the hero hanging from the torch of the Statue of Liberty in SABOTEUR (Truffaut 1968: 122), the outcome – in which the villain falls to his death – is typical. Fry's fall here is echoed in Valerian's off Mount Rushmore in NORTH BY NORTH-WEST: in each case the hero witnesses the death fall of the figure whose crime (the opening act of sabotage; the murder of Townsend) has been blamed on him. This pattern may also be seen in To CATCH A THIEF. Foussard, who planned the crimes (the cat burglaries), is killed in a similar manner; his daughter Danielle, who executed them, is caught by Robie as she slips from a roof gutter, and is held by him over the drop to the ground until she confesses. Likewise in STRANGERS ON A TRAIN: in the climactic fight on the runaway merry-go-round, Bruno tries violently to force Guy off, but is then himself killed in the ensuing crash.

Symbolically it would seem that the villain/double here dies 'carrying away' the guilt attributed to the hero. As Fry clings on with his fingertips, he says to Barry, 'I'll clear you', which is precisely what Robie demands of Danielle. As Bruno lies dying in the merry-go-round wreckage, Guy asks the same of him and, although Bruno refuses, as he dies he releases Guy's cigarette lighter: the signifier of his guilt. The outcome of the climactic struggle between Charlie and her uncle/double on the train in SHADOW OF A DOUBT is similar – Uncle Charlie, attempting to kill his niece, is the one who falls in front of a passing train – and here, too, one could argue that his death 'carries away' Charlie's guilt: her incestuous desire for him. But when Judy in VERTIGO witnesses the fall from the bell tower of Madeleine, her double, the terms are reversed: Judy herself is implicated in Madeleine's murder, and here the fall serves, rather, to imprint her with guilt (➤ THE CORPSE). Another film in which the material is reworked is REAR WINDOW. Although it climaxes with a fight between Jeff and Thorwald, his double, it is Jeff who is thrust out of the window into a dangerous fall. Those endings in which the double/villain dies falling away from the protagonist suggest the shedding of a burden, as if the bad part of the protagonist – or his evil

tormentor – has been despatched into the depths. But Jeff is denied this, which
lends an unresolved quality to the ending here.

Also relevant to some of these examples is Hitchcock's penchant for having
certain *sorts* of villain die in a fall. Fry's climb up and fall from the Statue of
Liberty may be seen as an allusion to his ambitions as a wartime saboteur: the
monument symbolises the very ideals which he has been seeking to destroy.
Similarly in JAMAICA INN: Sir Humphrey, a wrecker of ships, climbs a ship's
rigging and throws himself from the yard-arm. The villain's climactic ascent of
that particular structure is like a symbolic expression of his overweening arro-
gance and pride, so that his fall echoes Lucifer's. A similar idea is in play in the
falls of Valerian and, later, Leonard from Mount Rushmore: again the monument is a symbol of the country which their espionage work has sought to undermine. I would not wish to suggest that Hitchcock is implicating the deity in
casting these villains into the depths, but the religious parallel has certain resonances.

There are even examples where it really does seem as if a villain's death fall
has overtones of divine punishment. When Rowley is killed falling from the
tower of Westminster Cathedral in FOREIGN CORRESPONDENT, this is like a punishment for his sacrilegious use of a church for a murder attempt. Looking at a
newspaper report of the fall, complete with a photograph of the tower and a
helpful dotted line to show the body's trajectory, Johnny comments: 'There but
for the grace of God….' I have described Uncle Charlie in SHADOW OF A DOUBT
as the film's 'dark angel' (➤ BED SCENE); it seems entirely appropriate that he
should die in a fall which annihilates him. Another example is Drayton in THE
MAN WHO KNEW TOO MUCH (1955), whose gun goes off, killing him, when Ben
knocks him downstairs. Not only is Drayton Ben's dark double (➤ DOUBLES),
but at one point he impersonates a clergyman, so that his death as he falls could
be seen as punishment for that crime. However, it would be difficult to argue
that Tracy's fall through the glass dome of the British Museum in BLACKMAIL
belongs with either of these groups of examples. It functions, rather, as a critique of the 'hero': Frank's relentless pursuit of Tracy makes the latter seem like
a scapegoat for Alice's killing of Crewe. Here the villain's fall contributes to this
film's lack of resolution (➤ PAINTERS). Ultimately, the fall is ironic: it leaves the
hero and heroine suspended over a *future* metaphorical abyss, with the strong
possibility that her guilt and his cover-up will eventually be found out.

In *The Interpretation of Dreams*, Freud distinguishes between dreams of falling
over and dreams of falling from a height. The former he identifies as sexual: 'If a
woman dreams of falling, it almost invariably has a sexual sense: she is imagining herself as a "fallen woman"' (Freud 1900/1954: 202). The latter, he suggests,
must in part stem from childhood sensations of being swung around, or
dropped and caught, by an adult. He mentions that, whereas such childhood

games frequently give rise to sexual feelings, in an adult's dreams these feelings are transformed into anxiety. But he admits that he does not know what other meanings become attached to these sensations when they do return in adulthood (271-73). It is this second type of example with which the Falling motif is concerned.

If Freud's theories do have relevance to examples of the motif in Hitchcock, those instances where the villain threatens the protagonist with a fall would seem to be likely candidates. In such cases, the villain could be seen in psychic terms as occupying the place of the bad parent, someone who does not merely fail to catch the child, but deliberately tries to make him or her fall. Some of the examples already mentioned may indeed be read this way. In FOREIGN CORRE-SPONDENT, Rowley's status as bad father figure is in fact intimated just before his murderous attack on Johnny. He holds a schoolboy over the drop to the ground in a highly dangerous manner, and the boy's cap flies off as an indication of what could happen to the boy himself. In REAR WINDOW, we could see Thorwald as the bad father figure who 'drops' the hero and the police as good father figures who rush to catch him. In NORTH BY NORTHWEST, when Leonard tries to make Roger and Eve fall from Mount Rushmore he is acting on behalf of Vandamm, the bad father figure; the couple are then saved by the intervention of the Professor, the 'good' father figure. In SHADOW OF A DOUBT, we could even imagine that, when Charlie was a little girl, her uncle had actually played the relevant childhood games with her. Moreover, as noted under HANDS (and discussed in detail by Rothman: 1986: 237-42), the climactic struggle between Charlie and her uncle is highly sexualised; it thus incorporates the other aspect of Freud's analysis: the transformation of the pleasurable sexual feelings of childhood into (here extreme) anxiety. Only in STRANGERS ON A TRAIN does a different dynamic seem to be in play.

Another example which fits such a Freudian reading is in REBECCA, where evil mother figure Mrs Danvers tries to tempt the heroine into committing suicide by jumping from a high window. Finally, THE MAN WHO KNEW TOO MUCH (1934) provides an explicit example, because a real parent/child relationship is involved. At the climax, the teenage Betty is on the roof being menaced by Ramon, and it is her mother Jill, in the street below, who saves her: when the police marksman has a failure of nerve, Jill takes his rifle and shoots Ramon. Here the good parent really does step in to save her child from a threatened fall at the hands of a malevolent parent figure.

All these examples suggest the relevance of Freud's theories to the fear of falling in Hitchcock; in other words, here too the roots of the fear go back to childhood. That the fear is associated with the unconscious is indicated by the way in which it is visualised in nightmares (Scottie in VERTIGO), hallucinations (Lina in SUSPICION), dreamlike film images (Mrs Verloc in SABOTAGE), hallucinatory flashbacks to childhood (J.B. in SPELLBOUND) and elliptical flashbacks to murder (Judy in VERTIGO). Behind these oneiric images, again and again, is a bad parent figure, but the images frequently also suggest the eruption of the protagonist's (repressed) guilt.

There are also two instances in which it is the hero who threatens a young woman with such a fall, which inevitably casts a disturbing light on these particular heroes. Because Danielle is a villain, Robie may feel that his insistence that she confesses before he hauls her to safety is excusable. Nevertheless, there is a sadistic edge to his demand, which is distinctly unsettling. The other example is even more sinister. At the climax of SUSPICION, Johnnie drives at breakneck speed along a corniche, and the passenger-seat door flies open, exposing Lina to a terrifying fall down the cliff. Johnnie does not slacken speed at all, but lunges at Lina, as if trying to push her out of the car. When, in response to her terror, he does finally stop the car, he tries to convince her that he was merely trying to close the door. That is not what his actions looked like: they looked like attempted murder. Although there is perhaps a degree of ambiguity in his lunges, I would maintain that this is indeed another example of Johnnie's murderousness towards Lina, and that his feeble attempts to explain his behaviour to her in the ensuing scene (➤ GUILT AND CONFESSION) are simply further examples of his lies.

The various manifestations of the hero's fear of heights in VERTIGO provide the most elaborate examples, in Hitchcock, of the Falling motif. Scottie's acrophobia can be interpreted in a number of ways, but whatever the reading – e.g. associating it with femininity (Modleski 1988: 90), impotence (Price 1992: 140), or the fear of 'falling in love' (Leitch 1991: 202) – the common denominator is a flaw in his masculine identity. In other words, the motif here is linked to a psychological weakness in the hero which has complex resonances. I discuss under STAIRCASES the sexual symbolism of Scottie's fears: it is one of the very few Hitchcock films in which ascents – or, in Scottie's case, the failure to complete ascents – may clearly be seen to have sexual overtones. VERTIGO may also be included within the parent figure/child figure paradigm of the Falling motif. In the opening scene, the policeman who falls to his death whilst trying to save Scottie (as he is suspended from the gutter) may be seen, symbolically, as a father figure. In the second scene, Scottie sets out to try and lick his acrophobia with Midge, who is explicitly designated as a mother figure. But even though she comforts Scottie when his attempt fails, Midge is unable to help with his deeper fears. Haunted by his acrophobia, Scottie becomes a man adrift in the world and, although by the end of the film he seems to be cured of his vertigo, it is at the cost of the life of the woman he loved.

SPELLBOUND is surprisingly similar to VERTIGO. The traumatic incidents which have resulted in J.B.'s amnesia – accidentally killing his brother as a child; being shot down during World War II over Rome; witnessing Dr Edwardes go over a precipice – are connected by the experience of falling. The moments in the film when he then suffers the threatened return of his repressed memories are complementarily connected by the presence of Constance and, implicitly, the threat of her sexuality (➤ *Food and sex*). Here, too, the film forges a link between the hero's threatened masculinity and a (repressed) fear of falling. But SPELLBOUND, unlike VERTIGO, allows the hero to work through his fears to a happy ending. As he recreates the circumstances which produced his amnesia – skiing down a mountain-side towards a precipice – he is accompanied by Constance. As they approach the precipice, J.B. remembers the childhood trauma, when he slid down a sloping wall to impale his brother on some railings (visualised as a flashback). He grabs Constance so that they fall down, averting the threat of going over the precipice. Read in the light of the earlier examples, we can now see the crucial importance of Constance: she represents the mother (figure) who, in the childhood incident, was not present to grab the young hero and so prevent the fatal accident.

In SPELLBOUND and VERTIGO, the Falling motif charts a psychological flaw in the hero, a flaw which may be related to his sexual anxieties. Both films may in fact be seen to have an implicit Oedipal structure: in the former the hero is 'saved' by the mother figure; in the latter, he is left desolate by the power of the father figure (➤ STAIRCASES). Again, the basic Freudian structure underpins the workings of the motif. But what about Judy in VERTIGO, who is the only heroine to die in a fall? I would like to integrate a discussion of her situation with an examination of four further examples for the heroines, grouping them in two pairs.

SABOTAGE and SUSPICION. In SABOTAGE, shocked and appalled that her husband has caused the death of her brother, Mrs Verloc goes into their cinema and sees part of a Disney film, WHO KILLED COCK ROBIN? In the extract, Robin is shot with an arrow, and the camera accompanies his body as it falls vertically from its perch. This imagery is then echoed in the moment in SUSPICION when Lina first suspects that her husband is a prospective murderer: we see her fantasised image of him pushing his friend Beaky off a cliff, and, again, the camera then accompanies the body in its vertical fall. In both cases, the fall itself seems to express the terrifying plunge in the heroine's own feelings, capturing the emotional shock of being precipitated into the metaphorical abyss of the chaos world. Mrs Verloc returns to the meal table and kills her husband (➤ *Food and murder*). Lina merely faints – but then, at the climax of the film, finds herself threatened with the very fate she had earlier imagined for Beaky.

The Cock Robin sequence in SABOTAGE is the subject of a close analysis by Susan Smith (2000: 11-14): she points out the double association of Robin's death – as a reminder to Mrs Verloc of Stevie's death; as an anticipation of her own killing of Verloc – and then goes on to discuss Mrs Verloc's own position within this fantasy. Noting that the cartoon murder takes place within an implicit sexual triangle, she relates this to the Oedipal overtones of the 'triangle' Mrs Verloc herself had been in, with Stevie as the son figure, eliminated by the 'jealous' husband. Overall, she suggests that the cartoon murder allows the expression of 'previously unacknowledged desires on [Mrs Verloc's] part' (14). Lina's fantasy in SUSPICION likewise seems to express her unconscious wishes, suggesting on the one hand that she herself wants to get rid of Beaky, on the other that she identifies with him at this moment, masochistically imagining herself as Johnnie's victim. Here the murdered, falling figure is not the charismatic son-figure but the unexciting father figure (the film makes a number of links between Beaky and Lina's father), so that the fantasy also hints at Lina's unconscious wish for patricide. In both these examples, the motif is condensed into an image which seems to have surged up from the heroine's unconscious. And in both cases, this gives us a sharp insight into her darker impulses.

These two examples may also be related to key aspects of the way the motif functions in VERTIGO. Whereas the heroine in these films sees – or imagines – the fall as happening to another figure, in Scottie's nightmare in VERTIGO, he himself becomes the falling figure. Under THE CORPSE, I argue that this arises out of his (unconscious) identification with 'Madeleine', an experience so disturbing that it precipitates his nervous breakdown, which may be seen as an internalised form of the chaos world. But if Scottie's plight is serious enough, Judy's is even worse. The moment when she sees Madeleine fall is likewise the equivalent of the imaginary falls in SABOTAGE and SUSPICION, but Madeleine is a real victim. For Mrs Verloc and Lina, it's as if the image of the falling body, as a metaphor for her own feelings, carries her down emotionally to a point where she can confront her inner demons. This leads to a highly traumatic climax – the killing of Verloc; the reckless car drive along the corniche – but the heroine does at least survive. Judy is never given this chance. Her climactic scene with Scottie in the bell tower is the equivalent of Lina and Johnnie's crisis on the corniche, but on this occasion the outcome is bleak: the heroine really does fall to her death.

YOUNG AND INNOCENT and MARNIE. In YOUNG AND INNOCENT, Erica, a chief constable's daughter, is fleeing with Robert (wanted for murder) from the police, when her car sinks into some old mine workings, almost taking her down with it. I have discussed this moment elsewhere, suggesting that 'The ground giving way under Erica ... may be seen, psychically, as the wrath of the father threatening her for what she's been doing' (Walker M. 1999: 192). In MARNIE, Marnie's fall from her horse Forio is caused by her panic at the sight of the bloody murder of a fox by the hounds. But the fox hunt occurs just after she has re-encountered Strutt, the man she stole from at the beginning of the film, and who she knows will try to seek revenge. The hunt followed by the savaging of the fox is like a displacement of Marnie's anxieties about Strutt, and her fall – which leads to the death of Forio – seems a further expression of her terror. As if to emphasise the nature of the underlying fear, when Erica gets home she is summoned before her father to account for herself and, when Marnie gets home, Mark is still trying to appease Strutt. In both these examples, the (threatened) fall would thus seem to arise from the heroine's fear of patriarchal punishment for her transgressive behaviour. Although Marnie's fall could also be read in different terms – as in some sense a reworking of her repressed childhood trauma, climaxing with her killing Forio as she killed the sailor – it is the fall as punishment notion I would like to stress here.

The heroine's fears in these examples may again be related to VERTIGO. In Scottie's case, Elster is the patriarchal figure, and Scottie's punishment at his hands – implicitly, for loving the woman Scottie thought was Elster's wife – extends far beyond Elster's disappearance from the narrative. The extent of Elster's domination is discussed under STAIRCASES, where I argue that even Judy's death at the end of the film may be seen as an example of his power. Judy's fall to her death is indeed like her punishment, and here Scottie is acting in the place of the patriarchal figure, bitterly blaming her for what she did. In YOUNG AND INNOCENT and MARNIE, the hero is on the heroine's side; in the former, saving her from the threatened fall into the depths of the mine; in the latter, standing up for her against the vengeful patriarchal figure. But in VERTIGO, the hero condemns her, and fails to save her when she falls.

It is perhaps not surprising that almost all the examples of the Falling motif in other films lead to VERTIGO. Theodore Price makes the valid point that 'when Hitch has a really favorite recurrent theme, it will eventually have a Film of Its Own' (Price 1992: 50). But there remains one final example which would seem at first sight to offer a radically different perspective on the motif, because it concerns someone who has no fear of heights: Fane in MURDER! Fane is a trapeze artist, but on the one occasion when we see his act, he ends by hanging himself, an action which Hitchcock films like a brutally truncated fall. However, there is an additional feature here, since Fane's trapeze act is also sexualised. William Rothman writes:

> The key to this sequence, which establishes a Hitchcock paradigm, is that it images Fane's act in sexual terms. The passage details Fane's passion and ecstasy as, absorbed in his act, he appears on the threshold, then in the grips, of orgasm.
>
> (Rothman 1986: 89)

During Fane's act, he seems to have two visions: of Sir John's face and of Diana's. The exact status of the former is, as Rothman notes, ambiguous, but I think we should read it as Fane imagining himself being watched by Sir John:

the latter's posture matches the way he is actually standing in the circus ring below. By contrast, Diana's image – looking into the camera, i.e. Fane's eyes – is pure fantasy. And so, when Fane then finishes his act and hangs himself, this would seem to be a response to the impossibility of the fantasy.

Although Fane is a villain, responsible for the crime for which Diana has been sentenced to death, his suicide is far more powerful and disturbing than any other villain's suicide in Hitchcock (➤ PUBLIC DISTURBANCES for its impact on the circus audience). The nature of Fane's performance – which I see as more anguished than Rothman does – together with the imagery which accompanies it, suggests why. He enters the circus ring in a feathered outfit which makes him look like a woman, but then 'opens his cloak and reveals himself as a man-wo-man' (Rothman 1986: 89). But what might in another context have been a cele-bration of androgyny turns instead into a lament for the irreconcilable tensions it has generated in Fane. The hallucinated image of Diana emphasises that it is only in fantasy that he can 'possess' the woman whom he says that he loves. His suicide may thus also be seen as a protest at his condition: a public statement of the impossibility of living like this. Diana has declared to Sir John that to love Fane is impossible because he is a half-caste, and there is also an ambiguity around his sexuality: the coding of the period would clearly suggest that he is gay. In other words, within the society of the time, he is inevitably condemned to be an outcast. Whereas the death of Sir Humphrey in JAMAICA INN – the only other suicide in this motif – is presented as that of a madman (➤ EXHIBITIONISM / VOYEURISM), Fane seems almost a tragic figure. For a villain, he is also unusually mourned: as his body is carried into his dressing room, a young woman, holding his feathered headdress, sobs in the fore-ground. Accordingly, I would suggest that, once again, we have a connection with VERTIGO. Fane can be related to both Scottie *and* Judy: to the former through the sense of being haunted by a condition which condemns him to loneliness; to the latter through the corrosive guilt of loving someone whom he/she has falsely implicated in another woman's death. The trapeze climax of MURDER! may thus be seen as yet another equivalent of the bell tower climax of VERTIGO, and here the parallel is both structural and emotional. In both cases, the scene lays out the impossibility for these figures of a happy ending, and captures the poignancy of their failure and loss.

Hitchcock's villains other than Fane function within the Falling motif primar-ily in relation to the hero or heroine: the villain's death by falling, or his sym-bolic role as a malevolent parent figure, is significant mainly insofar as it says something about the protagonist's psyche. This sense that the motif serves above all to express the inner world of the protagonist is crucial. For a heroine, the motif usually marks a moment of dizzying fall into the chaos world; either one from which she can, ultimately, rescue herself, or (Judy) one which haunts her until she herself dies. For a hero, the motif tends to function as a measure of his mastery. Those who save the heroines from a threatened fall – in YOUNG AND INNOCENT, NORTH BY NORTHWEST and, after a nasty pause, TO CATCH A THIEF – demonstrate their potency as heroes. But in SPELLBOUND and VERTIGO, the motif, elaborated throughout the film, serves to express deep anxieties in the hero, anxieties which, at root, are sexual. It is in these two films, especially VERTIGO, that we can see the richness and complexity of the motif: the sheer density of the implicit meanings. The bell tower climax of VERTIGO, where these meanings find their fullest expression, is one of the most powerful and disturbing scenes in all cinema.

Heights, falling and the police

When someone falls, or is threatened with falling, the police or their equivalents are more often than not present. In THE MANXMAN (Kate's suicide attempt), REAR WINDOW and NORTH BY NORTHWEST, they save the heroine and/or hero from a potentially fatal fall. In SABOTEUR, they help reunite hero and heroine after the villain's fall. In THE MAN WHO KNEW TOO MUCH (the assassin's death in both versions), JAMAICA INN and TO CATCH A THIEF, they are witnesses to the villain's death or, in TO CATCH A THIEF, her confession. In BLACKMAIL, YOUNG AND INNOCENT and STRANGERS ON A TRAIN, they are responsible for the pursuit – and, in the last film, the chaos – which led to the fall, which casts them as harassing rather than helpful, but only in BLACKMAIL is their mistake not recognised by the end of the film.

On all these occasions, the presence of the police as witnesses emphasises their status as the figures who oversee the restoration of order. In FOREIGN CORRESPONDENT, the witnessing role is assumed by two nuns, who cross themselves at the sight of Rowley's dead body. This reinforces the Christian theme implicit in this fall. More rarely, the police actively intervene, thereby counteracting the malevolent villain by acting as good parent figures, seeking to protect the beleaguered hero and/or heroine (➤ ENDINGS AND THE POLICE). Accordingly, the death of the father figure policeman in the opening scene of VERTIGO depicts a world which is, for Hitchcock, seriously awry. It is not surprising that, when the heroine apparently falls to her death in a like manner, Scottie should succumb to the death drive.

HOMOSEXUALITY

Fig. 33. Still: ROPE: Homosexuality. As Rupert (James Stewart) produces the rope, Phillip (Farley Granger) half hides behind Brandon (John Dall).

Critical positions

There are widely differing opinions about the prevalence of homosexuality in Hitchcock, and it would be useful, first, to look at what are probably the two extremes: the essentially conservative assessment of Robin Wood in *Hitchcock's Films Revisited* (1989), and the far more radical one put forward by Theodore Price in *Hitchcock and Homosexuality* (1992). In his chapter 'The Murderous Gays: Hitchcock's Homophobia', Robin Wood begins by looking at the claim that many of Hitchcock's psychopaths are coded as gay (Wood 1989: 336-57). In certain cases – Fane in MURDER!, Mrs Danvers in REBECCA, Brandon and Phillip in ROPE and Bruno in STRANGERS ON A TRAIN – Wood is prepared to go along with this; in others – Uncle Charlie in SHADOW OF A DOUBT, Norman Bates in PSYCHO and Rusk in FRENZY – he questions it. However, he agrees that there are strong links between all these characters. In particular, he suggests that most of them are 'fascinating, insidiously attractive Hitchcock villains who constantly threaten to "take over" the films… not only as the center of interest but even, for all their monstrous actions, as the center of sympathy' (347-48). This emphasises Hitchcock's ambivalence about such figures and, by extension, about homosexuality, and Wood explores the complex resonances this sets up in the films. He also discusses in detail the Brandon and Phillip relationship, and analyses ROPE in terms of both the attitude towards homosexuality at the time and the problems of representing gayness under the Production Code (349-57).

Leonard in NORTH BY NORTHWEST is another murderous gay, and although Wood does not mention him here, he refers to the character's homosexuality in his original chapter on this film (Wood 1989: 133). In fact, Hitchcock cues us to connect the Vandamm-Leonard relationship with the Guy-Bruno one when he repeats the direct punch at the camera delivered by the seemingly straight character at the gay one. In each case – Guy hitting Bruno after the public disturbance at Senator Morton's party; Vandamm hitting Leonard when the latter exposes Eve's treachery – it's as if the (officially) straight character is angrily warding off the sexual threat of the gay one.

Robin Wood also includes the valet Latour in THE PARADINE CASE as a character who is probably gay, but then comments that, if he is, 'he is certainly the only gay character in Hitchcock who is neither neurotic nor villainous' (Wood 1989: 346). I discuss Latour later, but I also believe that he is not the only positive gay character in Hitchcock. When Lina and Johnnie in SUSPICION go for dinner at the novelist Isobel Sedbusk's house, there are two other guests. One is Isobel's brother Bertram; the other is a woman who is dressed in a manner which is clear 1940s coding for a lesbian: jacket, tie, tightly drawn back hair. It is fairly clear that she is not Bertram's companion. Isobel calls her 'Phil' (in the credits, she's Phyllis Swinghurst) and she in turn calls Isobel 'Izzy'; surely Hitchcock is implying that the two are a (completely unneurotic) gay couple.

Although Robin Wood's discussion of homosexuality in Hitchcock is careful and considered, he seems a little cautious in his overall estimate of the number of such figures. Theodore Price, by contrast, is quite reckless. Setting aside the issue of his book's many mistakes and annoying repetitiveness, the real problem with Price's argument is its insistence. Any sexual reluctance or inhibition on the part of a character (SPELLBOUND, REAR WINDOW, MARNIE, TORN CURTAIN) signifies gayness. (Because I am summarising points which are scattered and repeated throughout the book, noting page numbers here would be very messy. The examples can readily be found by using Price's extremely thorough index.) If a man comes from an English upper-class background (THE LODGER, DOWNHILL, EASY VIRTUE) or even just speaks in a posh voice (Crewe in BLACK-MAIL), he is effeminate/campy/gay; likewise if a man becomes dizzy (YOUNG AND INNOCENT, SPELLBOUND, Commodore Gill in STAGE FRIGHT, THE WRONG MAN, VERTIGO), this signifies effeminacy. Unlike Robin Wood, Price has no qualms about identifying Uncle Charlie, Norman Bates and Rusk as gay. He is even more alarming on what signifies that a woman is a whore, which seems to be either that she has had sex at some point in her life or that she is a model, showgirl, actress, barmaid or 'paid companion'. Thus the heroine of REBECCA is described as an 'apprentice prostitute' and Mrs Van Hopper as her madam (Price 1992: 159-63), and Marnie is a lesbian who used to be a prostitute (211-25). In some of these cases, Price may have a point, but in most of them he is simply making nonsense of the complexities of the characters concerned. For example, there are good arguments for thinking that Marnie could be a lesbian, but extending this to insisting that she is also a prostitute is simply ludicrous.

One of Price's more plausible arguments concerns I CONFESS. He begins with the premise that 'the priesthood is a metaphor-euphemism for homosexuality' (Price 1992: 270), and goes on to suggest that the details of the plot frequently lend themselves to such an interpretation. In particular, he seeks to link specific elements in I CONFESS to equivalent elements in each of what he calls the 'Touchstone films', i.e. the four Hitchcock films which clearly do have a homo-sexual theme: MURDER!, ROPE, STRANGERS ON A TRAIN and THE PARADINE CASE (271-73). Although some of the imputed links are dubious and others are simply examples of Hitchcock's authorship, applicable to his films in general, there are nevertheless enough intriguing correspondences for Price to build a suggestive case for a homosexual subtext to the characterisation of Father Logan and the tensions between him and the sacristan Keller. My own position, more cautious than Price's, is mentioned under LIGHT(S).

I am entirely in sympathy with Price's project, but much less happy with its execution. Despite the moments of insight in the book, overall it is simply too undisciplined. Time and again, Price flattens out nuances, casts aside qualifica-tions and thereby undermines what is at heart a very compelling case: that there are indeed strong traces of a homosexual subtext in a significant number of Hitchcock films.

With the development of Queer Theory, there have been several publications over recent years which look much more rigorously than Price at the issue of Hitchcock and homosexuality. For example, *Out in Culture: Gay, Lesbian and Queer Essays on Popular Culture* (1995) includes a 'Dossier on Hitchcock' subsec-tion (Creekmur and Doty 1995: 183-281), with essays on REBECCA, STRANGERS ON A TRAIN and MARNIE, together with a reprint of Robin Wood's 'Murderous

Gays' chapter. I would like to look at just one of these essays, Lucretia Knapp's 'The Queer Voice in MARNIE' (Knapp 1995: 262-81), since it offers a far more thoughtful approach to the film than Price.

In the *Bed Scene* in Part I, I suggest that there is a lesbian reading of Marnie's childhood trauma: first, it may be seen as a version of the Oedipal crime in which the daughter kills the father figure; second, it's as if the killing occurred so that Marnie would not be displaced from her mother's bed. Under KEYS AND HANDBAGS, I also mention Marnie's interest in the handbag of Susan, Mark's secretary. Knapp also refers to this scene, drawing attention to the looks that pass between Marnie and Susan as well their mutual interest in the handbag (Knapp 1995: 270). She also points out that, in the same scene, Marnie averts her gaze when Lil, Mark's sister-in-law, first enters and looks at her. Lil then asks Mark 'Who's the dish?' (275).

'I will not argue that Marnie is a lesbian character, although her resistance to compulsory heterosexuality could … define her as such' (Knapp 1995: 265). In fact, I believe that Knapp makes quite a compelling case for such an argument, focusing in particular on what goes on between Marnie and Lil. It is Lil who steps in and wakes Marnie after her nightmare at Wykwyn. When Marnie's horse Forio is badly injured, it is Lil who takes the 'male role' and offers to shoot him for Marnie (271). Indeed, I would go further than Knapp in the second scene. It begins with a struggle between Marnie and an older woman, Mrs Turpin – Marnie is trying to force her way into Mrs Turpin's house to get a gun – which echoes that between Marnie's mother and the sailor in Marnie's childhood trauma, and it ends with a direct parallel between Marnie's shooting of Forio and her childhood killing of the sailor: her response, 'There, there now.' In other words, Lil arrives into a part re-enactment of the childhood trauma as someone who seeks to protect Marnie from the awful responsibility of having to kill again. But it is crucial to Marnie's cure that she does kill again, and so she tears the gun from Lil and herself shoots Forio. This scene, in which all three characters are women, thus prepares the way for the film's climactic scene, when the struggle between Mark and her mother prompts Marnie to recall the childhood trauma (➤ *Bed Scene* in Part I). Heterosexual dynamics are restored, but only after 'passing through' a homosexual version.

Gay undercurrents

There are two main ways in which homosexuality is registered in Hitchcock's films: some of his characters are coded as gay, and some of the same-sex relationships in his films have a charged erotic undertow, which may remain at a

suppressed or playful level, but which is subtextually suggestive. Such gay undercurrents are in fact quite common in his films, and I have left my comments
about many of these examples under other motifs, rather than grouping them
here. In part, this is to draw attention to the ways in which aspects of certain
motifs seem to 'support' the homosexual theme in Hitchcock's work. The most
significant of these motifs is LIGHT(S). As well as Keller in I Confess, there I
mention Mrs Danvers, Bruno and Phillip, and discuss the rather more oblique
gay undercurrents in Secret Agent and Jamaica Inn. Other motifs where gay
characters and undercurrents in Hitchcock are discussed include *Cigarette case/
lighter* (Bruno and Guy) and the *Bed Scene* (Mrs Danvers) in Part I; CONFINED
SPACES (Secret Agent), THE CORPSE (Brandon and Phillip); BED SCENE
and KEYS AND HANDBAGS (Bruno), ENTRY THROUGH A WINDOW and
HEIGHTS AND FALLING (Fane) and DOUBLES (Guy and Bruno).

One gay character who has received inadequate attention in the Hitchcock
literature is Latour. Accordingly, I would like to use him as my main example
here. First, the evidence for his gayness. When he visits Tony late at night in the
Lake District Inn, there are clear hints in the dialogue.

> Tony: What can I do for you?
> Latour: It's not a question very easy to answer.

Tony then establishes that Latour watched the inn for some time to ascertain
which was his room, waited until the household had gone to bed and then
came in the back way in order not to disturb anyone else. He asks why Latour
didn't come earlier:

> Latour: I didn't care to come earlier, sir.
> Tony: Why not?
> Latour: I leave that to you, sir.

Tony suddenly becomes concerned about the fact that Latour is not his witness
in the Paradine Case, and tries to insist that, when he went earlier that day to
Hindley Hall, it was not to see Latour himself:

> Tony: I came on you purely by chance.
> Latour: But you wanted to come on me.

This last is the most outrageous *double entendre* in the scene, and it provokes
Tony into a heated denial. It's as if the (presumably straight) Tony is hastily
warding off the increasingly sexual tenor of Latour's responses. The film obviously could not make this explicit, but Latour's comments in the scene are
charged with the sense that he has come to see Tony in this manner at this time
to test whether Tony's interest in him is sexual. When Tony then refers to Mrs
Paradine as his 'former mistress', Latour's reaction is again telling:

Fig. 34. Still: THE PARADINE CASE: Homosexuality. Latour (Louis Jourdan) visits Tony (Gregory Peck) in the Lake District Inn.

Latour: Beg pardon, sir. She was not my mistress. Col. Paradine was my master... I would never have served a woman. It is not in my character to do that.

The dialogue in the scene is remarkable enough, but it is not all. Latour is wearing a leather jacket, and even though his comments are careful, his manner is poised: he is not disturbed by the idea of a clandestine rendezvous. Tony, by contrast, moves around restlessly, as if seeking to cope with a situation he is finding increasingly uncomfortable. During this, Hitchcock's camera performs some very striking movements. Using the low-hanging central light in the room as a sort of visual anchor, the camera sweeps around in a manner most untypical of the era. In *American Cinematographer* September 1948, Bart Sheridan mentions how Hitchcock took advantage of a newly invented crab dolly (Sheridan 1948: 304-305 & 314). Although the shot Sheridan describes here did not survive as an extended take into the finished film (which was cut by Selznick by eighteen minutes), the scene between Tony and Latour shows the virtuosity of Hitchcock's use of the dolly. The emphasis on the central light is also highly suggestive. Throughout the first half of the scene, it is an insistent visual presence in almost every shot. But in the second half, when we deduce (again, this is necessarily coded) that Latour has concluded that Tony's purpose in wanting to see him was not sexual, the light is no longer used in this way. This is one of the strongest examples in Hitchcock's work of the association of 'lights' with (coded) homosexuality (➢ LIGHTS).

There are several later references in THE PARADINE CASE which corroborate the coding of Latour as gay. During the court case, both his devotion to Col. Paradine and his indifference to women are repeatedly stressed. Unfortunately, like so many gay characters in the movies, Latour, like Fane, ends by committing suicide. However, just as I feel that Fane's suicide has a tragic dimension (➢ HEIGHTS AND FALLING), so the reasons behind Latour's merit a closer look. Theodore Price's reading is that, 'As a woman-hating homosexual [Latour] cannot live with the knowledge and memory of having gone to bed with a woman... and so he kills himself' (Price 1992: 13). That is not how I see the film. As the trial of Mrs Paradine for her husband's murder proceeds, Tony keeps trying to implicate Latour in his master's death. Latour denies this vehemently, but Tony's insinuations do finally provoke him into admitting that he had sex with Mrs Paradine and that Col. Paradine found out. But Latour blames Mrs Paradine: she made him disloyal to his master and he suffered agonies of remorse. Although we are dealing with competing versions of the past, this seems the more plausible one. So Latour must have realised that Mrs Paradine poisoned her husband in the hope of being with him, Latour. Hence his comment 'I can't live with the memory of what I've done' refers not to sex with a woman, but to the consequences of the sex, which led to the murder of the man he loved. The next day, we hear that he has committed suicide. This in turn causes Mrs Paradine to admit on the stand that she loved Latour and that she did indeed poison her husband, and to vilify Tony for his treatment of Latour (➢ GUILT AND CONFESSION).

I would argue that Latour commits suicide out of a sense of loss and of guilt at that loss: it was his own failure of integrity which initiated the chain of events which led to his beloved master's murder. This is quite a different reading from Price's. Its focus is only secondarily on a rejection of heterosexuality; it is mainly an affirmation – if such a term can be used of a suicide – of the intensity of his love for his master. That Latour commits suicide at all is a problem, but at least he does so for 'honourable' reasons.

Espionage and the look

Theodore Price ends his book with a chapter on Torn Curtain, which he seeks to enlist into his thesis by arguing that Michael's journey to East Germany is a metaphor for crossing over to homosexuality (Price 1992: 367-80). He follows Donald Spoto in assuming that Hitchcock's wish to base the story on the Guy Burgess and Donald MacLean defections of 1951 would require a plot involving 'unrequited love and homosexuality' (Spoto 1988: 487). However, Spoto had already tweaked Hitchcock's comments to Truffaut (Truffaut 1968: 259): it was Mrs MacLean's story Hitchcock was interested in and MacLean was not (so far as we know) homosexual, though Burgess was. Moreover, although with the casting of Paul Newman and Julie Andrews, Spoto notes 'the homosexual sub-theme had to be dropped' (Spoto 1988: 488), Price tries to insist that it is nevertheless present in the subtext. He gets himself into a terrible muddle. First, he states that the defection ends the forthcoming marriage between Michael and Sarah (Price 1992: 371). But Michael does not defect, and, as I argue under THE MACGUFFIN, he comes out of East Germany with a secret formula which will make him potent again (what does Price think Michael and Sarah are doing behind the blanket at the end?) Second, Price suggests that Gromek is the equivalent of the homosexual blackmailer: the Bruno figure. But Gromek is suspicious of Michael, not convinced that he is a genuine defector – read, a homosexual – and Price has to admit that Gromek is right (373). Yet he still interprets the murder of Gromek as a scene of displaced homosexual rape (374-75). It is perhaps possible to argue that what we have here are fragments of a once coherent subtext. In the film as it stands, they fail to jell at any level whatever.

Nevertheless, although Price has picked the wrong film, I think that he is on to something significant. Under CONFINED SPACES, I quote Marty Roth: 'the espionage thriller [is] a genre that is always on the verge of a homosexual subtext' (Roth 1992: 37), and I then discuss the bathroom scene in Secret Agent along such lines. I would like here to look at a particular feature of Hitchcock's spy movies: male-male voyeurism. When a man spies on other men, there frequently tend to be homosexual undercurrents to what he sees, especially if he looks through an optical device. Two early examples: Hannay in The 39 Steps looking through opera glasses during the Palladium climax, and Ashenden in Secret Agent watching through an observatory telescope at Caypor's murder on a mountain. What Hannay sees is Professor Jordan arranging a secret rendezvous with Mr Memory. But when Mr Memory then starts to talk about the organisation of spies called the '39 Steps', Jordan shoots him: this is not something one mentions in public. In SECRET AGENT, Ashenden knows that the General is going to murder Caypor, and he has deliberately removed himself from their company out of a sudden distaste for the matter. But he cannot resist watching. He looks through the telescope twice and, as in THE 39 STEPS, we share his point of view. On the first occasion, the General, standing behind Caypor, jokes with him, placing his hand on Caypor's upper arm; on the second, the General repeats the gesture in order to push Caypor off the mountain. In other words, what Ashenden sees is a distinctly camp man come up behind another man and lull him into a false sense of security in order to assault him.

Although these are both oblique, even tentative examples, they illustrate the principle. On the relatively few occasions in Hitchcock where a man spies on other men and we share his point of view, the scene he witnesses tends to have a suppressed sexual charge. Either it hints at a certain sort of intimacy, or it suggests a displacement from a sexual encounter. Nevertheless, we should be careful about how we read such overtones. In 'Masculinity as Spectacle', Steve Neale argues that, when male spectators look at men in the cinema:

> the erotic elements involved ... have constantly to be repressed and disavowed. Were this not the case, mainstream cinema would have openly to come to terms with the male homosexuality it so assiduously seeks to denigrate or deny. As it is, male homosexuality is constantly present as an undercurrent, as a potentially troubling aspect of many films and genres.
>
> (Neale 1983: 15)

These scenes in Hitchcock go a stage further: a man is spying on another man within the diegesis. In such examples, the repressed eroticism to which Neale refers 'returns'. In SECRET AGENT, one could perhaps link this scene with others (➤ CONFINED SPACES) and argue that it is part of a developed homosexual subtext around the hero. It would be more difficult to make this case in THE 39 STEPS. The overtones arise, rather, from the way that Hitchcock has staged the scenes, and they could be used as striking illustrations of Neale's thesis about the sexualisation of 'the look' in the cinema.

Since both these witnessed scenes culminate in a murder, they also support Robin Wood's position: even heavily coded (unconsciously registered?) homosexuality would seem to be associated with murderousness. This is also implicit in another oblique example in FOREIGN CORRESPONDENT. When Johnny enters the dream-like interior of the windmill (➤ STAIRCASES), the first thing he sees is Krug, in a white polo-necked sweater, paying off the assassin, who for no apparent reason is naked from the waist up. There is, at least, a hint here of payment for sexual services. But the explicit motivation for the payment is for a murder. However, when Johnny then hides out in the room at the top of the mill, we have a more playful example, with the mill itself joining in the action: it starts to tear off his clothes.

Crucial to these examples is that we share the point of view of the spying hero. In Strangers on a Train, where we see Bruno watching Guy from the latter's point of view, the dynamic is different. Although there are clear gay overtones to this, they derive from the sense that Bruno represents a regrettable episode from Guy's past which has come back to haunt him. In the hero as spy examples, by contrast, we are the figures looking into the world of the enemy agents (or whoever), and Hitchcock tends to sexualise what we see, just as he does when men spy on women.

With the arrival of the Cold War spy movies, the examples become more developed. When Roger in North by Northwest first starts to spy on the enemy agents – the auction scene – what he sees is a *menage à trois*: Eve, Vandamm and Leonard. But he betrays his presence and gets no further in his understanding. On the next occasion, when he spies unseen through the window of Vandamm's house, he learns a great deal more. First, Leonard's homosexuality and his hostility to Eve are both made explicit in this scene: he himself refers to his 'woman's intuition'; Vandamm accuses him of being 'jealous' of Eve. But Roger also learns about the MacGuffin, which is a secret that Vandamm and Leonard have kept from Eve: the statuette of the Tarascan warrior they bought at the auction contains, in Leonard's words, 'a belly full of microfilm'.

I find this distinctly suggestive. It's as if the statuette is symbolically pregnant with Vandamm and Leonard's child: the MacGuffin is their baby. In the auction scene, it is Leonard who prompts Vandamm to buy the statuette; during the climactic struggle on Mount Rushmore, it is Leonard and Eve who end up fighting for it. That Leonard seeks not merely to repossess the statuette, but also to kill Eve, his rival, is quite explicit here: he tries to push her down the cliff-face; he grinds Roger's fingers in order to make both him and Eve fall. Accordingly, when Leonard is shot and drops the statuette so that it breaks, this is like a miscarriage. Such symbolism is strengthened by the birth symbolism associated with the Cuban MacGuffin in Topaz, which is hidden in a dead chicken and is extracted in a parody of childbirth (➤ FOOD AND MEALS).

The sense that the MacGuffin is not just a political, but also symbolically a sexual secret is a feature of this motif in Hitchcock's films (➤ THE MACGUFFIN). Another example which has homoerotic overtones occurs in Topaz, and it, too, is integrated into a sequence which includes the hero spying on two men whose behaviour is highly suggestive. Outside the Hotel Theresa, André watches his agent DuBois, posing as a journalist, bribe Rico Parra's secretary Uribe in order to gain access to secret documents in Rico's briefcase. Hitchcock films this scene from André's position across the road, using point-of-view editing with the subjective shots filmed through a telephoto lens. We cannot hear what DuBois and Uribe are saying, but their little routine looks exactly like a gay pickup: DuBois approaches Uribe cautiously in the hotel lobby, then takes him outside to proposition him and, when he resists, wins him over by offering money. Moreover, these overtones continue in the scenes between the two men inside the hotel. DuBois and Uribe first meet in the latter's bathroom, where a naked light bulb is prominent in the foreground between them: another example linking this motif to homosexuality. Then, when Uribe has obtained the briefcase, he takes it back to his room and DuBois photographs the contents on the bed. Rico interrupts them and, as DuBois jumps out the window, fires shots after him. Again the scene is sexualised: it looks exactly as if Rico has interrupted an illicit encounter on the bed, obliging the lover figure to flee for his life. As DuBois runs along the pavement, he knocks André over in order to give him the camera, and the way he falls on top of André is like an echo of the sexual overtones of the secret hotel encounter.

The contents of the film that DuBois passes on to André here – the first of the film's MacGuffins – are thus charged with overtones of 'gay sex': a record of DuBois's illicit activities with Uribe on the bed. Again, however, I do not think that we are invited to see either of these characters as necessarily gay – as we are with Leonard. Once more, the gay overtones arise from the way that Hitchcock has filmed the whole sequence, as if he were unconsciously registering the undertones to such a rendezvous. A technical detail which strengthens this argument is that, in contrast to the examples in THE 39 STEPS and SECRET AGENT (and the many 'optical device' shots in REAR WINDOW), the telephoto lens shots here are not diegetically motivated: André would not be able to see the scene this way. But an effect of the lens is to draw us closer to the observed action, to involve us more. Together with the staging of the scene, this emphasises that it is Hitchcock's own investment in the material which has led to the scene's undertones.

A final point which links most of these examples is that either the hero is too far away to hear what the men are saying, or they communicate purely by gesture (THE 39 STEPS), or they are speaking a foreign language (FOREIGN CORRESPONDENT). Accordingly, he and we are forced to interpret what's going on from behaviour alone; this automatically introduces ambiguity. It is an ambiguity which nevertheless leans in a certain direction: implying a special understanding (THE 39 STEPS) or involving proximity and touching (DuBois and Uribe are constantly touching each other). In other words, when the conditions lend themselves to ambiguity, Hitchcock tends to shift the interaction between the men in a sexualised direction: as if the absence of the anchoring function of language serves as a licence to open up more coded, oneiric possibilities.

If this is a consistent feature of Hitchcock's work, it would obviously also need to apply to REAR WINDOW. This aspect of the film has in fact already been explored by Robert Samuels (1998). The premise of Samuels's book is that 'Hitchcock's subjects are inherently bisexual and that the director's own identifications represent multiple forms of desire and identification' (Samuels 1998: 4). In his chapter on REAR WINDOW (109-21), Samuels analyses Jeff's obsessive watching of Thorwald in terms of a repressed homosexual desire. Jeff's reluctance to marry Lisa has occasionally prompted critical speculations about his sexual proclivities, e.g. by Theodore Price. Samuels looks at a range of features in the film, focusing in particular on Jeff's personal anxieties about Thorwald, e.g. 'His constant attempts … to avoid having the killer see him … represent his attempts at avoiding the acknowledgement of his repressed homosexuality' (116). He also suggests that, in the climactic confrontation between the two men, Jeff's behaviour is 'indicative of the type of homosexual panic that Eve Kosofsky Sedgwick outlines in her book *Between Men: English Literature and Homosocial Desire*' (Samuels 1998: 116). I would in fact go further: when Thorwald hurls Jeff from his wheelchair onto the bed, the attack is redolent with overtones of homosexual rape.

The presence of such overtones to the 'hero as spy' examples supports my conviction that the famous cases of homosexuality in Hitchcock are only the tip of the iceberg. Although I disagree with the insistence of Theodore Price's observations, if one thinks, rather, in terms of traces or overtones of homosexuality, a different picture emerges: these do indeed seem to be widespread in the director's work.

Ivor Novello

Finally, the 'problem' of Ivor Novello. In Novello's films generally – not just those with Hitchcock – it is hard to ignore the insistent registering of his well-known homosexuality. I mention under HANDCUFFS AND BONDAGE the sense that the Lodger may be secretly aroused by the thought of being handcuffed, and then saved, by the manly Joe. In addition, the intertitle 'I'm glad he's not keen on the girls' seems like an extra-textual joke, designed to amuse Novello's 'knowing' fans. However, DOWNHILL – which was scripted (under a pseudonym) by Ivor Novello and Constance Collier from their play – is more problematic. In the public school scenes, one senses that the joking inflection predominates. Roddy laughs when Mabel, the local girl who has set her sights on him, invites him to kiss her. Then, when she later identifies him as the boy who made her pregnant, he absolutely roars with laughter – until the Headmaster's castrating stare silences him. It is because Roddy/Novello reacts to the suggestion that he has had sex with a young woman with such hilarity that I feel the film does not really sustain the DOUBLES motif which is implicit in its structure.

It is the later scenes, however, which are the problem. Throughout these, women are the primary source of Roddy's downfall: Mabel is merely the first of a line. A theatre actress, Julia, marries him when he inherits £30,000 and promptly proceeds, with her lover Archie, to fleece him of this money. He is next seen as a gigolo in a Paris dance hall, where he is controlled by a strong-willed patronne. He ends up, penniless and seriously ill, on the Marseille docks. His ensuing hallucinations during his feverish journey by boat back to London are particularly revealing (➤ BED SCENE). Charles Barr notes the misogyny in these images: '[The women] sit around a table together, leering or grimacing at him like vampires or witches from a horror movie, and he reels back in revulsion' (Barr 1999: 46). Moreover, in Roddy's unspecified illness there are links with the fate of the eponymous victims in *White Cargo*, a 1923 play by Leon Gordon, made into a British film in 1929 and a Hollywood film in 1942. Blatantly racist, *White Cargo* blames the native woman Tondelayo for turning her sexual conquests – all male British colonists – into 'white cargo', senseless beings carried out of the African rubber plantation to be shipped back home. Miscegenation, in other words, degrades and poisons a white man. Since Roddy's feverish and delirious state is identical to that of Tondelayo's victims, the message would seem to be that heterosexuality degrades a nice English public school boy like Roddy. It seems not irrelevant that the film ends with the hero, albeit playing for the 'old boys', back in the safe environment of his public school.

It should be apparent that I am attributing this aspect of DOWNHILL to its star, rather than its director. Although there is a critique of heterosexuality across Hitchcock's work, it centres on male domination, not female exploitation. I should also note that Michael Williams's recent study of Ivor Novello reads Roddy's delirium as symbolising the state of shell-shocked soldiers returning home after World War I (Williams 2003: 142-44). I do not deny the validity of such a metaphorical reading – which is developed by Williams across a number of Novello films – but this does not erase the misogyny. It is perhaps significant that DOWNHILL was Hitchcock's final collaboration with Novello, and that he cast Isabel Jeans (Julia) as the victim of patriarchy in EASY VIRTUE, his next film. Perhaps he, too, was uneasy about the misogyny and sought to make amends.

The subject of Hitchcock and homosexuality has generated a lot of interest in recent years, and I cannot claim to have covered all the angles. Overall, although I am to an extent sympathetic to Robert Samuels's argument about the bisexuality of Hitchcock's characters, it seems to me that homosexuality for

Hitchcock is a disturbing force. In Steve Neale's phrase, it functions in his films as a troubling undercurrent, fascinating but disavowed, an undercurrent which constantly threatens to rise and disturb the films' surface.

Homosexuality and the police

There are two contrasting ways in which Hitchcock links homosexuality and the police. In DIAL M FOR MURDER, where Chief Inspector Hubbard stops his colleague walking down the street with a handbag dangling from his arm, the matter is treated as a joke (➢ *Keys, handbags and the police*). But in STRANGERS ON A TRAIN, the reference is coded, and thus darker. We could read the ways in which the police doggedly watch Guy as a further allusion to the film's homosexual subtext: as if they are checking for suspicious liaisons. Certainly, when Guy finally goes to Metcalf to rendezvous with Bruno, he mobilises a massive police presence. Moreover, at the moment when he leaps on the merry-go-round to grab hold of Bruno, a policeman becomes so excited that he shoots: we cannot have that sort of thing going on. It is this feverish overreaction which precipitates the merry-go-round crash (➢ *Public disturbances and the police*). In short, the crash may be understood, subtextually, as the consequence of police paranoia and repressiveness concerning homosexuality.

JEWELLERY

Fig. 35. Still: NOTORIOUS: Jewellery. Prescott (Louis Calhern) fastens Alicia (Ingrid Bergman)'s necklace for her; excluded, Devlin (Cary Grant) pretends to read.

In films generally, as in life, jewellery has a wide range of possible associations. These may be romantic: in two early Garbo films – THE TEMPTRESS (Fred Niblo, 1926) and FLESH AND THE DEVIL (Clarence Brown, 1926) – she and the hero signal their love by exchanging rings. But, as a gift from a man to a woman, jewellery may equally connote the man's sense of his own status and wealth, as in the familiar situation of a husband wanting his wife to wear the expensive jewellery he has bought her. Such jewellery may have little sentimental value: RANDOM HARVEST (Mervyn LeRoy, 1942) nicely contrasts the expensive emerald pendant the hero gives the heroine when he is a famous politician with the much more highly valued cheap necklace he gave her during his amnesiac period, when he genuinely loved her. Similarly, both the engagement and wedding rings, with their familiar connotations, have been used in films to signal such matters as the owner's feelings about the relationship symbolised by the ring, or a woman's sacrifice in giving it up, as in GONE WITH THE WIND (Victor Fleming, 1939).

From early in his career, Hitchcock has used jewellery in his films, but almost invariably with illicit or sinister overtones. These may be summarised under a series of subheadings, listed here in approximate order of increasing importance.

Greed

In DOWNHILL, Julia's fleecing of the naïve Roddy is symbolised by the box of jewels she has – among other possessions – converted his inheritance into; her lover Archie advises her to put the jewels in the bank to prevent Roddy getting at them. In FAMILY PLOT, Adamson, a jeweller and kidnapper, insists on each of his ransom demands being met by payment in a single, massive diamond. Greed, however, is not really a Hitchcock preoccupation. Support for his indifference may be found in the cavalier treatment of the diamond necklace in NUMBER SEVENTEEN. As Charles Barr argues, the necklace functions in the film exactly like the (later very familiar) MacGuffin (Barr 1999: 125) (➤ THE MACGUFFIN). In FAMILY PLOT, Hitchcock seems less interested in the value of a diamond than in its visual qualities, which enables it to be hidden 'where everyone can see it' – on a chandelier. He ends his career with a close-up of a diamond on the chandelier – the credits of the film come up over this shot – but it is the way the diamond sparkles which gives the shot interest. Until Hitchcock freezes the shot, it seems to be winking, as Blanche has just done.

Status

In SABOTEUR, to get himself out of a difficult spot – a gun is trained on him – Barry changes his intended public exposé of the fifth columnists at Mrs Sutton's social gathering to an announcement that their hostess will auction some of her famous jewellery for charity. To her chagrin, Mrs Sutton is obliged to go through with the performance. The issue here is that of a wealthy middle-aged woman and her jewellery, which Hitchcock seems to take malicious delight in parting her from. That he sees such a woman's loss of her jewellery as amusing is evident from the opening shot of TO CATCH A THIEF, as a middle-aged woman in face cream screams that her jewels have been stolen. The joke is then continued through repetition: a succession of early morning screams from women in French Riviera hotel rooms who have similarly had their jewellery stolen. However, Uncle Charlie's dinner-table speech about wealthy widows in SHADOW OF A DOUBT gives a much more sinister twist to Hitchcock's implicit hostility to these women's obsession with their jewellery. Uncle Charlie pours out his contempt: 'these useless women... drinking the money, eating the money, losing the money at bridge... smelling of money. Proud of their jewellery but nothing else. Horrible. Faded, fat, greedy women.' Although one would certainly not wish to attribute such virulent misogyny to Hitchcock, Uncle Charlie's sentiments are an extension of Hitchcock's own attitude in the other films. In order for a wealthy woman to redeem herself in Hitchcock's eyes, she needs to be able to give up her jewellery, like Francie's mother in To CATCH A THIEF, who is unperturbed when her jewels are stolen. The key example of this is when Connie in LIFEBOAT finally surrenders her diamond necklace – which had been her passport out of the slums of South Side, Chicago – for fish bait. This is a rare example of a positive use of the jewellery motif, and what makes it positive is the loss; the fact that Connie can bring herself to part with the necklace for the sake of the common good.

Female desire

In THE RING, the snake bracelet given to Mabel by Bob is juxtaposed with her wedding ring – most strikingly, during the wedding ceremony itself – as a signifier of her adulterous desire for Bob (➤ WATER). When she returns to her husband Jack at the end, she discards the bracelet. In To CATCH A THIEF, Francie offers Robie – an ex-jewel-thief – her diamond necklace to steal; when he declares that it's imitation, she replies 'I'm not'. What she is really offering him is herself, a playful use of the motif which Hitchcock unfortunately spoils with his crude cuts to exploding fireworks. Nevertheless, female desire is most certainly a Hitchcock preoccupation, and these are merely two of many ways in which he has dramatised it.

Female beauty / male power

In NOTORIOUS and UNDER CAPRICORN there are parallel scenes which begin with two men waiting for Ingrid Bergman as heroine to appear, dressed to go to an important social function: dinner at Sebastian's and a ball respectively. One of the men has an expensive necklace in his hands, which he wants her to wear to the function. In NOTORIOUS, the CIA official Prescott simply tells Alicia that he wants her to wear the (specially hired) diamond necklace, and she asks him to fasten it for her. Devlin stands impotently by during this; it is Prescott who is in control and who is orchestrating Alicia's performance for her evening of espionage on Sebastian and his associates. In UNDER CAPRICORN, Sam has secretly bought a ruby necklace to give to Hattie to wear to the ball, but when he tentatively suggests this as Hattie descends the stairs, Charles is scathing: 'Do you want your wife to look like a Christmas tree?' Here, the issue is one of taste, and Sam's lower-class sensibilities are mocked by the aristocratic Charles – Sam hides the necklace. It is Charles who is in charge of Hattie's evening, taking her to the ball, and here it is Sam who stands by impotently. The status of the dominant male in each case is symbolised by his control over the heroine's jewellery. When Prescott fastens the necklace, he not only shows his power over Alicia, but also over Devlin, whom she has conspicuously not asked to do this for her. Similarly, when Charles obliges Sam to conceal the fact that he has bought the rubies, he reduces him to the role of onlooker – he barely gives Hattie time even to say goodbye to him.

Male murderousness

Two of Hitchcock's psychopathic killers wear similar tie-pins: Bruno's in STRANGERS ON A TRAIN is in the form of his name; Rusk's in FRENZY in the shape of an R. Evidently, Hitchcock wished to connect the two characters in certain ways: their flamboyance; their close relationship with their mothers (Bruno's tie-pin was indeed a gift from his mother). But Bruno's tie-pin is otherwise of significance only in enabling Anne to recognise him when she sees him for the second time, whereas Rusk's becomes a developed motif. Seized by Babs as he was strangling her, it obliges him to return to her body to retrieve it, leading to one of the most grotesque sequences in Hitchcock, as Rusk struggles with Babs's body in a potato sack on the back of a moving lorry (➤ CONFINED SPACES). Although Rusk is desperate to repossess the pin because it could identify him as her murderer, symbolically, it's as if Babs has unmanned him, and his fight with her intransigent corpse is like a blackly comic attempt to recover his purloined manhood (Conrad 2000: 86).

There are also two films in which a murderer gives himself away by stealing his victim's jewellery. In SHADOW OF A DOUBT, the emerald ring Uncle Charlie gives his niece belonged to one of his victims, and the initials engraved on it

Fig. 36. Still: SHADOW OF A DOUBT: Jewellery. Uncle Charlie (Joseph Cotten) gives Charlie (Teresa Wright) the ring of one of his murder victims.

serve to identify him to Charlie as the Merry Widow murderer. In REAR WIN-DOW, the presence of Mrs Thorwald's jewellery in the apartment after she herself has disappeared becomes the key to establishing that her husband murdered her.

There are both contrasting and linked points here. Uncle Charlie's gift of the ring has no equivalent in REAR WINDOW: symbolically, it suggests betrothal (Rothman 1986: 192) and is thus a feature of the film's Oedipal incest theme (➤ DOUBLES). Otherwise, however, the rings in the two movies function in essentially similar ways. Even though the murderer may try and hide the incriminating jewellery (to protect himself, Uncle Charlie subsequently repossesses the ring from Charlie), the heroine is able to find it. It's as if the ring in some sense 'represents' the woman to whom it belonged, and when the heroine puts it on and displays it, she is like the murdered woman's surrogate, exposing the killer. Both these scenes are surprisingly close: Charlie comes down the stairs, displaying the ring to her uncle as a way of telling him that she has the evidence to convict him; Lisa signals to Jeff – watching from across the courtyard – that she has Mrs Thorwald's wedding ring by pointing to it on her finger. REAR

WINDOW also has additional overtones at this point: as Truffaut points out (Truffaut 1968: 188) Lisa is also reminding Jeff of her wish to marry him. Finally, as if to emphasise the link between the jewellery and murderousness, the heroine's wearing of the ring then provokes the villain into further, irrational, murderousness – directed at herself in SHADOW OF A DOUBT; displaced to the hero in REAR WINDOW. The importance of the ring in REAR WINDOW is restated in the ensuing climactic confrontation between hero and villain: it is when Thorwald demands the ring back, and Jeff says 'the police have it by now' that Thorwald crosses the room to try and murder Jeff. All these points combine to suggest the ring as symbolically representing, on the one hand, the murderer's guilt, which refuses to go away, and on the other, the murdered woman's spirit, which refuses to rest.

These five subcategories summarise the broad range of Hitchcock's use of the jewellery motif. The first two are relatively minor, but the other three are major – they are issues to which Hitchcock repeatedly returns in his films. The motif helps articulate these issues in the films; in this respect, it is characteristic of the use of an elaborated motif. Overall, however, the most striking feature is the almost total absence of any 'romantic' connotations to Hitchcock's use of the motif, the sort of connotations that occur frequently in films generally, particularly when the jewellery is a gift. There are examples in other films which parallel some of Hitchcock's: as Robin Wood has pointed out to me, the notion of an older, powerful figure placing a necklace around a woman's throat as a way of demonstrating control over her is also found in LETTER FROM AN UNKNOWN WOMAN (Max Ophuls, 1948) and THE WINGS OF THE DOVE (Iain Softley, 1997). Nevertheless, I suspect that no other director who has used the motif in a significant number of films has consistently presented it so unromantically.

Other examples of this motif in Hitchcock tend to be single instances of a particular use, e.g. the assassin in THE MAN WHO KNEW TOO MUCH (1934) presenting Jill with her kidnapped daughter's brooch (a figure of a girl skier) as a way of warning her to keep quiet. Carlotta's necklace in VERTIGO is a more developed example. The necklace was originally given to Carlotta by the rich man who drove her to suicide; it then passed down through Carlotta's female descendants to the real Madeleine Elster, which enabled Elster to give it to Judy after he had murdered his wife. The necklace is thus, once more, associated with male power and murderousness. But not only does Judy keep it, after she and Scottie have first had sex, she puts it on when she dresses to go out. As Scottie fastens it for her, he recognises it from the portrait of Carlotta.

Critics have tended to focus on Scottie's reaction: the way the necklace reveals to him that Judy and 'Madeleine' are the same person – which leads him to begin to discern the murder plot. But what about Judy: why does she put on the necklace at this particular point? We could perhaps see her act as a

'Freudian slip'; now that she has finally succeeded in winning Scottie's love, unconsciously she wants him to learn the truth. But I think a more important point is that her wearing the necklace here suggests female desire. And this revelation of Judy's desire is highly problematic. Like Elster before him, Scottie has now become her lover – is she unconsciously linking the two men? Did Elster like her to dress up as Madeleine before having sex with her? Did she herself like to do this? Or is it Carlotta she is unconsciously identifying herself with: the female victim of male 'freedom and power' (➤ PAINTINGS)? After Scottie, in his rage at what was done to him, has forced Judy back up the bell tower, he says of the necklace: 'That was where you made your mistake, Judy. You shouldn't keep souvenirs of a killing. You shouldn't have been (his voice breaks); you shouldn't have been that sentimental.' James Stewart's delivery conveys, very movingly, Scottie's realisation that it is he himself who has been sentimental, but why did Judy keep the necklace? And the grey suit? Scottie is clearly tormented by the fact that she loved Elster to the point of becoming his accomplice in a murder plot: is the film hinting that she still loves him? Certainly, the necklace seems to carry a curse: Carlotta committed suicide, the real Madeleine Elster was murdered and Judy is wearing it when she falls to her death.

In summary, we can see in the use of the necklace in VERTIGO not only each of the three major subcategories of the jewellery motif, but also the suggestion of even more associations, both potentially perverse (what, exactly, did Elster and Judy get up to?) and fatalistic: the sense of the necklace carrying a curse. That many of these associations present themselves as questions rather than answers is a measure of the complexity of the film. Overall, however, the necklace is typical of the jewellery motif in Hitchcock, in the way it reveals the film's deep pessimism about desire.

Jewellery and the police

Except when they are searching for stolen (NUMBER SEVENTEEN, TO CATCH A THIEF) or ransomed (FAMILY PLOT) jewellery, the police have little to do with this motif. The one occasion when a policeman does otherwise make a pronouncement about jewellery is in REAR WINDOW. As support for Jeff's position that Mrs Thorwald has been murdered, Lisa tries to explain to Lt. Doyle that a woman wouldn't leave her jewellery behind when going on a trip. Doyle is dismissive: 'Look, Miss Fremont, that feminine intuition stuff sells magazines but in real life it's still a fairy tale.' In due course, Lisa proves him wrong, but at considerable risk to both herself and Jeff.

KEYS AND HANDBAGS

Fig. 37. Still: MARNIE: Key. Marnie (Tippi Hedren) locking away evidence of her previous identity as Marion Holland. In a few seconds, she will throw away the key.

In a stimulating discussion of objects in Hitchcock, Susan Smith uses the circulation of the wine cellar key in NOTORIOUS as a major example. Alicia takes it from her husband Alex's key-ring, gives it to Devlin, and he uses it to explore the wine cellar, where he finds the MacGuffin (a mysterious ore in a wine bottle). But Alex then notices its absence from and subsequent return to the key-ring, which alerts him to what has been going on and exposes Alicia as an

American spy. Smith points out that the key is used both as a structuring device
throughout the sequence (Smith 2000: 97) and, together with other objects (the
champagne bottles; the wine bottle containing the ore), as a mechanism to generate suspense (98).

In this example, Susan Smith looks at significant aspects of Hitchcock's use of
one key in one film. A fuller consideration of keys in Hitchcock's films opens up
a much broader set of concerns. Not only is there more to be said about the
circulation of the cellar key in NOTORIOUS, it may also be related to other examples of the motif in Hitchcock's films. In discussing these, I also want to include
a consideration of handbags in Hitchcock. Handbags complement keys: both in
the ways that they function in (some of) the films and because, in Freudian
terms, they are as familiar a female symbol as keys are a male symbol. In addition, handbags in Hitchcock are the subject of an excellent article by Sarah Street
(1995-96: 23-37), whose ideas I also wish to discuss.

KEYS

In the British films, there are several examples in which the locking and unlock-
ing of doors is given dramatic focus (e.g. through close-ups), but it is not until
NOTORIOUS that keys in Hitchcock function as an elaborated motif. There are, in
fact, two sets of keys in the film (the first is the house keys) and both only become an issue after Alicia has married Alex Sebastian. The keys in NOTORIOUS
may then be linked to those in UNDER CAPRICORN, where the house keys are in
effect symbols in a power struggle between Hattie, as the nominal mistress of
the house, and the housekeeper Milly, a power struggle which is ultimately over
Hattie's husband Sam. In DIAL M FOR MURDER, keys are a crucial feature in the
execution and then the investigation of Tony's plot to murder his wife Margot,
so that identification of him as the true criminal hinges on his knowledge of the
keys. It can be seen that the keys in all these films are linked to tensions in a
marriage. But the motif also proves to be richly suggestive in the details of its
operation in the individual films.

When Alicia moves in to the Sebastian house, Mme Sebastian has charge of
the house keys. In response to Alicia's request for them, Alex goes into his
mother's room, and the raised voices which we then hear are a sign of Mme
Sebastian's resistance to surrendering them. This is a sketched-in version of a
conflict which is much more developed in UNDER CAPRICORN: the heroine in
conflict with a dominant female figure over the question of who controls the
keys, i.e. runs the household. But the house keys only permit Alicia access to
neutral spaces, such as closets. Alex himself keeps the key to the wine cellar –

which Alicia suspects contains his political secret – hence her need to steal it. A wife stealing her husband's key in order to give it to her lover has obvious Freudian overtones: it is not therefore surprising that the scene in which Alicia obtains the key is 'overdetermined'. At the very moment that she is handling his keys, Alex, in the bathroom, is talking to her about Devlin's loving her. He then comes out and apologises. The ensuing little drama in which Alicia contrives to hide her possession of the key is discussed under HANDS; the tension and suspense of the scene bear testament to the nature of the wife's transgressive behaviour. Secret Beyond the Door and Sudden Fear (David Miller, 1952) also include a scene in which the heroine steals her husband's keys preparatory to entering his 'forbidden room', and, again, each scene is fraught with tension: see 'Secret Beyond the Door' in Movie 34/35, where I discuss the 'persecuted wife cycle' to which these films – as well as Rebecca, Suspicion and Notorious – belong (Walker M. 1990: 16-30).

In Notorious, we then have one of Hitchcock's most famous shots: a crane down from the upper landing to Alicia and Alex welcoming their party guests, a crane which ends with a big close-up of the key in Alicia's nervous hand. She is waiting to hand it to Devlin, who is late. Throughout the party sequence, the necessity for Alicia and Devlin to liaise, and then to meet secretly, charges their behaviour as spies with the overtones of a clandestine romance, and it is not surprising that Alex, both suspicious and jealous, should eventually catch them out. In fact, it is Devlin who ensures this. When Alex sees the couple outside the cellar, Devlin gets Alicia to kiss him, claiming that this will cover the real purpose of their rendezvous (➤ SPY FILMS / THE LOOK under EXHIBITIONISM / VOYEURISM). But, noting the absence and return of the key, Alex himself searches the cellar, and he finds traces of the espionage: particles of ore; pieces of a broken bottle. He goes to his mother's room a second time and tells her that he is married to an American agent. Structurally, this scene matches the earlier one, with Mme Sebastian now delighted at the opportunity to turn the tables on Alicia (➤ BED SCENE).

In my discussion of the persecuted wife cycle, I suggest that the forbidden room in these films contains, symbolically or otherwise, the husband's psychological secret, which is often sexual (Walker M. 1990: 29-30). Unica on the cellar key hints at Alex's impotence (eunuch) (➤ THE MACGUFFIN). The emphasis on keys draws attention to the cycle's links with the Bluebeard legend, where it is a key which reveals to the husband that his wife has entered the forbidden room. In Alicia's tampering with the keys there is in fact an overlap between the Freudian overtones (the symbolic emasculation of the husband) and the ideological implications. A woman manipulating her husband's keys would seem to set up a disturbance to patriarchal control, and in this case her punishment – the poisoning – is indeed severe.

In UNDER CAPRICORN, Milly's status as the figure who runs the Flusky house-hold is focused explicitly on the house keys: she wears them attached to her waist, like a badge of office. Their positioning evokes the westerner's revolver, an association supported by Helen Simpson's novel, where she writes: 'as she walked they rang authoritatively, like spurs' (Simpson 1937/1949: 53). This phal-lic inflection of the motif is also stressed in DAY OF WRATH (Carl Dreyer, 1943), where the heroine's tyrannical mother-in-law wears the keys in the same man-ner. It is because Hattie is alcoholic and incapable that Milly runs things, but we later discover that Milly herself has been feeding Hattie's alcoholism. There is thus a more sinister connection between her and Mme Sebastian: secretly in love with Sam, Milly too resorts to slow poisoning to get rid of her rival. But Hattie is completely unaware of this. Indeed, when Charles begins to rehabili-tate her, and insists that she is the one who should be wearing the keys and running the kitchen, Hattie protests: Milly would be furious. Hattie is right. Having overheard Charles's plan, Milly promptly arranges to sabotage it. When Hattie asks for the keys, Milly humiliates her: she displays the signs of her alcoholism – empty bottles – in front of the kitchen staff whom Hattie was trying to control. The women burst into laughter, and Hattie flees to the sanctu-ary of her room – and to drink.

This is, however, merely the first stage in a battle over the keys which con-tinues throughout much of the film. The marriage between Sam and Hattie, the groom and the lady, is riven with class tensions, and there is a sense that what is going on in the Flusky household is a class war, cleverly orchestrated by Milly. Humiliating Hattie is front of the kitchen staff is part of this. At one point, Milly leaves the household, enabling Hattie to regain her self-confidence: she shows that she can control the kitchen staff, and Sam rewards her by giving her the keys. However, Milly's withdrawal was merely a tactical retreat: she returns, and uses Sam's hatred of gentlemen to insinuate that Charles and Hattie are having an affair. This precipitates a whole series of marital crises, with two cli-maxes: Sam's accidental shooting of Charles and his violent rejection of Hattie. Milly thinks that she has won: Hattie will be sent back to Ireland to be tried for killing her brother (➤ GUILT AND CONFESSION), and Milly herself can then secure Sam as husband. Again proudly wearing the keys, she goes so far as to sit opposite him in Hattie's fireside chair. (Lesley Brill points out that 'The sym-bolism of the connubial chairs goes back in Hitchcock's movies at least as far as THE FARMER'S WIFE': Brill 1988: 261, and he discusses examples of this motif throughout his book.) But when she hears that Sam intends to accompany Hattie to Ireland, Milly decides to hasten the poisoning of her mistress. This leads to a three-way confrontation in Hattie's bedroom and here, too, the keys are important props. When Hattie finally grasps what Milly has been doing, Milly angrily takes the keys from her waist to assault Hattie with them. Her use of the keys as a weapon serves to literalise what has been going on all along, and we note that it is Sam who stops her, emphasising his role as the patriarchal figure who controls the keys. This is then re-stated in the way the scene ends. Milly so insults Hattie that Sam is provoked into striking at her, but what he in fact does is tear the keys from her. This robs Milly of her symbolic power; defeated, she flees downstairs and out of the film.

Also attached to her waist, Milly wears a small bag, in which she carries a sleeping draught, her final poison. Her third prop is a shrunken Aboriginal head, which she has been placing in Hattie's bed so that Hattie will be terrified and others will think that she is having the DTs. In other words, the keys are part of a network of objects which are charged with perverse associations: medicine transformed into poison; an anthropological artefact into an object of terror. These are typical Gothic transformations, emphasising this aspect to the film. An effect, however, is to charge the keys with similar overtones. They are not simply a sign of status, but also a licence to tyrannise: Milly's first significant act in the film is to go into the kitchen and whip the staff. This raises the crucial issue of how much Sam, albeit unconsciously, is permitting Milly to degrade Hattie, to keep her drunk and incapable of functioning as the mistress of the house. Florence Jacobowitz discusses this in 'UNDER CAPRICORN: Hitchcock in Transition', concluding that 'Milly's slow poisoning, which is accelerated by the turn of events, is presented consistently as an acting out of Flusky's fears and rage' (Jacobowitz 2000: 25).

Looked at slightly differently, then, the keys symbolise Milly's power over Sam. So long as she wears them, he is giving her permission to run the household and control Hattie. As Florence Jacobowitz points out: 'Flusky's curious domestic helplessness, his wilfully obscured vision and passive complicity – he cannot see what a newcomer like Adare or the new "gentleman" servant Winter see plainly, straight away' is a corollary of Milly's role: she 'functions as a sort of alter ego, giving voice and shape to Sam's subjective fears' (Jacobowitz 2000: 24).

We could, therefore, see the keys as the marker of an unspoken contract between Sam and Milly: this is why it is vital that he finally repossesses them from her. When she left earlier, we did not see her relinquish them. The keys are a status symbol, but within patriarchal culture, women may officially wear them only with the permission of a man. In NOTORIOUS, it is obvious that Alex has to mediate in the transfer of the keys from his mother to Alicia, but the same principle applies in UNDER CAPRICORN: Hattie cannot demand the keys from Milly; Sam has to effect the transfer.

In both NOTORIOUS and UNDER CAPRICORN the keys are associated with a husband's domination of his wife, a domination which extends to poisoning her: directly in NOTORIOUS; by proxy in UNDER CAPRICORN. The role of the lover figure in this unstable marital situation is to provoke a disturbance to the existing conditions pertaining to the keys: Devlin tells Alicia to steal the cellar key; Charles tells Hattie that she should be wearing the house keys. (The bottles which come into play in both films at this point may be seen as a linked motif: symbolically, they refer to a guiltily guarded secret, a sign of what is wrong with the marriage.) Charles's motive here seems decidedly more altruistic than Devlin's, but Florence Jacobowitz unravels his deeper motives: the more he returns Hattie to her earlier status as 'a lady', the greater the class difference between her and Sam (Jacobowitz 2000: 25-26). In UNDER CAPRICORN, the equivalent of the locked forbidden room is Hattie's bedroom, which Charles flamboyantly enters – through the window – in front of Sam. The moment when he kisses her in this scene (➢ ENTRY THROUGH A WINDOW) is thus the equivalent of Devlin and Alicia's kiss outside the forbidden room. In each case, the lover figure is asserting his romantic power over the heroine at the husband's expense. But he is, strictly, a usurper. Ultimately, it is the husband who controls the keys, and the wife who suffers because of this.

In DIAL M FOR MURDER, the underlying premise seems to be the same, but here the husband's control of the keys is criminal, not patriarchal, which destabilises his control. Provoked by Margot's past infidelity with Mark, Tony decides to murder her for her money. He blackmails the criminal Swann into becoming his agent for the murder and then steals Margot's house key and leaves it hidden outside the flat so that Swann can gain entrance. When his plan goes wrong and Margot kills Swann in self-defence, Tony quickly recovers the situation. By making the killing look like murder, he frames Margot, and she is tried and sentenced to death. But he made a mistake: he thought Swann's key was Margot's and transferred it from the corpse to her handbag; it is this mistake which enables the police – when they finally identify the key – to catch him out.

The film's use of the keys is taken directly from Frederick Knott's play (Knott also wrote the screenplay): for a detailed discussion of the differences between play and film, see Peter Bordonaro: 'DIAL M FOR MURDER: A Play by Frederick Knott/A Film by Alfred Hitchcock' (Bordonaro 1976: 175-79). But Hitchcock has also introduced his own embellishments; in particular, this is also a film in which the handbags motif comes into play. Indeed, the scene in which Tony first steals Margot's key from her handbag in order to leave it for Swann is not only handled quite differently in the film, but is Sarah Street's opening example. Accordingly, I would like to mention some of her ideas before looking further at the operation of the keys motif in DIAL M FOR MURDER.

Keys and handbags

Sarah Street suggests that handbags function in contrasting ways in Hitchcock's films, depending on whether the woman is married or single. A married woman is vulnerable to her husband's intrusion into her handbag, as in this scene in DIAL M FOR MURDER. Her description of the scene captures the implicit tensions:

> As [Tony] opens [Margot's] bag without asking, she protests, 'Hey, you leave my bag alone!' She is worried about his interest in her 'private space' where we already know she keeps her love letters… [Tony] tries to stop her taking the bag from him by holding it behind his back, forcing her to embrace him in a desperate attempt to continue the struggle. We see a close-up of his hand groping for the key, opening the small black purse which contains it, and its eventual removal. Throughout the awkward tussle the pair maintain a semblance of superficial humour and civility which pervades their dialogue throughout the film, a form of communication which has presumably enabled them to keep secrets from each other: her affair and his pretence of being a loving husband.
>
> (Street 1995-96: 24-25)

Street summarises: 'As her husband, Tony takes advantage of domestic familiarity to invade (Margot's) property: married couples are not supposed to have secrets' (25). Moreover, this scene is also a close reworking – with the sexes reversed – of that in NOTORIOUS when Alicia hides her possession of Alex's key by embracing him. Once again, Hitchcock has staged a moment of marital duplicity around the lifting of a key. But the use of the handbag undoubtedly sexualises the scene in DIAL M FOR MURDER. That there are two 'pouches' to open suggests the labia, and Tony's deft fingering would seem to hint at foreplay, with the key as the clitoris. After the completion of the little tussle, Margot offers him money, as if in payment. He (gallantly) refuses it. Spice is added to Tony's triumph through the risk that Mark, who has gone to get a taxi, may return at any second. In effect, Tony has secretly demonstrated his sexual mastery over the duped lover.

Why should Tony be so anxious to secure Margot's key for his murder plot: why not have a copy cut, and thus reduce the risks all round? Or, as in Mark's reconstruction of the crime, why not leave his own key? Is it simply because this would spoil the whole elaborate artifice of the plot? Or is it symbolic: like the husbands in the other two movies, Tony wants to dominate his wife, and he deprives her of her key in the same way – by stealing from her handbag – that he earlier deprived her of her love letter from Mark. The fact that he 'lends' the key to Swann is also significant. Swann functions as Tony's alter ego: he was at

Cambridge with Tony; he already is a woman murderer. Swann may thus be
seen as the equivalent of Milly, given the household key(s) as a licence to 'take
care of' a problem wife.

Although the keys in DIAL M FOR MURDER do not have the resonances of
those in the two earlier movies, they are not without symbolic interest. Here,
too, they are related to a husband's murderousness towards his wife, and her
possession of the key(s) is controlled by him. For example, Margot insists to
Chief Inspector Hubbard that Swann could not have come in through the front
door, because there are only two keys: 'My husband had his with him and mine
was in my handbag – here'. She takes it out, and Hitchcock highlights the moment by a reverse angle shot, in which her disembodied hand holds the key
away from the camera and towards the group of men in front of her. Margot
cannot imagine that her story has been undermined by her husband's manipulation of the evidence, including the keys (this is Swann's key, not hers); this is
the opposite of NOTORIOUS, and Hubbard's assumption that Margot is lying
confirms the strength of patriarchal thinking: it is the woman who is unreliable,
not her husband.

By framing the shot this way, Hitchcock constructs it, on behalf of the audience, as an accusation directed at the three men, and all of them fail her,
Hubbard and Mark because – at this stage – they are unable to see the logic of
her story: that her husband has been trying to kill her. As Sheldon Hall points
out, this shot is symbolically answered when, towards the end of the film, Hubbard takes her own key out of its hiding place under the stair carpet (where it
has been hidden since Swann returned it there before his murder attempt) and,
to show it to Margot and Mark, holds it towards the audience ('DIAL M FOR
MURDER' in *Unexplored Hitchcock*, ed. Ian Cameron, forthcoming). If the film is
seen in 3-D, this answering moment is given particular emphasis: it is one of
only two moments when Hitchcock uses the striking (and usually much
abused) device of visualising something come out of the screen into the audience. The other occasion, too, emphasises a Hitchcock motif: when Margot is
being strangled by Swann, she reaches out desperately for an object to defend
herself with: the Hands motif.

The ways in which the keys function in these three films confirms their status
as a male symbol, in the patriarchal as well as the sexual sense. A woman's
control over the keys is nearly always precarious, and unauthorised access to
them can be highly dangerous. Even Hitchcock's matriarchal figures do not necessarily enjoy complete control over the keys. REBECCA confirms this principle
by omission. Throughout the film, there is no reference whatever to any house
keys, so that the conflict between the heroine and a powerful female figure
within the house (here Mrs Danvers) is not expressed in the same terms as in
NOTORIOUS and UNDER CAPRICORN. On the one hand, Danvers's power is such

that the issue of who has the keys never arises: the heroine is simply too meek to raise it. On the other, the very fact that the keys are never mentioned protects Maxim's status as patriarch: Danvers's power is not a threat to him.

Even a minor example of a circulating key in Hitchcock can have resonances. Pursuing his scheme to get Guy to murder his father, Bruno in STRANGERS ON A TRAIN sends him a sketch plan of the family house and encloses the front door key. Giving Guy the key seems foolish; were he to carry out the murder, the police would quickly suspect that it was an inside job. But as an aspect of the film's gay subtext, the gift makes perfect sense. The scene in which Guy visits the house at night and uses the key is discussed in terms of such a subtext under BED SCENE. After Bruno has surprised Guy in his father's room, he questions him: 'Am I correct, Mr Haines, in assuming that you have no intention of going ahead with our arrangement?' When Guy confirms this, Bruno asks for his key back. As with other details in the scene, it's as though Bruno has sent Guy the key to come and visit *him*, and when Guy refuses the 'arrangement', Bruno wants the key returned. In other words, the key, passed between two men, is yet another signifier of the film's homosexual theme.

HANDBAGS

Given that handbags are a female symbol, do they operate in a complementary way to keys? Sarah Street suggests that, for single women, the handbag usually functions in a progressive manner:

> Perhaps surprisingly, in view of the standard claim that women in Hitchcock films are passive victims, the handbag is a signifier of female assertiveness rather than frivolity or passivity. The way it is used consistently demonstrates that in Hitchcock films femininity can be a powerful force to be reckoned with, often consuming the male protagonist with both fascination and fear.

(Street 1995-96: 24)

The main films she uses to support her argument are REAR WINDOW (Lisa's overnight case as an expression of her sexual forwardness: 26), VERTIGO (despite Elster and then Scottie's success in transforming Judy into 'Madeleine', there is a failure on both their parts to deal with the problem of her handbag; this is contrasted with Judy's own 'genuine' handbag: 27), and PSYCHO and MARNIE (in each, the heroine keeps the stolen money, symbol of her transgression against patriarchy, in her handbag: 28-30). I would like to look further at some of these examples, but also extend the discussion by considering others, including those from earlier in Hitchcock's work.

Fig. 38. Still: REAR WINDOW: the elegant handbag. Lisa (Grace Kelly) brings her overnight case to Jeff (James Stewart)'s apartment to show him that she is staying the night. Jeff's gesture indicates the subject of their conversation: the jewellery that was in Mrs Thorwald's handbag.

In a number of cases, Hitchcock sexualises the motif. William Rothman observes that, 'In Hitchcock's films, a woman's purse is an emblem of her sexuality' (Rothman 1982: 359, note 7) and mentions two examples. In BLACKMAIL, Alice takes a torn menu with Crewe's rendezvous note out of her handbag. Rothman points out that the tear is such that '"Nippy" Cocktails' has become '"Nippy" Cock' (351, note 13). In SHADOW OF A DOUBT, Rothman suggests that 'Mrs Potter's jewelled handbag glitters' (200) when she first meets Uncle Charlie. There are further examples. In THE 39 STEPS, the one useful item Pamela produces from her handbag is a (phallic) nail file, and Hannay's rhythmic use of it on the handcuffs sends her to sleep (➢ HANDCUFFS AND BONDAGE).

In SUSPICION, Johnnie puts his hand into Lina's handbag in the film's first scene (to extract a stamp); after their tussle on the hillside (➢ HANDS), she firmly shuts her handbag to signal that she does not want him to kiss her. As with Lisa's displaying the contents of her overnight case to Jeff, most of these sexual intimations seem to be quite consciously intended. But, to qualify Street's thesis, the woman who owns the handbag is not necessarily in control of the various situations. Later that evening Crewe's 'nippy cock' is no longer a joke:

Fig. 39. Still: Suspicion: the violated handbag. In the opening scene on a train, Johnnie (Cary Grant) puts his hand into Lina (Joan Fontaine)'s handbag in order to extract a stamp. The ticket collector (Billy Bevan) watches.

he tries to rape Alice. Likewise, Mrs Potter is later set up to be Uncle Charlie's next 'Merry Widow' victim. Lina is decidedly uncomfortable with Johnnie's over-familiarity with her. When Lisa is in the kitchen, her overnight case – now open to display her nightdress and slippers – becomes the focus of repeated looks from the cop Doyle, looks which carry enough of a salacious edge for Jeff to warn him. It's as if a woman's handbag can release sexual undercurrents which can subsequently prove disturbing, even dangerous, to her.

In those examples where a man gets his hands into a woman's handbag, this may suggest a displaced sexual threat, but may also reflect the other aspect of Tony's thefts from Margot's handbag: the wish to dominate. The fact that Johnnie presumes to help himself to something from Lina's handbag when he has only just met her is a warning about his future intentions. The scene in which Hubbard takes the key from Margot's handbag (which Street does not discuss) is remarkable for the way his control of both handbag and key seems to lend him authority over her (➤ *Keys, handbags and the police*). The final example in Hitchcock's films of a man taking something from a woman's handbag is particularly disturbing. In Frenzy, after Rusk has murdered Brenda, he helps himself to the money in her handbag. It is an unpleasant ending to a very unpleasant scene, and its significance for the motif is also negative: Blaney had also received money from the same handbag, and Brenda's face powder on the money helps incriminate him. The example is extreme, but one senses that the distaste communicated by the context in which Rusk steals from Brenda's handbag serves as a general comment on this particular male offence: it is striking that, with the exception of Hubbard, the men who violate a woman's handbag are all actual or potential murderers.

Likewise in REAR WINDOW. Lisa's overnight case is not the only significant bag; equally important is Mrs Thorwald's handbag. (In a later article, Sarah Street mentions this handbag and relates it to Margot's: Street 2000: 98.) The handbag becomes a focus of interest after Mrs Thorwald's disappearance from her flat, a disappearance which Jeff believes points to her murder. As he spies on Thorwald to gather evidence, he watches him make a phone call, during which Thorwald takes items of jewellery from the bag, as if discussing their value. Lisa is quick to realise the significance of this: that Mrs Thorwald would not have gone away and left her handbag and jewellery behind, particularly if one of the items was her wedding ring (➤ JEWELLERY). Equally, it is the very callousness of Thorwald's behaviour in treating his wife's possessions in this way which helps convince Jeff and Lisa that he is guilty. He is betrayed by his lack of understanding, as a man, of the psychic importance of the handbag. This example supports Street's thesis, and aligns the two motifs: Thorwald's tampering with a handbag gives him away, just as Alicia is exposed by her tampering with the keys.

Handbags and keys

To look at Sarah Street's ideas more closely, I should like to use PSYCHO, which is one of her examples and which is particularly useful because it also includes the keys motif. Street argues that Marion's theft of the $40,000 is a transgression against patriarchy:

> ... the money she has stolen belongs to a rich tax-evader who will use it as a wedding present for his daughter 'who has never had a day's unhappiness'. Marion's 'transgression', therefore, is not just stealing, but stealing money which has a clear patriarchal function.
>
> (Street 1995-96: 28)

Marion arrives at the Bates Motel with most of the stolen money still in her handbag. As she signs in under an assumed name, Norman asks her to include her home town. Prompted by a newspaper headline protruding from her handbag, she says 'Los Angeles'. As if reacting to this, Norman selects the key to cabin number one. We subsequently realise the significance of the choice: he puts Marion in this cabin so that he can spy on her through a peep-hole in the wall. However, Norman's voyeurism then triggers the murderousness of 'Mrs Bates', and Marion ends up slaughtered in the shower. In William Rothman's words, it's 'as if it were Marion's own guilty lie at this moment that seals her fate' (Rothman 1982: 271).

When Marion is in her cabin, she then takes the money from her handbag, wraps it in the newspaper and places it on the bedside table. It is at this point that Hitchcock introduces 'Mrs Bates', whose voice is suddenly heard shouting 'No!' Again, Rothman notes the link between Marion's act and the external event: 'The simultaneity of the intrusion of this voice and Marion's guilty gesture is uncanny, as though the voice emanated from Marion's imagination' (Rothman 1982: 274).

Despite the fact that, in both cases, Rothman suggests that it is Marion's guilt which prompts the linked external event, he does not connect these two moments. But V.F. Perkins has argued that certain elements during Marion's car drive to the Bates motel (the rain on the car windscreen; the 'slashing' windscreen wipers) may be seen as pre-echoes of her murder in the shower. His conclusion is that '[Marion] is destroyed by an explosion of forces existing within her own personality' (Perkins 1972: 113). These two 'guilty' moments are similarly suggestive. In each case, it is as though the film's narrative is responding to Marion's guilt with the introduction of something which will place her in jeopardy: her occupation of cabin number one; 'Mrs Bates'. Elements in the film may thus be seen as projections of Marion's unconscious, an unconscious which is insisting, in these instances, on her being punished for her transgression.

The cabin key may thus be seen as initiating the chain of events which leads, inexorably, to Marion's murder. In parallel to this, as Sarah Street notes, after Marion has taken the money from her handbag, 'she and her bag are less powerful' (Street 1995-96: 29). But it is also significant that this is where the film introduces 'Mrs Bates'. We do not see Marion hold her handbag again, and the switch to the money on its own as a focus of interest produces 'Mrs Bates' as the superego figure whose shout of 'No!' seems to be directed at Marion. At this stage, it is unclear what Marion might have done to provoke such a reaction. However, after her conversation with Norman in the parlour, Marion decides to take the money back; it is then that 'Mrs Bates' kills her. Symbolically, it's as if the murder is to *stop* her returning the money, suggesting that the earlier 'No!' was a warning of some kind, with 'Mrs Bates' – as, here, the voice from Marion's unconscious – protesting at her separating the money from her handbag. Whilst such a feminist, transgressive 'Mrs Bates' is only a hypothetical construct, the fact that the film can be read this way does suggest conflicting impulses in Marion's unconscious.

We do not know whether Marion, before her shower, locked the door to her cabin. However, when Norman cleans everything up after the murder, we see him pick up a key from the floor, and its positioning suggests that it had been in the lock. Norman pockets it. But he subsequently takes something from the dresser which he also pockets and which looks like another key: the one he gave to Marion. This means that the key on the floor was the duplicate: that Marion probably had locked the door and that 'Mrs Bates' had needed the duplicate to enter. This highlights the power of 'Mrs Bates': through Norman, she also controls the keys. Marion's handbag, together with all her possessions, goes with her corpse into the swamp. But the keys to cabin number one are pocketed by Norman for a future occasion.

I would argue that what happens in PSYCHO summarises the overall situation: that keys are ultimately the more potent of the two motifs. Handbags can indeed express a woman's independence or transgression, but this is not usually permitted to last too long. Marion's handbag serves its purpose as a symbol of her transgression for some 45 minutes, but she is then killed and her threat thereby neutralised. The keys, by contrast, go back into circulation.

MARNIE is similar. Hitchcock stresses the handbag as symbol of the heroine's transgressive power here by actually beginning the film with a shot of Marnie's yellow handbag, bulging with Strutt's $9967. Throughout the first section of the film, Marnie's handbags, like Marion's, then continue to symbolise her transgression. In addition, she is pretty handy with keys. When she divests herself of her previous identity, she locks a suitcase of her old clothes in a left luggage locker, and then drops the key down a drain. Hitchcock shows the act of getting rid of the key in precise detail, as if stressing it as a symbolic gesture: Marnie's rejection of the phallus? Then, when Marnie is employed at Rutlands, she watches closely as her new colleague Susan opens her handbag and takes out a key. Again Hitchcock emphasises the incident, which we see from Marnie's point of view as she stands next to Susan. In his discussion of the Hands motif in MARNIE, Joe McElhaney considers that there is a 'poised, almost ritualistic quality to [Susan's] hand movements and to the fetishistic impact of the opening of the leather purse and the tiny key held in [her] hand' (McElhaney 1999: 91). Here the precise detail is motivated by the fact that this is the key that Marnie needs to steal in order to get into the safe. But this is also, I believe, the only moment in Hitchcock where a woman shows interest in the contents of another woman's handbag. If we link this moment to the first key scene and view the keys and Susan's handbag in Freudian terms (the first key as phallic; the second as clitoral), this suggests yet another coded reference to the film's enigmatic lesbian subtext (➤ HOMOSEXUALITY).

After Mark has tracked Marnie down – about 50 minutes into the film – there are however no more significant examples of the handbags motif. Moreover, when, late in the film, Marnie takes Mark's office keys, she is unable to go through with the theft. I take Sarah Street's point that, at the end of the film, Hitchcock returns to the children's chant about the 'lady with the alligator purse' who said that nothing was wrong with the subject of the rhyme (symbolically, Marnie) (Street 1995-96: 31). But I should also mention that, on this occasion, the line about the lady's diagnosis is not heard: the rhyme is cut off.

As with a number of motifs, FAMILY PLOT provides a most satisfying coda to the operation of these two examples. About 30 minutes into the film, there is a scene in which George and Blanche search hurriedly for her car keys. During this, George picks up Blanche's handbag from the desk at the precise moment when Blanche herself finds the keys in a drawer: she gives him the keys; he drops the handbag back on the desk. It happens in a flash, but its purpose would seem to be to link the two motifs *without* the violation of Blanche's handbag. Then, towards the end of the film, the motifs recur. George discovers Blanche's car parked outside Adamson's garage door, and when he sees the keys in the ignition, he knows that something is wrong. He then notices a line of fresh white paint under the garage door, like a spoor showing him the way. He breaks in and, in the garage, finds Blanche's handbag, with spots of blood on it. The three items – keys, white paint, bloody handbag – are like a series of clues, a trail leading him to the site of Blanche's abduction. All three items are the result of Adamson's carelessness or violence: he used Blanche's keys to move her car; the spilt paint and blood were the consequence of her struggle when he injected her to render her unconscious. The white paint echoes the black oil which marked Maloney's earlier sabotage of Blanche's car; it, too, spilled to form a line on the road. In the same spirit, the syringe which was used to inject Blanche came out of Fran's black handbag, and – in a sinister example of the Hands motif – passed in close-up from Fran's hand to Adamson's black-gloved hand. But now the incriminating elements work against the villains, and Hitchcock's inclusion of Blanche's keys and (light-coloured) handbag combines these two motifs to a common purpose. When Blanche and George's beautifully choreographed double act results in Adamson and Fran being themselves locked in the 'forbidden room' (➤ BED SCENE), George signals their success by holding up the key to the room with a triumphant 'Got 'em'. His possession of the villain's key is then complemented by Blanche's discovery of the villain's blackmail diamonds (➤ STAIRCASES). In Hitchcock's final film, then, the keys and handbags motifs ultimately work together, and celebrate the reuniting of the hero and heroine and the defeat of the villains.

In his brief entry on keys in the original *Cahiers du Cinéma* article on Hitchcock's motifs, Philippe Demonsablon notes the significance of a key for Freudians, but declines to apply such symbolism to the films, merely observing that keys in Hitchcock are a sign of power (Demonsablon 1956: 22). It has been my purpose here to argue that matters are much more complicated than that. A key may function in the Freudian sense only on occasions in Hitchcock, but it is nevertheless a major motif, with complex resonances. Likewise with handbags. Here the perceptions of Sarah Street's article have provided a valuable starting point, but again I have sought to extend her observations, and a Freudian reading of some of Hitchcock's handbags has been a part of this. It is, I believe, a measure of the 'gender balance' in Hitchcock's films that both these motifs are of similar significance to the workings of the narratives, and if keys, ultimately, have an ideological edge, that is a reflection of the gender imbalance in the culture, not of a bias in the films.

Keys, handbags and the police

When Chief Inspector Hubbard questions Margot about the key in her handbag, he begins politely: 'May I have your bag a moment?' However, once she has surrendered the bag, he becomes quite dominating. He takes the key out, holds it up to ask her whose it is, continues to hold it whilst he goes and fetches Tony's (now empty) briefcase, and then returns it to the purse and the purse to the bag with a theatrical flourish. At this point, with no more explanation, he simply commandeers the handbag, sending it with a colleague, Pearson, back to the police station. Absent-mindedly, Pearson sets off with the handbag dangling from his arm. Hubbard is quite alarmed: 'Wait a minute, you clot: you can't walk down the street like that, you'll be arrested.' To avoid this embarrassing eventuality, the potentially incriminating handbag is safely hidden in a briefcase.

First, Hubbard's holding the key as he strides around the apartment would seem to lend him authority. Second, although he commandeers Margot's handbag, he also has to ensure that it is not displayed in a provocative manner to policemen out in the street. It would seem that, to the police, the key is an object which empowers, whereas the handbag, signifier of femininity, is one which is potentially so disturbing that there are occasions when it needs to be concealed from public view. The distinction serves as a comment both on the contrast between the motifs and the thinking of the police. But something else is going on. Although Margot is the owner of the handbag, she is completely sidelined. Nor is this corrected at the end of the film. When Tony enters the flat to discover

Margot, Mark and Hubbard all waiting for him, he is carrying both the handbag and Margot's key. She does not receive either, but Tony makes a point of presenting Hubbard with her key, as if identifying him as the patriarchal figure who controls the keys.

Fig. 40. Still: DIAL M FOR MURDER: Key, handbag and the police. Chief Inspector Hubbard (John Williams) asks Margot (Grace Kelly) whether the key he has taken from her handbag is hers. Mark (Robert Cummings) looks on with some concern.

LIGHT(S)

Fig. 41. Still: I Confess: candlelight reveals a murderer. Father Logan (Montgomery Clift) discovers Keller (O.E. Hasse) in the church. Keller will shortly confess to Vilette's murder.

Vampires and blinding

About fifteen minutes into The Lodger, there is a close-up of a light in the Buntings' lodging house growing dim: money needs to be inserted in the meter. This theatrical device – as William Rothman points out, like lowering the house lights (Rothman 1982: 14) – is in fact to cue Ivor Novello's star entrance. When he appears on the doorstep, wearing a hat and with a scarf over his mouth, he is intended to look like descriptions of the Avenger. But there is another association, missed by Rothman, though since noted by Richard Allen (1999: 223). With his pale face and darkened eye sockets, Novello also evokes Max Schreck's eponymous vampire in NOSFERATU (F.W. Murnau, 1921), an association reinforced when he reacts nervously to the brightening of the lights as a coin is inserted. Nor was this the first time that Novello's star image had been linked to Dracula: in THE MAN WITHOUT DESIRE (Adrian Brunel, 1923), his character spends two hundred years in a state of suspended animation in a tomb. This is an early example of one of Hitchcock's most complex and elusive motifs: the symbolic use of light/lights, which occurs in many of his films, but nearly always allusively.

JAMAICA INN indicates how allusively. First, as Mary approaches the inn in a coach, the driver's refusal to stop at such a cursed place is another oblique reference to NOSFERATU. Second, the wreckers, who operate at night, cause the shipwrecks by removing the cliff-top beacon, thereby consigning the sailors to a darkness which kills them. As in NOSFERATU, the evil spreads out over the terrain, extending to the beaches where any sailors who survive the wrecks are promptly murdered. Eliminating the light thus leads to mass murder; what Mary is required to do in the climactic scene is restore the light and thereby save the sailors' lives.

JAMAICA INN also preserves one of the most significant features of the Dracula myth: the fear of daylight. Neither Joss, the leader of the wreckers, nor Sir Humphrey, the mastermind behind them, is ever seen outside during the day, and nightfall arrives abruptly at one point in order to sustain this. In other films the myth is evoked without this restriction. James McClaughlin looks in detail at the scenes in SHADOW OF A DOUBT where Uncle Charlie is linked to vampire imagery: the way he is suddenly energised when the landlady at the beginning draws the blind; the way he disappears 'supernaturally' when pursued by the two detectives; the way Charlie seems to 'summon' him telepathically; the extensive nighttime scenes (McLaughlin 1986: 142-43). Tying in with this, and also anticipating another of the associations of the motif, is the moment when Uncle Charlie is photographed by the detective Saunders. The moment is signalled by the flash of the camera's bulb, and Uncle Charlie's insistence that Saunders give him the film connects the flash with the fear of detection. But there is also the anomaly (oversight?) that, although the photograph is still sent East for identification, nothing more is heard of it; the film ends with knowledge of Uncle Charlie's guilt confined to Charlie and her policeman boyfriend. Could we infer that the photograph turned out blank; that Uncle Charlie, like a supernatural figure, really couldn't be photographed, and that his insistence on having the film was to stop others learning this?

STRANGERS ON A TRAIN also has Dracula overtones. In Part I, I mention the distorted image of Bruno's hands in the murder scene: another reference to NOSFERATU. Then, as the film approaches its climax, it too has an apparent anomaly: after all the suspenseful cross-cutting between Guy playing tennis and Bruno reaching down the drain for the lighter, Bruno waits until dark before setting out to plant the lighter on the island. However, as Theodore Price has noted (Price 1992: 334 – though he gets the details badly wrong), the very emphasis on the setting of the sun here (which is seen with both Bruno in the fairground and Guy on the train) evokes the vampire myth. Even DOWNHILL contains a trace of the myth in the effect of daylight on the features of Roddy's hitherto not unattractive female companion: the daylight does not kill, as in the myth, but it does lead to what looks like a sudden, dramatic ageing. That Hitchcock had Dracula in mind here is reinforced by an apparent mistake in the Truffaut interview: he says that, at this point, 'through the open window we see people passing by carrying a coffin' (Truffaut 1968: 43). No coffin exists in any print I've seen, but Hitchcock's comment refers to another familiar example of vampire iconography.

In these examples, the Lights motif is employed, more or less subtly, to evoke the relatively familiar connotations of the vampire myth. This may be seen as a generic use of the motif: often delicately employed, but otherwise relatively conventional. Philippe Demonsablon takes a different tack. Restricting his examples to flashes of light, he suggests that these suggest 'the revelation of an unbearably vivid truth; the criminal confronted with a living awareness which is no longer dissociated from its crime'. Thus, when Uncle Charlie is photographed, Demonsablon suggests that the flash freezes him, so that he seems to be thunderstruck (Demonsablon 1956: 22).

Although Demonsablon's argument only works up to a point, it is strengthened by an example from a film made after his article was published. Lightning frightens Marnie, and we learn at the end that this is because it is associated in her unconscious with her 'crime': the killing of a sailor. In addition, Demonsablon makes a pertinent connection between flashes of light and eyes. He cites YOUNG AND INNOCENT, where the first scene ends with the future murderer Guy outside in a storm, his facial twitch illuminated with flashes of lightning (➤ RAIN), and the film's climactic revelation occurs at the end of a long crane shot across a dance hall which ends on a big close-up of Guy's twitching eye. Although it is the second scene which catches Guy at the moment when he is confronted with 'the revelation of an unbearably vivid truth' relating to his crime (➤ GUILT AND CONFESSION), the two moments are structurally linked, and the lightning at the beginning is certainly connected to Guy's crime: immediately afterwards, he kills Christine Clay.

I would like to move on to an association which arises out of Demonsablon's examples: the notion of 'blinding', i.e. the physical pain of experiencing a light in one's eyes. The most famous instance of this is in REAR WINDOW, where Jeff tries to ward off Thorwald by blinding him with flashbulbs, and we experience

Thorwald's temporary loss of vision through a series of point-of-view shots. On this occasion, the act is self-revelatory: in effect Jeff is projecting onto his alter ego a symbolic version of the voyeur's punishment (blinding) Stella mentioned at the beginning of the film. It is because Jeff is himself a voyeur that the nature of this attack on Thorwald is so significant.

SABOTAGE includes a different sort of example. The opening act of sabotage puts out the lights of London, consigning the city to darkness. As Verloc, the saboteur, then returns home to lie on the marital bed in the darkness, again Dracula is perhaps fleetingly invoked. More striking, however, is the ensuing scene when his wife enters the room and shines a torch in his eyes, temporarily blinding him. If we take it that a saboteur is like a spy, a political voyeur, then Mrs Verloc's act is, symbolically, both threatening to expose her husband (he lies about his whereabouts) and punishing him by 'blinding'. Whilst this reading of the motif is only implicit in SABOTAGE, it occurs more overtly in FOREIGN CORRESPONDENT, where the spies torture the statesman Van Meer by – inter alia – shining bright lights in his eyes; again shown in point-of-view shots.

As in REAR WINDOW, it's as if Hitchcock's spies/voyeurs gravitate to the eyes to inflict pain because of their own obsession with looking. Even an innocuous (non-painful) example – Dr Koska examining Michael's eye with an optician's light in TORN CURTAIN – has its place here in that Michael is a spy and Dr Koska then proceeds interrogate him about his plans. Just as the returned look – e.g. Thorwald in REAR WINDOW – catches out the voyeur, so the probing light seeks to break down his resistance.

When not linked to espionage, the chain of connections eyes-voyeurism-light-pain can be varied. In PSYCHO, dazzled by the lights of the oncoming cars (and disorientated by the rain), Marion gets off the main road and arrives at the Bates Motel, thus entering the chaos world. As Robin Wood points out, eyes are a motif running through the movie, and Marion's murder is in effect framed by two close-ups of eyes: Norman's voyeuristic eye and Marion's dead eye. At the climax, a swinging light bulb in the cellar – knocked by Lila in her terror at the sight of Mrs Bates's skull – causes light to play over the eye sockets in the skull and seems to animate them: 'the mocking "eyes" of a long-dead corpse... the eyes of living death, eyes that move without seeing, the true eyes of Norman' (Wood 1989: 149). But this is also the image which takes us – in the dissolve from the skull to the County Court House – out of the chaos world. Thus the chaos world, too, is 'framed' by the eyes motif: just as we enter it when Marion's seeing eyes are 'blinded', so we leave it when Mrs Bates's unseeing eyes are apparently animated. Moreover, the animation is prophetic. Whereas Marion is killed in the chaos world, 'Mrs Bates', through Norman, lives on. At the end of the film, it is her voice that we hear, and her stare that we see.

Murder and homosexuality

In PSYCHO, the combination of the 'blinding' lights and the rain in effect causes Marion to lose her way, which ultimately proves fatal. The relevance of the rain here is discussed under RAIN, but the blinding lights are perhaps equally significant. In YOUNG AND INNOCENT and MARNIE, flashes of light (lightning) are linked more directly to murder. And there is one almost literal example of this association in Hitchcock: in FOREIGN CORRESPONDENT, the fake Van Meer is shot by an assassin posing as a photographer, so that the victim is blinded by the flash of the bulb as he is killed. It looks as if he is 'shot by' the flashbulb, which is indeed how Demonsablon describes the moment (Demonsablon 1956: 22). It is yet another measure of Hitchcock's sophistication with motifs that this 'blinding' is then echoed in the 'blinding' of the real Van Meer during the torture scene.

An implicit association between 'lights' and murder is not however confined to flashes of light. Towards the end of REBECCA, we see a light moving through Manderley at night from window to window; familiar Gothic imagery to indicate the sinister. Then Hitchcock cuts inside the house: Mrs Danvers, with a candle, walks through the darkness, up to the heroine asleep in a chair. She then turns away, her face by candlelight registering cunning. She has just been told by Favell that the doctor's evidence that Rebecca had cancer will confirm her death as suicide, so that 'Max and that dear little bride of his will be able to stay on at Manderley and live happily ever after'. In setting fire to Manderley, Danvers is obviously seeking to destroy this happiness, which confirms the generic reading: her intentions are indeed sinister. But there is another factor in play here. Mrs Danvers is coded as a lesbian, and we could read her arson as revenge on the heterosexual couple; revenge stemming from sexual jealousy.

What is at stake here is thus a certain sort of murderousness; one which has gay overtones. Similarly in STRANGERS ON A TRAIN. The first dramatic use of a light in the film is when Miriam, fleeing from her boyfriends on the Magic Isle, comes into close-up; her face is then illuminated by Bruno striking Guy's lighter to confirm her identity before strangling her. (Again there is a focus on eyes: it will be the reflection of the lighter flame in Miriam's spectacles which subsequently haunts Bruno: ➤ SPECTACLES.) Not only is Bruno here killing Miriam 'for' Guy – the gay subtext – but the Lights motif is reused when Guy enters Bruno's father's bedroom in the dark and Bruno switches on the light to reveal himself, not his father, in the bed. I argue under BED SCENE that Bruno waiting for Guy in bed is also a reference to the film's gay subtext, and again there is a link to murderousness: Bruno's plan was that Guy would enter his father's bedroom this way and shoot him. As in REBECCA, here, too, it is the gay character

Fig. 42. Still: FOREIGN CORRESPONDENT: Light flash and murder. Posing as a photographer, the assassin (Charles Wagenheim) is about to shoot the fake Van Meer (Albert Basserman) – the camera flash goes off as he fires. Johnny (Joel McCrea) in the middle.

who is murderous. This is confirmed when Guy throws down the gun Bruno had sent him: Bruno promptly picks it up and threatens to use it.

ROPE also includes moments – admittedly fleeting – which hint at the double association. Twice Phillip asks for a lamp which has just been switched on – by Brandon at the beginning; by Rupert later – to be turned off. We assume that Phillip's fear is that the light will somehow expose his guilt, but I argue under THE CORPSE that the guilt the young men feel for the murder is equally guilt for their homosexuality. Although a character fearing that light will expose him or her to scrutiny and so reveal guilt is clearly a commonplace, in Hitchcock it is not usually as simple as this: there tends to be something else going on. The light is like a marker of a certain sort of secret, one concerning 'forbidden' sexuality, or murderous intent.

Even JAMAICA INN, commonly held to be one of Hitchcock's least resonant films, has suggestive overtones. As the stagecoach races past the inn at the beginning, the driver comments cryptically 'There's queer things goes on there', repeating 'Queer things' to emphasise this to his companion. Although 'queer' as an adjective did not connote homosexual in the nineteenth century when the film is set, it did in the late 1930s when it was made. We note that Joss's signal for Sir Humphrey to visit him at night is a candle in the window (discreetly hidden behind some curtains). It's as if Jamaica Inn is 'the repressed' behind the Pengallan mansion, and just as the official reason for Sir Humphrey's visits is to plan mass murder, so there are hints of a subtextual sexual reason: as if Sir Humphrey comes to see Joss at the inn late at night for a 'bit of rough'. Like Latour in THE PARADINE CASE (➢ ENTRY THROUGH A WINDOW and HOMOSEXUALITY), he comes in the back door. Under HANDCUFFS AND BONDAGE, I mention another detail: at one point, Joss pretends to tie Sir Humphrey up, like an echo of their hinted-at practices elsewhere.

There are also two suggestive church scenes in Hitchcock. In SECRET AGENT, Ashenden and the General enter a church to make contact with the organist, who is sitting at the organ playing a chord. To attract his attention, they go to a shrine and light three candles, and the way Hitchcock films them, behind the candles, kneeling side by side, looks like a parody of a wedding ceremony. When they then approach the organist, they discover that he has been strangled. SECRET AGENT is one of the Hitchcock films in which there is quite an elaborate gay subtext (➢ CONFINED SPACES; HOMOSEXUALITY) and the way that the candles are linked on the one hand to the suggestion of a gay relationship and on the other to a murder is yet another example of this combination of elements in his films.

Similarly in I CONFESS. Early in the film, Father Logan carries a candle down the aisle to discover Keller sitting in the darkness. Here one of the men is himself a murderer: Keller has just come from killing Vilette, and confesses as much to Logan. But does the scene also have a gay subtext? The links with both SECRET AGENT and the Bed Scene in STRANGERS ON A TRAIN are suggestive, and – if Spoto is correct about O.E. Hasse (Spoto 1988: 340) – both actors were gay. Moreover, I CONFESS is one of Theodore Price's more convincing candidates for a film with a homosexual theme (➢ HOMOSEXUALITY). Just as Bruno kills Miriam for Guy, subtextually it seems as though Keller has killed Vilette for Logan, and what is unspoken in his confession – which, as Price points out (Price 1992: 271-72), echoes the scene behind the barred gate when Bruno confesses to Guy – is his desire for Logan.

In most of these examples linking murder and homosexuality through the Lights motif, a gay character is a murderer, or at least has murderous intentions (Mrs Danvers). Only in SECRET AGENT does the murder derive from a third party, and even here, (a) the General is patently murderous, advancing on the organist with his knife at the ready and (b) Theodore Price also includes the actual murderer, Marvin, in the film's gay subtext, and I'm inclined to agree with him (Price 1992: 54). We are thus back once again with the association in the Hitchcockian unconscious between murder and homosexuality (➤ HOMOSEXUALITY). In a significant number of cases, the Lights motif serves to focus this notion in Hitchcock's work.

To an extent, I am being selective in my examples. There are a lot of light sources in any Hitchcock film, and not all will have these sort of resonances. Candles are perhaps a special case: they do indeed seem to be used suggestively more often than not. However, with the other light sources I am making claims for, there are certain basic criteria: they are lights which are suddenly switched on, or which are foregrounded in the image in some way, like the naked light bulb in the bathroom in TOPAZ (➤ HOMOSEXUALITY). On these occasions, the dramatic introduction of a light very frequently alludes to troubling undercurrents in the films.

I would maintain that, on those occasions when Hitchcock does give a light source an unusual emphasis in some way, there is almost always an allusion to such darker undercurrents. Another example is when, immediately after Bruno has informed him about Miriam's murder, Guy is in his apartment on the phone to Anne. Hitchcock films the shot from a low angle, and frames it so that an illuminated table lamp next to Guy is given a similar visual prominence to Guy himself. Again much the same subtextual elements are present: the reference to Miriam's murder (Guy is holding her spectacles), the troubling gay overtones to this (Bruno's motivation and his attitude to Guy) and Guy's need to keep all this a secret from the woman to whom he is speaking.

There is even one example where the light itself is hidden, but in such an ostentatious way that it is at the same time visually emphasised: the light in the milk in SUSPICION. Towards the end of the film, Hitchcock repeats the Gothic light imagery from REBECCA: Johnnie carries a glowing glass of milk up the stairs to Lina in bed. As is now well known, Hitchcock made the milk glow by putting a light in it. This – and the sleeping/bed association – draws the connection. In REBECCA, the candle also suggests the means whereby Danvers will set light to the house, and part of her motivation is to kill the heroine. By putting the light in the milk, Hitchcock is in effect saying that it, too, embodies the same sort of threat to the heroine. There are no gay overtones in this case, but there is certainly an intimation of murderousness: as I have already argued (➤ *Milk* in Part I), we are surely meant to assume that the milk is poisoned.

Vampires and blinding, murder and homosexuality, and behind these, the fear of discovery – this is a heady mixture. What ties most of them together is the sense of the repressed and the forbidden. Whereas light – like water – normally has positive connotations in the culture, and it is shadows which are used to suggest the sinister, in Hitchcock lights frequently seem to carry the same sort of negative associations as shadows. Even the very properties of light can be harmful: dazzling, disorientating, exposing, 'blinding', attracting attacking birds (Melanie's flashlight in the attic bedroom). It is regrettable that homosexuality is tied into this nexus of associations in such a negative sense, but when it is invoked through the use of the motif, it is almost always seen as malevolent. The motif is yet another which highlights the darkness of Hitchcock's vision: even light comes to be associated, primarily, with the sinister and the violent.

Not always, however. Sometimes a light is given a different sort of expressive function: Charles Barr has written eloquently of the sweeping lighthouse beam in THE MANXMAN – producing an alternating pattern of light and dark – as an image symbolising dividedness and uncertainty in the characters at different points in the narrative (Barr 1999: 69-70). In REAR WINDOW, Lisa switches on one or more lamps in Jeff's apartment on a number of occasions. The first is part of Grace Kelly's star entrance: as Lisa moves around the room, switching on three lamps, she is self-consciously displaying herself to Jeff in her $1100 gown. The repetition of the motif is then used to open up the associations: Lisa becomes the figure who brings light into Jeff's apartment, just as Thorwald is the figure who brings darkness into his own apartment. In SPELLBOUND, the light under the door of the hero's room is like a source of attraction for Constance: she goes in, J.B. wakes up, and their love affair begins. The shot of the light under the door is then echoed towards the end of the film, when the villain has repossessed the room; now it would seem that the early positive associations have been usurped. Again, however, Constance's entry is beneficial: she exposes Murchison as the murderer. Finally, in Johnny's stirring propaganda speech – broadcast from London to America – at the end of FOREIGN CORRESPONDENT, darkness is imaged as the result of Nazi bombing, but he sees hope in the lights of America. In contrast to the earlier uses of the motif in the film, now the associations of light are entirely positive. The film ends, as Johnny and Carol are plunged into total darkness, with his voice ringing on: 'Fellow Americans, hang on to your lights, they're the only lights left in the world.' Of course, the rhetoric here has everything to do with the film's time of production, but it is powerful stuff, nevertheless. However, these positive examples of the Lights motif are rare in Hitchcock. They have their place and importance, but the darker manifestations are much more prevalent.

See also APPENDIX I.

Lights and the police

In both Saboteur (Pat in the circus wagon) and To Catch a Thief (Robie on the roof at the climax), the police shine a light on someone. This does not help; they still get it wrong. In Saboteur, they fail to realise that they are looking at the young woman they are seeking; in To Catch a Thief, they've got the wrong man and, to make matters worse, they start shooting at him. However, it is also true that, in the later example, they stop shooting when they see that Robie is not alone on the roof. The arrival of the hero's double here gives the police pause.

The light the police use in To Catch a Thief is an arc light, as if lighting a film set. As Robie holds Danielle over the drop to the ground to make her confess, he extends the metaphor: 'You've got a full house down there – begin the performance.' Danielle thus confesses under the glare of the police searchlight, but the duress comes not from the light, but from Robie's bullying treatment of her. He makes her repeat both parts of her confession more loudly, to make sure that the police can hear. It's as if the very obtuseness of the police goads him into risking the life of a young woman in order to establish his innocence. The performance that the hero and his double enact in the public glare of the light may finally resolve the question of the identity of 'the Cat', but it also exposes the hero's ruthlessness.

THE MACGUFFIN

Fig. 43. Still: NORTH BY NORTHWEST: the MacGuffin. Roger (Cary Grant) and Eve (Eva Marie Saint) hold the Tarascan warrior which contains the microfilm as they clamber across the face of Mount Rushmore.

The concept of the MacGuffin in Hitchcock is more slippery than may, at first, be apparent. To Truffaut, Hitchcock defines it as the secret or documents the spies are after, distinguishing between his own point of view and that of the characters in the film: these items 'must seem to be of vital importance to the characters. To me, the narrator, they're of no importance whatever' (Truffaut

1968: 111-12). To illustrate this last point, he says that the uranium MacGuffin in
NOTORIOUS had troubled the producer (Selznick), so he had offered to replace it
with industrial diamonds (138). (I am not concerned with the accuracy of this
story, which Leonard J. Leff disputes [1988: 194], but with the point Hitchcock is
making: the nature of the MacGuffin is unimportant.) After the success of the
film, he claims further to have chided another producer who had rejected the
project because of the uranium: 'You were wrong to attach any importance to
the MacGuffin. NOTORIOUS was simply the story of a man in love with a girl
who, in the course of her official duties, had to go to bed with another man and
even had to marry him' (Truffaut 1968: 138). Here Hitchcock introduces a third
point of view on the MacGuffin: that of the audience. Even though the uranium
MacGuffin is, in fact, the secret of the atomic bomb, Hitchcock is saying that the
audience is simply not interested: it is the personal story which counts, and the
MacGuffin is merely a means to an end.

Other examples of the MacGuffin in his spy movies would certainly support
this. We are simply not interested in the nature of the 'state secrets' (or whatever) in these movies: the formula for an aircraft engine in THE 39 STEPS; the
secret clauses in THE LADY VANISHES and FOREIGN CORRESPONDENT; the government secrets in NORTH BY NORTHWEST; the formula for an anti-missile missile in TORN CURTAIN. Nevertheless, the implications of such a lack of interest
obviously merit discussion. I would like to look at this aspect of the MacGuffin
first.

Robert J. Corber argues, not unreasonably, that Hitchcock's indifference to the
nature of the MacGuffin serves to depoliticise the films. Corber suggests that
Hitchcock adopted this stance as an aspect of his project as artist: he 'discour-
aged critics from politicizing his films by situating them historically. He wanted
to ensure their canonization as great works of art' (Corber 1993: 200). Corber
has his own project – to argue that Hitchcock's post-war films are shot through
with political undercurrents – and he wishes to question this 'depoliticisation'.
But with the film he is discussing here, NORTH BY NORTHWEST, he displaces his
focus from the actual MacGuffin to a consideration of Roger's activities as
American agent, calling that the MacGuffin. This muffles the problem. Similarly
with NOTORIOUS. Wishing to question the way that 'critics have tended to celebrate the way in which the film supposedly reduces the discovery of the uranium ore to the status of a MacGuffin' (Corber 1993: 203), Corber points out that

> Devlin and Alicia's formation as a couple is contingent upon their discovering the
> source of the uranium ore... [Similarly, their] inscription within the discourses of na-
> tional security enables the American government to regulate and control the most
> personal aspects of the construction of their subjectivity, including the organization
> of their sexuality.
>
> (Corber 1993: 203)

Fine, but this does not affect Hitchcock's point: that he could have replaced the uranium ore with something else without changing the way the film works. There is a deeper problem here.

In his discussion of the MacGuffin in NORTH BY NORTHWEST, George Wilson seems to me closer to the spirit of Hitchcock's purpose. The government secrets are on strips of microfilm inside a pre-Columbian statuette of a Tarascan warrior, and the strips make an appearance at the film's climax on Mount Rushmore, when Leonard – trying to make Roger and Eve fall – is shot, and drops the statuette so that it breaks. Wilson comments:

> Here then *is* the ultimate MacGuffin. The crucial object at the heart of all this film's hallucinatory action, the goal that locks the opposing forces in loony cold war conflict, is no more and no less than a piece of the stuff that films are made of. In a context such as NORTH BY NORTHWEST, where films are the stuff that reality is made of [this refers to Wilson's argument in this chapter], there is nothing else that the Tarascan Warrior could contain.

(Wilson 1986: 81)

Wilson's use of the adjective loony is highly suggestive: it imputes a detached, cynical attitude to the political imperatives in these films. This, surely, is Hitchcock's position, and it is expressed in NORTH BY NORTHWEST by Roger's speech to the CIA's Professor: 'If you fellows can't lick the Vandamms of this world without asking girls like her to bed down with them and fly away with them and probably never come back, perhaps you ought to start losing a few cold wars.' From this point of view, the MacGuffin matters only as some Cold War trifle the heroine has been risking her life for.

This is made much more poignant in TOPAZ, because the heroine – among others – really does give her life to obtain the MacGuffin. Based on the real-life 1962 Cuban missile crisis – which brought the world to the brink of nuclear war – TOPAZ raises the stakes with regard to the MacGuffin. There are in fact two MacGuffins in the film: the 'aide memoire' in Rico Parra's briefcase which DuBois photographs with Uribe's help in the Hotel Theresa, and the microfilm showing the presence of Soviet missiles in Cuba. The former is obtained for the West in a typical MacGuffin-centred suspense sequence: it's enjoyably exciting, because none of the good guys gets hurt (➤ HOMOSEXUALITY). The latter, however, is a different matter, since it leads to the torture – and, we assume, execution – of the Mendozas, a married couple who took the espionage photographs, and to the murder of Juanita. But Hitchcock takes things further. He shifts the events from Leon Uris's novel – in which André's mission to Cuba was sufficiently in advance of the crisis to alert the USA to the danger – by having the mission take place after the American spy planes had obtained the necessary information, and even after President Kennedy had delivered his ultimatum to Krushchev, the Soviet leader. The former is noted by Lesley Brill (1988: 186-87); the latter may be deduced from the headline and date of the newspaper André reads as he flies into Cuba. The date is 22 October 1962, and the headline refers to Kennedy's forthcoming TV address, in which he told the world that the Soviet Union had placed missiles on Cuba and he was going to instigate a 'quarantine' around the island to stop further missiles arriving. In short, Hitchcock makes the sacrifices of the Western agents on Cuba pointless. This emphasises the pessimism of the film. In this case, the information being sought by the agents could not readily be replaced by something else, and Hitchcock was obviously aware of this. Instead, he made the whole business of obtaining it unnecessary, thus constructing a bitter indictment of Cold War politics.

The dangerousness of the quest for the MacGuffin is not, however, confined to Topaz; it is also apparent, for example, in the poisoning of Alicia in NOTOR-IOUS. Hitchcock's point about the importance of the MacGuffin to the characters is thus crucial. The MacGuffin is not simply a device to dramatise tensions between the characters, but – like the object of a quest in a myth or folktale – an overvalued object which draws the characters who seek to possess it into life-threatening situations. TOPAZ's most painful scene is the torturing of the Mendozas, and the most powerful one Rico's shooting of Juanita (➤ HANDS). Both scenes are a direct consequence of these characters' attempts to obtain the MacGuffin and to get the information out of the country.

In a myth or folktale, the object of a quest would normally bestow status and/ or power on its possessor. In Hitchcock's spy movies, the MacGuffin usually only delivers such power to those at the top of the political hierarchy: figures whom we do not meet. TOPAZ is not concerned with President Kennedy agonising over what to do with the information about the missiles. There is, however, an exception to this general rule: where the information concerns a projected assassination, as in the two versions of THE MAN WHO KNEW TOO MUCH. Their knowledge of the assassination confers on the married hero and heroine the power to prevent it, and Hitchcock explores the tensions which arise when, for personal reasons, they refuse to pass on this knowledge to the appropriate authorities, i.e. the relevant Home Office or Scotland Yard officials. This illustrates the ideological function of the MacGuffin: the characters we care about are supposed to set aside their personal wishes and feelings and act in the service of the state. In that the tensions which can arise under such circumstances are also dramatised in NOTORIOUS and NORTH BY NORTHWEST, we should explore this a little further.

The world of espionage is a typical example of the Hitchcock chaos world. The MacGuffin has its place here as a symptom – and symbol – of that world: overvalued (except to the spymasters), dangerous to pursue, the MacGuffin symbolises the heartlessness of the state. That is why it does not matter what it is: it's a symbol. In effect, through its insistence on the importance of the MacGuffin, the state creates the chaos world; or, at least, creates it in conjunction with another state, which similarly overvalues the MacGuffin. When Leonard is shot, urbane spymaster Vandamm quips to patrician spymaster the Professor: 'That wasn't very sporting, using real bullets.' In the meantime, all Vandamm's henchmen are dead and Roger and Eve are still clinging desperately to the face of Mount Rushmore.

Critics have sought to extend the notion of the MacGuffin beyond the spy movies, suggesting that it is possible to have a 'crime MacGuffin', e.g. the diamond necklace in NUMBER SEVENTEEN. Charles Barr notes that although we have no interest in the necklace as such, 'it has motivated and made possible the narrative. It is the pure prototype for the MacGuffin which became so celebrated a part of the Hitchcock strategy and the Hitchcock legend' (Barr 1999: 125). However, because there is no ideological charge attached to the necklace, it is much less significant as a device. Similarly with other objects which we might consider to be crime MacGuffins: the stolen jewels in TO CATCH A THIEF; the ransom diamonds in FAMILY PLOT. Because the quest for these objects is motivated purely by greed, their role is strictly structural. But there is more to be said about the spy MacGuffins, and this is to do with their positioning in the narratives of the movies.

The key examples are NOTORIOUS, NORTH BY NORTHWEST and the Cuban section of TOPAZ. In each, (1) the heroine is between the hero and the villain: she loves the former, but is sexually involved with the latter; (2) the triangle is implicitly Oedipal, and the MacGuffin is a part of this: it is the villain's secret, and the heroine – in NOTORIOUS and TOPAZ in collusion with the hero – is seeking to obtain it from him, and (3) there is a scene in which the three principals are brought together by the MacGuffin, resulting in a sexually charged confrontation.

In NOTORIOUS, this last scene occurs when Alex catches Alicia and Devlin outside the cellar where they have just discovered the uranium MacGuffin in a wine bottle. To pretend to Alex that their rendezvous was motivated by romance rather than espionage, Devlin gets Alicia to kiss him (➤ SPY FILMS / THE LOOK under EXHIBITIONISM / VOYEURISM). This leads Alex to discover that his wife is a spy, and he begins to poison her. In NORTH BY NORTHWEST, the equivalent scene is at the auction, when Roger sees Vandamm and Eve together for the first time. Here the hero has no knowledge of the heroine's undercover role, but his making such a fuss about her in front of Vandamm nevertheless serves a very similar function to Devlin's kissing Alicia: it begins to raise the villain's suspicions about the heroine. During this, prompted by Leonard, Vandamm bids for and purchases the Tarascan warrior.

The MacGuffin's entry into the narrative in this film is thus timed even more precisely to mark the point at which the hero and villain come face to face over the question of the heroine's 'loyalties'.

In TOPAZ, there are, strictly speaking, two scenes which integrate the MacGuffin in a similar way. As André first arrives at Juanita's hacienda, she comes out to greet him accompanied by Rico Parra, who places a proprietorial arm around her shoulders. During the ensuing scene on the doorstep, André hands her a boxed gift, declaring that it's nylons; in fact it contains electronic surveillance equipment. Although this is not the MacGuffin, it is the means to discover the MacGuffin: we could see this moment as the equivalent, in NOTORIOUS, of Alicia secretly handing Devlin the cellar key. The scene also echoes the one in the auction room: this is André's first sight of Juanita with Rico; the latter's proprietorial gesture is the same as Vandamm's; here, too, the heroine's loyalties are as yet unclear.

However, it is the second scene with these three characters which more closely matches the confrontation scenes in NOTORIOUS and NORTH BY NORTHWEST. This occurs after the Mendozas' spy photographs have been secretly delivered to Juanita, and also after Rico has discovered that André is a spy. He arrives at Juanita's hacienda to order André out of the country, only refraining from arresting and executing him because he seeks – at this point – to protect Juanita. The MacGuffin is not directly involved here, but the dead chicken in which it was smuggled into Juanita's house has just been consumed and appreciated by herself and André, so that it is there, in effect, by proxy.

If the doorstep scene in TOPAZ is also included, we can see that one role of the MacGuffin in these scenes is to mark a moment of Oedipal tension for the hero. His desire for the heroine has brought him into conflict with the villain who functions as an Oedipal rival in two senses: he considers that he has a sexual claim on the heroine, and his role as a (ruthless) political villain gives him power over the hero. The MacGuffin is a symbol of that power, albeit a sometimes ambiguous one. In TOPAZ, where the MacGuffin is knowledge of the Soviet missiles, we can readily Freudianise the hero's quest as an attempt to steal the villain's phallus. But in NOTORIOUS, the MacGuffin invites a less flattering reading. William Rothman suggests that the cellar contains the secret of Alex's relationship with his mother:

> The suggestion is that the key marked *Unica* (union, eunuch) which unlocks the [Devlin/Alicia] relationship ... unlocks as well the secret that [Alex] is sexually not really a man, that the wine bottle in his cellar is dry, containing not liquid but dust.
>
> (Rothman 1975: 908-909)

I discuss the symbolism of the NORTH BY NORTHWEST MacGuffin under HOMOSEXUALITY, where I argue that it refers, primarily, to the Vandamm-

Leonard relationship. As in NOTORIOUS, this is a sexual secret which lies buried under the political aspects, and which adds another twist to the Oedipal overtones.

In all cases, however, the MacGuffin is far more dangerous for the heroine. When the villain discovers that his secret is known, and that the heroine has been a party to this, it is she who is threatened with murder (NOTORIOUS; NORTH BY NORTHWEST), even killed (TOPAZ). The villain reacts like the betrayed husband or lover that he is, but because the betrayal is also political, he feels empowered to kill the heroine: the status of the MacGuffin authorises this. Even in NOTORIOUS, where Alex sets out to murder Alicia primarily to protect himself, the earlier fate of his fellow Nazi Emile – killed for drawing attention to the hiding place of the MacGuffin – shows that here, too, the same thinking prevails. In the name of the MacGuffin, the agents of the state are licensed to kill.

One could argue that there is in fact a third MacGuffin in TOPAZ: the identity of Topaz, a communist mole in the French government. However, to extend the notion of the MacGuffin to a person – another example would be the secret German agent Marvin in SECRET AGENT – is problematic. It is true that the heroine in both these films is deceived by the enemy agent, and that this prompts her to 'leave' the hero for him. But there is no real charge set up by these 'people MacGuffins': even the resulting sexual triangles seem superficial. When the MacGuffin is an object or message, Hitchcock is able to condense the concerns of the film into scenes in which it is prominent. A person lacks the flexibility to be used in this manner. I think it is more useful to conceptualise the way in which these figures function in the plots as in some senses like a MacGuffin, but in others, very different.

The role of the MacGuffin in the other main group of films is rather different. In THE 39 STEPS, THE LADY VANISHES, FOREIGN CORRESPONDENT and TORN CURTAIN, the MacGuffin is inside the head of someone. But there are no sexual tensions between the protagonists and these characters; indeed, they are more like elderly parent figures to the hero and heroine. Nevertheless, two of the films can be seen to have links with those already discussed; I would like to consider these first.

TORN CURTAIN echoes NOTORIOUS. Again, the MacGuffin concerns a secret weapon being developed by the enemy, and here the hero steals the actual formula on which the weapon is based. Michael's theft of this from Professor Lindt is motivated by his wish to regain the position he lost when, unable himself to find the formula, he was demoted from Washington research to teaching. The restoration of his status will also facilitate his marriage to Sarah: again, the MacGuffin symbolises the phallus, its theft enabling the hero to recover his potency. Lindt functions in this drama as the intellectual father figure who is outwitted by the scheming son, and, on this occasion, the MacGuffin genuinely lends the hero personal power.

Similarly, as is well known, THE 39 STEPS anticipates NORTH BY NORTHWEST. Links relevant to the MacGuffin are that an enemy agent is seeking to get it out of the country, that a major problem is to discover where it is hidden, and that the climax of each film is built around the saving of the MacGuffin for democracy and the formation of the romantic couple.

Mr Memory's role in this last has already been discussed by Slavoj Žižek. He points out that Mr Memory's public answer to Hannay's question, 'What are "the 39 steps"?' releases Hannay from the role of the falsely accused man and enables the police to capture the master spy, Jordan – who shoots Mr Memory to shut him up. Žižek comments: 'There is something of the fairy tale in this figure of a Good Dwarf who must die in order that the liaison of the amorous couple finally be established' (Žižek 1992: 100). It's as if the figure who has carried the MacGuffin as such a burden – a point implicit in Mr Memory's dying words – needs to die in order to relieve the hero of *his* burden. Mr Memory's garbled recitation of the MacGuffin to Hannay here is like a confession. Then, as Žižek indicates, the formation of the romantic couple is sealed: silently watching the crowd gather around Mr Memory's dead body, Hannay and Pamela in the foreground reach to hold hands.

The ending of NORTH BY NORTHWEST is surprisingly similar. As he hangs on to the face of Mount Rushmore with Eve, Roger proposes. In the ensuing action, first Valerian is killed in a fall (➤ HEIGHTS AND FALLING), then Leonard is shot, leaving Roger and Eve suspended over the abyss. At this point, Hitchcock magically rescues them: in a famous – and miraculous – match cut, he contrives to have Roger pull Eve straight from the face of Mount Rushmore up to the upper berth in a train sleeping car. As in THE 39 STEPS, the concluding handclasp confirms their romantic future together: here, they are already on their honeymoon.

Both happy endings are preceded by the same three events: (1) the arrest of the master spy, (2) the spilling out of the MacGuffin (verbally; physically) in front of the hero and heroine, and (3) the death of the figure who had it in his possession. We would anticipate that the matter of the MacGuffin has to be settled before the hero and heroine can have a 'happy ending'. But the spilling out of the MacGuffin at the end of these two movies goes further: it's a way of turning it into the garbage that Hitchcock has all along considered it to be. At the same time, the contrasting fates of the two spies in each film is a succinct comment on the hierarchy of power in the espionage organisations. Yet, at least in Mr Memory's case, Hitchcock also signals regret that his foolish involvement with the MacGuffin has led to his death. Also implied in the staging of the ending is that Hannay and Pamela are silently mourning his passing.

The final two films, THE LADY VANISHES and FOREIGN CORRESPONDENT, can be considered as a pair. In each, the person who has memorised the MacGuffin is kidnapped by enemy agents: either to shut her up (THE LADY VANISHES) or to make him talk (FOREIGN CORRESPONDENT). Much of the plot is then taken up with the protagonists' attempts to track down and rescue this character, thereby ensuring that the MacGuffin gets back to England (THE LADY VANISHES) or that it remains out of the enemy's hands (FOREIGN CORRESPONDENT). Because the character is on the same side as the protagonists in these films, a shift occurs: their priority is to take care of her/him. In THE LADY VANISHES, Gilbert and Irene work together to find and rescue Miss Froy, and the film ends with her joining hands with them as if to unite them. Again the ending emphasises the formation of the couple, here mediated through the benevolent mother figure whose adventures have served to bring them together. In FOREIGN CORRESPONDENT, although the equivalent character – the Dutch diplomat Van Meer – seems more peripheral to the love story, he is still significant. Here the heroine's father, Fisher, is one of the kidnappers, which means that the fulfilment of the romance is dependent on freeing the heroine from him. In this respect, Van Meer's role is crucial. It is when he is rescued and tells his story that a chain of events is set in motion which includes Fisher's confession to Carol, his own suicide and the reuniting of the hero and heroine. Albeit behind the scenes, Van Meer, too, creates the conditions which enable the formation of the couple.

Collectively, these endings indicate that it is the very quest for the MacGuffin – or concern for the bearer of the MacGuffin – which has served to bring the hero and heroine together. The death of Juanita in TOPAZ may be seen as a rare, tragic outcome, but even here the ending of the film conforms – however unsatisfactorily – to the pattern, in that it reunites André and Nicole. At least, that was Hitchcock's plan, visible in the film's first two endings. The more familiar third ending reveals its cobbled-together nature by not including their reunion. But this function of the MacGuffin is purely structural: one finds the same pattern in all those films in which the hero and heroine share a quest for something, e.g. the raincoat and the man with the twitching eye in YOUNG AND INNOCENT. What is special about the MacGuffin-centred quests is the role of the competing state agencies in determining the outcome. The MacGuffin is a state secret, and hence is surrounded with the apparatus of state paranoia: the espionage networks, the security measures and the ruthless, even brutal, practices built up around them. The fates of the Mendozas and Juanita demonstrate just how brutal these can be. Perhaps the strongest argument for including Marvin in SECRET AGENT and Granville in TOPAZ as 'people MacGuffins' is that the same practices come into play around these figures, resulting in the murder of (the in fact innocent) Caypor in the former and of Jarre in the latter.

There are two contrasting ways in which the hero and heroine engage with the quest for (and/or protection of) the MacGuffin. In NOTORIOUS, NORTH BY NORTHWEST and TOPAZ, it is associated with an Oedipal villain, and its theft symbolically emasculates him. If we also include TORN CURTAIN in this group, we can see that for these four films Corber's point about the state regulating the protagonists' sexuality has some relevance. The films operate on a continuum in this respect; from the murderous finality of the state intervention in TOPAZ (the killing of Juanita) to the implicit escape from the demands of the state at the end of NORTH BY NORTHWEST, with the fate of couples in NOTORIOUS and TORN CURTAIN somewhere in between.

In the other group of films, the characters who carry the MacGuffin in their heads are oddly endearing eccentrics, and the protagonists are usually more or less protective of them. Here the MacGuffin itself is even more irrelevant, and the focus shifts from it to these symbolic parent figures. Yet they, too, become victims of state-sponsored violence. Again, TORN CURTAIN is an exception on both these counts: Michael's mission has not been sanctioned by the US authorities, and he shows no concern whatever for Lindt's welfare. But in the other films, the protagonists bear witness to the violence meted out in the interests of the state against these figures: the kidnapped and mummified Miss Froy; the kidnapped, drugged and tortured Van Meer; the ruthlessly shot Mr Memory. These figures' knowledge of the MacGuffin is like a curse, condemning them to suffer, even die, for knowing too much.

This helps to locate the functioning of the MacGuffin in the two versions of THE MAN WHO KNEW TOO MUCH. In a reworking of the kidnap plots in THE LADY VANISHES and FOREIGN CORRESPONDENT, it is a child who is kidnapped, and the parents refuse to talk to the authorities because of the harm which could come to their child. The projected assassination victim is an elder statesman; as a father figure to his country, he belongs to the group of figures who are treated with some solicitude by the protagonists in the other movies. The hero and heroine are thus emotionally divided by a powerful impulse (to save their child) and an equally powerful imperative (to save a seemingly benevolent statesman's life). According to the theories of Robert B. Heilman, this dividedness in the protagonist is the stuff of tragedy (Heilman 1973: 27-31). In each version of THE MAN WHO KNEW TOO MUCH, it is the heroine in particular who experiences this. As discussed under PUBLIC DISTURBANCES, the tension builds in her until she emits a highly dramatic scream during a concert at the Albert Hall. At an obvious level, her scream represents both a release of tension – her response to the unbearable pressure of the inner conflict – and her protest at the impossible situation she is in. It may also be read as a rather striking substitute-formation. She cannot reveal the MacGuffin: what she knows about the planned assassination. Instead, she involuntarily releases a scream which is so timed that it has the same effect as if she had talked. She does not divulge the MacGuffin, but she does save the statesman's life.

In these two films, the assassin's bullet merely wounds. More often, at the end of the quest for the MacGuffin, there is an actual political killing, in which the agents of one state or the other 'deal with' a spy or spies. This also applies to SECRET AGENT, where the British spymaster 'R' orders the bombing of a whole train to eliminate one enemy agent (➤ TRAINS). One is tempted to use the word execution. We can thus see another reason why Hitchcock originally wanted to end TOPAZ with a duel between André and Granville (➤ DOUBLES). Just as first Uribe and then Juanita are 'executed' by Rico Parra, so in this scene Granville is 'executed' by a Soviet sniper in the stands of the stadium. This was Hitchcock's last spy film, and one feels that he was finally able to express what he really felt about the world of espionage and its preoccupation with the MacGuffin. The tone is bleak indeed.

The MacGuffin and the police

In the communist countries, the police take the MacGuffin very seriously. They are prepared to torture (Munoz in TOPAZ), even to machine-gun bus passengers and costume baskets (TORN CURTAIN) in their efforts to prevent it getting out of the country. The British and American police, by contrast, are much too busy pursuing the falsely accused hero to be of practical use in such matters. Discussing the role of the police in the theatre at the climax of THE 39 STEPS (they won't listen to Hannay's story, and seek to usher him away), Charles Barr nevertheless suggests that 'through a combination of stupidity and temperamental sympathy, [they are] on the fascist side' (Barr 1999: 160). This is, perhaps, a little harsh. Only moments later, the police do their stuff and arrest the master spy. Similarly, at the end of NORTH BY NORTHWEST, the forest ranger shoots Leonard, thereby saving both the MacGuffin *and* the romantic couple. In general, however, one would have to admit that the MacGuffin is really too weighty a matter for the British or American police; state secrets are not their territory.

MOTHERS AND HOUSES

Fig. 44. Still: THE BIRDS: the middle-class mother in her house. Waiting for the birds to attack, Lydia (Jessica Tandy) sits close to Mitch (Rod Taylor) and the portrait of her husband; Melanie (Tippi Hedren) looks after Cathy (Veronica Cartwright).

My concern here is with Hitchcock's representation of middle-aged mothers and mother figures. His young mothers are presented sympathetically: Kate in THE MANXMAN, Jill and Jo in each version of THE MAN WHO KNEW TOO MUCH, Jennifer in THE TROUBLE WITH HARRY, Rose in THE WRONG MAN. But his older maternal figures are a much more mixed bunch. The general consensus is that such figures in Hitchcock's films are usually viewed negatively, but that this is restricted to the American period. 'Throughout his British films, Hitchcock's maternal figures are loving, sympathetic and attractive, even when they are slightly ridiculous' (Leitch 1991: 133). Even Robin Wood writes that the fussy, bossy Aunt Margaret in YOUNG AND INNOCENT is 'the closest figure in the British films to the monstrous mothers of the American period' (Wood 1989: 284). Not so. Hitchcock's malevolent mothers go back to EASY VIRTUE. As soon as we see Mrs Whittaker at the top of the stairs, about to descend to meet her son's bride, Larita, we recognise her instantly as the prototype of Mrs Danvers (REBECCA) and Mme Sebastian (NOTORIOUS): her whole demeanour signals hostility and repressiveness. At the end of Larita's first day in the Whittaker mansion, an inter-title informs us 'During the days that followed, Mrs Whittaker made Larita's life a burden to her – in private. But she was all smiles and sweetness with her – in public.'

Mrs Whittaker's hostility stems from her conviction that the woman her son has married is unsuitable, even though it is not until later that she uncovers any evidence that Larita has a 'scandalous' past. What galls her is Larita's air of sophisticated irony, which is focused in the latter's retrospectively unfortunate habit of smoking incessantly. THE MANXMAN has a similar figure in Philip's repressive aunt, who has brought him up and who informs him that Kate, a pub landlord's daughter, is not suitable for a man who is destined to become Deemster (judge). It is the aunt's opposition which is crucial in rendering the love affair furtive and so prompting the consequent disaster. In THE SKIN GAME, Jill's mother Mrs Hillcrist is the main source of the trouble between the two families. Her insistence on treating the nouveau riche Hornblowers as social inferiors hardens Hornblower's intransigence, and her ruthless use of blackmail material against them results in disaster: Chloë Hornblower attempts suicide.

In all these cases, the mother or mother figure is a snob, and her hostility is directed at a woman whom she can feel contempt towards because of her background or social position. By contrast, Hitchcock's lower-middle or working-class mothers – in the British films, at least – are generally sympathetic. Indeed, Juno in JUNO AND THE PAYCOCK is in effect the heroine and the focus of the film's melodrama of suffering.

Lying behind the actions of the hostile mothers is a deeper purpose; what they are really defending from the intruding woman is the home: the family position or tradition. This is the key to the power of Hitchcock's mothers: with only the rarest exceptions, hostile mothers are linked to the home. This helps explain why the forthright and unpretentious Jessie Stevens in To CATCH A THIEF (on holiday in Europe with her daughter Francie) is viewed favourably by Robie – until, at the end, Francie threatens to move her into his home. Equally, the most sinister and powerful of the threatening mother figures (Mrs Danvers; Milly in UNDER CAPRICORN) may only be servants, but their association with the hero's house dramatically enhances their power.

Despite the precedents of EASY VIRTUE and THE SKIN GAME, there is nevertheless no question that, in the Hollywood movies, the representations of Hitchcock's mothers and mother figures are in general more negative. REBECCA – in which the heroine suffers at the hands of a series of mother figures – and

MARNIE – in which Marnie's mother is to a large extent responsible for her psychological problems – are discussed under the *Bed Scene* in Part I. But there are also mother-son relationships which are pathologised, most famously Mme Sebastian and Alex in NOTORIOUS and 'Mrs Bates' and Norman in PSYCHO. In each case, the mother rules over the house she occupies and her emasculated son with formidable power, and she is sufficiently hostile to the intruding heroine that she tries to kill her in NOTORIOUS and does so in PSYCHO.

PSYCHO is a special case: Norman is insane, and 'Mrs Bates' is entirely a creation of his psychosis. The repressed guilt he feels for her murder has turned her, in his imagination, into a monster, bullying him and murdering any young woman whom he happens to desire. The relationship between Norman and his 'mother' has been discussed at length in the Hitchcock literature, although there is one feature which is usually overlooked: the fact that Norman has desexualised his mother by turning her into an old woman. This makes sense as Norman's unconscious internalisation and transformation of Mrs Bates's actual state as a corpse, but it is also a measure of the sophistication of the characterisation.

Certain aspects of PSYCHO are anticipated in REBECCA. In each film, the powerful mother(figure) is in fact dead, killed by a jealous husband/son. Nevertheless, her power lives on through a figure in the present (Mrs Danvers; Norman); it's as if she 'possesses' this figure, who seeks to keep her – in some sense – alive. This Gothic theme is also found in the way that the house continues to reflect the personality of the dead woman. Manderley may be Maxim's family mansion, but it is Rebecca's mark the heroine keeps coming across: an embroidered 'R' on everything from table linen to stationery. The sense of Rebecca as a powerful presence within the house is focused in particular on her bedroom. When the heroine plucks up the courage to go into the bedroom, she discovers that it has been kept by Mrs Danvers as a shrine to Rebecca's memory. Mrs Danvers then intimidates the heroine by taking her on a guided tour of the room's delights, including Rebecca's furs and her underwear, made for her, in one of Hitchcock's great jokes, by 'the nuns in the Convent of St Claire'.

Similarly in PSYCHO. Robin Wood discusses the ways in which 'Mrs Bates's' personality dominates the house, suggesting that 'The Victorian décor, crammed with invention, intensifies the atmosphere of sexual repression' (Wood 1989: 147). One feels strongly that this is the original décor, faithfully preserved by Norman. And here, too, it is the bedroom which registers the mother's pervasive presence most strongly. Lila's exploration of Mrs Bates's bedroom is like a compressed version of the heroine's of Rebecca's, even including some of same features, but transformed by the contrasting personalities of the two women. Instead of expensive furs, Mrs Bates's wardrobe contains dowdy, shapeless dresses; her dressing-table, too, is neatly laid out with a prominent hairbrush, but in place of the husband's photograph is a bronze sculpture of a woman's folded hands, a much more elusive image. Whereas Rebecca's bedroom is full of flowers and light, Mrs Bates's is sealed off from the outside world, with a cold, unlived-in atmosphere. Indeed, when Lila first enters it, the Victorian décor makes it seems as if she is stepping into the past. This is, nevertheless, the master bedroom, far more imposing than Norman's attic room. His subordinate position is summarised in the glimpse we have of him in this room: Marion's first view of the house, as Norman, dressed as his mother, walks past the window. In effect, Norman has become his 'mother's' puppet.

This moment, too, was anticipated in REBECCA, where, before going into Rebecca's bedroom, the heroine glimpses a figure at the bedroom window. Although we know that this must be Mrs Danvers, she seems for a moment to be Rebecca's ghost. All these links between REBECCA and PSYCHO emphasise that just as it is Norman who has turned his mother into a monster, so it is Mrs Danvers and Maxim – in their different ways – who have turned Rebecca into a monster.

In the *Hitchcockian levels* section of STAIRCASES, I discuss the ideas of Dennis Zirnite, who argues that the upper level in Hitchcock's houses functions as the 'malignant domain' (Zirnite 1986: 4). The location of the mother's bedrooms in particular on this level is a feature which supports Zirnite's thesis. In NOTORIOUS, Alicia's initial encounter with Mme Sebastian is when she descends the staircase from this upper domain. Likewise, when Alex Sebastian discovers that Alicia is an American agent, he goes timidly to his mother's bedroom to seek her advice on what to do about her (➤ BED SCENE). But the mother-son relationship in this film is much more developed than the other examples – apart from the special case of PSYCHO – and merits further discussion.

From the first scene in which we see them together, Mme Sebastian dominates Alex, both in the way she interrupts and tells him what to do, and in the mise-en-scène. For example, when Alex informs her that he is marrying Alicia, Hitchcock frames Mme Sebastian, embroidering, in the foreground of the shot, whilst Alex himself is a markedly smaller figure in the background. He accuses his mother of jealousy towards Alicia – i.e. he does at least try and resist her domination – but Mme Sebastian's implacability as well as her visual prominence undermine his efforts. In the Bed Scene, Alex is weak, defeated by his discovery; here Mme Sebastian becomes more and more assertive, first sitting up in bed so that she looks down on his slumped figure, then getting out of bed and standing over him, telling him what they will do. They begin to poison Alicia, who becomes bed-ridden. Mme Sebastian's triumph is now registered in the way she sits in Alicia's room like a prison guard; again, she is embroidering, and effectively she has replaced Alex, whom we do not see again in his wife's room. The embroidering is another element which is echoed in PSYCHO. One of the many small details Hitchcock includes in Mrs Bates's bedroom is an embroidery frame close to the dressing-table.

Imprisoned and poisoned, Alicia is like the victimised princess in a fairy tale, and it is necessary for Devlin as the (reformed) prince figure to enter the malignant domain and rescue her. This has a dramatic effect on Mme Sebastian's power. At the climax of the film, as Devlin guides Alicia down the stairs and out of the house, Mme Sebastian and Alex walk down with them, but cannot do anything to stop them. Alex tries to leave with Devlin and Alicia, knowing that, if he stays, he will be exposed by his Nazi colleagues and killed. But Mme Sebastian does not even try. The house is her domain, and we only once see her outside it. And, after Devlin has shut Alex out of his car, Alex, too, has to go back into the house. The final closing door signals Alex's doom, but one cannot imagine that Mme Sebastian will escape the same fate. Alex will die because he was foolish enough to love the wrong woman, but Mme Sebastian is doomed by her quasi-incestuous devotion to her son.

NOTORIOUS and PSYCHO show the Hitchcock mother-son relationship at its most perverse, but in each case there is an additional feature which enables us to see these as special cases. Just as it is Norman's insanity which has turned 'Mrs Bates' into a monster, so the fact that Alex Sebastian and his mother are Nazis provides both a rationale for their behaviour and a mechanism for their punishment: Nazis kill people. This means that we should be careful of reading too much into these particular examples: they are not typical.

The fact that PSYCHO is the first of a trilogy of films in which the mother is a dominant and dominating figure has also led to certain misapprehensions, such as grouping the films together from this point of view. This is implicit in Paula Marantz Cohen's comment: 'in PSYCHO, THE BIRDS and MARNIE the destructive potential of the mother is taken seriously and made central to the plot' (Cohen 1995: 143-44). In fact, the representation of the mother in each of these films is quite different, and the differences are more important than the similarities. As with the example of THE CORPSE, where the motif is inflected quite differently depending on which of the three main figures – hero, heroine or villain – we are dealing with, so too with the mothers.

In PSYCHO, as in NOTORIOUS, she is the villain's mother, which particularises her monstrosity. In THE BIRDS, Lydia Brenner is the hero's mother, and she mellows during the course of the film. At first, she seems like Mrs Whittaker in EASY VIRTUE, anxious to protect her son from a sophisticated 'woman with a past'. But Lydia is far more complex and developed a character. Despite the schoolteacher Annie's story of the failure of her own relationship with Mitch (in which Lydia features as the main problem), Melanie gradually develops a tentative relationship of trust with Lydia. This begins in the film's main Bed Scene, when Melanie takes Lydia tea in bed after the latter's traumatic encounter with

Dan Fawcett's corpse. Lydia begins to talk about herself, her children and her loss of her husband and makes a point of asking Melanie to stay so that she can get to know her better. This communication between the hero's mother and the heroine completely bypasses Mitch himself (there is no indication that he even hears about it), and the sense that in Lydia Melanie finds a surrogate mother to replace her own wayward one is then sealed by the moving use of the Hands motif at the end of the film (➤ HANDS).

In MARNIE, where Bernice Edgar is the heroine's mother, the representation is much more negative. In fact, Mrs Edgar is one of Hitchcock's rare unsympathetic working-class mothers. No doubt partly in response to her earlier life as a prostitute (which she has kept from Marnie), Mrs Edgar hates men, and she is as vehement in seeking to protect her daughter from them as Hitchcock's earlier mothers were to protect their sons from women. Again, the mother's home becomes the setting for the most important stage of the conflict: it is when Mark finds himself wrestling with a hysterical Mrs Edgar that Marnie begins to recall her repressed childhood trauma (➤ *Bed Scene* in Part I).

PSYCHO illustrates another Hitchcock principle: where there is a psychotic or psychopathic killer, there is usually a mother (mother figure in SHADOW OF A DOUBT) in the background. In SHADOW OF A DOUBT, Emma Newton is the elder sister of the murderer, but she pampers him in much the same way as an over-indulgent mother. In STRANGERS ON A TRAIN, Mrs Antony is no less devoted to her delinquent son, and refuses to believe the heroine when the latter tries to tell her Bruno is a murderer. At the same time, each of these men reveals his (repressed) hostility towards his indulgent mother/mother figure by killing (the 'Merry Widows') or almost killing (Mrs Cunningham in STRANGERS ON A TRAIN) her substitutes. In FRENZY we see Rusk's mother only briefly, when she cheerily pops her head out of his flat window. But the flat, with mother's photograph on the mantelpiece, later becomes the centre of the film's chaos world: it is where Babs is murdered, Blaney is framed and arrested, and the film's climactic confrontation staged.

Dominating mothers not linked to houses occur only in the comedies, where they can be satirised and ultimately forgotten about: the heroine's, Mrs Krausheimer, in MR AND MRS SMITH; the hero's in NORTH BY NORTHWEST. Mrs Krausheimer is last seen as a comic figure, sitting on her bed in curlers and affecting distress at her son-in-law's behaviour; Roger's phone call to his mother from Grand Central Station (➤ CONFINED SPACES) is the last we hear of her.

Mansions without mothers or mother figures are also uncommon. Even in MARNIE, where the upper-class mansion of the hero is presided over by the benevolent if weak figure of his father, the hostile role of the mother has simply been passed down a generation to Mark's sister-in-law Lil, who behaves to-

Fig. 45. Still: MARNIE: the working-class mother in her house. Mark (Sean Connery) confronts Mrs Edgar (Louise Latham) over what happened to Marnie (Tippi Hedren, on the stairs) when she was a little girl. In the background, the dog and puppy painting.

wards the 'intruding' heroine with a similar hostility to Mrs Whittaker, Mrs Danvers and Mme Sebastian (➤ EXHIBITIONISM / VOYEURISM).

A particularly striking set of examples of houses with matriarchal figures is supplied by the spies' mansions. In THE 39 STEPS, the house in the Scottish Highlands does indeed have a resident mother, Mrs Jordan, and although she is a background figure, she is clearly privy to her husband's activities. Played, like the chilling Mrs Hillcrist, by Helen Haye, Mrs Jordan is quite unfazed when she walks into a room and sees her husband preparing to shoot Hannay. In SABOTEUR, the New York mansion used by the fifth columnists is run by a woman, the dowager Mrs Sutton. Mme Sebastian presides over the mansion used by the Nazis for their nefarious purposes; Townsend's mansion in NORTH BY NORTHWEST is protected from exposure as a spy hideout by a highly plausible performance by a fake Mrs Townsend. These women are also all characterised as hostesses, holding parties, dinners, balls. Implicit, here, is the spy/saboteur as cultured bourgeois, with a matriarchal figure as a guarantee of respectability. The association of matriarchal figures and espionage extends even to maids. In both Tobin's ranch in SABOTEUR and Vandamm's house in NORTH BY NORTH-

WEST there is a moment when a middle-aged woman produces a gun and threatens the hero on behalf of the master saboteur/spy.

In the spies' residences in the West, this matriarchal figure functions primarily as part of the spies' cover, but in the communist countries, she becomes more involved herself in espionage. The difference is encapsulated in the contrast in TOPAZ between the two women in André Devereux's life: his wife Nicole, who is also a mother, is part of his cover as a Washington 'commercial attaché'; his mistress Juanita in Cuba actually runs a spy network from her hacienda. It is true that Juanita is not a mother figure, but her power could be seen as like that of a matriarch: in Rico Parra's words, 'She is a widow of a hero of the revolution.' In TORN CURTAIN, the first woman Michael contacts for information about the secret anti-communist organisation pi – an anonymous farmer's wife – is structurally like a mother figure (➤ THE CORPSE); the second – Dr Koska – questions him (➤ LIGHTS) and is then revealed to have a young daughter. Dr Koska's role as a mother is especially noteworthy in that her daughter is the only child in the film.

It's as if there is a link, in the Hitchcockian unconscious, between spying and matriarchy, a link which is strengthened by the sheer watchfulness of most of his mothers/mother figures. This rather unusual sub-motif in his films may set against the observations under SPY FILMS / THE LOOK (➤ EXHIBITIONISM / VOYEURISM) about the problem of the woman's look. There would seem to be a tension in Hitchcock's work: matriarchal figures are frequently highly observant, but the idea of women actually spying is problematic. The presence in the spies' mansions of such figures emphasises their unsettling powers of observation, but contains it by restricting it to the domestic sphere, where either the heroine (NOTORIOUS) or the hero (Roger spotted by the maid Anna in NORTH BY NORTHWEST) is the subject of their scrutiny. The one obvious exception to this strategy of containment is Miss Froy in THE LADY VANISHES, but (a) she is one of our spies, and hence benevolent, and (b) when we actually see her obtain secret information, she does it as women in Hitchcock most frequently do, by eavesdropping.

There is one group of mothers who have received little attention in the Hitchcock literature: those who have both husbands and daughters. They are found particularly in the British films. The mothers in EASY VIRTUE (Mrs Whittaker also has daughters), THE SKIN GAME and THE 39 STEPS have already been mentioned in other contexts. But there is also another set of examples which shares significant features with an equivalent set of Hollywood movies. The British films are THE LODGER, THE MANXMAN, BLACKMAIL and JUNO AND THE PAYCOCK; the Hollywood ones SUSPICION, SHADOW OF A DOUBT and STAGE FRIGHT. In all these films, the daughter – who in all but JUNO AND THE PAYCOCK is also the heroine – is attracted to a man from a different background to herself who is usually in some sense dangerously unknown. However, the fact that the families belong to different classes in each period means that both the representations of the mothers and the mother-daughter relationships differ across the periods.

In the British films, the daughter's family is petty-bourgeois or working-class, and in each of the films she rejects a boyfriend from her own class in favour of someone who seems to her more glamorous. Here the mother – whose daily routine seems restricted to menial tasks around the home – would seem to represent the sort of future the daughter consciously or unconsciously rejects. But these mothers are all presented as essentially sympathetic, hard-working figures, who have the best interests of their daughters at heart. Where the mother misjudges the man the heroine prefers – as in THE LODGER (➤ BED SCENE) and JUNO AND THE PAYCOCK – this is not her fault, but a consequence of the man's deceptiveness.

Among these films, JUNO AND THE PAYCOCK includes perhaps the most positive representation of a mother. Here the family initially welcomes the outsider, Charles Bentham – who claims to be an English lawyer – because he brings news of an inheritance. However, not only does the inheritance fall through, but Bentham seduces Mary Boyle and makes her pregnant. But Juno does not abandon her daughter. Alone with Mary in their empty home – the furniture has all been repossessed – Juno tells her that the two of them will leave the useless Boyle and go off together, so that Mary's child will have 'what's better [than a father], it will have two mothers'. After Mary has left, Juno then mourns her murdered son (➤ PAINTINGS). This is the only Hitchcock film to end with the mother, and although it is untypical of his work, the tough pragmatism of the mother here is also found in Sara Allgood's other Hitchcock mother, Mrs White in BLACKMAIL. At the same time, the fact that Juno is Irish would seem to permit a more resolute mother than is commonly found in Hitchcock's English families.

In the Hollywood films, the daughter's background is (sheltered) middle-class, and she is attracted to a man who seems to have a more exciting life-style than her own. Here, however, Hitchcock raises the stakes: the man seeks to murder the heroine. And her mother is not someone to whom she can turn for help; cocooned in her middle-class world, her mother would be quite unable to make sense of such a 'perverse' relationship. In effect, the heroine's discovery of the true nature of the charismatic man dramatically alters her hitherto untroubled relationship with her mother.

In SUSPICION, Lina's father dies during the course of the film, and so, when she has to face up to the strong possibility that her husband is trying to kill her, there is only her mother with whom she can seek refuge. Although Mrs McLaidlaw is probably the most sensible of these middle-class mothers, as

Thomas Leitch perceptively points out in his entry on 'Mothers' in *The Encyclo-pedia of Alfred Hitchcock*, '[Lina] can't go home again [to mother] because it is impossible to unlearn or retreat from the experience of Johnnie' (Leitch 2002: 219). She is forced, by Johnnie's manipulations, to return home with him. How-ever, Leitch also includes Charlie in SHADOW OF A DOUBT in the same argument, and I don't think this works. From the moment that she learns the truth about her uncle, Charlie is determined to protect her mother: Emma must not find out that her own brother was a serial killer. Here, although the heroine has a terrible secret which she cannot divulge, she can at least go home.

Mrs Gill in STAGE FRIGHT is in certain respects quite similar to Emma Newton: kindly and well-meaning, but rather too trusting. But in her case, it seems un-likely that Eve and her father will be able to keep from her that the young man who stayed in their house was in fact a murderer. It is true that Mrs Gill also possesses an absent-minded scattiness, which enables her – like Mrs Antony – to be selective in what she chooses to notice or accept. Nevertheless, one feels that, once again, the heroine's experience of the charismatic man will cast a shadow over her future relationship with her mother: there will be matters which it is best not to discuss.

When Lina leaves the family home to elope with Johnnie, her mother, too, is embroidering. Most of the middle-class mothers in the Hollywood movies seem to be wrapped up in their own circumscribed worlds to a remarkable degree, and Mrs Antony's hobby of painting (➤ PAINTERS) at least suggests a more adventurous turn of mind. Lydia Brenner's lament to Melanie that she does not really know what to do with herself now that her husband is dead (➤ *Food and marriage*) can be seen as a comment on the lack of a role for mothers outside the family. Hitchcock evidently recognises the problems attendant on this lack.

The one actress who has played mothers for Hitchcock twice in the Holly-wood films is Jessie Royce Landis – in TO CATCH A THIEF and NORTH BY NORTH-WEST – and her mothers are different from the more familiar home-bound fig-ures. They are more direct and out-spoken, but they are also characterised by an ironic amusement: each treats Cary Grant's hero as a naughty boy, flirting with him in the former (where she is the heroine's mother), lecturing him in the latter (where she is his own mother).

In FAMILY PLOT, as in PSYCHO, the mother is dead but her influence is never-theless crucial. In fact, the films have a number of parallels. Although Adamson, like Norman, committed matricide, here too this did not get rid of the mother. Her return in the form of Norman's psychosis has been much-discussed; FAMILY PLOT represents an alternative 'return'. Adamson does not know this, but he was adopted, and the couple he murdered when he was a teenager were his adopted parents. Years later, his real mother, Harriet Rainbird, died. But then her sister Julia – who had insisted, when the illegitimate son was born, that the

Fig. 46. Still: To CATCH A THIEF: the (seemingly) haughty Hitchcock blonde and her scheming mother. As Francie (Grace Kelly) affects indifference to Robie (Cary Grant), Jessie Stevens (Jessie Royce Landis) eyes him appreciatively. Hughson (John Williams) on the right.

family name be preserved by having him adopted – began to suffer from nightmares in which Harriet tormented her for this past deed (➤ GUILT AND CONFESSION). Just as Julia's action in the past echoes that of Hitchcock's early oppressive mothers, so her action in the present – seeking to make amends by finding the missing son and making him heir to the family fortune – initiates the train of events which will end with the criminal Adamson in jail. And it was his mother's restless spirit which began it all.

When critics generalise about Hitchcock's mothers, they tend to mean the middle-class, middle-aged figures, who can seem rather similar: either bossy, interfering figures like Mrs Whittaker, Mrs Krausheimer and, in a more sinister vein, Mme Sebastian, or kindly but rather ineffectual figures like Emma Newton and Mrs Gill. Mrs Antony represents a rather more daffy version of the second type. There is, indeed, a sense of silliness to some of these figures, and this would apply to other middle-class, middle-aged women in Hitchcock, such as Mrs Atwater in ROPE and Mrs Cunningham in STRANGERS ON A TRAIN.

However, the range of representations of Hitchcock's mothers is much greater than this. Not only are his petty-bourgeois or working-class mothers in general viewed sympathetically, but there are also differences within the middle-class mothers: the Jessie Royce Landis mothers, Mrs McLaidlaw, Lydia Brenner. Finally, there is even one film where the hero's mother shows him the way. In THE WRONG MAN, Manny's Italian mother moves in with him and his sons when Rose is committed to a mental hospital, and as Manny begins to despair, she asks him if he has prayed. In the next scene, Manny prays to a portrait of Christ as the Sacred Heart, a prayer which, on my reading of the scene, Hitchcock answers (➤ PAINTINGS).

Mothers and the police

In SPELLBOUND, as Constance and J.B. wait for Dr Brulov to return home, they are in the same room as two police officers. Mindful, no doubt, that they are in the house of a psychoanalyst, Sgt. Gillespie asks Lt. Cooley about his mother. Cooley reports that she has been complaining of rheumatism, and wants him to transfer to Florida. A good son, Cooley took this up with his superior. But the latter was most unsympathetic, and 'made some crack about me being a mama's boy'. Unfortunately, this riveting conversation is interrupted at this point by the phone ringing.

PORTRAITS, PAINTINGS AND PAINTERS

Fig. 47. Still: SUSPICION: the patriarchal portrait. Lina (Joan Fontaine) and Johnnie (Cary Grant) address the portrait of General McLaidlaw (Cedric Hardwicke), her father.

Paintings in Hitchcock's films are not simply part of the décor; they inform us about the characters who own them and/or those who look at them. On occasions, the paintings may simply be appropriate to the household in question. In STAGE FRIGHT, for example, Charlotte's house is full of portraits of herself (the narcissistic theatre star), whereas the house where Eve lives with her mother contains the sort of traditional bourgeois family portraiture often found in a well-to-do middle-class British household. However, Jonathan's flat contains modernist paintings, the connotations of which are more subtle (➤ *Modern art*). Similarly, the Vladimir Tretchikoff reproductions in Rusk's flat in FRENZY place him in a certain cultural context: in the 1960s, the prints were so popular in petty-bourgeois and working-class households that they were seen by the 'educated classes' as almost as naff as plaster flying ducks on the wall ('Tretchikoff prints are as lowbrow as art gets': Lesley Gillilan 2000: 15). In placing them behind Rusk when he is acting most ostentatiously as a false friend to Blaney, Hitchcock is clearly getting in a dig at him for his taste in art. The large sentimental dog and puppy picture in Marnie's mother's house conveys a similar irony about her tastes. In all these examples, one senses Hitchcock's sensitivity to the connotations of the different paintings/reproductions. A proper consideration of Hitchcock and art would entail detailed discussion, but a few key points may be made. For convenience, I will divide the paintings into portraits, other representational art and modern art and, since portraits have played a significant role in films generally, begin by looking at their traditional associations.

PORTRAITS

A painted portrait given visual prominence in a film is typically used to signify one of a limited number of ideas:

1. the power of a patriarchal (more rarely, matriarchal) figure, e.g. the dead father as Great White Hunter in THE SPIRAL STAIRCASE (Robert Siodmak, 1945); the fathers who founded industrial empires in WRITTEN ON THE WIND (Douglas Sirk, 1956) and WHILE THE CITY SLEEPS (Fritz Lang, 1956);
2. the power of family tradition, e.g. the gallery of military ancestors in THE FOUR FEATHERS (Zoltan Korda, 1939);
3. a lost loved one, e.g. dead wives in John Ford movies, such as THE LAST HURRAH (1957) and DONOVAN'S REEF (1963);
4. the desire of the beholder. Such connotations apply particularly where the portrait is of a young woman, and those who gaze at it are men, e.g. LAURA (Otto Preminger, 1944); THE WOMAN IN THE WINDOW (Fritz Lang, 1944). Where the portrait is painted during the course of the film, desire is the most common association, even when the sexes of male artist and female model are reversed, as in CAGE OF GOLD (Basil Dearden, 1950).

For each of these four key categories, the dominant idea is the sense of the subject of the portrait as having a continuing presence or importance. Many of the subjects are dead, or die during the film – so that the portrait can then continue to represent them.

The importance of the portrait in these traditional associations resides primarily in its significance for the figure(s) who observe it. But there is a further frequent association which relates to the subject of the portrait and/or the artist: the linking of a portrait to (attempted) suicide or (attempted) murder. This is, in particular, a 1940s inflection of the motif, but there are many examples. Suicidal painters are discussed later, but there are also demented painters who murder – or attempt to murder – their models, especially where these are young women, as in BLUEBEARD (Edgar G. Ulmer, 1944), SCARLET STREET (Fritz Lang, 1945) and THE TWO MRS CARROLLS (Peter Godfrey, 1947). In other films, a portrait of the heroine is linked to a possessive husband (or husband figure) who sets out to murder her out of jealousy, as in HISTORY IS MADE AT NIGHT (Frank Borzage, 1937), EXPERIMENT PERILOUS (Jacques Tourneur, 1944) and LAURA. In these films, the heroine survives the murder attempt, but other subjects of portraits are not so lucky. In GASLIGHT (George Cukor, 1944), WHIRLPOOL (Otto Preminger, 1950) and THE HOUSE ON TELEGRAPH HILL (Robert Wise, 1951) we see portraits of women who have been murdered. Finally, suicidal models are no less common than suicidal painters, and here the range of examples is greater, including films from different countries, e.g. IL NODO (Gaston Ravel, Italy, 1921), LADIES OF LEISURE (Frank Capra, USA, 1930), THE SEVENTH VEIL (Compton Bennett, UK, 1945) and LE PLAISIR (Max Ophuls, France, 1952). PANDORA AND THE FLYING DUTCHMAN (Albert Lewin, 1951) includes, in one film, many of these morbid inflections of the motif. When Pandora (Ava Gardner) first meets the Dutchman (James Mason) on his ship, he is painting 'her' portrait – in fact, a portrait of her double, the wife he murdered centuries ago – and their story ends with her dying with him in order to release him from his curse.

There are many literary antecedents to this association of the painted portrait with a violent or morbid death. Writers in an issue of *Iris* devoted to 'The Painted Portrait in Film' (1992) trace these antecedents in works by Edgar Allan Poe (*The Oval Portrait*), Emile Zola (*L'Oeuvre*), Gabriele D'Annunzio (*Joconda*), Dmitrii Merezhkovski (*Leonardo da Vinci*), Robert Browning (*My Last Duchess*) and Oscar Wilde (*The Picture of Dorian Gray*): see the articles by Susan Felleman, Yuri Tsivian, Thomas Elsaesser and Réda Bensmaïa (all 1992). In particular, Thomas Elsaesser comments on the sense of fatality which hangs over so many painted portraits in the cinema:

> … the genres of the fantastic, the uncanny, the gothic are almost invariably present whenever there is a painted portrait in a film, insofar as it casts a radical uncertainty around what is alive and what is dead, it installs at the heart of the filmic representation a *memento mori*.
>
> (Elsaesser 1992: 148)

More specifically, for a young woman (especially) to have her portrait in a film is a highly dangerous enterprise. It's as if her portrait generates passions and jealousies, especially in the artist, or in a man who considers he has a claim on her, and these erupt in the form of destructive or self-destructive violence. On occasions, the portrait brings a particular dynamic into play – other men may now gaze without censure on the woman's beauty – and the violence of the artist or the possessive male may be seen as a response to the sense of inadequacy he then feels. This, clearly, is exacerbated if the woman favours another man: the portrait serves as a mocking reminder of what the artist/possessive man has lost. But sometimes one senses a more elusive rationale: as if the portrait functions as a double of the woman, a double which usurps her status within the narrative, threatening her with expendability – an idea literalised in Poe's *The Oval Portrait* (1842).

Painted portraits in Hitchcock's films fit into these traditional associations, but also take things further. Not only do the four key categories occur in his films, but in his examples there tends to be a greater closeness between the portrait and the person who views it; as if the portrait were a projection of a part of the character, or bound to him/her in a peculiarly intimate or intense way. This supports Peter Wollen's view (➤ Part I) of the crucial importance of the visual in conveying the inner world of Hitchcock's characters. Equally, the association of a painted portrait with a violent or morbid death occurs both directly (Col. Paradine's in THE PARADINE CASE) and indirectly (Caroline de Winter's in REBECCA) in Hitchcock's films, so that overall the various connotations to this inflection of the motif are more diverse.

General McLaidlaw's portrait in SUSPICION both signifies patriarchal power and illustrates the sort of psychic closeness one finds in Hitchcock between a portrait and its viewer. Lina and Johnnie each addresses it as if talking to the General, and after learning that the General in his will has left Lina the portrait rather than an inheritance, Johnnie actually defers to it: 'You win, old boy.' It also operates like a superego to Lina: after her father's death, she continues to respond to the portrait's forbidding presence as though it were criticising her for her 'rash' marriage. It's as if the General is still managing to exercise control over his daughter, and the portrait is his way of doing this.

The sense of a portrait in Hitchcock having a heightened importance for the one who views it is also found with photographs. When the Lodger first moves into his room, he reacts badly to the portraits of fair-haired women, first turning them to face the wall, then ordering their removal. At the time, this helps suggest that he could be the Avenger. But when he is arrested, a different backstory emerges. Joe finds the photograph of a young woman hidden in the Lodger's bag, and we learn that she was the Lodger's murdered sister. She is a 'lost loved one', but it is also implied that the Lodger's feelings for her were rather more than fraternal. The photograph is only shown in close-up when the Lodger subsequently tells Daisy about her murder, but we see then how attractive she was, and in the arrest scene the Lodger is most upset that Joe should see her photograph. Together with the story the Lodger tells Daisy (➢ GUILT AND CONFESSION), these details hint at a more subversive feature to the use of the sister's portrait: it helps connote the Lodger's incestuous desire. In THE RING, when her husband Jack hurls the mounted photograph of her (assumed) lover Bob across the room, Mabel not only retrieves it but, when Jack angrily tears off the top of her dress, holds it across her breasts to cover herself. Her gesture enhances the sexual meaning of the photograph, and provokes Jack to go out and assault Bob. In these cases, too, an image of someone becomes charged with intense subjective feelings for the hero or heroine.

An early example of Hitchcock's use of a portrait to indicate the power of family tradition is relatively conventional. In THE MANXMAN, when Kate comes to Philip's office to tell him he must choose between her and his career, we see a portrait of a stern-looking man whom we take to be one of Philip's Deemster ancestors. Philip is thus confronted with the familiar choice between love and duty: as in THE FOUR FEATHERS, the family tradition is seen as an oppressive weight on the shoulders of the young man who is expected to follow it. However, although Philip tries to choose duty, he cannot follow this through (➢ GUILT AND CONFESSION), and he ends by rejecting the tradition symbolised by the portrait.

A later example of this sub-motif is more complex. In REBECCA, the dress in the portrait of Caroline de Winter was copied first by Rebecca, then, without realising this, by the heroine. Unwittingly, the heroine thus imitates Rebecca, which brings on one of Maxim's tantrums. In effect, each of his wives reproduced the dress worn by one of his ancestors as a way of identifying herself with the family tradition, and his reaction is to bawl out the one who does this innocently rather than the one who does it cynically. But the heroine's act of copying the dress emphasises the sense of an unusually close bond between the portrait and its viewer. As we see in her secrecy surrounding what she is doing and her wearing the dress to the ball (➢ EXHIBITIONISM / VOYEURISM), she has a great deal of emotional investment in her project, and its failure almost drives her to suicide.

Susan Felleman connects the use of the portrait here – the idea of the heroine inadvertently imitating Rebecca, symbolically the mother figure – with the way Lina relates to the General's portrait in SUSPICION. Felleman suggests that, in each case, the use of the portrait serves to register a blockage in the heroine's Oedipal development. The heroine in REBECCA thinks that she is asserting her own identity, but – Felleman is following Tania Modleski's argument (Modleski 1988: 49) – she finds that she is merely re-presenting 'the mother'. In SUSPICION, the General's portrait serves to emphasise how Lina is inhibited, in her relationship with Johnnie, by her father's psychic dominance over her (Felleman 1992:

Fig. 48. Still: Rᴇʙᴇᴄᴄᴀ: Portrait of an ancestor. Mrs Danvers (Judith Anderson) suggests to the
heroine (Joan Fontaine) that her ball dress could be a copy of the one in the portrait of
Caroline de Winter.

193-94). The argument is an intriguing one, raising the possibility that portraits
elsewhere in Hitchcock may also have Oedipal significance.

The portrait in Rᴇʙᴇᴄᴄᴀ also functions like that in Lᴀᴜʀᴀ: it conjures up the
dead. In Lᴀᴜʀᴀ this is done directly. At the beginning of the film, Laura (Gene
Tierney) is believed to have been murdered, but her portrait mesmerises Mark
McPherson (Dana Andrews), the detective investigating her murder, and one
night he falls asleep in front of it. At this point, Laura herself walks into the
room – it wasn't she who had been shot, but a romantic rival. But Preminger
articulates her return so that it is as if Mark has dreamt her up from the portrait.
In Rᴇʙᴇᴄᴄᴀ, the heroine's imitation of the dress in the portrait not only makes

her appear, to Maxim and his sister Beatrice, like the ghost of Rebecca, but actually seems to conjure up Rebecca herself: that same night the boat containing Rebecca's body is found. And although Rebecca in death is still an extremely potent figure, the discovery of her body does prompt Maxim into a confession, a confession which finally reveals to the heroine that, far from loving Rebecca, as she had believed, Maxim hated her. In both films, then, the association of the portrait with death ultimately serves, for hero and heroine, a therapeutic function, bringing them together.

Carlotta's portrait in VERTIGO may also be related, in its use, to Caroline de Winter's. First, it, too, depicts a woman from the past who has psychic resonances for figures in the present, and in this case the woman committed suicide, reinstating the sense of fatality so often attached to portraits in films. Second, here, too, the portrait is imitated by the two women in the hero's life. Judy as 'Madeleine' adopts certain elements in the portrait (the bouquet; the hairstyle) as part of her masquerade for Scottie; Midge actually copies the portrait, with her own face in place of Carlotta's. Whilst Midge's motive in doing this is by no means innocent, she underestimates the extent of Scottie's obsession with 'Madeleine'; when he sees her imitation, he does not throw a fit, like Maxim, but he still rejects her. But the portrait of Carlotta proves even more damaging for Judy. When, towards the end of the film, she puts on Carlotta's necklace, Scottie remembers it from the portrait (➤ JEWELLERY) and so realises that Judy and 'Madeleine' are the same person. The portrait's apparent psychic effect on 'Madeleine', originally a fake – her 'possession' and 'suicide' – now becomes a reality, as Scottie's demented reaction to what he has just realised leads to Judy's death. In both REBECCA and VERTIGO, the portrait is thus used as much for its psychic associations for the hero as for the heroine(s), and the violence with which he reacts to these associations is a terrible comment on his inability to cope.

THE PARADINE CASE includes three significant portraits. Two are given special emphasis: Col. Paradine's in the London house; Mrs Paradine's in the Lake District house. The former is shown in the opening scene, when the police come to arrest Mrs Paradine for her husband's murder; she even points it out to them. We do not know at this stage that she is indeed the murderer, but her reference to the skill with which the artist has captured the blind man's look could be seen, in retrospect, as significant: as if she is reassuring herself that her husband's unseeing look means that the portrait cannot be subjecting her to an 'accusing' stare. Normally, when a murderer looks at a portrait of his/her victim, we would expect a degree of agitation, as in GASLIGHT. Mrs Paradine's comment suggests that she is seeking to ward off her anxiety.

By contrast, when Tony looks at Mrs Paradine's portrait in her bedroom, Hitchcock places great emphasis on the looks: that of Tony himself, gazing repeatedly at the portrait, and that of Mrs Paradine in the portrait, whose eyes, looking straight out at the viewer, seem to follow Tony round the room. Embedded in the headboard of Mrs Paradine's bed, the portrait dominates the room. Moreover, since Col. Paradine was blind when Mrs Paradine married him, and the valet Latour resistant to her charms, the implication is that Tony is the first man to gaze at her portrait with desire. For each portrait, then, Hitchcock stresses the subjective charge for the character who looks at it. This point is reinforced by the presence of the third portrait: of Tony's wife Gay. Although the portrait is clearly visible in at least two scenes in Tony's study, no-one looks at it; it has simply become part of the décor. Picturing Gay in eighteenth-century costume à la Gainsborough, the portrait suggests a psychic investment in a certain sort of English past: the wealthy bourgeois. It helps construct Mrs Paradine as 'other': dark, foreign, exotic, mysterious and, above all, sexual.

PSYCHO also includes a portrait over a bed. When Lila explores Mrs Bates's bedroom, amongst the Victorian décor (➤ MOTHERS AND HOUSES) is a portrait over her bed. Eric S. Lunde and Douglas A. Noverr identify it as that of a 'Victorian youth' (Lunde and Noverr 1993: 104), but I think it is a girl or young woman. The fact that it is very similarly positioned to Mrs Paradine's suggests that it could be Mrs Bates herself as a girl. If so, our sense that Norman alone would have looked at it reinforces the Oedipal overtones of the mother/son relationship. Moreover, since this is a blocked Oedipal relationship – Norman is still in thrall to his 'mother' – this would also fit Felleman's argument.

Although the evidence for considering the portrait to be a youthful Mrs Bates is purely circumstantial, it contributes to the enigma of Mrs Bates's bedroom, and its Victorian style adds to the general sense of a Victorian oppression in the room. By contrast, a photograph of a woman glimpsed on the mantelpiece looks modern. Hitchcock's camera does not dwell on either picture, but the portrait over the bed is similar in style to the Victorian photograph Uncle Charlie in SHADOW OF A DOUBT carries of his mother (as well as one of his father), and the mantelpiece is where Rusk keeps a picture of his mother. In relation to Hitchcock's other disturbed killers, then, Norman is being implicitly inserted into both a Victorian and a modern heritage of 'matriarchal oppression'.

Portraits of men play a minor role in Hitchcock, with one exception: military officers. In their case, an imposing portrait is de rigueur. General McLaidlaw's portrait is a prominent motif throughout SUSPICION; Col. Paradine's portrait dominates the living-room in the London house. In SECRET AGENT, we are introduced to the hero, Captain Edgar Brodie, through his portrait. Only the portrait of Col. Burgoyne, the heroine's father, in YOUNG AND INNOCENT is an understated rather than an emphatic presence (it can be glimpsed in his study). Although we would assume that such portraits are a signifier of class background (all the subjects are upper middle-class British), Hitchcock also seems to have seen these men as peculiarly narcissistic. This can be seen in details such as General McLaidlaw leaving only his portrait to Lina in his will, and Col. Paradine only having his painted after he'd gone blind.

The portraits of General McLaidlaw and Col. Paradine also refer, in different ways, to the association of portraits and (violent) death. SECRET AGENT offers a comic reinflection of this idea. The film begins in Brodie's Mayfair rooms with mourners paying respects at his coffin. But after they have left, a burlesque routine by a one-armed batman reveals that the coffin is empty. The batman then turns to look up at Brodie's portrait. A zoom in to the portrait cues the introduction of Brodie himself who, in the next scene, arrives to complain to spymaster 'R' about a newspaper report of his death. He is informed that he has been declared officially dead in order to be reincarnated as the spy Ashenden. Here the portrait-death connection is used playfully, signalling the hero's 'death' as Brodie before his 'rebirth' as Ashenden.

PAINTINGS

In PSYCHO, the painting which covers Norman's voyeur's spy-hole is of Susanna and the Elders, showing two elderly men assaulting a naked woman. Lunde and Noverr suggest that the Apocryphal story of Susanna 'reveals several themes elucidated in PSYCHO: voyeurism, wrongful accusation, corrupted innocence, power misused, secrets, lust and death' (Lunde and Noverr 1993: 101). I would focus, rather, on the significance of the painting for Norman. The voyeurism theme (the elders first spy on Susanna) is certainly relevant, but in the original story Susanna resists their sexual assault, and the elders take revenge by accusing her of adultery with a youth. It would be more accurate to describe the painting as depicting a rape fantasy, a fantasy which is unfulfilled; hence its particular relevance for Norman.

On the one occasion when Hitchcock makes significant use of a Catholic painting – the picture of Christ as the Sacred Heart in THE WRONG MAN – that, too, becomes invested with a strong sense of psychic closeness. As Manny prays to it, his prayer is answered: superimposed over his face a man with an uncanny resemblance to him – the real robber – walks towards the camera until the two faces merge. The significance of this is that the robber then attempts a hold-up and is caught, and this leads to his being correctly identified by the witnesses who had earlier misidentified Manny, which is the first stage of Manny's release from his nightmare.

In JUNO AND THE PAYCOCK, two Catholic statues are used with equal psychic force. Johnny sees the ghost of Robbie Tancred, the man whose death he was responsible for, in front of the first (unseen) statue, 'the wounds bleeding in his breast'. As Robbie's coffin then passes by outside, Johnny looks up at the statue of the Virgin Mary over the fireplace – as if the statue were judging him. Then as Johnny himself is taken off to be executed, Hitchcock superimposes non-diegetic machine gun fire over a shot of the same statue, signalling Johnny's death by the snuffing out of the statue's candle. Here the statues are so closely associated with death that at the end of the film Juno, Johnny's mother – echoing the earlier words of Mrs Tancred – appeals to the one of the Virgin Mary: 'Where were you when me darlin' son was riddled with bullets?'

Religious paintings and imagery are a special case: it is not surprising that, on occasions, they have similar significance for Hitchcock's characters to portraits. But other representational art rarely has the same sort of significance. Such paintings may well hang in the houses of the characters – and so tell us something about the occupants – but they have usually become a part of the background. A rare exception is the sailing ship on the living-room wall in Fred and Emily Hill's house in RICH AND STRANGE: in the first scene between them (➤ *Food and marriage*), it helps express Fred's dream of the sort of life he would like to lead. When they return home at the end after their adventures, the painting – looked at by Fred after a gale warning on the radio – seems more ironic.

A more sophisticated example of a painting being integrated into a scene through comments about it occurs in Elster's office in VERTIGO. Elster remarks to Scottie that the city has changed: 'The things that spelled San Francisco to me are disappearing fast.' Scottie turns and walks towards a painting of nineteenth-century San Francisco on the wall: 'Like all these?' As Scottie contemplates the painting, Elster continues: 'Yes, I should have liked to have lived here then: colour, excitement, power, freedom.' Because 'power' and 'freedom' are cited throughout the film, that element of Elster's speech has been much-quoted, beginning with Robin Wood. But the use of the painting to relate Elster's remark to Scottie has not, I think, been noted. As Robin Wood observes: 'We shall see how important for Scottie are a nostalgia for the past and a desire for "freedom" and "power"' (Wood 1989: 112).

Modern art

Diane Waldman has suggested that the attitude towards modern art in films and literature of the 1940s is nearly always hostile (Waldman 1982: 52-65). Hitchcock's attitude towards modern art seems to me more ambivalent. On the one hand, Salvador Dalí did the sketches for the dream in SPELLBOUND, the hero in THE TROUBLE WITH HARRY is a modernist painter, and the one person to disparage modern art in his films is a buffoon: Maxim's brother-in-law Giles in REBECCA. Such positive associations are also found in TOPAZ, where the fact that both André (in his Washington house) and Juanita (in her Cuban hacienda) have modernist paintings suggests a cultural affinity between them. On the other hand, Hitchcock is equally likely to locate modernist paintings in the houses of somewhat suspect figures, e.g. Johnnie in SUSPICION (a cubist painting in the hall which fascinates a police sergeant), the murderers in ROPE and Jonathan in STAGE FRIGHT.

A surrealist painting in Jonathan's flat illustrates Hitchcock's ambivalence. In part, it is used to poke fun at Jonathan (and/or Richard Todd). As he talks on the phone to Mrs Gill, the heroine's mother, an upturned spiralling building in the painting behind him seems to stick out of his ear like a joke hearing aid, a point underlined when, exasperated at his apparent slowness, Mrs Gill asks him, 'Didn't you hear?' But the painting also invokes the world of the unconscious from which the surrealists drew much of their inspiration and this, in its suggestion of a confusion of thoughts and feelings in Jonathan's mind, also makes him seem more sympathetic. Indeed, it is even possible that the painting is telling us something about Hitchcock's unconscious. At the centre of it is the final shot from NORTH BY NORTHWEST, ten years before he filmed it.

PAINTERS

Male painters in the cinema tend to be an emotional, gloomy lot: some go mad (BLUEBEARD, SCARLET STREET, THE TWO MRS CARROLLS); some commit suicide (A WOMAN OF PARIS, Charles Chaplin, 1923; THE LIGHT THAT FAILED, William Wellman, 1939; THE LOCKET, John Brahm, 1946); some do both (Van Gogh/Kirk Douglas in LUST FOR LIFE, Vincente Minnelli, 1957). In addition, most of them fall in love with their female models, or indeed their male models, as in MIKAEL (Carl Dreyer, 1924).

In fact, MIKAEL seems to have been a specific influence on Hitchcock, since crucial elements from Dreyer's film may be discerned in the Hitchcock-scripted THE BLACKGUARD (Graham Cutts, 1925). Both young heroes are called Michael and each film has early scenes in which he is an artist's model. In MIKAEL, it subsequently becomes apparent that, whereas the painter Zoret (Benjamin Christensen) is gay and loves Mikael (Walter Slezak), Mikael does not reciprocate: he is seduced away from Zoret's influence by a Russian princess (Nora Gregor). He first meets her in Zoret's apartment: both of them look at the naked

figure in Zoret's painting 'Victor' and she recognises Mikael as its model. In THE
BLACKGUARD, the painter-model scenes are also eroticised (Michael poses naked
but for a discreet towel), but, because at this stage he is only a boy, the overtones, however fleetingly, are paedophilic. Here, Michael first meets the future
heroine Maria when she, too, is a child and he is actually posing; as an adult, he
then re-meets her after she has just re-seen the painting of him as a youth. She,
too, turns out to be a Russian princess. But only in MIKAEL is the full melodrama of the suffering artist played out. Zoret's reaction to the loss of Mikael is
typical of an 'abandoned' artist: he does not commit suicide, but he dies of a
broken heart. After these early scenes, THE BLACKGUARD follows a different narrative path: the artist moves into the background, and the significant father figure in Michael's life becomes his violin teacher, Lewinski (➤ STAIRCASES).

Although the gay overtones of MIKAEL are not really followed through in THE
BLACKGUARD, another notion – a painting of a man/boy as the subject of the
eroticised gaze of a woman/girl – is common to both films. In fact, this has two
stages in THE BLACKGUARD: it is (the almost naked) Michael himself that the girl
Maria first looks at; the painted portrait she later sees as an adult is essentially a
reminder of this moment. Such an inversion of the far more familiar situation of
a man looking with desire at a woman's portrait is quite striking, and in both
films it is the woman rather than the man who then becomes the pursuer. Once
again, it is as if there is an erotic power to a portrait of a young, beautiful person, whatever the sex.

Claude in EASY VIRTUE is the first painter in a Hitchcock-directed film, and he
follows the familiar pattern. His story is told in flashback, by Larita, from the
courtroom where Filton is seeking a divorce from her; although he has already
committed suicide, Claude is named as the third party. The story Larita tells is
of a man who tried to rescue her from her drunken, violent husband, climaxing
in a violent confrontation between the men in which Claude shot and wounded
Filton and the latter, after beating Claude savagely with his cane, collapsed.
Claude was then so frightened by the imminent arrival of the police, he shot
himself. This is a particularly strong example of the ways in which the passions
involved in the painting of a portrait can lead to violence: in effect, Larita in-
flames both men to the point where they try to kill one another. Because this
scene of violence is introduced at an earlier stage than in the other movies – the
portrait is still being painted – the film suggests that it is in the nature of the
artist-model relationship for the former to be aroused, and the husband is
goaded into such a violent reaction by his awareness of this. But because of
censorship, the film can only hint at what we assume lies behind the artist's
passion: his repeated and intense contemplation of the 'suggestively dressed'
model.

None of this material is in the Noel Coward play on which the film is based. Nevertheless, key aspects are in the first of Franz Wedekind's Lulu plays, *Der Erdgeist* (1895), filmed in 1923 – with Asta Nielsen as Lulu – by the famous Weimar theatre director Leopold Jessner (➤ STAIRCASES). In *Der Erdgeist*, the passions aroused by the heroine as artist's model are even more extreme than in EASY VIRTUE. In the first act, Lulu poses as a model for Schwarz, the artist, and, as she romps with him in his studio, her husband Goll forces his way into the studio by literally smashing down the door, and then promptly has a fatal heart-attack. In the second act, Schwarz is now married to Lulu, but when he hears from her old protector Schön about her infidelities, he commits suicide. Hitchcock has often commented on the influence of his work of the Weimar cinema; this play/film and MIKAEL would seem to be two lesser-known examples.

The suicidal tendencies of painters are not easy to explain: within the examples cited there is a range of motives. Nevertheless, apart from the special case of Van Gogh, a common thread is that each artist has painted a young model who in life itself eludes him. This suggests that what lies behind the suicides is a sense of inadequacy; the painting may be brilliant, but the model is 'capricious'. The nature of this capriciousness varies from film to film – we may indeed, as in EASY VIRTUE, find the model conspicuously more sympathetic than the artist – but at heart is a clash between the artist's control over his art and his lack of control over the woman (in MIKAEL, the man) who inspired his art. From the artist's point of view, all these works dramatise the elusiveness, indeed unknowability, of woman (or, in MIKAEL, the fickleness of youth). But Claude, like the artist in A WOMAN OF PARIS, is a weak figure, and his suicide also reflects this. The heroine trapped between a highly unpleasant husband and a besotted but weak artist is replayed in ABWEGE (G.W. Pabst, 1928), a Weimar film which could perhaps have been influenced in turn by Hitchcock.

BLACKMAIL makes the artist unambiguously the villain: when Crewe tempts Alice to undress on the pretext of becoming his model, his intention is to rape her. Again, a violent death ensues, as Alice, defending herself, stabs Crewe with a knife. The terms have shifted from EASY VIRTUE, but not greatly: the heroine is still faced with a choice between two deeply unsatisfactory men, and Hitchcock's use of the artist's studio as, once more, the setting for the violence emphasises the highly charged emotions which can be generated in the artist-model dynamic. The one Hitchcock hero who is a painter, Sam in THE TROUBLE WITH HARRY, escapes from the problems generated by these earlier artists by (a) being in a comedy, (b) concentrating for the most part on non-representational art and (c) not having the heroine as his model. But he still has sex on his mind; at the end of the film, it is revealed that the payment he requested for his paintings from the millionaire was a double bed. There is also a Hitchcock mother who paints – Mrs Antony in STRANGERS ON A TRAIN – and here this signifies both her own weirdness (she claims her wildly expressionist portrait is of St Francis) and her son's craziness (Bruno roars with laughter: 'That's father all right').

Although Claude was painting Larita's portrait, we see little of it and it does not otherwise function in the narrative. In BLACKMAIL, by contrast, a painting by Crewe and a sketch are crucial to the plot. The former is of a jester, pointing its finger at the viewer and laughing: this could be another oblique echo of *Der Erdgeist*, in which Lulu poses for Schwarz in a Pierrot's costume. The sketch is of a naked woman, done with Crewe guiding Alice's hand. Although Alice pretends to be shocked when Crewe does this, she nevertheless adds her name to the sketch, signalling her identification with it. Before Crewe's death, both works are seen by Alice as 'fun'; after it, both seem much more sinister. Now the jester seems to be mocking her, and she tears the painting, getting paint on her fingers (in the place of Crewe's blood). Equally, now her name on the sketch is a giveaway, and she anxiously obliterates it.

However, both works turn up later as police evidence and, at the end, Alice watches them – like signifiers of her guilt – being taken past her into New Scotland Yard. She stares with trepidation at the jester, and the sense of it as mocking her is here enhanced by the off-screen laughter of the two policemen in the scene. Elisabeth Weis perceptively observes: 'It is no accident that the figure is specifically a jester, for the painting evokes the Elizabethan jester, whose function was to provoke laughter while revealing truths too unpalatable to be stated without the indirection of parable or art' (Weis 1982: 49). The implication is that the investigation is not over; that the sketch with Alice's (surely detectable) name on it, together with her fingerprints on the bread knife, may yet serve to incriminate her. (The earlier references to fingerprints – the fingerprinted man in the prologue; the film that Frank wanted to see – support the sense that Hitchcock wished us to bear this in mind.) Lacking the sense of closure which almost all classical films possess, this is one of Hitchcock's most powerful endings.

I would like to conclude by returning to the issue of portraits being linked to violent or morbid deaths. If all the examples in Hitchcock's films are included, we can see that here, too, there is a surprisingly high number. The artists in EASY VIRTUE and BLACKMAIL both die violent deaths in their studios. Sam in THE TROUBLE WITH HARRY does not, of course, die, but the one portrait we see him do is of Harry, who has himself just dropped dead. In TOPAZ, François, a journalist, does sketches of the subjects he writes about. The two which are singled out in the narrative are of Uribe and Jarre, both of whom are subsequently murdered. One of the two main portraits in THE PARADINE CASE depicts a murderer; the other, her victim. The Lodger's sister was also recently murdered. In VERTIGO, Carlotta committed suicide, and her portrait seems to act like a curse on

Fig. 49. Still: BLACKMAIL: Painting. After she has killed Crewe in self-defence, Alice (Anny Ondra) stands in front of his painting of a jester which she has just torn.

Judy, who dies shortly after she has unconsciously betrayed her link to it. In SECRET AGENT, the association is present symbolically: Brodie's portrait serves to mark his 'death' as Brodie. Even Bruno's misidentification of St Francis as his father is relevant: Bruno is at that moment planning his father's murder. To these examples should be added the more oblique references in REBECCA and JUNO AND THE PAYCOCK, where a portrait (REBECCA) or a statue (JUNO AND THE PAYCOCK) is linked within the narrative to a violent death, or deaths.

There is, therefore, something fitting about the lack of closure at the end of BLACKMAIL. At issue is the violent death of an artist, and two of his works are still in circulation as potential clues as to 'what really happened'. In other words, the survival – and circulation – of a work of art after the artist has died can have powerful repercussions. It is only to be expected that in a Hitchcock film these repercussions are to do with the question of innocence and guilt concerning an alleged murder.

Portraits, paintings and the police

It is apparent that Hitchcock's police do not understand art. In SUSPICION, Sgt. Benson does not contemplate Johnnie's cubist painting out of aesthetic appreciation, but out of bafflement. This is echoed in REAR WINDOW when Lt. Doyle makes a face at Jeff's slightly bizarre still life over his fireplace.

This lack of artistic appreciation is shown most clearly in THE TROUBLE WITH HARRY. Calvin Wiggs, part-time deputy sheriff and the film's sole representative of the law, is dismissive of Sam's paintings. Then Sam's 'pastel drawing' of the dead Harry's face comes to his attention. Since Calvin has not seen the dead body, but has been given a description of it, he seizes on the drawing as evidence that it existed. Concerned, at this stage, that Calvin should not take this further, Sam promptly amends the drawing whilst mystifying Calvin with a mock-learned discourse on art. Calvin watches dumbfounded, only commenting when Sam has finished: 'You know what you just did... You just destroyed legal evidence.'

PUBLIC DISTURBANCES

Fig. 50. Still: NORTH BY NORTHWEST: Public disturbance. The auction room: after his erratic bidding has led to the summoning of the police, Roger (Cary Grant) livens things up to ensure that he is arrested. The onlookers are shocked.

Perhaps the most familiar examples of Hitchcock's public disturbances are those bourgeois social occasions which are suddenly disrupted by an 'improper' event, e.g. Bruno almost strangling Mrs Cunningham during Senator Morton's party in STRANGERS ON A TRAIN, or Roger making a nuisance of himself in the auction room in NORTH BY NORTHWEST. There seems little doubt that Hitchcock enjoys the confusion and embarrassment such disruptions provoke – we could indeed see them as illustrating Hitchcock the practical joker, amusing himself at the expense of bourgeois stuffiness. However, if we take a public disturbance to include any disruption which causes a group of onlookers to react en masse, then there are a number of different categories to consider. The bourgeois disturbances, for instance, may be contrasted with their lower-class equivalents, in which a group of working-class men suddenly begin brawling. This occurs at the beginning of THE 39 STEPS, when a commissionaire tries to eject one of the noisy crowd at the music hall bar, and in YOUNG AND INNOCENT, when Erica's questions in a transport café cause the patrons to fall out over how much information to give her. In other words, there is a class distinction in Hitchcock's disturbances: inherently unruly, working-class crowds are readily prone to outbreaks of violence; inherently constrained by social propriety, bourgeois groups require a more or less outrageous triggering event to upset them.

Another distinction may be drawn between an event which prompts a crowd to gather out of alarm or curiosity (e.g. Mary Hearn's hysterics in THE FARMER'S WIFE, when Sam is rude to her after she rejects his proposal), and one which provokes panic, with people fleeing to escape (e.g. when, moments later in THE 39 STEPS, a gun is fired by someone in the audience). We could call these centripetal and centrifugal public disturbances: in each case, there is an event which provokes a crowd reaction, but in opposite directions. Specific examples of this second pair may overlap with the first: Mary Hearn's attack occurs during a pretentious tea party, so a bourgeois occasion is also being disrupted; in THE 39 STEPS, it's as if the panic of the audience fleeing the music hall has arisen directly out of the violence which began at the bar.

THE LODGER includes three of these four distinct categories of disturbance, but they are darker than the norm. The murder of the Lodger's sister disrupts a bourgeois social event – her coming-out dance – and prompts the guests to rush and form a circle around her body. This shocked centripetal movement is then echoed in the murderousness of the mob which pours out of a pub (i.e. their violence, too, is linked to drink) to pursue the Lodger with the intention, it would seem, of lynching him (➤ HANDCUFFS AND BONDAGE). Except for the rather special case of the collective murder of Willi in LIFEBOAT, this is the only example in Hitchcock of a crowd turning genuinely murderous, and the Lodger's ordeal is extremely harrowing.

With only a few exceptions, later examples of public disturbances in Hitchcock's British films (at least) are more light-hearted. Even the machine-gun fire interrupting a political speech to a gathered crowd at the beginning of JUNO AND THE PAYCOCK is not shown to cause any deaths, and Hitchcock includes such comic touches as a cat streaking up a lamppost, and the men tumbling into a pub – and on top of one another – as a way of playing down the violence. The fights in THE 39 STEPS and YOUNG AND INNOCENT are also essentially comic. And in the Hollywood films, with a shift to more middle-class settings, working-class fights no longer occur. There is a working-class disturbance in the flower market in TO CATCH A THIEF, but it is focused on the comical wrath of an elderly female flower seller, enraged that Robie and the police have damaged her wares. Centripetal and centrifugal disruptions still take place – especially the latter – but otherwise the emphasis is on public disturbances which violate bourgeois propriety, from David giving himself a nose bleed in the fancy restaurant in MR AND MRS SMITH, to Blaney losing his temper in Brenda's club in FRENZY. Like JUNO AND THE PAYCOCK, FRENZY also includes an opening political speech which is rudely interrupted, but the interruption here is more in keeping with the darkly comic bourgeois examples: outside County Hall on the Thames, a politician is making ringing pronouncements about cleaning up the river, when a naked female body is spotted floating by.

Apart from THE LODGER, perhaps the most traumatic example of a public disturbance in Hitchcock's British period is the moment when Fane hangs himself in front of the circus audience in MURDER! This example may also be used to illustrate a general point about these public disturbances: that many are dramatised through rapid editing – a quick montage of shots vividly capturing the reactions of onlookers to an event which upsets them, or causes them to panic or flee. The impact of Fane's suicide is captured in 15 shots lasting a mere 28 seconds, interspersing shots of the swinging rope with such reactions as the audience jumping up, rushing forward, women screaming, a horse rearing, a clown looking on impassively, a woman fainting, a group being held back, plus the rather disturbed reactions of Sir John and Markham, whose presence has prompted the suicide. In the penultimate shot, the circus master orders the band to play, just as Mr Memory gets the band to play to calm the brawling men in THE 39 STEPS. In neither case do we see a positive outcome to this manoeuvre: in THE 39 STEPS, the disturbance continues; here Hitchcock terminates the sequence with a fade to black. Hitchcock's most powerful public disturbances would seem to affect the crowds which experience them like a fever, and the rapid montage serves to convey the ways in which the surge of emotion translates into a series of sudden, largely involuntary reactions. To explore this further, it is useful to refer to some of Elias Canetti's ideas in *Crowds and Power* (1973), a work which is specifically concerned with the nature of different kinds of crowd.

Fane's suicide provokes a centripetal disturbance: the circus audience reacts by rushing forward *into* the ring. More common are the centrifugal disruptions, when a crowd tries to flee. Canetti distinguishes between the two main types of crowd here: (1) a 'panic crowd', when a crowd disintegrates in an enclosed space: archetypally, theatre-goers trying to flee from a fire (Canetti 1973: 28-30), and (2) a 'flight crowd', where a crowd flees from danger in more open terrain, e.g. city streets (60-63). The reaction of the music hall patrons to the firing of a gun in THE 39 STEPS is one example of a panic crowd; later examples occur in the cinema towards the end of SABOTEUR, when Fry and the police exchange shots, and in the theatre in TORN CURTAIN, when Michael deliberately creates a panic by shouting 'Fire!' Similarly, the machine-gun fire in JUNO AND THE

PAYCOCK creates a flight crowd; a later example occurs when Keller shoots his wife Alma in the crowd outside the courthouse in I CONFESS. By contrast, when Van Meer's double is assassinated on the steps in Amsterdam in FOREIGN COR-RESPONDENT, the onlookers do not flee but rather huddle together (under their umbrellas), as if seeking communal protection from the still shooting assassin. I do not think that Canetti mentions this type of crowd, which would suggest that it is rare. Although the crowd's behaviour obviously derives from that of certain animal packs under threat, it is made possible here, one feels, because of the umbrellas, which seem to confer the appearance of anonymity and protection.

Canetti says that it is in the nature of a panic crowd for everyone to fight with everyone else in order to get out of the auditorium (Canetti 1973: 29). We see this in THE 39 STEPS in the way the usherettes are brutally swept aside as the crowd surges through the exit doors. This example also has a structural function: as Hannay is swept out with the crowd, he finds himself caught up with Annabella Smith – who later identifies herself as the source of the shots – a 'chance encounter' which takes him into the chaos world (➤ CAMEO APPEAR-ANCES). In other words, here the panicking crowd acts like a gateway to the chaos world. TORN CURTAIN reverses this notion: Michael creates a panic in the theatre as a way of escaping from the chaos world. Under the Production Code until 1956, cries of 'Fire!' in a film were in fact banned; presumably on the grounds that those asleep in the audience might wake up at this point and panic. Hitchcock refers back to this prohibition not only by including such a moment in the film, but also by setting the scene itself in a theatre, in effect doubling the offence. (See Mogg 2002: 28 on the issue of the legality of falsely shouting 'Fire' inside a theatre.) The 'fire' Michael dramatically points to is a stage representation (paper flames wafting aesthetically), but the audience panic in exactly the way they are supposed to: fighting to get to the exits; jamming the aisles; violently pushing aside obstructions. But since the figures at the exit doors in this instance are not usherettes but East German policemen with automatic rifles, the crowd's panic works in favour of Michael and Sarah's escape.

The public disturbance created in the cinema in SABOTEUR is the most developed of these panic crowd examples. First, Hitchcock mixes gunfire in the film on the screen (which the audience find funny) with real shots being fired by the escaping Fry, one of which hits a man in the audience. In effect, the diegetic audience is being shocked by the eruption of 'the real' into the harmless fantasy of screen entertainment. As the audience rush for the exit, Hitchcock then furthers the connection between the on-screen film and their reaction by accompanying their flight with the exhortation 'Come on, get out!' from the irate screen husband. It is his wife's lover that he is shouting and shooting at. In the

Fig. 51. Still: TORN CURTAIN: Public disturbance. After Michael has shouted 'Fire!', members of the audience fight to get out of the theatre. Sarah (Julie Andrews) is visible in the middle; Gerhard (Hansjoerg Felmy) at the top left.

psychic economy of Hitchcock's films, he thus assumes the form of a punishing superego. In her discussion of the nature of the superego, Kaja Silverman argues that it possesses one component which

> is formed through the introjection of the symbolic father... the internalization of the father as Law, gaze, voice-on-high. This element of the superego has no necessary relation to any historical figure, but its gender is irreducibly masculine... It is, quite simply, the paternal function, and the ego is always already guilty in relation to it – guilty by virtue of Oedipal desire.

> (Silverman 1993: 41)

Here Hitchcock has found an external correlative of this component, and the guilt Silverman mentions could be seen to exacerbate the audience's panic.

In I CONFESS, the disturbance caused by Keller shooting his wife is, in fact, the climax of an extended sequence which begins in the court room, with Father Logan being found not guilty of Vilette's murder, the crime for which Keller is responsible. The judge signals his disapproval of the verdict, and Logan's walk through the corridor and down the stairs is filmed like his Via Dolorosa, with hostile crowd members lining his route, vilifying him, whilst others wait outside to voice further disapproval. The crowd outside the courtroom is indeed so dense that the police have to assist Logan in making his way through it: the crowd begin to manhandle him, pushing him against a car which causes him to break its window. Witnessing all this, Alma becomes more and more upset, finally rushing forward through the crowd to declare that Logan is innocent. But when she turns to identify her husband as the killer, Keller shoots her. It is this which causes the crowd to flee, but Hitchcock is less interested in this than in Alma's fate. The material is a reworking of the lynch mob sequence in THE LODGER: the hostile crowd, the Christian overtones, and an innocent victim who, in this case, really is dying. Here the shooting serves to scatter away the hostile crowd, leaving the dying Alma to beg Logan to forgive her. Amongst so many overwrought, violent and even hysterical outbursts that characterise the public disturbance motif in Hitchcock, this is an unusually private, moving moment.

The famous disruption of an Albert Hall concert in the two versions of THE MAN WHO KNEW TOO MUCH illustrates another kind of public disturbance. The heroine knows that a foreign diplomat/prime minister in the audience is under the threat of assassination, but she is constrained from warning him because the assassins have kidnapped her child. After a long build-up, the tension in her is released in a scream so powerful that it disturbs the assassin's aim. The heroine screams despite herself, and the disruption of the performance – dramatised more effectively in the remake, where the hero traps the assassin and causes him to fall from a balcony into the stalls – is accompanied by the usual excitement and concern from the bourgeois audience: Hitchcock has found a very impressive arena in which to stage his climax. But the focus, here, is less on the audience than the heroine: in effect, Hitchcock has built the tension to the point where it is released in the 'hysteria' of her body. This also occurs in REBECCA, when the heroine faints during the inquest just at the point where Maxim's irritability is about to give himself away as Rebecca's killer. These examples, too, contrast with Alma's fate in I CONFESS. In rushing forward to help Logan, Alma is also reacting to an unbearable tension, but by taking a more active role than simply screaming or fainting, she brings about her own death.

Mary Hearn's hysterics in THE FARMER's WIFE constitute the most extended example of hysteria in Hitchcock, and the scene itself may be seen as an elaborated example of those public disturbances which violate bourgeois propriety. Here it is the hysteria itself which spreads like a fever: the hostess, Thirza, starts to become hysterical, but then decides to faint; the maid really does have hysterics. The tea party collapses under the strain of keeping up the pretence of bourgeois refinement and chaos ensues.

In a discussion of the elements in Hitchcock's films which reflect the director's petty-bourgeois upbringing, Colin McArthur looks at certain scenes in his films which dramatise the notion of 'making an exhibition of oneself'. He relates such scenes to the cartoons of H.M. Bateman, popular in British publications from the 1910s to 1930s, especially Bateman's famous 'The Man Who...' cartoons, which depict the embarrassment of a petty-bourgeois whose social gaffe shocks the upper middle class. Three of the scenes McArthur mentions are relevant to the public disturbances motif: the murderer Guy's breakdown on a bandstand at the climax of YOUNG AND INNOCENT, David Smith's embarrassment at finding that the date he was going to use to make his wife jealous is a 'floozie' (the self-inflicted nosebleed is his attempt to escape from the situation), and Sam Flusky's entrance into the Irish Society Ball in UNDER CAPRICORN, where he is rude to the Governor and literally throws his money around (McArthur 2002: 22-25).

In fact, each of these scenes fits the Bateman paradigm obliquely. It is the fear of detection which causes Guy, a drummer, to draw attention to himself by his erratic drumming (➤ GUILT AND CONFESSION), and the reaction of the dancers is concern rather than scorn. No-one notices David's predicament until he makes a fool of himself, and the only people to be embarrassed by this are David himself – he becomes the recipient of his date's enthusiastic first aid – and Ann, obliged to witness the little comedy. In UNDER CAPRICORN, Sam is too worked-up to be embarrassed, and the Governor manages to retain his dignity; the only person who is really upset by Sam's outburst is Hattie. Nevertheless, McArthur's focus on the inherent class tensions and on the 'petty-bourgeois scopophobia' (the fear of being looked at) in such scenes is valid. Although the bourgeoisie may manage to keep its cool, what is at stake here is a threat to its sense of social decorum by a potentially disruptive lower-class intrusion and an anxiety on the part of the intruder – or an associated figure – about being the centre of attention.

In SABOTEUR the disruption is blocked before it even occurs. When Barry sets out to announce to the guests at Mrs Sutton's society party that they are in the midst of fifth columnists, he is discreetly silenced with the threat of being shot. He switches to an announcement which chimes in with the social occasion: Mrs Sutton will auction some of her jewellery for charity (➤ JEWELLERY). Even Bruno's more spectacular disruption is swiftly contained. Having almost strangled Mrs Cunningham, he passes out and crashes to the floor. But his unconscious body is quickly removed to another room, Anne equally promptly takes the distraught Mrs Cunningham upstairs, and an army officer dismisses the disturbance: 'She was just frightened; I think they were playing a game of some sort.' All this is shown in one shot, with Hitchcock's camera tracking forward, past these examples of the restoration of order, to end on Barbara, whose distress at what has occurred has passed unnoticed by everyone else (➤ SPECTACLES).

In short, Hitchcock also shows the social cohesion of the upper-middle class: it is extremely good at recovering from threats to harmonious social discourse. The one occasion in which the intruder succeeds in seriously disrupting such a bourgeois occasion is probably the auction in NORTH BY NORTHWEST, when Roger deliberately upsets the proceedings with erratic bidding and mocking remarks so that he will be arrested and thereby escape from the spies. This is perhaps Hitchcock's most extended public disturbance, and it includes a whole range of responses to Roger's outrageous behaviour: ignoring him, insulting him, pleading with him to enter into the spirit of the occasion, asking him to leave. Throughout the scene, bourgeois propriety is most definitely under strain, as the auctioneer does his best to continue despite Roger's calculated attempts to confuse and rattle him. Dazzlingly constructed so that, alongside the comic effects of the disturbance itself, we can see the success of Roger's hidden agenda – the upsetting of the spies; the summoning of the police – the sequence illustrates the density of Hitchcock's best sequences, in which several narrative threads are being orchestrated at once.

Throughout these examples, Hitchcock demonstrates that the response of onlookers to a public disturbance is essentially emotional, especially if there are sufficient of them to constitute a crowd. This can lead, on occasions, to serious misapprehensions, as with the lynch mob in THE LODGER. Likewise with the first public disturbance in NORTH BY NORTHWEST: when Townsend is knifed in the back in the United Nations, Roger foolishly plucks the knife out, thereby encouraging excited onlookers to see him as the murderer (➤ THE CORPSE). But this capacity of witnesses to misread what they have seen is then brilliantly utilised in the third such example in the film (the auction room scene is the second). In a crowded cafeteria beneath Mount Rushmore, Roger – pretending to be the government agent Kaplan – pulls Eve away from Vandamm and starts to get aggressive with her, whereupon she pulls a gun and shoots him. The onlookers react on cue: they scream, jump up, run forward, creating precisely the sort of disorder necessary for Eve to escape and the Professor to position himself as 'the doctor' who attends the body and indicates – for Vandamm's benefit – that 'Kaplan' won't live. Whereas in the United Nations scene the onlookers were unintentionally misled, here they are deliberately fooled by a piece of expertly choreographed theatre: Eve's bullets were blanks.

Canetti's theories only cover some of the examples discussed here. Overall, Hitchcock's focus is different: his concern is less with the nature of crowds, and more with the impact of a certain sort of event on onlookers. His elaboration of this motif – and it is, indeed, one of his most wide-ranging – could nevertheless be seen as pointing to a fundamental feature of his cinema. His dramatisation of situations in which the onlookers – the diegetic audience – jump at his bidding is a reflection of his general approach to cinema audiences. In orchestrating the different responses of his diegetic audiences – fear, shock, panic, excitement, anger, outrage, amusement, embarrassment, confusion, sympathy, distress – he shows, once more, his mastery of 'the cinema of emotions'.

Public disturbances and the police

Usually, Hitchcock's police do their best when involved in a public disturbance. At the end of THE 39 STEPS, when Professor Jordan shoots Mr Memory on stage at the Palladium, they are quick to move in and capture the killer. They efficiently clear the cinema when a saboteur threatens to blow it up in SABOTAGE. They are less successful in SABOTEUR, where they return Fry's fire in the crowded cinema and make matters worse. But when a trigger-happy cop shoots at Guy as he leaps on the merry-go-round at the climax of STRANGERS ON A TRAIN, this *creates* the public disturbance. The bullet hits the machine's operator, he falls on the lever governing the speed, and the merry-go-round goes out of control. Eventually it crashes, and although we do not see the extent of the casualties, it is highly unlikely that Bruno was the only fatality. Accordingly, one feels this is an emblematic Hitchcock moment: the police shoot at one wrong man, hit and apparently kill another wrong man, and release a chaos in which children, surely, are killed.

SPECTACLES

Fig. 52. Still: SPELLBOUND: Spectacles. The intellectual woman: Constance (Ingrid Bergman) as doctor.

Of all the motifs considered here, this is the one which smacks most heavily of cliché. Hitchcock has his characters wear spectacles for a limited number of reasons, almost all of them familiar from a thousand other films. For both men and women, there are six or so broad types who wear spectacles, although the types are somewhat different for each of the sexes. For men, a wearer of spectacles is either:

1. highly intelligent, e.g. the psychoanalyst Dr Brulov in SPELLBOUND, the nuclear scientist Professor Lindt in TORN CURTAIN, or
2. comically absent-minded, e.g. Robert's lawyer in YOUNG AND INNOCENT, Dr Greenborough in THE TROUBLE WITH HARRY, or

3. kindly, well-meaning, but somewhat ineffectual, e.g. Alice's father in BLACK-MAIL, Charlie's father's friend Herb in SHADOW OF A DOUBT, or

4. financially grasping, e.g. Cousin Bob in MARNIE, who complains to Lil about Mark's extravagances, or

5. a nuisance, e.g. Mr Fortesque in STAGE FRIGHT, who keeps approaching Eve in the pub to impose himself on her when she is trying to attract the attention of Det. Insp. Smith, or

6. sinister – which covers a range of characters, from the dentist in THE MAN WHO KNEW TOO MUCH (1934) to Mr Drayton in the remake, and includes some of Hitchcock's more colourful villains, such as the soft-spoken Freeman in SABOTEUR and Thorwald in REAR WINDOW. A visual effect Hitchcock sometimes uses to emphasise bespectacled villainy is to reflect the set lights in the lenses, so that the character's eyes are masked by a battery of reflections: for a good example, see the scene between Freeman and Barry at the dam.

Although there is a range of representations here, only the intellectuals are viewed reasonably positively. Otherwise, the characterisations tends towards the comic or the sinister, and – apart from the villains – these are usually minor characters. Occasionally, Hitchcock will mix two categories. Thus, at Isobel's dinner party in SUSPICION, her brother Bertram, a Home Office pathologist – whose spectacles make him look sinister – entertains the other guests with a story of traces of arsenic in a body as he carves into a quail, so that the juxtaposition of his appearance, his actions and his story has a comic effect. Even figures who might seem to be exceptions are only partial ones. Although Mr Kentley in ROPE does not really fit these categories, he is 'bookish', keen on first editions; in the early scenes of TORN CURTAIN, Karl Manfred's spectacles assist in making him *seem* sinister, even though later events qualify this.

On a woman, spectacles signify that she is either:

1. intelligent/bookish but spinsterish, e.g. Pamela in THE 39 STEPS, Lina in SUSPICION, Constance in SPELLBOUND, or

2. conspicuously less glamorous than the heroine, e.g. Miriam and Barbara in STRANGERS ON A TRAIN, Midge in VERTIGO, or

3. financially grasping, e.g. Charlotte's maid Nellie in STAGE FRIGHT, or

4. a nuisance, e.g. the cruise busybody Miss Imrie in RICH AND STRANGE, or

5. a secretary, e.g. the lawyer O'Connor's secretary in THE WRONG MAN, or

6. sinister, e.g. one of the women guarding the Nazis' London hideout in FOREIGN CORRESPONDENT, the Drayton's assistant Edna in THE MAN WHO KNEW TOO MUCH (1955).

With women, Hitchcock is also more likely to refer to their short-sightedness without spectacles. When Mrs Atwater arrives at the party in ROPE, she mistakes Kenneth for the murdered David, which so shocks Phillip that he breaks a glass in his hand (➤ HANDS). Miss Lonelyhearts in REAR WINDOW has to wear her spectacles in order to see to put on her makeup; this is then comically inverted in STAGE FRIGHT, where Eve tries wearing her mother's reading glasses as part of her disguise as a maid and promptly finds that, looking in a mirror, she cannot even see the effect. This variation of the motif finds its most entertaining example in NORTH BY NORTHWEST. When Roger enters through the window into the room of an anonymous hospital patient, she switches on the light, sits up in bed and calls out 'Stop!' as a reflex. But when she has put on her spectacles and sees that it is Cary Grant, no less, who has miraculously turned up in her room, she says 'Stop!' in a very different tone of voice.

That the wearing of spectacles is essentially symbolic is shown most clearly with the first group of women. Pamela, Lina and Constance are the films' heroines, and when we first meet them we are shown that they need to wear spectacles in order to read. But we do not, I think, see Pamela wear them again, and Lina does not put them on for the scene in which she (a) writes her farewell letter to Johnnie and (b) reads the telegram informing her of her father's death. With Constance, Hitchcock is more careful to remember that she is supposed to be long-sighted, so that, when she reads a note without her spectacles, we see the writing shift into focus. But Hitchcock conformed to the ideological thinking of the period: spectacles make a woman seem more intelligent but less attractive. Hence, no heroine wears them because she is short-sighted (or, in order to see properly, she would need to wear them all the time, like Midge), and each of his long-sighted heroines finds less need for them as her relationship with the hero takes her away from her books.

The ideological thinking is shown very neatly in a brief scene in THE 39 STEPS. When Hannay arrives at the Professor's house in Scotland, the latter's daughter Hilary is having a party. Hannay is in fact introduced to both the Professor's teenage daughters: Patricia, described in the screenplay as 'a tailored, rather intellectual type' and then Hilary, described as 'younger, more modern, pretty and vivacious'. Patricia wears spectacles; Hilary does not.

Significantly, the (unpublished) screenplay of THE 39 STEPS is by Charles Bennett and Alma Reville. In other words, it would seem that Alma Hitchcock shared the same views about a woman wearing spectacles as her husband. In photographs of the two of them, it is striking that Alma wears spectacles when she is working (where it would have been essential that she could see clearly), but not when she is socialising – except in her later years.

Another revealing moment occurs in the second pub scene in STAGE FRIGHT, as Eve bribes Nellie to take over the latter's role as Charlotte's maid for a few days. When Eve says that she can act the part, Nellie is not convinced. Character acting is involved, and Nellie belittles Eve's idea of what this entails: 'I see: all you've got to do is put on some of the old clothes and make yourself look common like me.' There is a self-reflexive quality to this remark: Kay Walsh, who plays Nellie, had just switched from playing leads to playing character parts (see McFarlane 1997: 593-95). But it wasn't old clothes Hitchcock put her into to make her look common, it was spectacles.

With children, there is a smaller range of examples, but much the same thinking applies. Thus two precociously clever children in Hitchcock – Erica's eldest brother in YOUNG AND INNOCENT, Charlie's kid sister Ann in SHADOW OF A DOUBT – both wear spectacles. In I CONFESS, Inspector Larrue and Robertson, the Crown Prosecutor, question two girls who say that they saw a priest leaving Vilette's house at the time of his murder. One of the girls wears spectacles, which may help give credence to her story, in that a child wearing spectacles is likely to be seen as observant. Here, it is not the girls who are to blame for the mistake, but the adults, who do not think to ask them whether they could simply have seen a man wearing a cassock. Hitchcock has even used spectacles to make a child seem sinister, as with the cub scout in STAGE FRIGHT, who confronts Charlotte on stage with a doll with a bloody dress (➤ EXHIBITIONISM / VOYEURISM). From Charlotte's point of view, the boy's spectacles add to the spooky effect of the apparition. Finally, THE BIRDS includes an example of the vulnerability of a child who wears spectacles: when the crows pursue the fleeing schoolchildren, the only one who falls is a girl wearing spectacles, and the image of the shattered lenses on the road adds impact to her tearful distress.

Only in STRANGERS ON A TRAIN is the Spectacles motif developed into something more substantial. I mention in Part I the expressionist effect achieved when Bruno strangles Miriam and Hitchcock films the murder reflected in one of the lenses of her spectacles, which have fallen off in the struggle. Both the spectacles themselves and the mental image Bruno carries of Miriam's face then recur in the narrative. The former he gives to Guy to show that he has carried out the murder; when Guy, minutes later, talks to Anne on the telephone, he holds the spectacles in front of him like a signifier of his guilt (➤ LIGHTS). The latter is prompted by Barbara's resemblance to Miriam, a resemblance focused on her wearing of spectacles.

Although I have argued that Bruno kills without feeling guilt (➤ GUILT AND CONFESSION), the moments when Barbara triggers his memory of Miriam suggest the return of a repressed guilt. On the first occasion, as Bruno looks at Barbara, Hitchcock tracks in to her face and 'echoes' the murder scene: reflections of the cigarette lighter are shown in her lenses and we hear the merry-go-round music and Bruno's words: 'Is your name Miriam?' On the second occasion, Bruno is about to demonstrate to Mrs Cunningham his preferred murder technique, strangling. As his hands fasten round Mrs Cunningham's neck, he looks up and sees Barbara. It's as if this re-creation of the circumstances of Miriam's murder conjures up Barbara – like Miriam's ghost. Here, Hitchcock simplifies the subjective effect – as the camera tracks in to Barbara's face, we just hear the music – but Barbara's shocked reaction tells us that she knows what is happening. After the disturbance Bruno causes here has been calmed down (➤ PUBLIC DISTURBANCES), Barbara is still shocked. She tells Anne: 'His hands were on her throat, but he was strangling me.' As she says this, she takes off her spectacles and holds them in front of her, asking, 'Why me?' Anne's reaction as she looks at them tells us in turn that she knows the answer: the spectacles have served to make her see.

The spectacles could be viewed as merely a shorthand way of connecting the two women, thereby enabling Hitchcock to further the plot. Bruno's swoon after the strangling episode and Anne's perceptive detective work both galvanise Guy into action: he goes to Bruno's house to talk to his father (➤ BED SCENE). However, there is a further crucial feature connecting Miriam and Barbara: both look at Bruno with a sexual interest, which is emphasised by showing each, from Bruno's point of view, looking directly at the camera. This has resonances both for the character – Bruno is threatened by a woman looking at him in this way: the gay subtext – and for patriarchal culture: women are supposed to be looked at, not to look. This gets to the heart of why, for generations, spectacles were considered to make a woman look less attractive. Apart from the connotations of 'cleverness' (in itself, a potential threat to a man), they also served both to draw attention to the fact that she was looking and lent her look a certain intensity; the sort of intensity that men, apparently, find disturbing. Mary-Ann Doane has written of this phenomenon:

> Glasses worn by women in the cinema do not generally signify a deficiency in seeing but an active looking, or even the fact of seeing as opposed to being seen. The intellectual woman looks and analyses, and in usurping the gaze she poses a threat to an entire system of representation.
>
> (Doane 1991: 27)

Hence, in contrast to men, no woman who wears spectacles in Hitchcock – so far as I can recall – becomes comically absent-minded, or even kindly but ineffectual. Women who wear them tend to be sharp, observant and often a little threatening, like Nellie. A woman who looks is supposed to be discreet about it, like Anne, not forward, like Miriam and Barbara. The use of the spectacles in STRANGERS ON A TRAIN does however go part way in unpacking the ideological thinking.

Spectacles and the police

Hitchcock's cameo in YOUNG AND INNOCENT (➤ *Cameos and the police*) is so scene-stealing that one might miss the fact that the sergeant barking orders also instructs the escaping Robert, who is wearing stolen thick-lensed spectacles as a disguise. Now it is true that the sergeant probably does not know what Robert looks like, but the spectacles obviously serve to make him seem quite unlike a potential fugitive. Even the fact that he cannot see in them, which means that he keeps walking sideways, passes unobserved.

By contrast, SPELLBOUND records an example of the powers of observation of the police. When Lt. Cooley (➤ *Mothers and the police*) is shown a photograph of Constance, he merely has to draw spectacles over her eyes to identify her to Sgt. Gillespie as the woman they met recently at Dr Brulov's. Tracking the fugitives from justice down is then irritatingly easy: 'You left a trail a mile wide,' Gillespie says to them as he and Cooley arrive to arrest J.B. Unsurprisingly, J.B is the wrong man, but this in no way detracts from Lt. Cooley and Sgt. Gillespie's excellent detective work.

STAIRCASES

Fig. 53. Still: VERTIGO: the emblematic Hitchcock staircase shot. Scottie (James Stewart) goes back down the stairs of the bell tower after witnessing Madeleine's fall.

The first shot of THE PLEASURE GARDEN shows chorus girls descending a spiral staircase as they come on stage. The penultimate shot of FAMILY PLOT shows Blanche sitting on the staircase in Adamson's house and winking at the camera. Staircases thus frame Hitchcock's entire directorial oeuvre. They are also one of his more famous motifs, mentioned quite often in the Hitchcock literature. Equally, however, they are familiar features not just of the cinema generally, but of cultural forms which preceded the cinema – myths, folk tales, art, drama – so that one needs to look at Hitchcock's use of the staircase in relation to its typical symbolic associations in other contexts.

The traditional associations of the staircase are summarised in *The Penguin Dictionary of Symbols* by Jean Chevalier and Alain Gheerbrant:

The stairway is the symbol of the acquisition of learning and of the ascent to knowledge and transfiguration. If it rises skywards, the knowledge is that of the divine world; if it leads underground, it is to knowledge of the occult and of the depths of the unconscious… This classic symbol of ascent can denote… a concerted elevation of the whole being… [It also] possesses a negative aspect of descent, falling, returning to Earth and even to the Underworld'.

(Chevalier and Gheerbrant 1996: 923-24)

In addition, the staircase has long been a feature of set design in the theatre. Apart from its potential for entrances, exits and visual staging generally, a staircase on stage also provides a ready-made setting for confrontations in which the positioning of the characters has symbolic significance. Hitchcock undoubtedly recognised the dramatic potential of creative set design; in his early years in the cinema, one of his jobs was as art director, and at least two of his sets – in THE PRUDE's FALL (Graham Cutts, 1924) and THE BLACKGUARD (Cutts, 1925) – have significant staircases. The expressionist influence is also relevant here: both THE BLACKGUARD and THE PLEASURE GARDEN were made in Weimar Germany. The prevalence of staircases in Weimar films has been well documented by Lotte Eisner in *The Haunted Screen* (Eisner 1973: 119-27). In these films, staircases were sometimes used in a manner familiar from the theatre, but also, reflecting the pervasive expressionist influence in the films, as an aspect of the landscape of the mind. In this capacity, they often suggest a sense of threat or menace, intimating the dangers which may lurk either on or at the top or bottom of the stairs. Hitchcock's staircases frequently evoke similar fears: famous examples would be Melanie going up the staircase in the dark in the Brenner house (THE BIRDS), and Lila going down into the cellar in the Bates house (PSYCHO). In both cases, we anticipate with dread the terrible encounter that the young woman is about to experience at the top/bottom of the stairs.

Hitchcock's staircase for THE BLACKGUARD was built at Ufa – the Berlin studio where most of the great Weimar films were made – and it illustrates, from the beginning of his career, the importance of the motif. On this film, Hitchcock was not only the art director, but also the scriptwriter and, according to John Russell Taylor, he even filmed some of the scenes. One of these required a massive staircase: having received a blow on the head, the hero Michael hallucinates going up a long staircase to Heaven. Taylor recounts how Hitchcock was quite ruthless in having the staircase built to the dimensions he required, going so far as to insist on the demolition of the existing forest set of Fritz Lang's recently completed DIE NIBELUNGEN (1924) – 'the pride and joy of the studio' – in order to achieve this (Taylor 1978: 57). Even before he officially became a director, Hitchcock was not going to have his vision compromised and, in this case, it was the staircase which was the focus of his vision. (One can see a strong echo of Hitchcock's staircase here in the one designed for A MATTER OF LIFE AND DEATH, Michael Powell and Emeric Pressburger, 1946.)

When Michael reaches the top of the staircase, St Peter instructs him: 'You will be the greatest violinist in the world, as long as you love only your art.' In effect, this is the defining moment, if not of Michael's life, at least of his career. He becomes haunted by St Peter's words, and deeply troubled that falling in love should distract him from his commitment to his art. His fears climax with a moment, late in the film, when he is fighting a sword duel with his castrating ex-teacher and father figure, Lewinski. Suddenly, he 'sees' Lewinski as St Peter and becomes transfixed, thereby incurring an almost fatal blow. Symbolically, he is punished for his failure to love only his art.

In line with the traditional associations of an ascent, we would anticipate that the hero's encounter with St Peter would be a transcendental experience. But it is in fact traumatic, endowing him with a burden that he is unable to carry, and which almost leads to his death. Critics have sometimes noted the refusal of the transcendental in Hitchcock's work, but it is nevertheless remarkable to find it so starkly in place at the very beginning of his career.

Michel Cieutat argues that the primary symbolic use of the staircase in Hollywood films is that embodied in the traditional associations of ascent expressing optimism, hope, etc. and descent the opposite (Cieutat 1991: 202-25); precisely the notion Hitchcock rejects in THE BLACKGUARD. Cieutat refers to the symbolism here as 'biblical', and he cites a number of examples which fit this notion – e.g. CABIN THE SKY (Vincente Minnelli, 1943) (ascent to Heaven is indeed transcendental) and SUNSET BLVD. (Billy Wilder, 1950) (Joe/William Holden's descent to be shot; Norma/Gloria Swanson's into madness) – but there are also many others which contravene it. The staircase is a much more ambiguous motif than this. The childhood fear of 'the dark at the top of the stairs' is frequently evoked in films with Gothic or horror overtones, charging ascents with trepidation. Melanie going up the stairs in THE BIRDS plays on these sorts of fears, as does Arbogast's ascent to Mrs Bates's bedroom in PSYCHO.

Another familiar use of the staircase which Cieutat does not mention is as a setting for the female star to make a (usually) impressive star (and/or social) entrance, descending to be greeted by her admirers at the foot of the stairs. In the BBC series, *Architecture of the Imagination*, which began with THE STAIRCASE, the psychologist James Hillman described this feature of Hollywood films as 'like a mythical moment: it's not just the descent of the film's main actress, it's the descent of Aphrodite or Venus into our human world… Heaven has opened up, and she's come down' (BBC2, tx 6/8/1993). (Or, as in THE PLEASURE GARDEN, they've come down.) The woman's film has many instances of this, and in the films of Bette Davis, the star's staircase descent is a recurring motif: e.g.

JEZEBEL (William Wyler, 1938), NOW, VOYAGER (Irving Rapper, 1942) and MR SKEFFINGTON (Vincent Sherman, 1944).

Hitchcock's use of the device is usually more problematic. A relatively conventional example occurs at the end of THE FARMER'S WIFE, when Minta comes down in her 'brave party frock' to be presented to the women now eager to marry Sam Sweetland as his fiancée. But most instances in his films are marked by problems or tensions. In EASY VIRTUE, Larita's entrance down the stairs in a low-cut gown is an act of defiance: she is deliberately setting out to scandalise the guests attending her stuffy in-laws' party. But she knows that the defiance will be short-lived: the family are about to expel her. In UNDER CAPRICORN, when Hattie descends the stairs in her ball gown to be complimented by Charles (excessively) and Sam (uncertainly), the moment is certainly a triumph for her, but I discuss under JEWELLERY the way in which the scene brings out the class tensions in the marriage. REBECCA contains the most devastating example of the heroine's entrance going wrong: the heroine descends the stairs in her ball gown fully anticipating her husband's delighted approbation, only to suffer his humiliating rejection (➢ EXHIBITIONISM / VOYEURISM). In I CONFESS, Ruth's flashback account of her romance with Michael Logan begins with her descent of a curved metal stairway to be kissed by him. Here, the extreme tilted camera angle, her billowing white dress, and the use of both slow motion and an operatic love ballad on the soundtrack all contribute to the sense of this as Ruth's highly romanticised view of the love affair. In all but the first of these examples, Hitchcock has taken a familiar motif of Hollywood cinema and, to a greater or lesser extent, problematised it.

In *Tales of Sound and Fury*, Thomas Elsaesser discusses the use of staircases in Hollywood melodramas, tracing this back to the *Jessnertreppe* of German theatre (Elsaesser 1972: 12 & 15 note 10), a reference to the stage staircases of Leopold Jessner, which Lotte Eisner mentions as a crucial influence on Weimar cinema (Eisner 1973: 47). Elsaesser refers primarily to the emotional ups and downs which can be achieved through ascents and descents of staircases, and his main examples, in which rushing downstairs is associated with joy and going back upstairs with humiliation provide further instances which go against Cieutat's thesis. Although the heroine does not rush, the scene in REBECCA is a good illustration of Elsaesser's version.

Directors of melodramas would also use staircases for their architectural and spatial properties, so that, for example, tensions between the characters are dramatised through the spatial dynamics, e.g. Jim (James Dean) in REBEL WITHOUT A CAUSE (Nicholas Ray, 1955) trapped between his dominant mother, above him on the stairs, and his weak father, sitting impotently at the bottom. In general, Hitchcock does not use his staircases this way: almost all his significant staircase scenes involve movement up or down. At the climax of NOTORIOUS, Devlin

Fig. 54. Still: NOTORIOUS: Staircase and the sinister mother. The climax: Devlin (Cary Grant) helps
the poisoned Alicia (Ingrid Bergman) downstairs and out of the Sebastian house: Alex (Claude
Rains) and his mother (Leopoldine Konstantin) accompany them, but are unable to intervene.

guides the poisoned Alicia down the stairs and out of the Sebastian house,
whilst Alex and his mother walk impotently beside them and the Nazis watch
suspiciously from the hallway below. This is a highly dramatic scene, brilliantly
edited to convey the tensions between the characters, but it is orchestrated by
Hitchcock primarily in terms of movement down the staircase rather than a
symbolic spatial positioning of the characters.

Hitchockian levels

In the Hitchcock literature relating to the staircase motif, there are two compet-
ing positions. The more familiar is the equivalent of Cieutat's 'biblical' inflection; this has been expressed most comprehensively by Lesley Brill:
- Of NORTH BY NORTHWEST: 'Counterpoising Thornhill's ascents to love and
  illumination are declivities in which he confronts confusion, evil and danger'
  (Brill 1988: 13).
- Of THE 39 STEPS, YOUNG AND INNOCENT, SABOTEUR and TO CATCH A THIEF:
  'Their plots are shaped by descents to infernal places and by ascents to truth
  and love...' (32).
- Of I CONFESS: 'The descents to danger and ascents to release that we expect
  of a Hitchcock film occur repeatedly as the story unfolds...' (100).

On the other hand, Brill recognises that, in some films, the associations are reversed:
- 'In Hitchcock's comic romances, ascents to love, light and understanding balance descents to threat and isolation. In THE WRONG MAN, such ascents are
  either absent, thwarted or parodied' (116).
- 'Characters ascend insistently in BLACKMAIL, but when they go up in this
  ironic film, they do not escape their woes or clarify their confusion but only
  discover or cause further misfortunes' (150).

Although not all these ascents and descents are effected by means of staircases,
the principle extends to them. With a few, rare, exceptions, Brill maintains that
associations of ascent are positive, of descent negative. However, in *Hitchcock,
on the Level: The Heights of Spatial Tension*, Dennis Zirnite proposes a model
which conflicts with Brill's. Zirnite argues that there are two dominant spatial
levels in Hitchcock's films, which he terms the main level and the upper level.
He summarises the associations of each as follows:

> 1) *The Main Level*: Generally characterized by banality, complacency and a shallow
> vigilance, this 'earth-bound' plane is personified by those who are impelled by a pre-
> carious sense of decency. Here we find ... the viewer representations who are, for the
> most part, socially accepted in the diegesis, making this level of existence the diegetic
> norm.
>
> 2) *The Upper Level*: This is the oppressive dominion of a malignant force, of human
> destructiveness; the 'overseeing' catalyst of moral instability. Typified by deceptive
> charm, a repressed misogyny, and an exuding seductiveness, this ascendant domain
> is incarnated by those who unleash the darkest human impulses.
>
> (Zirnite 1986: 4)

Zirnite's main examples to illustrate his thesis are THE LODGER (the Lodger, both seductive and seemingly sinister, lives upstairs: 4-6); BLACKMAIL (Crewe's studio is at the top of the stairs: 6-7); NOTORIOUS (Mme Sebastian's domain is upstairs; Alicia is confined there to die: 8-9); SHADOW OF A DOUBT (Uncle Charlie 'takes over' Charlie's bedroom: 10), VERTIGO ('the bell tower is a veritable locus of damnation': 15), PSYCHO (Mrs Bates's bedroom is upstairs; the motel below: 16-17) and FRENZY (both Brenda and Babs are murdered by Rusk on the upper level: 19). With REAR WINDOW, he suggests that Miss Torso and Thorwald (upper level) are related to the darker impulses in Jeff, whereas the sculptress and Miss Lonelyhearts (lower level) represent the more mundane features of his personality, which Zirnite summarises as vigilance (the sculptress) and decency (Miss Lonelyhearts) (12-13). Another example is Guy going up to 'Bruno's domain' in STRANGERS ON A TRAIN (17).

I would qualify Zirnite's reading in the case of THE LODGER (➤ *Staircases and the police*), but otherwise his argument is compelling. Brill does not cite PSYCHO as one of his exceptions, but Arbogast and, later, Lila going up to Mrs Bates's bedroom clearly do not fit his notion of ascent being beneficial: they are heading towards the highly dangerous malignant domain. Equally, the climactic descent in NOTORIOUS is patently a liberation, an escape from the malignant upper level. Such inversions of the Brill structure lend weight to Zirnite's thesis: there does indeed seem to be an upper level which is harmful to heroes, heroines and others who are associated with the 'main level'. Whereas, for the villainous characters – those associated with the upper level – both descents from and ascents to this level will carry connotations of the sinister. Thus, in NOTORIOUS, Alicia's first sight of Mme Sebastian is when the latter comes down the stairs and across the hallway to greet her. Filmed in one take from Alicia's point of view, the shot communicates unease: Hitchcock hints from this first meeting that Mme Sebastian, descending from her domain, is a threat to Alicia, something which is amply confirmed by subsequent events. Although the connotations here conform to Brill's model, Zirnite's analysis is different: he maintains that the descent is sinister because a villainous figure carries the associations of the upper level down with her/him. Similarly in PSYCHO, where 'possessed by [his mother's] virulent spirit, Norman descends under its dictates to destroy … the "innocent" main-level figures' (Zirnite 1986: 17).

An example Zirnite cites of a villain's sinister *ascent* is Johnnie bringing Lina the glass of milk in SUSPICION: Hitchcock, he points out, wanted the milk to be poisoned. In fact, I maintain that the milk *is* poisoned (➤ *Milk* in Part I), which supports Zirnite's reading. A parallel example is in NOTORIOUS, when Alex comes up from the cellar, having discovered that his wife is an American spy. The camera films his ascent from the top of the main staircase, and Zirnite draws the connection with Suspicion, pointing out that Alex will shortly be a party to his mother's plan to poison Alicia (Zirnite 1986: 8).

Zirnite's model gains weight from the fact that Hitchcock's bedrooms are usually on the upper level, which brings in the host of negative features associated with the beds (➤ BED SCENE). His examples also draw attention to the fact that the room itself – rather than the bed – may be the site of the threat, as in the bird attack on Melanie in the attic bedroom. Similarly with Rusk's bedsit in Frenzy: each time we see a character go up the stairs to the room, something terrible happens. In Babs's case, we know that she is about to be murdered, and here, as Rusk shuts the door on the two of them, Hitchcock's camera withdraws back down the stairs and into the street. Cieutat uses this as an example of descent being linked to villainy (Cieutat 1991: 203). Zirnite's argument is more sophisticated. Whilst recognising the understated power of the shot as a displacement from the murder, he argues, in effect, that the movement stands in for the one which Babs, now, will never make: 'here, through the inexorable darkening of Hitchcock's vision, the figure of decency never makes it back down' (Zirnite 1986: 19).

In his conclusion, Zirnite links the form of the threat to the 'main level figures' to the nature of their characters:

> they have ... proved to be characterized by a parochial vision and a dearth of introspection. Consequently, the threat to these figures, the malignant impulse, is seen as excluded, alien, present only at another level of existence ... 'evil' is dissociated, detached from the self, and from those within our immediate social sphere who reflect and affirm the self. But as the impulse resides at a level of spatial superiority, it is removed in the sense of a deity, pervasive yet elusive, like the free-floating anxiety charging the atmosphere of every Hitchcock work...
>
> (Zirnite 1986: 19)

He also argues that the birds in The Birds and the plane which attacks Roger in North by Northwest are further manifestations of such a malevolent 'overseeing power' (18).

It is tempting to Freudianise Zirnite's model in terms of a malevolent superego, which is less an embodiment of 'free-floating anxiety' than a hostile force which seeks to punish characters who ascend to the 'forbidden zone' at the top of the stairs. If one traces the motives for those 'main level' characters who go up the stairs, it can be seen that very few are genuinely innocent. Usually, they are impelled by a rather suspect curiosity; some – Arbogast in Psycho; Lisa in Rear Window climbing into Thorwald's apartment – are breaking the law. Only Babs seems entirely innocent; a reflection of the bleakness of Frenzy. In addition, some of the figures most closely associated with the upper level may indeed be seen as personifying a virulent, punishing superego: Mme Sebastian,

'Mrs Bates', perhaps Elster in VERTIGO. A similar argument has been made about the birds in THE BIRDS: see Horwitz 1986: 279-87.

Zirnite points out that, in Elster's first scene, he walks up a short flight of stairs to a level in his office above Scottie, as he begins to involve the latter 'in the initial stage of his lethal intrigue', and that this anticipates Elster's position above Scottie in the bell tower (Zirnite 1986: 3). In fact, VERTIGO is even more remarkable in this respect: from Elster's first appearance here to his final appearance at Madeleine's inquest, we never see him on the main level.

Where the upper level figures are young male psychopaths (Uncle Charlie, Bruno, Rusk, perhaps Crewe in BLACKMAIL), a different structure would seem to apply, but it is striking that most of these young men, implicitly or explicitly, are 'mama's boys': Uncle Charlie in the sense that his older sister Emma indulges him like a over-fond mother (➤ MOTHERS AND HOUSES). This suggests that, in the 'Hitchcockian unconscious', the malignant upper level is most frequently the domain of the mother figure, either in person or – the PSYCHO syndrome – in the perverted form of her mentally disturbed son (brother in SHADOW OF A DOUBT). There are exceptions, but there are also more examples: Mrs Danvers in Rebecca's bedroom; Milly in Hattie's bedroom feeding her alcoholism (UNDER CAPRICORN); Mrs Edgar standing in the bedroom doorway as if overseeing Marnie's nightmare before tapping her way downstairs (➤ Part I). Finally, ROPE – which takes place entirely on the malignant upper level – could be included as another variation on this structure.

In effect, Zirnite's model locates the heart of the chaos world in these films in a malignant domain upstairs, a domain which is usually presided over – in some sense – by a more or less malevolent female presence. Where the dominant figure is a young man, usually he is under the sway of such a presence. This summarises the core of my argument about MOTHERS AND HOUSES, and the specific inflections of 'maternal malevolence' are discussed under that motif. One association here is with the prototypical 'madwoman in the attic' in Charlotte Brontë's *Jane Eyre* (1847), a Gothic motif. But Hitchcock has expanded the range of associations. Indeed, in some of his films, the malevolent figure associated with the upper level is an older man: SPELLBOUND, REAR WINDOW and VERTIGO. SPELLBOUND is precise about the different levels: Murchison's rooms are located upstairs; Constance's downstairs. Here the fact that the malevolent presence is male fits the overall structure of the film, in which traditional gender norms are reversed: the hero is the weak figure who needs to be saved/cured; the heroine is the active agent who effects this. It is Constance who goes up to Murchison's room at the climax of the film and defeats him. REAR WINDOW also preserves elements of this reversal (again it is the heroine who is active, and who enters the villain's domain), but mainly because of the hero's physical incapacity. More relevant here, I think, is that the hero himself occupies an upper-level domain, and Thorwald may in certain respects be seen as his alter ego (➢ DOUBLES).

The sense that the source of the malevolence associated with the upper level is so often a parent figure emphasises that this is, at root, a childhood construction, often Oedipal in its overtones. We have here a specific inflection of the childhood dread of 'the dark at the top of the stairs': that it hides a threatening adult monster, who in some cases exercises a tyrannical control over the fortunes of the protagonist; in others threatens a terrifying violence. The violent (young) men who are likewise associated with the upper level are like agents of this monster: it's as if it possesses them. Once again, a Hitchcock motif would seem to dramatise childhood fears.

Political variations

In FOREIGN CORRESPONDENT, the malignant domain is associated with Nazi terror. Both the Dutch windmill and the Charlotte Street house in London (where the Nazis later operate) are relevant here, and I would like to look at the two buildings and their staircases together. We enter the former with Johnny in his pursuit of the assassin of 'Van Meer'. Cobwebbed and dusty, charged with menace, the mill's interior is peculiarly oneiric. The huge cogged wheels are an insistent, grinding presence; there is almost nowhere to hide. With three villains already inside and two more approaching, Johnny is obliged to go up, across a free-standing staircase which traverses the mill in full view of the men below. However, as in a dream, the men move to permit his ascent by standing under the staircase; he thus steps literally over their heads. At the top of the stairs, he enters the malignant domain and finds the real Van Meer, a kidnap victim. Van Meer explains that the murdered man was a double, killed to buy the Nazis time in order to force him to reveal the secret clause of a treaty (the MacGuffin). But Van Meer is also drugged, and Johnny learns nothing more from him. As men come to collect Van Meer, Johnny escapes through a window, only to find himself clinging on the outside of the mill with no way down. He is obliged to go back inside, which means once more negotiating the exposed staircase. Again, the villains below unwittingly cooperate: the one facing in Johnny's direction pulls a jumper over his head to give Johnny the vital seconds he needs. He descends the staircase and gets out and away.

The two moments when Johnny traverses the staircase are symptomatic. Hitchcock's spy movies crucially include the risk to the spying figure of being him- or herself caught, and the exposed staircase here obliges the hero to negotiate this risk in a very direct way; in effect, with the literalness of a dream. The killing of the false Van Meer on the Conference Hall steps (a murder *on* a staircase) may now be seen as a piece of theatre, staged by the villains to fool the world. Johnny has to go into the dream world of the mill, and ascend the dream staircase to the malignant domain, to uncover this secret. The nature of his exposure on the staircase is later echoed when he climbs out of his hotel window and across to the heroine's (➤ ENTRY THROUGH A WINDOW), and when he is at the top of Westminster's Cathedral's tower (➤ HEIGHTS AND FALLING). Throughout the film, Johnny is a man repeatedly on the edge of an abyss, but he keeps his cool and handles the dangers of the chaos world with some aplomb. A similar sense of the hero repeatedly on the edge of abyss occurs in NORTH BY NORTHWEST, particularly after Roger has agreed to impersonate the fictitious spy Kaplan. The hero traversing the mill staircase in FOREIGN CORRESPONDENT may thus be seen as a metaphor for the dangers of the espionage world.

Van Meer is taken to a house in London, once more incarcerated in an upper room, and now actually tortured to reveal the MacGuffin. On this occasion we enter the house with the heroine's father Fisher, who is secretly working for the Nazis. The echoes of the mill sequence are striking. Again, the interior is 'made strange': here by a clutter of ladders and planking – workmen are redecorating. Again, the mix of villains inside is much the same: three are upstairs 'taking care of' Van Meer; two control the entrance (both here are women). Again, the staircase up to the malignant domain is emphasised: here by a crane as Fisher ascends. This shot required a double for Herbert Marshall going up the stairs (a general problem in his films because of his wooden leg), but when the crane reaches the upper landing, Marshall himself is shown 'arriving'. Since the crane is continuous, this needed careful orchestration: that Hitchcock took this sort of trouble indicates that he wanted the emphasis on the staircase and the ascent. But here there is no danger, just a strategic use of shadows. The fact that the villain going up the stairs is blended into them is also a comment on his character.

The link between the mill and the house is doubly emphasised: when Fisher first enters, he walks under a plank between two ladders, and a workman stands literally over his head, so that the trajectory of Johnny's progress through the mill is inverted (as is appropriate for a villain). The inversion is re-emphasised when Fisher enters the upstairs room and sees Van Meer in a bed being tortured: whereas Johnny sought to help the man, Fisher is obliged to witness the brutal consequences of his own involvement with the Nazis enacted in front of him. One can thus infer an implicit rationale for Hitchcock wanting Fisher to be seen ascending the stairs: it is to emphasise his own moral implication in the malignant domain.

In both these buildings, the domain to which the staircase leads is peculiarly evil because the figures who control it are Nazis. Similarly with the poisoning of

Fig. 55. Still: FOREIGN CORRESPONDENT: Staircase and the threat of being seen. The oneiric interior of the mill. Johnny (Joel McCrea) on the staircase; the assassin (Charles Wagenheim) and Krug (Eduardo Ciannelli) underneath it.

Alicia in NOTORIOUS. As noted under the BED SCENE, the Nazis in both films turn the bed itself into a site of agony. Nevertheless, the domain is still on the upper level: fascism is thus integrated into the dominant structural patterns of Hitchcock's work. However, with his two films which include scenes set in communist countries, matters are quite different.

In Juanita's hacienda in Cuba in TOPAZ, the upper level is associated with romance, the lower with murder, and the staircase is foregrounded as the link between the two. When Rico Parra's troops storm up the stairs as they search the house, Juanita is at the top, and she fights desperately to stop them getting past her into the bedroom. Rico is below, and orders her to come down. As she descends, we hear other troops forcing their way past her servants into the secret pantry. This confirms to Rico, now holding her, that she is a spy. He shoots her. Whereas in virtually all the other main examples in Hitchcock, from BLACK-MAIL to FRENZY, it is *ascents* of the stairs which lead to attack/murder, here it is the reverse.

There is an equivalent inversion in TORN CURTAIN. In Leipzig, Michael finally realises that he has to take Sarah into his confidence, and reveal his plan to steal atomic secrets from the East Germans. To do this, he takes her to the top of a hillock, whilst his minders look on from below. The scene is a clear reworking of the one in STRANGERS ON A TRAIN where, with Hennessy (Guy's minder) watching from across the road, Guy confesses to Anne that Bruno killed Miriam. In TORN CURTAIN, the location of the confession – which renews the romance – at the top of a hill emphasises the symbolic shift: as in TOPAZ, the lower level is associated with malevolent (communist) forces; the upper with the hero and heroine's love affair.

In communist countries, Hitchcock thus inverts the moral parameters of the two levels found elsewhere in his work. The inversion is more striking in TOPAZ, because when the Cuban delegation stay in the Hotel Theresa in New York, they are installed on the second floor, conforming to the usual pattern. Moreover, Rico Parra may be seen here – from the Western point of view – as the malevolent superego figure, guarding the 'forbidden zone' from unwelcome intruders. But in the communist countries of both films, there is no symbolic space above the lovers for the superego figures to occupy. The ideological thinking would seem to be clear: it is communism which creates the chaos world and that is located firmly down below.

Although traditional ('biblical') ascent and descent symbolism continues to apply in certain Hitchcock films, Zirnite's model has, overall, a more wide-ranging application. However, the significance of the spatial levels in Hitchcock is only one aspect of the way his staircases function. Very often in his films, a staircase itself generates unease, in the audience if not the characters in the film. Ascending or descending a staircase in Hitchcock is rarely a neutral act: it ratchets up the tensions of the plot. In other words, the expressionist notion of the staircase as a source of threat or menace is rarely far away. This, too, is relevant to the effectiveness of the motif and needs to be explored.

Sinister staircases

In VERTIGO, when Scottie races up the bell tower to try and stop 'Madeleine' committing suicide, the expressionist shots Hitchcock uses to convey his vertigo (combining a zoom out and track in) make it seem as if the staircase itself has a malignant power, preventing the hero from getting to the top. This is perhaps the most overt example of a 'sinister' staircase in Hitchcock, but the shot he uses when, moments later, Scottie goes back down the staircase has a wider application to his work. Scottie's descent is shown in a vertical shot down through the stairwell. Although it only occurs in relatively few of his films, this is probably Hitchcock's emblematic staircase shot, going back to THE LODGER. In most cases, the stairwell includes several flights of stairs, so that the banister rails descend away from the camera in a spiral, drawing the eye down and creating a slightly giddy effect – it is no accident that Hitchcock uses the shot almost exclusively for descents. In BLACKMAIL and VERTIGO, the person descending the stairs is traumatised: Alice has just killed Crewe; Scottie thinks he has failed to save 'Madeleine's' life. Here the shot conveys the sense of a descent *into* the chaos world. The protagonist's traumatic experience of the malignant domain at the top of the stairs was only the beginning: she/he is now plunged into a much more engulfing chaos world, one which takes over her/his entire life. The everyday world has become the chaos world: shortly afterwards, we see the protagonist in the grip of hallucinations (BLACKMAIL) and nightmares (VERTIGO).

In THE LODGER, the overhead shot shows the Lodger descending the lodging house stairs to go out late on a Tuesday night, the night when the Avenger strikes. At this stage, we do not know his intentions, and it is indeed possible that he is himself the Avenger (➤ BED SCENE). Certainly the shot makes his descent seem furtive: all we can see of the Lodger is his hand, ghost-like, gliding down the banisters. Even after he has told Daisy the 'real reason' for his nocturnal excursions – to hunt for the Avenger – the unsettling effect of the overhead shot is not diminished. Although, again, the shot signals the character's descent into the film's chaos world, the Lodger's clandestine manner makes it seem as if he is a part of that world. In other words, the shot here suggests a disturbance around the nature of the hero, a disturbance which may be related to Hitchcock's well-known wish to leave the question of the Lodger's innocence or guilt ultimately unresolved: see Truffaut 1968: 38.

In PSYCHO, there are two examples of the overhead shot. The first occurs at the point when 'Mrs Bates' comes out of her bedroom to assault Arbogast at the top of the stairs. This heralds Hitchcock's most brutal scene on a staircase: knifed at the top of the stairs, Arbogast falls back down them, and is savagely

'finished off' at the bottom. Here the overhead shot serves to dramatise a theatrical moment of bloody violence. The second example is when Norman carries
his mother downstairs to hide her in the fruit cellar. This shot is the culmination
of a slow crane up the stairs, during which (a) Norman, swinging his hips, ascends the stairs and (b) he and his 'mother' argue off-screen in her bedroom. As
the camera completes its ascent, it assumes the position of the earlier overhead
shot. We know, now, that Hitchcock filmed Norman carrying his mother from
this angle partly to conceal the fact that she is a corpse, but in context the shot
serves to increase the mystery surrounding 'Mrs Bates'. The image of her here, a
pathetic figure unable to prevent Norman from taking her down into the cellar,
contrasts melodramatically with her appearance as psychotic killer in the earlier
overhead shot. In PSYCHO, the overhead shots work together to create an enigma; an enigma which concerns the nature of the mother and son relationship
within the house.

Overhead shots are inherently powerful, and Hitchcock's use of them for his
staircases should ideally be considered in conjunction with the other occasions
when he films vertically down on a scene. Lesley Brill discusses such shots
throughout his book, relating them to 'The depths of the [films'] lower worlds'
(Brill 1988: 13). But such shots are by no means the only way in which Hitchcock
makes his staircases seem sinister. Staircases can become charged with the associations of the buildings in which they appear. The houses in both NOTORIOUS
and PSYCHO not only contain a staircase which goes up to the malignant domain, but also another which goes down to the cellar. In *The Poetics of Space*,
Gaston Bachelard characterises the cellar as 'the *dark entity* of the house, the one
that partakes of subterranean forces' (Bachelard 1969: 18). In these two films,
the whole house is a dark entity, and the staircases, leading both up and down,
serve to connect the different realms into a malignant unity. Just as the main
staircase leads up to the mother's domain, which is associated with poisoning
(NOTORIOUS) and murder (PSYCHO), so the one going down leads to the male
occupant's dark secret, discovery of which puts a young woman in mortal danger. The end of NOTORIOUS emphasises that the house is in itself a malignant
entity: Devlin and Alicia escape from it, but Alex is summoned back inside, and
we know, as he slowly ascends the steps to the front door, that he is going to his
death. It's as if he is going up the steps of the scaffold.

Other examples of sinister staircases are not difficult to find. Even though I
would qualify Zirnite's reading of the levels in the house in THE LODGER,
Hitchcock still uses the staircase in a manner which anticipates the darker examples: ➢ HANDCUFFS AND BONDAGE for an example of a sexually
charged scene which is staged around the stairs. In REBECCA, the main staircase
at Manderley goes up to all the bedrooms, but it is used most dramatically in
two scenes: when the heroine ascends to Rebecca's room and when her entrance

at the ball goes disastrously wrong. In Guy's clandestine ascent of the staircase in the Antony house in STRANGERS ON A TRAIN, he has to make his way past a Great Dane guarding the stairs, a scene which has led Donald Spoto to invoke a mythical analogy: the dog 'is the classical Cerberus, the guardian dog of the underworld' (1976, p 216). The staircase in Vandamm's house in NORTH BY NORTHWEST becomes in itself a trap: when Roger descends it he is caught and held prisoner on it at gunpoint by Vandamm's maid. Even in NUMBER SEVENTEEN, where Hitchcock plays around with the idea of the spooky staircase in the deserted house in an overtly parodic way, the hero Barton is nevertheless shot on the stairs. In all these examples, ascending or descending a staircase is in itself associated with unknown dangers or with terrible experiences.

Even when the house itself lacks a sense of menace, the staircase can become charged with sinister overtones. In the second half of SUSPICION, Hitchcock makes the stairs in the hero and heroine's house seem visually sinister, casting a 'spider's web' of shadows over them. Three times the effect is associated with Johnnie's seemingly baneful impulses: when he turns nasty towards Lina for questioning his highly suspect business practices; when they return home after the dinner at which he had shown such an interest in the 'untraceable poison' (➤ *Food and marriage*); and when he brings Lina the (poisoned) glass of milk. In each case, either the couple or Johnnie is ascending the staircase, and however one reads the 'spider's web' effect – as a symbolic expression of either Lina's fantasies about Johnnie or of his genuinely murderous designs on her – it suggests the nightmare at the heart of the marriage.

In SHADOW OF A DOUBT, Uncle Charlie is on the front stairs when he has his moment of realisation about Charlie: that, even if the police believe him innocent, she knows that he is guilty. He then tries to kill her by sawing through the back stairs. Here, too, the villain's malevolent power seems woven around the stairs, so much so that Charlie's chosen method to drive him from the family home is to make a dramatic entrance down the stairs wearing the incriminating ring (➤ JEWELLERY). In these last two examples, a charismatic man enters the house, moves into – or shares – the heroine's bedroom and begins to pervert the household by his presence. The importance of the staircase in this operation would seem to reside in its symbolic status as the 'spine of the house', to use the term employed by production designer Stuart Craig in THE STAIRCASE episode of *Architecture of the Imagination*. (He is discussing the use of the staircase in the house in THE SECRET GARDEN, Agnieszka Holland, 1993.) It is on the staircase where the villain's sinister power is most explicitly signalled, and on the staircase where the heroine is first subjected to this.

Freudian overtones

Absent from the symbolic functioning of the staircases in these films are the familiar Freudian dream associations: 'Steps, ladders or staircases, or, as the case may be, walking up or down them, are representations of the sexual act' (Freud, 1900/1954: 355). The absence is particularly noteworthy in SHADOW OF A DOUBT. Uncle Charlie's occupation of Charlie's bedroom is by no means 'innocent': Robin Wood cites a whole series of details through which Uncle Charlie's desire for his niece is symbolically indicated, e.g. the way he becomes erect when he first sees her, or the moment when he takes a flower for his button-hole on entering her bedroom, an implicit reference to 'deflowering' (Wood 1989: 300). But none of this symbolism in the film is associated with the stairs. Given the highly Freudian nature of Hitchcock's work, this seems surprising, and raises a general question about Hitchcock's staircases: do any of them function in the Freudian manner? I believe that only rarely is this the case, and that the absence of such an inflection of the motif in SHADOW OF A DOUBT is the rule, not the exception. However, given my argument that the motif of ENTRY THROUGH A WINDOW *is* highly sexualised, a corresponding absence of sexualisation of the staircase motif clearly requires discussion.

First, the examples which could be characterised as sexual in the Freudian sense. In UNDER CAPRICORN, Hattie calls down to Charles from her bedroom door, saying that there is something on her bed. Hitchcock emphasises Charles's ascent of the stairs by craning up with him; he goes into Hattie's room and, to relieve her fears, discharges his pistol, pretending to shoot whatever it was she saw. There is little doubt that this scene can be read in sexual terms: the lover-figure races up the stairs, enters the heroine's bedroom and fires his pistol into her hearth. In SHADOW OF A DOUBT, when Uncle Charlie first enters Charlie's bedroom – an equivalent moment – the staircase ascent is elided, which further emphasises its significance in UNDER CAPRICORN. Nevertheless, throughout this little drama, Hattie remains nervously outside the door. The scene thus contrasts strongly with Charles's later, uninvited entry into Hattie's room (➢ ENTRY THROUGH A WINDOW). Charles goes into Hattie's bedroom twice, and each entry is associated with a different motif. But whereas his entry through a window leads to an overtly sexual scene, the scene which follows his ascent of the staircase is marked by sexual displacement: the absence of the woman; the use of the pistol.

The only other significant example of a Freudian inflection to the staircase motif that I am aware of occurs in VERTIGO. I would like to look at this in conjunction with another feature of the film: the function and status of Elster as the film's malevolent superego figure. Scottie's inability to ascend the bell tower staircase – because of his acrophobia – is crucial in both narrative and symbolic terms. In narrative terms, his failure – as he sees it – to prevent 'Madeleine's' 'suicide' leads to his year-long nervous breakdown (➤ THE CORPSE). But the failure also lends itself to a Freudian reading. In *Hitchcock at Work*, Bill Krohn writes: 'As any Freudian dreambook would have told Hitchcock, dreaming that you can't go up a flight of stairs is a symbol of impotence' (Krohn 2000: 190). Scottie's attack of vertigo on the stairs symbolises his sexual failure with 'Madeleine', a failure which Elster foresaw. Elster thus assumes the status of a castrating father figure, and our retrospective discovery that he was above Scottie in the bell tower emphasises his symbolic power.

There is, however, an earlier example of the staircase motif in the film. During the period when Scottie is following 'Madeleine', he sees her enter the McKittrick Hotel and then appear at an upstairs window. But when he goes into the hotel to investigate further, he is told by the manageress that she has not been in today and he finds her room empty. Her disappearance is eerie, and here the staircase to the upper floor suggests an ascent not to a malignant domain, but to an uncanny one. 'Madeleine' has become like a ghost. This, too, is a reflection of Elster's power: she vanishes from the McKittrick Hotel because he decreed it, just as she later disappears – Scottie thinks that she is dead – as a part of Elster's plot to murder his wife. 'Madeleine's' appearance at the upstairs window here is later echoed in Judy's appearance at the upstairs window of her hotel. In both cases, we are seeing her from Scottie's point of view, and the imagery likens her to an imprisoned princess in a fairy tale. But the figure who in effect has imprisoned her, Elster, is simply too powerful for her to be rescued.

Elster's dominance over Scottie echoes Murchison's over J.B. in SPELLBOUND: in each case, the villain exploits the hero's psychological weaknesses to his own malevolent ends. However, Elster's power is the greater in that the heroine, too, is subject to it. Even though Elster uses and then rejects Judy, he continues to cast a shadow over her life. It is when Judy wears Elster's gift – Carlotta's necklace – that she inadvertently reveals the murder plot to Scottie (➤ JEWELLERY). This prompts Scottie to take Judy back to the bell tower and force her up the staircase to the site of Madeleine's murder. Marked by the inner conflicts driving the hero, this is one of Hitchcock's great sequences. On the one hand, Scottie insists that this is his second chance; that he wants to stop being haunted. If he makes it to the top, his vertigo – linked, now, to his obsession with 'Madeleine' – will be cured. On the other, he is also impelled by a barely suppressed murderous rage towards Judy, forcing a confession out of her by violently manhandling her up the stairs. Again, Krohn invokes Freud: noting that this scene takes place after Scottie and Judy have finally made love, he says that it is 'logical' that Scottie should now be able 'to drag Judy to the top of the tower … although the violent manner in which Scottie completes his "cure" resembles a rape' (Krohn

2000: 190). But the tragic outcome to the ascent – Scottie does make it to the top, but Judy is then killed – re-emphasises Elster's power. My reading of the ending is that Judy, racked with guilt, interprets the sudden appearance of a nun as Madeleine's ghost, and this so frightens her that she falls to her death (≻ GUILT AND CONFESSION). It's as if Elster's power is quasi-supernatural: just as he made 'Madeleine' seem like a ghost to Scottie, here, in the malignant domain of the bell tower, he has such psychic dominion that Judy thinks that she sees the ghost of Madeleine.

Insofar as the staircase ascents in VERTIGO may be read in sexual terms, they chart first Scottie's sexual failure and then his (sexual) violence. The negative overtones are typical. In MURDER!, Fane's climactic trapeze act begins with his ascent of a rope ladder, and the act itself has been read by William Rothman in sexual terms (≻ HEIGHTS AND FALLING). But it ends with Fane's suicide. The most emphasised ascent of a staircase in Hitchcock is the crane with Alice and Crewe as they go up five flights to his studio. Crewe, one feels sure, is imagining a sexual outcome to the ascent. But the scene at the top of the stairs ends with him being stabbed to death. There are occasional staircase ascents by a couple which are signalled as leading to sex, but they are rare. And, so far as the symbolism of staircases – or ladders – is concerned, sexual overtones in Hitchcock are very rare indeed, and all the examples seem to be either negative (VERTIGO; MURDER!) or inconclusive (UNDER CAPRICORN).

The contrast with ENTRY THROUGH A WINDOW is striking. In Hitchcock's films, entering a building through a window is repeatedly associated with sexual transgression, whereas going up the stairs inside a building is generally not. The staircase thus emerges as one of Hitchcock's darker motifs, in which the sinister aspects of the motif are so strong that they suppress the Freudian sexual overtones – unless these are negative. Hitchcock's staircases are predominantly sites of – or sites which lead to – danger and threat. There is, however, one final group of examples in which the motif opens up somewhat, introducing positive elements which may even counteract the more sinister associations. The examples in this group all concern couples.

Couples and staircases

The key examples so far mentioned of a couple ascending the stairs together – BLACKMAIL, SUSPICION and the climax of VERTIGO – are negative. Others, however, are different. An unusual example occurs in the embassy towards the end of THE MAN WHO KNEW TOO MUCH (1955). Knowing that their kidnapped son Hank is being held prisoner somewhere in the building, Jo and Ben McKenna use a social occasion as a means to find and rescue him, and the embassy staircase is structurally integrated into this process. As Jo sings 'Que Sera Sera' to the embassy guests, Hitchcock cuts steadily up the stairs, Jo's voice becoming fainter, until the camera reaches the room where Hank is imprisoned. Encouraged by Mrs Drayton, who is officially guarding him, Hank whistles a response. Ben hears him, and arrives to rescue him. But the rescue is interrupted by Mr Drayton, and Ben and Hank are taken back down the stairs at gunpoint. During the descent, Ben knocks Drayton downstairs, and the gun goes off, apparently killing him. As the guests gather round Drayton's body at the foot of the stairs, the family is reunited.

This staircase sequence may be seen as a variation on its equivalent at the end of NOTORIOUS, a variation in which husband and wife work together to effect the rescue from the upper level. The shots in which Jo's voice seems to travel up the stairs are answered by Ben and Hank's descent of the stairs, a descent which includes the despatch of the kidnapping villain. It is striking, here, that we do not see Ben's ascent of the stairs: Hitchcock evidently wanted the shots accompanying Jo's singing to serve the structural function of marking the ascent, a feature which further emphasises the rescue as a joint operation between husband and wife. Uniquely, in Hitchcock's work, a *song* goes up the stairs and acts, as if magically, to link mother and son. The stairs are like a stage on which the resolution of the conflict is played out, and there is an almost transcendental quality to these shots. Robin Wood has written, 'The shots of Doris Day's voice traveling up the stairs (so to speak) are among the most moving in the whole of Hitchcock' (1989, p 370). Nevertheless, the happy ending is only possible because of Mrs Drayton's change of heart: correctly reading Jo's singing as a mother's attempt to find her son, she gets Hank to send a reply. It is she who thus brings about the family reunion. But her husband's (apparent) death on the stairs is rather hastily glossed over: there is nothing here of the power of the last shot of NOTORIOUS. We do see Mrs Drayton gazing down from the stairs on the crowd around her husband's body. We are not told what she feels.

The other examples linking couples and staircases in Hitchcock are more conventional. Michel Cieutat notes that staircases in Hollywood films are also used for the discussion of a couple's problems: he mentions VIOLENT SATURDAY (Richard Fleischer, 1955) (Cieutat 1991: 205); ALL I DESIRE (Douglas Sirk, 1953) furnishes another good example. Although Cieutat does not say this, the appropriateness of the setting relies in part on the obvious point that stairs lead up to bedrooms: it is implied, after both these scenes, that the partners then seal their new-found togetherness by sleeping together. There is one example in Hitchcock which fits this scenario: Hattie and Sam have a magnificent reconciliation on the stairs towards the end of UNDER CAPRICORN, and they, too, end by going upstairs together. And a closely equivalent scene occurs at the end of

MARNIE: Marnie is sitting at the bottom of the stairs when she suddenly remembers, and narrates to Mark, what happened to her as a child. Both these are moments of renewal, when a couple whose marriage has been almost destroyed by past events experiences an emotional breakthrough.

The scene in UNDER CAPRICORN also has great symbolic power, because throughout the film the staircase has functioned to express the 'great gulf' (Sam's phrase) between husband and wife. Hattie spends most of her time in her bedroom upstairs, and is very uneasy when she descends to the main level. By contrast, until the reconciliation scene, Sam never goes upstairs. And so the staircase here helps dramatise the structural divide in the marriage; a divide further highlighted by Charles's own ascent of the staircase. In the meantime, the housekeeper Milly moves easily between the two levels, a sign of her power within the household. She is the figure who has transformed Hattie's bedroom into the malignant domain (➤ BED SCENE). It is thus crucial that the final confrontation with Milly should occur with both Sam and Hattie in the latter's bedroom, and that Milly's expulsion from the house should be signalled by her going back downstairs (➤ KEYS).

In THE PARADINE CASE, Tony and Gay Keane first meet on the stairs: he enters the house boyishly wet, having neglected both raincoat and umbrella, and she runs down to greet and then mother him. The meeting is structurally very similar to that in UNDER CAPRICORN: the wife comes down the stairs; the husband goes up. Here, however, there is no symbolic distinction between the two levels in the house, and the relaxed way in which the couple go into the bedroom to discuss the day's events points to a sexual marriage, a rare phenomenon in Hitchcock. Later, Gay actually makes a statement – 'It's time we were in the gondola' – which, followed by the couple beginning to go up the stairs, signifies quite clearly, in a Production Code euphemism, that they are going to bed together. The staircase is also used to register the strain on the marriage brought about by Tony's subsequent obsession with Mrs Paradine. When Tony ascends it in a later scene, shadows of the banisters create an enveloping cage effect, and when he goes into Gay's room on this occasion, she signals that she does not want him to spend the night with her. Here the prison-like imagery around the staircase alludes to the transformation that Tony's infatuation has wrought on his home and marriage.

Hitchcock's final staircase is in Adamson's house in FAMILY PLOT. It is first ascended when Adamson and Fran go to bed after coming home with their ransom diamond. As the camera tracks in to the diamond hidden in the chandelier, Adamson is refusing to tell Fran where it is: 'You'll have to torture me first.' Fran: 'I intend to; in a few minutes.' Here the two kidnappers, sexually aroused by their successful crime, are about to celebrate with some mutually consenting sado-masochism. This scene is then answered by a contrasting scene at the end of the film. After Blanche and George have successfully locked Adamson and Fran in their own secret room (➤ BED SCENE), Blanche seems to go into a trance, and leads George up the cellar steps and then to a point, halfway up the front stairs, where she can point to the diamond in the chandelier. George is most impressed, telling her that she is psychic, but as he goes to phone the police Blanche sits on the stairs and winks directly at the audience. The implication is that she is not psychic; that she overheard where the diamond was hidden.

This is the final scene of Hitchcock's final film, and its staircase ascent is in complete contrast not only with the savage climactic ascent of the stairs in VERTIGO, but also with the first Hitchcock ascent in THE BLACKGUARD. Here the tone is light-hearted, and the scene itself quite charming. With George as her audience, Blanche enacts her ascent of the stairs as a piece of theatre, and the hint of a heavenly choir on the soundtrack both ironises and supports her performance. Unusually for Hitchcock, here the traditional associations of an ascent really do seem to apply: as if the couple were going up to a better realm. The joke – that Blanche was putting it all on – is part of the charm: she is leading George so that she gets him just where she wants him. As with the BED SCENE, it is heartening that Hitchcock's last example of the staircase motif should be so optimistic.

This example is, however, untypical. Although the staircase is a highly elaborated – and frequently recurring – Hitchcock motif, it is more often a focus for anxiety. The prevalent sense of a malignant domain located at an upper level invests Hitchcock's buildings in general and houses in particular with menace. Especially in the Hollywood films, relatively few buildings in his films are 'safe', a refuge from the dangers of the world. Their terrible secrets are a source of danger, their bedrooms frequently places of torment, they may even be invaded by hostile forces from without. As the spine of the building, the staircase is the point of transition between its different zones and both ascents and descents become charged with the frequently disturbing associations of the building itself. Those secrets contained in the rooms at the tops or bottoms of stairs, and the traumatic experiences of the characters who seek to penetrate them (both the rooms and the secrets); those anxieties attendant upon mounting or descending the stairs; those moments when an awful calamity happens on the stairs – these are the typical ways in which Hitchcock's staircases function.

Staircases and the police

In THE LODGER, the policeman Joe usually enters the Bunting's boarding-house by coming down the back steps into the basement parlour: he feels at home there. With each level that he ascends, he is less comfortable. On the ground floor, he tries to charm Daisy, but is rather clumsy: his kisses are interrupted; he crudely handcuffs her. When he ascends to the Lodger's room, he is plainly ill at ease, which he masks by being authoritarian and aggressive. The second time, he is also carrying out the crucial police role of arresting the wrong man. Here the policeman's relationship to the levels in the house is in terms of class: Joe is a working-class figure, and his behaviour shows this. For this reason, and because the Lodger himself is not a threat within the home, I feel Zirnite's argument about the film should be modified. The class hierarchy, I would maintain, is more significant in characterising the levels of the house.

In later Hitchcock films, the relationship between the police and staircases is a more familiar story. Only in the opening sequence of BLACKMAIL does an ascent lead to the arrest of someone who is probably guilty (when interrogated, he confesses); only at the end of SABOTEUR do we see the police in their benevolent role, reuniting the hero and heroine (➤ ENDINGS AND THE POLICE). Otherwise, we have the usual collection of disasters: they chase an innocent man up a staircase to his death (BLACKMAIL); they photograph a suspect at the top of the stairs and so blow their cover (SHADOW OF A DOUBT); they are tripped on the stairs by an old woman, enabling the hero and heroine to escape (TORN CURTAIN); they come up the stairs and arrest the wrong man (FRENZY).

TRAINS AND BOATS / PLANES AND BUSES

Fig. 56. Still: THE 39 STEPS: encounter on a train. Hannay (Robert Donat) meets Pamela (Madeleine Carroll) and asks her to help him; she turns him over to the police.

Donald Spoto has recorded that, as a boy, Hitchcock

constructed a huge wall chart, showing the positions each day of virtually every British ship afloat… But most of all he loved timetables… Perhaps they corresponded to

his training in tidiness and orderliness, everything regulated and on schedule; and perhaps, too, they corresponded to a wish to be somewhere else.

(Spoto 1988: 20)

Hitchcock's boyhood obsession was equally with the means of transport themselves, and this preoccupation shows clearly in his films. There are relatively few of his films in which cars are the dominant mode of transport, and these are mostly late in his career. Hitchcock's characters tend to travel quite a lot, but journeys of any length are more usually undertaken by public transport. As a consequence, there are many scenes in his films set on trains and boats in particular. Planes and buses feature less prominently, but they are still sufficiently popular to each constitute a motif. With trains and boats, I have concentrated on scenes which actually take place on the means of transport, excluding for the most part mere arrivals or departures. With planes and buses, for reasons which will be discussed, I have extended the examples.

TRAINS

Although in three of his films the hero and heroine first meet on a train, this does not mean that Hitchcock considers it a romantic setting. In THE 39 STEPS, Hannay enters Pamela's compartment and kisses her in order to try and fool the pursuing police, but she promptly turns him in anyway. Johnnie's emergence out of the darkness created by a train tunnel at the beginning of SUSPICION hints at his suspect persona, amply confirmed by later events. Roger and Eve's love scene on the train in NORTH BY NORTHWEST is followed by the revelation that she is (apparently) working for the villains. A meeting with a glamorous 'stranger on a train' in a Hitchcock movie is invariably full of risk: one cannot be sure how trustworthy the stranger is. The same is true of Guy's meeting with Bruno in STRANGERS ON A TRAIN: later Guy discovers that Bruno took their conversation as approval for his plan that they 'swap murders'.

In NORTH BY NORTHWEST, the glamorous stranger, Eve, first seduces Roger and then sends a message to the spy Vandamm and his gay henchman Leonard – in another compartment – asking what to do with Roger in the morning. The outcome of this is the attempt on Roger's life by the cropdusting plane. This material is a close reworking – with key roles reversed – of that on the train at the climax of SECRET AGENT. With the train passing through enemy territory during World War I, here it is the villain, Marvin, who is vamped by the beautiful blonde spy, Elsa, whilst the men she is officially working for – elsewhere on the train – are the hero Ashenden and his camp henchman, the General. The outcome of this, too, is a plane attack: ordered (in effect) by Ashenden, but blamed by Marvin on Elsa, British planes attack the train. And, just as Eve is upset about sending Roger off to be killed, so Elsa turns out to be unexpectedly protective of Marvin when Ashenden and the General come to kill him. She holds them off at gunpoint and the situation is only resolved when the plane attack precipitates a train wreck in which Marvin is mortally wounded. The plane crashing into the oil tanker in NORTH BY NORTHWEST is the equivalent of this moment, with the important difference that Roger, as the hero, escapes (➢ CONFINED SPACES).

These parallel examples indicate the potential hazards of rail travel in Hitchcock. Even though the wreck in NORTH BY NORTHWEST is displaced away from the train, it arises out of the events on the train journey. The hazardousness of rail travel goes back to NUMBER SEVENTEEN, Hitchcock's first extended train sequence (there is a minor, elliptical one in EASY VIRTUE). At the film's climax, the villains make their getaway on a ferry goods train, and the undercover cop Barton pursues them in a hijacked Green Line coach. Five of the film's main characters have boarded the train: three villains; Nora, a mystery woman who has now turned against the villains, and Ben, Barton's working-class helper. These characters argue and fight with one another, and pursue one another up and down the train, but to little dramatic effect. Nevertheless, the comic incompetence of the villains does result in a spectacular train wreck: they shoot the fireman; the driver promptly faints and they then cannot stop the train, which smashes into the ferry, tearing it from its moorings. Not only does the wreck represent a collision between two transport categories, train and boat, it also serves as the reformed Nora's traumatic event (➢ WATER).

In Hitchcock's most comprehensive train movie, THE LADY VANISHES, the hero and heroine meet in the hotel before catching the train. Although the encounter is typically hostile (➢ BED SCENE), their mutual differences are set aside on the train itself in the interests of solving the mystery of Miss Froy's disappearance. In *English Hitchcock*, Charles Barr analyses the events on the train – or, at least, the first 45 minutes of them – in terms of Iris's inner conflicts. She is hit by a falling flowerpot just before boarding the train, and spends much of the early part of the journey drifting in and out of consciousness. Barr suggests that there is an oneiric dimension to this part of the film:

> From the moment the flowerpot strikes her and we are given her blurred point of view as she lapses into unconsciousness, the film could *be* the dream of Iris, working through her eve-of-marriage preoccupations: her doubts about Charles [her fiancé], her attraction to Gilbert, and her lack of a mother.
>
> (Barr 1999: 197)

From this point of view, the train journey is through the terrain of Iris's unconscious, and the characters and events on the train are embodiments of her fears and phantasies.

What happens on the train is also threatening. Here it is not at first apparent that the (fictitious) country through which the train is travelling is in fact enemy territory, and that Miss Froy is a British spy. But as Gilbert and Iris search the length of the train for her, a highly effective paranoid atmosphere is created: foreigners are duplicitous, situations fraught with danger and the other English travellers too insular to be of much help. Here, too, there is a glamorous stranger, Dr Hartz, who turns out to be particularly untrustworthy: it was he who kidnapped Miss Froy and he becomes murderous when his plans are thwarted. The characters and events on the train are like a projection of English suspicions about both Europeans and each other, in which the outcome suggests that the only safe place for the English to be is back home.

The initial meeting between Bruno and Guy in STRANGERS ON A TRAIN not only sets up the plot, but also establishes a structural pattern: a lot of train journeys are made during the course of the film, but the ones we see all involve Metcalf, Guy's home town. Situated between Washington, D.C. (where Bruno and Guy both live) and New York (where Guy goes to play tennis), Metcalf is the only station where we see anyone disembark – Guy and Bruno each arrives twice – as if the important train journeys all involve going there. Even the one train scene which does not involve someone travelling to Metcalf is linked to the town: after his murder of Miriam, Bruno in Metcalf looks at his watch; cut to Guy on a train en route to Washington looking at his watch. Later, Guy seeks to use his ensuing conversation with a maths professor on this train as his alibi, but the Metcalf police are not convinced: they calculate that he could have murdered Miriam and still caught the same train. Metcalf, it would seem, is inescapable. The town is thus both the chaos world – symbolised, above all, by the fairground and the Magic Isle – and a site of compulsive return, repeatedly drawing the film's central characters back to it. With Bruno, Hitchcock takes the transport motif further. When he first goes to Metcalf, he travels by a succession of different means of transport: train to Metcalf, bus to the fairground, boat to the Magic Isle. Each is smaller and more intimate than its predecessor, and the overall journey is symbolic, taking Bruno by stages into the darkness of the chaos world. It is on the Magic Isle that he murders Miriam.

SHADOW OF A DOUBT and SPELLBOUND both include two train journeys, and in each film they show a protagonist (Uncle Charlie; Constance) going to and then away from a place associated with his/her past. In the earlier film, Uncle Charlie pretends to be ill during his journey to Santa Rosa – another example of duplicity on a train – but immediately perks up when he disembarks and sees the waiting Newton family. This is Hitchcock's most celebrated train arrival.

Robin Wood comments on the black smoke which clouds the image as the train pulls into the station (Wood 1989: 298); Roger Greenspun writes: 'The day Uncle Charlie arrived, nobody else had gotten off the train at Santa Rosa, and he brought with him the world, its riches, its sparkling wine, its knowledge, its murders' (Greenspun 1991: 22). In the matching departure scene at the end of the film, Uncle Charlie again reverts to his sinister persona: he is planning to murder Charlie, and grips her wrists until the train starts to move (➤ HANDS). Once the train has gathered speed, he tries to throw her off, but Charlie miraculously turns the tables on him, so that it is he who is hit by a train speeding in the opposite direction.

In SPELLBOUND, as Constance and J.B. travel to Rochester to stay with her old mentor Alex Brulov, she continues to probe into his repressed past. In fact, she is successful on this journey: her questions prompt J.B. to remember the least repressed element of that past: being shot down during the war over Rome. Despite the achievement, he still becomes very angry with her, and on the journey away from Rochester, he is sufficiently disturbed not even to talk to her (➤ *Food and sex*). The hostile look he gives her on the train then continues throughout their subsequent downhill ski which almost results in both of them going off a precipice. At the climax of this, J.B. remembers his repressed childhood trauma, and the fact that this is to do with falling links this climactic moment with that of the death of Uncle Charlie (➤ HEIGHTS AND FALLING).

It is true that NORTH BY NORTHWEST ends with Roger and Eve's honeymoon on a train, but the happy ending is only just achieved: in the previous shot Eve was hanging precariously from Roger's hand on Mount Rushmore. This ending, and the climactic 'falls' in SHADOW OF A DOUBT and SPELLBOUND, summarise what happens to Hitchcock's couples who meet or travel together on a train. Either the relationship is severed by death (SECRET AGENT, SHADOW OF A DOUBT, STRANGERS ON A TRAIN – where the couple are Guy and Bruno and the merry-go-round crash stands in for a train wreck), or there is a climax, usually to do with the threat of falling, in which death is narrowly averted (THE LADY VANISHES, SUSPICION, SPELLBOUND and NORTH BY NORTHWEST). THE 39 STEPS is the only exception to this rule; even NUMBER SEVENTEEN, where Barton and Nora do not travel together on the train, has the same climax. Hitchcock's train journeys almost always lead his couples into potentially fatal situations, so that, even if death is avoided, the film includes a cathartic climax in which its threat is confronted and overcome.

BOATS

Fig. 57. Still: I Confess: confession on a boat. On the ferry, Ruth (Anne Baxter) tells Father Logan
(Montgomery Clift) that she loves him.

Partly because it includes all kinds of boats, and not just those used for public
transport, this is by far the most common of these four motifs: around twenty
Hitchcock films have ship or boat scenes, and Lifeboat is set entirely on a boat.
In order to see how his use of the setting is distinctive, one could begin by in-
voking a familiar generic use of the sea voyage: the 'shipboard romance'. In the
cinema generally, this one of romantic melodrama's most potent narratives:
One Way Passage (Tay Garnett, 1932), Now, Voyager (Irving Rapper, 1942),
An Affair to Remember (Leo McCarey, 1957), Titanic (James Cameron,
1997). In each of these films, the romance is unusually intense, and results in a
complete transformation in the lovers' lives.

By contrast, although four of Hitchcock's films include the typical setting and
appropriate characters for a shipboard romance, in each case this is deeply ironised. In Champagne, seasickness and a lovers' tiff intervene as soon as the
situation between the Boy and the Girl shows signs of becoming serious. In
Rich and Strange, the husband, Fred, is also extensively seasick, and when he

does recover and has a 'romance' with a 'Princess', she turns out to be a fake who is after his money. In the meantime, his wife, Emily, has what seems to be a genuine shipboard romance with Commander Gordon, but she feels that she has to give him up when she learns how Fred has been deceived. In MARNIE, Mark and Marnie's honeymoon takes place on a pleasure cruiser, but it is highly traumatic for both of them: she refuses to have sex; he eventually rapes her – leading to her attempted suicide. Finally, the opening voyage in TORN CURTAIN does at least provide Michael and Sarah with a scene in bed, but this is troubled by his detachment from her: planning to pretend to defect to East Germany, he had not even wanted her to come with him on the trip. And for their second voyage, (a) they are confined to theatre costume baskets and (b) they only just escape being machine-gunned before reaching safety.

The failure of Hitchcock's shipboard romances is of a piece with his scepticism about love affairs in general: like sex, romance in his films is almost always problematic and difficult. The only Hitchcock film to include a genuinely romantic love scene set on a boat is FOREIGN CORRESPONDENT, but the scene occurs on the windswept deck of a Channel ferry, once more ironising any sense of the ship as a romantic setting. Indeed, as soon as a boat journey in his films extends to the point where sleeping and beds are involved, the traumas associated with the latter come to the fore (➤ BED SCENE). For Hitchcock, ships and boats can be very uncomfortable places. Even in the opening scene of TORN CURTAIN, the ship's heating has broken down, so that Michael and Sarah are in bed together as much for warmth as for sex. Cruises can, in addition, be socially claustrophobic, so that it becomes difficult to avoid irritating fellow passengers (e.g. the cruise busybody Miss Imrie in RICH AND STRANGE) and the forced proximity tends to exacerbate the tensions already in a relationship (e.g. MARNIE).

There is one group of boat scenes which is rather different, in that it involves a woman declaring her love to a man. Danielle and Robie's scene in a motorboat in TO CATCH A THIEF is the light-hearted version: although she suggests that he take her to South America, she knows that he is not interested; she's just flirting with him. The scenes in SECRET AGENT (Elsa and Ashenden on a riverboat) and I CONFESS (Ruth to Father Logan on a ferry) are, by contrast, surprisingly intense. First, both are imbued with the fraught circumstances of the woman's declaration. Elsa is semi-hysterical, having just learnt that the man the General killed – with Ashenden's connivance – was not the spy they had assumed. In I CONFESS, Ruth is relatively calm, but she is also fully aware that they are probably being watched by the police. Both scenes are also charged with guilt: Elsa is compromised by her own involvement in Ashenden's mission; Ruth insists on declaring her adulterous love for a priest. In effect, both scenes become like confessions.

In THE MANXMAN, the material is handled differently. In this case, the couple are on the seashore, and the ship – bringing home Pete, Kate's fiancé – is in the background, inexorably approaching the port. Here the couple have already consummated their relationship and, although this occurred when they thought that Pete was dead, the boat serves as a powerful metaphor for the return of the guilt which they had disavowed but which they now feel. REBECCA takes this a stage further. Here the discovery of Rebecca's boat with her body in it is like the return of the repressed for Maxim, her killer. In this case, the return of the boat prompts a full-scale confession to the heroine, which Hitchcock again situates on the shore (in the boathouse).

In JAMAICA INN – adapted, like REBECCA, from a Daphne du Maurier novel – the ships function more in a generic sense: the film is concerned with wreckers; the ships and the sailors are their victims. The film also climaxes on a ship: Mary is rescued from Sir Humphrey and he himself, exposed as the mastermind behind the wreckers, commits suicide. With the wreckers themselves already apprehended, his fall from the yard-arm thus guarantees that no more ships and sailors will be sacrificed to his demented ambitions. SABOTEUR has a similar notion: in the climactic act of sabotage Fry blows up a ship as it launched; later, it is seen lying on its side in the dock. And here, too, the ship-destroying villain dies by falling from a great height: in Fry's case, from the top of the Statue of Liberty (➤ HEIGHTS AND FALLING).

Apart from the special case of LIFEBOAT, Hitchcock's most traumatic boat journey is Roddy's 'five days and nights in a world of delirium' from Marseille to London in DOWNHILL (➤ BED SCENE). It is possible to see Roddy's ordeal as in certain respects a metaphor for Hitchcock's extended boat journeys. Whether or not they include an actual illness, they are often like a period of sickness, but with a (usually) beneficial outcome. Roddy's journey at least serves to bring him home. Fred and Emily's return journey after their unfortunate cruise includes surviving a ship-wreck, losing all their possessions and eating cat meat, but it brings them together as a couple: when they arrive home, Emily is pregnant. The honeymoon sequence in Marnie at least serves to make Marnie's fears known to Mark: it initiates the long process of her recovery. Hitchcock's ordeals on boats are generally ultimately therapeutic.

This occurs, too, with some of the other examples. Setting the final scene of JAMAICA INN on a ship helps heal the earlier traumatic associations. Like RICH AND STRANGE, CHAMPAGNE includes a later ship scene in which the couple's relationship is renewed. Even the peculiarly fraught confession scenes either on or associated with boats indicate that boats serve to release what has hitherto been suppressed. And in two cases, this is directly beneficial: Elsa's outburst initiates her romance with Ashenden; Maxim's confession renews his marriage.

LIFEBOAT would seem to be darker. As well as the trials arising from the ocean setting itself (➢ WATER AND RAIN), the journey includes the deaths of Mrs Higley and her baby, the amputation of Gus's leg and then the death, too, of Gus. When the others realise that the U-boat Captain Willi was responsible for Gus's death, they turn on him like a pack of wild animals and murder him; only the black steward Joe refrains from joining in. Nevertheless, the experience of surviving together also changes the characters in a positive way. By the end, the radio operator Sparks and the nurse Alice are engaged, the famous correspondent Connie has come to terms with the loss of her valuables, and the industrialist Ritt says that he'll honour his poker losses to the stoker Kovac. When another German sailor climbs aboard and tries to command them, they are more sanguine about what to do with him. Here, too, the journey is an ordeal, but for the survivors it is also therapeutic.

See also APPENDIX I.

PLANES

The first and the last plane journeys in Hitchcock's films are nicely contrasting examples. In CHAMPAGNE, the Girl commandeers her father's plane in order to pursue the transatlantic liner her boyfriend is on, getting the pilot to ditch the plane in the sea alongside the liner so that they'll be 'rescued' and taken aboard. Given that she is an American heiress, who has done all this in defiance of Daddy's orders, what we have here – some six years before the genre was assumed to have begun – is like the opening of a screwball comedy. In FAMILY PLOT, Fran commandeers a helicopter in order to take the pilot to her kidnap victim. On this occasion, the young woman has a very different agenda. It still involves her boyfriend, who is waiting with the victim, but it also includes the couple making a successful getaway with the ransom diamond. Yet once again she is the figure in charge of the flight, defying, in this instance, the law itself.

Apart from these examples, planes only appear in a significant sense in Hitchcock's spy movies. The most extended plane sequence is in FOREIGN CORRESPONDENT when, at the outbreak of World War II, Nazi spy Fisher flies with his daughter Carol from England to the USA and Johnny and Scott ffolliott catch the same plane. Learning from a telegram that he'll be arrested on arrival in New York, Fisher confesses to Carol, shortly after which the plane is shot down by a German ship and Fisher is drowned (➢ GUILT AND CONFESSION). In NOTORIOUS, a plane journey from the USA to Rio de Janeiro is likewise the setting for the heroine to learn about her enemy agent father: in this case, that he has committed suicide in jail. In both cases, the hero, who has

Fig. 58. Still: NORTH BY NORTHWEST: the malevolent plane.
Roger (Cary Grant) pursued by the crop-dusting plane.

opposed the father on political grounds, is with the heroine on the plane. The
flight would thus seem to be symbolic. Since the death of the father occurs as
the heroine flies out of the country he has betrayed, it is as if a new life for her is
being marked out not just romantically but also politically. But if this applies in
FOREIGN CORRESPONDENT, it is ironised in NOTORIOUS. Here the hero is a much
more ambiguous figure and thanks to him the heroine is taken back into her
father's corrupt world.

There are three plane flights in TOPAZ, each marking a stage in the development of the film's espionage plot. For the Kusenov family's defection, as the

plane flies west, Hitchcock visualises it as going into the sunset; a cliché image which, in its excess, seems ironic. For André's flights to and from Cuba, there is a much more powerful irony. On the flight there, a newspaper headline and its date alert us to the fact that he is too late to find out anything which could possibly influence the political events; on the flight back, having heard of Juanita's death, he discovers her farewell gift to him: the microfilm hidden in a book. He has secured the MacGuffin, but the lateness of his mission means that her death was unnecessary (➤ THE MACGUFFIN). In TORN CURTAIN, the one plane scene is more enigmatic: we only realise in retrospect that Michael's apparent defection to East Germany is a mask for his pursuit of the MacGuffin. But Sarah has learned of Michael's plans to fly to East Berlin and has followed him on the plane; the staging of the scene is thus primarily about his failure to take her into his confidence: indeed, he is so rude to her here that he reduces her to tears.

Espionage is a very nasty business, and it is not surprising that the plane scenes in these movies reflect this. The betrayals are often personal as well as political: a father betrays a daughter (FOREIGN CORRESPONDENT); the hero and his boss collude to make use of the heroine (NOTORIOUS); the hero reveals that he does not trust his fiancée (TORN CURTAIN); the hero leaves his wife to visit his mistress and his mission leads to the latter's death (TOPAZ). Overall, the scenes also comment on the destructiveness of the espionage world on those closest to the figures directly involved in that world.

The association of planes with spies and spying is so strong in Hitchcock's work that it extends to plane attacks (those noted under TRAINS in SECRET AGENT and NORTH BY NORTHWEST are ordered by the spies) and even to airport scenes. It is at Chicago airport that Roger in NORTH BY NORTHWEST finally meets the Professor, who explains to him the CIA background to the mystery of George Kaplan and Eve's role as a secret agent. Similarly, it is at East Berlin airport that Sarah learns of Michael's stated aim to defect. The second ending to TOPAZ (now available on video) is set at Orly airport and shows Soviet spy Granville escaping by plane to Moscow whilst French spy André and his wife catch a plane back to Washington, D.C. An apparent exception occurs in THE MAN WHO KNEW TOO MUCH (1955), when Ben and Jo McKenna disembark from a plane at London airport. But Hitchcock includes this scene in order to emphasise that their movements are being monitored: the Draytons' assistant Edna observes their arrival and makes a phone call to report this. They, too, are being spied on.

The opening pair of examples for this motif are the exceptions. In the symbolic system of Hitchcock's films, planes generally function in a peculiarly negative sense. In the way the flights connect countries, the motif tends to refer to the international-political themes in Hitchcock's work, which are almost always given a sinister twist in the way they are characterised by suspicion, espionage and even war. But even in the Midwest cornfields of the USA, a plane is a threat. On top of these general associations, the additional, more personal ones are similarly dark. During the plane flights in FOREIGN CORRESPONDENT and NOTORIOUS, the heroine either experiences or learns of the death of her father. In TOPAZ, the hero has just learnt of the death of his lover. In TORN CURTAIN, the hero and heroine's relationship is jeopardised by his behaviour. In FOREIGN CORRESPONDENT, the plane is shot down into the sea. Finally, it is by *not* taking the plane at the end of NORTH BY NORTHWEST that the heroine avoids being murdered by the villain.

BUSES

One way in which buses function in Hitchcock is as part of a transport chain which has a violent, even catastrophic climax. It's as if the pursuit of a train by a bus in NUMBER SEVENTEEN *causes* the climactic crash between train and boat. The transport chain in STRANGERS ON A TRAIN, which takes Bruno into the chaos world, also involves Miriam: she takes a bus, then a boat, to her death. There is also a chain in NORTH BY NORTHWEST: Roger travels by train to Chicago and by Greyhound bus to the Midwest Prairie Stop, where he is attacked by a plane. In NUMBER SEVENTEEN and NORTH BY NORTHWEST, the chain ends with a spectacular crash, and in STRANGERS ON A TRAIN, the merry-go-round crash can be seen as a delayed version of the same idea. Bruno and Miriam also ride on the merry-go-round before taking boats to the Magic Isle, thereby in effect incorporating the fairground attraction into the transport chain.

In these three examples, although the bus is not involved in the actual crash, its presence in the chain would seem to increase the likelihood of a violent outcome. But what about isolated bus journeys in Hitchcock? Setting aside Hitchcock's cameo next to Robie on a bus in the South of France in TO CATCH A THIEF (➢ CAMEO APPEARANCES), there would seem to be three major and two minor examples. In SABOTAGE, the schoolboy Stevie boards a London bus whilst unwittingly carrying a bomb, and everyone on board is killed when the bomb goes off. This, clearly, is an even more destructive example of the motif: in Joseph Conrad's *The Secret Agent* (1907) on which the film is based, the bomb goes off when Stevie is in Greenwich Park, and he alone is killed. For all Hitchcock's subsequent insistence that it was a mistake to have Stevie in the film killed in this manner (➢ CHILDREN), it is nevertheless striking that he should situate the climactic explosion on a bus in the heart of London. In his films, nowhere seems safe: even travelling on a London Transport bus in the West End is dangerous.

Although the other Hitchcock bus scenes are in themselves less violent, they are usually followed by violence. In the opening scene of THE MAN WHO KNEW TOO MUCH (1955), the McKennas meet Louis Bernard, a mysterious stranger, on a coach to Marrakech. The next day, Louis is murdered: it transpires that he was a secret agent. It may seem excessive to implicate the bus journey in this, but the same outcome to a bus journey occurs in THE 39 STEPS. Hannay meets secret agent Annabella Smith at the Music Hall, they take a bus back to his apartment, and she is promptly killed – like Louis, with a knife in her back – by unknown enemy agents. Although the fact that these two murders are preceded by bus journeys may be simply coincidence, bus journeys in Hitchcock would seem to be peculiarly dangerous if spies or other secret agents are involved. The final major bus scene in his films is like an elaborated version of this idea. In TORN CURTAIN, Michael and Sarah travel from Leipzig to Berlin on a special bus used to transport fugitives from communism. Although they and the other passengers survive the journey, it is extremely hazardous, involving an attempted armed robbery by army deserters, the intervention of the East German police and climaxing with the police firing machine guns at them all as they flee from the bus at the end of the journey. A further feature relevant to the negative aspects of the bus motif is that this bus, strictly speaking, is an impostor, and the scheduled bus, which gradually catches them up, thus assumes the status of a malevolent pursuer. When it does finally catch them up, the machine-gunning begins.

The final example of bus travel in Hitchcock is in DOWNHILL: Roddy travels home on an open-topped double-decker and is drenched by the rain (➤ RAIN). His discomfort should be linked with the examples of commuting on the London Underground in Hitchcock. In BLACKMAIL, he himself is harassed by a small boy (➤ CAMEO APPEARANCES); in RICH AND STRANGE, Fred has an uncomfortable (crowded, jolting) journey home after work. The point may not be profound, but the examples are consistent: commuting in London is stressful.

Despite my comments about the therapeutic outcome of some of the boat scenes, travelling by these four means of transport in Hitchcock is still a pretty perilous business. In his films overall, there are five shipwrecks (one an act of sabotage), two train crashes, two plane crashes (plus a ditched plane in CHAMPAGNE) and one blown-up bus. One should not forget that Hitchcock's first Hollywood project was to have been THE TITANIC.

The means of transport are also the settings for murders, attempted murders, a kidnapping, a rape and an attempted suicide. Strangers met on trains and boats are for the most part duplicitous and/or murderous; boats carry the extra hazard of seasickness, and bus journeys tend to lead to murders or murder attempts. Trains in particular often seem to be the settings for a condensed or extended version of the chaos world: a murder attempt by a beloved uncle; a seduction which leads directly to a murder attempt (NORTH BY NORTHWEST); the dangers of war-time or other espionage activities (SECRET AGENT, THE LADY VANISHES).

One could argue that such incidents are part and parcel of Hitchcock's world in general, and that one could make a similar case for the dangerousness of car journeys. Nevertheless, Hitchcock seems to be registering a particular anxiety about the hazardousness of travel by public transport. When Marnie comes out of the station on her arrival in Philadelphia, she walks into close-up, and Hitchcock makes a point of tilting down to show the exposed part of the head-line on the folded newspaper she is carrying. It says, 'Crash Kills 118'. Roger Greenspun may be right that this is probably referring to a plane crash (Greenspun 1991: 19), but it could alternatively be seen as a warning about rail travel: we do not see Marnie travel by train again.

Marnie's train journey at this point is also structurally significant. A number of Hitchcock films begin on a means of transport, but it is far more common for a crucial transport scene to occur at the end of the first scene or the first act, as here. Whether by train (THE 39 STEPS, THE LADY VANISHES, SHADOW OF A DOUBT), ship (RICH AND STRANGE, Johnny leaving New York in FOREIGN COR-RESPONDENT) or plane (NOTORIOUS, TORN CURTAIN, the Kusenovs defecting in TOPAZ), the journeys involved at this point are substantial. In THE LADY VANISHES and RICH AND STRANGE, the journey itself takes up most of the rest of the film; in the other examples, the journey is to the place where the most sig-nificant action then takes place. Given that Hitchcock's cameos also frequently occur early in a film at a point of transition (➤ CAMEO APPEARANCES), it is somewhat surprising that only one of these journeys (SHADOW OF A DOUBT) is in fact the setting for his cameo. Perhaps, when a major journey is involved, he would rather not involve himself. Or, with those journeys to London, he would rather wait until the protagonist(s) arrived there (THE LADY VANISHES; FOREIGN CORRESPONDENT). London was, after all, home.

The importance of an early transport scene in Hitchcock is enhanced by the fact that three of his films include a small boat scene at the same structural point. Again, Danielle taking Robie along the coast to Cannes in TO CATCH A THIEF is the light-hearted version; nothing particularly dramatic happens when he goes ashore: he simply fails to notice the film's introduction of the heroine Francie, watching him as she suns herself on the beach. The other two examples are more significant. Bruno's boat journey across to the Magic Isle ends with Miriam's murder. Melanie's across the bay to deliver the love birds in THE BIRDS ends, as she returns to the wharf, with the first bird attack (➤ SPY FILMS / THE LOOK under EXHIBITIONISM / VOYEURISM). Bruno's boat is even called

Pluto, likening his journey to crossing the Styx to the Underworld. In both films, these are crucial transitional moments for each character: not only is this the point where Bruno and Melanie go into the chaos world, they also never escape from that world.

Trains and boats and the police

On the rare occasions when the police take the trouble to pursue someone on to public transport, they usually mess things up. In THE 39 STEPS, they break the safety regulations and stop the train on the Forth Bridge, thereby enabling Hannay to get away. In NORTH BY NORTHWEST, they fail to realise that Eve, whom they question in her compartment, could be hiding Roger (➤ CONFINED SPACES). But there is one example of a successful police operation on a boat. In I CONFESS, when Father Logan mentions to Ruth on the ferry that the police are probably watching, there are three shots, from Ruth's point of view, of possible suspects. One turns out to be Sgt. Farouche, who in the next scene reports to his superior, Inspector Larrue. Unfortunately, Sgt. Farouche's triumph in tracking down the woman in the case is rather undermined by Ruth's declaration in this scene that she has already decided to go to the police with her story.

WATER AND RAIN

WATER

Fig. 59. Still: THE SKIN GAME: Water and a (probable) corpse. Having thrown herself into the garden pond, Chloë (Phyllis Konstam) is pulled out by Hillcrist (C.V. France) and her husband Charles (John Longden). Jill (Jill Esmond) looks on from the left; Rolf (Frank Lawton) from the right. We are not told whether or not Chloë survives.

Hitchcock seems to have had a fascination with water, particularly the sea. Almost half his films include a coastal setting and/or a sea voyage: ➢ BOATS for a discussion of the latter. At the same time, water – especially the sea – is most often a source of threat. There are various inflections of the motif.

1. Suicides and suicide attempts in water. Most of the Hitchcock characters who try to drown themselves are women; his men prefer more violent deaths. Men also occur in this motif more often as murderers. The female suicide/ male murderer distinction is present from Hitchcock's first film. Rejected by the dissolute Levet, the native woman in THE PLEASURE GARDEN walks into the sea, evidently to commit suicide. Levet follows her; she assumes he has changed his mind and joyfully reaches out to him; he drowns her. The scene is extremely powerful, and one of many features in the film which demonstrate Hitchcock's early mastery of the medium. Attempted suicides in which a woman is rescued from drowning then occur in THE MANXMAN (Kate from the harbour) and MARNIE (Marnie from the ship's swimming-pool). Although there is only one definite female suicide by drowning in Hitchcock (Mrs Higley follows her dead child into the ocean in LIFEBOAT), when Chloë is pulled from the Hillcrists' garden pond at the end of THE SKIN GAME, she may well still die and we are told that her unborn child has been killed. In VERTIGO, there is another variation: Judy as 'Madeleine' fakes a suicide attempt in San Francisco Bay so that Scottie will rescue her. By contrast, there are no attempted male suicides by drowning in Hitchcock and just one successful one: Fisher in FOREIGN CORRESPONDENT (➢ GUILT AND CONFESSION).

2. Murders, murder attempts and bodies disposed of in water. THE PLEASURE GARDEN has been mentioned. In YOUNG AND INNOCENT, Christine Clay's body is washed up on the beach; in JAMAICA INN, sailors who survive the wrecks are murdered as they try to reach the shore. Rebecca's body was sunk by Maxim in her boat at sea; in LIFEBOAT, Willi pushes Gus into the sea to drown and is himself brutally forced into the sea when the other survivors take revenge. In REAR WINDOW, Thorwald disposes of his wife's body off-screen in the East River; in FRENZY, Rusk's first murder victim is seen floating naked in the Thames. Early in NORTH BY NORTHWEST, the villains attempt to kill Roger by placing him, totally inebriated, in a car and sending him along a winding corniche above the sea; towards the end of the film, Vandamm imagines Eve's death: 'This matter is best disposed of from a great height over water.'

3. The threat of drowning. At the climax of NUMBER SEVENTEEN, Nora is trapped in a sinking goods wagon, handcuffed, and she would surely have drowned but for the swift action of Barton who swims out to rescue her. In RICH AND STRANGE, Fred and Emily are trapped in their cabin when the ship starts to sink, and are only saved when it stops sinking long enough for them to be rescued by a passing Chinese junk. In FOREIGN CORRESPONDENT, when the transatlantic clipper is shot down into the sea, most of the passengers are trapped inside and drown; only a few escape onto the wreckage to be

rescued. In LIFEBOAT, the survivors are at the mercy of the weather (in one scene Sparks is swept overboard and the boat almost swamped) and of an enemy ship, which almost runs them down.

In the first group, the water tempts a woman (usually) with the oblivion of death – a surrender to the death drive which is imagined in fantasy as a return to the womb. But it is a destructive womb, as is emphasised in those cases where the water also 'takes' a baby or foetus. Nevertheless, if the woman is saved – as in THE MANXMAN and MARNIE – there is a sense in which a new life is now possible for her. This is certainly not rendered unproblematically, but Kate's appearance before Philip in court forces him to confront the way he has treated her (➤ GUILT AND CONFESSION), and the outcome of Marnie's suicide attempt is that the terms of her marriage to Mark are redrawn: they return home; he makes no more sexual demands on her; he reunites her with Forio, her beloved horse, and seeks to find other ways to help her.

In the second group, the water is more like a symbol for the unconscious: the killer has attempted to repress his crime by submerging the body under water, but the repressed returns. REBECCA has already been discussed from this point of view under THE CORPSE. THE PLEASURE GARDEN offers an even more direct example: after the murder, Levet hallucinates the ghost of the native woman coming back to haunt him (➤ BED SCENE). The sense that a corpse disposed of in water is likely to return in some form even extends to corpses left *by* water, as in STRANGERS ON A TRAIN (➤ SPECTACLES). LIFEBOAT includes another inflection: Willi's murder is followed by the appearance out of the sea of another German sailor, like Willi's psychic replacement. A sense of the 'return of the repressed' is also suggested in THE MANXMAN. When Kate is brought into court, her head is covered and she has refused to give her name. She then looks up at Philip, the judge, like a silent accusing figure. Philip is certainly not a murderer, but he is responsible for Kate's plight, and she appears before him as a similar manifestation of his suppressed guilt.

In the third group, existential anxiety is uppermost. In a dangerous, unpredictable world (two of the films are set during World War II), disaster can strike suddenly and death occur arbitrarily. It is not the disaster which is so remarkable in these films but the rescue: as if Hitchcock were prepared, on occasions, to imagine a benevolent providence. This is felt most strongly in RICH AND STRANGE: with the door jammed, and the porthole under water, Fred and Emily resign themselves to being drowned. But they wake up the next morning and discover that not only has the ship stopped sinking, but the porthole is no longer under water: they can escape on to the deck. Sparks managing to get back into the lifeboat also seems miraculous: just as one wave sweeps him over, it seems that another sweeps him back.

Connecting the second and third groups is another feature: Hitchcock's villains are very often associated with water. In LIFEBOAT, for example, we see the Allied survivors approach the lifeboat – swimming or on wreckage – but Willi seems to emerge out of the sea itself, a sense reinforced by Ritt's puzzled reaction: 'Where'd he come from?' The association is also found in other movies. The fact that Rebecca's body is at the bottom of the sea in no way diminishes her power: her presence still dominates Manderley. Moreover, at one point Hitchcock dissolves the image of Mrs Danvers into the sea, as if merging her with the power of Rebecca. In SABOTEUR, Tobin emerges out of a swimming-pool on his first appearance; in SABOTAGE, Verloc meets with a fellow anarchist in the London Zoo Aquarium. In NUMBER SEVENTEEN, it is the villains' stupidity that precipitates the train into the harbour, drowns two of them and almost drowns Nora; in To CATCH A THIEF, it is only when Foussard is killed and his body falls into the sea that it becomes apparent that he was a villain.

The suggestion of a 'new life' for the heroines who are immersed in water and then rescued is a rare positive inflection of this motif. This is perhaps most explicit in NUMBER SEVENTEEN. When Barton pulls Nora from the water, this is like a symbolic rebirth, signalled in her change of costume: she sheds her expensive fur coat, signifier of her criminal past, and at the end – as she passes into 'the hands of the law' – wears a much more modest borrowed one. Her loss anticipates Connie's in LIFEBOAT, who loses all her valuables, including her fur coat, into the sea. Likewise, when Kate and Marnie are rescued from an attempted suicide in water, this marks at least the beginnings of a new life. In VERTIGO, Scottie's rescue of 'Madeleine' may be compromised, not least because she was only pretending to try to drown herself, but his act does serve to bring the two of them together, and when they later kiss against crashing waves – restating the water motif, if in rather clichéd terms – this is genuinely passionate. In TORN CURTAIN, Michael and Sarah's swim from a communist ship to Swedish land is another positive example of the motif, symbolising their crossing back to the 'free world'.

The examples thus far concern large amounts of water – large enough, at least, to swim in. Apart from the separate rain motif, and despite the occasional bath or shower, this is the dominant form of the water motif in Hitchcock. But there is one film in which water is used as an element rather than as an expanse. In THE RING, water as a motif recurs throughout the film, and since it is linked to another motif – the snake bracelet – I shall look at both together.

A sexual triangle develops early in THE RING, with Mabel engaged to Jack, a fairground boxer, but attracted to the more glamorous Bob, a boxing champion. Water makes a fleeting appearance in a curious scene in which Mabel wipes Jack's face as if he were a little boy: we are invited to see this as typifying the mother-child nature of their relationship. In the next scene, Bob gives Mabel the

bracelet, but she hides this from Jack. Water and bracelet are then brought together when Jack shaves beside a small pond, using the water to see his reflection. Mabel joins him, and as Hitchcock films the two of them reflected in the
water, they kiss. Immediately, the snake bracelet slips down Mabel's arm into
the water, breaking their reflection.

In the superstitious milieu of the fairground – Mabel has already had her
cards read by the resident gypsy fortune-teller – breaking a reflection of someone is not a good omen, particularly since it is the lover figure's gift which does
this. Mabel tries to cloud the issue of Bob's having given her the bracelet by
saying to Jack that the money came indirectly from him, but Jack is not convinced. Moreover, she continues to wear the bracelet throughout the film, and
it even slips down her arm during her actual wedding to Jack. It would seem
she wants both men. After her marriage, she continues to flirt outrageously with
Bob, and she has his photograph provocatively on the piano. It is not certain
that she actually has an affair with him at this stage – one feels that she would
be more discreet if this were the case – but when Jack is provoked into a rage by
her behaviour (➤ PORTRAITS), he goes out and assaults Bob. Mabel leaves
him, and now it is indeed implied that she becomes Bob's mistress.

The film's climax is a fight in the ring between the two men. Mabel is in the
audience, and her status as Bob's girl is conveyed through her fur-lined coat.
However, when Bob starts to get the better of Jack, she changes sides, shedding
the coat as she goes to Jack's corner. By now, Jack is too dazed to realise that she
is beside him, reassuring him that she's back, but as he looks down at his pail of
water, he sees her reflection. In fact, Hitchcock films this subjective image ambiguously: since Mabel's image in the water dissolves into a reflection of Jack
looking at himself, it is not certain that her reflection really is there or whether
Jack has conjured it up from hearing her voice. But the crucial point is that he
sees her return to him *through* the water. When he sees that she is also there in
the flesh, he is sufficiently inspired to win the fight. Then, just before the fade-
out on them as a couple, Mabel discards the bracelet.

Again a woman symbolically shedding an expensive coat is, albeit obliquely,
linked to the water motif. Otherwise, this is one of the more subtle examples of
the motif. On the one hand, the connection between Mabel and water suggests
her elusiveness: she becomes as difficult to hold on to as her reflection. On the
other, this is one of the rare examples in Hitchcock of an essentially positive link
between water and 'the mother', a highly prevalent association in mythology
(see Walker B.G. 1983: 1066). Not only does the water motif help define Jack as
a child figure who needs mothering, it suggests that Mabel is someone who can
perform this function without the usual traumatic outcome. The symbolism of
the bracelet locates Bob as the serpent figure, who seduces Mabel into his more
glamorous world. But she returns at the end to the mothering role: it is when

Jack is being hurt that she rushes to his side. Her return through the water strengthens this notion.

Although the associations of water in Hitchcock can, as here, be positive, such examples are outnumbered by those which are negative. In her word association game with Mark, Marnie's responses to 'water' are variations on the familiar Baptist notion of water as cleansing (➤ *Bed Scene* in Part I). Famously, Hitchcock sets up this notion when Marion steps into the shower in Psycho: she has decided to return the stolen money, and so here her shower is like a symbolic cleansing. But she's brutally murdered.

RAIN

Fig. 60. Still: I Confess: Rain. Ruth (Anne Baxter)'s flashback: she and Logan (Montgomery Clift) caught in the rain, which results in their spending an illicit night together.

In his autobiography, Frank Capra writes 'In practically every picture I've made there are scenes in the rain – especially love scenes. It's a personal touch. Rain, for me, is an exciting stimulant, an aphrodisiac' (Capra 1971: 199). This romantic use of rain is very common in films, but not in Hitchcock. As with water, the dominant associations of rain in his films are negative. At the same time, there are certain sequences in which the elements seem to be an expression of the inner turmoil of his characters. This connection is crucial to an understanding of the effectiveness of this motif in Hitchcock. Whilst setting a violent scene to the accompaniment of a raging thunderstorm (for example) could seem something of a cliché, Hitchcock repeatedly transcends the cliché by the imaginative relationship he establishes between character and nature.

In YOUNG AND INNOCENT, a storm rages outside during the opening row between Christine and Guy. Guy then goes out into the rain and stands on a balcony overlooking the sea: he turns to look at the camera and his nervous tic (a crucial identifying feature) is illuminated by flashes of lightning. In other contexts, we could imagine a man in his situation going out into the rain to cool off, but Hitchcock conveys precisely the opposite: the turbulent waves below, the malevolent stare, the lightning flashes all combine to suggest a man about to erupt into violence. Like Frankenstein's monster, it's as if he is being charged by the storm. The next morning, Christine's body is washed up on the beach.

In LIFEBOAT, having discovered that Willi has a compass, and so has been knowingly deceiving them about the boat's direction, the Allied survivors argue about what to do with him. With Kovac and Gus saying that he should be killed, and the others opposing this, the argument becomes very heated and, as if in response, the wind whips up the waves with steadily increasing ferocity. The argument is only halted when a huge wave sweeps Sparks overboard and the boat seems in danger of being swamped. Immediately, Willi moves astern to take Sparks's place on the tiller; in effect, assuming control of the boat. Although there is little, if any, rain, this is undoubtedly a storm, and it seems to express the villain's power, creating the precise conditions of chaos which enable him to assert mastery. This is the point when he speaks English for the first time, and what he does is give orders. Gus is the quickest to catch on: 'What do you know: we've got a Führer.'

In I CONFESS, Ruth narrates in a fragmented flashback the story of her romance with Michael Logan. When Logan returned from the war, they arranged to meet in the countryside for what Ruth hoped would be a romantic reunion. But when she kissed him she realised (in the words of her voice-over) that 'the war had changed him'. Immediately, it began to rain heavily, and they were obliged to seek shelter in a summerhouse. As Logan gently brushed Ruth's hair, we come out of the flashback for a close-up of Ruth saying, 'It stopped raining in the morning.' The interruption of the flashback at this point, the way she speaks these words, and their expressions when we return to the flashback the next morning, all suggest that sex has occurred. Here, the rain seems prompted by Ruth's wish to seduce Logan.

In MARNIE, the first storm occurs when Marnie goes to Mark's study at Rutlands to do some typing. It seems to increase in intensity in proportion to Marnie's own panic, climaxing with a tree crashing through a window. Occurring behind Mark, sitting at his desk, the storm is thus like an oneiric projection of Marnie's fears of male sexuality, with the tree smashing the window as a terrifying image of symbolic rape. At the end of the film, when we learn of the childhood trauma which has made Marnie so terrified of storms, we can see that the sexual symbolism here is entirely appropriate. The incident occurred during a thunderstorm and was charged with the five-year-old Marnie's sexual fears , climaxing with her killing the sailor who awakened them (➤ *Bed Scene* in Part I).

Murderous violence and the assertion of mastery for the men; seduction and sexual fears for the women: this is fairly standard Hitchcock material. Yet each of the examples is different, and collectively they testify, once more, to the director's inventiveness. Nor do these summaries exhaust the symbolic meanings. It has often been noted that certain sorts of narrative mimic the sex act: rising to an orgasmic climax, followed by quiet and calm. These sequences are good illustrations: the storms reach a powerful climax and then, suddenly, they are over. In YOUNG AND INNOCENT and I CONFESS the downpour is followed by the striking contrast of the peacefulness of the morning after. But in I CONFESS, where sex is indeed implied during the storm, the morning after also produces guilt in the form of Vilette, who recognises Ruth as Mme Grandfort and promptly begins to blackmail her.

In MARNIE, the storm suddenly quietens after the window has been shattered and, as Marnie clings to Mark, he gently kisses her, as if post-coitally. He then says, 'It's over – all over; you're all right', exactly as if she has just experienced the shock of her first experience of sex and he is reassuring her. The destructiveness of the storm has also served another function: the tree smashed the cabinet in which Mark kept the pre-Columbian statues which had belonged to his dead wife. It's as if Marnie's unconscious also summons up the storm to destroy these reminders of Mark's marital past.

LIFEBOAT makes the sexual analogy even sharper. The storm continues for some time after Sparks is swept overboard, and it really does seem as if the boat is going under. The climax is reached when the mast breaks off: the equivalent of the falling tree in MARNIE. At this point, Kovac says to Connie, 'Might as well die together, eh Connie?' and she responds by passionately kissing him. Over the crashing waves, Hitchcock then dissolves to the boat in a peaceful sea. Connie is now draped over Kovac's semi-naked body in a posture of quite remarkable (for 1944) erotic abandon: exactly as if she is sexually satiated.

I would characterise these four sequences as the paradigmatic examples of the motif. In each case, the rain or storm is related to the inner world of one of the characters: the storm would seem to arise out of the desires or tensions felt by the character at this point, expressing them in a violent form. Hence the sense, in LIFEBOAT and MARNIE at least, of the storm getting out of control; like forces from the unconscious being unleashed on the characters. To appropriate the famous metaphor from FORBIDDEN PLANET (Fred M. Wilcox, 1956), the storm is the 'Monster from the Id'.

There are also examples in Hitchcock where the rain is less significant in itself than as a part of the film's structure. DOWNHILL and RICH AND STRANGE are quite close structurally: we could see them as two versions of a similar plot, one focusing on a single man (Roddy); the other on a married couple (Fred and Emily). In each, there is a scene in which the hero journeys home through the rain, arriving to receive a letter which promises him money: Roddy's inheritance from his godmother; Fred's from his uncle. The films then chart what happens as a result of the newly acquired wealth. In both cases, the outcome is double-edged: it enables the hero to fulfil his dream, but it also lays him open – among other misfortunes – to a predatory woman, who makes off with most of the money. Both stories also take the protagonist(s) far from home, and he/they end up having to make a traumatic journey, by sea, back to London.

A substantial part of each of these stories – in DOWNHILL, a little over half the film; in RICH AND STRANGE, most of it – is bracketed between the rain early on and the traumatic encounter with the sea towards the end. Here the water and rain motif is woven into film's structure: as if, once a character has journeyed through rain, the water motif is liable to return into the narrative later in a heightened, melodramatic form. There is also a variation of this idea in MARNIE: the traumatic storm is echoed in an even more traumatic honeymoon on a pleasure cruiser, during which (a) Marnie really is raped and (b) she attempts suicide in water.

In REBECCA and PSYCHO the structural pattern is found in the heroine's story. In each film, as she first approaches the building at the centre of the narrative, she observes it – in a point-of-view shot – through a car windscreen in the rain. Here the motif is used more precisely: it is through the rain that the heroine first sees the terrible house/motel which is the source of danger. But the other elements are darker. First, the danger in the building is embodied in a monstrous mother (figure). The association of such a figure and water is here much more sinister: Rebecca and Mrs Danvers seem to derive malevolent power from the sea (➤ WATER); 'Mrs Bates' murders Marion in the shower. Second, although the heroine's journey through rain results in a later return of the water motif, this return is linked to death. In REBECCA, the outcome for the heroine is in fact more positive: the flares which signal a shipwreck – which in turn leads to the discovery of Rebecca's sunken boat and body – also save the heroine's life. Mrs Danvers was on the point of persuading her to commit suicide out of the window, and the dramatic interruption stops this. Equally, the flares mark the beginning of the end of Rebecca's power association with the sea: once her corpse has been returned to land, it ceases to be so potent. But in Psycho, the water motif recurs much more negatively: by the time the shower is turned off, Marion is dead, and her body is condemned to the swamp outside.

Saboteur reworks this material in the context of an espionage/thriller format. After Barry has emerged from the river (➤ *Water and the Police*), he is then doubly soaked, because he is caught in the rain. His journey through the rain takes him to Philip Martin's isolated house, where he meets Pat, the heroine. Accordingly, we could see this, too, as a symbolic rebirth – the water here contrasting with the fire which consumed Barry's friend Ken and in effect leading him to the heroine. Nevertheless, the subsequent return of the water motif is more sinister: restating the association already established through Tobin in his swimming pool, it is associated with the activities of the villains. First, there is a scene in which the saboteurs and Barry stop beside the dam the former were planning to blow up; then Barry re-encounters Fry in the New York docks, where the latter sabotages a ship as it is launched into the water. Although these examples seem less striking than those in the other movies, they point, again, to the density of Hitchcock's narratives.

Other examples of the rain motif in Hitchcock's films would seem to be more conventional. In The Pleasure Garden and Suspicion, it rains on the heroine's wedding day, which is a bad sign. (In fact, a very bad sign: her husband will ultimately try to kill her.) The use of rain for the assassination of Van Meer's double in Foreign Correspondent seems prompted mainly by the striking imagery Hitchcock achieves in his overhead shots of the cluster of umbrellas on and around the steps where the assassination occurs, imagery repeated during the garden party in Stage Fright. When Ann and Jeff are trapped in the rain on the parachute ride in Mr and Mrs Smith, they merely get wet and miserable, and any romantic developments which might have occurred when they finally get back to Jeff's apartment are firmly checked by his Southern gallantry.

A final example of Hitchcock's use of rain is more allusive. In Rear Window, it rains on the night Thorwald takes his wife's body – in pieces – out of his apartment. Rear Window is famous for its oneiric quality: it begins and ends with shots of Jeff asleep, and the apartment block opposite can be understood as a sort of dream screen, on to which Jeff's fears and phantasies are projected (➤ DOUBLES). This sequence goes a stage further. First, the sequence itself is bracketed by shots of Jeff asleep at his window, like a dream within the dream. Second, because of the point-of-view editing, the rain here intervenes into the space between Jeff and 'dream screen' opposite: Jeff has to look through the rain, as if through a transparent barrier. In the rest of the film, there is nothing mediating between Jeff and the dream screen, but here there is. Just as the film begins with the curtains in Jeff's apartment being raised, and ends with them being lowered, so we can see the rain as another curtain: the curtain of the unconscious. This clarifies the dream structure of the whole film. Behind the blinds to Thorwald's apartment is the unconscious, repressed material: the murder and dismemberment of Thorwald's wife – which may be seen as the expression of Jeff's hostility towards Lisa. But this repressed material is then represented in a displaced, more innocent form – through the analogy with the latent and the manifest content of a dream – by the events which Jeff witnesses outside the repressed space.

Almost immediately after Lisa has angrily left Jeff's apartment, he hears the noises which stand in for the murder: a woman's scream, her voice crying 'Don't', and the crash of an object breaking on the floor. Still at the window, he then falls asleep; the storm wakes him. The first thing he sees is the dog-owning couple who sleep on their balcony being caught by the downpour and making an undignified scramble back through the window into their apartment. Within the narrative, this comic little scene directly precedes Thorwald's first trip – i.e. it is some time after the murder – but what it symbolises (and masks) is the murder itself. The smashing of the couple's alarm clock echoes the smashed object, but also, because it is a clock, symbolises death. (Hitchcock himself introduces the 'clock motif' into the evening's events by appearing earlier adjusting the songwriter's clock: ➤ CAMEO APPEARANCES.) The problems the couple have with their mattress (Mrs Thorwald would almost certainly have been killed in bed; later her mattress is rolled up on the bed), and the way in which the husband falls in through the window on to the bedding (and possibly his wife) may likewise be seen as translating the material of the murder into burlesque. The incident is accompanied by a highly ironic rendering of the Richard Rodgers-Lorenz Hart tune 'Lover' (from LOVE ME TONIGHT, Rouben Mamoulian, 1932), which sounds as if it is being played, diegetically, on a cinema organ. It's like a silent movie accompaniment, as if Hitchcock were suggesting that the incident was like a movie scene watched by Jeff. This does not undermine the sense that the incident could also be interpreted oneirically: REAR WINDOW allows both readings (➤ DOUBLES). But it does emphasise the comedy of the incident, thereby helping to mask its darker implications.

As soon as the couple are back in their apartment, Jeff sees Thorwald go out with his sample case for the first time. It is 1.55 a.m. Forty minutes later, Thorwald returns, but then goes out again. The next morning, before any of the additional suspicious-looking actions have occurred, Jeff discusses these trips with the nurse Stella. She speculates that Thorwald, a salesman, was out on business. Jeff interprets the trips differently: Thorwald was taking something out of the apartment, and the likeliest explanation was that he was preparing to leave his wife. In other words, even Jeff's 'innocent' interpretation of Thorwald going out in the rain makes sense as an expression of his own feelings about Lisa. Then, at the end of the film, we learn the true, 'repressed' meaning of the trips. In another example of a journey through rain leading to an (again, sinister) introduction of the water motif, we hear that Thorwald went to the East River to dump the body parts of his wife.

The rain in REAR WINDOW may be linked to the earlier paradigmatic examples through the notion of dream displacement. But whereas the storms in the other films could be seen as arising out of the inner world of one of the characters, here the rain works rather differently. Jeff cannot confront his own unconscious murderousness towards Lisa, but the rain creates an arena in which his repressed desires are alluded to in a distorted (censored) form. As well as the incident with the middle-aged couple and Thorwald's trips, Jeff also witnesses two other little vignettes during this four minute sequence, and they, too, can be related to his ambivalent feelings towards Lisa. First, the songwriter returns home drunk and signals his frustration about his composition by swiping at his music sheets. Earlier that evening, Lisa had imagined that his song was being written for her and Jeff, so that his apparent blockage here satisfies Jeff's wish that their relationship should remain, in Jeff's words, 'status quo'. Then Miss Torso returns home, and we see her fight to close the door on the man who escorted her. Since Jeff had compared Miss Torso's popularity with men to Lisa's, this action satisfies his contradictory feelings of possessiveness about Lisa: Miss Torso demonstrates her faithfulness. But if these two vignettes seem relatively mild in their coded implications, the middle-aged couple are treated more ignominiously. Does Jeff harbour an unconscious hostility towards them? Are they symbolically the parents or, in Freudian terms, the superego? If so, their propulsion back into their apartment is surely significant: it removes them from their position over Thorwald's point of exit, so that he can come and go freely, without someone there to hear – and hence, potentially, monitor – his movements. Like a defence mechanism, the rain masks Jeff's true thoughts: unconsciously, he wants Thorwald to get away with murder.

The use of rain in Hitchcock is quite diverse, ranging from examples in which it seems to express unresolved tensions within and between characters to those where its function is more structural, linking different features of the film together. Nevertheless, the rain in REAR WINDOW would seem to operate at a different level of complexity. Integrated into an oneiric structure, it assumes a much more resonant form. I would argue that this is true of other motifs, and that this underlines the sense that a psychoanalytical approach is the most productive way of analysing Hitchcock's motifs.

Water and the police

In SABOTEUR, Barry manages to escape from the deputy sheriffs who have hand-cuffed him, and he leaps off a bridge into a river. As the deputies hunt up and down the bank, he hides behind some rocks. The most macho of the deputies (who hangs his pistol over his genitals, like a sporran) stands on the rocks, baffled at Barry's disappearance. Barry views him from under the water (a rare Hitchcock point-of-view shot through water) and then pushes him into the river. As the deputy, evidently not a champion swimmer, is swept downstream, a friendly lorry-driver, who has been enjoying the whole show immensely, shouts to those on the bank, 'There he goes.' He thus enables Barry to get away. For a brief moment, the Hitchcock thematic is inverted: the policeman becomes the 'wrong man'; the hero escapes. And it is dunking the cop in water that does it.

Appendix I: TV Episodes

Given the restricted format of Hitchcock's television work as director – seventeen 25-minute episodes for his long-running series *Alfred Hitchcock Presents*; three 50-minute episodes for other series – a different cross-section of themes and motifs from his films is only to be expected. The most frequently recurring motif in the *Alfred Hitchcock Presents* episodes is corpse disposal, with the plot corollary of a character seeking to avoid blame for murder in a variety of ingenious ways. This motif is actually referred to in a feature film, THE GAZEBO (George Marshall, 1959). Taken from a play by Alec Coppel – the co-writer of VERTIGO, who also wrote on occasions for *Alfred Hitchcock Presents* – the plot involves a television writer, Elliott Nash (Glenn Ford), who finds himself with the body of a blackmailer to bury (in the foundations of the gazebo) and no shovel. At this point, Hitchcock phones to enquire about the progress of a script Elliott is writing for him, and so Elliott asks his advice – pretending that it is the script rather than an actual corpse that he needs help with. We do not actually hear Hitchcock speak, but his suggestion – use the shovel from the fireplace – solves the hero's problem. Towards the end of the film, the corpse is disinterred and deposited back in the house, prompting Elliott's wife Nell (Debbie Reynolds) to ask him: 'Couldn't you call Hitchcock again?'

To correct a common misapprehension: this is not a Hitchcock cameo. We do not see or hear the director, and so this figure in the plot is in effect a fictitious character 'Alfred Hitchcock' who is based on the real-life director. Nevertheless, Coppel's use of the familiar Hitchcock persona is a nice tribute. When the gazebo is erected over the body, Elliott toasts Hitchcock and comments that he is sure that the director would have approved.

In some cases, a particular television episode is in effect built around one of the key motifs. It is these episodes, and a few others where a given motif is otherwise prominent which are considered here. The episodes are in motif order; all are from *Alfred Hitchcock Presents*. Hitchcock presents this series – which ran weekly from 1955 to 1962 – in that he himself appears before and after each episode to deliver usually jokey introductory and concluding remarks. When the latter refer to subsequent developments to the story we have just seen, we are invited to be sceptical: some of these outcomes are implicit in the material, but some are to appease the censors and some are clearly a joke, and the last two possibilities may be combined. They are only mentioned here if they seem relevant to the discussion of the motif.

BED SCENE

The entire episode of 'Poison' (1958) may be seen as an extended version of the Bed Scene. On a Malayan rubber plantation, Timber Woods (Wendell Corey) arrives home to find his roommate Harry Pope (James Donald) lying without moving on the bed, insisting that a poisonous snake is asleep under the sheet on his stomach. Timber is casual about the crisis – he considers Harry a drunk, prone to delusions – but he manages to contact the local doctor just before the latter leaves on holiday. As they wait for the doctor to arrive, Timber takes the opportunity, whilst Harry is incapacitated, to raise some of the matters between them: he mentions Julie, who has come from Paris to see Harry; now Timber may not have to wait for her to find out that Harry is a lush. He also confesses that it was he himself who made Harry into a drunk, so that he could take the business away from him. In other words, he is talking as if Harry were going to die, which, we take it, is what he really wants.

On arrival, the doctor (Arnold Moss) injects Harry with a serum, but its efficacy is not guaranteed, and so he decides that they need to anaesthetise the snake as it sleeps. This requires sending Timber back to his house for chloroform. All these delays inevitably build suspense: throughout the whole period, Harry has been afraid to move. Finally, however, the chloroform is poured in, and after a fifteen-minute wait for it to take effect, the doctor and Timber carefully peel back the sheet. At this point – to avoid the potentially censorable complication of the other men poking around in his pyjamas – Harry stands up on the bed and jumps around: no snake. Harry insists that it was there, but Timber says mockingly to the doctor: 'it wouldn't be the first time he'd had the DTs.' As Timber sees the doctor out, Harry sits sullenly on the bed; at this point, Hitchcock cuts to show the snake hiding under the pillow. Returning, Timber is now openly laughing, ironically offering Harry a drink: 'Let's drink to friendship.' Harry throws it in his face. Timber takes this as another example of Harry's lack of self-control and, still laughing, lies down on the bed. He is promptly bitten. In close-up, terrified, he begs Harry to send for the doctor. Harry watches him impassively: 'The doctor's gone, Timber.' The episode ends with the camera on Harry, as Timber's voice pleads with him to hurry.

Apart from the obvious point that the bed, typically of Hitchcock, is a site of trauma, is this also a gay allegory? The details of Harry's alcoholism – not least, the fact that the unseen Julie does not know about it – would make sense as a cover for a homosexual relationship which Harry, now, is seeking to escape from: 'I'm not going to drink anymore.' Hence the significance of his throwing the drink in Timber's face, and Timber's reaction of laughing and lying down on the bed. It is the snake itself which most strongly suggests such a reading; its poisonousness a reflection of the dominant ideological view of homosexuality at the time. Hitchcock says in his concluding comments that Harry went to jail for failing to call a doctor, but we heard during the episode that the bite was fatal within minutes; Harry couldn't possibly have caught up with the doctor's car in time. The implication would seem to be that Harry had to go to jail for something else. Although this reading is speculative, it supports Robin Wood's point that Hitchcock's gay characters are usually viewed negatively (➢ HOMOSEXUALITY). Here the subtext suggests that homosexuality is both deadly and incriminating.

CHILDREN

'Bang! You're Dead' (1961) is the main example in Hitchcock's work of a narrative which enters into the world of a child: that of five-year-old Jackie Chester (Billy Mumy). The episode begins with a close-up of a hand inserting bullets into a revolver; only when we hear boys' voices do we realise that this is a toy gun. Its owner dismisses Jackie's gun as 'cheesy', and won't let Jackie play with him and his friend: 'This is our war, I told you: go on home.'·

What happens next seems from Jackie's point of view to be perfect wish fulfilment. His uncle Rick (Steve Dunne) comes back from 'the wars' in Africa and, noticing Jackie's gun, asks, 'You got your own war on?' In his room, Rick happily allows Jackie to stick him up for money and then tells him that he has a surprise for him. He won't say what it is. Asked by his father Fred (Biff Elliott) to unpack for Rick, Jackie finds a six-shooter in the suitcase. Assuming that this is the surprise, he takes it and puts his own gun in its place. Also discovering a box of shells, he loads one, puts the revolver in his holster and the other bullets in his pocket and goes back downstairs. Spinning the cylinder before he fires – so that he is inadvertently playing Russian roulette – Jackie moves among the adults and shoots twice at his mother Amy (Lucy Prentiss). His parents shoo him out of the house; before he goes he thanks Rick for the surprise. Rick is puzzled by the comment, but does not grasp its significance.

Sticking up the mailman en route, Jackie goes to the supermarket. It is at this point that Rick discovers what has happened and the three adults begin a frantic search. Meanwhile, Jackie loads a second bullet and, annoyed at being displaced from a mechanical horse by a father with a spoilt daughter, almost shoots them (close-ups show the bullets moving round into the firing position). The adults track Jackie to the supermarket, but Amy keeps being interrupted as she tries to communicate the urgency of the situation to the store personnel. This adds suspense, as does the fact that Jackie, unseen, now pauses to load all six chambers. After various false alarms, he makes his way back home. The adults are still searching.

In the house, the maid Cleo (Juanita Moore) is too busy to play with Jackie, and he laments: 'Nobody will play war with me.' When he then says that he'll shoot her, Cleo says she doesn't mind: 'I've made my peace with the Almighty.' He pulls the trigger as the other adults burst into the house; the bullet shatters the mirror beside Cleo. His father grabs the gun; a terrified Jackie runs into his mother's arms.

In his introductory and concluding comments, Hitchcock presents this episode in a more serious manner than is his wont, referring to the real-life problem that it depicts. At a basic level, the episode does indeed carry a strong message about the dangers of adult carelessness with guns. More, however, is going on. The repeated references to playing war; the sense that Jackie is re-enacting American imperialist history (carrying a Western gun; wearing a cowboy hat); the tolerance of the adults towards being shot at; the failure to realise that the gun Jackie is pointing at everyone is real; the wish-fulfilment structure of the episode – all these point to a climate in which the gun is simply too much a part of everyday American culture for the adults to grasp what's happening in front of their eyes. In the supermarket, when Jackie points the now fully loaded gun at point blank range at a sales promoter, she cheerfully says, 'You wouldn't shoot a girl, would you?' and checks his aggressive response – 'Sure I would' – by popping sweets into his mouth. A few moments later, the same young woman sees one of the bullets he has dropped and realises that it is real. But when Jackie almost shot her, she simply didn't notice the danger.

There is also the sense that Jackie is acting out tensions which stem from the adult world. There are three main topics of conversation between the adults in the early scenes: the state of the African country Rick was in ('blowing sky high'); a witch doctor's mask he brought back with him (left over after a 'blood bath') and the lateness of Cleo, who is black. The first accounts for the gun: although only a salesman in Africa, Rick slept with one under his pillow. The second is associated with something more elusive. It seems to introduce a sense of unease into the house: it gives Amy 'the willies', and in the last shot, just as Fred grabs the gun, Rick grabs the mask, as if it is equally implicated in the near disaster. At one level, the implication is that both the gun and the mask, imported from Africa, bring the violence of the 'dark continent' into the American small town. However, just as this is complicated by the blindness of the adults to Jackie's dangerousness, so what happens around Cleo also points to troubling cultural undercurrents. It is Amy who is worried about her lateness, but it is Fred who shoos Jackie out of the house with the words: 'See if you can go outside and bring down a real live maid.'

Much of the dialogue in these early scenes is in fact cryptic, as if to avoid being too precise about the intimations of political instability in Africa. But since the episode climaxes with Jackie coming very close indeed to 'bringing down a real live maid', the shot he fires would seem to carry some disturbing overtones. Fred's comment sounds like a Freudian slip: since he has been busy reassuring Amy about Cleo's reliability, perhaps he meant to say 'bring back a real live maid'. Nevertheless, when the three adults and Jackie first enter the house, Fred comments to Rick: 'You think that you're the only one who has trouble with the natives – oh, brother', a comment which is particularly mystifying. Its ostensible point of reference is the buffet which has been laid out for the party that they are giving for Rick. But we simply do not know who 'the natives' are.

When Jackie first comes downstairs with the part-loaded revolver, Hitchcock's camera moves down to a child's eye level, and remains there for most of the scenes in which Jackie is the central figure. When Jackie is threatening to shoot Cleo, Hitchcock repeats the point-of-view shot along the barrel of the gun from the penultimate scene of SPELLBOUND. In other words, we are seeing things from Jackie's perspective. Moreover, as he comes downstairs, he enters into the middle of a conversation about the mask which is simply indecipherable – indeed, Pinteresque – without the context of its first part. Could it be that the conversations between the adults are confusing because they are also mediated by the child's perspective? If so, this would be remarkably sophisticated for mainstream television in early 1960s USA.

Both gripping as a narrative and complex in its resonances, 'Bang! You're Dead' is one of the most impressive examples of Hitchcock's television work. It is also one of the occasions when a Hitchcock work quite explicitly refers to the ideology of the culture, intimating the tensions under the surface of petty-bourgeois small-town America. And it achieves this primarily through adopting the 'innocent' perspective of a child.

CONFINED SPACES

'Breakdown' (1955), the first TV episode Hitchcock filmed – although the second to be aired – begins with business tycoon Callew (Joseph Cotten) on holiday in Miami. Over the phone, he confirms the firing of an employee, Hubka (Forrest Stanley), and is disgusted that Hubka should be so upset as to cry: 'I hate that kind of weakness.'

Driving back to his business in New York, Callew is involved in an accident on a side road which leaves him trapped in his car, paralysed. He cannot move or speak; cannot even close his eyes. His crashed car attracts first some local labourers, then two escaped convicts; but everyone assumes that he is dead. The labourers steal two tyres and his suitcases; the convicts free him from under the steering wheel, but simply so that they can take his clothes – including his identification papers. By nightfall, the authorities have also turned up, but they, too, assume that he is dead and take him to the city morgue. Although Callew can in fact move one finger, no-one notices. He's left overnight under a sheet, waiting for the coroner. When the coroner (Harry Shannon) does examine him, Callew finds that his hand is trapped under his body, so that he cannot even move his finger. In despair, he starts to cry, thereby signalling that he is alive.

Throughout the long period of Callew's paralysis, we hear his voice-over and from time to time see events from his limited point of view. His corpse-like state generates a restricted narrative which emphasises his impotence. But his state also echoes those inflections of the Confined Spaces motif which show characters confined but visible. I argue there that this is in effect a paranoid construction, in which the threat of the police repeatedly emerges as the fear lying behind the visibility. Here, where the protagonist is rich and powerful, the threat manifests itself as criminals who strip Callew of both his possessions and his identity: they scavenge from his body. The police should have turned up as saviours but, once again, the sheriff who shines a torch on the protagonist fails to see what he is looking at (➤ *Lights and the police*). What finally saves Callew from being buried alive is the very sign of weakness he so derided in his employee.

When Callew crashes his car, he is heading towards a group of convicts being supervised by guards. But it is the guards who are hit and killed by the car. This, too, accounts for the variation in the inflection of the Confined Spaces motif. With the guards – the superego figures – killed, the prisoners escape: Callew in effect unleashes 'chaos'. It is one form of this chaos – criminality – which 'returns' to threaten him.

Equally, however, Callew's fate may be read as another sort of breakdown. His hostility to signs of 'male weakness' could be seen as a hysterical defence against stereotypical signs of homosexuality (crying signifying effeminacy). But now the defence has broken down. Callew becomes helpless, and this produces the sort of bodily invasion he so desperately dreads. The people who converge on his car are all men, and two of them strip off his clothes. What's more, this feminises him. It is as if his final tears are his inner acceptance of what he has been resisting all his life.

THE CORPSE

'The Crystal Trench' (1959) is like a companion piece to 'Breakdown': whereas in the earlier episode the paralysed hero is treated as a corpse, here the lives of the hero and heroine are 'moulded and shaped' (in the words of the hero's voice-over) by a corpse which is both preserved and given eerie life through being embedded in a drifting glacier: the crystal trench itself. Although there are a lot of corpses in the TV episodes, this is the key example. Most of it is narrated, in voice-over flashback, by Mark Cavendish (James Donald). In 1907, forty years ago, he was on a climbing holiday in the Alps. On arriving at his hotel, he was told that a young Englishman, Michael Ballister, died while making a foolhardy climb on the Schwarzhorn. Mark was asked to inform Ballister's widow Stella (Patricia Owens) of her husband's death; he then went with his friends to retrieve the body. But the body slipped from their grasp and fell down the mountain into a glacier. When Stella left the hotel, Mark, now falling in love with her, went with her – ultimately, back to England. Already Stella was beginning to live in the past, declaring that, in her memory, she would expand each moment of her six month's marriage into a month, or a year, so that, 'Even if I live to be eighty, I shall never live long enough to recapture all of it.' Back in London, Mark continued to see her, and eventually proposed. She turned him down, and took him to a geologist so that he could understand her reasons. Knowing the glacier's rate of drift, the geologist had calculated exactly when Michael's body would arrive at its foot: on 21 July 1947: 'You see, Mark, I shall have Michael back after all.' The flashback ends with Mark's voice-over: 'I realised then that Stella had made her choice, and for the next forty years she intended to wait for Michael, just as I knew I must wait for Stella.'

On the predicted date, Mark and Stella return to the foot of the glacier. Only as Michael's still youthful face emerges out of the ice do we see the ageing faces of first Stella and then Mark; Michael's preserved youth seems, at that moment, to embody Stella's idealised memory of him. However, as the ice around Michael melts way, Mark discovers a locket around his neck, and inside it a portrait of a woman who is not Stella. He tries to pretend that it is, but Stella does not even have to look at it: 'He had no locket with a portrait of me.' She throws it back into the ice, and the episode ends with the sad faces of the two of them turning away from the glacier.

Just as VERTIGO is about a man who is obsessed with a woman who is dead (or so he thinks), so 'The Crystal Trench' is about a woman who is obsessed with a man who is dead. But in this case, the corpse of the loved one is preserved, and the woman waits patiently for the day when she can be reunited with it. The scenario is no less perverse than that of VERTIGO, and the ending no less bleak: Stella has wasted forty years her life – and of Mark's – living with the memory of a great love which turns out to have been false. Mark's reactions all along have served to emphasise that, even without the final twist, Stella has been living her life in fantasy. The problem is the corpse. Because Mark had failed to retrieve it, and Stella had been unable, in her own words, 'to look at him once more … to touch him again', and because she suspects that his climbing companions abandoned Michael to die, she is unable to mourn and move on. The psychic connection between protagonist and corpse that I argue exists in VERTIGO (Judy and Madeleine's corpse) and PSYCHO (Norman and his mother's corpse) is here prolonged through forty years, with Stella's emotions, in effect, remaining frozen as the body is frozen in the glacier.

Stella's ageing is signalled, most dramatically, through her hair. When Mark tells her that her husband is dead and his body is on the Schwarzhorn, they are standing on the hotel balcony; in a reflex, Stella turns to look towards the mountain. As she holds the pose, Hitchcock favours her with one of his most distinctive shots: a track in to the back of her head, emphasising the lustrous coils of her pinned-up hair. (Only a privileged few of his actresses were treated to this undeniably fetishistic shot: ➤ BLONDES AND BRUNETTES.) Then, at the beginning of the final shot of the episode, again we see Stella from behind. And in this shot, her hair looks identical to Mrs Bates's in the fruit cellar. Audiences seeing *The Crystal Trench* when it was first televised – 4 October 1959 – could not have drawn the connection: PSYCHO was still in pre-production. But in retrospect it is a chilling moment. It is as if Stella's obsession with her dead husband has turned her into a replica of Mrs Bates.

DOUBLES

'The Case of Mr. Pelham' (1955) is Hitchcock's most developed treatment of the double, and is indeed modelled on Dostoyevsky's early novella *The Double* (1846). The episode begins as investment broker Albert Pelham (Tom Ewell) consults Dr Harley (Raymond Bailey) for advice. The story that Pelham tells – visualised as a series of flashbacks – is that he has discovered that he has a double, who at first merely turned up in his club when he was not there, but later did the same in his apartment and his office. In all cases, the double acted much as Pelham would have done: Pelham's manservant Peterson (Justice Watson) and his secretary Miss Clement (Kay Stewart) both assumed that he was Pelham, and the letters that he dictated were written in Pelham's style and showed the same knowledge of Pelham's affairs as Pelham himself. Pelham tried changing the locks, but the double mysteriously possessed a duplicate key; he even altered his signature, but the double followed suit. Because of the flashback structure, the narrative sustains for some time the possibility that there could be a 'rational' explanation, along the lines of Otto Rank's analysis of Dostoyevsky's novella as depicting 'with an unsurpassable skill' the 'onset of mental illness in a person who is not aware of it' (Rank 1971: 27). The possibility of such a Dostoyevskian reading is signalled when, after concluding his story, Pelham goes home that evening and finally meets his double. Obliged to choose between them, Peterson decides that the double is the real Mr Pelham. The double then says to Pelham, with a smile: 'You're mad, you know.' Pelham breaks down. But we then have a coda, where we learn that Pelham was put away: 'I don't think that he'll ever be right again' says the double. In shifting the narrative away from Pelham's consciousness to suggest that the double really does have an independent existence, the episode moves beyond Dostoyevsky into the supernatural realms of *The Twilight Zone*.

The double here is characterised as more assertive and dominant than the hero, a paranoid projection which bears testament to the hero's felt inadequacy. It's as if the double appears because the hero, although moderately successful, lacks the necessary drive to do really well. In the final scene 'Pelham' is playing billiards with fellow club member Tom Mason (Kirby Smith), who mentions that 'Pelham' must be a millionaire by now. In addition, the absence of any woman in Pelham's life – bachelor apartment; manservant; no girlfriend – enables the episode also to be read, like many of the examples Rank analyses, as dealing with repressed homosexuality. Much of the action – the talk with the doctor, several minor scenes, the coda – takes place in Pelham's club, with its all-male clientele. Twice Peterson tells Pelham that 'he' – i.e. the double – was in the apartment just now, and on both occasions Pelham reacts by going to look at his bed, as if that was where he would expect to see the double. Despite the absence of a rational explanation, the fantastic narrative of the episode may be seen as dealing, in a displaced form, with contemporary male anxieties.

The casting of Tom Ewell furthers this. In THE SEVEN YEAR ITCH (Billy Wilder, 1955), released only months before the episode, Richard Sherman (Ewell) has fantasies of himself as a suave seducer; these are visualised, and contrast hilariously with the fumbling efforts of the real Sherman. The two Pelhams in the episode are not as distinct as the two Shermans in Wilder's movie, but the double still possesses something of the fantasy Sherman's sense of style, here offered as more of a critique of the unassertiveness of the familiar Ewell persona. By the end of the episode, the real Pelham has had a breakdown because he could not cope, and his place has been taken by his tougher, more dominant alter ego. The male anxieties are not just sexual, but are also to with power and success in the business world.

FOOD AND MURDER / ENDINGS AND THE POLICE

There are two episodes which, although seemingly dealing with rather different situations, in fact go together neatly as a pair: 'Lamb to the Slaughter' (1958) and 'Arthur' (1959). The material in each is also relevant to the same two motifs.

In 'Lamb to the Slaughter', policeman Patrick Mahoney (Allan Lane) informs his pregnant wife Mary (Barbara Bel Geddes) that he is leaving her for another woman. In a state of shock, Mary says that she'll get his supper, and fetches a joint of lamb from the freezer. As Mahoney continues to insist that he is leaving, she pleads with him not to, then says: 'I won't let you.' He challenges her: 'Try and stop me.' She walks up behind him with the joint and hits him over the head with it, killing him. She then puts the joint in the oven to cook, goes to the store to buy vegetables and, when she returns home, messes up the room to make it look as if there has been a struggle and calls the police.

Led by Lt. Noonan (Harold J. Stone), Mahoney's colleagues come round and begin to investigate. Noonan is suspicious about a number of details – he does not believe that there really was a struggle – but he shows no signs of suspecting Mary. A particularly puzzling feature is the nature of the murder weapon, and the fact that the police cannot find it. As Noonan questions Mary and his men gather evidence, the joint cooks, whereupon Mary invites them all to eat it. As the detectives sit round the kitchen table, finishing the joint off – even the bone will go to one of their dogs – Mary is sitting unobserved in the living room; the camera tracks towards her. The police are still discussing the missing murder weapon, and we hear Noonan comment: 'For all we know, it might be under our very noses.' Mary bursts into suppressed laughter.

'Arthur' goes a stage further: it is not the murder weapon which is eaten but, indirectly, the corpse. The episode begins with Arthur Williams (Laurence Harvey), the owner of a New Zealand poultry farm, directly addressing the camera as he kills and then cooks a chicken for dinner, commenting on how superb it is. In voice-over flashback he then tells the story of how he got away with murder. His girlfriend Helen (Hazel Court) left him to marry a rich man, but returned a year later, having discovered what a 'beast' her husband was. Now enjoying his bachelorhood and irritated by Helen's sluttishness, Arthur wanted nothing to do with her. But with nowhere else to go, Helen said that she would rather die than be thrown out. Arthur took this literally and strangled her. He then managed to dispose of her body so successfully that, even though the police suspected him of her murder, they could not find it, which meant that they could not charge him. One of the policemen, Sgt. Theron (Patrick Macnee) was an old friend, and Arthur sent him a brace of cockerels for Christmas. As we come out of the flashback, Arthur mentions that Sgt. Theron was so pleased with the cockerels that he asked for details of the 'special diet' Arthur had fed them with; Arthur gave him all the ingredients but one. It is quite clear that the missing ingredient was Helen's body, ground into small pieces by Arthur's food-mixing machine.

After each of these episodes, Hitchcock comes on and placates the censors by saying that the protagonist did not, after all, get away with it: Mary was caught when she tried to kill her second husband the same way, not noticing that the lamb wasn't frozen; Arthur received his just desserts when the chickens which had been fed on his special diet grew to an enormous size and – Hitchcock breaks off at this point with protestations about how horrible it was, but obviously he is implying that they ate Arthur. Both these tacked on moral endings seem to me a joke, the latter quite explicitly so. Within the episodes, Hitchcock ends, rather, with a joke at the expense of the police, which is where his real inclinations lie.

In 'Lamb to the Slaughter', a wife kills a faithless husband; in 'Arthur', a man kills a faithless girlfriend, and in each case the murderer takes the last thing the victim says as a challenge or licence to carry out the killing. As well as ending on a food joke at the expense of the police, each episode also involves the cooking and eating of a substantial meal. In 'Lamb to the Slaughter', it is the cooking which extends for most of the episode; in 'Arthur', it is the consumption of the meal: Arthur tells his story as he eats his chicken dinner. In each episode, the police are searching for something which, if found, would enable them to identify the murderer. The twist in both cases is that the missing something is eaten.

'Lamb to the Slaughter' also has a couple of details which fit in with other examples discussed elsewhere. First, typically of those cases in which a woman kills someone, Mahoney's body remains for some time as an 'insistent presence' on the floor (➤ THE CORPSE). Second, the police also follow their colleagues in the movies in that they fail to see what is in front of their noses (➤ *Corpses and the Police*).

'Arthur' also goes further than those feature films which suggest the idea of symbolic cannibalism, ROPE and FRENZY, since it shows actual cannibalism at one remove. It is thus one of Hitchcock's most extreme narratives, and the levity of his opening and closing remarks is presumably intended to try and defuse the gruesome aspects of the story. Nevertheless, what we see at the end of each of these episodes is a successful murderer smiling with the cleverness of her/his plan. Moreover, throughout each episode, not only are we invited to identify with the murderer, but the police are ineffectual. The structure here is thus the opposite of those built around the familiar falsely accused figures in Hitchcock's feature films. The episodes also suggest Hitchcock's revenge on the police elsewhere in his work.

LIGHTS

The first and the last shot of 'One More Mile to Go' (1957) is of a light. The first is 'innocent': the lighted window of a house at night viewed from across some fields. The last is incriminating: a close-up of the dodgy taillight on Sam Jacoby (David Wayne)'s car blinking. It is blinking because his wife's weighted corpse in the trunk is catching on the wiring, and since Sam is here being led by a high-way patrolman (Steve Brodie) to police headquarters – where the trunk will be opened – he is about to be exposed as his wife's murderer. It's as if the blinking taillight mockingly 'refers to' the association of the motif with murder.

Equally, the opening shot leads into the scene of the murder. From it, Hitchcock cuts to a shot framing the window, then tracks forward to emphasise the couple inside, Sam and his wife Martha (Louise Larabee). Sam is sitting, trying to read a newspaper; Martha is angrily berating him. This is the start of a long (80-second) take, throughout which the camera remains outside the window. We cannot hear Martha's words. She tears the paper from Sam and throws it on the fire. He stands, she backs away, then the argument continues. As Sam pokes the newspaper more safely on to the fire, Martha continues to rail at him; by now, with the newspaper blazing behind him, he is arguing back. She slaps him. As things get even more heated, Sam snaps and hits her with the poker; at this point, Hitchcock cuts inside the house to a close-up of Sam's face. He has killed her.

Throughout this astonishing take, Hitchcock's camera repeatedly changes position, both to keep the couple in shot and to emphasise other elements in the scene. The fire clearly has symbolic significance, blazing up to intimate Sam's increasing rage, but the lights in the room could also be seen as having dramatic import. In retrospect from the ending, and with the associations from Hitchcock's feature films in mind, the first light we see – a lamp just above Sam's head – could be read as 'marking' Sam as a potential murderer. When he stands and the couple move left to the other side of the fireplace, the shift in camera position cuts out this light and brings a table lamp into shot. As the argument continues, with Sam now answering back, Hitchcock tracks forward to position this lamp precisely between the couple. It's as if he is using the lamp as well as the fire to dramatise the building aggression: with the lamp at waist level, both Sam and Martha's faces are illuminated from below. By now, Sam is gripping the poker belligerently; it is here that Martha slaps him. Still arguing violently, the couple move further to the left; again Hitchcock pivots the camera to follow them. It is as they move past another table lamp that Sam raises the poker with such a threatening gesture that Martha turns to flee, and it is then that he strikes and kills her.

Although the use of the lights here does not tell us anything that is not otherwise evident from the violence of the quarrel, it is nevertheless striking that the episode overall is structured around the Lights motif, and that they are used in this opening sequence as an aspect of the mise-en-scène to help dramatise the escalating tensions. Moreover, as the episode continues, a case could also be made for the relevance of the other dominant association of the motif – hinting at homosexual undercurrents.

Having put his wife's body in the trunk, Sam drives with great care to a site where he can dump it. He never arrives; the patrolman sees to that. The latter makes his first appearance in Sam's rear-view mirror, when the lights from his motorcycle signal his approach and his siren signals that he is a cop. At this stage, the patrolman's pursuit of Sam could be put down to duty: he stops a motorist with a defective taillight. But he continues, quite obsessively, to keep after Sam. He sends the latter to a local gas station to get the light fixed, and then follows him there. He then hangs around watching Sam until an opportunity presents itself for him to come over and supervise the light fixing; as he passes Sam, his hand falls casually on Sam's shoulder. It is he who identifies the source of the problem as something in the trunk, which leads him to become preoccupied with getting into it. When Sam pretends not to have the key, the patrolman tells the gas station attendant Red (Norman Leavitt) to fetch him a crowbar. The light on a gas pump behind Sam now comes prominently into shot, and remains in shot as the patrolman's vigorous exertions with the crowbar prompt the taillight to come on again.

Relieved, Sam thinks that he can escape. Yet once again the patrolman follows him; this time with the excuse that Sam was in such a hurry that he forget his change. Since, earlier, the patrolman made a point of finding out where Sam lived, he knows that Sam is not driving home, which also interests him. And now, since the tail-light has gone out again, he has an excuse to get Sam where, it would seem, he has wanted to get him all along: at police headquarters. Since we could read the little scene at the gas station as indicating that what Sam's light needs to get it going is a friendly cop with a nifty crowbar poking at the trunk, it all seems distinctly suggestive.

Although, once again, the structure of the episode leads us to identify with a murderer at the expense of the police, in this case the latter triumph – albeit by chance. But if the episode seems relatively simple in its moral, the Lights motif points to some intriguing undercurrents.

BOATS

The entire episode of 'Dip in the Pool' (1958) takes place on a transatlantic liner. William and Ethel Botibol (Keenan Wynn and Louise Platt) are travelling to Europe for a holiday, but disagree about their itinerary: she wants to visit art galleries and cultural sites; he the Folies-Bergère and casinos. From an on-board acquaintance, Mr Renshaw (Philip Bourneuf), Botibol learns about the ship's pool, in which passengers bet on how far the ship will sail in twenty-four hours. Tempted, he quizzes the purser (Ralph Clanton) on the way the mileages on offer are worked out, and calculates that, because of the bad weather, the lowest figure is the most likely. But to secure this mileage, he has to bid for it in the daily auction, which results in his spending almost $1000 – most of their holiday money. Then the bad weather clears up during the night, and so Botibol decides, before the time is up, that he has no chance of winning unless the ship is delayed for some reason. He concludes that the only way to ensure this is to jump overboard, so that a delay will occur when he is rescued. Unfortunately, the woman, Emily (Doreen Lang) whom he chooses to witness his jump is, unknown to him, under psychiatric care, and her story that a man has jumped off the stern of the ship is not believed.

After the episode, Hitchcock comes on and adds a moral ending: the ship was subsequently delayed by engine trouble, so that Ethel Botibol, in her husband's absence, won the pool, and she and her second husband had a good time with it. It is only in this narrated ending that the 'therapeutic' theme of the voyage is apparent: Ethel loses a boorish husband and gains $10,000 – and another, one trusts more sympathetic husband. Typically of Hitchcock's voyages, what occurs within the episode is much darker. Botibol believes he can emulate Renshaw's success as a Wall Street financier by applying the latter's practice: reduce the odds by gambling with 'inside information'. That he is unsuccessful is a comment in part on the dangers of gambling – Ethel mentions at one point that Botibol always loses – but more interestingly on the aspirations of a certain sort of American petty bourgeois. The casting of Keenan Wynn – and his contrast with the patrician Philip Bourneuf – is crucial to the project. Mrs Renshaw (Fay Wray) comments, snobbishly but accurately, on Botibol's vulgar dress sense: plaid dinner jacket and flashy bow-tie. Wynn plays Botibol as a loudmouth imitation bon viveur, lying to Renshaw about his lifestyle and making a point of throwing his money around, but not even letting his wife know that he is not drinking the martinis that he so ostentatiously orders because he is fighting seasickness. In short, he is a phoney, but a peculiarly American one: he despises his wife for her wish to absorb European culture, but is so convinced that he can beat the odds that he gambles almost all their money before they even get to Europe.

The function of the voyage – the place of the episode in the motifs – would seem to be to emphasise the flaws in the marriage by exaggerating Botibol's irrational behaviour to the point where it kills him. In gambling their holiday money, he shows his simmering hostility to the trip: he is quite prepared to sabotage it, and the only thing that really worries him is that he will have to tell his wife. The fever metaphor that I suggest could be applied to Hitchcock's boat journeys can be seen here in a condensed form in the pool auction itself. As with Hillcrist in THE SKIN GAME, Botibol goes on bidding compulsively, long after the amount has exceeded what he was originally prepared to pay. But in carrying the gamble to the point where he loses his life, he illustrates – as black comedy – the death drive which could perhaps be seen to lie at the heart of the compulsive gambler. When Botibol dives off the stern of the liner and disappears into the foam, one can sense Hitchcock's amusement that the man is such a complete fool. Therein, I think, lies his wish to reward the wife with a happy ending.

It will be apparent that there is one motif which keeps recurring as a subtext in this short survey of the TV episodes. Given that the episodes were shown on prime time to a family audience, we should perhaps call it the motif that dare not speak its name. The fact that no less than four of the nine episodes considered here would seem to allude to it is quite astonishing, although one notes that one of the representations is clearly hostile ('Poison'), two are ambiguous ('The Case of Mr Pelham', 'One More Mile to Go') and only one is implicitly positive ('Breakdown'). Nevertheless, these four episodes should also be taken as further evidence in support of my comment under HOMOSEXUALITY: that the famous cases of homosexuality in Hitchcock are only the tip of the iceberg.

Appendix II: Articles on Hitchcock's motifs

The first lexicon of Hitchcock's motifs was published in *Cahiers du Cinéma* 62: *Lexique mythologique pour l'oeuvre de Hitchcock* by Philippe Demonsablon (1956: 8-29 & 54-55). The motifs listed there are Jewellery (subdivided); Cats; Dogs; Falls (subdivided); Keys; Knives; Flashes of Light (lightning; flash bulbs); Children; Geography (in effect, countries); Drinks; Spectacles and Optical devices; Hands; Handcuffs; Eggs; Shadows; Paintings; Telephones; Theatre; Trains; Disguises. For each motif, there is a brief assessment of its symbolic import, but for the most part this is a – fairly thorough – listing of these elements in Hitchcock's films up to THE MAN WHO KNEW TOO MUCH (1955).

The only other article I have found on Hitchcock's motifs generally is by Hartmut W. Redottée: 'Leid-Motive: Das Universum des Alfred Hitchcock' (Redottée 2000: 19-50). Redottée begins by looking at some more general Hitchcock features: Suspense; Montage; Loss of Identity (including the falsely accused figures). He then settles into a brief consideration of a number of different motifs and other recurring features of the films: The Abyss (essentially the threat of falling), in which hands reaching out for one another is a linked motif; Staircases; the Uncanny House; Bars-Grilles-Shadows (film noir lighting; images of imprisonment; threatening shadows); Cages (prison cells; cars; telephone boxes – the equivalent of CONFINED SPACES); Back projection; Colours (e.g. red); Meals; Kisses; Mothers; Portraits; The Look, including Optical devices and Eyes; Symbols, including iconic buildings (The British Museum, Statue of Liberty, The Golden Gate; Windmills etc.) and the use of plans, maps and drawings; Animals.

There is certainly more discussion here than in Demonsablon's article, but the range of films Redottée covers is fairly limited and the points he makes are mostly familiar from the Hitchcock literature. Nevertheless, he does convey the darkness of Hitchcock's cinema. For example, he suggests that, in general, Hitchcock's houses do not protect, but contain secrets, puzzles, danger, isolation and decay (Redottée 2000: 31-32). The introduction to the section on Kisses gives the flavour of his approach:

> Human relationships are the central issue in all Hitchcock films: trust that can turn to mistrust, suspicion, uncertainty; the longing for love and the fear of losing it; feeling threatened and feeling relieved – all these appear again and again in his films in multiple variations and combinations, together with the loss of identity and the ensuing search for it. Kisses are the attempt to make sure of one another, to experience one of

the rare moments of happiness, but at the same time they are often imbued with the fear that the happiness could be an illusion, at any time the abyss underneath could open up again. Nobody has ever produced kisses so ecstatic and at the same time so desperate as Hitchcock.

(Redottée 2000: 40)

Thomas Leitch's *The Encyclopedia of Alfred Hitchcock* (2002) includes entries on 'themes, motifs and topics of general interest'. However, since the book is readily available, I will simply list those categories he includes which relate to what happens in the films, and note that his comments are concise, thoughtful summaries of these features in Hitchcock's work: birds; blondes; brandy; cameo appearances; Catholicism; children; colour; comedy; death scenes; doubles; dreams; eating and drinking; expressionism; eyes; families; fathers; fear and pleasure; fetishism; film noir; games; gaze; guilt; homes; homosexuality; identification; identity, public and private; ideology; irony; long takes; MacGuffin; masculinity; mirrors; montage and découpage; mothers; murder; normalcy; performance; police; psychoanalysis; pure cinema; staircases; suspense and surprise; 3-D; thrillers; voyeurism; wit.

Appendix III: Definitions

There are two frequently used terms I would like to clarify.

Diegesis

The narrative world of the film, conceived as a unity. The two main areas in this study where a distinction has been made between the diegetic and the non-diegetic are with the soundtrack and the audience. Music or sounds which are diegetic can be heard by the characters within the film. A soundtrack added to the film afterwards will normally be non-diegetic: Marion does not hear the pounding violins in PSYCHO. But sound effects may also be non-diegetic: the characters in JUNO AND THE PAYCOCK do not hear the machine gun shots which punctuate the breaks between the film's acts. By contrast, sound emanating from *any* source within the diegesis – whether or not we can see the source, which may be off-screen – is diegetic. Similarly, a diegetic audience refers to an audience within the film, and is referred to in that manner to distinguish it from an audience watching the film.

In fact, Hitchcock also includes visuals which are non-diegetic, albeit rarely. The shots of dancers swirling to 'The Merry Widow Waltz' which punctuate the narrative of SHADOW OF A DOUBT from time to time are not, say, flashbacks or what Uncle Charlie is imagining (if that were so, they would be diegetic). They are outside the narrative world, and so are non-diegetic.

Point-of-view editing

Following David Bordwell in *Narration in the Fiction Film* (Bordwell 1985: 60), when describing shots in a film, I have restricted point of view to mean optical point of view. In other words, what we see on the screen corresponds to the subjective view of someone within the diegesis: the camera is placed where the person is situated and angled to show what he/she sees. Occasionally Hitchcock will cut in closer along the axis of the look to emphasise something (REAR WINDOW includes shots like this), but this is relatively rare: he usually respects the necessary distance. Point-of-view editing is an elaboration of point-of-view shots into a specific sort of sequence. A point-of-view shot of what a character sees (alternatively called a subjective shot) is followed by a reaction shot – usually in medium shot or close-up – of the person looking, which is followed by another point-of-view shot and then another reaction shot and so on. Scottie trailing 'Madeleine' in his car around San Francisco in VERTIGO is one of many examples in Hitchcock of point-of-view editing. In REAR WINDOW, point-of-view editing also includes sequences filmed through optical devices, e.g. Jeff's telephoto lens. Hitchcock employed this technique from his first film; no other director uses it so extensively.

Hitchcock also uses point-of-view editing with the camera moving with a walking character. The nature of the movement of the camera gives this a different feel to point-of-view editing from a moving car: I call it track-and-reverse point-of-view editing. A point-of-view shot tracking forward with a character shows what she/he is looking at, this is then followed by a reverse-angle shot of the character which tracks back in front of her/him – in the direction of movement – as she/he continues to walk forward. Another point-of-view track forward is then followed by another reverse-angle track back and so on. In most cases, the point-of-view shots look ahead, e.g. when Lila is heading up the hill to the Bates house in PSYCHO, she is looking at the house ahead of her. But there are exceptions. When Melanie walks along the Brenner jetty to deliver the love birds in THE BIRDS, she is looking at the barn over to her right, and so her point-of-view shots are lateral tracks. The flow of the sequence is exactly the same, but Melanie's concern is whether Mitch, who is in the barn, will come out and see her. Her point-of-view shots register that concern.

References

Richard Allen (1999): 'Hitchcock, or the Pleasures of Metaskepticism' in Allen and Ishii-Gonzalès (1999)

Richard Allen and S. Ishii-Gonzalès (Eds) (1999): *Alfred Hitchcock: Centenary Essays* (British Film Institute, London)

John Atkins (1984): *The British Spy Novel: Styles in Treachery* (John Calder, London)

Dan Auiler (1999): *Hitchcock's Secret Notebooks* (Bloomsbury, London)

Gaston Bachelard (1969): *The Poetics of Space* (Beacon Press, Boston)

Barbara M. Bannon (1985): 'Double, Double: Toil and Trouble', *Literature/Film Quarterly* Vol. 13 No. 1, Winter

Charles Barr (1999): *English Hitchcock* (Cameron & Hollis, Moffat)

Sabrina Barton (1995): '"Crisscross": Paranoia and Projection in *Strangers on a Train*' in Creekmur and Doty (1995)

Sabrina Barton (2000-01): 'Hitchcock's Hands', *Hitchcock Annual* 2000-2001

Raymond Bellour (1969/2000): 'System of a Fragment (on *The Birds*)' in Bellour (2000)

Raymond Bellour (1975/2000): '*Le Blocage Symbolique*', *Communications* 23, Paris, translated and reprinted as 'Symbolic Blockage (on *North by Northwest*)' in Bellour (2000)

Raymond Bellour (1977/2000): 'Hitchcock, the Enunciator', *Camera Obscura* 2, Fall; reprinted as 'To Enunciate (on *Marnie*)' in Bellour (2000)

Raymond Bellour (2000): *The Analysis of Film*, edited by Constance Penley (Indiana University Press, Bloomington, IN)

Raymond Bellour and Guy Rosolato (1990): 'Dialogue: Remembering (This Memory of) a Film' in E. Ann Kaplan (Ed): *Psychoanalysis & Cinema* (Routledge, New York)

John Belton (Ed) (2000): *Alfred Hitchcock's* Rear Window (Cambridge University Press, Cambridge)

Réda Bensmaïa (1992): 'La Figure d'inconnu ou l'inconscient épinglé: *Le Portrait de Dorian Gray* d'Albert Lewin', *Iris* 14-15, Autumn

Basil Bernstein (1973): *Class, Codes and Control* (Paladin, St Albans)

Peter Bogdanovich (1997): *Who the Devil Made It: Conversations with Legendary Film Directors* (Ballantine, New York)

David Bordwell (1985): *Narration in the Fiction Film* (Methuen, London)

Peter Bordonaro (1976): 'Dial M for Murder: A Play by Frederick Knott/A Film by Alfred Hitchcock', *Sight and Sound*, Summer

Laurent Bouzereau (1993): *The Alfred Hitchcock Quote Book* (Citadel, New York)

Lesley Brill (1986): 'Hitchcock's *The Lodger'* in Deutelbaum and Poague (1986)

Lesley Brill (1988): *The Hitchcock Romance: Love and Irony in Hitchcock's Films* (Princeton University Press, Princeton, NJ)

Andrew Britton (1986): 'Hitchcock's *Spellbound*: Text and Counter-Text', *CineAction* 3/4, January

Peter Brooks (1976): *The Melodramatic Imagination: Balzac, Henry James, Melodrama, and the Mode of Excess* (Yale University Press, London)

Stella Bruzzi (2000): 'Grace Kelly' in Stella Bruzzi and Pamela Church Gibson (Eds): *Fashion Cultures: Theories Explorations and Analysis* (Routledge, London)

Barbara J. Buchanan (1935/1995): 'Alfred Hitchcock Tells a Woman that Women are a Nuisance' in Gottlieb (1995)

Elias Canetti (1973): *Crowds and Power* (Penguin, Harmondsworth)

Frank Capra (1971): *The Name Above the Title: An Autobiography* (MacMillan, New York)

Stanley Cavell (1986): 'North by Northwest' in Deutelbaum and Poague (1986)

Jean Chevalier and Alain Gheerbrant (1996): *The Penguin Dictionary of Symbols* (Penguin, London)

Michel Cieutat (1988): *Les grands thèmes du cinéma américain, tome 1* (Les Éditions du Cerf, Paris)

Michel Cieutat (1991): *Les grands thèmes du cinéma américain, tome 2* (Les Éditions du Cerf, Paris)

Paula Marantz Cohen (1995): *Alfred Hitchcock: The Legacy of Victorianism* (University Press of Kentucky, Lexington, KY)

Herbert Coleman (with Judy Lanini) (2003): *The Hollywood I Knew: A Memoir: 1916-1988* (Scarecrow Press, Lanham, MD)

Peter Conrad (2000): *The Hitchcock Murders* (Faber and Faber, London)

Robert J. Corber (1993): *In the Name of National Security: Hitchcock, Homophobia and the Political Construction of Gender in Postwar America* (Duke University Press, Durham, NC)

Corey K. Creekmur and Alexander Doty (Eds) (1995): *Out in Culture: Gay, Lesbian and Queer Essays on Popular Culture* (Cassell, London)

Philippe Demonsablon (1956): 'Lexique Mythologique pour l'oeuvre de Hitchcock', *Cahiers du Cinéma* 62, August/September

Steven DeRosa (2001): *Writing with Hitchcock: The Collaboration of Alfred Hitchcock and John Michael Hayes* (Faber and Faber, New York)

Marshall Deutelbaum (1986): 'Finding the Right Man in *The Wrong Man*' in Deutelbaum and Poague (1986)

Marshall Deutelbaum and Leland Poague (Eds) (1986): *A Hitchcock Reader* (Iowa State University Press, Ames, IA)

Mary Ann Doane (1991): *Femmes Fatales: Feminism, Film Theory, Psychoanalysis* (Routledge, London)

Raymond Durgnat (1974): *The Strange Case of Alfred Hitchcock* (Faber and Faber, London)

Raymond Durgnat (2002): *A Long Hard Look at 'Psycho'* (British Film Institute, London)

Richard Dyer (1979): *Stars* (British Film Institute, London)

Lotte Eisner (1973): *The Haunted Screen* (Secker & Warburg, London)

Thomas Elsaesser (1972): 'Tales of Sound and Fury', *Monogram* 4

Thomas Elsaesser (1992): 'Mirror, Muse, Medusa', *Iris* 14/15, Autumn

John Fawell (2001): *Hitchcock's* Rear Window: *The Well-Made Film* (Southern Illinois University Press, Carbondale and Edwardsville, IL)

Susan Felleman (1992): 'The Moving Picture Gallery', *Iris* 14/15, Autumn

Otto Fenichel (1946): *The Psychoanalytic Theory of Neurosis* (Routledge & Kegan Paul, London)

Jack Foley (1978): 'Doubleness in Hitchcock: Seeing the Family Plot', *Bright Lights* 7

J.G. Frazer (1957): *The Golden Bough: A Study in Magic and Religion*, Abridged Edition (MacMillan, London)

Sigmund Freud (1900/1954): *The Interpretation of Dreams* (George Allen & Unwin)

Sigmund Freud (1905/1977): 'Three Essays on the Theory of Sexuality' in *On Sexuality*, Vol. 7, Pelican Freud Library (Penguin, Harmondsworth, 1977)

Sigmund Freud (1913/1985): 'Totem and Taboo' in *The Origins of Religion*, Vol. 13, Pelican Freud Library (Penguin, Harmondsworth, 1985)

Sigmund Freud (1916/1973): 'Symbolism in Dreams' in *Introductory Lectures on Psychoanalysis*, Vol. 1, Pelican Freud Library (Penguin, Harmondsworth, 1973)

Sigmund Freud (1919/1985) 'The Uncanny' in *Art and Literature*, Vol. 14, Pelican Freud Library (Penguin, Harmondsworth, 1985)

Northrop Frye (1957): *Anatomy of Criticism* (Princeton University Press, Princeton, NJ)

Ed Gallafent (1988): 'Black Satin – Fantasy, Murder and the Couple in *Gaslight* and *Rebecca*', *Screen* Vol. 29, No. 3, Summer

Lesley Gillilan: 'Twenty Quid Genius' in *The Guardian* Space 12 October 2000

Sidney Gottlieb (1995): *Hitchcock on Hitchcock: Selected Writings and Interviews* (Faber and Faber, London)

Martin Grams Jr. (1999): 'The Short Story Anthologies' in Mogg (1999)

Roger Greenspun (1991): '"Beats Flying, Doesn't It?": The Train in Hitchcock' in *Junction and Journey: Trains and Film* (Museum of Modern Art, New York)

Elizabeth Grosz (1990): 'The Body of Signification' in John Fletcher & Andrew Benjamin: *Abjection, Melancholia and Love: The Work of Julia Kristeva* (Routledge, London)

Elizabeth Grosz (1992): 'Voyeurism/Exhibitionism/The Gaze' in Elizabeth Wright (Ed): *Feminism and Psychoanalysis: A Critical Dictionary* (Blackwell, Oxford)

Patricia King Hanson (Ed) (1988): *The American Film Institute Catalog of Motion Pictures Produced in the United States: Feature Films 1911-1920* (University of California Press, Berkeley)

Patricia King Hanson (Ed) (1993): *The American Film Institute Catalog of Motion Pictures Produced in the United States: Feature Films 1931-1940* (University of California Press, Berkeley)

Patricia King Hanson (Ed) (1999): *The American Film Institute Catalog of Motion Pictures Produced in the United States: Feature Films 1941-1950* (University of California Press, Berkeley)

Ina Rae Hark (1991): 'Revalidating Patriarchy: Why Hitchcock Remade *The Man Who Knew Too Much*' in Raubicheck and Srebnick (1991)

Joan Harrison and Robert E. Sherwood (1940/1959): *Rebecca* (screenplay) in John Gassner and Dudley Nichols (Eds): *Great Film Plays* (Crown Publishers, New York)

Molly Haskell (1974): *From Reverence to Rape: The Treatment of Women in the Movies* (Penguin, Harmondsworth)

Ben Hecht (1946): *Spellbound* (screenplay) in John Gassner and Dudley Nichols (Eds): *Best Film Plays 1945* (Crown Publishers, New York)

Robert Bechthold Heilman (1973): *The Iceman, the Arsonist, and the Troubled Agent: Tragedy and Melodrama on the Modern Stage* (George Allen & Unwin, London)

Robert Hichens (1933/1958): *The Paradine Case* (Ernest Benn, London)

Alfred Hitchcock (1931/1995): 'How I Choose My Heroines' in Gottlieb (1995)

Alfred Hitchcock (1937/1995): 'Direction' in Gottlieb (1995)

Alfred Hitchcock (1938/1995): 'Nova Grows Up' in Gottlieb (1995)

Alfred Hitchcock (1939/1995): 'What I'd Do to the Stars' in Gottlieb (1995)

Alfred Hitchcock (1949/1995): 'The Enjoyment of Fear' in Gottlieb (1995)

Alfred Hitchcock (1959): 'Entretien avec Alfred Hitchcock par Jean Domarchi et Jean Douchet', *Cahiers du Cinéma* 102, Décembre

Margaret M. Horwitz (1986): '*The Birds*: A Mother's Love' in Deutelbaum and Poague (1986)

Florence Jacobowitz (2000): 'UNDER CAPRICORN: Hitchcock in Transition', *CineAction* 52, June

E. Ann Kaplan (Ed) (1990): *Psychoanalysis & Cinema* (Routledge, New York)

Lucretia Knapp (1995): 'The Queer Voice in *Marnie*' in Creekmur and Doty (1995)

Richard P. Krafsur (Ed) (1997): *The American Film Institute Catalog of Motion Pictures Produced in the United States: Feature Films 1961-1970* (University of California Press, Berkeley)

Bill Krohn (2000): *Hitchcock at Work* (Phaidon Press, London)

J.L. Kuhns (1998-99): 'Hitchcock's *The Mountain Eagle*', *Hitchcock Annual* 1998-1999

J. Laplanche and J-B. Pontalis (1973): *The Language of Psycho-Analysis* (Hogarth Press, London)

Leonard J. Leff (1988): *Hitchcock and Selznick* (Weidenfeld & Nicholson, London)

Thomas M. Leitch (1991): *Find the Director and Other Hitchcock Games* (University of Georgia Press, Athens, GA)

Thomas M. Leitch (2002): *The Encyclopedia of Alfred Hitchcock* (Checkmark Books, New York)

Richard Lippe (1986): 'Kim Novak: A Resistance to Definition', *CineAction* 7, December

Erik S. Lunde and Douglas A. Noverr (1993): '"Saying it with Pictures": Alfred Hitchcock and Painterly Images in *Psycho*' in Paul Loukides and Linda K. Fuller (Eds): *Beyond the Stars: Studies in American Popular Film: Volume 3: The Material World in American Popular Film* (Bowling Green State University Popular Press, Bowling Green, OH)

Colin McArthur (2000): 'The Critics Who Knew Too Much: Alfred Hitchcock and the Absent Class Paradigm', *Film Studies* 2, Spring

Joe McElhaney (1999): 'Touching the Surface: *Marnie*, Melodrama, Modernism' in Allen and Ishii-Gonzalès (1999)

Brian McFarlane (1997): *An Autobiography of British Cinema* (Methuen, London)

Patrick McGilligan (2003): *Alfred Hitchcock: A Life in Darkness and in Light* (John Wiley and Sons, Chichester)

James McLaughlin (1986): 'All in the Family: Alfred Hitchcock's *Shadow of a Doubt'* in Deutelbaum and Poague (1986)

Tania Modleski (1988): *The Women Who Knew Too Much: Hitchcock and Feminist Theory* (Methuen, New York)

Ken Mogg (1999): *The Alfred Hitchcock Story* (Titan Books, London)

Ken Mogg (2002): 'Odd Spot', *The MacGuffin* 28, May

Ken Mogg (2004): 'Hitchcock's THE PLEASURE GARDEN (1925) and FAMILY PLOT (1976): Basically English', *The MacGuffin* 29, January

Christopher D. Morris (2002): *The Hanging Figure: On Suspense and the Films of Alfred Hitchcock* (Praeger, Westport, CT)

Laura Mulvey (1975): 'Visual Pleasure and Narrative Cinema', *Screen* Vol. 16, No. 3, Autumn

Kenneth W. Munden (Ed) (1997): *The American Film Institute Catalog of Motion Pictures Produced in the United States: Feature Films 1921-1930* (University of California Press, Berkeley)

Steve Neale (1983): 'Masculinity as Spectacle', *Screen* Vol. 24, No. 6, Nov/Dec

Bill Nichols (1981): *Ideology and the Image: Social Representation in the Cinema and Other Media* (Indiana University Press, Bloomington, IN)

Pat Hitchcock O'Connell and Laurent Bouzereau (2003): *Alma Hitchcock: The Woman Behind the Man* (Berkley Books, New York)

Iona & Peter Opie (1959): *The Lore and Language of Schoolchildren* (Oxford University Press, London)

Camille Paglia (1998): *The Birds* (British Film Institute, London)

James Reid Paris (1983): *The Great French Films* (Citadel Press, Secaucus, NJ)

V.F. Perkins (1972): *Film as Film: Understanding and Judging Movies* (Penguin, Harmondsworth)

V.F. Perkins (1990): 'Film Authorship: The Premature Burial', *CineAction* 21/22, November

Theodore Price (1992): *Hitchcock and Homosexuality* (Scarecrow Press, Metuchen, NJ)

Otto Rank (1971): *The Double: a Psychoanalytic Study*, translated and edited by Harry Tucker Jr (Meridian Books, New York)

Walter Raubicheck and Walter Srebnick (Eds) (1991): *Hitchcock's Rereleased Films: From ROPE to VERTIGO* (Wayne University State Press, Detroit)

Hartmut W. Redottée (2000): 'Leid-Motive: Das Universum des Alfred Hitchcock' in Sabine Lenk (Ed): *Obsessionen: Die Alptraum-Fabrik Des Alfred Hitchcock* (Schüren Verlag, Marburg)

Eric Rohmer and Claude Chabrol (1957): *Hitchcock* (Éditions Universitaires, Paris). Translated into English (1979) by Stanley Hochman as *Hitchcock: The First Forty-Four Films* (Ungar, New York)

Marty Roth (1992): 'Hitchcock's Secret Agency', *Camera Obscura* 30, May

William Rothman (1975): 'Alfred Hitchcock's *Notorious*', *The Georgia Review*, Fall

William Rothman (1982): *Hitchcock - The Murderous Gaze* (Harvard University Press, Cambridge, Mass)

William Rothman (1988): 'The Unknown Woman in Vertigo' in *The 'I' of the Camera: Essays in Film Criticism, History and Aesthetics* (Cambridge University Press, Cambridge)

William Rothman (1999): 'Some Thoughts on Hitchcock's Authorship' in Allen and Ishii-Gonzalès (1999)

Richard Roud (1960): 'The French Line', *Sight and Sound*, Autumn

Victor Sage (1987): Entry on 'Theme' in Roger Fowler (Ed): *Modern Critical Terms* (Revised Edition) (Routledge & Kegan Paul, London)

Robert Samuels (1998): *Hitchcock's Bi-Textuality: Lacan, Feminisms and Queer Theory* (State University of New York Press, Albany, NY)

Bart Sheridan (1948): 'Three and a Half Minute Take...', *American Cinematographer*, September

Kaja Silverman (1993): 'Masochism and Male Subjectivity' in Constance Penley and Sharon Willis (Eds): *Male Trouble* (University of Minnesota Press, Minneapolis)

Helen Simpson (1937/1949): *Under Capricorn* (Pan, London)

Jane E. Sloan (1995): *Alfred Hitchcock: A Filmography and Bibliography* (University of California Press, Berkeley, CA)

Susan Smith (1997): 'Cinematic Point of View in the Films of Hitchcock (PhD thesis, University of Sunderland)

Susan Smith (1999): 'Disruption, Destruction, Denial: Hitchcock as Saboteur' in Allen and Ishii-Gonzalès (1999)

Susan Smith (2000): *Hitchcock: Suspense, Humour and Tone* (British Film Institute, London)

Donald Spoto (1979): *The Art of Alfred Hitchcock* (Doubleday & Company, New York)

Donald Spoto (1988): *The Dark Side of Genius: The Life of Alfred Hitchcock* (Frederick Muller, London)

Robert Stam and Roberta Pearson (1986): 'Hitchcock's *Rear Window*: Reflexivity and the Critique of Voyeurism' in Deutelbaum and Poague (1986)

Sarah Street (1995-96): 'Hitchcockian Haberdashery', *Hitchcock Annual* 1995-1996

Sarah Street (2000): '"The Dresses Had Told Me": Fashion and Femininity in REAR WINDOW' in Belton (2000)

John Russell Taylor (1978): *Hitch: The Life and Work of Alfred Hitchcock* (Faber and Faber, London)

Klaus Theweleit (1989): *Male Fantasies Volume 2: Male Bodies: Psychoanalyzing the White Terror* (Polity Press, Cambridge, UK)

François Truffaut (1968): *Hitchcock* (Martin Secker & Warburg, London)

Yuri Tsivian (1992): 'Portraits, Mirrors, Death: On Some Decadent Clichés in Early Russian Films', *Iris* 14/15, Autumn

James M. Vest (1998-99): 'The Controller Controlled: Hitchcock's Cameo in TORN CURTAIN', *Hitchcock Annual* 1998-1999

James M. Vest (1999-2000): 'Alfred Hitchcock's Cameo in *Marnie*', *Hitchcock Annual* 1999-2000

Diane Waldman (1982): 'The Childish, the Insane and the Ugly: The Representation of Modern Art in Popular Films and Fiction of the Forties', *Wide Angle* Vol. 5, No. 2

Barbara G. Walker (1983): *The Woman's Encyclopedia of Myths and Secrets* (Harper Collins, New York)

Barbara G. Walker (1995): *The Woman's Dictionary of Symbols and Sacred Objects* (Pandora, Harper Collins, London)

Michael Walker (1982a): 'Alfred Hitchcock', *Film Dope* 24, March

Michael Walker (1982b): 'Melodrama and the American Cinema' , *Movie* 29/30, Summer

Michael Walker (1982c): 'Ophuls in Hollywood', *Movie* 29/30, Summer

Michael Walker (1990): 'Secret Beyond the Door', *Movie* 34/35, Winter

Michael Walker (1999): 'The Stolen Raincoat and the Bloodstained Dress: *Young and Innocent* and *Stage Fright*' in Allen and Ishii-Gonzalès (1999)

Marina Warner (1995): *From the Beast to the Blonde: On Fairy Tales and Their Tellers* (Vintage, London)

Elisabeth Weis (1982): *The Silent Scream: Alfred Hitchcock's Soundtrack* (Associated University Presses, East Brunswick, NJ)

Estela V. Welldon (1988): *Mother, Madonna, Whore: The Idealization and Denigration of Motherhood* (Free Association Books, London)

Michael Williams (2003): *Ivor Novello: Screen Idol* (British Film Institute, London)

George M. Wilson (1986): *Narration in Light: Studies in Cinematic Point of View* (Johns Hopkins University Press, Baltimore, MD)

D.W. Winnicott (1971): *Playing and Reality* (Tavistock Publications, London)

Peter Wollen (1969): 'Hitchcock's Vision', *Cinema* 3, Cambridge, June

Peter Wollen (1999): '*Rope*: Three Hypotheses' in Allen and Ishii-Gonzalès (1999)

Robin Wood (1989): *Hitchcock's Films Revisited* (Columbia University Press, New York)

Maurice Yacowar (1977): *Hitchcock's British Films* (Archon Books, Hamden, CT)

Dennis Zirnite (1986): 'Hitchcock, on the Level: The Heights of Spatial Tension', *Film Criticism* Vol. 10 No. 3, Spring

Slavoj Žižek (1992): *Looking Awry: An Introduction to Jacques Lacan through Popular Culture* (MIT, Cambridge, MA)

Filmography

This filmography includes all the feature films Hitchcock directed plus his other work which is discussed in this book, i.e. *The Blackguard* (1925) and the nine TV episodes of *Alfred Hitchcock Presents* covered in Appendix I. It is not comprehensive, but it is designed to provide the main production credits for each film and a listing of the cast members so that readers can look up the actors for all the characters cited in the book. The primary sources are Charles Barr's *English Hitchcock* (1999) for the English films, and the multi-volume *AFI Catalog of Motion Pictures Produced in the United States* (Hanson 1993 & 1999; Krafsur 1997) for the Hollywood features. Barr is extremely detailed on the sources of the films, and most of my information on these is from his excellent notes. In general, I have also followed Barr's practice of transcribing from the screen what the credits actually say, but have not indicated the difference between on-screen credits and those found from (reliable) sources elsewhere. Equally, just as Barr has checked the English films, I have also checked the Hollywood films to weed out the many errors which have crept into Hitchcock filmographies over the years. I have also standardised the listings as follows:

1. where the technical contributions are the same from film to film, the same term is used throughout, e.g. Photography for Director of photography; Music for Musical score; Sound for the various alternatives such as Sound recording, Recording or Recorded by;
2. the date preceding the title of the film is the copyright date, visible on the film itself (this cannot be done for the British films, and I have followed Barr and cited the release date); the release date is only mentioned if in a later year;
3. the company in brackets after the title is the production company, and the distributor is only mentioned by name (under Released through) if different;
4. director, producer and screenplay are in that order at the head of the credits; AH stands for Alfred Hitchcock;
5. the hierarchy of names and the designated technical contributions are usually otherwise as on-screen, but square brackets indicate spelling mistakes in the credits, and an i.e. in square brackets means that the credits are simply wrong: the character so named is called by another name in the film;.
6. if the aspect ratio is not mentioned, it is Academy, i.e. 1:1.33. The VistaVision films from To Catch a Thief to North by Northwest all have a recommended aspect ratio of 1:1.85. Other ratios are cited.

7. for the extant silent films, I have followed the practice adopted by Le Gior-
nate del Cinema Muto, citing the source of the print and the running time in
relation to a specified projection speed in fps (frames per second). Few silent
films survive in their full original lengths, but prints of all the extant
Hitchcock silents were screened during the 1999 festival in Sacile, Italy. The
lengths cited here are those of the prints shown, which were probably the
best surviving versions. Future restorations could result in longer versions.

English period: Silent features

1925 THE BLACKGUARD (DIE PRINZESSIN UND DER GEIGER) (Ufa/Gainsbor-
ough Pictures)

Director: Graham Cutts. Producer: Michael Balcon. Assistant producer: Erich
Pommer. Scenario & assistant director: AH. From the novel by Raymond Paton.
Photography: Theodor Sparkuhl. Art director: AH. NFTVA print 96' at 18 fps.
Cast: Walter Rilla (Michael), Jane Novak (Princess Maria Lobanoff), Bernhard
Goetzke (Lewinski), Fritz Alberti (Painter), Martin Herzberg (Michael as a boy),
Rosa Valetti (Michael's grandmother), Dora Bergner (Maria's aunt), Robert
Schotz (Grand Duke Paul), Frank Stanmore (Pomponard, Michael's impressar-
io), Alexander Murski (Antique dealer Vollmark).

1926 THE PLEASURE GARDEN (IRRGARTEN DER LEIDENSCHAFT) (Emelka/
Gainsborough)

Director: AH. Producer: Michael Balcon. Scenario: Eliot Stannard. From the
1923 novel by Oliver Sandys (pseudonym of Marguerite Florence Barclay).
Photography: Baron Ventimiglia. Assistant director: Alma Reville. NFTVA
print 75' at 18 fps.
Cast: Virginia Valli (Patsy Brand), Carmelita Geraghty (Jill Cheyne), Miles Man-
der (Levet), John Stuart (Hugh Fielding), George Snell (Oscar Hamilton, Pleasure Garden proprietor), C. Falkenburg (Prince Ivan), Ferdinand Martini (Mr
Sidey), Florence Helminger (Mrs Sidey).
Note: The actress playing the 'native woman' is usually listed as Nita Naldi.
Charles Barr questions this and I would definitely maintain she is not Naldi. A
differently edited version of THE PLEASURE GARDEN (sometimes called the
Rohauer version) has been screened in various countries on TV. It runs 61' at a
faster projection speed (probably 24 fps) which means it is in fact longer than

the NFTVA print, but each version contains scenes not in the other. For a discussion of the two versions, see Mogg 2004: 16-20.

1926 **THE MOUNTAIN EAGLE** (DER BERGADLER) (Emelka/Gainsborough)

Director: AH. Producer: Michael Balcon. Scenario: Eliot Stannard. Photography: Baron Ventimiglia.
Cast: Bernard Goetzke (Pettigrew), Nita Naldi (Beatrice), Malcolm Keen (John Fulton, known as Fearogod), John Hamilton (Edward Pettigrew).
A lost film. See Barr (1999: 216-17) and Kuhns (1998-99: 31-108).

1926 **THE LODGER: A STORY OF THE LONDON FOG** (Gainsborough)

Director: AH. Producer: Michael Balcon. Scenario: Eliot Stannard. From the 1913 novel by Mrs Belloc Lowndes. Photography: Baron Ventimiglia. Assistant director: Alma Reville. Art directors: C. Wilfrid [Wilfred] Arnold & Bertram Evans. Editing & titling: Ivor Montagu. Title designs: E. McKnight Kauffer. NFTVA print 98' at 18 fps.
Cast: Ivor Novello (the Lodger), June (Daisy Bunting), Malcolm Keen (Joe, police detective), Marie Ault (Mrs Bunting), Arthur Chesney (Mr Bunting).
Hitchcock appears in a newspaper office early in the film, but this was not planned as a cameo (see Truffaut 1968: 42). Truffaut and others also maintain that Hitchcock is in the crowd assaulting Ivor Novello on the railings at the climax; I agree with Charles Barr (1999: 218) that this figure is probably not Hitchcock.

1927 **DOWNHILL** (Gainsborough)

Director: AH. Producer: Michael Balcon. Scenario: Eliot Stannard. From the 1926 play by David L'Estrange (pseudonym of Ivor Novello & Constance Collier). Photography: Claude McDonnell. Art director: Bert Evans. Assistant director: Frank Mills. Editor: Lionel Rich. Script/editing associate: Ivor Montagu. NFTVA print 103' at 20 fps.
Cast (in order of appearance): Ivor Novello (Roddy Berwick), Ben Webster (Dr Dowson, Headmaster), Norman McKinnel (Sir Thomas Berwick), Robin Irvine (Tim Wakeley), Jerrold Robertshaw (Rev. Henry Wakeley), Sibyl Rhoda (Sibyl Wakeley), Annette Benson (Mabel), Lilian Braithwaite (Lady Berwick), Isabel Jeans (Julia), Ian Hunter (Archie), Hannah Jones (Dresser), Barbara Gott (Madame Michet), Violet Farebrother (Poetess), Alf Goddard (Sailor).

1927 **EASY VIRTUE** (Gainsborough)

Director: AH. Producer: Michael Balcon. Scenario: Eliot Stannard. From the 1926 play by Noel Coward. Photography: Claude McDonnell. Art director: Clifford Pember. Assistant director: Frank Mills. NFTVA print 72' at 20 fps.
Cast: Isabel Jeans (Larita Fulton), Franklin Dyall (her husband), Eric Bransby Williams (the Co-respondent/artist), Ian Hunter (Plaintiff's Counsel), Robin Irvine (John Whittaker), Violet Farebrother (Mrs Whittaker), Frank Elliott (Col. Whittaker), Dacia Deane (Marion Whittaker), Dorothy Boyd (Hilda Whittaker), Enid Stamp Taylor (Sarah), Benita Hume (switchboard operator).
Hitchcock appears walking out of a tennis court past Larita in the south of France.

1927 **THE RING** (British International Pictures)

Director: AH. Producer: John Maxwell. Scenario: AH. Photography: John J. Cox. Assistant director: Frank Mills. Art director: C.W. Arnold. NFTVA print 108' at 20 fps.
Cast: Carl Brisson ('One round' Jack Sander), Lilian Hall Davis (Mabel), Ian Hunter (Bob Corby), Forrester Harvey (James Ware, the Promoter), Harry Terry (the Showman), Gordon Harker (Jack's trainer), Clare Greet (Gypsy fortune-teller).
Note: No producer is credited on the BIP pictures Hitchcock directed. I have followed most earlier compilers of Hitchcock filmographies in assuming that the Studio Head, John Maxwell, fulfilled that function.

1928 **THE FARMER'S WIFE** (British International Pictures)

Director: AH. Producer: John Maxwell. Screenplay: Eliot Stannard. From the 1916 play by Eden Phillpots [Phillpotts]. Photography: John J. Cox. Art director: C. Wilfred Arnold. Assistant director: Frank Mills. NFTVA print 117' at 20 fps.
Cast: Jameson Thomas (Samuel Sweetland), Lilian Hall-Davis (Minta, his housekeeper), Gordon Harker (Churdles Ash, his handyman), Gibb McLaughlin (Henry Coaker), Maud Gill (Thirza Tapper), Louie Pounds (Widow Louisa Windeatt), Olga Slade (Mary Hearn, postmistress), Ruth Maitland (Mercy Bassett), Antonia Brough (Susan, Thirza's maid), Haward Watts (Dick Coaker), Mollie Ellis (Sibley Sweetland).

1928 **CHAMPAGNE** (British International Pictures)

Director: AH. Producer: John Maxwell. Scenario: Elliot Stannard. Adapted by AH from an original story by Walter C. Mycroft. Photography: John J. Cox. Art director: C.W. Arnold. Assistant director: Frank Mills. NFTVA print 118' at 18 fps.
Cast: Betty Balfour (the Girl, Betty), Jean Bradin (the Boy), Theo von Alten (the Man), Gordon Harker (the Father), Clifford Heatherley (Cabaret Manager), Hannah Jones (Cabaret maid).

1929 **THE MANXMAN** (British International Pictures)

Director: AH. Producer: John Maxwell. Scenario: Eliot Stannard. From the 1894 novel by Sir Hall Caine. Photography: Jack Cox. Assistant director: Frank Mills. Art director, C.W. Arnold. Editor: Emile de Ruelle. NFTVA print 101' at 20 fps.
Cast: Carl Brisson (Pete Quilliam), Malcolm Keen (Philip Christian), Anny Ondra (Kate Cregeen), Randle Ayrton (Caesar Cregeen), Claire [Clare] Greet (Mrs Cregeen).

English period: Sound features

1929 **BLACKMAIL** (British International Pictures)

Director: AH. Producer: John Maxwell. From the 1928 play by Charles Bennett. Adapted by AH & Michael Powell. Dialogue by Benn Levy (sound version). Photography: Jack Cox. Art director: C.W. Arnold. Assistant director: Frank Mills. Editor: Emile de Ruelle. Music (sound version): Campbell & Connelly, compiled and arranged by Hubert Bath & Harry Stafford. British International Symphony Orchestra. Conductor: John Reynders. 86'.
Cast: Anny Ondra (Alice White) (voice spoken by Joan Barry), John Longden (Frank Webber), Donald Calthrop (Tracy, the blackmailer), Cyril Ritchard (Crewe, the artist), Sara Allgood (Mrs White), Charles Paton (Mr White), Hannah Jones (Crewe's landlady), Sam Livesey/Harvey Braban (Chief Inspector), Phyllis Konstam/Phyllis Monkman (Gossiping neighbour), Ex-Det. Sgt Bishop (Det. Sgt), Percy Parsons (Arrested man), Johnny Butt (Desk Sgt., New Scotland Yard).
Note: BLACKMAIL was also filmed and released in a silent version, hence the doubling of two of the actors. See Barr 1999: 81-97 on the film's complex production history and the casting complications.

Hitchcock plays a passenger on the London Underground harassed by a small boy as Alice and Frank travel to the Lyons Corner House.

1929 JUNO AND THE PAYCOCK (British International Pictures)

Director: AH. Producer: John Maxwell. From the 1924 play by Sean O'Casey. Adapted by AH, scenario by Alma Reville. Photography: J.J. Cox. Art director: J. Marchant. Assistant director: Frank Mills. Sound: C. Thornton. Editor: Emile de Ruelle. 96'.

Cast (in order of appearance): Barry Fitzgerald (the Orator), Maire O'Neil (Mrs Madigan), Edward Chapman (Captain Boyle), Sidney Morgan (Joxer Daly), Sara Allgood (Juno Boyle), John Laurie (Johnny Boyle), Dave Morris (Jerry Devine), Kathleen O'Regan (Mary Boyle), John Longden (Charles Bentham), Denis Wyndham (the Mobiliser), Fred Schwartz (Mr Kelly).

1930 MURDER! (British International Pictures)

Director: AH. Producer: John Maxwell. From the 1928 novel *Enter Sir John* by Clemence Dane (pseudonym of Winifred Ashton) & Helen Simpson. Adapted by AH & Walter Mycroft. Scenario by Alma Reville. Musical director: John Reynders. Assistant director: Frank Mills. Art director: J.F. Mead. Sound: Cecil V. Thornton. Editor: Rene Marrison, under the supervision of Emile de Ruelle. 104'.

Cast: Herbert Marshall (Sir John Menier), Norah Baring (Diana Baring), Phyllis Konstam (Doucie Markham), Edward Chapman (Ted Markham), Miles Mander (Gordon Druce), Esme Percy (Handel Fane), Donald Calthrop (Ion Stewart), Esme V. Chaplin (Prosecuting Counsel), Amy Brandon-Thomas (Defending Counsel), Joynson Powell (Judge), S.J. Warmington (Bennett, Sir John's facto-tum), Marie Wright (Miss Mitcham, Diana's landlady), Hannah Jones (Mrs Didsome, Markhams' landlady), Una O'Connor (Mrs Grogram, landlady with children). Members of the jury: R.E. Jeffrey (Foreman), Alan Stainer, Kenneth Kove, Guy Pelham Boulton, Violet Farebrother, Clare Greet, Drusilla Wills, Robert Easton, William Fazan, George Smythson, Ross Jefferson, Picton Roxborough.

Hitchcock walks past the camera with a female companion as Sir John and the Markhams converse in the background outside the house where the murder occurred.

Note: A German version of MURDER! entitled MARY (SIR JOHN GREIFT EIN!) was filmed simultaneously with Alfred Abel, Olga Tschechowa, Paul Graetz and Lotte Stein in the main roles.

1931 **THE SKIN GAME** (British International Pictures)

Director: AH. Producer: John Maxwell. From the 1920 play by John Galsworthy. Adapted by AH. Scenario: Alma Reville. Photography: J.J. Cox. Assistant director: Frank Mills. Sound: Alec Murray. Art director: J.B. Maxwell. Editors: A. Cobbett & R. Marrison. 88'.
Cast: *The Hillcrists*: C.V. France (Mr Hillcrist), Helen Haye (Mrs Hillcrist), Jill Esmond (Jill). *The Hornblowers*: Edmund Gwenn (Mr Hornblower), John Longden (Charles), Phyllis Konstam (Chloë), Frank Lawton (Rolf). Herbert Ross (Mr Jackman), Dora Gregory (Mrs Jackman), Edward Chapman (Dawker, Hillcrist's agent), R.E. Jeffrey (First stranger), George Bancroft (Second stranger), Ronald Frankau (Auctioneer).

1931 **RICH AND STRANGE** (British International Pictures)

Director: AH. Producer: John Maxwell. From the 1930 novel by Dale Collins. Adapted by AH. Scenario: Alma Reville & Val Valentine. Photography: John Cox & Charles Martin. Assistant director: Frank Mills. Sound: Alec Murray. Art director: C. Wilfred Arnold. Music: Hal Dolphe. Musical direction: John Reynders. Editors: Rene Marrison & Winifred Cooper. 83'.
Cast: Henry Kendall (Fred Hill), Joan Barry (Emily Hill), Percy Marmont (Commander Gordon), Betty Amman ('the Princess'), Elsie Randolph (Miss Imrie), Hannah Jones (Mrs Porter, charwoman).

1932 **NUMBER SEVENTEEN** (British International Pictures)

Director: AH. Producer: John Maxwell. From the 1925 play by J. Jefferson Farjeon, produced by Leon M. Lion. Scenario: Alma Reville, AH & Rodney Ackland. Photography: John J. Cox & Bryan Langley. Assistant director: Frank Mills. Art director: Wilfred Arnold. Sound: A.D. Valentine. Editor: A.C. Hammond. Music: A. Hallis. 63'.
Cast: Leon M. Lion (Ben), Anne Grey (Nora), John Stuart (Barton), Donald Calthrop (Brant), Barry Jones (Henry Doyle), Ann Casson (Rose Ackroyd), Henry Caine (Ackroyd, her father), Garry Marsh (Sheldrake).

1934 **WALTZES FROM VIENNA** (Gaumont-British Picture Corporation)

Director: AH. Producer: Tom Arnold. Scenario: Guy Bolton & Alma Reville. Based on the 1931 stage musical by Heinz Reichert, Dr A.M. Willner & Ernest Marischka, and the musical arrangement of Julius Bittner & E.W. Korngold. The music of Johann Strauss (father and son) adapted for the screen by Hubert Bath,

under the direction of Louis Levy. Production manager: Henry Sherek. Unit manager & assistant director: Richard Beville. Photography: Glen McWilliams. Art director: Oscar Werndorff. Editor: Charles Frend. Sound: Alfred Birch. 80'.
Cast: Jessie Matthews (Rasi), Edmund Gwenn (Johann Strauss the Elder), Fay Compton (the Countess), Esmond Knight (Schani Strauss), Frank Vosper (the Prince), Robert Hale (Ebeseder, Rasi's father), Charles Heslop (the Valet), Hindle Edgar (Leopold), Marcus Barron (Dreschler, music impresario), Betty Huntley Wright (Lady's maid), Sybil Grove (Mme Fouchet).

1934 THE MAN WHO KNEW TOO MUCH (Gaumont-British)

Director: AH. Associate producer: Ivor Montagu. Scenario: Edwin Greenwood & A.R. Rawlinson. Based on an original story by Charles Bennett & D.B. Wyndham Lewis. Additional dialogue: Emlyn Williams. Photography: Curt Courant. Art director: Alfred Junge. Editor: Hugh Stewart. Sound: F. McNally. Unit production manager: Richard Beville. Music: Arthur Benjamin. Musical director: Louis Levy. 75'.
Cast: Leslie Banks (Bob Lawrence), Edna Best (Jill Lawrence), Peter Lorre (Abbott), Frank Vosper (Ramon), Hugh Wakefield (Clive), Nova Pilbeam (Betty Lawrence), Pierre Fresnay (Louis Bernard), Cicely Oates (Nurse Agnes), D.A. Clark Smith (Insp. Binstead), George Curzon (Gibson), Henry Oscar (Dentist), S.J. Warmington (Gang member), Frederick Piper & Frank Atkinson (PCs during siege), Betty Baskcomb (Young woman displaced from her bed), Charles Paton (Shopkeeper).
Note: For the Gaumont British films up to SABOTAGE, Michael Balcon was Studio Head, and so functioned as an Executive Producer.

1935 THE 39 STEPS (Gaumont-British)

Director: AH. Associate producer: Ivor Montagu. From the 1915 novel by John Buchan. Adaptation: Charles Bennett. Continuity: Alma Reville. Dialogue: Ian Hay. Photography: Bernard Knowles. Art director: O. Werndorff. Editor: D.N. Twist. Sound: A. Birch. Wardrobe: Marianne. Dress designer: J. Strassner. Musical director: Louis Levy. 86'.
Cast: Robert Donat (Hannay), Madeleine Carroll (Pamela), Lucie Mannheim (Annabella Smith), Godfrey Tearle (Professor Jordan), Peggy Ashcroft (Margaret, crofter's wife), John Laurie (John, Crofter), Helen Haye (Mrs Jordan), Frank Cellier (Sheriff), Wylie Watson (Mr Memory), Jerry Verno, Gus McNaughton (Commercial travellers on train), Peggy Simpson (Maid), Frederick Piper (Milkman), S.J. Warmington (Detective in Palladium), Miles Malleson (Palladium manager).

Hitchcock walks past the camera with a male companion outside the Music Hall as Hannay and Annabella board a bus in the background.

1936 **SECRET AGENT** (Gaumont-British)

Director: AH. Associate producer: Ivor Montagu. Screenplay: Charles Bennett. From the play by Campbell Dixon, based on two of the stories ('The Traitor' and 'The Hairless Mexican') in *Ashenden, or the British Agent* (1928) by W. Somerset Maugham. Dialogue: Ian Hay. Continuity: Alma Reville. Additional dialogue: Jesse Lasky Jr Photography: Bernard Knowles. Art director: O. Werndorff. Editor: Charles Frend. Sound: Phillip Dorté. Dresses: J. Strassner. Musical director: Louis Levy. 86'

Cast: John Gielgud (Brodie, then Ashenden), Peter Lorre (the General), Madeleine Carroll (Elsa), Robert Young (Marvin), Percy Marmont (Caypor), Florence Kahn (Mrs Caypor), Charles Carson ('R'), Lilli Palmer (Lilli), Tom Helmore (Liaison officer), Michel Saint-Denis (Coachman), Howard Marion Crawford (Carl, Lilli's boyfriend).

Note: Charles Barr (1999: 236) has been unable to find any evidence that the play by Campbell Dixon was either published or produced.

1936 **SABOTAGE** (Gaumont-British)

Director: AH. Associate producer: Ivor Montagu. Screenplay: Charles Bennett. From the novel *The Secret Agent* (1907) by Joseph Conrad. Dialogue Ian Hay & Helen Simpson. Continuity: Alma Reville. Additional dialogue: E.V.H. Emmett. Photography: Bernard Knowles. Editor: Charles Frend. Art director: O. Werndorff. Sound: A. Cameron. Dresses: J. Strassner. Wardrobe: Marianne. Musical director: Louis Levy. Cartoon sequence WHO KILLED COCK ROBIN? by arrangement with Walt Disney. 76'.

Cast: Sylvia Sydney [Sidney] (Mrs Verloc), Oscar Homolka (Verloc), Desmond Tester (Stevie, Mrs Verloc's brother), John Loder (Ted Spencer), Joyce Barbour (Renee, ticket office), Matthew Boulton (Supt. Talbot), S.J. Warmington (Hollingshead), William Dewhurst (the Professor), Clare Greet (Mrs Jones, Verloc's cook), Aubrey Mather (Greengrocer), Martita Hunt (Professor's daughter), Peter Bull & Torin Thatcher (Conspirators), Austin Trevor (Vladimir, Verloc's paymaster), Charles Hawtrey & Betty Baskcomb (Aquarium visitors), Frederick Piper (Bus conductor).

1937 **YOUNG AND INNOCENT** (Gaumont-British)

Director: AH. Producer: Edward Black. Screenplay: Charles Bennett, Edwin Greenwood & Anthony Armstrong. Based on the novel *A Shilling for Candles* (1936) by Josephine Tey. Dialogue: Gerald Savory. Continuity: Alma Reville. Photography: Bernard Knowles. Sound: A. O'Donoghue. Editor: Charles Frend. Art direction: Alfred Junge. Musical director: Louis Levy. Wardrobe: Marianne. Songs: Lerner, Goodhart & Hoffman. 83'.

Cast: Nova Pilbeam (Erica Burgoyne), Derrick de Marney (Robert Tisdall), Percy Marmont (Col. Burgoyne), Edward Rigby (Old Will, the china-mender), Mary Clare (Aunt Margaret), John Longden (Det. Insp. Kent), George Curzon (Guy, the drummer), Basil Radford (Uncle Basil), Pamela Carme (Christine Clay), George Merritt (Det. Sgt. Miller), J.H. Roberts (Solicitor), Jerry Verno (Lorry driver), H.F. Maltby (Sgt.), John Miller (PC)

Hitchcock is trying to take a photograph outside the courthouse when Robert goes on the run (see Fig. 8).

1938 **THE LADY VANISHES** (Gainsborough for Gaumont-British)

Director: AH. Producer: Edward Black. Screenplay: Sidney Gilliatt [Gilliat] & Frank Launder. Based on the novel *The Wheel Spins* (1936) by Ethel Lina White. Continuity: Alma Reville. Photography: Jack Cox. Editors: R.E. Dearing & Alfred Roome. Sound: S. Wiles. Settings: Vetchinsky. Musical director: Louis Levy. 96'.

Cast: Margaret Lockwood (Iris Henderson), Michael Redgrave (Gilbert), Paul Lukas (Dr Hartz), Dame May Whitty (Miss Froy), Cecil Parker (Mr Todhunter), Linden Travers ('Mrs Todhunter'), Naunton Wayne (Caldicott), Basil Radford (Charters), Mary Clare (Baroness), Emile Boreo (Hotel Manager), Googie Withers (Blanche), Sally Stewart (Julie), Philip Deaver (Signor Doppo), Zelma Vas Dias (Signora Doppo), Catherine Lacy [Lacey] ('the Nun'), Josephine Wilson (Madame Kummer), Charles Oliver (the Officer), Kathleen Tremaine (Anna, the maid).

Hitchcock appears on Victoria Station when the train arrives at the end, shrugging his shoulders to a male companion.

1939 **JAMAICA INN** (Mayflower)

Director: AH. Producer: Erich Pommer. (Mayflower was Pommer & Charles Laughton's production company.) Screenplay: Sidney Gilliat & Joan Harrison. From the 1936 novel by Daphne du Maurier. Dialogue: Sidney Gilliat. Continuity: Alma Reville. Additional dialogue: J.B. Priestley. Photography: Harry

Stradling, in collaboration with Bernard Knowles. Settings: Tom Morahan. Costumes: Molly McArthur. Music: Eric Fenby. Musical director: Frederic Lewis. Sound: Jack Rogerson. Editor: Robert Hamer. Special effects: Harry Watt. Make-up artist: Ern Westmore. Production Manager: Hugh Perceval. 108'.

Cast: Charles Laughton (Sir Humphrey Pengallan), Maureen O'Hara (Mary), Leslie Banks (Joss Merlyn), Marie Ney (Patience Merlyn, Mary's aunt), Robert Newton (Jem Trehearne), Emlyn Williams (Harry the Pedlar), Wylie Watson (Salvation Watkins), Morland Graham (Sea lawyer Sydney), Edwin Greenwood (Dandy), Mervyn Johns (Thomas), Stephen Haggard (the Boy), Horace Hodges (Chadwyck, Pengallan's butler), Hay Petrie (Pengallan's groom), Frederick Piper (Pengallan's agent), Basil Radford (Lord George), George Curzon (Capt. Murray), Bromley Davenport (Ringwood), Jeanne de Casalis, Mabel Terry Lewis (Pengallan's guests), Herbert Lomas, Clare Greet, William Devlin (Pengallan's tenants), Aubrey Mather (Coachman).

Hollywood period: Features

1940 **REBECCA** (Selznick International Pictures, Inc.)

Director: AH. Producer: David O. Selznick. Screenplay: Robert E. Sherwood & Joan Harrison. Adaptation: Philip MacDonald & Michael Hogan. From the 1938 novel by Daphne du Maurier. Photography: George Barnes. Music: Franz Waxman. Art director: Lyle Wheeler. Interior designer: Joseph B. Platt. Special effects: Jack Cosgrove. Interior decorator: Howard Bristol. Supervising editor: Hal C. Kern. Associate editor: James E. Newcom. Scenario assistant: Barbara Keon. Sound: Jack Noyes. Assistant director: Edmond Bernoudy. Released through United Artists. 130'.

Cast: Laurence Olivier (Maxim de Winter), Joan Fontaine (Mrs de Winter), George Sanders (Jack Favell), Judith Anderson (Mrs Danvers), Gladys Cooper (Beatrice Lacy), Nigel Bruce (Major Giles Lacy), Reginald Denny (Frank Crawley), C. Aubrey Smith (Colonel Julyan), Melville Cooper (Coroner), Florence Bates (Mrs Van Hopper), Leonard Carey (Ben), Leo G. Carroll (Dr Baker), Edward Fielding (Frith), Lumsden Hare (Tabbs), Forrester Harvey (Chalcroft, publican), Philip Winter (Robert).

Hitchcock's cameo outside a phone booth whilst Favell phones Mrs Danvers towards the end of the movie (see Fig. 9) was cut, presumably on Selznick's orders. He can, however, still be glimpsed walking by in the background in the ensuing scene when Favell argues with a policeman on the pavement.

1940 **FOREIGN CORRESPONDENT** (Walter Wanger Productions, Inc.)

Director: AH. Producer: Walter Wanger. Screenplay: Charles Bennett & Joan Harrison. Dialogue: James Hilton & Robert Benchley. Special production effects: William Cameron Menzies. Music: Alfred Newman. Art director: Alexander Golitzen. Associate art director: Richard Irvine. Photography: Rudolph Maté. Special photographic effects: Paul Eagler. Supervising editor: Otho Lovering. Editor: Dorothy Spencer. Interior decorator: Julia Heron. Costumes: I. Magnin & Co. Assistant director: E.F. Bernoudy. Sound: Frank Maher. Released through United Artists. 119′.

Cast: Joel McCrea (Johnny Jones, pseudonym Huntley Haverstock), Laraine Day (Carol Fisher), Herbert Marshall (Stephen Fisher), George Sanders (Scott ffolliott), Albert Basserman (Van Meer), Robert Benchley (Stebbins), Edmund Gwenn (Rowley), Eduardo Ciannelli (Mr Krug), Harry Davenport (Mr Powers, *Globe* editor), Martin Kosleck (Fake tramp at windmill), Frances Carson (Mrs Sprague [i.e. Mrs Appleby]), Ian Wolfe (Stiles, Fisher's butler), Charles Wagenheim (Assassin), Edward Conrad (Latvian), Charles Halton (Bradley), Barbara Pepper (Dorine, Stebbins's date), Emory Parnell (*Mohican* captain), Roy Gordon (Mr Brood), Gertrude Hoffman (Mrs Benson), Martin Lamont (Clipper captain), Barry Bernard (Clipper steward), Holmes Herbert (Assistant commissioner ffolliott, New Scotland Yard), Leonard Mudie (Insp. McKenna), John Burton (English announcer).

Hitchcock appears reading a newspaper in the street outside Johnny's London hotel at the moment Johnny hears the doorman greet Van Meer.

1941 **MR. & MRS. SMITH** (RKO Radio Pictures, Inc.)

Director: AH. Executive producer: Harry E. Edington. Story and screenplay: Norman Krasna. Music: Edward Ward. Photography: Harry Stradling. Special effects: Vernon L. Walker. Art director: Van Nest Polglase. Associate art director: L.P. Williams. Gowns: Irene. Set decorator: Darrell Silvera. Sound: John E. Tribby. Editor: William Hamilton. Assistant director: Dewey Starkey. 95′.

Cast: Carole Lombard (Ann Krausheimer Smith), Robert Montgomery (David Smith), Gene Raymond (Jeff Custer), Jack Carson (Chuck Benson), Philip Merivale (Mr Custer), Lucille Watson (Mrs Custer), William Tracy (Sammy), Charles Halton (Harry Deever), Esther Dale (Mrs Krausheimer), Emma Dunn (Martha, cook), Betty Compson (Gertie), Patricia Farr (Gloria), William Edmunds (Proprietor, Momma Lucy's), Adele Pearce (Lily, maid), Georgia Carroll (Glamorous woman, Florida Club), James Flavin (Jealous escort, Florida Club).

Hitchcock appears outside David and Ann's apartment after David has insulted Jeff and the men have walked off in opposite directions along the pavement. The cameo – allegedly directed by Carole Lombard – is visually emphasised by a track back at 90 degrees to the pavement: Hitchcock walks left to right across the space revealed.

1941 **SUSPICION** (RKO Radio Pictures, Inc.)

Director: AH. Executive producer: Harry E. Edington. Screenplay: Samson Raphaelson, Joan Harrison & Alma Reville. Based on the novel *Before the Fact* (1932) by Francis Iles (pseudonym of Anthony Berkeley Cox). Music: Franz Waxman. Photography: Harry Stradling. Special effects: Vernon L. Walker. Art director: Van Nest Polglase. Associate art director: Carroll Clark. Gowns: Edward Stevenson. Set decorator: Darrell Silvera. Sound: John E. Tribby. Editor: William Hamilton. 100'.

Cast: Cary Grant (Johnnie Aysgarth), Joan Fontaine (Lina McLaidlaw), Cedric Hardwicke (General McLaidlaw), Nigel Bruce (Beaky Thwaite), Dame May Whitty (Mrs McLaidlaw), Isabel Jeans (Mrs Newsham), Heather Angel (Ethel, Aysgarths' maid), Auriol Lee (Isobel Sedbusk), Reginald Sheffield (Reggie Wetherby), Leo G. Carroll (Captain George Melbeck), Violet Shelton (Mrs Barham), Carol Curtis-Brown (Jessie Barham), Faith Brook (Alice Barham), Clyde Cook (Photographer), Leonard Carey (Jenner, McLaidlaws' butler), Kenneth Hunter (Sir Gerald), Rex Evans (Mr Bailey, estate agent), Hilda Plowright (Postmistress), Lumsden Hare (Insp. Hodgson), Vernon Downing (Benson), Billy Bevan (Ticket collector), Gavin Gordon (Bertram Sedbusk), Nondas Metcalf (Phyllis Swinghurst), Rita Page (Melbeck's secretary), Alec Craig (Receptionist, Hogarth Club).

Hitchcock posts a letter in the background of an establishing shot of the village, immediately after the scene which ends with Beaky's choking fit.

1942 **SABOTEUR** (Frank Lloyd Productions, Inc./Universal Pictures Company Inc.)

Director: AH. Producer: Frank Lloyd. Associate producer: Jack H. Skirball. Original screenplay: Peter Viertel, Joan Harrison & Dorothy Parker. Photography: Joseph Valentine. Art director: Jack Otterson. Associate art director: Robert Boyle. Editor: Otto Ludwig. Assistant director: Fred Frank. Set decorator: R.A. Gausman. Set continuity: Adele Cannon. Musical director: Charles Previn. Music: Frank Skinner. Sound: Bernard B. Brown. Sound technician: William Hedgcock. Released through Universal. 108'.

Cast: Priscilla Lane (Pat Martin), Robert Cummings (Barry Kane), Otto Kruger (Tobin), Alan Baxter (Freeman), Clem Bevans (Neilson), Norman Lloyd (Fry), Alma Kruger (Mrs Sutton), Vaughan Glazer [Glaser] (Mr Miller [i.e. Philip Martin, Pat's uncle]), Dorothy Peterson (Mrs Mason, Ken's mother), Ian Wolfe

(Robert, Mrs Sutton's butler), Frances Carson (Society woman), Murray Alper
(Truck driver), Kathryn Adams (Tobin's daughter). *Circus troupe*: Pedro de
Cordoba (Bones), Billy Curtis (Midget), Marie Le Deaux (Fat Woman), Anita
Bolster (Lorelei [i.e. Esmeralda]), Jeanne Romer, Lynn Romer (Siamese twins).
Jean Trent (Blonde plant worker), Virgil Summers (Ken Mason), Belle Mitchell
(Adèle, Tobin's maid), Matt Willis (First deputy who arrests Barry), William
Ruhl (Second deputy), Oliver Blake (Mac, driver of deputies' car), Dorothy
Parker (Woman in car: 'They must be terribly in love'), Charles Halton (Sheriff),
Hans Conried (Edward, Mrs Sutton's major-domo), Paul Everton (Elderly
guest), Gene O'Donnell (Jitterbug), Cyril Ring (Enemy guest), Frank Marlowe
(Newsreel truck driver), Pat Flaherty (George, saboteur), Emory Parnell (Film
husband), Margaret Hayes (Film wife), Milton Kibbee (Shot spectator), Claire
Adams (His wife).
Hitchcock makes a fleeting appearance outside the New York drugstore as the
car with Freeman and Barry pulls up next to the store, which is the saboteurs'
back entrance to the Sutton mansion. He is apparently conversing with a female
companion in sign language.

1942 **SHADOW OF A DOUBT** (Skirball Productions/Universal)

Director: AH. Producer Jack H. Skirball. Screenplay: Thornton Wilder, Sally
Benson & Alma Reville. From an original story by Gordon McDonell. (Thornton
Wilder also receives a special acknowledgement for 'contribution in the pre-
paration of this production'.) Photography: Joseph Valentine. Music: Dmitri
Tiomkin. *Merry Widow Waltz* by Franz Lehar. Art director: John B. Goodman.
Associate art director: Robert Boyle. Sound: Bernard B. Brown. Sound techni-
cian: Robert Pritchard. Set decorator: R.A. Gausman. Associate set decorator: E.
R. Robinson. Musical director: Charles Previn. Set continuity: Adele Cannon.
Editor: Milton Carruth. Assistant director: William Tummel. Teresa Wright's
gowns: Adrian. Costumes: Vera West. Released through Universal January
1943. 108'.
Cast: Teresa Wright (Charlie Newton), Joseph Cotten (Uncle Charlie Oakley),
Macdonald Carey (Jack Graham), Henry Travers (Joseph Newton), Patricia
Collinge (Emma Newton), Hume Cronyn (Herb Hawkins), Wallace Ford (Fred
Saunders), Edna May Wonacott (Ann Newton), Charles Bates (Roger Newton),
Clarence Muse (Railroad porter), Janet Shaw (Louise Finch, 'Til Two Bar),
Estelle Jewell (Catherine, Charlie's friend), Frances Carson (Mrs Potter),
Constance Purdy (Mrs Martin, Uncle Charlie's landlady), Minerva Urecal (Mrs
Henderson, postmistress), Edwin Stanley (Mr Green, bank manager), Isabel
Randolph (Mrs Margaret Green), Earle S. Dewey (Mr Norton, traffic cop), Eily

Malyon (Miss Cochrane, librarian), Grandon Rhodes (Reverend MacCurdy), Ruth Lee (Mrs MacCurdy).

Hitchcock appears on the train on which Uncle Charlie travels to Santa Rosa, holding an unbeatable bridge hand of all the spades.

1944 LIFEBOAT (Twentieth-Century Fox)

Director: AH. Producer: Kenneth Macgowan. Screenplay: Jo Swerling. Based on a story by John Steinbeck. Original story idea: AH. Photography: Glen MacWilliams. Art directors: James Basevi & Maurice Ransford. Set decorator: Thomas Little. Associate set decorator: Frank E. Hughes. Editor: Dorothy Spencer. Costumes: Rene Hubert. Make-up: Guy Pearce. Special photographic effects: Fred Sersen. Technical adviser: Thomas Fitzsimmons. Sound: Bernard Freericks & Roger Heman. Music: Hugo W. Friedhofer. Musical director: Emil Newman. 97'.

Cast: Tallulah Bankhead (Constance Porter), William Bendix (Gus Smith), Walter Slezak (Willi), Mary Anderson (Alice Mackenzie), John Hodiak (Kovac), Henry Hull (C.J. 'Ritt' Rittenhouse), Heather Angel (Mrs Higley), Hume Cronyn (Stanley 'Sparks' Garrett), Canada Lee (Joe Spencer).

Hitchcock's cameo is in two photographs for an advertisement (in a newspaper read by Gus) for the (fictitious) diet aid 'Reduco', showing him in profile, before and after the diet.

1945 SPELLBOUND (Selznick International Pictures, Inc.)

Director: AH. Producer: David O. Selznick. Screenplay: Ben Hecht. Adaptation: Angus MacPhail. Suggested by *The House of Dr Edwardes* (1927) by Francis Beeding (pseudonym for John Leslie Palmer and Hilary St. George Saunders). Photography: George Barnes. Music: Miklos Rosza. Art director: James Basevi. Associate art director: John Ewing. Supervising editor: Hal C. Kern. Associate editor: William Ziegler. Production assistant: Barbara Keon. Special effects: Jack Cosgrove. Interior decorator: Emile Kuri. Assistant director: Lowell J. Farrell. Sound: Richard De Weese. Dream sequence based on designs by Salvador Dalí. Psychiatric adviser: May E. Romm. Released through United Artists. 111'.

Cast: Ingrid Bergman (Dr Constance Peterson), Gregory Peck (John Ballyntine, known first as Anthony Edwardes, then as J.B.), Michael Chekhov (Dr Alex Brulov), Leo G. Carroll (Dr Murchison), Rhonda Fleming (Mary Carmichael), John Emery (Dr Fleurot), Norman Lloyd (Garmes), Bill Goodwin (House detective, Hotel Empire), Steven Geray (Dr Graff), Donald Curtis (Harry, Green Manors' attendant), Wallace Ford (Masher, Hotel Empire), Art Baker (Lt. Cooley), Regis Toomey (Sgt. Gillespie), Paul Harvey (Dr Galt), Erskine Sanford (Dr

Hanish), Jacqueline de Wit (Nurse, Green Manors), Janet Scott (Norma Cramer, Edwardes's secretary), Victor Kilian (Sheriff), Dave Willock (Bellboy, Hotel Empire), Irving Bacon (Gateman), George Meader (Hallett, railroad clerk), Matt Moore (Policeman at railroad station), Constance Purdy (Brulov's charwoman), Joel Davis (J.B. as a boy), Teddy Infuhr (J.B.'s brother), Edward Fielding (Dr Anthony Edwardes).

Note: in every cast listing consulted, including the published script (Hecht 1946), the roles played by Paul Harvey and Erskine Sanford are credited the wrong way round.

Hitchcock, carrying a violin (case), exits from a lift in the Hotel Empire lobby when Constance first arrives at the hotel.

1946 **NOTORIOUS** (RKO Radio Pictures, Inc.)

Director-Producer: AH. Screenplay: Ben Hecht. Production assistant: Barbara Keon. Photography: Ted Tetzlaff. Special effects: Vernon L. Walker & Paul Eagler. Art directors: Albert S. D'Agostino & Carroll Clark. Set decorators: Darrell Silvera & Claude Carpenter. Music: Roy Webb. Musical director: C. Bakaleinikoff. Orchestral arrangements: Gil Grau. Editor: Theron Warth. Sound: John E. Tribby & Terry Kellum. Miss Bergman's gowns designed by Edith Head. Assistant director: William Dorfman. 101'.

Cast: Cary Grant (T.R. Devlin), Ingrid Bergman (Alicia Huberman), Claude Rains (Alexander Sebastian), Louis Calhern (Paul Prescott), Mme Leopoldine Konstantin (Mme Sebastian), Reinhold Schunzel ('Dr Anderson', pseudonym for Otto Renzler), Ivan Triesault (Eric Mathis), Alex Minotis (Joseph), Wally Brown (Mr Hopkins), Sir Charles Mendl (Commodore), Ricardo Costa (Dr Senor Barbosa), Eberhard Krumschmidt (Emile Hupka), Fay Baker (Ethel), Frederick Ledebur (Mr. Knerr), Peter von Zerneck (William Rossner), Lenore Ulrich (Senora Ortiza), Fred Nurney (John Huberman).

Hitchcock appears taking a drink of champagne during Alicia and Sebastian's party, at the point when Devlin and Alicia first show concern that the champagne might run out.

1947 **THE PARADINE CASE** (Vanguard Films, Inc.)

Director: AH. Producer: David O. Selznick. Adaptation: Alma Reville & James Bridie (pseudonym for Osborne Henry Mavor). Screenplay: David O. Selznick. Additional dialogue: Ben Hecht. Based on the 1933 novel by Robert Hichens. Photography: Lee Garmes. Music: Franz Waxman. Production designer: J. McMillan [MacMillan] Johnson. Art director: Tom Morahan. Gowns: Travis Banton. Supervising editor: Hal C. Kern. Associate editor: John Faure. Scenario assistant: Lydia Schiller. Sound director: James G. Stewart. Recordist: Richard Van Hessen. Interiors: Joseph B. Platt. Set decorator: Emile Kuri. Assistant director: Lowell J. Farrell. Unit manager: Fred Ahern. Special effects: Clarence Slifer. Hair styles: Larry Germain. Released through Selznick Releasing Organization, Inc. January 1948. 114'. (Premiered at approx. 132'; shortened by Selznick for general release.)

Cast: Gregory Peck (Anthony Keane), Ann Todd (Gay Keane), Charles Laughton (Lord Thomas Horfield), Charles Coburn (Sir Simon Flaquer), Ethel Barrymore (Lady Sophie Horfield), Louis Jourdan (André Latour), [Alida] Valli (Mrs Maddalena Paradine), Leo G. Carroll (Sir Joseph Farrell), Joan Tetzel (Judy Flaquer), Lester Matthews (Insp. Ambrose), Pat Aherne (Sgt. Leggett) (arresting officers), Isobel Elsom (Innkeeper), Phyllis Morris (Mrs Carr, Housekeeper at Hindley Hall), John Williams (Barrister).

Hitchcock, carrying a cello (case), follows Keane out of the Lake District station.

1948 ROPE (Transatlantic Pictures Corporation)

Director-Producer: AH. (Transatlantic was AH and Sidney Bernstein's production company.) Screenplay: Arthur Laurents. From the 1929 play by Patrick Hamilton. Adaptation: Hume Cronyn. Photography: Joseph Valentine & William V. Skall. Technicolor. Technicolor color director: Natalie Kalmus. Art director: Perry Ferguson. Set decorators: Emile Kuri & Howard Bristol. Production manager: Fred Ahern. Editor: William H. Ziegler. Assistant director: Lowell J. Farrell. Make-up: Perc Westmore. Sound: Al Riggs. Lighting technician: James Potevin. Musical director: Leo F. Forbstein. Music based on the theme *Perpetual Movement No. 1* by Francois Poulenc. Miss Chandler's dress by Adrian. Released through Warner Bros. 80'.

Cast: James Stewart (Rupert Cadell), John Dall (Brandon), Farley Granger (Phillip), Sir Cedric Hardwicke (Mr Kentley), Constance Collier (Mrs Atwater), Joan Chandler (Janet Walker), Douglas Dick (Kenneth Lawrence), Edith Evanson (Mrs Wilson), Dick Hogan (David Kentley).

Hitchcock's cameo is in a neon outline of his face, visible on the New York skyline between Kenneth and Janet as they are about to leave the apartment. It is just possible to read that this is another advertisement for 'Reduco' (see LIFEBOAT cameo).

1949 UNDER CAPRICORN (Transatlantic Pictures Corporation)

Director-Producer: AH. Screenplay: James Bridie. Adaptation: Hume Cronyn. Based on the 1937 novel by Helen Simpson and an unpublished dramatic version by John Colton & Margaret Linden. Photography: Jack Cardiff. Technicolor. Technicolor color director: Natalie Kalmus. Associate color director: Joan Bridge. Production designer: Thomas Morahan. Costume designer: Roger Furse. Production manager: Fred Ahern. Unit manager: John Palmer. Editor: A. S. Bates. Assistant director: C. Foster Kemp. Sound: Peter Handford. Continuity: Peggy Singer. Make-up: Charles Parker. Set dresser: Philip Stockford. Music: Richard Addinsell. Musical director: Louis Levy. Released through Warner Bros. 117'.

Cast: Ingrid Bergman (Lady Henrietta Flusky), Joseph Cotten (Sam Flusky), Michael Wilding (Hon. Charles Adare), Margaret Leighton (Milly), Cecil Parker (The Governor), Denis O'Dea (Mr Corrigan, Attorney General), Jack Watling (Winter), Harcourt Williams (The Coachman), John Ruddock (Mr Cedric Potter), Bill Shine (Mr Banks), Victor Lucas (The Reverend Smiley), Ronald Adam (Mr Riggs [i.e. Rigg]), Francis de Wolff (Major Wilkins), G.H. Mulcaster (Dr Macallister). Kitchen staff at Flusky's house: Olive Sloane (Sal), Maureen Delaney (Flo), Julia Lang (Susan), Betty McDermott (Martha).

Hitchcock appears in period costume on the steps of the Government House talking to two other men in the background as Charles first arrives by carriage at the mansion.

1949 **STAGE FRIGHT** (A Warner Brothers-First National Picture)

Director-Producer: AH. Screenplay: Whitfield Cook. Adaptation: Alma Reville. Additional dialogue: James Bridie. Based on a novel by Selwyn Jepson. (See *note*.) Photography: Wilkie Cooper. Art director: Terence Verity. Editor: E.B. Jarvis. Sound: Harold King. Make-up: Colin Garde. Production supervisor: Fred Ahern. Music: Leighton Lucas. Musical director: Louis Levy. 110'.

Cast: Jane Wyman (Eve Gill), Marlene Dietrich (Charlotte Inwood), Michael Wilding (Det. Insp. Wilfred 'Ordinary' Smith), Richard Todd (Jonathan Cooper), Alistair [Alastair] Sim (Commodore Gill), Sybil Thorndike (Mrs. Gill), Kay Walsh (Nellie Goode), Miles Malleson (Mr Fortesque), Hector MacGregor (Freddie Williams), Joyce Grenfell ('Lovely Ducks', shooting gallery attendant), André Morell (Inspector Byard), Patricia Hitchcock (Chubby Bannister), Ballard Berkeley (Sgt. Mellish), Irene Handl (Mrs Mason, Mrs Gill's maid), Arthur Howard (Groves, Charlotte's butler), Alfie Bass (Man in theatre with mike), Micky Valios (Cub).

Note: Selwyn Jepson's novel was published as *Man Running* (London, 1948), as *Outrun the Constable* (New York, 1948) and as *Killer by Proxy* (Bantam, New York, 1950.)

Hitchcock turns to look at Eve in the street as she is on her way to Charlotte's house, rehearsing out loud what she will say.

1951 **STRANGERS ON A TRAIN** (Warner Bros. Pictures, Inc.)

Director-Producer: AH. Screenplay: Raymond Chandler & Czenzi Ormonde. Adaptation: Whitfield Cook. From the 1950 novel by Patricia Highsmith. Music: Dmitri Tiomkin. Photography: Robert Burks. Art director: Edward S. Haworth. Editor: William Ziegler. Sound: Dolph Thomas. Set decorator: George James Hopkins. Wardrobe: Leah Rhodes. Make-up: Gordon Bau. Special effects: H.F. Koenekamp. Production associate: Barbara Keon. Musical direction: Ray Heindorf. 101'
Cast: Farley Granger (Guy Haines), Ruth Roman (Anne Morton), Robert Walker (Bruno Antony), Leo G. Carroll (Senator Morton), Patricia Hitchcock (Barbara Morton), Laura Elliott (Miriam Haines), Marion Lorne (Mrs Antony), Jonathan Hale (Mr Antony), Howard St. John (Captain Turley), John Brown (Professor Collins), Norma Varden (Mrs Cunningham), Robert Gist (Det. Hennessy), John Doucette (Det. Hammond), Ed Clark (Miller, Music Store owner), Tommy Farrell, Roland Morris (Miriam's boyfriends), Louis Lettieri (Boy with balloon), Al Hill ('Ring the gong' barker), Murray Alper (Boat hirer), John Butler (Blind man), Mary Alan Hokanson (Louise, secretary), Odette Myrtil (Mme Darville), George Renevant (M. Darville), Charles Meredith (Judge Donahue), Laura Treadwell (Mrs Anderson), Jack Cushingham (Fred Reynolds, tennis player), Harry Hines (Man under merry-go-round), Dick Ryan (Minister on train).
Note: A slightly different version of Strangers on a Train – labelled 'British version' – was discovered in 1995 in the Warner Bros. Collection at UCLA archives in Los Angeles. Internal evidence would suggest that this is an earlier cut of the 1951 release version. It lacks the final scene of Guy, Anne and the Minister on the train, but includes additional material in the early scene between Guy and Bruno on the train and also a couple of extra shots as Guy sneaks out of his apartment at night to visit the Antony house. Its running time is 103'. It is now included with the original release version on the Warner Bros. DVD of the film.
Hitchcock, carrying a double bass (case), gets on the train as Guy gets off on his visit to Miriam in Metcalf.

1953 **I CONFESS** (Warner Bros. Pictures, Inc.)

Director-Producer: AH. Screenplay: George Tabori & William Archibald. Based on the 1902 play *Nos Deux Consciences* by Paul Anthelme. Music: Dmitri Tiomkin. Photography: Robert Burks. Art director: Edward S. Haworth. Editor: Rudi Fehr. Sound: Oliver S. Garretson. Set decorator: George James Hopkins. Wardrobe: Orr-Kelly. Production supervisor: Sherry Shourds. Production associate: Barbara Keon. Make-up: Gordon Bau. Assistant director: Don Page. Technical advisor: Father Paul LaCouline. Music director: Ray Heindorf. 95'.

Cast: Montgomery Clift (Father Michael Logan), Anne Baxter (Ruth Grandfort), Karl Malden (Insp. Larrue), Brian Aherne (Crown Prosecutor Willie Robertson), O.E. Hasse (Otto Keller), Roger Dann (Pierre Grandfort), Dolly Haas (Alma Keller), Charles Andre (Father Millais), Judson Pratt (Sgt. Murphy), Ovila Légaré (Vilette), Gilles Pelletier (Father Benoit), Henry Cordon (Sgt. Farouche), Carmen Gingras, Renee Hudson (Schoolgirls).

Hitchcock appears in the opening shots of the film, walking right to left across the top of a flight of steps.

1954 **DIAL M FOR MURDER** (Warner Bros. Pictures, Inc.)

Director-Producer: AH. Screenplay: Frederick Knott, as adapted from his 1952 play. Music: Dmitri Tiomkin. Photography: Robert Burks. Warnercolor. (Filmed in 3D, but only released briefly in that format.) Art director: Edward Carrere. Editor: Rudi Fehr. Sound: Oliver S. Garretson. Set decorator: George James Hopkins. Wardrobe: Moss Mabry. Make-up: Gordon Bau. Assistant director: Mel Dellar. 105'.

Cast: Ray Milland (Tony Wendice), Grace Kelly (Margot Wendice), Robert Cummings (Mark Halliday), John Williams (Chief Insp. Hubbard), Anthony Dawson (C.J. Swann, pseudonym Captain Lesgate), Patrick Allen (Pearson, Hubbard's assistant).

Hitchcock appears in a photograph of Tony and Swann at a Cambridge reunion dinner.

1954 **REAR WINDOW** (Patron, Inc.)

Director-Producer: AH. (Patron was AH and James Stewart's production company.) Screenplay: John Michael Hayes. Based on the 1942 short story by Cornell Woolrich. (See *note*.) Music: Franz Waxman. Photography: Robert Burks. Aspect ratio: 1:1.66. Technicolor. Color consultant: Richard Mueller. Art directors: Hal Pereira & Joseph MacMillan Johnson. Special effects: John P. Fulton. Set decorators: Sam Comer & Ray Moyer. Assistant director: Herbert Coleman. Editor: George Tomasini. Costumes: Edith Head. Technical adviser: Bob Landry. Make-up: Wally Westmore. Sound: Harry Lindgren & John Cope. Released through Paramount Pictures Corporation. 112'.

Cast: James Stewart (L.B. 'Jeff' Jeffries), Grace Kelly (Lisa Carol Fremont), Wendell Corey (Thomas J. Doyle), Thelma Ritter (Stella), Raymond Burr (Lars Thorwald), Judith Evelyn (Miss Lonelyhearts), Ross Bagdasarian (Composer), Georgine Darcy (Miss Torso), Sara Berner & Frank Cady (Couple on fire escape), Jesslyn Fax (Sculptress), Irene Winston (Mrs Thorwald), Rand Harper & Havis Davenport (Honeymooners), Ralph Smiley (Carl, '21' waiter), Anthony

Warde (Detective in Jeff's apartment at end), Benny Bartlett (Stanley, Miss Torso's boyfriend).

Note: Cornell Woolrich's short story was first published as *It Had to be Murder* in *Dime Detective*, February 1942. Its first book appearance – as *Rear Window* – was in *After-Dinner Story* by William Irish, Woolrich's pseudonym, 1944.

Hitchcock appears in the composer's apartment on the first evening, adjusting the latter's clock.

1954 **TO CATCH A THIEF** (Paramount Pictures Corporation)

Director-Producer: AH. Screenplay: John Michael Hayes. Based on the 1952 novel by David Dodge. Photography: Robert Burks. VistaVision. Technicolor. Color consultant: Richard Mueller. Art directors: Hal Pereira & Joseph MacMillan Johnson. Second unit photography: W. Wallace Kelly. Special photographic effects: John P. Fulton. Process photography: Farciot Edouart. Set decorators: Sam Comer & Arthur Krams. Editor: George Tomasini. Assistant director: Daniel J. McCauley. Make-up supervisor: Wally Westmore. Sound: Harold Lewis & John Cope. Music: Lyn Murray. Second unit director: Herbert Coleman. Costumes: Edith Head. Dialogue coach: Elsie Foulstone. Released September 1955. 106′ (UK); 97′ (USA).

Cast: Cary Grant (John Robie), Grace Kelly (Francie Stevens), Jessie Royce Landis (Mrs Jessie Stevens), John Williams (H.H. Hughson), Charles Vanel (Bertani), Brigitte Auber (Danielle Foussard), Jean Martinelli (Foussard), Georgette Anys (Germaine, Robie's cook), René Blancard (Commissaire Lepic), Jean Hebey (Mercier, Lepic's assistant), Roland Lesaffre (Claude, young man on beach), Lewis Charles (Man with milk in kitchen), Paul 'Tiny' Newlan (Vegetable man in kitchen), Adele St. Maur (Woman with bird cage).

Hitchcock appears sitting beside Robie on a bus, early in the film – but is only identifiable if the film is viewed in widescreen.

1954 **THE TROUBLE WITH HARRY** (Alfred J. Hitchcock Productions, Ltd)

Director-Producer: AH. Screenplay: John Michael Hayes. Based on the 1949 novel by Jack Trevor Story. Associate producer: Herbert Coleman. Music: Bernard Herrmann. Photography: Robert Burks. VistaVision. Technicolor. Color consultant: Richard Mueller. Art directors: Hal Pereira & John Goodman. Editor: Alma Macrorie. Special photographic effects: John P. Fulton. Set decorators: Sam Comer & Emile Kuri. Assistant director: Howard Joslin. Costumes: Edith Head. Make-up supervisor: Wally Westmore. Sound: Howard Lewis & Winston Leverett. Released through Paramount January 1956. 99′

Cast: Edmund Gwenn (Captain Albert Wiles), John Forsythe (Sam Marlowe), Shirley MacLaine (Jennifer Rogers), Mildred Natwick (Miss Ivy Gravely), Mildred Dunnock (Mrs Wiggs), Jerry Mathers (Arnie Rogers), Royal Dano (Calvin Wiggs), Parker Fennelly (Millionaire), Barry Macollum (Tramp), Dwight Marfield (Dr Greenwood), Philip Truex (Harry Worp), Leslie Woolf (Art critic).

Hitchcock makes a distant appearance – from Mrs Wiggs's point of view inside her store – walking past the stall exhibiting Sam's paintings as the millionaire first inspects them. Wearing a raincoat, he is not clearly identifiable.

1955 **THE MAN WHO KNEW TOO MUCH** (Filwite Productions, Inc.)

Director-Producer: AH. (Filwite was AH's own company.) Screenplay: John Michael Hayes and Angus MacPhail (see *note*). Based on a story by Charles Bennett & D.B. Wyndham-Lewis. (A remake of AH's 1934 film.) Associate producer: Herbert Coleman. Music: Bernard Herrmann. Photography: Robert Burks. VistaVision. Technicolor. Color consultant: Richard Mueller. Art directors: Hal Pereira & Henry Bumstead. Special photographic effects: John P. Fulton. Process photography: Farciot Edouart. Set decorators: Sam Comer & Arthur Krams. Technical advisers: Connie Willis & Abdelhaq Chraibi. Editor: George Tomasini. Costumes: Edith Head. Assistant director: Howard Joslin. Make-up supervisor: Wally Westmore. Sound: Paul Franz & Gene Garvin. *Storm Cloud Cantata* by Arthur Benjamin & D.B. Wyndham-Lewis. Performed by London Symphony orchestra. Conducted by Bernard Herrmann. With Covent Garden chorus & Barbara Howitt, soloist. Songs: Whatever Will Be and We'll Have Love Again by Jay Livingstone & Ray Evans. Released through Paramount June 1956. 119'

Cast: James Stewart (Dr Ben McKenna), Doris Day (Jo McKenna), Brenda de Banzie (Lucy Drayton), Bernard Miles (Edward Drayton), Ralph Truman (Buchanan), Daniel Gélin (Louis Bernard), Mogens Wieth (Foreign Ambassador), Alan Mowbray (Val Parnell), Hillary Brooke (Jan Peterson), Christopher Olsen (Hank McKenna), Reggie Nalder (Assassin), Richard Wattis (Assistant manager, Albert Hall), Noel Willman (Woburn), Alix Talton (Helen Parnell), Yves Brainville (French police inspector), Carolyn Jones (Cindy Fontaine), Abdelhaq Chraibi (Arab), Gladys Holland (Bernard's date), Betty Baskcomb (Edna, Drayton's accomplice), Harry Fine (Insp. Edington), George Howe (Ambrose Chappell Sr.), Richard Wordsworth (Ambrose Chappell Jr.), Frank Atkinson & John Barrard (Workmen in Chappell's shop), Leo Gordon (Drayton's chauffeur), Pat Aherne (Drayton's accomplice), Walter Gotell (Embassy guard), Bernard Herrmann (Orchestra conductor), Alexis Bobrinskoy (Foreign Prime Minister).

Note: An account of Angus MacPhail's contribution to the structuring of the script is in Dan Auiler: *Hitchcock's Secret Notebooks*, 1999: 176-197.

Hitchcock enters the shot to stand with Ben and Jo at the back of the crowd as they watch a troupe of acrobats in Marrakech.

1956 **THE WRONG MAN** (Warner Bros. Pictures, Inc.)

Director-Producer: AH. Screenplay: Maxwell Anderson & Angus MacPhail. Story by Maxwell Anderson. (Source: see *note*.) Associate producer: Herbert Coleman. Music: Bernard Herrmann. Photography: Robert Burks. Aspect ratio: 1:1.66. Art director: Paul Sylbert. Editor: George Tomasini. Assistant director: Daniel J. McCauley. Sound: Earl Crain Sr. Set decorator: William L. Kuehl. Technical advisers: Frank D. O'Connor, District Attorney, Queens County, New York & George Groves, Sgt, NYPD, Retd. Released January 1957. 105'.

Cast: Henry Fonda (Christopher 'Manny' Balestrero), Vera Miles (Rose Balestrero), Anthony Quayle (Frank D. O'Connor), Harold J. Stone (Lt. Bowers), Charles Cooper (Det. Matthews), John Heldabrand (Tomasini, Assistant DA), Esther Minciotti (Manny's mother), Doreen Lang (Mrs Ann James), Laurinda Barrett (Constance Willis), Norma Connolly (Betty Todd), Nehemiah Persoff (Gene Conforti), Lola D'Annunzio (Olga Conforti), Kippy Campbell (Robert Balestrero), Robert Essen (Gregory Balestrero), Richard Robbins (Daniell, the guilty man), Werner Klemperer (Dr Banay), Sherman Billingsley (Himself: Stork Club proprietor).

Note: The title of the story by Maxwell Anderson on which the film was based is usually credited as *The True Story of Christopher Emmanuel Balestrero*. However, Marshall Deutelbaum notes that there were two earlier accounts of the story (1) *A Case of Identity* by Herbert Brean, published in *Life* Magazine, 29 June 1953 and (2) *A Case of Identity*, a TV dramatisation scripted by Adrian Spies, broadcast on 'Robert Montgomery Presents Summer Stock Theater' on 11 January 1954, with Robert Ellenstein and Florence Anglin as Manny and Rose (Deutelbaum 1986: 208, 209 & 217). Deutelbaum does not account for the film being credited to yet a third source, which may indeed be no more than Anderson's story treatment for Hitchcock.

Hitchcock introduces the film as the dramatisation of a real-life case.

1958 **VERTIGO** (Alfred J. Hitchcock Productions, Inc.)

Director-Producer: AH. Screenplay: Alec Coppel & Samuel A. Taylor. Based on the 1956 novel *D'Entre les Morts* by Pierre Boileau & Thomas Narcejac, translated into English by Geoffrey Sainsbury as *The Living and the Dead*. Associate producer: Herbert Coleman. Music: Bernard Herrmann. Conductor: Muir

Mathieson. Photography: Robert Burks. VistaVision. Technicolor. Color consul-
tant: Richard Mueller. Art directors: Hal Pereira & Henry Bumstead. Special
photographic effects: John P. Fulton. Process photography: Farciot Edouart &
Wallace Kelley. Set decorators: Sam Comer & Frank K. McKelvy. Titles design:
Saul Bass. Editor: George Tomasini. Assistant director: Daniel McCauley. Make-
up supervisor: Wally Westmore. Hair style supervisor: Nellie Manley. Sound:
Harold Lewis & Winston Leverett. Costumes: Edith Head. Special sequence:
John Ferren. Released through Paramount. 128'.

Cast: James Stewart (John 'Scottie' Ferguson), Kim Novak (Judy Barton/
'Madeleine Elster'), Barbara Bel Geddes (Midge), Tom Helmore (Gavin Elster),
Henry Jones (Coroner), Raymond Bailey (Doctor), Ellen Corby (Hotel
McKittrick manager), Konstantin Shayne (Pop Liebel), Lee Patrick (Mistaken
identity at car), Fred Graham (Falling policeman), Rolando Gotti (Maître D',
Ernie's), William Remick (Jury foreman), Paul Bryar (Det. Capt. Hanson),
Joanne Genthon (Carlotta Valdes), Julian Petruzzi (Flower vendor), Margaret
Brayton (Ransohoff's saleslady), Molly Dodd (Beautician), Sara Taft (Nun in
tower).

Hitchcock, carrying a horn (case), walks past Elster's shipyard as Scottie arrives
there.

1959 **NORTH BY NORTHWEST** (MGM – Loew's Incorporated)

Director-Producer: AH. Screenplay: Ernest Lehman. Associate producer: Her-
bert Coleman. Music: Bernard Herrmann. Photography: Robert Burks. Vista-
Vision. Technicolor. Production designer: Robert Boyle. Art directors: William
A. Horning & Merrill Pye. Set decorators: Henry Grace & Frank McKelvey. Spe-
cial effects: A. Arnold Gillespie & Lee LeBlanc. Titles design: Saul Bass. Editor:
George Tomasini. Color consultant: Charles K. Hagedon. Sound: Franklin
Milton. Hair styles: Sydney Guilaroff. Make-up: William Tuttle. Assistant direc-
tor: Robert Saunders. 136'.

Cast: Cary Grant (Roger Thornhill), Eva Marie Saint (Eve Kendall), James
Mason (Phillip Vandamm), Jessie Royce Landis (Clara Thornhill, Roger's
mother), Leo G. Carroll (The Professor), Josephine Hutchinson ('Mrs
Townsend', Vandamm's sister), Philip Ober (Lester Townsend), Martin Landau
(Leonard), Adam Williams (Valerian), Edward Platt (Victor Larrabee, Roger's
attorney), Robert Ellenstein (Licht), Les Tremayne (Auctioneer), Philip Coolidge
(Dr Cross, Glen Cove Police Station), Patrick McVey (Sgt. Flamm, Chicago po-
lice), Edward Binns (Capt. Junket, Nassau County detective), Ken Lynch
(Charley, Chicago police), Doreen Lang (Maggie, Roger's secretary), Frank
Wilcox (Herman Weltner), Carleton Young (Fanning Nelson), Nora Marlowe
(Anna, Vandamm's housekeeper), John Beradino (Sgt. Emile Klinger), Paul

Genge (Lt. Hagerman, Glen Cove Police Station), Robert B. Williams (Patrolman Waggoner, Klinger's partner), Alexander Lockwood (Judge Anson B. Flynn), Maudie Prickett (Elsie, maid, Plaza Hotel), James McCallion (Valet, Plaza Hotel), Doris Singh (Main receptionist, United Nations), Sally Fraser (Public Lounge receptionist, United Nations), Larry Dobkin (Cartoonist/Intelligence agent), Harvey Stephens (Stockbroker/Intelligence agent), Madge Kennedy (Mrs Finley/Intelligence agent), Walter Coy (Reporter/Intelligence agent), Ned Glass (Ticket agent), Malcolm Atterbury (Man at Prairie Stop), Patricia Cutts (Woman in hospital bed).

Hitchcock appears at the end of the opening credits sequence, just missing a bus.

1960 **PSYCHO** (Shamley Productions, Inc.)

Director-Producer: AH. (Shamley was the production company for Hitchcock's TV films.) Screenplay: Joseph Stefano. Based on the 1959 novel by Robert Bloch. Music: Bernard Herrmann. Assistant director: Hilton A. Green. Pictorial consultant: Saul Bass. Photography: John L. Russell. Aspect ratio: 1: 1.66. Art directors: Joseph Hurley & Robert Clatworthy. Set decorator: George Milo. Unit manager: Lew Leary. Titles design: Saul Bass. Editor: George Tomasini. Costume supervisor: Helen Colvig. Make-up supervisors: Jack Barron & Robert Dawn. Hair styles: Florence Bush. Special effects: Clarence Champagne. Sound: Waldon O. Watson & William Russell. Released through Paramount. 109'.

Cast: Anthony Perkins (Norman Bates), Janet Leigh (Marion Crane), Vera Miles (Lila Crane), John Gavin (Sam Loomis), Martin Balsam (Milton Arbogast), John McIntire (Sheriff Al Chambers), Simon Oakland (Dr Richmond), Vaughn Taylor (George Lowery), Frank Albertson (Tom Cassidy), Lurene Tuttle (Mrs Chambers), Pat Hitchcock (Caroline), John Anderson ('California Charlie', car salesman), Mort Mills (Highway patrolman).

Hitchcock, wearing a Stetson, stands outside Lowery's Real Estate office as Marion enters it.

1963 **THE BIRDS** (Alfred J. Hitchcock Productions, Inc.)

Director-Producer: AH. Screenplay: Evan Hunter. Based on the 1952 short story by Daphne du Maurier. Photography: Robert Burks. Technicolor. Aspect ratio: 1:1.85. Production designer: Robert Boyle. Assistant director: James H. Brown. Miss Hedren's costume designer: Edith Head. Electronic Sound Production and Composition: Remi Gassmann & Oskar Sala. Sound consultant: Bernard Herrmann. Editor: George Tomasini. Production manager: Norman Deming. Special photographic adviser: Ub Iwerks. Special effects: Lawrence A.

Hampton. Pictorial designs: Albert Whitlock. Sound: Waldon O. Watson & William Russell. Make-up: Howard Smit. Hairstyles: Virginia D'Arcy. Assistant to Mr Hitchcock: Peggy Robertson. Set decorator: George Milo. Script supervisor: Lois Thurman. Wardrobe supervisor: Rita Riggs. Bird trainer: Ray Berwick. Titles: James S. Pollak. Released through Universal Pictures. 119'.

Cast: Rod Taylor (Mitch Brenner), 'Tippi' Hedren (Melanie Daniels), Jessica Tandy (Lydia Brenner), Suzanne Pleshette (Annie Hayworth), Veronica Cartwright (Cathy Brenner), Ethel Griffies (Mrs Bundy), Charles McGraw (Sebastian Sholes), Doreen Lang (Mother in Tides Restaurant), Ruth McDevitt (Mrs MacGruder, Pet shop proprietor), Lonny Chapman (Deke Carter, proprietor of Tides), Joe Mantell (Salesman in Tides), Doodles Weaver (Man who hires boat), Malcolm Atterbury (Deputy Al Malone), John McGovern (Postal clerk, Bodega Bay), Karl Swenson (Drunk in Tides), Richard Deacon (Mitch's neighbour), Elizabeth Wilson (Helen Carter), William Quinn (George, Dan Fawcett's farmhand).

Hitchcock appears at the beginning of the film, being led out of the pet shop by his two West Highland Terriers, Geoffrey and Stanley, as Melanie goes in.

1964 **MARNIE** (Geoffrey Stanley Inc.)

Director-Producer: AH. (Geoffrey Stanley was Hitchcock's own company: see his cameo for *The Birds*.) Screenplay: Jay Presson Allen. Based on the 1961 novel by Winston Graham. Music: Bernard Herrmann. Photography: Robert Burks. Technicolor. Aspect ratio: 1:1.85. Production designer: Robert Boyle. Assistant director: James H. Brown. Unit manager: Hilton A. Green. Miss Hedren and Miss Baker's costumes: Edith Head. Miss Hedren's hair styles created by Alexandre of Paris. Editor: George Tomasini. Pictorial designs: Albert J. Whitlock. Sound: Waldon O. Watson & William Russell. Make-up: Jack Barron, Howard Smit & Robert Dawn. Hair styles: Virginia D'Arcy. Assistant to Mr Hitchcock: Peggy Robertson. Set decorator: George Milo. Script supervisor: Lois Thurman. Camera operator: Leonard South. Costume supervisor: Vincent Dee. Women's costumes: Rita Riggs. Men's costumes: James Linn. Released through Universal Pictures. 130'.

Cast: Sean Connery (Mark Rutland), 'Tippi' Hedren (Marnie Edgar), Diane Baker (Lil Mainwaring), Martin Gabel (Sidney Strutt), Louise Latham (Bernice Edgar), Bob Sweeney (Cousin Bob), Milton Selzer (Man at racetrack), Mariette Hartley (Susan Claborn, Ward's secretary), Alan Napier (Mr Rutland), Bruce Dern (Sailor in flashbacks), Henry Beckman (First detective), S. John Launer (Sam Ward), Edith Evanson (Rita, Rutland cleaner), Meg Wyllie (Mrs Turpin), Louise Lorimer (Mrs Strutt), Rupert Crosse (Rutland caretaker).

Note: In UK prints of the film, a small section of dialogue has been deleted from Mrs Edgar's account, in the last scene, of Marnie's conception. This dialogue is present in North American prints. The missing dialogue, and an account of the reasons for the deletion, may be found in Auiler 1999: 524.

Hitchcock appears about five minutes into the film, exiting from a hotel room after a black-haired Marnie and a bellboy have passed down the corridor, looking first towards Marnie, then at the camera.

1966 **TORN CURTAIN** (Universal Pictures)

Director-Producer: AH. Screenplay: Brian Moore. Additional dialogue Keith Waterhouse and Willis Hall. Production designer: Hein Heckroth. Miss Andrews's costumes: Edith Head. Music: John Addison. Photography: John F. Warren. Technicolor. Aspect ratio 1:1.85. Art director: Frank Arrigo. Unit production manager: Jack Corrick. Pictorial designs: Albert Whitlock. Sound: Waldon O. Watson & William Russell. Editor: Bud Hoffman. Assistant director: Donald Baer. Set decorator: George Milo. Costume supervisor: Grady Hunt. Assistant to Mr Hitchcock: Peggy Robertson. Camera operator: Leonard South. Script supervisor: Lois Thurman. Miss Andrews's hair styles: Hal Saunders. Hair styles: Lorraine Roberson. 128'.

Cast: Paul Newman (Professor Michael Armstrong), Julie Andrews (Sarah Sherman), Lila Kedrova (Countess Kuchinska), Hansjoerg Felmy (Heinrich Gerhard), Tamara Toumanova (Ballerina), Wolfgang Kieling (Hermann Gromek), Ludwig Donath (Professor Gustav Lindt), Günter Strack (Professor Karl Manfred), David Opatoshu (Mr Jacobi), Gisela Fischer (Dr Koska), Mort Mills (Farmer), Carolyn Conwell (Farmer's wife), Arthur Gould-Porter (Freddy, Copenhagen bookshop proprietor), Gloria Gorvin (Fraulein Mann, complaining bus passenger).

Hitchcock appears, with a baby on his knee, in the foyer of the Hotel D'Angleterre, Copenhagen. His movement of the child and gestures indicate that he has been subjected to a wetting.

1969 **TOPAZ** (Universal Pictures)

Director-Producer: AH. Screenplay: Samuel Taylor. Based on the 1967 novel by Leon Uris. Associate producer: Herbert Coleman. Music: Maurice Jarre. Production designer: Henry Bumstead. Costumes: Edith Head. Fashioned in Paris by Pierre Balmain. Photography: Jack Hildyard. Technicolor. Aspect ratio: 1:1.85. Editor: William Ziegler. Photographic consultant: Hal Mohr. Sound: Waldon O. Watson. Unit production manager: Wallace Worsley. Assistant directors: Douglas Green & James Westman. Special photographic effects: Albert J.

Whitlock. Set decorator: John Austin. Script supervisor: Trudy Van Trotha. Make-up: Bud Westmore & Leonard Engelman. Hair styles: Larry Germain & Nellie Manley. Assistant to Mr Hitchcock: Peggy Robertson. Camera operator: William J. Dodds. Men's costume supervisor: Peter V. Saldutti. Cuban technical advisor: J.P. Mathieu. French technical advisor: Odette Ferry. 125'. A recent Universal video release of *Topaz* has restored the film to its original length of 142' (i.e. 136' on video).

Cast: Frederick Stafford (André Devereaux), Dany Robin (Nicole Devereaux), John Vernon (Rico Parra), Karin Dor (Juanita de Cordoba), John Forsythe (Michael Nordstrom), Michel Piccoli (Jacques Granville), Philippe Noiret (Henri Jarre), Claude Jade (Michèle Picard), Michel Subor (François Picard), Per-Axel Arosenius (Boris Kusenov), Roscoe Lee Browne (Philippe Dubois), Edmon Ryan (McKittrick, CIA interrogator), Sonja Kolthoff (Mrs Kusenov), Tina Hedstrom (Tamara Kusenov), John Van Dreelen (Claude Martin, NATO official), Don Randolph (Luis Uribe), Roberto Contreras (Munoz, Cuban secret police), Carlos Rivas (Hernandez, Parra's aide), Roger Til (Jean Chabrier), Lewis Charles (Pablo Mendoza), Sandor Szabo (Emile Redon), Anna Navarro (Carlotta Mendoza), Lew Brown (CIA official), John Roper (Thomas, Juanita's servant), George Skaff (René d'Arcy), Ben Wright (French General, Washington D.C.).

Hitchcock appears in a wheelchair, pushed by a nurse, at the New York airport just before Michèle and François meet André and Nicole. He steps out of the wheelchair in order to shake the hand of a man and walks off with him.

1972 **FRENZY** (Universal Pictures Ltd.)

Director-Producer: AH. Screenplay: Anthony Shaffer. Based on the 1966 novel *Goodbye Piccadilly, Farewell Leicester Square* by Arthur La Bern. Music: Ron Goodwin. Associate producer: William Hill. Photography: Gil Taylor. Technicolor. Aspect ratio: 1:1.85. Editor: John Jympson. Assistant director: Colin M. Brewer. Production designer: Syd Cain. Art director: Bob Laing. Production manager: Brian Burgess. Camera operator: Paul Wilson. Continuity: Angela Martelli. Sound mixer: Peter Handford. Sound recording: Gordon K. McCallum. Sound editor: Rusty Coppleman. Wardrobe supervisor: Dulcie Midwinter. Assistant to Mr Hitchcock: Peggy Robertson. Casting: Sally Nicholl. Special photographic effects: Albert Whitlock. Make-up: Harry Frampton. Hairdresser: Pat McDermott. Set dresser: Simon Wakefield. 116'.

Cast: Jon Finch (Richard Blaney), Alec McCowen (Chief Inspector Oxford), Barry Foster (Bob Rusk), Billie Whitelaw (Hetty Porter), Anna Massey (Babs Milligan), Barbara Leigh-Hunt (Brenda Blaney), Bernard Cribbins (Felix Forsythe), Vivien Merchant (Mrs Oxford), Michael Bates (Sgt. Spearman), Jean

Marsh (Monica Barling, Brenda's assistant), Clive Swift (Johnny Porter), John Boxer (Sir John), Madge Ryan (Mrs Davison, Blaney bureau client), George Tovey (Mr Salt, Blaney bureau client), Elsie Randolph (Glad, receptionist, Coburg Hotel), Jimmy Gardner (Bertie, porter, Coburg), Gerald Sim (Mr Usher, pub customer), Noel Johnson (Pub customer), June C. Ellis (Maisie, barmaid), Rita Webb (Mrs Rusk).

Hitchcock appears, wearing a bowler hat, in the crowd listening to Sir John's speech outside County Hall at the beginning of the film.

1976 **FAMILY PLOT** (Universal Pictures Ltd.)

Director-Producer: AH. Screenplay: Ernest Lehman. Based on the 1972 novel *The Rainbird Pattern* by Victor Canning. Photography: Leonard J. South. Technicolor. Aspect ratio: 1:1.85. Music: John Williams. Production designer: Henry Bumstead. Costume designer: Edith Head. Editor: J. Terry Williams. Special visual effects: Albert Whitlock. Set decorator: James W. Payne. Assistant to Mr Hitchcock: Peggy Robertson. Unit production manager: Ernest B. Wehmeyer. First assistant director: Howard G. Kazanjian. Second assistant director: Wayne A. Farlow. Sound: James Alexander & Robert L. Hoyt. Script supervisor: Lois Thurman. Make-up: Jack Barron. Production illustrator: Thomas J. Wright. Titles & optical effects: Universal Title. 120'.

Cast: Karen Black (Fran), Bruce Dern (George Lumley), Barbara Harris (Blanche Tyler), William Devane (Arthur Adamson, pseudonym of Eddie Shoebridge), Ed Lauter (Joseph Maloney), Cathleen Nesbitt (Julia Rainbird), Katherine Helmond (Mrs Maloney), Warren J. Kemmerling (Grandison, FBI), Edith Atwater (Mrs Clay, Adamson's assistant), William Prince (Bishop Wood), Nicholas Colasanto (Constantine), Marge Redmond (Vera Hannagan, department store assistant), John Lehne (Andy Bush, Bureau of Inspectors), Charles Tyner (Wheeler, stonemason), Alexander Lockwood (Parson, Maloney's funeral), Martin West (Floyd Sanger, FBI), Louise Lorimer (Ida Cookson).

Hitchcock appears as a silhouette through the frosted glass of the Registrar of Births and Deaths office when George goes to check on Eddie Shoebridge's death.

TV Episodes: *Alfred Hitchcock Presents*

Shamley Productions, Inc. Director-Producer: AH. Associate producer: Joan Harrison. Photography (unless otherwise shown): John L. Russell Jr. Art director (unless otherwise shown): John Lloyd. Editorial supervisor (until final episode): Richard G. Wray. Editor: Edward W. Williams. 25'.

2 Oct 1955 REVENGE (ep. 1)

13 Nov 1955 **BREAKDOWN** (ep. 7)

Teleplay: Francis Cockerell, Louis Pollock. Based on a story by Louis Pollock. Art director: Martin Obzina. Assistant director: Jack Corrick. Music supervisor: Stanley Wilson.
Cast: Joseph Cotten (William Callew), Raymond Bailey (Ed Johnson), Forrest Stanley (Hubka), Lane Chandler (Sheriff), Harry Shannon (Doc Horner, Coroner), James Edwards (Convict).

4 Dec 1955 **THE CASE OF MR PELHAM** (ep. 10)

Teleplay: Francis Cockrell. Based on a story by Anthony Armstrong. Assistant director: Jack Corrick. Music supervisor: Stanley Wilson.
Cast: Tom Ewell (Albert Pelham), Raymond Bailey (Dr Harley), Justice Watson (Peterson, Pelham's manservant), Kirby Smith (Tom Mason), Kay Stewart (Miss Clement, Pelham's secretary), Norman Willis (Ray, bartender), Jan Arvan (Harry, billiard room attendant), Richard Collier (Necktie salesman).

4 March 1956 BACK FOR CHRISTMAS (ep. 23)

30 Sept 1956 WET SATURDAY (ep. 40)

23 Dec 1956 MR BLANCHARD'S SECRET (ep. 52)

7 Apr 1957 **ONE MORE MILE TO GO** (ep. 67)

Teleplay: James P. Cavanagh. Based on a story by F.J. Smith. Assistant director: Hilton Green. Music supervisor: Stanley Wilson.
Cast: David Wayne (Sam Jacoby), Steve Brodie (Highway patrolman), Louise Larabee (Martha Jacoby), Norman Leavitt (Red, gas station attendant).

20 Oct 1957 THE PERFECT CRIME (ep. 79)

Future episodes: Producer: Joan Harrison. Associate producer: Norman Lloyd.

13 Apr 1958 **LAMB TO THE SLAUGHTER** (ep. 104)

Teleplay: Roald Dahl, based on his story. Assistant director: Hilton Green.
Cast: Barbara Bel Geddes (Mary Maloney), Harold J. Stone (Lt. Jack Noonan), Allan Lane (Patrick Maloney), Ken Clark (Mike, detective), William Keene (police officer), Thomas Wild (Doctor).

1 June 1958 **DIP IN THE POOL** (ep. 111)

Teleplay: Robert C. Dennis. Based on a story by Roald Dahl. Photography: John F. Warren. Assistant director: Hilton Green.
Cast: Keenan Wynn (William Botibol), Louise Platt (Ethel Botibol), Philip Bourneuf (Renshaw), Fay Wray (Mrs Renshaw), Doreen Lang (Emily), Doris Lloyd (Emily's companion), Ralph Clanton (Purser), Owen Cunningham (Auctioneer), Barry Harvey (Steward).

5 Oct 1958 **POISON** (ep. 118)

Teleplay: Casey Robinson. Based on a short story by Roald Dahl. Assistant director: Hilton Green.
Cast: Wendell Corey (Timber Woods), James Donald (Harry Pope), Arnold Moss (Doctor).

3 May 1959 BANQUO'S CHAIR (ep. 146)

27 Sept 1959 **ARTHUR** (ep. 154)

Teleplay: James P. Cavanagh. Based on a story by Arthur Williams. Assistant director: Hilton Green. Music supervisor: Frederick Herbert.
Cast: Laurence Harvey (Arthur Williams), Hazel Court (Helen Braithwaite), Robert Douglas (Insp. Ben Liebenberg), Patrick Macnee (Sgt. John Theron), Barry G. Harvey (Constable Barry).

4 Oct 1959 **THE CRYSTAL TRENCH** (ep. 155)

Teleplay: Stirling Silliphant. Based on a story by A.E.W. Mason. Photography: John F. Warren. Assistant director: Hilton Green. Music supervisor: Frederick Herbert.
Cast: James Donald (Mark Cavendish), Patricia Owens (Stella Ballister), Ben Astar (Hotel Manager), Werner Klemperer (Herr Ranks), Oscar Beregi (Tourist), Harald O. Dyrenforth (Frederick Blauer), Frank Holms (Hans Blauer), Patrick Macnee (Prof. Kersley, Geologist).

27 Sept 1960 MRS BIXBY AND THE COLONEL'S COAT (ep. 191)

14 Mar 1961 THE HORSEPLAYER (ep. 213)

17 Oct 1961 **BANG! YOU'RE DEAD** (ep. 231)

Teleplay: Harold Swanton. Based on a story by: Margery Vosper. Art director: Martin Obzina. Assistant director: Wallace Worsley. Editorial department head: David J. O'Connell. Music supervisor: Joseph E. Romero.
Cast: Steve Dunne (Rick Sheffield), Biff Elliott (Fred Chester), Lucy Prentiss (Amy Chester), Juanita Moore (Cleo), Billy Mumy (Jackie Chester), Marta Kristen (Jiffy Snack girl), John Zaremba (Market manager), Karl Lukas (Mailman), Olan Soulé (Darlene's daddy), Craig Duncan (Marker clerk), Thayer Burton (Cashier).

Other TV episodes directed by Hitchcock

30 Sept 1957 FOUR O'CLOCK (for SUSPICION) 50'.

5 Apr 1960 INCIDENT AT A CORNER (for FORD STARTIME) 50'.

11 Oct 1962 I SAW THE WHOLE THING (for THE ALFRED HITCHCOCK HOUR) 50'.

List of illustrations

Stills 4, 14, 53, 55, 59 courtesy of BFI Stills, Posters and Designs.
Stills 7, 13, 15, 37, 38, 42, 46 courtesy of Bob Baker.

Stills 11, 19, 20, 23, 25, 39, 41, 45, 47, 49, 50, 51, 60 courtesy of Richard Lippe. The remainder are from the author's own collection.

Index of Hitchcock's films and their motifs

Entries next to a motif under a film title show where the motif is discussed in relation to that film. In most cases, the motif will be in the film, but there are a few negative examples, and also some instances where I question critical assertions made elsewhere about the motif and the film. Other references to the film are listed separately after the film's title.

Where this is possible, e.g. with 'Trains and boats/ planes and buses', grouped motifs have been split into their separate components. Where it is not possible, e.g. with 'Blondes and brunettes', the full motif is quoted for each entry.

Under 'Dogs', a cross-reference to Charles Barr's entry in *English Hitchcock* is noted on the occasions when he mentions the motif and I don't.

Rather than strict alphabetical order, the motifs are listed in the order they are in the book, with the three motifs in Part I first, with any 'split' motifs in their alphabetical *group* position and with 'The police' at the end. This last covers references to the police *other* than those in 'Endings and the police' for that film.

'Espionage' is indexed under 'Exhibitionism/ voyeurism', 'Homosexuality' and 'Planes'.

'The look' is indexed under 'Exhibitionism/ voyeurism' and 'Homosexuality'.

The motifs in the TV episodes are indexed at the end.

Entries in *italics* indicate stills; entries in **bold** the filmography.

General index

This index covers all entries other than Hitchcock's films. Films, novels and plays are indexed under both title and (when cited in the text) director or author. Critical, theoretical and other non-fiction works are indexed purely by author. Actors in the TV episodes are not indexed; other actors cited in the text, including those in Hitchcock's films, are indexed.

Themes and motifs additional to those in the index of Hitchcock's films are listed under Hitchcock.

Page numbers for stills are shown in *italics*; for the TV episodes' credits in **bold**.

Film Culture in Transition
General Editor: *Thomas Elsaesser*